T0358437

SHARING POWER

LEARNING-BY-DOING IN CO-MANAGEMENT OF NATURAL RESOURCES THROUGHOUT THE WORLD

SHARING POWER

LEARNING-BY-DOING IN CO-MANAGEMENT OF NATURAL RESOURCES THROUGHOUT THE WORLD

Grazia Borrini-Feyerabend, Michel Pimbert, M. Taghi Farvar,
Ashish Kothari and Yves Renard

with Hanna Jaireth, Marshall Murphree,
Vicki Pattemore, Ricardo Ramírez and Patrizio Warren

Published by Earthscan in the UK and USA in 2007

For a full list of publications please contact:

Earthscan
2 Park Square, Milton Park, Abingdon, Oxon OX14 4RN
711 Third Avenue, New York, NY 10017

Earthscan is an imprint of the Taylor & Francis Group, an informa business

Copyright © 2004 Grazia Borrini-Feyerabend and Michel Pimbert. Reproduction of this publication for educational or other non-commercial purposes is authorized without any prior written permission from the copyright holders provided the source is fully acknowledged. Reproduction of this publication for resale or other commercial purposes is prohibited without prior written permission by the copyright holders.

The designation of geographical entities in this publication and the presentation of the material do not imply the expression of any opinion whatsoever on the part of the sponsoring organizations concerning the legal status of any country, territory, or area, or of its authorities, or concerning the delimitation of its frontiers or boundaries. The views expressed in this publication do not necessarily reflect those of the sponsoring organizations.

All rights reserved. No part of this book may be reprinted or reproduced or utilised in any form or by any electronic, mechanical, or other means, now known or hereafter invented, including photocopying and recording, or in any information storage or retrieval system, without permission in writing from the publishers.

Notices
Practitioners and researchers must always rely on their own experience and knowledge in evaluating and using any information, methods, compounds, or experiments described herein. In using such information or methods they should be mindful of their own safety and the safety of others, including parties for whom they have a professional responsibility.

Product or corporate names may be trademarks or registered trademarks, and are used only for identification and explanation without intent to infringe.

ISBN-13: 978-1-84407-497-6 (pbk)
Layout and artwork by Jeyan Farvar (jeyran@cenesta.org) and Fabrice Prati (pratigraphe@bluewin.ch)

Cover design by Andrew Corbett

The pictures reproduced and used for the artwork inside the book are all by Grazia Borrini-Feyerabend except the ones on pages 48 and 337 by Maryam Rahmanian, pages 54, 188, 273, 289 and 342 courtesy Wet Tropics Management Authority, page 74 by unknown author, pages 91 and 191 by Josiane Olff-Nathan, page 95 courtesy of North York Moors National Park Authority, Page 109 by O. Andre, pages 115 and 270 by Jose Pablo Jaramillo for the Asociación de Cabildos Tandachiridu Inganokuna, page 129 by Jean Larivière, pages 136 and 140 by Linda Norgrove, page 144 by Hal Noss, page 146 by Patrizio Warren, page 153 by Randall K. Wilson, page 156 by Pierre Campredon, page 200 by Jean Marc Garreau, page 228 by P. Khosrownezha, page 231 by Stan Jones, pages 245, 296 and 400 by Ashish Kothari, page 251 by Bernard Toutain , page 281 by Stéphane Boujou, page 285 by Cristina Eghenter, page 305 by Doriano Franceschetti, page 328 by P. Khosronezhad, page 338 by Juan Mayr, pages 341 and 392 by Maurizio Farhan Ferrari, page 364 by Ralph Buss, page 370 by Christian Chatelain, page 384 by Ahmed Reza Slapoosh, page 389 by Patricia Pinto de Silva, page 414 coutesy Regole di Cortina d Ampezzo and page 423 by Ajit Pattnaik.

A catalogue record for this book is available from the British Library

Library of Congress Cataloging-in-Publication Data has been applied

This book is dedicated to the memory of the many thousands of people, most of them unknown by us and the world at large, who offered their feelings and intelligence, their time, resources, their health and too often their life, in solidarity with their communities and in the struggle to conserve the wonders of life.

CONTENTS

Foreword by Juan Mayr Maldonado   XIX

Preface and acknowledgements   XXI

Introduction   XXVII

Part I. TOWARDS A CONTEXTUAL FRAMEWORK   1

Chapter 1. Managing natural resources: a struggle between politics and culture   3

1.1   From local livelihood strategies to global agro-industrial markets   3

     Livelihood systems   10

1.2   The interface between indigenous/ local NRM systems and the modern/ a-local agro-industrial market system: five field examples   17

     Field example 1.1   The Shuar and the colonisation frontier   19

     Field example 1.2   Erosion control, indigenous know-how and economic change in Oued Sbahiya watershed   21

     Field example 1.3   The Qashqai: nomadic pastoral livelihoods against all odds...   23

     Field example 1.4   Managing the sustainable use of wildlife   27

     Field example 1.5   Don Emiliano's farm   31

1.3   Contemporary indigenous NRM systems and co-management   33

Chapter 2. Actors, entitlements and equity in natural resource management   37

2.1   Management actors   37

     Indigenous and local communities   43

2.2   Entitlements to manage natural resources   47

2.3   Equity in managing natural resources   52

Chapter 3. Co-management of natural resources   64

3.1   What is in a name?   64

3.2   Practising co-management   71

     ... in agriculture   71

     ... in water and watershed management   73

     ... in agricultural research   75

     ... in rangeland management   76

     ... in forest management   78

     ... in the management of coastal resources   81

     ... in the management of freshwater wetlands   84

     ... in fishery management   86

     ... in mountain environments   88

     ... in managing migratory wildlife   90

     ... in managing protected areas   93

     ... for private property under stewardship conditions   98

... promoted by conservation and development projects 99

... with indigenous peoples 100

3.3 The characteristics of co-management systems 103

Part II. TOWARDS EFFECTIVE PROCESSES 109

Chapter 4. A point of departure 110

4.1 What is to be managed? Who is to be involved? 110

The natural resource management unit 117

The relevant social actors 124

4.2 Is co-management needed? Is co-management feasible? 128

The feasibility analysis 133

4.3 Gathering resources and creating a Start-up Team 135

4.4 The special case of indigenous peoples: can co-management help them assert their rights to land and natural resources? 140

Chapter 5. Preparing for the partnership 146

5.1 Gathering relevant information and tools and promoting social communication 146

Gathering information and tools 147

Social communication 151

5.2 Engaging the partners in participatory action research 157

5.3 Assisting local communities to organise 164

Acquiring specific capacities 168

Developing an internal agreement on their own values, interests and concerns about the territory or natural resources at stake 172

Appointing a representative to convey the "internal agreement" to the negotiation forum 175

5.4 Preparing for the negotiation meetings: procedures, rules, logistics and equity considerations 178

Procedures, rules and logistics 178

Equity considerations 182

Chapter 6. Negotiating the co-management agreement and organisation 188

6.1 Agreeing on the rules and procedures of negotiation 188

The first procedural meeting 191

The role of the facilitator 193

Fairness, conflicts and power differentials 195

6.2 Developing and "ritualising" a common vision of the desired future 197

6.3 Developing a strategy to approach the common vision 203

6.4 Negotiating and legitimising the co-management agreement and organisation 210

Agreements, disagreements, consensus and compromise 213

Managing conflicts 219

Taking the process to a productive close 222

Part III. TOWARDS EFFECTIVE INSTITUTIONS — 233

Chapter 7. Co-management agreements — 234

7.1	Customary and non-notarised agreements	236
7.2	Formal legal agreements	243
7.3	The components of a co-management agreement	251
	Title	251
	Preamble and statement of purpose	251
	Definitions	252
	Scope of authority of the parties in the agreement	253
	General covenants	254
	Powers and responsibilities of co-management organisations	258
	Dispute resolution and amendment procedures	258
	Information, communication and confidentiality clauses	260
	Specific clauses	262
7.4	Recognition of efforts and commitment	262
7.5	Crucial issues for indigenous peoples and local communities	265
7.6	Crucial issues for government agencies	274

Chapter 8. Co-management organisations — 278

8.1	Types and characteristics of co-management organisations	279
	Functions	280
	Composition	283
	Scope of authority	286
	Size and level of operations	287
8.2	Examples of co-management agreements and organisations	289

Chapter 9. Learning-by-doing in co-management institutions — 296

9.1	Making the agreement functional	297
	Providing fair support for the parties to join the agreement	297
	Recognising and building upon local resources, technologies and natural resource management systems	299
	Letting the agreement specify the co-management organisation, and not vice-versa	302
	Fostering relatively small, diverse, committed and accountable management bodies	304
	Pursuing timeliness, clarity, accountability... but also conviviality and warm human relationships	306
	Publicising the agreement until it is widely known	307
	Dealing fairly with conflicting interpretations of the agreement	308
	Ensuring compliance and effective enforcement of the agreement	309
9.2	"Learning by doing" through monitoring and evaluation	311
	Assessing the preparatory phase	315
	Assessing the negotiation phase	315
	Assessing the implementation phase	316
	Assessing the co-management results	317
	Who evaluates success?	321

9.3   Promoting effective and sustainable co-management institutions   325

Developing goodwill among the parties   325

Maintaining flexibility and fostering social experimentation   325

Allowing the management partnership to mature   327

Promoting people-centred organisational culture   328

Promoting participatory approaches and learning attitudes at various levels   330

Encouraging "champions" with enabling attitudes and values   336

Ensuring transparency in the distribution of benefits   337

Striving for equity   337

Part IV. TOWARDS AN ENABLING SOCIAL CONTEXT   341

Chapter 10. Natural resource policy and instruments   342

10.1   Enabling policies at the national level   345

Constitution and basic civil law   346

Natural resource management policy   348

Decentralisation, delegation and devolution policies   356

Policies that support the organisation of civil society   359

Policies that strengthen cultural identity and customary governance systems   359

Policies that secure natural resources access and tenure rights   362

Policies that recognise and respond to the rights of indigenous peoples   364

Policies that set the rules and conditions of participation and co-management   366

Financial and economic policies   370

10.2   Enabling policies at the international level   376

Chapter 11. Empowering civil society for policy change   384

11.1   The politics of policy   384

11.2   Methods and approaches for participatory policy processes   389

A glimpse of history   389

Participatory methods for inclusive deliberation   393

Linking deliberative inclusive processes to broader policy change   399

Ensuring safeguards for quality and validity   401

11.3   Strengthening civil society   407

A stronger voice for civil society   408

Federations, networks and policy influence   415

11.4   The challenge of participatory democracy   418

Equity, gender and voice   418

Safe spaces for participation and people's knowledge   420

Deepening democracy in the age of globalisation   422

Concluding remarks   428

References   432

FIGURES

2.1   Towards social actors empowered and responsible in natural resource management   56
2.2   Including equity considerations in the process towards empowered and responsible social actors   63
4.1   The Ring around the Central Desert as the "management unit" for the Asiatic Cheetah in Iran   121
4.2   Phases of a collaborative management process   139
6.1   The co-management setting for the Galapagos Marine Reserve   218
6.2   Composition of the Local Management Structure for Takiéta Forest Reserve, Niger   225

CHECKLISTS

2.1   Categories of social actors possibly relevant in natural resource management   41
2.2   The roots of entitlements: examples of grounds to claim a "title" to manage natural resources   50
2.3   Forms of power that shape and affect environmental entitlements   51
4.1   A snapshot of the interests and concerns at stake   124
4.2   A snapshot of the capacities and comparative advantages at stake   125
4.3   Co-management of natural resources: potential benefits   131
4.4   Co-management of natural resources: potential costs and obstacles   132
4.5   Investigating the co-management feasibility in a specific context   133
5.1   Questions and ranking exercises to engage the relevant social actors in the CM process   162
5.2   Procedures and logistics for the negotiation meetings   180
5.3   Example of rules for the negotiation process   182
5.4   Promoting equity in co-management: some examples and ideas   183
5.5   Evaluating the outcome of a settlement on the basis of its fairness   184
5.6   Some ideas for truly "levelling the playing field"   184
6.1   Qualities and tasks of a good facilitator/ mediator for a co-management process   194
6.2   Methods and tools to identify the components and objectives of a common strategy   204
6.3   Methods and tools to agree on a course of action   212
6.4   Ideas for managing conflict   221
7.1   Questions to address in tourism-related agreements   274
9.1   Examples of process and result indicators to assess the CM preparatory phase   315
9.2   Examples of process and result indicators to assess the CM negotiation phase   316
9.3   Examples of process and result indicators to assess the CM implementation phase   317
9.4   Characteristics of effective indicators   318
9.5   Is co-management "successful"? Does it have a positive social impact?   320
9.6   Towards successful co-management organisations: some implications of going large-scale   334
10.1 Devolving to whom? What kind of organisations can manage common property resources?   357
11.1 A selection of methods that can be used in deliberative inclusive processes for policy-making   393
11.2 Some features of deliberative and inclusionary processes (DIPs)   395
11.3 Criteria and safeguards for public acceptance and effectiveness of a CM process   401
11.4 Broad principles for deliberative and inclusive processes related to policy development   406
11.5 Transforming organisations for deliberative democracy and citizen empowerment   421

TABLES

1.1	Agro-industrial market system and indigenous NRM systems compared	18
2.1	Relevant social actors in Rajaji National Park, India	42
2.2	Local stakeholders in Aveto Regional Park, Italy	45
2.3	Categories of institutional actors	53
2.4	Users of coastal resources in Tanga, Tanzania	54
3.1	Concepts and terms used to understand and describe collaboration in managing NR	65
4.1	Relevant social actors in Kikori watershed, Papua New Guinea	126
4.2	Developing a CM setting in the Sierra Tarahumara (Mexico): are the conditions in place?	135
4.3	Four co-management "models" in Australia	143
6.1	A strategy to reach the shared vision of Wenchi district (Ghana)	206
6.2	Benefit sharing: a company-community agreement in Cameroon	226
6.3	Five Principles of Good Governance	229
8.1	Co-management agreements and organisations	290
9.1	Soil and water conservation in southern Zimbabwe	319
9.2	Indicators to monitor agreements suggested by indigenous knowledge systems	322
9.3	Participatory methodologies and approaches: the spectrum of CM current practice	331
11.1	Examples of deliberative and inclusive processes in environmental policy making	396

BOXES

definitions & general considerations   examples from the South   examples from the North

1.1	Natural resources, property and access regimes	7
1.2	The Beni Halba Tribe– accommodating "foreigners" in resource management	9
1.3	Community tapping and management of ground water in Asia	14
2.1	Institutional actor (also "relevant social actor" or "stakeholder")	40
2.2	Indigenous peoples and mobile indigenous peoples	43
2.3	Entitlements in natural resource management	49
2.4	Social groups organised to manage forests in India	58
2.5	Forms of representation	59
2.6	Asymmetrical rights in Joint Forest Management in India	61
3.1	Co-management of natural resources	69
3.2	The boneh– a co-management system based on crop-sharing in Asia	71

3.3 Cultural co-management in Bali ... 73

3.4 Participatory research with women farmers in dry-land agriculture ... 75

3.5 Forole, the sacred mountain of the Galbo people (Ethiopia/ Kenya) ... 77

3.6 Conserving their palm groves: the pride of Gaya communities, Niger ... 79

3.7 Devolving power: a way to promote management partnerships (Madagascar) ... 80

3.8 Co-managing the Sian Ka'an Biosphere Reserve (Mexico) ... 81

3.9 Marine Co-management in Soufrière (St. Lucia) ... 83

3.10 Community based river conservation in Mandailing (North Sumatra, Indonesia) ... 85

3.11 Fishery co-management in the Mekong– Khong district (Lao PDR) ... 88

3.12 Ambondrombe (Madagascar): caring together for a sacred mountain ... 90

3.13 Private and community conservancies in Namibia ... 92

3.14 Tayna Gorilla Reserve (Democratic Republic of Congo) ... 95

3.15 The contractual approach to manage forest resources in Mali ... 99

3.16 Gwaii Haanas: the bright spot among Canada's co-managed Parks ... 101

3.17 Contested reefs in the Miskito Coast of Nicaragua: no co-management in sight! ... 105

4.1 Decentralisation? What type of decentralisation? ... 111

4.2 A natural disaster gives birth to solidarity, partnerships and participatory democracy in the Andes ... 112

4.3 Balancing the powers in Makuleke land (South Africa) ... 114

4.4 Alto Fragua Indiwasi National Park (Colombia): co-management secures land tenure and rights ... 116

4.5 "Natural" geographic units in aboriginal management systems (Canada) ... 119

4.6 Conservation of the Asiatic Cheetah in Iran– defining the management "ring" ... 120

4.7 By splitting the area into five, problems do not hamper progress in Limingalahti Bay (Finland) ... 122

4.8 The co-management conveners ... 138

4.9 Mayan resistance in Totonicapán– a gentle reverberating echo in the volcanic altiplano ... 141

4.10 The new Indigenous Protected Area model (Australia) ... 143

4.11 The Kaa-ya Iya National Park: ensuring indigenous territorial recognition in Bolivia ... 145

5.1 Participatory mapping in the Brazilian Amazon ... 148

5.2 Examples of People's Biodiversity Registers (India and Costa Rica) ... 150

5.3 Informal contacts between actors are important! ... 151

5.4 Social communication for co-management ... 152

5.5 Accompanying a new perception of problems, actors, resources and opportunities in Madagascar ... 154

5.6 Participatory land and resource mapping as an empowering, capacity building process (Venezuela) ... 158

5.7 Community organising: a powerful NRM tool in Mongolia ... 166

5.8 Organising of the Maya, between tradition and modernity (Guatemala) ... 167

5.9 What makes an organisation capable of participating in co-management? The answer of CANARI ... 169

5.10 Collective learning on collaborative management of natural resources in the Congo Basin ... 171

5.11 Community consensus on fishing rules found essential in Lao PDR ... 173

5.12 The elusive nature of the "fishing sector" in Galapagos (Ecuador) 173

5.13 Twelve tribes need twelve representatives... not ten and not fifteen! (Sudan) 176

5.14 Traditional jirga as a model for round-table meetings (Pakistan) 178

5.15 Strengthening social actors before the negotiation: the case of the Baka People of Dja (Cameroon) 185

5.16 Towards more gender- and equity-sensitive representation in Joint Forest Management (India) 186

6.1 Bicultural co-management in New Zealand 189

6.2 Setting up a partnership to manage a watershed in the USA 190

6.3 Conflict management– Chinese style 196

6.4 Conflict management– Iranian style 197

6.5 A vision for Wenchi district (Ghana) 198

6.6 A vision for Molokai (USA) 200

6.7 Involve the stakeholders and pursue a common vision! 201

6.8 Fusing the traditional and the modern to ritualise a co-management vision (Republic of Congo) 202

6.9 Leaders in the Napa Valley Watershed (California, USA) 209

6.10 Mutual trust built on the respect for local knowledge and practices in Tanga (Tanzania) 210

6.11 Consensus decision-making for aquatic resource co-management in Khong district (Lao PDR) 214

6.12 Zoning as a product of a participatory GIS in the Amazons 216

6.13 Consensus in a co-management board: a key incentive for the Galapagos Marine Reserve 217

6.14 Common themes and considerations in conflict management 220

6.15 Enhanced productive use of natural resources helps solving conflicts in Itoh (Cameroon) 222

6.16 The process we followed in Takiéta: developing a co-management setting in Niger 223

6.17 Developing an integrated, participatory development plan in Richtersveld (South Africa) 228

7.1 Customary management agreements for indigenous agriculture in the Peruvian Andes 236

7.2 Indigenous peoples' "social agreements" on natural resource management (Africa, Pacific, Amazon) 237

7.3 Resource management agreement: who has the right to speak in the Solomon Islands? 239

7.4 Village law and co-management of aquatic resources in Khong district (Lao PDR) 240

7.5 The Protocol for the Community Biodiversity Development and Conservation Programme 241

7.6 The Awa Federation and research agreements (Ecuador) 242

7.7 Conservation easements in the USA 244

7.8 "Les ententes": resource management agreements in Upper Guinea 245

7.9 Gender supportive articles in the local contract/ convention of N'Dour N'Dour (Senegal) 246

7.10 Co-management of landscapes through negotiated territorial charters in France 246

7.11 Gurig National Park (Australia) 247

7.12 The forest use agreement between Mt.Elgon and the people of Ulukusi Parish (Uganda) 249

7.13 The Agreement between Canada and the USA on the conservation of the porcupine caribou herd 250

7.14 Substantial flexibility in NRM agreements accommodates ethnic governance systems 253

7.15 An inclusive management body with consultative power for Retezat National Park (Romania) 253

7.16 Detailed co-management agreements developed for sylvo-pastoral zones in southern Mali 254

7.17 Protecting the investment 256

7.18 Canadians set priority criteria for resolving disputes about resource management 259

7.19	Co-management, the oil and gas industry and indigenous empowerment in Kaa Iya (Bolivia)	266
7.20	The 5th World Parks Congress recommendations on indigenous peoples and protected areas	272
8.1	A co-management organisation with a high-level "brokering" role (Canada)	279
8.2	An innovative co-management organisation for Waza National Park (Cameroon)	280
8.3	A new organisation co-manages a woodland in Scotland	282
8.4	Fishing associations and the co-management of freshwater ecosystems in Sweden	282
8.5	Representation of stakeholders in co-management organisations: two examples from India	283
8.6	The Dayak people co-manage the Kayan Mentarang National Park: a first in Indonesia!	284
8.7	Historical/ institutional change in the management of national forests in the western USA	286
8.8	Co-management organisations with different decision making powers: examples from Australia	287
8.9	A large scale co-management organisation in Australia's Wet Tropics World Heritage Area	287
9.1	"Levelling the playing field" for the Maori to participate...	297
9.2	Financial support from the government helps implement co-management agreements in Australia	298
9.3	The making of unsustainable livelihoods: eroding the landscape of the Oromo-Borana (Ethiopia)	300
9.4	Restoring the traditional tribal organisation– towards a Community Conserved Area in Iran	301
9.5	From social communication to negotiation to co-management in Conkouati (Republic of Congo)	303
9.6	Build on small successes in the USA	306
9.7	Signing and publicising a CM agreement in Bwindi Impenetrable National Park (Uganda)	307
9.8	The International Covenant on Civil and Political Rights	309
9.9	Enforcing co-management agreements in coastal areas: an example from the Philippines	310
9.10	Local enforcement of forest management rules in India	310
9.11	Enforcing regulation and awareness raising: two faces of the same coin (Lao PDR)	311
9.12	Learning from poor practice in participatory monitoring and evaluation	313
9.13	McKenzie Watershed Council– action at the sub-watershed level in Oregon (USA)	314
9.14	A good impact indicator: percent nutrient reduction for bay tributaries in Chesapeake Bay	318
9.15	Monitoring and evaluation of the CM agreement in Bwindi National Park (Uganda)	321
9.16	Watching for unintended and unexpected consequences...	321
9.17	Government foresters and resource management institutions in Tanzania	323
9.18	The elements of strengths of the participatory management of Galapagos Marine Reserve	323
9.19	Learning by doing in co-managing aquatic resources in Khong district (Lao PDR)	326
9.20	Villagers regenerate miombo woodlands in Tanzania	327
9.21	Debunking myths on people-environment interactions	329
9.22	Co-management of natural resources in Gujarat (India): village to village extension	332
9.23	Integrated pest management in Indonesia	333
9.24	How to spoil conservation: CM clashes against the repressive approach (Republic of Congo)	335
9.25	Learning transparency from Mahenye Ward (Zimbabwe)	337
9.26	Women design their own Public Distribution System in Andhra Pradesh, India	339

10.1   Policies defined   343

10.2   Co-management of forests and protected areas in Haiti   345

10.3   Extracts from the Constitution of Ecuador   347

10.4   Constitutional amendments encourage more devolution and subsidiarity in India   348

10.5   The National Biodiversity Strategy and Action Plan, India   349

10.6   Reforming national protected area systems   350

10.7   The Inuvialuit Agreements in the North West Territories of Canada   353

10.8   Provisions made in national legislation and specific co-management agreements   356

10.9   More perspectives on decentralisation and devolution   357

10.10 Examples of government decentralisation policies   358

10.11 Back to the marga? Reversing destructive forestry policies in Sumatra (Indonesia)   360

10.12 Discovering and recognising the cultural dimension of natural resource management   361

10.13 The demarcation and titling of indigenous land: a duty of the state?   366

10.14 The Aarhus Convention– promoting access to information, public participation and justice   367

10.15 The Tagbanwa strive for their Community Conserved Area in Coron Island (The Philippines)   368

10.16 Concentration in agri-food business sectors   373

10.17 Regulating corporations involved in natural resource sectors: some initiatives   374

10.18 Policy for local governance   375

10.19 Key rights affirmed by the UN Draft Declaration on the Rights of Indigenous Peoples   378

10.20 Ecosystem approach principles adopted as part of the Convention on Biological Diversity   380

11.1   Defining civil society   385

11.2   A history of trial by jury   391

11.3   Prajateerpu– a citizens jury/ scenario workshop in Andhra Pradesh (India)   398

11.4   Oversight and transparency in the participatory assessments of policy futures for Andhra Pradesh   402

11.5   Joint planning approaches   410

11.6   New forms of accountability   410

11.7   Participatory budgeting in Porto Alegre (Brazil)   410

11.8   Towards more inclusive representation in local government   411

11.9   The MASIPAG experience (The Philippines)   412

11.10 The Regole of the Ampezzo Valley (Italy) maintain their autonomous status for a 1000 years   414

11.11 Producer organisations, collective action and institutional transformation in West Africa   416

11.12 The Peasant Rights Movement and policy change in Indonesia   417

11.13 Beyond good governance: participatory democracy in the Philippines   418

11.14 Knowledge and power   420

11.15 Civil society imagining other possible worlds   425

ABBREVIATIONS

BATNA	Best alternative to a negotiated agreement
BR	Biosphere reserve
CAMPFIRE	Communal Areas Management Programme for Indigenous Resources
CANARI	Caribbean Natural Resources Institute
CARE	Cooperative for Assistance and Relief Everywhere
CBD	Convention on Biological Diversity
CBO	Community-based organisation
CCA	Community conserved area
CEESP	Commission on Environmental, Economic and Social Policy
CENESTA	Iranian Centre for Sustainable Development
CIPM	Community integrated pest management
CM	Co-management
CMNR	Co-management of natural resources
CMPA	Co-managed protected area
CMWG	Collaborative Management Working Group
COP	Conference of Parties
DANIDA	Danish International Development Agency
DGIS	Dutch Development Cooperation Agency
DIP	Deliberative and inclusionary processes
EPA	Environmental Protection Agency
EU	European Union
FAO	Food and Agriculture Organisation of the United Nations
FD	Forestry department
FPC	Forest protection committee
GEF	Global Environment Facility
GIS	Geographic information system
GM	Genetically modified
GMO	Genetically modified organism
GPS	Global positioning system
GTZ	German Development Cooperation Agency
ICCPR	International Covenant on Civil and Political Rights
ICDP	Integrated conservation and development project
IDS	Institute of Development Studies
IFAD	International Fund for Agricultural Development
IFOAM	International Forum for Organic Agriculture
ICESCR	International Covenant on Economic, Social, and Cultural Rights
IIED	International Institute for Environment and Development
ILO	International Labour Organisation
IPA	Indigenous protected area
IPM	Integrated pest management
IPR	Intellectual property right
IRRI	International Rice Research Institute
IUCN	The World Conservation Union
JFM	Joint forest management
JPAM	Joint protected area management

MAB	Man and the Biosphere
NBSAP	National biodiversity strategy and action plan
NEAP	National environmental action plan
NGO	Non-governmental organisation
NR	Natural resource
NRM	Natural resource management
OECD	Organisation for Economic Cooperation and Development
PA	Protected area
PAR	Participatory action research
PDR	People's Democratic Republic
PIC	Prior informed consent
PLA	Participatory learning and action
PMA	Park management authority
PNR	Parc naturel régional
PO	Producer organisation
PRA	Participatory rural appraisal
PRSP	Poverty reduction strategy paper
R&D	Research and development
RRA	Rapid rural appraisal
SAM	Special area management
SIDA	Swedish International Development Agency
SWOL	Strengths, weaknesses, opportunities and limitations
SWOT	Strengths, weaknesses, opportunities and threats
TNC	Trans national corporation
TRIP	Trade related intellectual property right
UDHR	Universal Declaration of Human Rights
UK	United Kingdom
UN	United Nations
UNCTAD	United Nations Conference on Trade and Development
UNDP	United Nations Development Programme
UNEP	United Nations Environment Programme
UNESCO	United Nations Educational, Scientific and Cultural Organisation
UNHCR	United Nations High Commission for Refugees
UNICEF	United Nations Children's Fund
US	United States
USA	United States of America
USD	United States dollar
WAMIP	World Alliance of Mobile Indigenous Peoples
WCS	Wildlife Conservation Society
WHA	World heritage area
WHO	World Health Organisation
WSSD	World Summit on Sustainable Development
WTO	World Trade Organisation
WWF	World Wide Fund for Nature

FOREWORD by Juan Mayr Maldonado

"Sharing Power" should be required reading for all of us who, in one way or another, are involved at the local, national or international level in the governance and management of natural resources. But this volume should also be read by those who gain economic benefits from natural resources at a distance thanks to the sophisticated technology of communications and marketing systems. Most of these people are deeply indebted to the labour and creativity of rural communities, whose livelihoods are inextricably related to the natural resources and ecosystems in the different regions of the planet. Above all this volume is a tribute and recognition to the traditional knowledge, rights, skills and institutions of indigenous peoples and local communities and to their daily struggles for a balance between their immediate needs and long term well-being, founded on the sound and sustainable management of our planet's natural wealth.

From a recollection of the political and socio-cultural history of human relationships with nature, the volume moves into a more conceptual analysis of actors, entitlements, equity and co-management itself. Through a series of illuminating examples characterised by cultural and regional diversity, the authors show us the impacts, tensions, inequalities and opportunities that inhabit the field of natural resource management and bear such important consequences for the livelihoods and quality of life of rural communities. Co-management as a process is then unpacked and explored in detail, from its roots in local systems of solidarity to the unlikely and very powerful "syncretic" merging of traditional practices and modern conservation expertise. As a matter of fact, when we are lucky enough to approach sound contemporary natural resource management, this looks more and more like a jigsaw puzzle of new and old knowledge, indigenous and modern elements, practices and values of different "cultural" origin. As in all processes of cultural change, we find in it contradictions and chaotic situations and, exactly because of this, the concept and practice of adaptive management become crucial. This should be appreciated in terms of both conceptual and practical relevance, as top-down inflexible and supposedly a-political decisions have indeed past their time.

For practitioners in search of an open and flexible guide to co-management practice on the basis of lessons learned in a variety of socio-ecological settings, this volume simply has no equal. The "phases" of the process– organising, negotiating, implementing agreements and learning by doing– as well as the agreements and organisations they usually end up developing, are described and appreciated through a wealth of examples, tools and sound advice. The authors have obviously in mind the real world, where nothing is univocal and fixed and where complications abound as well as unexpected opportunities. The product is a creative tension between realities and visions, what is and what could be, especially in response to external forces and the continual demographic, social, economic and cultural changes that affect both local communities and other actors, and natural resources. If anything, one could fault the authors for being too positive, for compelling us to believe that, even in the worst possible situation, change is possible. But this may be more a consequence of the invigorating feeling that the reader carries away from the reading than of the content of the volume in itself. Examples of problems and failures, in fact, abound, and they are candidly recounted....

It is on the basis of a world perceived in a state of evolution and creative tension that the political proposal for co-management illustrated in this volume– because this is what it is– becomes most compelling. Co-management can involve the gradual harmonising, balancing and adjustment of the interests, aspirations and capacities of a variety of actors both within rural communities and in the world at large. The lamp-posts are intelligence, care and equity– the exact opposite of situations in which the stronger forces impose their will on the weaker ones without regard to understandings, results or even meaning, let alone sustainability. The practices that are here described to make a difference are a careful assessment of issues, dialogue, negotiation, the active mediation of conflicts and the nurturing of joint learning. But we would be wrong if we would think that this applies only to specific contexts where local actors are concerned, let us say, with a specific forest, a pastoral landscape, a rare species of wildlife or a rich coastal fishery. "Sharing power" makes a compelling case that continuous engagement of actors and learning must extend to the policy arena, beyond the command and control operations of policy specialists and non-participatory elected leaders.

"Sharing Power" is an important contribution to environmental thinking and reflection, at a time of great political and economic challenges throughout the world. It invites us to, and equips us for, a dialogue among different cultures, being those of neighbours or of distant actors, in a respectful and equitable search for new forms of natural resource management. I do not advise you to read this volume cover-to-cover– although you may want to!– but I definitely advise you to go through it, be inspired to understand what it contains, and keep it on your desktop. You will find yourself consulting it over and over again when you need inspiration and practical help about more cooperative ways of managing natural resources.

Juan Mayr Maldonado

Member of the Blue Ribbon Panel for environmental policy advice to the President of the IDB
Member of the Panel of Eminent Advisors to the UN Secretary General
on UN-Civil Society Relationships
Former Minister of Environment, Colombia
President of the Extraordinary Session of the Convention on Biological Diversity–
Cartagena Protocol on Biosafety
Deputy Chair of IUCN Commission on Environmental, Economic and Social Policy

PREFACE & ACKNOWLEDGEMENTS

This volume had a long gestation. It was conceived in the first half of the 1990s, at a time when the social innovations introduced by the 1992 Earth Summit of Rio were timidly percolating amidst the conservation community. A large part of such community, actually, was still openly weary of participatory processes, let alone co-management settings. Discussing issues of equity and power-sharing in conservation was an uphill job, and social advocacy was barely tolerated. The heart of conservation institutions and resources remained solidly in the hands of conservation businessmen, agency bureaucrats and biological scientists.

It was in this context that Grazia and Michel, at the time staff of the World Conservation Union (IUCN) and the World Wide Fund for Nature (WWF International),[1] decided to gather experiences in collaborative management (CM) of natural resources and derive from those some concrete lessons for action. They felt that unspecific advocacy about "community participation" was not sufficient and potentially even damaging. At the same time, the promises as well as the limitations of integrated conservation and development programmes (ICDPs) were becoming apparent, as was the need to utilise more specific methods and tools to engage a variety of social actors in conservation. Crucial issues were not only "participation" (how can people be effectively engaged in conservation?) but also the meeting of local needs in the areas to be conserved, and how to do so in a way that is sustainable in the long term.[2] Interestingly, community empowerment, social justice and human rights, which were the origin and essence of those concerns, could barely be mentioned in an open way. Such terms were not well received in conservation organisations and speaking them was a sure way to raise a backlash.

> ...unspecific advocacy about "community participation" was not sufficient and potentially even damaging.

The first step towards this volume was a questionnaire which was sent, in three languages, to hundreds of field practitioners of both organisations. The inquiry was about the kind of information and tools sought by IUCN and WWF field practitioners. What would practically help them in their tasks, when dealing with social concerns in conservation? It was also about the experiences and lessons they wished to pass on and share with others. In the meantime, the IUCN was heading towards its first World Conservation Congress, in Montreal in 1996. In the preparatory process, about fifty IUCN members joined efforts to draft and table a Resolution on Collaborative Management for Conservation, which was then approved by the Congress.[3] As part of this, ideas, case examples and reflections on CM were gathered, some of which in the form of papers to be presented

---

[1]   Grazia was then Head of the IUCN Social Policy Programme, and Michel was Head of the Biodiversity, Protected Areas and Species Conservation Policy Programme at WWF International.

[2]   These are dealt with at length in Pimbert and Pretty,1995; Borrini-Feyerabend, 1997; Ghimire and Pimbert, 1997.

[3]   IUCN Resolution 1.42 on Collaborative Management for Conservation, 1st World Conservation Congress, Montreal, 1996.

[Concepts of] community empowerment, social justice and human rights... were not well received in conservation organisations....

at the Congress in a dedicated workshop that attracted hundreds of participants. A Panel of IUCN Commission members interested in collaborative management was also created at the Congress, with Fikret Berkes and Yves serving as its first Co-chairs. Ashish was also importantly involved in the Congress workshop and in the CM Panel. The replies to the questionnaire, the papers, the relevant correspondence and the results of literature searches carried out also with the help of members of the IUCN Commission on Environmental, Economic and Social Policy (CEESP) working as consultants, volunteers and interns were consolidated in a small CM resource centre at the IUCN Headquarters.

Very many people played an important role in gathering and consolidating information and encouraging work in the early stages described above. Among them we would like to thank in particular Fikret Berkes, Christian Erni, Don Gilmour, Pascal Girot, Magnus Ngoile, Hanna Jaireth, Vicky Pattemore and Patrizio Warren. Their early encouragement and the specific experience and insights they shared with us were extremely precious. Many others were also variously involved and we are most grateful for the important ideas and advice they provided. They include Anil Agarwal, Janis Alcorn, Ivannia Ayales, Demba Baldé, Siddarta Bajracharya, Tom Barton, Michael Beresford, Anupam Bhatia, Seema Bhatt, Jessica Brown, Michael Brown, Dianne Buchan, Claudio Carrera Maretti, Monica Castelo, Michael Cernea, Carol Colfer, Gloria Davis, Alex de Sherbinin, Charles Doumenge, Gay Duke, Eduardo Fernandez, Bob Fisher, Krishna Ghimire, Lyle Glowka, Meghan Golay, Hugh Govan, Biksham Gujja, Roy Hagen, Narpat Jhoda, Kirsten Hegener, Peter Hislaire, Michael Horowitz, Chris Horrill, P. Horsey, Ruud Jansen, Sally Jeanrenaud, Andrew Inglis, Aban Kabraji, Graeme Kelleher, Elisabeth Kemf, Omar Asghar Khan, Larry Kholer, John Krijnen, Michel Kouda, Patricia Larson, Connie Lewis, Ken MacDonald, Jeff McNeely, Patricia Madrigal, Juan Mayr Maldonado, Rowan Martin, Robert Monro, Arthur Mugisha, Marshall Murphree, James Murombedzi, Jackson Mutebi, Gayl Ness, Samuel-Alain Nguiffo, Krishna Oli, Elinor Ostrom, Gonzalo Oviedo, Adrian Phillips, Mark Poffenberger, Tom Price, Ricardo Ramírez, Per Ryden, Bob Pomeroy, Darrell Posey, Mohammad Rafiq, Gabriella Richardson, Guillermo Rodriguez-Navarro, Rodney Salm, Richard Sandbrook, Madhu Sarin, Lea Scherl, Steve Selin, Andrea Simoncini, Vivienne Solis, Andrej Sovinc, Achim Steiner, Chip Temm, Petr Tengler, Anada Tiega, John Thompson, Jim Thorsell, Edgardo Tongson, Jan Teun Vissher, Joyce Wafula, Lini Wollenberg, Jacques Weber, Liz Wily, Nick Winer, Sejal Worah, Barbara Wyckoff-Baird and Marija Zupancic Vicar.

On the basis of the collected materials, Grazia, Michel and Ashish produced a draft of this volume at the end of 1997. The document was widely circulated in 1998 and the comments received were poignant and useful for the versions to come. Among those, we have the great pleasure of acknowledging the reviews by Carmen Aalbers, Anil Agarwal, Ed Barrow, Marcus Cochester, Christo Fabricious, Andrea Finger, Ian Scoones, Neena Singh, Vital Rajan and Peter Schachenmann. Grazia, Michel and Ashish set to revise the work on the basis of the received comments but the task proved more difficult than expected. Both Grazia and Michel– some say precisely because of the key interests and concerns they brought into their jobs– were no longer employed by IUCN and WWF, which rendered the book a full labour of volunteer love. More importantly, a staggering amount of relevant experiences and lessons was accumulating in the field. Co-management was literally growing under our eyes, and taking on new connotations at every turn. The human rights dimensions of conservation, environmental entitlements, social communication, conflict management, public participation in policy development and many other subjects were being explored in detail by specific constituencies. The subject of our book was dangerously (but excitingly) enlarging....

It was then that the second phase of our work began. On the eve of the second World Conservation Congress (Amman, 2000), which reconfirmed the importance of co-management approaches for conservation,[4] Grazia, Michel, Yves and Taghi– newly elected Chair of CEESP– had a meeting in Switzerland to review the fate of the earlier work on co-management. Over a decade earlier, Taghi had been one of IUCN's earliest and strongest advocates of communities as key actors in natural resource management and conservation. With him as Chair of CEESP, they all felt more hopeful that community concerns could be incorporated in the work of the Union, and were encouraged to proceed with the book. They agreed to gather and synthesise as much new relevant material as they could, privileging field-based lessons for action over theoretical analyses. From the institutional point of view they were going to be supported by the International Institute for Environment and Development (IIED), for which Michel was then working and, as all were long-time members of CEESP, they could also take on writing as volunteers or semi-volunteers for the Commission. Eleven chapters were thus "re-conceived", and the book took its final form.

> The subject of our book was dangerously (but excitingly) enlarging.

Grazia took responsibility for Chapters 1 to 6 and weaved in the contributions by Marshall Murphree, Patrizio Warren, Ricardo Ramírez and Taghi. Michel took responsibility for Chapters 7 to 9, in contact with Hanna Jaireth and Vicky Pattemore. Yves and Michel took responsibility for Chapters 10 and 11, in which they also incorporated the work originally prepared by Ashish and some more recent comments from him. Taghi and Yves, and then Grazia, revised and harmonised the whole. The work for the book proceeded slowly– not least because all the authors were engaged in much CM-related work, in policy and in practice. It was punctuated by a handful of meetings, but most communication proceeded via e-mail. All throughout, invaluable stirring and inspiration were provided by many colleagues through the "sounding board" of the Collaborative Management Working Group (CMWG) of CEESP– a body now encompassing nearly 400 people from over 40 countries dedicated to learning, mutual support and action on co-management.[5]

Among the CMWG members and other colleagues we have consulted and worked with in these last years, we would like to acknowledge with gratitude Cherif Abdellatif, Yéyé Abdoulaye, Mady Abdhoulanzis, Peter Abrams, Abdul Rahman Al Eryani, Janis Alcorn, Inayat Ali, Will Allen, Miguel Altieri, Thora Amend, Bruce Amos, Alejandro Argumedo, Karin Augustat, Didier Babin, Ian Baird, Richard Baker, Tariq Banuri, Chip Barber, Solon Barraclough, Ed Barrow, Christian Barthod, Marco Bassi, Seema Bhatt, Eléonore Béchaux, M'hamed Bendanoon, Judithe Bizot, Tom Blomley, Luigi Boitani, Gianfranco Bologna, Juan Bottasso, Mohamed Nagy Ould Bouceif, Steve Brechin, Dan Brockington, Pete Brosius, Jessica Brown, Michael Brown, Nicole Brown, Martin Bush, Ralph Buss, David Butz, Pierre Campredon, Christian Castellanet, Claudio Carrera Maretti, Michael Cernea, Moreno Chiovoloni, Christian Chatelain, Dawn Chatty, Purna Chhetri, Brian Child, Maurilio Cipparone, Marcus Colchester, Steve Collins,

---

4   IUCN Resolution 2.15 on Collaborative Management for Conservation Programme, 2nd World Conservation Congress, Amman, October 2000.

5   See http://www.iucn.org/themes/ceesp/Wkg_grp/CMWG/CMWG.htm

...invaluable stirring and inspiration were provided by many colleagues through the "sounding board" of the Collaborative Management Working Group....

Gordon Conway, Gillian Cooper, Roger Croft, Alex de Sherbinin, David E. De Vera, Nelson Diaz, Chimère Diaw, Antonio Carlos Diegues, Joanna Durbin, Olivier Dubois, Nigel Dudley, Cristina Eghenter, Azizou El Hadj Issa, Barbara Ehringhaus, Christian Erni, Arturo Escobar, Maria Fernanda Espinosa, James Everett, Kirsten Ewers, Maurizio Farhan Ferrari, Andrea Finger-Stich, Bob Fisher, Phil Franks, Kathryn Furlong, Roberto Gambino, Norbert Gami, Chachu Gangya, Julia Gardner, Jean Marc Garreau, Eric E. Garret, Tighe Geoghegan, Krishna Ghimire, Mario González Martín, Hugh Govan, Christiane and Diego Gradis, Jacques Grinevald, Salah Hakim, Mark and Maria Halle, Olivier Hamerlynck, Kirsten Hegener, Augusta Henriquez, Abdellah Herzenni, Ced Hesse, Pippa Heylings, Thea Hilhorst, Mark Hockings, Tarita Holm, Clarisse Honadia Kambou, Jon Hutton, David Hughes, Mark Infield, Andrew Inglis, Jeremy Ironside, Tilman Jaeger, Sally Jeanrenaud, Jim Johnston, Brian Jones, Marilee Kane, Graeme Kelleher, Sandra Kloff, Andrea Knierim, Michel Kouda, Juliette Koudenoukpo Biao, Roger Kouokam, Vijay Krishnarayan, Franco La Cecla, Sarah Laird, Alain Lambert, Patricia Lamelas, Charles Lane, Jean Larivière, Jannie Lasimbang, Andrew Long, Stefano Lorenzi, Marc and Jacqueline Lucet, Andres Luque, Ken MacDonald, Rolf Mack, Francine Madden, Patricia Madrigal, Luisa Maffi, Will Maheia, Abdul Karim Mamalo, Kathy Mangonès, Sheldon Margen, Kwabena Mate, Aldo Matteucci, Juan Mayr Maldonado, Jeff McNeely, Ricardo Melendez, Kenton Miller, Saliou Miscouna, Andrew Mittleman, Rob Monro, Oliviero Montanaro, Antonino Morabito, James Murombedzi, Kawar (Rani) Mumtaz, Alejandro Nadal, Nahid Naghizadeh, Anoushirvan Najafi, Vincent Ndangang, Gayl Ness, Linda Neuhauser, Daniel Ngantou, Jean Claude Nginguiri, Maryam Niamir-Fuller, Léon Nkantio, Josiane Olff-Nathan, Krishna Oli, Elinor Ostrom, Gonzalo Oviedo, Pierre Oyo, Diane Pansky, Neema Pathak, Tonino Perna, Adrian Phillips, David Pitt, Darrel Posey, Thomas Price, Hanta Rabetaliana, Aghaghia Rahimzadeh, Maryam Rahmanian, Claudine Ramiarison, Ricardo Ramírez, Vololona Rasoarimanana, Shah Rehman, Juan Carlos Riascos, Liz Rihoy, Juan Rita Larrucea, Hernan Rodas, Dilys Roe, Guillermo Rodriguez Navarro, José Sanchez Parga, Park Poffenberger, Madhu Sarin, Trevor Sandwith, David Satterthwaite, Peter Schachenmann, Lea Scherl, Sabine Schmidt, David Sheppard, Ole Simel, Allan Smith, Dermot Smyth, Lars Soeftestad, Hadi Soleimanpour, Vivienne Solis Rivera, Sayyaad Soltani, Andrej Sovinc, Erika Stanciu, Achim Steiner, Rick Steiner, Sue Stolton, Boku Tache, Giuliano Tallone, Marcel Taty, Martjin ter Heegde, Jan Tersdad, Ibrahim Thiaw, Anada Tiega, Camilla Toulmin, Alex Triantafyllidis, Manuel Valdés-Pizzini, Ileana Valenzuela, Jorge Varela, Kit Vaughan, Sonia Vermeulen, Gill and Kees Vogt, Pier Carlo Zingari, Marjia Zupancic-Vicar, Patrizio Warren, Michael Watts, Jacques Weber, Webster Whande, Nathalie Whitfield, Clive Wicks, Andy Wilson, Liz Alden Wily and Nick Winer.

We are very grateful to all the sponsors of this volume. Early work was made possible thanks to the support provided by the Danish Development Agency (DANIDA) to the then Social Policy Programme of IUCN. Most subsequent work was carried out on a volunteer or semi-volunteer basis as part of the initiatives of the IUCN Commission on Environmental, Economic and Social Policy (CEESP). This publication is made possible by grants from the Swedish International Development Agency (Sida) and the Dutch Development Cooperation (DGIS) in support to IIED's work on the co-management of biodiversity and natural resources as part of on-going action research on food, agriculture and livelihood security and by a grant from the German Technical Cooperation Agency (GTZ) to

CMWG/ CEESP as part of their on-going encouragement to learning the lessons of collaborative management of natural resources in several regions of the world.

We also warmly thank Jeyran Farvar and Fabrice Prati for art work and layout and Hoonam Publishing Services in Tehran, which did the lithography and printing under the technical supervision and management of CENESTA– the Iranian Centre for Sustainable Development– host to the IUCN Commission on Environmental, Economic and Social Policy.

Our special gratitude and admiration go the multitude of indigenous peoples, local communities and enlightened government and NGO staff who have shown the way to wise co-management of natural resources and who have provided the rich base of experience, practice and policy we have documented here. We hope to have done at least partial justice to their efforts and work.

After these several years of gestation, we confide this volume to print and to its readers with joy and some sense of relief. May it be useful!

Grazia Borrini-Feyerabend,
Michel Pimbert,
Taghi Farvar,
Ashish Kothari,
Yves Renard

INTRODUCTION

The natural and social calamities pass away. Whole populations are periodically reduced to misery and starvation: the very springs of life are crushed out of millions of men, reduced to city paupers; the understanding and the feelings of the millions are vitiated by the teachings worked out in the interest of the few. All this is certainly part of our existence. But the nucleus of mutual support institutions, habits and customs remains alive with the millions; it keeps them together…. In the practice of mutual aid, which we can retrace to the earliest beginning of evolution, we see the origins of our ethical conceptions; and in the progress of man, mutual support– not mutual struggle– has had the leading part. In its wide extension, even at the present time, we find the best guarantee of a still loftier evolution of our race.

– Petr Kropotkin, 1902

Nothing truly valuable can be achieved
except by the unselfish cooperation of many individuals.

– Albert Einstein, 1940

The history of mutual aid and collective action in social and ecological affairs is as ancient as human life. For many thousands of years, human communities established their livelihoods by gathering, hunting and fishing in a collective fashion. Human collaboration within small groups was essential to recognise edible and medicinal plants as well as to overpower animals, build shelter or find and carry water. Through time, "communities" gained their livelihoods by dealing together with the natural threats and opportunities in their surroundings, by developing productive technologies and practices and by producing knowledge and culture in the same process. A feature of most traditional human societies throughout the world is to retain under common property– thus common care and "management"– pasture, forests, fisheries, wildlife and wetlands, including lakes and rivers. Such communal resources are subjected to a variety of rules and regulations devised by the communities themselves, usually embedded in institutions that prove their worth through centuries of trial and errors. For the distant past much of this is inferred from indirect data, but in time closer to us historical evidence abounds of human associations for various livelihood enterprises. In Mutual Aid, first published in 1902, Petr Kropotkin draws from the history of guilds and unions in Europe, from travel and colonial accounts

...the more difficult the natural environment, the more necessary is cooperation among the members of a species to be able to survive and prosper.

outside Europe, from the experience of village communities everywhere and even from the biological realm at large, to show how collaboration and mutual support are at the heart of whatever makes our species successful. As a biologist, he stressed that, the more difficult the natural environment, the more necessary is cooperation among the members of a species to be able to survive and prosper.

Negotiated agreements on the roles, rights and responsibilities of different actors in a common enterprise are at the heart of the forms of collaboration described by Kropotkin and celebrated by some of the most imaginative and engaged members of the human race. We have been moved and inspired by the immense richness of the human experience that stirred these insights, and brought to explore contemporary forms of group collaboration and lessons learned along the way. This volume is the result of our efforts in bringing together accounts and reflections on a variety of partnerships for the management of natural resources in different social and ecological contexts, based on both our own experiences and the very rich experience of others. The volume has inevitable limitations and we are aware that we have just touched upon the wealth of existing relevant experiences and insights. We still hope, however, to have provided a stepping stone towards a better understanding of co-management (CM) of natural resources (NR) for conservation, livelihoods, and development purposes.

Social organisation for the management of natural resources is a fundamental attribute of human communities. Not all social responses to resource management challenges, however, achieve appropriate or effective results. Violent conflicts, extreme inequities in access to natural resources, instances of people scrambling for resources in open access situations or major development schemes delivering environmental and human tragedies too often do occur, ushering in human and environmental tragedies. What do we know about the root causes of such tragedies? What distinguishes social progress from destructive change?

The analysis of the experiences collected in this volume seems to suggest that problems often arise when change is imposed by force or is hurried through, without the benefit of slow advances and testing through time. Many such changes are part of a socio-political shift of historical proportion currently well advanced throughout the world. From the early agrarian and industrial revolutions to the current dominance of the global agro-industrial-market system, peasants have been progressively reduced in relative numbers, involved in cash crop production and grown dependent on mechanised implements, oil, pesticides, fertilisers and abundant water. Nomadic pastoralists have been forced to settle and become dependent on imported feed for their animals. Hunter-gatherers have also been constrained to settle, become farmers (or "poachers") and link to market economies. The loss of power of local communities has corresponded to a rise in power of national states and private individuals and corporations. New state bureaucracies and economic enterprises, associated with monolithic views of progress and rational order, have expropriated from indigenous and local communities many of the decisions and privileges that used to be their own.[1] From the "scramble for Africa" to the top-down declaration of state jurisdiction on forests, rangelands, waters and coastal resources in Asia, from the state collectivisation of farms and natural resources in the Soviet Union to the imposition of huge-agribusiness ventures upon the common lands of Latin America, from

...problems often arise when change is imposed by force or is hurried through, without the benefit of slow advances and testing through time. Many such changes are part of a socio-political shift of historical proportion currently well advanced throughout the world.

---

[1]   See the very pertinent analysis of Scott, 1998.

the forced resettlement of nomadic populations in Iran, Turkey, Central Asia and East Africa to the destruction of ancient villages to make room for obscenely anonymous apartment complexes in Rumania– rural communities[2] have been dis-empowered and, in the words of Banuri and Amalric,[3] "de-responsibilised" of taking care of much of their own environment and livelihoods. The phenomenon can be seen as part of the "great transformation" described by Karl Polanyi,[4] by which an idealised economic rationality has been slowly but steadily negating and crushing a whole range of other human and social values and areas of autonomy. Other authors emphasised the scope of this historical process of sweeping and authoritarian domestication of people and nature, highlighting how it influenced biological and cultural diversity, local (community) knowledge and skills, human well being, "common sense" and even the nature of scientific inquiry.[5]

The "great transformation" brought about a variety of consequences throughout the world, among which the fact that many customary and community-based natural resource management (NRM) systems have been overlooked, negated or simply crushed in the name of modernisation and development. Nature has become a collection of "natural resources", to be "managed" through "dismembering" and extreme biological and social simplification in the interest of producing commodities.[6] Many rural communities are no longer in charge of managing their natural resources, and, importantly, they are not "trusted" by state bureaucracies to be able to do so.[7] Their inventiveness and autonomy are brushed aside in the name of state rationality, economic development and conservation. Their viable, relatively simple to operate, modest and time-tested solutions to natural resource management problems, embedded in unique local knowledge and skills, are substituted by powerful and locally-untested solutions, based on a-local ("scientific") understanding of how nature should be managed and "conserved". While the character of rural environments changes under these forces, urban environments are also created or enormously expanded, resulting in new demands and challenges for people. Increasingly, in both rural and urban systems, success is defined in economic terms and the collateral damages in terms of human and cultural losses[8] are perceived as inevitable side effects.

> Many rural communities are no longer "in charge" of managing their natural resources, and... not "trusted" by state bureaucracies to be able to do so.

Is the phenomenon unstoppable and irreversible? Should we all resign ourselves to it? But also: is the phenomenon entirely negative and destructive? Or are there also positive changes brought about by the rise of national states, private enterprises, new technologies and globalisation? As always in human phenomena, matters are not sharply defined and history presents us with a never-ending coex-

---

2   We understand as "community" a human group sharing a territory and involved in different but related aspects of livelihoods– such as managing natural resources, producing knowledge and culture and developing productive technologies and practices. Communities are by no means homogenous, and harbour complex socio-political relations, with diverging and sometimes conflicting views, needs and expectations. Yet, they have major common concerns which, in healthy situations, lead towards various forms of collaboration and cohesion. Examples may be found in Ralston et al., 1983; Reader, 1990; Ghai and Vivian, 1992; Pye Smith et al., 1994; Western and Wright, 1994; Borrini-Feyerabend et al., 2004, (in press); and in this volume.

3   Banuri and Amalric, 1992.

4   Polanyi, 1944.

5   Gramsci, 1947; Goodman and Goodman, 1947; Farvar and Milton, 1972; Georgescu-Roegen, 1971; Mumford, 1971; Illich, 1973; Schumacher, 1973; Berger, 1976; Dupuy and Robert, 1976; Foucault,1977; Hyden, 1980; Merchant, 1980; Franke and Chasin, 1980; Bookchin, 1982; Bodley, 1982; Ralston et al., 1983; Watts, 1983b; Jackson et al., 1984; Richards, 1985; Escobar, 1985; Crosby, 1988; Lindblom, 1988; Gould, 1989; Harvey, 1989; Hacking, 1990; Appfel Marglin and Marglin, 1990; Rosaldo, 1993; Netting, 1993; Altieri, 1995; Scott, 1998; Feyerabend, 1999; Colchester, 2003.

6   Merchant, 1980; Bookchin, 1982; Scott, 1998.

7   This is one of the important insights masterly illustrated by Scott (1998). As a result of this active disempowering, which in some places has been going on for a long time, human communities may have become all but capable of managing their environments and/ or sharing management rights and responsibilities with others.

8   See the lucid description by Berger (1976).

istence of tragedies and miracles of ingenuity and personal and collective strength. In this volume we refrain from interpreting or judging phenomena of historical proportions. We rather wish to point at specific examples of "values in action", instances in which people and nature found remarkable ways of organising their co-existence. Indeed, despite adverse forces of great proportions, local communities are still able to discern and adjust, they can merge their unique heritage with innovations and new structural conditions, they can "re-organise" themselves, re-conquer memories, skills, information, rights. These communities adapt themselves, develop new capacities and weave political and economic alliances with new actors, including state governments, international organisations, individual and corporate businesses. New and at times experimental partnerships are central to these phenomena, involving extensive dialogue and action-research and the recognition, understanding and reconciliation of a multiplicity of capacities and comparative advantages. Traditional knowledge and skills, in particular, are set to work within changed environmental, political and social contexts, including "science-based" innovations. Instead of witnessing the death of local communities in natural resource management we witness at times the birth of many forms of social "syncretism" and synergy– the wise merging of features from different origins. This is at the heart of what we understand as "co-management" in this volume– a process of collective understanding and action by which human communities and other social actors manage natural resources and ecosystems together, drawing from everyone's unique strengths, vantage points and capacities.

> Instead of witnessing the death of local communities in natural resource management we witness at times the birth of many forms of social "syncretism" and synergy– the wise merging of features from different origins.

This said, we should also stress that our understanding of co-management is not restricted to state-community partnerships. Co-management approaches can be and are applied among and within communities as well. For indigenous peoples in particular, co-management processes, albeit rarely described with this name, are part of traditional ways of relating with common property natural resources and with community conserved areas.[9] In such indigenous versions of co-management, the national state is often not present as a partner because it is perceived as non-legitimate or irrelevant or antithetical to indigenous peoples' self-determination. In this volume, therefore, we do not necessarily refer to co-management as a state-led or even a state-involving process. While we include such cases, we also bring in many instances of cooperative decision-making concerning natural resources held in common property regimes among two or more communities, or between communities and private, NGO, or international actors, or including only interest groups within a local community.

We believe our "open" understanding of the co-management concept is helpful to situate it in a historical context and to avoid using it in a restrictive sense, which is a real possibility as the term, along with the term "partnership", is becoming accepted jargon and even a buzzword. In this sense, we wish to contribute to an empowering adoption of the approach by national decision-makers and, most of all, by indigenous and local communities and civil society at large. We wish this volume to contribute to disseminating valuable experiences, enhancing reflection and capacities, and promoting inter-cultural and international comparison and cross-fertilisation. As "explicit" partnerships to manage natural resources are a growing phenomenon throughout the world[10] and as critical environmental and social situations clamour for action, we believe that our attempt to systematise the co-management concept and practice has a chance to be useful.

---

9   Posey, 1999; Kothari, 2004; Borrini-Feyerabend et al., 2004 (in press).
10 But they are not a new phenomenon, as described in Chapter 1.

An idea whose time has come

Several reasons help to explain the current interest in the co-management of natural resources for both conservation and livelihood purposes. Among those:

1. Extensive conflicts in the development and conservation arena. Top down, imposed development and conservation schemes all too often entail huge social and ecological costs, especially in areas where people are directly dependent on natural resources for their livelihoods. For instance, a growing body of evidence indicates that many state-based development and conservation projects have brought serious adverse effects on the food security and livelihoods of people living in and around major infrastructures or protected areas and wildlife management schemes.[11] Local communities have faced loss of land and restrictions in their use of common property resources for food gathering, harvest of medicinal plants, grazing, fishing, hunting, collection of wood and other wild products from forests, wetlands and pastoral lands. Development enterprises, infrastructures or national parks have denied local resource rights, turning local people overnight from hunters, pastoralists, sea nomads and cultivators into "poachers", "invaders" and "squatters".[12] Resettlement schemes for indigenous peoples removed from areas earmarked for development or conservation have had devastating consequences.[13] No wonder, there are serious conflicts between indigenous and local communities and development managers or park authorities. Such conflicts are burning in many contexts, too often side by side precious natural resources, biodiversity and ecosystem services that should be carefully used and conserved. Co-management processes often provide answers to these conflicts or at least a forum where different views can be vented and confronted, and where conciliation can be attempted.

2. Increased complexity and uncertainty of ecosystem and natural resource management questions. Policy processes and resource management regimes involve making decisions under conditions of uncertainty, being largely unable to predict the effects of different courses of action. Indeed, many past and current conflicts in development and conservation have come from the failure of management agencies to accept and embrace this complexity and this uncertainty even in "simple" systems. The science of parts (reductionism), as opposed to knowledge and ways of knowing that integrate the parts, has largely failed to come to terms with dynamic complexity[14] and variation within and among ecosystems. Global environmental change and human-made risks, such as climate change or interactions among genetically modified organisms (GMOs) and the environment at large, exacerbate these variations and uncertainties.[15] In addition, the perceptions of both problems and solutions are value laden and differ enormously within society,[16] and "experts" seem no longer better equipped than any other groups to decide on questions of values and interests. All of the above emphasises the need for flexible responses and adaptive management of natural resources, which can best be

> At the heart of what we understand as "co-management" ...[is] a process of collective understanding and action by which human communities and other social actors manage natural resources and ecosystems together, drawing from everyone's unique strengths, vantage points and capacities.

---

11 Cernea, 1985; Kothari et al., 1989; West and Brechin, 1991; Wells and Brandon, 1992; IIED, 1995; Pimbert and Pretty, 1995; Ghimire and Pimbert, 1997.

12 McIvor, 1997; Koch, 1997; Colchester, 2003.

13 Cernea and Schmidt-Soltau, 2003.

14 Variation in response to the same change is enormous in both organisms and biological systems, with daily, seasonal and longer term modifications apparent from the broad landscape to the small cultivated plot. See Gunderson et al., 1995; Holling et al., 1998.

15 The conventional approaches of risk management and cost benefit analysis become more apparently inadequate when "we don't know what we don't know" and where "we don't know the probabilities of possible outcomes".

16 Pimbert and Wakeford, 2001a.

grounded on customary practices and participatory learning and action.[17] In facing these challenges, co-management processes and flexible institutional agreements are increasingly sought to assure new forms of dialogue and participatory decision-making, responsive to the particular contexts.[18]

3. Globalisation and decentralisation phenomena. Local resource users and their communities are increasingly caught in the contradictions of global governance systems. Whilst some trends towards devolution and decentralisation foster local awareness and empowerment processes, the global rules of the World Trade Organisation (WTO), the agreements of the Trade Related Intellectual Property Rights (TRIPs) such as for patents on seeds and medicinal plants, the concentration of economic power in the hands of trans-national corporations (TNCs) and finance markets, and the current widespread privatisation trends related to land, water, forests and public services add to the undermining of community control over natural resources, knowledge and institutions.[19] In the conservation arena, while protected areas demand high management investments by governments and sacrifices by local communities, the majority of benefits accrue to national and international businesses active in tourism, hunting, pharmaceuticals or water-hungry agriculture and industrial production. National states are challenged from both "above", by trans-national corporations and elements of state power acting on their behalf, and below, by local communities. Co-management attempts provide a promising, if uncertain, balancing act among contrasting needs, for instance by setting up "contracts", "agreements" and "partnerships" with various social actors, including local communities, corporations and non governmental organisations (NGOs). Such attempts "legitimate" and guarantee the new roles assumed by the new actors and increasingly blur the conventional divide between the local and global.

4. Emerging interest in good governance principles and processes. Governance in general and governance of natural resources in particular are gaining attention in the national and international debates on conservation. Experiences in the governance of natural resources have even proven to be good vehicles for the promotion of local governance in other spheres of social and economic development. On the one hand, governments seek to implement their policies and programmes in so-called cost-effective ways and look for social actors with whom they can share their burdens of responsibility. On the other, civil society demands more influence on decisions affecting their lives and, as appropriate, the redressing of past injustices. Indigenous peoples and local community organisations, non-governmental organisations with environment and development goals, trans-national corporations, bodies of international and national law, scientific and local expert groups and professional associations– all clamour for attention and are actively engaged in influencing policies. Among their results are the increased recognition of the legal basis for the rights of indigenous peoples and the demand for effective access to information and the representation of civil society interests in policy and decision-making. In this dynamic situation, conventional governance structures and roles, based on a centralised and hierarchical authority, appear increasingly inadequate. More flexible institutional arrangements, characterised by interdependence among the actors and shared authority, are being tested both within

---

[17] Gunderson and Holling, 2002; Berkes et al., 2003.

[18] Richards, 1985; West and Brechin, 1991; Netting, 1993; Borrini-Feyerabend, 1996; Leach and Mearns, 1996; Pimbert and Pretty, 1999; Posey, 1999; Gunderson and Holling, 2002; Berkes et al., 2003.

[19] Korten, 1995; Passet, 2000; Bertrand and Kalafatides, 2002.

national governments and between governments and society.[20] These include various forms of collaboration among local communities, government, business and other actors ("public interest partnerships") with increasing reference to the respect of human rights and the United Nations (UN) principles of good governance ("participation and voice", "accountability", "equity", "direction" and "performance")[21] as reference benchmark. In this sense, co-management can be seen as empowering for some of the social downtrodden, as it helps them find a place at the decision-making forum. Whether that is enough to overcome their problems is a very open question.

A variety of concepts and terms are used to describe partnerships for the management of natural resources. As mentioned, we will use in this volume a comprehensive rather than narrow understanding of what co-management is about, emphasising the following in particular:

1. Collaboration as a form of self-defense. Many indigenous peoples and local communities in a changing world need more than ever strong internal and external forms of cooperation to be able to withstand the dangers of environmental degradation and socio-cultural impoverishment.

2. Collaboration as a response to complexity. As a result of complex historical developments, the management of natural ecosystems and the natural resource base of livelihoods generally cut across a variety of political, administrative, cultural and social boundaries: a multiplicity of concerned social actors exists for most ecosystems and natural resource units.

3. Collaboration for effectiveness and efficiency. Different social actors possess complementary capacities and comparative advantages in management, which, while respecting customary and existing rights, can be profitably harnessed together.

4. Collaboration for respect and equity. A fair sharing of the costs and benefits of managing natural resources and ecosystems is essential for initiatives aiming at human development and conservation with equity.

5. Collaboration through negotiation. Most institutional arrangements among relevant actors have at their core formal and/ or informal co-management plans, agreements and organisations. Such arrangements need to be negotiated through a fair process and subsequently adjusted in a learning-by-doing mode.

6. Collaboration as social institution. The harnessing of complementary capacities and the fair share of the costs and benefits of managing natural resources are the natural roots of many institutional arrangements.

The aim of this volume

This book is designed to support professionals and others attempting to understand collaborative management regimes and interested in supporting them in policy and developing them in practice. The relevant understanding and lessons learned are evolving, and this book is only a stepping stone. Whilst we draw from a large variety of examples of co-management partnerships throughout the

...we wrote this volume to promote action....

---

20   Calame, 2003; Fung and Wright, 2003.
21   UNDP, 2002; Graham et al., 2003; Hickey and Mohan, 2004 (in press).

world, there is no claim or hope to be exhaustive. We only attempt to overview relevant experiences and concerns and, from those, synthesise some key CM features, important steps in developing those and lessons learned regarding management institutions and the evolution of a favourable policy context. There is no "recipe" to develop a co-management partnership capable of fitting the variety of existing contexts and requirements. While recognising this, we wrote this volume to promote action, and thus offer a practical menu of examples, considerations to learn from, tools and reminder checklists. We hope these can be useful and inspiring. The specific co-management path, unique for every context, can only be made by the ones who will decide to walk it.

A guide to this volume

The overall structure of this volume is designed to both draw from and help support co-management practitioners in "learning by doing" in a variety of field contexts.

Towards a contextual framework

In Part I of this volume we explore natural resource management at the historical interface between traditional and "modern" societies and illustrate some complex combinations of the old and the new devised by local communities as a response to current challenges. Five case examples offer a glimpse of the complexities that abound in specific contexts, while pointing at a general pattern of generating syncretic solutions. We then discuss issues of actors, entitlements and equity in natural resource management, setting a conceptual foundation to our analysis. Various types of actors are described, with attention to the unique entitlements of indigenous peoples and local communities and why they are more akin to rightholders than stakeholders. Entitlements are social constructs that find meaning only within the society that created them. In this sense, we explore a number of arguments that have been used to claim entitlements to manage natural resources as well as their interplay with various forms of power. Pathways to move from potential to empowered and responsible actor, and to do so with specific attention to equity, are sketched and illustrated. Ways by which the actors can represent themselves in negotiation or be represented by others are discussed, as well as the development of co-management concepts through the last decades.

Part I closes with a panorama of contemporary forms of co-management in different places and cultures. Examples deal with pastoral societies, forest resources, fisheries and coastal resources, mountain environments, management of wildlife and protected areas, agriculture, agricultural research, and water management. Various common successful characteristics are highlighted but we also include cases in which co-management did not succeed in taking off. The rest of the book analyses in some more detail the constituent elements (components) of co-management: the co-management process, the co-management institution and the social context that makes them possible.

Towards effective processes

A co-management process is the series of events by which a management partnership develops and unfolds. Its key aim is to develop a consensus among the relevant partners on "what to do" about the ecosystem and natural resources at stake. The term "consensus" is often misunderstood as to convey a sense of total satisfaction achieved by everyone involved. This is not what it represents. A consensus may just imply that a compromise has been achieved by which each party renounced some of its desires but satisfies others. The term consensus means that the phase of negotiation achieved an agreement that everyone "can live with". In Part II of this volume, we begin by describing a number of points of departure and occasions for the co-management process to start. We then explore several preparatory requirements to the negotiation phase and lessons learned during negotiation. We offer a variety of methods and tools, including several checklists. By comparing contexts and examples, we emphasise the need to bend and adjust the process steps in the light of particular situations and conditions. Broadly, such process steps accompany a variety of social actors in organising, expressing and defending their interests and concerns, negotiating the agreement, setting up one or more pluralist management organisations, and learning by doing while implementing their agreement.

These steps are mostly valid for modern and formal contexts and possibly less so for other contexts, where co-management can be practiced in a variety of culture-specific ways (for instance, without developing a written agreement). In the latter cases the process we outline may not be entirely applicable or some of the steps may merge together. In all, no general procedure is applicable to all cases, but we can still examine a number of important experience-based recommendations. Regardless of context, a co-management process is rarely entirely smooth, often complex and lengthy, and sometimes arduous. It may involve changes of plans, surprises, contradictory information and the need to retrace one's own path and re-iterate a number of steps.

Towards effective institutions

The co-management agreement and organisations negotiated among the parties spell out the consensus reached through the co-management process and are, basically, as good as the process that generated them. In general, the co-management agreement includes a management plan but also accords or initiatives that do not immediately and directly relate to natural resources but complement the plan by creating the conditions that make sound management possible. It may consist of oral understandings or written documents, including project contracts, letters of intent, local by-laws, etc. The co-management plan, whether written or non-written, usually defines the essential management elements for the relevant area and natural resources, including objectives, priorities, expected results, the recognised relevant actors, their functions, responsibilities, entitlement, etc. The agreement often foresees the setting up of one or more co-management organisations,[22] i.e., multi-party bodies with defined functions in the management setting (e.g., an advisory council, a management board, an executive secretariat) usually including the key relevant actors at stake.

Together, the co-management plan and complementary accords represent the overall efforts of the parties to fairly share the relevant management functions, entitlements and responsibilities, and thereby create a co-management institution. And yet, a real institution is more than the sum of its parts. An institution includes expectations and routine reflexes (in particular the sense of shared responsibility in managing natural resources), social norms (such as the habit of discussing decisions with various relevant actors, and accepting that all points of

The co-management agreement and organisations... are, basically, as good as the process that generated them.

---

[22] We understand as organisations "groups of individuals or customary social groups bound by a common purpose to achieve objectives". See also North (1990).

view are valuable) and the use of specific terms and concepts in everyday life (such as co-management, but also entitlements, equity, linking of benefits and responsibilities, seeking good governance in resource management). Agreeing on a co-management plan and setting up a pluralist management board are crucial but not sufficient steps towards institutionalising a co-management regime. This will be achieved only when, besides and beyond rules and organisations, behaviours and ideas become spontaneously pluralist and respectful of a variety of entitlements and concerns in society. For this to be achieved, one of the crucial ingredients of a social institution is time. Only a day-by-day experience through time can give people the sense of normality and the confidence associated with a spontaneous, acquired behaviour and the associated social values. Other essential ingredients are the stability and resilience of the rules and organisations, which need to merge into normal life.

The forms and functioning of co-management agreements and organisations are examined in Part III of this volume, along with the dynamics of institutionalising co-management. We offer several examples of co-management agreements and organisations and discuss what makes them effective and sustainable. We then explore the experience of social actors engaged in "learning by doing" as part of co-management institutions.

Towards enabling policies

A social context favourable to co-management allows the co-management process to take place and fosters the development of co-management institutions. In some cases, key features are specific legislation and policy, while in others political and economic conditions are determining elements. No social pre-condition is always and absolutely necessary for effective co-management regimes, which are largely the products of the wider environment of which they are parts, but can also contribute to shaping and reforming that environment. In other words, practice can be ahead of policy, and co-management processes can have significant impacts on policy environments. In some countries, context-specific changes in natural resource governance towards increased participation and empowerment have even inspired and informed broader processes of decentralisation and democratisation.

Part IV of this volume is concerned with the policy contents and instruments helpful to make co-management work. We focus on the types and content of enabling policies and institutions and seek to address the real problems encountered by policy-makers, managers and social actors. We discuss how a supportive and coherent policy environment can comprise elements at various levels, from the specific deeds of local level bureaucrats and leaders to the founding principles of national constitutions and the carefully crafted wordings of global conventions. International and national policies that enable collaborative approaches to natural resource management and sustainable development are described, and the diversity of possible pathways is emphasized. Far from delivering standardised recommendations, we stress that policies and institutions need to adapt to local and national contexts, although possibly on the basis of an in-depth analysis of what has worked or failed elsewhere. We affirm the importance of local history in co-management processes, and stay away from standardised prescriptions and a "one—size-fits-all" approach.

In the final chapter of Part IV we discuss the policy-making process and specific ways to change and improve it with an emphasis on participatory democracy, civil society deliberation and mechanisms for social inclusion. In any given society it is important to ask whose perspectives, knowledge and aspirations are embedded in policies, and whose are excluded. Recognising that policies usually reflect and reinforce the interests of the powerful, we describe some of the methods and approaches that foster greater inclusion and democratic pluralism in policy making. After highlighting ways of strengthening civil society, we reflect on key challenges for deepening participatory governance of both natural resources and the broader conditions of social life.

Finally, in the Concluding Remarks, we draw from our own field experience to offer the reader our personal observations and heartfelt commentary.

Part I.   TOWARDS A CONTEXTUAL
FRAMEWORK

Chapter 1. MANAGING NATURAL RESOURCES: A STRUGGLE BETWEEN POLITICS AND CULTURE

1.1 From local livelihood strategies to global agro-industrial markets

Filder is at work in the family's shamba. She is harvesting cassava today, and worrying about the disease that seems to have attacked so many of the new plants. Wondering what she could do to prevent further spreading, she resolves to discuss the problems with some of her village friends later in the day. In her mother's shamba on the outskirts of Kampala, cassava still grows well. Perhaps she could walk there, one of these days, and get some of her mother's cuttings to try in her own fields.

The new portable machine has been set under a shack on the side of the grazing fields and Tobias is gathering the cows for milking. The machine could easily service many more cows than he has, but his quota for the year is already filled. Fortunately, the farmers' political lobby in Switzerland is very strong. Tobias and colleagues just celebrated their most recent victory against a motion to lower agricultural subsidies in the country. With subsidies at the current level, twenty cows are enough to gain an excellent income.

Erika has just survived one of the two annual meetings of the Consultative Council of the Protected Areas Authority of which she is in charge. She is exhausted but satisfied. The discussion was lively and the people had so much to say. The new local administrators seemed not entirely at ease, but the representative of the cattle owners and the one of the environmentalists were extremely vocal and everyone now clearly knows where they stand. She goes back in her mind to the pictures of the degraded areas she showed in the afternoon, against the backdrop of the whitest peaks and one of the most untouched old-growth forests in Romania. These were impressive images and she is sure they will be discussed by the working group in charge of developing a draft management plan in their forthcoming meeting, just a week from now.

The minga, a weekly day of communal work, has just ended. Colourful people scatter back home on the chequered green and brown landscape of the Andean hills. Rosario and twenty other people representing all the village households gathered in the morning to plant lentils and oats in the plot of hard soil they are all recuperating together. For some months they moved the earth and fertilised it with animal manure, and are now halfway into the process. Once the oat and lentils are harvested, they will mix the remains into the soil, and add some more manure. In the next growing season they will be able to plant maize and potatoes. They will finally have managed to add some productive land to the meagre resources of their community.

This is one of the most important deals of Mark's stockbroker career in New York. He puts down the phone having reached an agreement that will change the price of cocoa for some time, and his client will profit from it. The new price will eventually encourage more people to produce and process cocoa, and the supply may rise too much in a not-so-distant future. This is not his immediate concern. He just needs to call his client and announce the good news of the deal.

Fatima had just gathered the yews and she-goats within the stone enclosure. As she milks the animals, she thinks about the quality of grass in the pasture. The nomadic pastoral elders are about to meet and decide the date, length, itinerary and size of the migrating herd for the entire Qashqai sub-tribe, one of the largest tribes in Iran. Some months ago she and several other women collected a good quantity of quality grass seeds. Tomorrow they will place them in perforated goatskins, and append those to the neck of the lead goat. As the animals roam, the seeds will come out gradually and will be ploughed under and fertilised by the marching flocks. The rangeland will improve after the next rains and better quality pasture will be available on their return from the summering grounds.

What do Erika and Filder, Fatima and Tobias, Mark and Rosario have in common? Not much, seemingly. Yet, the daily work and decisions of all of them impact upon the natural environment. They are all "natural resource managers".

For some of them, the interaction with natural resources and the environment is a direct and intimate affair. Learned in the household and the community, it is an integral part of what makes life normal, convivial and safe, what makes them a member of a group and a culture. For others it is an acquired and rather distant power, mediated by technology, sophisticated information systems and big money.[1] Still for others, in rapidly growing numbers in the urban sprawls of the

> For some [natural resource managers], the interaction with natural resources and the environment is a direct and intimate affair.... For others, it is an acquired and rather distant power....

---

[1]   We do not wish to express judgments here on the relative merits of one or the other type of interaction, but some cultural critics and environmentalists do, at times very powerfully. See, for instance, Wes et al., 1983; and Berry, 1990.

world, that interaction is both distant and relatively uninformed. Many of us eat food we have not grown, consume electricity unaware that it comes from burning fossil fuels or from nuclear power plants, use and pollute water without considering that we are subtracting it from environmental functions with no known alternative.

For the vast majority of time in which our species roamed the planet, the interaction between humans and the environment has been of the first kind. Early groups of Homo sapiens may have impacted upon the environment in a substantial manner (mostly through the use of fire)[2], but were also in the front-line to see and feel the results of their own action. More recently, modern technology and the globalisation of the economy allowed for some on the planet to have an interaction with natural resources that is at the same time very powerful and very remote. This is a unique characteristic of modern times, built up in recent millennia through social diversification, the diffusion of travelling and exchanges, the intensification of agricultural and industrial production and the progressively imposed domination of the market economy.[3] Below we will discuss, on the basis of field examples, how such intimate and remote interactions with the environment co-exist today, and how they clash or integrate with one another. To arrive at that, however, we will start from some general considerations.

A human culture is a set of institutions, practices, behaviours, technologies, skills, knowledge, beliefs and values proper to a human community. As such, a human culture is usually received, lived, refined, and reproduced at any given moment in history. In traditional societies, many of the features proper to a culture can be interpreted primarily as a response to the specific natural environment where they need to gain their livelihood. Much of what differentiates Ugandan peasants from Mongolian herders, French wine makers, or Japanese fisher-folks can be traced back to environmental factors such as landscape, climate, water availability, type of soil and the existing flora, fauna and mineral wealth. By no means are these the only determinants of the cultures that developed in their midst, but they provided the crucial set of external conditions around which different cultures developed their characterising features. Among those features are the organisations, rules, practices, means, knowledge and values allowing communities to exploit and conserve their natural resources. We will refer to these as "natural resource management (NRM) systems". Another term used to represent the set of conditions that regulate the reproduction and use of natural resources is "NRM institutions". In this work we will use the term "institutions" with reference to NRM systems strongly characterised by social rules and organisations.

[Many cultural differences can be interpreted in the light of specific] environmental factors, such as landscape, climate, water availability, type of soil, and the existing flora [and] fauna....

An NRM system regulates the interplay between human activities and the natural environment. Its major outputs include:

- human survival and the satisfaction of economic needs through productive activities, such as hunting, fishing, gathering, agriculture, animal raising, timber production and mining;
- the transformation of portions of the natural environment into a domesticated environment, more suited to being exploited (e.g., clearing of agricultural land, irrigation, management of grazing land and forests);
- the control of natural environmental hazards (e.g., preventing floods, fighting vectors of disease, distancing dangerous animals from human communities);
- the control of degradation and hazards caused by human pressure on the envi-

---

[2] Simmons, 1989.
[3] See the far-looking analysis of Polanyi, 1944. See also Esteva, 1992; and Farvar and Milton, 1972.

ronment, through more or less intentional forms of conservation of biodiversity and sustainable use of natural resources.

The technological and social capabilities to exploit natural resources (in particular food resources) are a major factor in shaping the size and density of human populations.

A feature closely related to NRM systems is the social regulation of population dynamics. The technological and social capabilities to exploit natural resources (in particular food resources) are a major factor in shaping the size and density of human populations. For instance, communities featuring an NRM system based on agriculture and animal husbandry are usually larger in size and more concentrated than hunting-gathering communities. In general, an increase in human productive capability may result in an increased community size. Yet, that same increase is one of the main problems NRM systems need to face. If a population grows beyond a certain limit, the existing territory may become unable to support it. Some common solutions involve the migration of a sector of a community towards uninhabited areas and the intensification of local production by adoption or invention of newer or more effective technologies and practices.[4] Dominant neo-Malthusian theories maintain that these solutions are far from being available to all communities, and many NRM systems are today stressing their environment, at times beyond the point of recovery. More balanced analysis would show, however, that in nearly all such cases, some social, economic and political factors outside of local control are playing a dominant role. Too often, unequal terms of trade, land grabs and natural resource alienation by governments and private actors impinge on the community NRM systems and drive them to stress their resources much beyond the traditional sustainable practices.

...control over land and natural resources– in particular closure and limitation of access and use– has also been a pervasive area of social struggle.

All NRM systems include elements explicitly addressing the conservation (including wise use) of natural resources, such as knowledge of the local environment, technology and know-how. Examples of these elements are hunters' knowledge of animal behaviour and self-restraint in time of mating and growing of the offspring, regulation of grazing and fishing rights in indigenous communities, modern farmer capacity to use fertilisers, and community– or state-promoted watershed management schemes.

Many conservation features embedded in NRM systems, however, are not explicitly meant for the purpose. Rather, they are embedded in other components of a culture (social organisation, magic and religious beliefs, prevailing values) but have a significant impact on the interaction between a human community and the environment. For instance, a religious taboo preventing hunting during the breeding season, on the surface not inspired by a preoccupation for the conservation of game, may still be an effective means to avoid over-hunting and over-fishing. A rule establishing distribution of the camel herd among the children of a Bedouin head of household may be meant to ensure a fair share of wealth among the community, but could also be useful to avoid unsustainable grazing in given locations. The belief that land is a "gift from God" is a religious sentiment, but it may also motivate farmers to practice sound land husbandry. A sweeping land reform may be a political move to pacify the rural and urban poor, but may also have important consequences on the type and intensity of agricultural practices.

...a religious taboo preventing hunting during the breeding period, on the surface not inspired by a preoccupation for the conservation of game, may still be an effective means of avoiding over-hunting.

In fact, the distinction between "natural resource management" and the rest of human life may make more or less sense according to the socio-cultural point of view. Most traditional societies formed relatively closed systems in which natural resources were managed though complex interplays of reciprocities and solidarities. These systems were fully embedded into local cultures and accommodated

---

4   Boserup, 1981.

for differences of power and roles, including decision-making, within holistic systems of reality and meaning. A telling example is described in Box 3.3, in Chapter 3 of this volume. In all cultures, on the other hand, one can also find some explicit social institutions directly related to the management of natural resources. These generally include:

- inclusion/ exclusion rules limiting access to natural resources to communities and individuals belonging to special groups based on kinship, residence, citizenship, economic capacity (ownership of land), personal skills or other criteria;
- customary regulations or written laws aimed at making individual use of resources compatible with collective interests (e.g., reciprocity and solidarity customs, taxation system, "polluter pays" principles);
- social organisations in-charge of establishing and enforcing rules, through persuasion, negotiation, coercion, etc.

Often, such elements coalesce around specific use regimes (Box 1.1)

Box 1.1   Natural resources, property and access regimes
            (Adapted from Murphree, 1997a)

Natural resources are those components of nature that are being used or are estimated to have a use for people and communities. In this sense, what is a "resource" is culturally and technologically determined. Cultures shape demand: until they create a use for it, a resource remains latent. Similarly, the development of technology can promote new uses and thus discover new resources (e.g., oil and natural gas). Demand and scarcity— perceived or actual, present or future— are the complementary and primary incentives to regulate resource use, and they are usually present side by side with the management and use regulations that characterise a society.

Property, or ownership, is the faculty of disposing of certain resources. Contrary to common interpretations of the term, however, ownership is never absolute. It is, rather, a set of entitlements to use a territory or set of natural resources with some limitations– different in different social settings– regarding the entitlements of others. Entitlements of longer duration ("tenure") and subject to fewer conditions are obviously stronger than others. The legitimacy and conditions of resource entitlements arise from a variety of social factors, including formal legislation, cultural norms, kinship, and socio-economic interaction. These multiple sources explain the frequent discrepancy between the de jure and de facto entitlements of resource users, i.e., between what is prescribed by norms and laws and what actually happens in real life. Types of property regime include:

Communal property
A common property regime under the jurisdiction of a community of users. The term "community" can be defined spatially, socially, culturally or economically. Often– although not always– it is used to refer to a residential group small enough for the sanction and pressure of peers to be significant in self-regulation. To be sustainable, communal property regimes must have a defined membership, with rules for inclusion and exclusion, and rules to regulate internal competition. In other words, they must have the institutional means to ensure that the collective good is not eroded by particular interests. Communal land property in peasant and pastoral nomadic societies and the kinship-based property of a well among dry land herders are examples in point. Common property has been the predominant form of land tenure in traditional societies.

The right of using, modifying and/ or selling the concerned land and resources according to the will and interests of the private (individual or corporate) owner. Other social actors are usually unable to have a say on the management and use of privately owned resources. Only in particular and rather extreme circumstances the neighbours or public bodies have negative rights, i.e., can forbid a private owner of a piece of land to use the resources in a certain way. For instance, they may forbid a landowner to build a skyscraper, raise dangerous animals or drain a unique wetland. Private property is the prevailing form of land tenure that regulates "modern" capitalist production systems (agriculture and industry).

State property

A common property regime under the jurisdiction of the state. In contemporary societies, this type of regime pertains to a great proportion of a country's forests, rivers, wildlife and mining resources. State property is also the legal foundation of most conservation laws. The may rent, sell or assign part of its natural resource wealth to other social actors. Forestry and mining concessions are typical examples of this kind of arrangement. In many socialist or other "statist" countries common or private property has been expropriated by the.

Open-access

Open-access resources are available to any one and effectively the property of no one. This condition arises when there is no demand for, or perceived scarcity of the resource concerned, and thus no collective attempt to control its use. Frequently, open access situations are the result of ineffective property regimes, which claim authority over a resource but lack the means to fulfil the responsibilities involved. This can apply to individual, communal or state property regimes, although a de facto open access situation is most frequent for state-owned resources that a state has not the capacity to manage.

...a basic feature of NRM systems is their continuous striving to adapt in response to demographic, economic, social and cultural changes affecting environments and human communities.

The inclusion/ exclusion rules are a fundamental feature of NRM systems but also an important source of problems. First, rules may work only to a limited extent. There is a need to survey that they are respected, and to enforce them if necessary. Second, rules may not ensure equity and fairness in access to resources. Sooner or later, such rules will be challenged by the excluded and disadvantaged, with both overt and hidden means. Third, new social and political subjects may enter the picture… and the rules may be challenged by them! In fact, NRM systems are a political arena par excellence, intertwined with social clashes fuelled by economic interests, ethnic and cultural differences, ideological and religious values. How do these clashes get solved?

In many traditional societies, social values such as caste, predestination, religious authority or historical continuity have determined NRM decisions and their relative sharing of costs and benefits among individuals and groups. In others, dialogue and discussion of field-based experience (what some, today, refer to as "co-management") were widely and effectively practiced. In most cases, culture-based relationships of solidarity and reciprocity, the prevalence of communal property regimes and the collective building of local knowledge and skills through extended experience in managing the resources, succeeded in producing cohesive and sustainable systems. But control over land and natural resources– in particular closure and limitation of access and use– has also been a pervasive area of social struggle.

Throughout history, wars and violent conflicts have produced innumerable changes and substitutions of one group by another in the control of natural resources. This has been mostly true between outsiders and insiders to a community, but at times also within a community, which could weaken and even split– sometimes also as a direct consequence of population expansion or accumulation of wealth. External actors, however, were the ones to intrude most often in a violent and uncompromising way. The expansion of the Roman Empire to control grain production in Northern Africa, cattle raiding among pastoralist groups in Madagascar, the recent wars in Kuwait and Iraq over oil fields, Israel's occupation of a joint Jordanian-Syrian dam site during the six-day war or the imposition of colonial rule or national government rule over community resources in countless countries are just some poignant examples. Outright violence, however, has not been the only way of gaining control over natural resources, nor has always succeeded. In many instances, the "weapons of the weak" included powerful non-overt means of resistance, such as hiding, deceiving, cheating, stealing, or spreading false rumours and ridicule.[5] These means allowed them to maintain access over at least part of the natural resources they needed. While this situation of conflict may be perceived as typical, there are, nonetheless, striking examples of societies based on relations of solidarity, hospitality, magnanimity and mutual aid. See Box 1.2 for one such example in south-western Sudan.

Box 1.2   The Beni Halba Tribe– accommodating "foreigners" in resource management
(field observations by M. Taghi Farvar, 1988-90)

Beni Halba is one of the Baggara (cattle pastoralist) tribes of South Darfur in Sudan. The tribe consists of 12 clans, one of which is composed of "foreigners"– immigrants, refugees and others who, throughout the ages, came to be welcomed and accepted locally. Rather than fighting them or depriving them of access to natural resources, the Beni Halba recognise the status of foreigners who come as refugees or through other events, and consider them as legitimate and equal partners with their original 11 clans. The chiefs of the 12 clans participate in the tribal Council and have common access to the rangelands and territories of the tribe that extend into neighbouring Chad.

The majority of NRM systems strive to be relatively efficient (i.e., capable of generating good results with acceptable effort) and sustainable (i.e., capable of maintaining a flow of benefits through time). Many, indeed, beautifully succeed. For instance, communal grazing has supported human livelihoods in very inhospitable natural environments generation after generation, and water-sharing systems have sustained for centuries abundant agricultural productions in dry lands. Yet, even successful natural resource management systems are not free from contradictions, inefficiencies, wastes and errors. Such imperfections make any management system much more of an experimental, trial and error process than a stable state of affairs. In fact, a basic feature of NRM systems is their continuous striving to adapt in response to the demographic, economic, social and cultural changes affecting all environments and human communities. For example, population growth may lead hunter-gatherers to engage in agriculture. The market economy may urge peasant communities to abandon a traditional labour sharing system. Overgrazing may lead cattle ranchers to adopt agro-forestry techniques. Concern for the preservation of biodiversity and the recreational value of wilderness, may lead a government to establish a National Park. In general, the necessary adjustments of NRM systems are done via progressive fine-tuning of interests, concerns, influences and decisions within any given community and/ or between community insiders and outsiders. This process needs to take advantage of con-

In an absolute sense, it is impossible to assess whether a management system has a positive or negative effect on the environment.

---

5   Scott, 1985.

sultation, negotiation and conflict prevention and resolution mechanisms, which in the ideal case are embedded in the relevant NRM institutions

...each property of an ecosystem may favour some interests and actors in society, but displease others.

In an absolute sense, it is impossible to assess whether a management system has a positive or negative effect on the environment. This is true because there is no "optimal" state in which a given environment could or should be. What does this mean? An ecosystem can be described by many properties, such as: capacity to sustain a certain quantity of biodiversity (many different species) or quality of biodiversity (presence of highly sensitive, endemic species), wildness (for instance as defined by low dependence on human interaction and extensive presence of endemic species), productivity for given species (including species capable of sustaining the life of human inhabitants), resilience after stress, structural variety, maturity (average age and size of some important species), matrix distribution of habitats, aesthetic values, and so on. Many of these properties can be optimised only one at a time, or even one at the expense of the other, but not all together. Thus, if we wish to maximise the total quantity of biodiversity we may do so at the cost of the quality of biodiversity, for instance the disappearance of a few species, endemic and fragile. If we opt to maximise productivity we may pay the price in terms of resilience or wildness. And so on.

The problem is compounded by the fact that each property of an ecosystem may favour some interests and actors in society, but displease others. For instance, the presence of important biodiversity in a given patch of forest may please some university researchers, herbal healers, and scouts of medicinal plants for pharmaceutical companies, but the local youth may be more interested in gaining revenue from an environment managed for the maximum production of coffee or cocoa. For some tourists it may be interesting to spend time in an unspoiled and wild tropical watershed, but for the urban planners it may be crucial to transform it into a water reservoir for energy production. Who should decide?

The question is particularly problematic as peasants and pharmaceutical companies, tourists and urban planners indeed belong to different "communities" and cultures. Within a self-contained society, existing institutions and cultural norms generally provide their unique answers to their internal conflicts of interests and concerns. When different cultures clash, however, matters are thorny and eminently political: management decisions end up reflecting the priorities of the most powerful parties in the controversy. Thus one option is the oligarchic or dictatorial control by the few (be they the "scientific experts", the ones with the guns, the rich, the conservationists, or the dominant elite). Another option is the pluralist/ dialogue/ democratic way. This is based on the acceptance of various entitlements in society, the gathering of the best available information on the consequences of various possible decisions and a negotiation process among the parties possessing entitlements, interests and concerns. This, at least in theory, is what collaborative management– the subject of this volume– is all about.

When different cultures clash… management decisions end up reflecting the priorities of the most powerful parties in the controversy.

Livelihood systems

For most of its existence on the planet, humankind got its subsistence from hunting, fishing and gathering. Some contemporary indigenous societies (such as the Kung bushmen of the Kalahari Desert, the Eskimos, fishing communities in remote islands in the Pacific and some Aboriginal communities in Australia) still rely on this livelihood system to a significant extent.

A hunting/ fishing and gathering economy is based on the exploitation of wild natural resources in a wide territory or sea area. The people do not control the reproduction of resources but they take advantage of everything nature can offer. Low population density, diversification of the diet (according to seasons and sites), and nomadism are common characteristics of hunter-gatherer societies. They are facilitated by a flexible social organisation, which allows human groups to change size according to food availability.

Hunters-gatherers possess an impressive knowledge of animals, plants, and local ecology, and some of their practices aim at preventing overexploitation of resources and facilitating the reproduction of significant species. This expertise– together with a highly co-operative attitude within human groups– is essential for their survival. As hunting and gathering activities do not always procure enough food, food security depends on the generous sharing of whatever has been gathered and hunted among the households in the same group.

In these egalitarian societies, access and use of natural resources are not regulated by any economically significant exclusion rule. Every member of a human community has the same right to exploit the hunting and gathering territory, and the same duty to contribute through his/ her activities to the common livelihood. A wide demographic dispersion diminishes competition over natural resources. As a consequence, relationships among hunter-gatherer groups are usually peaceful. Contact with more aggressive human groups is avoided. At times, this may even involve abandoning a well-known territory and moving into a new one.

Throughout millennia, most of the world's hunting-gathering societies have transformed themselves into societies based on agriculture and animal husbandry. This has been a complex process, which proceeded at different paces in different environments. Indigenous tropical forest societies in the Amazon, Central Africa, Asia and Papua-New Guinea represent some contemporary examples of a "transitional" situation in which hunting and gathering still play a key role.

As hunting and gathering activities do not always procure enough, food security depends on the generous sharing of whatever has been gathered and hunted among the household in the same group.

The subsistence of tropical forest societies is based on a mix of shifting horticulture (tuber-focused), which provides the caloric basis of nutrition, and of hunting, fishing and gathering activities, which supply proteins, other qualitative elements of the diet, fuel and raw materials. This livelihood strategy is usually associated with a relatively sedentary settlement pattern. Communities live in long houses or clusters of long houses, hosting about 150-200 people each, scattered over a wide area. Each human settlement includes the dwellings, the surrounding fields, and a hunting territory.

The NRM systems of tropical forest hunters-horticulturists usually include strict territorial control through feuding and warfare (often ideologically promoted by complex, highly elaborate rituals such as headhunting or witchcraft). Such strong exclusion mechanisms limit human pressure on the forest. Often the buffer territory between one community and another becomes a de facto "no man's land" where game and other forest resources reproduce without human disturbance. These undisturbed territories and their own sophisti-

cated knowledge of soils, species and ecotypes allow tropical forest hunters-horticulturists to make sustainable use of the fragile tropical forest ecosystem and resources.

About eight thousand years ago, many human communities started to concentrate their productive effort on cereal and leguminous cultivation (often coupled with small-scale animal raising). This peasant way of life is practised today by innumerable rural communities, in both developing and industrial countries. In comparison with hunter-gatherers, tropical forest hunter-horticulturists, and nomadic pastoralists, peasants feature a more intensive way of exploiting the natural environment. Their technology and know-how allow them to get all they need for survival from a small but efficiently exploited territory. Furthermore, in the absence of special catastrophic events such as droughts, floods, famines or major wars, peasant societies are also able to accumulate surpluses relatively rapidly. This may provide livelihood opportunities for larger and more concentrated human communities.

Most nomadic pastoral societies ...rely on complex pasture and water tenure regulations, which usually include rangeland conservation measures. The enforcement of these measures is entrusted to tribal elders and authorities, called to act as mediators in conflicts that may arise among local groups.

Traditional peasant NRM systems focus on arable land. The arable land surrounding a settlement is usually under some form of communal property regime. Plots are periodically assigned for cultivation by village authorities such as the Councils of Elders, according to kinship and other customary rules. Often, these authorities are also in charge of conserving and enhancing productivity of common land. To this end, for instance, communities mobilise to implement erosion control and flood prevention or management works (the agricultural areas of Hadramaut in Yemen are an excellent example of this). Land husbandry regulations (such as respect of fallow time, crop rotation or terracing) are promoted and, when necessary, enforced. Similar practices are sometimes extended to the near-by forests and grazing areas, which are kept in a state of semi-cultivation similar to that advocated by modern agro-forestry practices. There the peasants collect fuel wood, fodder and other wild natural resources. Peasant cultures deliberately seek to transform the natural environment into a human-made environment. At times, this includes attempts to control unpredictable factors (such as weather and climate) through magic and religious means.

Most peasant NRM systems are not stable. For instance, under the pressure of climatic change between 9000 and 3000 years ago, groups of Central Asian farmers were forced onto horseback to experiment nomadic pastoralism, a livelihood strategy which was subsequently adopted in many arid areas of the world. Nomadic pastoral societies (such as those existing in Southwest Asia, Central Asia and North, sub-Saharan and East Africa) base their economy on the exploitation of domesticated animals, such as cattle, horses, camels or sheep and goats. Their NRM system is geared towards providing the herds with a constant supply of fodder and water and thus they adopt a mobile life-style, which allows them to track rangelands and water resources throughout the year. Seasonal displacements are often combined with cyclical migrations taking place over longer periods, which distribute grazing pressure over a large territory. Overgrazing is prevented also by the periodic sub-division of human communities into smaller sub-units, a phenomenon that facilitates the de-stocking of the animal herd. Needless to say, the sedentarisation policies of many national governments severely disrupt this livelihood system, with resulting extreme social and environmental stress.

Nomadic pastoral communities usually possess impressive capabilities in managing the constraints and hazards of the semi-arid environment, as well as the health of their animals. Their NRM systems, however, can function only if strong social control is ensured over rangeland and water resource use. Most nomadic pastoral societies, in fact, rely on complex pasture and water tenure regulations, which usually include rangeland conservation measures. The enforcement of these measures is entrusted to tribal elders and authorities, called to act as mediators in conflicts that may arise among local groups. If negotiations are not successful, open struggles for the control of water and pasture may ensue.

Peasants who do not adopt pastoral nomadism are usually forced by population growth to expand and intensify the exploitation of arable land. This exposes them to environmental hazards and conflicts with neighbouring villages. To overcome the above limitations, some peasant communities join in confederations of rural villages ruled by a common authority, which can regulate land tenure conflicts and ensure a region-wide control over land husbandry practices. In the ancient world, this process took an especially rapid pace on the shores of the Nile, the Tigris, the Euphrates, the Indus, the Ganges and the Yellow River.

In these areas, the quality of soil was high (benefiting from river water and sediments), a fact that prompted peasants to solve land disputes locally rather than disperse (a common response in areas were natural resources are distributed over large territories). In addition, the advantages of a central authority are rather evident among the inhabitants of large river watersheds, where public works are necessary to control the floods and to make water available outside the natural edges of the alluvial plain.

Starting from 4,000 BC, the village confederations of the south-west Asian rivers developed fairly stable "hydraulic states", which acquired their legitimacy from their capability of implementing flood-control and irrigation works. A variant of this watershed management-based form of state is the one developed by some Andean civilisations such as the Inca. Due to the specific ecological conditions of their territories, the water management activities promoted by the Inca focused on erosion control, rather than on water-stream control. A huge amount of peasant labour was mobilised to establish impressive terracing works– the still observable and functioning andenes– which made suitable for agriculture the steep hills of the Andes, highly prone to erosion. The hydraulic states also entailed the development of complex sets of rules for access to land and resources (especially water), legislation for water management (often encoded in religion)[6] and the rise of a centralised bureaucracy and military force in charge of enforcement and defence. In this process, individual, community, and state property were differentiated and many NRM systems were institutionalised, i.e., codified in specific rules and organisations under central control. This notwithstanding, local knowledge, skills and institutions continued to be central to the water and irrigation systems, at least in the oriental world (see Box 1.3).

...the advantages of a central authority are rather evident among the inhabitants of large river watersheds, where public works are necessary to control the floods and to make water available outside the natural edges of the alluvial plain.

---

6   See Box 3.3 Chapter 3.

Box 1.3   Community tapping and management of ground water
           (Adapted from CENESTA, 2004)

The land of west and central Asia is dotted with an ingenious community-managed technology for the tapping of ground water. Known as Karez (Afghanistan, Iran and Chinese Turkistan), Qanat (Iran), Fouggara (North Africa), Surangam (India) and Falaj (Arabian Peninsula), this ancient technique has supplied water for irrigation and social life for millennia. Tapping into the renewable hydrological reserves of the hills and mountain, the karez provides abundant water for local uses under the control of local community councils and often in defiance of the central authority.

Even the water of the centrally-organised irrigation systems of the great rivers (the so-called hydraulic states), once flowing in secondary and tertiary irrigation canals, has been treated the same way as the water from the ground. The karez system, initially transferred by the Arabs to the Spaniards, can be found today in places as far apart as the Philippines (the sanjeras system), Mexico and Peru.

In other areas, possibly less characterised by very important river basins, the focus of state development and expansion was more urban than rural. Confederations of peasant villages developed into states that progressively expanded their area of influence through warfare and built vast political units. This was the case for the Roman Empire (and for the development of most states in continental Europe), which made some effort to plan agricultural exploitation in selected rural areas of Italy, Southern France, Spain and Tunisia, but always perceived its expansion as a process of colonisation, based on road building, military control, collection of tributes, trade, and pillage of local resources. The Empire was in need of progressively larger agricultural harvests to sustain its densely populated towns. This was achieved through the introduction and extension of technological innovations (e.g., diffusion of crops from one place to another, small-scale irrigation schemes, and progressive improvement of tools) rather than via major public works and state-controlled policies. This approach was consistent with the overwhelming importance attributed to private property in Roman laws.

An early momentous role... was played by the appropriation and partition of common lands by private individuals and, later, by the state...[this] goes under the name of "enclosure of the commons".

In more recent times, the emphasis on technological innovation and private (or corporate) land property has become an overwhelming characteristic of natural resource management in the Western world. A case in point is the transformation of most European rural inhabitants into urban proletarians or overseas settlers that took place in the last couple of centuries and was closely intertwined with the development of capitalist agriculture. Technological innovations– originally coming to Europe from the East– became very important, including the practice of crop rotation, improved crop varieties and breeds and safer storage systems. Later on, new methods such as mechanical cultivation and harvesting, more sophisticated irrigation techniques and new crops (e.g., potato, tomato and maize) tended to minimise losses, decrease the need for labour and increase the overall output of the productive process for a given unit of land.

An early momentous role in this process of transformation was played by the appropriation and partition of common lands by private individuals and, later, by the state. The phenomenon, which goes under the name of "enclosure of the commons", was a by-product of the monetisation of feudal life. It started in England as early as the 13th century and reached its climax in the late 18th and early 19th centuries, when half of the arable land of England, previously held as feudal commons and used by peasants to grow food crops or graze their flock, was "enclosed" and reserved for cash-oriented production (initially mostly for sheep rearing and, later, also for tillage) for the benefit of the landowner aristocracy.[7] Trees were cleared, marshes were drained, efforts were made to improve the fertility of the soil and large portions of land were offered for lease at competitive rents. Among the consequences of the enclosures was an increase in economic productivity of the land, coupled with benefits for the landlords and the ones who could afford to buy or lease land. In parallel, however, the human cost for the small peasants reached tragic proportions. In some estates nine-tenths of the peasant population were forced to leave the land and went to feed a mass of wandering poor– the labour pool for the industrial revolution to come and for the migrations to the "New World". This wrenching human dislocation proceeded at different pace throughout the European continent and did not go without rebellions. Thousands of peasants were slaughtered in the process, which was at times slowed down by the intercession of kings and the Church and even by specific legislation, but basically never stopped. As aptly described by Polanyi[8]:

"Enclosures have appropriately been called a revolution of the rich against the poor. The lords and nobles were upsetting the social order, breaking down ancient laws and customs, sometimes by means of violence, often by pressure and intimidation. They were literally robbing the poor of their share in the common, tearing down the houses which, by the hitherto unbreakable forces of custom, the poor had long regarded as theirs and their heirs'."

The "enclosure" model, centred on private property, a monetary economy and efforts to increase land productivity has not remained confined to the lands of noble aristocracy. Policies of deforestation and "enclosure" by order of the state have been the rule in European countries throughout recent centuries. In northern Italy, for instance, the new national state did not spare efforts at alienating, splitting up and privatizing the collective property of the village communities (woods, pastures, etc.), a process still in the making as late as 1927.[9] This was sooner or later accepted for the land most suited to the profit-oriented agriculture in the plains (with consequent creation of important landowning possessions), but encountered fierce resistance for the more mountainous and marginal lands of the upland communities, to the point that some special legislation was carved to allow some of them to maintain a collective, solidarity-oriented– and, incidentally, very successful– form of control over those resources.[10]

The "enclosure" model has not remained confined to Europe either. It was well applied in the colonies, with individual land conquest and appropriation as a pathway (e.g., for the haciendas of South America[11]), but also with land appropriation by the colonial powers as an explicit effort to "scientifically manage" the so-called wastelands of India.[12] In Africa, the colonial triad of taxation, export cropping and monetisation took care of tearing apart local peasants from their kin and community affiliations and obligations in the commons, creating

The new post-colonial independent states are also extremely comfortable with the practice of "enclosures"....

...changes in natural resource management... lead towards the expansion of cultivated land at the expense of forests and wildlife habitats, the replacement of use values by market/monetary values and the substitution of experience-based, culture-embedded and often highly productive production systems by the "science-based" decisions of merchants, bureaucrats and experts.

---

[7]   Heilbroner, 1968.

[8]   Polanyi, 1944.

[9]   On this date the Italian government passed Act No. 1766 aimed at liquidating collective property: the woods and pastures had to be handed over to the communes and the agricultural land to the farmers.

[10] Merlo et al., 1989. Many of these collective property systems continue to this day (see Box 11.10 in Chapter 11).

[11] Burbach and Flynn, 1980.

[12] In 1865 the Indian government passed such legislation with the Indian Forest Act, which expropriated the individual and collective rights of local communities.

the social and environmental crises at the roots of many modern famines.[13] The new post-colonial independent states are also extremely comfortable with the practice of "enclosures", which they have set to work without much re-thinking or change. In Kenya, for instance, the Registered Land Act makes the individual title deeds to prevail over all sorts of customary collective rights[14] considered contrary to modernisation. In West Africa, where cultural resistance to land privatisation is strong, the state policies have favoured state ownership or individual ownership of agricultural land also with the support of foreign aid projects.[15] State control, however, too often revealed itself a euphemism for unregulated, "open access" regimes through which both the state and others appropriate resources with no concern for sustainability. In Nepal, for instance, unqualified state control of village forests prompted a break down of traditional management practices that damaged both the resources and the people.[16] Likewise, in Iran, Syria, Jordan and other countries, the "nationalisation" of rangelands have caused their alienation from the nomadic pastoralists and the further degradation of these productive, albeit marginal, natural resources.

The last centuries have thus seen progressive changes in natural resource management all over the world. Prompted by technological innovations and the enclosure of the commons, these changes lead towards the expansion of cultivated land at the expense of forests and wildlife habitats, the replacement of use values by market/ monetary values and the substitution of experience-based, culture-embedded and often highly productive production systems by the "science-based" decisions of merchants, bureaucrats and experts. In parallel, a progressively smaller percentage of the population of a country remained employed and/ or in control of agricultural production. This "taming of nature" obtained spectacular results but also left behind degraded soil and water, polluted air, depleted resources because of excessive extraction (first among all from the sea and forests) and a sustained loss in biological diversity (habitats, species, and genetic variety).

Far from being a mere economic or environmental phenomenon, this is principally a political one. It happened first as a consequence of the expansion of the power of landed aristocracy, then through colonisation and colonial enterprises and later as a consequence of the globalisation of the world economy and the coming to dominance of one, or a few, superpowers. In this, subsistence peasants have been progressively involved in cash crop production, nomadic pastoralists have been forced to settle and hunters-gatherers have been constrained to become farmers. In other words, many existing customary and community-based rights and traditional NRM systems have been overlooked, negated or simply crushed in the name of the "higher" goals of modernisation and development.

Today, the agro-industrial-market system is the dominant, "modern" NRM system at the global level. Every day, the international trade and market system moves huge financial resources (real and virtual) that have all too real effects on land and resource uses and practices. This process is effectively dominated by a few countries, a few international corporations and a few banking giants. Many countries are seriously dependent on foreign imports of food and other natural resources (raw or processed) and virtually exist under the patronage of the few who dominate their markets. Crucial resources, such as oil, are internationally and nationally controlled, by virtue or vice. In fact, specialisation of local production and

...a progressively smaller percentage of the population of a country remained employed and/ or in control of agricultural production.

...customary and community-based rights and traditional NRM systems have been overlooked, negated or simply crushed in the name of the "higher" goals of modernisation and development.

13 Watts, 1983a and 1983b.
14 In fact, a registered land owner in Kenya is immune to challenge, no matter how the property was obtained, a fact discussed by Alden Wily and Mbaya, 2001.
15 Franke and Chasin, 1980.
16 See the story of a specific village masterly narrated in Kuchli, 1997.

local dependence on inputs from outside increasingly appear as the two faces of the same coin. These phenomena sprout in part voluntarily and in part imposed by a variety of socio-economic constraints. They have in part healthy results, such as increased communication and friendly relationships among people belonging to different backgrounds and histories, and in part pernicious results, such as loss of autonomy, diversity and sense of people's identity and culture.

The "collateral ecological damage" intrinsic to the taming of nature is possibly the most ominous consequence of the agro-industrial market system. Only recently, as environmental damage began to affect private and collective interests throughout the world, environmental concerns have come to the fore. Principles such as "polluter-pays" start clamouring for attention, as societies become conscious of the costs of un-regulated exploitation of natural resources. Some state-enforced conservation and sustainable use policies are slowly becoming part of the modern agro-industrial NRM system. Societies are not even close, however, to the extent and depth of change they should make in order to reverse and repair existing negative trends. In addition, too often even the positive measures remain as far from the interests and concerns of local communities as the economic motivations that force them to plant one crop as opposed to another or spray all of them with pesticides. Decisions taken in capital cities or even distant continents have a dominant influence on the interaction people have with their local environment.

To a significant extent, the history of contemporary rural development efforts can be seen as the history of the encounter– or clash– between the indigenous NRM system and the modern, agro-industrial market system.

1.2 The interface between indigenous/ local NRM systems and the modern/ a-local agro-industrial market system: five field examples

To a significant extent, the history of contemporary rural development efforts can be seen as the history of the encounter– or clash– between the indigenous NRM system and the modern, agro-industrial-market system. Such a clash originates in the profound differences existing between the two in terms of goals, values and means (see Table 1.1). It also originates in the power struggles that accompany the process, cutting across both the centre and the periphery of the world order.

Table 1.1 Agro-industrial market system and indigenous NRM systems compared

Agro-industrial market system	Indigenous NRM systems
Supra-national/ international; global, large-scale, similar everywhere	Local, relatively small-scale, many context-depending features
Focus on the generation of private, corporate or state wealth	Focus on community livelihoods
Innovative, often recently tested only outside the area in different social and environmental settings	Traditional, tested at the local level, in the relevant area, for a long time
All market-oriented	Mostly subsistence-oriented
Based on the control of energy sources (e.g., oil), mineral sources and water.	Based on the control of land, biological resources and water.
Requires sophisticated technological inputs and major capital investments, including for transportation	Based on soft technology and small capital investment, including for transportation
Tenure and use of natural resources focus on private and state property regimes, regulated by written law	Tenure and use of natural resources focus on communal property regimes, regulated by customary laws
Promoted by the state and private businesses and backed by military power	Supported by the social organisation of communities and by forms of reciprocities with other communities
Managers are economically-tied individuals, corporate or state decision-makers, dispersed and acting on a global scale	Managers are tightly knit social organisations, closely interacting with society and acting in the local sphere
Separation between exploitation and conservation	Integration of exploitation and conservation (conservation-by-use approach)
Politically and economically powerful on the large scale	Politically and economically weak on the large scale
Mostly explicit, i.e., based on intentional strategies	Mostly implicit, i.e., working on the basis of feedback from other cultural elements
Aims at relatively short-term, precisely measurable results	Aims at long-term sustainable livelihood (defined in a rather general sense)
Based on "objective science" aiming at the reduction of subjective decisions and uncertainties	Based on local knowledge and skills, the recognition of indeterminacies, risk-aversion behaviour and an emphasis on experimentation and adaptation
Conservation mostly understood as preservation of biodiversity and maintenance of ecosystems for aesthetic, recreational and scientific purposes	Conservation mostly understood as sustainable production to sustain livelihoods
Little religious or symbolic value attached to nature	Important religious and symbolic value attached to nature

Nothing is more illustrative of the interaction, or clash, between modern and indigenous NRM systems, than some actual field examples. Five such examples are given below.

Field example 1.1 The Shuar and the colonisation frontier[17]

The Shuar are a 40,000 people Amerindian group settled along the rugged valleys of the Upano, Morona, Santiago, Zamora and Pastaza rivers, in the Ecuadorian Amazon. Since the beginning of the last century, they have been known as Jívaros, a term that in Ecuadorian Spanish denotes fierce, rebel and savage people. This reputation relates to head-hunting, raiding, witchcraft feuding, and indomitable hostility against outsiders, which– after a brief period of Spanish rule between 1549 and 1599– made the Indian territory off-limits to Ecuadorians and travellers for about three hundred years.

By the beginning of the nineteenth century, the Shuar were living according to their tropical forest hunting-horticulturist pattern. They were settled in clusters of 5 — 10 long houses, scattered over an immense and de-populated region and separated by rather large "buffer" areas. Each long house cor-responded to an extended family and each cluster to a local group of about 150 persons. Each group was named after a Big Man acting as a military and ritual leader in headhunting (against non-Shuar Indians) and feuding (against other Shuar settlements). They practised a subsistence economy based on manioc and plantain horticulture, pork breeding and hunting. Most technology was indigenous, with the exception of iron tools, introduced during the sixteenth century, which were bought from mestizo traders settled on the Western border of Indian Territory. Pigs, handicraft (e.g., baskets, blow-guns), forest products (e.g., dart-poison), and small agricultural surplus were bartered with imple-ments such as machetes, knifes, axes, and, after 1920, muzzle-load shotguns and powder.

In the early 1930s, gold was discovered in Western Shuar territory. Gold miners coming from the Azuay highlands used gifts, alcohol, fraud and violence to make their presence accepted. Once the gold fever was over, several miners settled in the area, established cattle ranches and started to employ Shuar labour. The Ecuadorian Army came to protect colonists' property and life, and mis-sions were opened to pacify the Jívaros.

In 1950, the Ecuadorian Government, with the aim of responding to highland peasants' claim for land– without affecting landowners' interests– started to actively promote the colonisation of the area. This process reached its climax in the sixties, when a special institution– the CREA (Centro de Reconversión Económica del Azuay, Cañar y Morona-Santiago)–was created to build the infrastruc-ture needed for a massive colonisation of the Shuar territory.

To resist this mounting pressure on the Western valleys, many Shuar migrated towards the inaccessi-ble region located east of the Kutukú Mountains, where it was still possible to practice their indige-nous way of life. Others, however, adapted to the new situation, seeking protection from the mission-aries against colonists' abuses. They converted to Catholicism, allowed some of their sons and daughters to learn Spanish and be "civilised" in boarding schools, and started to combine indigenous slash-and-burn agriculture with cattle breeding on behalf of the church fathers. Some of them became traders and supplied the "wild Shuar" of Transkutukú with an increasing quantity and variety of western goods. This, of course, increased Eastern Shuar dependence on trading relationships with the frontier. Thus, in one way or another, all the Shuar became increasingly involved in the national market and society.

---

[17]   This case example has been provided by Patrizio Warren. See also Warren, 1992; and Warren, 1996.

By the mid-sixties, some "educated" Shuar started to realise that little chance was left to their people to escape this process. Based on this awareness, an ethnic organisation called the Shuar Federation was founded. Its objectives were defending indigenous land rights, ensuring that benefits of development would be made available to Shuar communities, and preserving indigenous cultural and ethnic identity.

With these goals in mind, the Shuar Federation (supported by missionaries and international non governmental organisations — NGOs) started to promote the modernisation of indigenous society through the following strategy: registration of Shuar settlements as legally acknowledged co-operatives (called Centros); procurement of agricultural land titles; provision of credit and technical assistance for extensive cattle breeding; provision of bilingual education, health and transport services.

During the following twenty years, the Federation was successful in achieving its development objectives. However, by the early 1990s, it became clear that the modernisation process was spoiling the indigenous NRM system, and, eventually, was having a negative impact on the physical and human ecology of most Indian communities. Why was this happening?

Since its establishment, the Shuar Federation had decided to work with the existing laws and procedures. Unfortunately, these were colonisation rules, based on the assumption that there was no "Indian land" in the Amazons but only state property, which could be distributed to individuals or legally recognised groups (i.e., colonisation co-operatives) in accordance with their exploitation capability. Among colonists, this policy had already made clearing the forest and opening pastures an especially popular (and inexpensive) way to get into the position to claim huge extensions of land.

By adopting the same tactics, the Shuar Federation was able to secure significant land titles to many Shuar Centros. This slowed down the occupation of indigenous land. Furthermore, cattle rearing helped people to create some savings, which could then be used to purchase commodities and basic services. Nonetheless, the substitution of forest cover with grassland had a major impact on bio-diversity and soil, and thus on indigenous subsistence practices. Game, forest materials (such as vines, thatching and poles), and good arable land were becoming scarce. An increasing amount of labour had to be invested in cattle raising and pasture management. Even in the eastern plains, where colonists were still few and large untouched forest areas persisted, men started lacking the time for hunting, fishing or looking for forest materials. As a result, tin roofs became less expensive than thatched roofs and nylon rope cheaper than jungle vines.

At the same time, the improvement in the standards of living, modern services and commodities were performing well in decreasing under-five mortality, which fell from 267 per thousand in 1976, to 99 per thousand in 1992. Related to this trend, the total population grew at a rate of about 4% a year. By the early 1990s, the population density was already 5.2 persons per square km of entitled land (i.e., four to five times higher than before contact with the frontier), and it was expected to reach 10.6 persons per square km in 2006. Nobody in the Federation really knew whether the land would be sufficient to sustain the livelihood of all these people. For sure, however, the poor quality of most Shuar soils and the increasing land tenure conflicts occurring among families and settlements suggested that hard times might be coming.

In the late 1990s, based on the above elements and under the influence of several co-operation agencies, the Shuar Federation included environmental sustainability as a major objective in its fight for development and cultural survival. Moreover, new Ecuadorian conservation laws allowed the Shuar Federation to negotiate their entitlements in two major national parks, in which they would be free to practice hunting, fishing and gathering in exchange for conservation works and surveillance. Currently, agro-forestry is also being promoted at the farm level and new income-generating activities based on indigenous know-how, and diversification of production are being tested. Family planning services are also being introduced, despite their poor cultural acceptability and missionary resistance.

All together, the above initiatives may be useful in improving the human ecology of the Shuar, and in preventing an environmental catastrophe. None of them will however be able to restore the demographic and ecological conditions on which the indigenous NRM system was originally based. After three centuries of strenuous resistance, the increased pressure of the national society and economy on their land brought the Shuar to adopt the particular variant of the "modern" NRM system promoted by the national government. This allowed them to survive as an ethnic group, to increase their wealth, and to get basic services, but did not prevent them from eventually clashing with the problems of demographic growth and unsustainable development.

The impact of the national economy and market on indigenous NRM strategies is not always as dramatic as in the Shuar case. Less comprehensive and abrupt changes take place when indigenous strategies are less culturally distant and can coexist with "modern" strategy with minor adjustments. Significantly enough, however, these adjustments often result in less sustainable use of natural resources. The following case, concerning a Mediterranean peasant community, provides a good example of how modernisation may spoil indigenous practices, without being able to replace them with feasible "modern" NRM solutions.

Field example 1.2 Erosion control, indigenous know-how and economic change
in Oued Sbahiya watershed[18]

Oued Sbahiya watershed is located in Zaghouan Governorate, Northern Tunisia. It is a small catchment of 62,000 ha, featuring highly deteriorated forest and rangeland areas in the upper part, and over-exploited agricultural land in the lowlands. It hosts a population of about 1,300 Arabic-speaking peasants who originally migrated from the fertile Zaghouan plain towards this less favourable area under the pressure of early twentieth century French colonisers.

Sbahiya inhabitants practice typical subsistence Mediterranean farming: they grow cereals (wheat, oats and barley) and leguminous crops (broad beans and green peas), cultivate olive and some fruit trees. They also breed sheep and goats, and tend small kitchen gardens. Dwellings are nucleated in small hamlets, according to lineage segments known as douars. Douars own collectively the arable land surrounding the settlement. Several small parcels (as small as 0.25 ha) are however assigned for exploitation to households.

Erosion is a major problem in the ecology of Oued Sbahiya, originated by both natural factors (such as slope, climate, and soil texture) and human-made factors (including population growth, over-

---

[18]   This case-example has been provided by Patrizio Warren.

exploitation of agricultural land, grazing, and firewood pressure on the forests). To tackle the problem, the Centre Régional de Développement Agricole (CRDA) of Zaghouan started in the early 1990s to promote soil management works in the area. Bulldozers were made available to the farmers for erosion control works on their land. This intervention, however, rapidly made soil conservation authorities unpopular with the peasants. Bulldozers were simply too big to operate efficiently in the patchwork of micro-parcels owned by Sbahiya peasants. Inter-property borders could not be respected and tracks scrapped away amounts of soil which (given the parcel size) farmers perceived as significant. Passive resistance mounted against the programme, which eventually led CRDA technicians to think that Sbahiya peasants were not aware of the consequences of erosion on their farming system, nor willing to take any measure to counteract it, unless forced by authorities.

In 1996, researchers from a participatory watershed management project supported by the Food and Agriculture Organisation of the United Nations (FAO) tried to face the issue from a different prospective. In the framework of a participatory appraisal exercise, the project team visited a highly eroded area together with a group of peasants and asked them what they knew about erosion. People defined erosion as "fertile soil going away, leaving bad land behind". This was related in part to the will of Allah, who created the djebels (mountains) and the steep slope; and, in part, to the behaviour of abdallah (literally, "Allah's servant", i.e., the peasant), who does not take appropriate care of his land.

The peasants were then asked to describe what could be done to avoid soil loss. They said that in the past they used to stabilise soil by constructing check-dams with stones and planting prickly pear cactuses on the gullies. They also used to build embankments made of tree branches and earth, consolidated through the plantation of fig trees, for collecting and deviating running water.

Technicians realised and agreed that these measures were sound and asked why they were abandoned. People explained that this depended on changes in their lifestyle. New needs (including agricultural inputs, household commodities, and expenses related to education and health) have made their households increasingly dependent on cash. Yet the price paid for their agricultural products is far less than the salaries that can be earned by masonry workers in the tourist areas of the coast, by wage labourers in big agricultural estates, or by migrants overseas. Moreover, city lights are attractive for youngsters. That's why most men (and some unmarried girls) migrate elsewhere in search of better chances, leaving the burden of agriculture on the shoulders of old people, women and children. In these conditions of local labour scarcity, the household economy can not anymore afford conservation works. The fields are worked as fast as possible, trying to squeeze out of them maximum yields with little concern for loss of fertility.

These considerations had a very practical immediate implication. The erosion control authorities were urged to consider the opportunity to reinvest part of the money allocated to mechanical erosion control works, to pay cash incentives to farmers willing to implement manual works in accordance with local know-how. It was also stressed that such an option would bring two additional benefits: contributing to lessening seasonal migration, and revitalising some elements of the indigenous farming system that are essential for sustainability.

The case, however, tells us more than that. It shows that current attitudes and behaviours of Sbahiya peasants towards land husbandry could not be considered independently from some embedding economic and political factors, such as land tenure policies, structure of the local market, and social marginalisation. The shrinking of arable land per household (related to population growth), the poor prices paid locally to local production, the increased social needs, and the presence of off-farm income generation opportunities, have all resulted in decreased availability of labour for indigenous soil conservation works. At the same time, the modern alternative (mechanical works) is not appropriate to the prevailing land tenure pattern. In other words, as far as land husbandry is concerned, Sbahiya peasants are stuck between the old and the new– between the indigenous and "modern" NRM systems– without being able to find a satisfactory solution to their soil conservation problem.

Modern influences on indigenous NRM systems do not always result in destruction (as in the Shuar case) or a loss (as in the Sbahiya peasants' case). The following example from Iran demonstrates the strength and resilience of some traditional NRM systems in the face of powerful agents of change.

Field example 1.3 The Qashqai: nomadic pastoral livelihoods against all odds…[19]

A hundred years ago, the Confederation of Qashqai Tribes was one of the largest nomadic pastoralist groups of Iran. At that time, most of the population of the country (probably over one-half) was composed of nomadic pastoralists. The most significant ethnic groups were the Qashqai, Shahsavan, Baluch, Turkmen, Bakhtiari and other Luri peoples. Besides them there were seven hundred large and small tribes and independent clans of pastoralists. Since time immemorial, the pastoralist tribes constituted the backbone of the political structures governing the region. Typically, a number of such tribes would form a coalition and take hold of political power in the land. The chief of the dominant tribe in the coalition would be named King of Kings and start a new dynasty. If people became unhappy with the ruling dynasty, a new coalition of tribes would take over and form a new dynasty. This is the essence of the political history of Iran over the past twenty five centuries. Some fourteen centuries ago, Arab tribes took over the land as part of the Islamic expansion. Having defeated the Sasanid dynasty, they took over the country and ruled it for four centuries until about 1,000 years ago, when some Turkish-speaking tribes liberated Iran from Arab colonial rule. Various Turkic tribes then ruled the country nearly all the time until about 1920 when the Pahlavi dynasty took over the Kingdom. This was the first non-tribal, non-pastoral dynasty to rule the country since the domination by Arab regimes had been overthrown.

The Qashqai tribes have likely been living in southern Iran for over a thousand years. For all practical purposes they are "indigenous" to several provinces in the south, including Fars, Bushire and Hormozgan. These pastoralists, like most of the others in Iran, have depended on grazing rangelands in an extensive manner, migrating from wintering grounds to summering grounds and back. The wintering grounds are usually lower planes and hillsides, while the summering grounds are higher up the mountains. The distance between these two ranges is usually several hundred kilometres. Most of the tribes have an agreed migration route through which they pass twice a year: in the spring and in the autumn.

The landscape over which these tribes migrate is held and managed under a typical common property regime. The allocation of land follows the customary laws and each unit of the tribe knows the territory over which it has the right of grazing. They take great care to insure that the rangelands are healthy. Men take care of larger animals that can move over large distances without water, while women take female and lactating animals grazing closer by. Women are also in charge of milking the animals twice a day and processing the milk into butter, yoghurt, and many other products. Children, too, are a productive part of the system, as they usually take the young animals to pasture. Managing the common property resources is the responsibility of the Councils of Elders, usually through a sophisticated and complex process. Barring unusual events and disasters, the system assured the sus-

---

[19]   This case example has been provided by M. Taghi Farvar.

tainable use of pasture for centuries, maintaining the ecosystem in a state of dynamic equilibrium.

In the 1920s and 1930s, however, the rule of Reza Shah brought drastic and disastrous changes. Reza Shah was not of nomadic origin. He actually held the nomads in contempt and thought that they were a huge impediment to his imitation of the style of development of Europe. In his mad rush to dominate and "modernise" the country (by modernisation he simply understood Europeanisation) he mimicked Ataturk, who was busy dismantling the traditional social structures of Anatolia at the same time. Reza Shah used military force against the nomadic pastoralists to smash any resistance to his designs, and did not hesitate to use treachery where he could not succeed by the use of force. The landscape of the Qashqai nomads is scattered with the reminders of this very unfortunate epoch. Most of these take the form of ruins of mud housing projects that the King ordered built in the middle of nowhere. Finding themselves confined at gunpoint to a very limited area for grazing, many pastoralist groups perished together with their livestock. The powerful rural police of Reza Shah managed to keep them effectively under the siege of forced sedentarisation.

With the abdication of the King in the middle of World War II, his son Mohammad Reza Shah took over. During the 1940s the nomadic pastoralists felt a relative lessening of the iron rule over them, which unfortunately was soon to be re-established. The Qashqai took full advantage of the temporary situation, as the government in Tehran was weak and ineffective: they simply took to their migration routes again! They collected the surviving sheep, goats, donkeys, horses and camels and started again to take care of their rangelands and flocks of livestock. They managed rather well until 1953, when a well known USA-UK-backed coup d'état ousted the nationalist and popular Prime Minister Dr. Mohammed Mosaddeq and brought the self-exiled Shah back to power. Throughout their history, the Qashqai have shown to be defenders of the land, particularly against British colonialism. In support of the popular deposed prime minister they actually took up arms and fought for the next ten years a hard war against the government of the Shah. In the end the Qashqai were defeated and their tribal chiefs expelled from the country.

Already in the 1950s, a new law for foreign aid had passed in the Parliament of the United States of America and an agreement of cooperation had been signed with the government of the Shah. A young man from the Qashqai tribe was recruited by the Point Four (foreign aid) Administration and taken to the United States of America. This young man, by the name of Bahman-Beygi, was shown the school system in the American Indian reservations, designed to assimilate the Indians into the American lifestyle and alienate them from their land and traditions. It was assumed that the nomadic pastoralists of Iran were equivalent to the "Indians" of the United States. Bahman-Beygi was instructed about how to brainwash the minds of the young students in order to alienate them from their tribes and implant in them an insatiable thirst for the modern, urban life far removed from the realities of nomadic pastoralism. He came back to Iran and convinced the Shah to let him organise an innovative tribal school system, based on mobile schools held in tents. The tents were white against the backdrop of the black tents of the nomads. The white tents were to symbolise, in the very words of Bahman-Beygi "purity and enlightenment against the darkness and ignorance of the evil black tents!"[20] The methods of learning were harsh and rote, reminiscent of a fascist system of education, and were inculcated into selected tribal teachers, recruited from the very tribes. Each teacher was given a white tent and was armed with tools for conditioning the innocent children. When hearing criticisms of his rote methods of learning, for instance that they were not conducive to encouraging thinking, Bahman-Beygi would retort: "these children are not supposed to think; they are simply supposed to carry out the programme I have implanted in them."[21] Mohammed Reza Shah had effectively replaced the bullets of his father with American-inspired chalks. Both were instruments for sedentarisation and the second was even more pernicious than the first in undoing the very basis of nomadism in Iran.

---

[20] Expressed publicly to M. T. Farvar by Bahman-Beygi in the 1977 National Seminar on Nomadism, Kermanshah, western Iran.
[21] Bahman-Beygi expressed these words to M. T. Farvar in 1977 in the same Seminar.

Two more events took place in these years and were extremely harmful to the life styles and livelihoods of the Qashqai nomads. The first was the exile of their chiefs, who took refuge in Germany until after the Islamic revolution of 1979. This amounted to the virtual beheading of the tribes. In their place the Shah's security apparatus appointed colonels from the dreaded SAVAK, the secret police, who controlled every movement of the tribe and commanded their migrations. The other was the much heralded land reform laws, which included among other things the nationalisation of all natural resources in Iran. According to these laws, forced through the handpicked parliament, all rangelands, which amounted to ninety percent of all usable land in the country and which had been treated and managed under a common property regime throughout history, became henceforth state property. Instead of dealing with rangelands as a collective responsibility and privilege, individuals had to apply for short term licenses for grazing and all customary rights and laws were ignored. This action was tantamount to removing the base of survival for the nomadic tribes of Iran.

As a matter of fact, even other national policies were designed without any consideration for the needs and capacities of pastoral societies, and had a powerful weakening effect on them. Animal products such as meat, skin, dairy products and even live sheep were imported from abroad for the benefit of national merchants, undercutting the production systems of the pastoralists who had been able to supply the needs of the country with much surplus for export to boot. With their chiefs exiled, the economic base seriously weakened and the minds of the young changed fundamentally, the once powerful tribes of Iran were firmly headed towards annihilation. One of the immediate consequences was that the integrity of the rangeland ecosystems, which they had so carefully maintained through time, began to erode. On a positive note, a number of groups, often based in universities, succeeded in early 1970s in designing and testing a different kind of mobile services for pastoral nomads. These included veterinary services (veterinary assistants recruited from the tribes and trained, returned to them to provide mobile epizootic and vaccination services) and mobile health services (health assistants, also called "barefoot doctors", recruited from the tribes and trained, returned to them to provide primary health care and a referral service to clinics and hospitals).

The 1979 Iranian revolution presented another chance for the nomadic tribes of Iran to exercise once again their freedom of movement. The Qashqai tribes took once again to migrate in their greatest glory. One should imagine the joy and sense of liberation of these people who were regaining their simple right to livelihoods. The Qashqai exiled chiefs had returned from Germany and were attempting to get back their functions in their tribes. Having lived for nearly two decades in the west, they had adopted new ideas, and included democratic governance into their world view. They talked about human development, and environmental integrity of the rangelands. They were also concerned about the social responsibility of tribal chiefs. One of them– the late Khosrow Qashqai– was eager to introduce the concept of ecodevelopment into the Qashqai tribes. This same chief was elected Member of Parliament. To his dismay, when he attempted to take his seat in Parliament, some extremist elements prevented him from doing so. Shortly afterwards he was kidnapped, submitted to summary justice and executed without the benefit of an appeal to the supreme leader, who would surely have protected him.

Under the new Islamic regime, the cultural intrusion continued via the same tribal schools mentioned above, now run by the national Ministry of Education. This meant even less autonomy for the tribal educational system. At this time, issues of natural resources, especially rangelands, were dealt with by the Forest and Rangeland Organisation (FARO) of the Ministry of Agriculture, which continued the alienation of the nomadic tribes through the endorsement of the practice of rangeland ownership by the state.[22] At that time, verses from the Holy Koran– originally dealing with the spoils of war (infal)– were interpreted by none other than the very progressive Grand Ayatollah Taleqani as applying to all natural resources, making them state property. No one understood at the time this was

---

22 This happened despite the fact that the late Imam Khomeini, in 1963, had led the rebellion against the land reform laws of the Shah, including the nationalisation of rangelands and other natural resources.

spelling out a sure breakdown in rangeland management and the further alienation of the nomadic pastoralists from their rightful heritage. The government finally realized something to this effect in the 1990s, but even then decided to privatise rangeland management rather than return it to its original rightful owners. Rangelands were and still are given away by FARO for everything– from military bases and oil refineries to urban development and speculative operators. One of the Governors-General of the province of Fars boasted in a public statement in 1991 that he had purposely caused the blocking and destruction of tribal migration routes in order to uproot nomadic pastoralism, which he considered a backward way of life. The same Governor admitted to playing a key role in the trapping and summary execution of Khosrow Qashqai, the popular tribal chief mentioned earlier.

While the technical capacity of government institutions, including FARO, was progressively weakened as a result of attrition and ideological purges of highly qualified personnel, when the Iranian Government finally realized the value of technical expertise, it was expertise of the wrong kind that was available. In the case of rangeland ecology and management, the old school promoted in Iran by the Utah State University– to whom the management of natural resources had been entrusted by the Shah– became the dominant ideology despite its repeated failures to respond to the needs of the Iranian ecology. The non-equilibrium ecosystem conditions that characterise most of Asian arid regions had not yet been understood by the relevant establishment of the country. Alien concepts of carrying capacity were applied, including for a major government project called "Livestock and Rangeland Equilibrium," imposed all over the country. The main purpose of this project was to reduce livestock on rangelands, and to eliminate many of the pastoral producers, obliging the nomads to settle permanently. The sedentarisation of nomads, in fact, became the main focus of the Organisation for Pastoralists Affairs (OPA), which had originally been created in the office of the Prime Minister to support nomadic pastoralism. Another post-revolutionary institution, called "Rural and Pastoral Service Centres", was later reduced to rural service centres only, and its job degenerated mainly into writing extravagant prescriptions for pesticides.

At the time of this writing the Iranian legislation is still not suited to meet the need of the pastoral communities. The important provision for Local Councils has not been enacted for pastoral communities, and a law in Parliament, which would allow for the creation of Tribal Councils, did not take into consideration the specificity of tribal nomadic societies and their traditional organisations. In the end, even this law was vetoed by the powerful Council of the Guardians that is charged with supervising the Parliament. Hopefully, the Fourth National Development Plan has a chance to remedy this ill and to respond in a positive vein to the needs of the nomads, who still number some 1.5 million souls and who can still play an invaluable role as the guardians of the semi-arid ecosystems that cover most of the country.

Despite the most discouraging experience of the past century, there are new seeds of hope among pastoralists. For instance, a recent agreement between the Iranian Government and the Centre for Sustainable Development, a national NGO, has made it possible for pastoral communities to start participatory planning sessions for sustainable livelihoods and rangeland conservation. This work brings together supporting agencies at the national and international levels and holds some hope for reversing some past negative trends. It is also encouraging that a group of national legislators are now interested in supporting pastoral communities in their quest for cultural survival and sustainable livelihoods. New models for the sustainable development of pastoral regions and communities are obviously needed and the Iranian NGO is promoting rangeland management based on concepts and practices of non-equilibrium ecosystem and community-based sustainable livelihoods tailored to the country's specific characteristics. As part of the mentioned project, one Qashqai sub-tribe has organised its own tribal council in March 2003 and hopes to register as a community-based organisation (CBO) endowed with a community investment fund. With the help of wealth generating activities a surplus is expected to be created, which will be used to help other sub-tribes jumpstart their own process of endogenous development. A nomadic pastoralist model for a community conserved area at the heart of their migratory route has also being elaborated by the sub-tribe currently leading the way and presented at the 2003 World Parks Congress in Durban (South Africa). All this does not mean that traditional nomadic pastoralism is continuing unchanged. Commercially acquired fodder is now part of the subsistence system of the herds and several habits of sedentary people have become widespread among the pastoralists. And yet, the diversification in the production system and the newly acquired habits do not seem to have altered the main character of the tribes' livelihood– herding as primary production, social solidarity, communal care for the pasture– nor their proven strength, resilience and pride.

In some instances, indigenous and rural cultures have been able to place market-oriented production at the heart of their traditional NRM system. The sustainable use of wildlife resources in Southern Africa provides a powerfully telling example.

Field example 1.4 Managing the sustainable use of wildlife[23]

Chapoto Ward is an administrative sub-unit of the Guruve district in Zimbabwe. It spans an area of 300 square kilometres and is sandwiched in between national parks estate land on the south and west, the Mozambique border on the east and the Zambezi River, which forms a boundary with Zambia, on the north. A meeting took place there, in February of 1998, between the Chapoto Ward Wildlife Committee and a few international visitors. The Wildlife Committee arises from the ward's inclusion in Zimbabwe's Communal Areas Management Programme for Indigenous Resources (CAMPFIRE) programme, a national programme that encourages rural development and sustainable natural resource use through the devolution of management responsibility and access rights to "producer communities".[24] To date, the expansion of the programme has rested largely on the exploitation of high-value species through sport hunting, with concessions leased to commercial safari operators. Although formally introduced in 1989, the programme did not achieve implementation momentum in Chapoto until 1992. By 1996 wildlife had become the largest collective economic enterprise of the ward with revenues at household levels equalling those of cash cropping. A party of two trustees and regional representatives of an international donor foundation constituted the visitors.

The chair of the Wildlife Committee opened the meeting by outlining the background and history of the Programme in Chapoto. Being an astute politician he put the programme forward in its best light. For decades of colonialism the people of Chapoto had suffered government neglect, without the roads, schools and clinics, which the communities closer to the capital had received. Living in an agriculturally marginal environment they had had to eke out an existence by cultivation of riverine alluvium, supplementing their diet with foraging and hunting. Even hunting was however difficult, since government claimed the wildlife which raided their fields and gardens as its own. Local hunters were subject to harassment and arrest by National Parks staff. Wildlife had become an unmitigated liability for all, except for the few poachers who were adept enough to evade detection.

With the coming of the CAMPFIRE programme things had changed. Wildlife became a collective asset, to be communally managed. Poaching dropped and wildlife populations increased, since individual off-takes became a theft of communal property and the community made use of its own knowledge and peer pressure mechanisms to suppress deviance. Revenues from the sale of wildlife

---

23   This case-example has been provided by Marshall Murphree. See also Murphree, 1997b.
24   See Metcalfe, 1994.

escalated annually and the community built a school, a clinic and a grinding mill from the proceeds. One of the foundation's trustees opened the question time. "We are pleased," she said, "to learn that you are getting large sums from your wildlife which has contributed dramatically to your development. But what is the impact of this exploitation on the biodiversity of your area? How do you count your animals to ensure that you are not driving certain species to extinction?"

After the interpreter attempted to translate the word "biodiversity" into the local language with some complex phrases, the chair rose to reply. With a smile he commented, "We know that you people from overseas want to count animals by aeroplane, and have many papers with figures before animals can be used. But I must be honest and tell you that we do not count each of our animals. Even if we had an aeroplane, we could not count animals in the thick bush here. But we know that wildlife populations have increased because we see more of them and they are raiding our fields more intensively than before." "But," he continued, "you should know that a general increase in wildlife is not our main concern. Yes, we like to see more kudu and bushbuck around, but they are not central for our management objectives. What we are really concerned with are two species: elephant and buffalo. They are our focus, because it is these two species that produce high safari revenues. Since they are so important we monitor them closely."

"The way we monitor them," he said, "is by watching trends. And to examine trends we look at trophy quality. Each trophy taken is carefully measured; for elephant it is tusk weight, for buffalo the horns are sized by Rowland Ward measurements. These measurements are taken in each instance by the safari operator, the National Parks staff and our own game scouts. Since 1992 we have kept these records and over time can determine trends in trophy quality. If you want to see a paper with lots of figures," he added with a twinkle in his eye, "we can show it to you."

By this time the chair was full stride. "Now," he said, "if we see that trophy quality is improving we increase the quota slightly for the following year. But if we see that it is dropping, we decrease the quota since quality is a greater determinant of our safari revenues than quantity. We want to continue to receive high wildlife revenues indefinitely, and limiting quotas is our investment in the future. In our last assessment," he went on, "we saw that buffalo trophies were continuing to improve and so we increased the quota. However, we saw that tusk size of elephant trophies was declining and so we have cut the quota."

"What about generating income from your wildlife through photographic tourism?" was the next question from the visitors. "By all means," replied another committee member, "but it is difficult to show the tourists elephant and buffalo in our thick bush. However, we can show them rare birds, and visitors are interested in the beauty and the fishing opportunities that they find on the Zambezi. We have already leased land on the river to two tourist operators and we are maintaining the riverine habitat and restricting settlement patterns." A number of other questions were posed on issues like problem animal control, strategies in times of drought, compensation for crop depredation, control of fishing and wood-cutting, the ivory trade and locally managed tourism. To each the community had a reply that showed insight and previous discussion.

"What are your other problems?" was the final question. "There are three main ones," was the reply. "Firstly, this business of managing wildlife takes time and transport. We have to constantly meet with the safari operator, the National Park staff and the District Council. Secondly, it is difficult to manage our money. We are not trained in book-keeping and there is no bank here." For the community, in fact, the biggest problem was uncertainty about the future. "We don't really know how long government will allow us to keep these animals and the revenues they generate. We don't know how long government will allow us to lease sites on the Zambezi and keep the proceeds. Government knows, as we have learned, that these things are extremely valuable and government may take them back. If that were to happen we would abandon our quotas and self-imposed restrictions and take what we can without being caught." With this the meeting closed.

The conversation did not cover all aspects of Chapoto's sustainable use programme. The Wildlife Committee's presentation did not reveal the internal divisions that exist within the community or the ongoing disputes it has with the District Council, since these are not matters to be discussed with visitors. However, the dialogue clearly illustrates some elements of cultural dissonance between the local people and their visitors, including at least five main areas.

The first of such areas is about values. The people of Chapoto were concerned with sustainable productivity. For rural farmers and pastoralists as they are, conservation is an investment (in direct or opportunity costs) for present and future value, the goal being the maintenance or enhancement of their livelihoods. The visitors were instead concerned with species preservation, "biodiversity" and "ecosystem maintenance" for aesthetic, recreational or scientific purposes. As a matter of fact, there is nothing inherently incompatible in the two sets of values. Dissonance arises, however, when one stance is accorded privileged status, as it is at present for international valuations. This does not work. Aside from their inherent merits, local perspectives have a powerful veto dimension. Unless they are accommodated, international values and goals will be subverted by local responses ranging from defiance to covert non-compliance. From an international perspective, conservation, sustainable use and equity are distinct and separate issues, with distinct associated activities while local perspectives roll these three into one interactive bundle. Programmatic interventions are unlikely to work if they are not responsive to this synthesis.

The second area is proprietorship. The devolution of a direct authority over the use and benefit of land and resources has been the catalyst to mobilise action in Chapoto. It stimulated a sense of responsibility and launched the community into a new mode of management requiring skills in handling the exchange values of their natural resources. The conferment of proprietorship had, however, been one of programme and not legal entitlement. It was therefore incomplete, lacking tenure or long-term security of access. This insecurity led the people of Chapoto into gloomy prognostications of the future. Without proprietorship their incentives for conservation would falter and fail. Unfortunately, this clashes with the bureaucratic mind, disposed to the centralisation of authority, against the technocratic mind, disposed to see devolution as the surrender of professional management to the vagaries of cost/ benefit decisions by unsophisticated peasants, and with the interests of the central political elite and their private sector allies. The answer lies neither in community autarky nor state autocracy. It lies instead in a redefinition and acceptance of complementary and mutually supportive roles. Local organisation can assume the authority and responsibility necessary to carry through local incentives. The state can take on a supra-local coordinative role with its arbitrative, regulatory and extension functions.

The third area of dissonance is science– what is it and how should it be used. International conservationism relies on high-tech quantitative modelling to monitor and predict ecological status. In the process, biological scientists gain a powerful clientele, while governments and agencies "seek to find a scientific algorithm to reduce subjective decision-taking and uncertainties". Rural farmers such as those in Chapoto have a similar goal. Dealing with uncertainty is a continuing factor in their lives and risk-aversion a pervasive feature of their farming strategies. When given the opportunity, they use a methodology of the highest scientific credentials: experimentation. Chapoto's monitoring of trophy trend is elegant in its simplicity, robust in its empiricism and striking in its tight application to management decisions. It is also pregnant with potential for the development of locally based environmental science, which moves beyond issues of species off-take. Such science, flexible in its foci and dynamic in its analysis, is far more important than the static domain of "indigenous technical knowledge," the box to which we condescendingly assign local insight and experience. People like those at Chapoto have problems with the scientific environmental "technicism". It involves for them a significant loss of control and can be applied to stop use, which their own science indicates is viable. And they have a healthy scepticism of its ability to produce the predictive certainties that are expected of it. (In this they have major allies amongst scientists concerned with evolutionary biology, system approaches and adaptive management.) Most environmental regulations demand certainty and when scientists are pressured to supply this non-existent commodity there is frustration, poor communication and mixed messages in the media. One can also add that this pressure is a perverse incentive for the integrity of science itself, since it carries with it the temptation to assert as definitive that which is tentative. Fortunately, both conservation biology and local science tend now to converge to acknowledge indeterminacy and emphasise experimentation and adaptation in NRM.

Potential "lack-of-fit" between social and ecological topography is another area of dissonance. The institutional requirements of a local natural resource management regime such as Chapoto include social cohesion, locally sanctioned authority and co-operation, and compliance reliant primarily on peer pressure. This implies a tightly knit interactive social unit spatially located to permit this. However, while social topography suggests "small-scale" regimes, ecological considerations tend to mandate "large-scale" regimes. This may arise from ecosystem needs or when key resources are widely dispersed or mobile, as in the case of Chapoto's elephant and buffalo. Economic considerations may also dictate "large-scale" regimes where market factors require that several owners of resource units manage and tender their resources collectively. There is no inherent reason why social and ecological topographies cannot be harmonised, although this requires context-specific institutional engineering through negotiation. Often this will involve nested systems of collective enterprise by owners of resource units. The units of management will have a built-in incentive to spread. Dissonance arises when larger ecosystem regimes are imposed rather than endogenous. Such impositions, often in the form of ecologically determined projects, concentrate on ecological sustainability at the cost of ignoring the institutional sustainability on which it depends.

Projects and programmes are the principal, though not exclusive, contexts bringing together international and local incentives for sustainable use. These contexts juxtapose two cultures of planning and implementation. The one is reductionist, bureaucratic, directive and contractual, operating through the rigid time and budget frames of a "project cycle." The other is incrementalist, personalised, suasive and consensual, operating through experiment and adaptation set in indeterminate time-frames. For various reasons governments and donor agencies typically operate in project cycles far more condensed in time than that required for the institutional learning which must take place before local regimes can harmonise their modes of implementation with those of external partners. Such institutional learning goes far beyond the impartation of knowledge and skills by external agents. More fundamentally it is about experiential adaptation of roles and norms in new circumstances within local social units themselves. Knowledge and skills required by individuals do not suffice on their own; institutional learning is a collective process of adaptive interaction responsive to external and internal change. It takes time. At whatever point in the learning curve we place Chapoto, we should bear in mind that their perspectives were the product of a nine year evolution in status and experience.

The demand for safari experiences– a phenomenon originating in countries and cultures very far from Chapoto, seems thus to have successfully integrated the local livelihood system of rural communities in Southern Africa. Technical innovations have also been integrated with relative success by indigenous and rural cultures in their traditional NRM system. This is especially true for rural cultures born from an encounter between native people and foreign colonists, which is a widespread phenomenon in Latin America and the Caribbean. The Ribereño farmers of the Peruvian Amazons are an excellent example.

Field example 1.5 Don Emiliano's farm[25]

The ethnic roots of the Ribereño people are heterogeneous in the extreme. Some of them are the heirs of the sixteenth and seventeenth century Spaniards and Indian river-people. Others originated from inland Indians, Peruvian Creoles, and European adventurers, who were involved in exploitation of different types of natural rubber in the period 1880-1950. Others are a mix of recently acculturated Indians, colonists coming from the upper course of the river, soldiers from other areas of Peru who married local women, indigenous protestant missionaries, and town-dwellers escaping from the law.

The Ribereño culture is a real melting pot of indigenous and exotic elements. The local language, for instance, is strongly influenced by Quechua (the Andean language spread in the Upper Amazon by Jesuits in the seventeenth and eighteenth centuries). The social structure includes both Indian features (such as cousins' marriage) and Spanish-Peruvian elements (such as ritual compadrazgo). Symbolic culture combines folk-Catholicism (or sometimes revivalist Protestantism), Amazonian shamanism, and elements of sixteenth and seventeenth century European magic, with a major interest in global media culture (all Ribereño households own a radio, and some own a colour TV).

This trend of mixing and melting different cultural influences is especially evident in the Ribereño farming systems, which are based on a combination of subsistence and market-oriented agriculture, hunting and fishing, cattle raising, and agro-forestry activities. An example of how the complex ecology of the Amazonian riverbanks is managed through such a diversified NRM strategy is provided by the farm owned by Don Emiliano (in Barranco, Marañon River).[26]

---

25   This case study has been provided by Patrizio Warren.
26   These observations were made by Patrizio Warren between 1982 and 1986.

As for any Ribereño household, the basis of Emiliano's household subsistence is the cultivation of plantains, manioc, and other tubers on never-flooded restinga lands. This activity is carried out with traditional slash and burn techniques of Indian origin, and according to the indigenous division of labour by gender lines (with men in charge of clearing the fields and women responsible for their cultivation). The fields (chacras) are cultivated for two or three years and, when weeding becomes too hard, are left to lie fallow during 5 to 10 years (depending on restinga's soil quality). These patches of secondary forest (purma) have always had a significant value for a household: they are a place where wild fruits, special materials, medicinal plants and narcotics can be collected.

Following the indigenous livelihood strategy, Don Emiliano's household complements its starch-rich tuber and plantain diet with river proteins. In times of shallow waters, Don Emiliano and his sons go fishing in the river and surrounding lakes, using a technology in part of indigenous origin (canoe, paddle, spear), in part introduced by the Spaniards (hook, tarafa net) and in part modern (nylon line, outboard motor). According to a practice of Spanish origin, part of the catch is salted to secure pango (the Ribereño fish and plantain soup) for the time of the flood, when fishing becomes difficult and dangerous. Unlike some of his neighbours, however, Emiliano has been resistant to engaging in commercial fishing and is against dynamite fishing because of its negative environmental impact. Rather, inspired by an ancient Indian practice he learned from a folk-tale, he experiments with river turtle breeding in a pond near his house.

Hunting is a marginal practice in Emiliano's subsistence strategy, because of the scarcity of game in the surroundings of the farm. This is due to the overexploitation of edible mammals (such as wild pork, tapir and deer) in the last 50 years by soldiers from the neighbouring military camp. However, during the flooding season, at night, Emiliano's sons hunt the big rodents, which haunt chacras to eat tubers. To this end, the Ribereño gun-and-lamp hunting technique (based on instinct of rodents to stop cold when sharp lights are focussed on them in the dark) is used, as well as pit-and-stakes traps, which Emiliano has learned to build from the Indians.

As in any other Ribereño household, Emiliano's family is engaged in income generating activities. The main business is supplying the military camp (and other customers) with beef and pork. To breed zebu cattle, the hill on the back of the house has been cleared from the forest and sown with gramalote fodder grass, a species recommended in the area for its soil retention capability, despite its low nutritional content. Applying extension information heard on the radio, Emiliano decided to leave a patch of primary forest on top of the hill. To prevent erosion, provide shading to the cattle, and fulfil household timber and fruit needs, he also planted valuable cedar specimens and fruit trees on the slope. Made aware by the same source of the low nutritional value of his pasture, Emiliano is striving to prevent his herd from increasing, by timely selling of calves.

In contrast with such a modern approach to cattle breeding, pig breeding is managed according to the indigenous pattern. In order to prevent pigs from spoiling crops, animals are kept on a small restinga (island in the middle of the river) where they can run free in search of food. A child brings household garbage to the pigs every day. According to Don Emiliano, daily feeding by humans is essential to prevent the animals from becoming wild and unmanageable at the time when it becomes necessary to catch them.

Finally, Emiliano and his family engage in cash cropping. To this end, as many other Ribereño households of the area, at every shallow water season they receive credit from the Agriculture Bank and sow rice on the fertile soil of river mud banks. This is a risky enterprise, because young rice is highly exposed to parrots and insects, and, what is worse, nobody in the Amazons can really foresee when the floods will come. However, with good luck, significant gains can be made through this activity.

Emiliano believes that this is a "crazy business, which is spoiling so many farmers." However, he allows his sons to engage in it, because, as he says, "the trunk of our farm is solid enough to afford the loss of some branches."

Don Emiliano's story illustrates the complexity and sophistication of the Ribereños' NRM system. It shows their diverse and specific uses of the Amazonian wetlands– the never flooded restingas, the rivers, the lake, the hills, the mud-banks– in accordance with seasons, subsistence needs, and market opportunities. It also shows how such diversification is promoted by the Ribereño cultural capacity to combine in a new synthesis elements originating in a variety of cultural environments and historical experiences. Emiliano's farming system is indeed a mix of reminiscences of pre-Colombian Amazonian wetland society, old Spanish and European legacies, contemporary Indian influences, twentieth century technology and modern agricultural extension advice. Its success witnesses the capability of contemporary Amazonian people to build an alternative to the development model which national colonisation agencies and the global market are striving to impose on them in the name of progress.

1.3 Contemporary indigenous NRM systems and co-management

From the field examples illustrated above, a few lessons can be derived concerning the structure of NRM systems currently practised by indigenous and local communities and their relevance for sustainable development and conservation initiatives.

The lesson here is that most NRM systems of contemporary indigenous and local communities are puzzles of old and new knowledge, practices, tools and values of different cultural origin. Building upon the characteristics of diverse political and economic contexts, the combination of indigenous and modern elements in these NRM systems varies and leads to different outcomes. The indigenous system may be almost completely replaced by a variant of the agro-industrial market system promoted by the state (as in the Shuar case). Change in the indigenous system could be only partial, but powerful enough to affect the community's capability to manage the local resources in a sustainable way (as in the Sbahiya peasants' case) or apparently overpowering but unable to destroy the heart of the livelihood system, as in Iran. Eventually, an innovative and more complex NRM system can develop by combining indigenous and modern elements (as for Chapoto's community and in Don Emiliano's farm and, to a certain extent also in Iran).

Process and outcome variations on this theme are indeed as diverse as human cultures and communities on earth. But– local differences notwithstanding– practically no NRM system observable in the field at the beginning of the 21st

...most NRM systems of contemporary indigenous and local communities are puzzles of old and new knowledge and practices, tools and values of different historical and cultural origin.

Century can be claimed to be purely "indigenous." On the contrary, NRM systems featured by contemporary ethnic and rural communities are syncretic constructions, i.e., more or less consolidated syntheses of knowledge and practices of different historical and cultural origins, which previously might have even been considered incompatible.[27] As such, they represent attempts made by local people to adapt indigenous NRM systems to cope with new environmental conditions, market economy requirements, and tenure regulations imposed by the national society and the state.

The merging of features from different cultural origins is not a unidirectional process. Elements of modern NRM systems are integrated into an indigenous background and, at the same time, the indigenous background contributes to shape the particular variant of the modern system that is actually implemented in the area. For instance, the shifting horticultural knowledge and practices of the Shuar (the only component of the indigenous NRM system still alive in the area) has substantially influenced the colonists' subsistence agriculture. Zaghouan soil and water management authorities are considering the opportunity of providing incentives to Sbahiya farmers to implement conservation works on the basis of indigenous know-how. Diversified exploitation of multiple ecosystems and ecotypes, as experimented in Don Emiliano's farm, is increasingly promoted among tropical forest farmers by rural development agencies and experts. The pragmatic approach to sustainable use of the Chapoto community has now been studied and advocated by the World Conservation Union's (IUCN) Sustainable Use Initiative and the pastoral practices of nomadic communities are being re-discovered as a most effective and careful way of managing rangelands in non-equilibrium ecosystems.[28]

> ...syncretic constructions [are] more or less consolidated syntheses of knowledge and practices of different historical and cultural origins, which previously might have even been considered incompatible.

As in any process of cultural change, the development of this syncretism is somehow chaotic and unsystematic. It mostly takes place through a trial and error process, whereby new elements are adopted, old elements dismissed, and system structures re-arranged. At times, and especially when trial and error is transformed into a more or less conscious form of "adaptive management"[29] this succeeds in identifying creative and effective solutions. Unfortunately, most contemporary indigenous NRM systems are not as well integrated, efficient or sustainable as the traditional ones. This is because most of them are in a phase of transition in which much testing takes place, often unsuccessfully. Furthermore, the rapid evolution of the relationship between local communities and the national society, new development and conservation policies, innovative technologies and the omnipresence of the global market, make the building of combined NRM systems a tricky endeavour under ever-changing rules. In some ways, the development of NRM systems that uniquely combine elements from different origins is a worldwide laboratory in which communities experiment with options for sustainable development. Everyone concerned

---

27 The term "syncretic" is used in religious and philosophical contexts to signify the merging of rather opposite positions, at times bordering on heresy.

28 See Behnke and Scoones, 1993; Niamir-Fuller, 1999; Farvar, 2003; Sullivan and Homewood, 2004.

29 Lee, 1993.

with sound environmental management– on matters of both policy and practice– may learn from these experiences while, hopefully, positively contributing to them.

Understanding and supporting the efforts made by communities to experiment and combine old and new elements as part of their NRM systems is essential for programmes or projects willing to improve the use of natural resources in a participatory way. Such combined (syncretic) NRM systems share with participatory natural resource management both the basic objective (i.e., improving the management of local natural resources according to people's needs, expectations and values) and methods (community driven processes, in which local actors play a major role in making decisions and taking action).

A second key lesson to consider regards indigenous knowledge and know-how. Many "modern" natural resource managers and sustainable development practitioners are now well aware of their importance. Unfortunately, however, several of them focus their attention and appreciation on the traditional wisdom of indigenous and peasant communities but neglect the new economic, political and environmental conditions in which indigenous knowledge and know-how exist today. As a result, the dynamics of change in indigenous NRM systems are overlooked in pursuit of an unrealistic and anachronistic purity of values, understanding and practices.

In fact, insistence on research on indigenous knowledge may lead far from the needs of the people. Shuar elders' knowledge of forest trees and plants is fascinating, but it is rather useless in a situation in which there is no more primary forest in the surroundings of the settlements, and no forest exploitation.[30] For sure, however, resources and time could be effectively spent in appraising what the last two generations of Shuar (and colonists) have learned on range management, agro-forestry and diversification of agricultural production. Furthermore, the "traditional wisdom" approach can lead to missing the structural conditions needed to turn indigenous knowledge into actual NRM practice. For instance, Sbahiya peasants' indigenous land husbandry cannot survive the shortage of agricultural labour affecting the household economy— tackling this problem is essential to adapting indigenous know-how to the new conditions and to making the syncretism viable. On the other hand, if the traditional livelihood system is resilient enough, it will withstand all sorts of blows, incorporate change and maintain its unique essence and sense of identity, as in the case of the Qashqai of Iran.

The third key lesson, linked and in fact derived from the above two, is the present opportunity to engage a multiplicity of social actors in a dialogue and joint action-research about natural resource management. Through it, a multiplicity of capacities and comparative advantages can be recognised, understood and hopefully harmonised and reconciled. Traditional knowledge and skills, in particular, can be set to work within changed environmental, political and social contexts, including the presence of the new social actors which historically emerged in the NRM scene. The safest route begins with a thorough understanding of the indigenous and traditional NRM systems, and only integrating modern practices into them in a careful and reversible way, if absolutely necessary. Some science-based innovations do not stand the test of time, and long-

...NRM systems that uniquely combine elements from different origins [are] a worldwide laboratory in which communities experiment with options for sustainable development.

...the dynamics of change in indigenous NRM systems [should not be] overlooked in pursuit of an unrealistic and anachronistic purity of values, understanding and practices.

---

30 This said, local knowledge should also be preserved for an unknown future, as the conditions of its usefulness may present themselves again. Losing such knowledge may be equivalent to losing entire livelihood alternatives.

term studies end up just confirming the wisdom of the traditional systems.[31] When the dialogue and action research are conducted with equity and integrity, however, they can produce concerted agreements and institutions capable of meeting the challenges of modernisation through the wise merging of features of different historical and cultural origins– what earlier we referred to as "syncretism". Such a process of dialogue and action-research– which we call "co-management"– is the very subject of this work.

---

[31] Cases in point are the nomadic lifestyle of Qashqai pastoralists-first denigrated and opposed and now re-evaluated (see case example 1.3 in this chapter), and the prohibition of grazing from Keoladeo National Park (Rajastan), later found to be essential for the birds habitat (see the discussion of freshwater wetlands in Chapter 3 of this volume).

Chapter 2. ACTORS, ENTITLEMENTS AND EQUITY IN NATURAL RESOURCE MANAGEMENT

2.1 Management actors

People have diverse perceptions of the same environment. A forest can be seen as an aggregate of trees waiting to be felled and sold, a place of rest and leisure, a source of food and firewood, the hiding nest of dangerous animals, the sacred home of water-giving gods, a place providing safe haven from pursuing enemies, a hiding place for insurgents against a government, or the habitat of a rare sub-species of pangolins. These different perceptions correspond to different under-standings of the values, opportunities and risks that the same environment has to offer. As a basic source of livelihood, the forest should be utilised and protected. As a place of leisure, it should be visited in the weekend in the company of friends. As an immobilised capital, it should be exploited. As a dangerous place, it should be avoided or cleared out. As a sacred place, it should be worshipped and respected. As a valuable ecological niche it should be enlisted as protected area as soon as possible....

In a broad sense, everyone on Earth could recognise opportunities and risks in the

...most people and organisations are principally concerned with the status and management of a specific, and usually local, natural environment.

whole planetary environment and in the management of all natural resources.[1] Via the physical cycles of water, air and energy, the movements of living organisms and people and the expanding global exchanges of goods and information, powerful linkages are established among distant ecosystems and the human and animal populations living therein. The most impressive example may be the enormous consumption of fossil fuels in the industrialised North, which is altering the chemical composition of the atmosphere and influencing the climate all over the globe. As a result, nomadic pastoralists in Niger may find that drier seasons will exacerbate their conflicts with sedentary peasants. Mozambicans may find themselves hit by exceptional flooding. And Maldives islanders may even lose their basic "living ground" because of the melting of Arctic ice. Thus, the residents of Niger, Mozambique and the Maldives can indeed have legitimate concerns about the propensity of North Americans and Europeans for a high-energy consumption lifestyle.

In practice, however, most people and organisations are principally concerned with the status and management of a specific, and usually local, natural environment. It may be the case of the territory in which they live and work, the resources that generate their sustenance and income, the land they own, have a right to use or a mandate to care for, or the territories to which they feel historically and culturally tied. And yet, even for local environments, recognising environmental values, opportunities and risks is not a simple matter. Some people may not be informed or aware of phenomena, activities and decisions affecting the territory or resources at stake. Others may lack the time, resources, self-confidence and organisation to articulate their concerns and express them forcefully. In addition, environmental interests may not be neatly defined (exceptions are private property borders, and borders of an area defined in the mandate of an institution), or their definition, while clear and binding to some, may seem hazy to others (such as the three stones put on top of each other to set out the exclosures of the nomadic pastoralists in Iran and Yemen). Commonly, however, borders are recognised in a generic and geographically fuzzy way. For instance, down-stream communities may be broadly interested in soil conservation "upstream", fishermen may be concerned with spawning grounds "all along the coast", and hotel owners may be interested in the preservation of the "landscape" that attracts tourists.

...bundles of [different values, opportunities and risks are recognised] for the same territory or resources... [a fact that] may generate all sorts of dilemmas.

What is more, individuals, groups and institutions do not usually recognise single values, opportunities and risks, but bundles of those for the same territory or resources at stake. This may generate all sorts of dilemmas. Local people may be willing to preserve their unspoiled scenery (aesthetic value) but also need a new road and the jobs provided by factories (economic opportunity). A conservation organisation may have a mandate to preserve a species habitat (ecological value) but also may recognise that, as a consequence, another interesting species may disappear from the territory (ecological risk). The local administration needs tourist revenues (economic value) but also knows that the tourists will introduce cultural and health problems in the area (cultural and health risks). The very recognition of certain environmental values, opportunities and risks and not others is a cultural phenomenon at the core of a society's world-view and of the body of knowledge, practices and technology that characterises its economy, politics and lifestyle. And it depends on inputs and capabilities that may not be under the control of the people concerned.

The above complexities notwithstanding, we will assume here that for any specif-

---

[1]   Lovelock, 1979.

ic territory or set of natural resources, some communities, organisations, groups and individuals will recognise some relevant values, opportunities and risks. Such communities, organisations, groups and individuals are the ones who, once properly organised, may effectively express their interests and concerns and become actively involved in management. The awareness of relevant opportunities and risks (i.e., interests and concerns) and some form of organisation to express those vis-à-vis others are necessary preconditions for any social action in natural resource management. Murphree (1994) postulates such prerequisites when he refers to the difference between individuals and groups, on the one hand, and "institutional actors" on the other:

"The concept of actor is a social construction rather than simply a synonym for individual. Nor is an institutional actor a synonym for group. An institutional actor is an entity organised for the interests of some group or set of goals. Groups and individuals are considered within the context of organised institutional arrangements."

Thus, according to Murphree, the difference between an institutional actor and a non-specified individual or group is that the institutional actor is organised for an interest or purpose. It is in this sense that we will use the term "institutional actor" or "relevant social actor" in this work. In the current literature, another term– stakeholder– is often employed to describe the same concept. We have purposefully chosen not to adopt such term in a prominent way in our analysis of co-management approaches. Although the term "stakeholder" is widely recognised, it is not accepted by all. Some recall that it derives from the times of land grabbing in North America, when ownership titles were distributed to people who would demarcate new lands with stakes. Stakeholders, then, were the individuals who ran with a stake in hand to cover as much land as possible within a given time. As pre-existing rights and concerns of indigenous inhabitants were not respected in those land appropriation processes, the term "stakeholder" carries a negative connotation for some people, especially in non-western cultures.[2]

The very recognition of certain environmental values, opportunities and risks, and not others, is a cultural phenomenon....

Another term applied in the literature (especially in French) is the one of "strategic groups" understood as "groups of social actors possessing the same interests with respect to a given issue". This concept is essentially empirical. The strategic groups cannot be defined a priori, even though some hypotheses may be made about how certain actors may react and behave with respect to a given issue. In fact, it is often the case that some unforeseen factors– such as a system of social and cultural ties, reciprocities, alliances, some political or personal rivalries– reveal themselves much more

2   Smitu Kothari, personal communication, 1998.

influent than other "objective" conditions in determining motivations and positions vis-à-vis NRM decisions.[3] For instance, in a village in Senegal the strategic groups identified a priori by the staff of a project included: the youth within a local cooperative; the youth outside of it; the adult population; the local elite; and the outside actors (governmental agencies and NGOs). What was later revealed in practice was that the key strategic groups were, in fact, only the lineage groups that had different access and tenure to specific landholdings. Another strategic group, the one of local women buyers of vegetables, became also apparent as time went by.[4] In contrast, a project among the Qashqai nomads of Iran dealing with rangeland biodiversity and sustainable livelihoods simply asked the local people to identify their own internal structures and subdivisions. They identified nomadic camps, clans and sub-tribes as institutional actors, and certainly not the externally promoted cooperatives– the only local actors recognised by the central government.

Box 2.1   Institutional actor (also "relevant social actor" or "stakeholder")

An institutional actor in a given subject or event is a bearer of specific interests and concerns organised to express them and carry them forward.

With reference to the management of natural resources, an "interest" refers to a recognised opportunity with potential origin in the natural resources or influence/ impact on them and a "concern" refers to a recognised risk also with potential origin in the natural resources or influence/ impact on the same.

The term "stakeholder" is at times used in place of "institutional actor". In this volume we have chosen to do so only rarely (e.g., when used by original authors), for reasons explained in the text. We will, however, report here some conceptual definition from recent literature:

"Stakeholder is a term which, over the last few years, has come into common usage by most donor organisations; it was first used in business management theory and has since been widely adopted as a further refinement of the user concept. It is an umbrella term, which covers all the people and organisations who have a stake in, and may be affected by, an activity, a development programme or a situation, or who may have an impact or influence on it. In some situations stakeholders may both "be affected by the intervention and also have an impact on the intervention." (Hobley, 1996)

"… the various institutions, social groups and individuals who possess a direct, significant and specific stake in the protected area will be referred to as its 'stakeholders'." (Borrini-Feyerabend, 1996)

"In the context of Bank-supported activities, stakeholders are those affected by the outcome– negatively or positively– or those who can affect the outcome of a proposed intervention." (World Bank, 1996)

Some authors include among "stakeholders" not only organised social actors, but also animals and plants (or wildlife in general) whose survival depends on the resources of a given area (Hobley, 1996, page 96). This approach is not taken here, as those animals and plants would still need some human advocate to foster their interests in co-management processes.

Which social actors are most likely to express interests and concerns in the management of a given territory, area or set of natural resources? Checklist 2.1 lists a typology of possibly relevant social actors, including communities, organisations, groups and individuals. Among the listed actors, only some will be willing and

---

[3]   Lavigne Delville, 2000.
[4]   Olivier de Sardan quoted in Lavigne Delville, 2000.

capable of investing their own time and resources, organising themselves, acting to get their interests and concerns socially recognised and taking on some NRM responsibility. Those will effectively become the "institutional actors" in the management of that territory, area or resources.

Checklist 2.1 Categories[5] of social actors possibly relevant in natural resource management

● Local actors, including the communities, organisations, groups and individuals who live and work close to the resources, the ones who possess knowledge, capacities and aspirations that are relevant for their management, and the ones who recognise in the area a unique cultural, religious or recreational value. (This is an ample category, including several sub-categories.)

● Natural resource users, including local and non-local, direct and indirect, organised and non-organised, actual and potential users, as well as users for subsistence and income purposes.

● National authorities and agencies with explicit mandate over the territory or resource sectors (e.g., ministries or departments of forests, freshwater, fisheries, hunting, tourism, agriculture, protected areas and, in some cases, the military).

● Sub-national administrative authorities (e.g., district or municipal councils) dealing with natural resources as part of their broader governance and development mandate.

● Non-governmental organisations and research institutions (e.g., local, national or international bodies devoted to environment and/ or development objectives) which find the relevant territories and resources at the heart of their professional concerns.

● Businesses and industries local, national or international (e.g., tourism operators, water users, international corporations) which may significantly benefit from natural resources in the area.

● Non-local actors, national and international, indirectly affected by local environmental management practices (e.g., absentee landlords, down-stream water users, environmental advocates or animal rights groups).

● Individual professionals employed in environment and development projects and agencies dealing with the management of natural resources in the area.

Institutional actors usually possess specific capacities (e.g., knowledge, skills) and/ or comparative advantage (e.g., proximity, mandate) for resource management, and are usually willing to invest specific resources (e.g., time, money, and political authority) for it.[6] Among them, traditional groups and organisations (e.g., a council of elders, a fisher folks society, or a peasant association) are particularly valuable. Traditional groups possess a tested structure and representation system and generally enjoy a broad social recognition– what some commentators called social capital– to take on an effective role in natural resource management.[7] Table 2.1 shows a list of relevant social actors for a specific National Park in India: eighteen major stakeholders, bearing different interests and concerns! The analysis of the relevant social actors was carried out by the staff of the governmental agency in charge of Park management and provides a telling example of the complexity of stakeholder differentiation.

---

5   These categories are obviously not exclusive, and some institutional actors may belong to more than one category.
6   Borrini-Feyerabend, 1996.
7   Ostrom and Ahn, 2001.

Table 2.1 Relevant social actors in Rajaji National Park (India) (adapted from Rathore, 1997)

Relevant social actors	Main interests/ concerns
Gujjar communities (more than 500 households, total population over 10,000, now semi-permanent residents)	Cattle rearing and marketing of milk (Gujjars depend entirely on park resources)
Ban workers (18 villages south of Dhaulkhand; prior to 1991, 6,707 households were allowed Bhabbar grass collection)	Bhabbar grass extraction from the park (average income: Rs700-800 per month)
Other dwellers in the surroundings of the Park (in all 57 villages, including the Ban workers)	Fuelwood, fodder collection, cattle grazing, water source for agriculture, theft for subsistence
Taungya villages (four in number, 250 Taungya workers)	Same as above
Tehri Dam oustees (occupy 48.56 hectares, more than ten houses constructed)	Maintaining their camps inside the park, along the elephants' movement route
Army ammunition dump	Defence requirements
Hydle Power Department	Irrigation in the command area
Railways and Road transport department	Providing surface transport facilities
District Administration in Hardwar/ Dehradun/ Pauri Garhwal	Space for headquarters construction on the park periphery, socio-economic uplifting of people dependent on park resources
Rajaji Park Management (8 Rangers, 15 Deputy Rangers, 22 Foresters, 66 Forest Guards and 49 Wildlife Guards)	Wildlife Conservation in Rajaji
Social Forestry Division, Hardwar (buffer zone east of Rajaji)	Productivity of the buffer forests and forest conservation
Forest Division in Shiwalik and Dehradun	Same as above
Township of Hardwar	Dependable supply of fuelwood and medicinal plants
NGOs	Representing and defending the interests of local people
Wildlife Institute of India.	Preserving Rajaji as a learning laboratory for researchers, faculty and trainee officers
Zila Parishad and Panchayats	Development of viable local institutions
Tourism Department	Promotion of tourism in Rajaji and elsewhere
State Forest Department and Ministry of Forest & Environment	Biodiversity conservation through the Protected Area concept
Doon Valley Integrated Watershed Management Project	Ecological restoration in Doon Valley

Indigenous and local communities

Indigenous peoples and local communities– including mobile communities (see Box 2.2)– have a central and pre-eminent role to play in natural resource management. Typically, they have long associations with nature and a deep understanding of it. Often they have made significant contributions to the maintenance of many of the earth's most fragile ecosystems, through their traditional sustainable resource use practices and culture-based respect for nature[8]. This argument has recently been forcefully brought to the fore,[9] countering years of theoretical and practical neglect of the rights, interests and capacities of local people vis-à-vis "scientific" management practices, agency decisions and national development schemes. Nonetheless, indigenous and local communities are not yet recognised as full partners in mainstream environment or development initiatives. In the best of cases, only their participation in activities identified by outside experts is recommended and has become an issue to tackle.

Indigenous peoples and local communities are social units that possess a strong, usually historical, relationship with a given territory and natural resources and are involved in the different but related aspects of local livelihoods.

Box 2.2   Indigenous peoples and mobile indigenous peoples
(adapted from ILO, 1989; and Dana Declaration, 2002)

According to the ILO Convention no.169 (1989) indigenous peoples include:

- tribal peoples in independent countries whose social, cultural, and economic conditions distinguish them from other sections of the national community, and whose status is regulated wholly or partially by their own customs or traditions or by special laws or regulations;

- peoples in independent countries who are regarded as indigenous on account of their descent from the populations which inhabited the country, or a geographical region to which the country belongs, at the time of conquest or colonisation or the establishment of present state boundaries and who, irrespective of their legal status, retain some or all of their own social, economic, cultural and political institutions.

According to the same Convention, self-identification as indigenous or tribal shall be regarded as a fundamental criterion for determining the groups to which the provisions of the Convention apply. Among the criteria used by indigenous peoples to identify themselves as such are: their own historical continuity with pre-colonial societies, the close relationship with the land and natural resources of their own territory, their peculiar socio-political system, their own language, culture, values and beliefs. In general, they do not belong to the dominant sectors of a national society, they see themselves as different from it and prefer to relate with the international networks of indigenous peoples.

The term mobile peoples (i.e., pastoralists, hunter-gatherer, sea nomads, shifting agriculturalists and other peoples with dynamic regular changing patterns of land and resource use) encompasses a subset of indigenous peoples whose livelihoods depend on extensive common property use of natural resources and whose mobility is both a management strategy for dealing with sustainable use and conservation and a distinctive source of cultural identity.

Indigenous peoples and local communities are social units that possess a strong, usually historical, relationship with a given territory and natural resources and are involved in the different but related aspects of local livelihoods. As this definition can apply to a range of sizes (e.g., is a city a community? Is the sum of all people

---

8   Beltrán, 2000.
9   See, for instance: Durning, 1989; Agarwal and Narain, 1989; West and Brechin, 1991; Western and Wright, 1994; Pye-Smith and Borrini-Feyerabend, 1994; Stevens, 1997; Ghimire and Pimbert, 1997; Kothari et al.,1998; Pimbert and Pretty, 1998; Posey, 1999; Borrini-Feyerabend et al., 2004 (in press); and, with specific regard to mobile indigenous communities: Scoones, 1994; Niamir-Fuller, 1999; Chatty and Colchester, 2002; and Farvar, 2003.

inhabiting a given watershed a community?), one could further specify the term to describe people likely to have "face-to-face" encounters and/ or direct influences in their daily life. In this sense, a rural village, a tribal group moving together in a transhumance path or the inhabitants of an urban quarter can be considered a "community", but not all the inhabitants of a district or town. A community usually possesses some form of social organisation– often based on the need for the management of a particular resource or set of resources– and its members share in varying degrees political, economic, social and cultural characteristics (in particular language, behavioural norms, values, knowledge, skills and technologies) as well as ethnic and health features. It is not usual, however, for communities to be recognised as micro-political bodies with administrative capacity.

Important processes in community life regard social integration (cooperation to address common needs) and cultural continuity. Mechanisms that promote integration in communities include patterns of reciprocity (like exchanges in labour, pooling resources, births, marriages and deaths, or economic trade) and redistribution (sharing resource or economic surpluses among individuals or households). Mechanisms that promote continuity are the acculturation of children in society and a variety of local organisations with specific tasks, responsibilities and rules of functioning. Many local communities thus constitute important cultural units, and the self-awareness, pride, sense of common identity and solidarity of their members often represent the last defence against massive socio-cultural change and incorporation by outside models and socio-economic forces.

> [Indigenous peoples and local] communities constitute important cultural units… the self-awareness, pride, sense of common identity and solidarity of their members often represent the last defense against massive socio-cultural change and incorporation by outside models and socio-economic forces.

In the sense just described, a local community can indeed be regarded as one actor for a variety of decisions concerning the territory and natural resources of its interest. And yet, for other decisions the communities may include a variety of different opinions and be willing to have them all expressed. As a matter of fact, communities are neither perfectly homogeneous bodies nor are they culturally static. On the contrary, they continuously grapple with cultural change and social conflict (for instance clashing of needs and wants among people belonging to different families or ethnic sub-groups). Thus communities need to continuously manage a balance between the opposite forces of integration and conflict, continuity and change. Their capacity to deal with contrasting socio-cultural phenomena as well as their capacity to gain a livelihood from a given environment provides us with a measure of their capacity to adapt and their social resilience.

No community can be regarded as homogeneous regarding all interests and concerns on the management of the local environment and resources. On the contrary, most of them, including traditional rural communities, are highly internally differentiated. Among the factors at the roots of different interests and concerns in environmental management within the same community are basic characteristics such as clan, ethnic group, gender, age, caste, social class, economic status, education, skills and profession. Ownership of land or other resources is a discriminatory factor but other factors are also important. These include place of residence, existence of cash savings in the household (or tent-hold), linkage to a particular party or religious group, access to means and sources of external information (e.g., technical or bureaucratic), social standing, physical ability, intra-household division of tasks, household surplus or scarcity of labour, presence of salaried people in the household, and so on.

One of the important innovations of the co-management approach is that it spotlights different interests and concerns not only between communities and other actors in society but within local communities as well. In this sense, one may speak of co-management when a community joins in management with external actors, but also in entirely community-based and community-run initiatives, as long as different interests and concerns within the community are recognised and represented.

Table 2.2 provides a typology of interest groups within a local community vis-à-vis the management of a regional park in Liguria (Italy). The expressed interests and concerns, although only schematically reported, illustrate the spectrum of interests and concerns that can exist within a small and relatively homogeneous local community. Noticeably, the information provided in Tables 2.1 and 2.2 is available because someone took the initiative to organise a meeting to discuss the management of the local park. The individuals who participated in the meeting introduced themselves as members of a given category (mostly related to resource ownership and profession) and spoke in the name of their categories. The spectrum of community interests and concerns would likely look different if someone else would have called the meeting and/ or different social groups (for instance the village elders or an association of women) would have participated and expressed their interests and concerns. It is important to keep this in mind, as often the "interest groups" get organised on the basis of an external impulse or occasion.

...one may speak of co-management [even for] entirely community-based and community-run initiatives, as long as different interests and concerns within the community are recognised and represented.

Table 2.2 Local stakeholders in Aveto Regional Park (Italy) (adapted from Triantafyllidis, 1996)	
Individuals, groups and organisations within the "local community"	**Key interests/ concerns**
Local authorities	Avoiding jurisdiction conflicts
Aveto Regional Park Committee	Respect of law; sound ecological management
Farmers	Cropping, breeding & forest harvesting
Cooperatives	Fair income for members
Hunters	Good hunting and fishing grounds available
Landowners	Maintaining property rights
Holders of Common Properties ("beni frazionali")	Maintaining property rights, harvesting and grazing included
Restaurants, hotels and shop owners	Enhancing commerce and tourism
Pro Loco (local association to promote tourism)	Enhancing tourist flow and revenues; social animation
Students (primary & secondary school)	Leisure and future involvement (jobs?)

The interests [and roles of women and men] in natural resources are usually different.... It may thus be inequitable and unwise to accept the voice of one gender group as representing a whole community....

Among the many categories of potentially different interests in a local community, two may be relevant nearly everywhere: age groups and gender groups. As such, they deserve particular attention. Younger people represent the future and, at least on that account, are supposed to have the most compelling interest in maintaining their environment viable and productive. There are, in fact, telling examples of effective involvement of adolescents and children in natural resource management.[10] But not all youngsters can be expected to be sensitive to environmental values or good managers of natural resources. In great part this is due to modern school systems, which, following the colonial legacy, often succeeded, over and above everything else, in alienating the young from their ancestral traditions and culture. Often, indeed, the "stakes of future generations" are most forcefully represented by the traditional elders of a community. In Yemen, the traditional systems of land and water management that assured for millennia the prosperity of the country are now rapidly falling in disarray. Most youth and adult men leave the rural villages in search of easy and lucrative jobs in the cities. The ones left behind to care for the land and preserve the ancient management systems, when they still succeed in doing so, are only the elderly and the women. This is the case in many so called developing societies.

With the possible exception of usually temporary living and working arrangements (e.g., labour camps, or villages abandoned by migrant workers), human societies always include men and women, and their interests in natural resources and roles in managing them are usually different. For instance, a survey of forest product uses was carried out in villages surrounding Mount Elgon National Park, in Uganda.[11] It was found that women were mostly interested in being able to gather firewood, vegetables, mushrooms, medicinal plants and bamboo shoots from the park's territory, while the men were keener on grazing permissions, and on collecting less frequently extracted resources, such as materials for house construction and maintenance. In addition, the men wished to gather bamboo shoots for sale, rather than for household consumption, as stated by the women.

For the communities living in the surroundings of Mount Elgon decisions that are pleasing or acceptable to the men may then be detrimental or unacceptable to the women, and vice-versa. A programme to protect wildlife may bring revenue to men (such as jobs as park guards) but more abundant wildlife may be only a cost to women, because of crop damage or increased danger in daily tasks. Forest protection may favour the commercial farmers who use water to irrigate their fields, but disfavour the women and children who have to walk much further to find fodder, poles or firewood. If only men or only women are allowed to negotiate resource management agreements for the whole community, the other gender group may find its interests poorly represented, if not outright neglected. It may thus be inequitable and unwise to accept the voice of one gender group as representing a whole community: both men and women should organise and participate in management.

Madhu Sarin, a most effective advocate of gender consideration in stakeholder analysis,[12] adds a further dimension to this point, and warns against generalisations and gender stereotypes. She stresses combinations of social characteristics (e.g., gender and caste, gender and socio-economic class) as main determinants of interests and concerns in resource management, and she recommends remaining open to surprises:

---

[10] Hart, 1997.
[11] Scott, 1994.
[12] Sarin, 1996; Sarin and SARTHI, 1996.

"...forest-related roles and responsibilities [of] women and men in Haryana's Shiwalik belt... vary dramatically within and between villages in terms of occupational, caste, economic and cultural characteristics.... Jat women do not go to the forest at all. While some Gujjar village women collect fodder from forest, in the majority of villages they do not do so. [Among the Banjaras] men harvest the grass from the forest [but] processing into ropes is done by women. In Bar Godam, only the men collect bamboo from the forest while in another Banjhida village, Kalka... the collection of bamboo from the forest was done by the women. The Lavana women of main Nada villages collect heavy headloads of both grass and tree leaf fodder for several months of the year.... [But] the stereotyped image of rural women carrying heavy head loads of firewood is extremely rare in Haryana's Shiwalik belt. Practically none of the women in the area's diverse communities are responsible for domestic firewood collection. Occasionally they do pick fallen twigs and branches while collecting fodder, but firewood collection in the belt is essentially a male task, done by either male children, adults or elders."

Combinations of social characteristics (e.g., gender and caste, gender and socio-economic class) are main determinants of interests and concerns in resource management....

2.2   Entitlements to manage natural resources

We have seen that the interests and concerns of different social actors in natural resource management can originate from a variety of roots. Some may live in close geographic proximity to the resources, or their ancestors may have been associated with them from times immemorial. Others may own the resources, either legally or by custom, or may have acquired some use rights on them. Some organisations may have been assigned a management mandate by the government. Some households may be totally dependent on natural resources for livelihood or income. And some individuals or groups may simply possess unique knowledge and skills applicable to the local environment. Such different interests and concerns, which can well coexist for the same territory or body of resources, may compel different social actors towards contrasting management options. Whose opinions should count? Who should decide?

The above questions are fundamental in co-management processes, and no single answers are appropriate or possible. Always, however, it is advisable to understand the "playing field" as thoroughly as possible. This involves an analysis of the relevant social actors (organised and non-organised), their mutual relationships, the context in which they live, their management claims and the justifications– foundations, motivations, historical roots– they put forth for them. Who are the social actors willing and organised to take part in management (the institutional actors)? What are their claims? How do they justify those claims? Can their different justifications be compared and weighted vis-à-vis one another?

In the analysis mentioned above– at times referred to as "stakeholder analysis"

...an entitlement... is a dynamic social construct that finds its meaning only within the social context that created it.

in current literature– we can utilise the concept of "entitlement" to great advantage. We understand here as an entitlement to manage a territory or set of natural resources a socially recognised (legitimate) claim to participate in one or several of its relevant management activities. Entitlements do not usually refer to exclusive or extreme powers (all or nothing). Rather, they cover some specific activities, such as using part or all of those resources, deriving indirect benefits from them, taking responsibilities on related tasks or speaking up and negotiating on management decisions. For instance, an entitlement to manage a given

territory could be a broadly recognised claim to speak up and negotiate with others in relevant decision-making processes. An entitlement to manage firewood and fodder from the local forest may be recognised as the right of a household to gather enough dry and green material to warm their home, cook and feed their animals. Gathering more than that, for instance gathering firewood for the market, would be seen as going beyond their entitlement, and would have to be negotiated.

In the working definition used in this volume, an entitlement does not need to be legally codified, and it is more a statement of facts ("what is") than a statement of norms ("what should be"). It can in effect be understood as the end result of a combination of determinants including both accepted normative values (see Checklist 2.2) and differentials of power (see Checklist 2.3). As such, it is a dynamic social construct that finds its meaning only within the social context that created it.

Different social actors are not all equally entitled to manage resources. On the contrary, some have most of the relevant decisions at their fingertips and others have almost none. In general, a mix of visible and hidden factors combines to generate a given distribution of the benefits and costs of management. In some cases, an open debate can take place on those matters and an adjustment of the respective positions and influences can be agreed upon. In others, poorly recognised social actors struggle for years to enhance their own measure of control over natural resources. Still in others, even attempting to put forth some interests and concerns may be a dangerous activity. A re-arrangement of the entitlements of different social actors can even be promoted and supported from outside the relevant context (e.g., by some conservation and development initiatives), but it is only within the local context that a new balance of entitlements must be achieved and sanctioned.

Box 2.3   Entitlements in natural resource management

An entitlement to manage a territory or set of natural resources is a socially recognised claim to partici-pate in one or several management activities, such as planning, advising, taking decisions, implement-ing plans, appropriating benefits (including using resources), assuming responsibilities, monitoring and evaluating results, etc.

An entitlement is a formal or informal title to do, a dynamic social construct that finds its full meaning only within the social context that created it. Sometimes it is codified by the legal system, but often it is not. It reflects facts ("what is") rather than norms only ("what should be"). It usually results from a combination of social determinants that include both accepted normative values and differentials of power. And it is an evolving social phenomenon, more akin to a process than to a fixed state of affairs.

The concept of entitlement owes a lot to the seminal work of Amartya Sen, for whom[13] "the word enti-tlement does not refer to people's rights in a normative sense– what people should have– but to the range of possibilities that people can have." Thus, entitlements are "the set of alternative commodity bundles that a person can command in society using the totality of rights and opportunities that he or she faces... based on processes such as production, own labour, trade, inheritance or transfer." In the words of Leach et al. (1997): "An extended entitlement approach sees entitlements as the outcome of negotiations among social actors, involving power relationships and debates over meaning rather than simply the result of fixed moral rules encoded in law."

Leach et al. (1997) provide a further analysis of the concept: "Environmental entitlements are the alter-native sets of utilities derived from environmental goods and services over which social actors have legitimate, effective command and which are instruments in achieving well being." Such entitlements "...enhance peoples' capabilities, which are what people can do or be with their entitlements. For example, command over fuel resources derived from rights over trees gives warmth or the ability to cook, and so contributes to well being." Also: "Entitlements are what social actors actually get in prac-tice.... By "legitimate" we refer not only to command sanctioned by a statutory system but also to command sanctioned by customary rights of access, use or control or other social norm."

In the words of de Graay Fortman (1997): "Entitlement is the possibility to make legitimate claims, i.e., claims based on rights. It is a function of both law and power. Power means opportunity, actual com-mand. Law legitimises and hence protects in case of dispute.... People continue to try to improve their entitlement positions. Hence, more than a given state of affairs, entitlement is... a process in society."

As entitlements are social constructs, we can attempt to understand their social roots and justifications. To begin with, there exist a variety of grounds for entitle-ments recognised as valid and legitimate on the basis of accepted normative val-ues in different societies (see Checklist 2.2). For any given society, such validity and legitimacy may be acknowledged in a more or less explicit way. For instance, they could refer to a body of written law, but also to customary law or to the basic tenets of social life. The latter may include the right to life and the other basic human rights of the United Nations (UN) Charter but also human solidarity, democracy, social equity, sustainability of the environment, or obedience to a cul-tural or religious credo. Some specific principles may be upheld by the large majority of a society, and thus become a sort of social norm. These may include "respect of law and order", pragmatism, adherence to "scientific principles", liber-alism, respect of free market and private property, basic fair play, affirmative action, patriotism, effectiveness and efficiency in management, and so on.

---

[13]   Quotes of A. Sen (1984) from Leach et al., 1997.

- legally recognised rights to land or resources (e.g., property rights, usufruct rights)

- customarily recognised rights to land or resources (e.g., use rights, communal property, ancestral domains of indigenous peoples)

- specific mandate by the state (e.g., statutory obligation of a given agency or governmental body)

- proximity to the resources (e.g., the residents of the local community)

- direct dependence for subsistence and survival (e.g., food, medicine, communication)

- direct dependence for basic economic resources

- historical, cultural and spiritual relations with the natural resources at stake (e.g., in the case of indigenous peoples)

- continuity of relationship (e.g., local communities and long-time resource users versus recently arrived immigrants, tourists, hunters from other areas)

- social equity (fairness) in access to resources and distribution of benefits from their use;

- number of people bringing forth the same interests and concerns

- unique knowledge and skills for the management of the resources at stake

- losses and damage incurred in the management process

- degree of commitment, effort and resources invested in natural resource management

- actual or potential impact of the activities of the social actor on the resource base

- general recognition of the value of the perspective/ position (e.g., "scientific validation", "fitting the local knowledge system", aiming at "sustainable use", following the "precautionary principle", etc.)

- compatibility with the country's policies and body of law (e.g., a Freedom of Information Act, the special rights of indigenous peoples)

- compatibility with international conventions and agreements (e.g., the Convention on Biological Diversity, the Ramsar Convention, the UN Convention to Combat Desertification).

In all, different "grounds", differently acknowledged and respected by different cultures, can be upheld and used by social actors as a justification for their claims to participate in managing natural resources. For instance, an indigenous community may claim a role in managing a territory within a state-controlled protected area on the basis of their customary rights. A local business may claim a right to use certain resources as in so doing it is providing jobs for local people. A governmental agency may impose some rule of access to a territory for the sake of national security. But this is not the whole story.

In many societies, the emergence of specific environmental entitlements has little to do with an explicit social consensus on claims and values, and more to do with the exercise of coercive physical power, power of position, economic power, household and group power, etc. (see Checklist 2.3). As some have put it:[14] "The history of environmental management systems shows that those are more a reflection of dominant socio-economic thinking than of the level of ecosystem knowledge." The social actors who can exercise various types of power, do so to overcome, distort or impose upon more legitimate claims. At times, however, one form or another of power is also utilised to back up a socially legitimate claim. For instance, coercive power may be necessary to prevent some people from hunting wildlife, even though the hunting ban may be fully inscribed in a country's environmental legislation. Or personal charismatic power may be necessary to advance the claims of an ethnic minority demanding a more equitable distribution of water rights within a community.

Checklist 2.3 Forms of power that shape and affect environmental entitlements (adapted from Lewis, 1997)

● power of position (having authority, being in a position to make or influence decisions)

● power of knowledge (having information unavailable to others)

● personal power (being personally forceful, persuasive)

● household power (being from a well-connected family)

● group power (being a member of an ethnic, religious or other type of group that has a dominant social position or, for example, being male in male-dominated society)

● economic power (commanding financial and other economic resources in overwhelming amount with respect to the resources of others)

● political power (having a powerful supportive constituency or access to political leadership)

● legal power (having strong expert legal council, or privileged access to courts)

● coercive physical power (having police or military backing or weaponry)

Another important kind of power– the power of passive non-compliance, subtle sabotage, evasion and deception– has been the route of escape for many of the disenfranchised (dis-entitled) throughout history.[15] At times, this has allowed them to survive and gather more environmental benefits than the established system of power would have allowed (the environmental impact of this type of behaviour is still in need of thorough investigation).

Whether today it is advisable for many under-privileged to continue on the route

---

14   Weber and Bailly, 1993. On this, see also the illuminating article by Ramírez (2001).
15   Scott, 1985.

[Some] societies...
cannot yet provide
the conditions that
would make
a transparent and
direct debate safer
and more
convenient than a
hidden search for
private advantages.

of passive non-compliance or attempt "developing their own entitlements" in a transparent and open struggle is still a matter of debate. In some societies characterised by large power disparities, the recent development of democratic systems and the state of law allowed a number of social movements, unions, consumer and minority groups to adopt a transparent and direct strategy of confrontation, sometimes even in a overtly legal manner. For example, a recent struggle in India, where the legal system has always favoured the literate gentry, led to the recognition by the Supreme Court of the right of a community elder to provide oral testimony in matters of customary law. Other societies, however, cannot yet provide the conditions that would make a transparent and direct debate safer and more convenient than a hidden search for private advantages. In fact, even in relation to the above example, the experience of many Indian community activists working on land rights issues shows they are constantly exposed to physical danger and repression.[16] This is by no mean an isolated case, as activists attempting to improve the NRM conditions of their communities are routinely singled out for violent repression[17] and non infrequently murdered.[18] This represents a most serious obstacle to the promotion and spreading of partnerships in natural resource management.[19]

2.3   Equity in managing natural resources

In the context of multiple social actors with conflicting interests and concerns or competing entitlements on the same territory or set of natural resources, is there a way (or are there many ways) of pursuing equitable management arrangements? One fairly obvious first consideration brings to the fore the essential distinction between equity and equality. Certainly not all social actors deserve the same entitlements to natural resources. We are far from the simple democratic rule of "one person, one vote", as the interests and concerns of different social actors with respect to the same resources can be enormously different in both quantity and quality. But who deserves a privileged position? Who should be considered a "primary stakeholder", and thus a rightful decision-maker versus an associate, an advisor, or simply someone to be kept informed about the decisions of others?

...distinguishing
between local and
non-local actors...

For some authors, one or more roots or grounds for environmental entitlements appear much more fundamental than others. Marshall Murphree, for instance, stresses that there is one major and most important distinctive characteristic among social actors with a claim on natural resources, and this is the distinction between local and non-local actors:[20]

"The danger is that this perspective [stakeholder analysis] can easily transform interests into a conceptual collective proprietorship by a vast and amorphous

---

16   Prabhu Pradip, personal communication, 2002.
17   One example among many is recounted in Varela, 2003.
18   Again, one example among many is illustrated in Henderson, 2000.
19   Borrini-Feyerabend, 1997.
20   Murphree, 1994.

circle of stakeholders. Those stakeholders who have invested most in professional expertise and monetary capital form the board of directors. But this accounting procedure is false. Communities' investment in their environments– their land, their resources, their labour, their local environmental knowledge, their managerial presence, and their stake in the future... is far higher than that of all external actors put together.... Community interests, responsibility and authority should be paramount."

Consequently, Murphree organises social actors into three categories (Table 2.3), according to their range of action and institutional affiliation, clearly distinguishing between local and non-local institutional actors (governmental and non-governmental) and stressing that the former should have a pre-eminent position in management decisions.

Table 2.3 Categories of institutional actors (from Murphree, 1994)

Community institutional actors	"Responsive to local relational dynamics, accountable to collective community interests, and able to articulate views and positions effectively with external institutional actors."
Government institutional actors	"State institutional actors derive much of their strength from their status as "gate-keepers": coercively backed authorities that determine what communities can and cannot do. They also derive strength from their ability to control the flow of fiscal and other resources from the centre to the periphery. Rarely do flows to communities offset what has been extracted from them. Finally, state agencies act as gatekeepers for donor grants and aid projects."
Non-Governmental institutional actors	"...focus on specific issues or problems. NGOs arise in response to perceived needs and their raison d'être falls away when the need (or the perception of it) changes. They can mobilise financial and personal resources comparatively quickly and efficiently. They have the money, personnel, and rapid-response capacity for programmes and projects, while national governments claim sovereignty and gate-keeping authority."

The distinction between local and non-local actors is not the only one possible. Elinor Ostrom offers another demarcation criterion between resource "appropriators" and resource "providers". The appropriators are the ones who simply harvest or pull out resource units. The providers are instead engaged in the process of creating, maintaining, or restoring a resource. Fishermen are usually appropriators but become engaged in provision when they change the structure of the seabed in order to improve the habitat for nesting. Irrigators are engaged in provision when they construct or maintain a canal. Many self-governed systems of common property resources provide their own rules as a result of extensive discussion, bargaining, and negotiation over what these rules should be, and only those rules ensure the long-term sustainability of the resource.[21] Obviously, the providers have stronger grounds to claim resource entitlements than pure appropriators do.[22]

... distinguishing between resource appropriators and resource providers...

A similar but not identical distinction is made by Gorman (1995) between primary and secondary users of coastal resources in Tanga (Tanzania). In Table 2.4,

[21] Elinor Ostrom, personal communication, 1998. See also Ostrom and Walker, 1997.
[22] For a given set of natural resources, providers and appropriators can mix, coincide or remain neatly separate.

...distinguishing
between primary and
secondary users of
natural resources...

primary users are defined as the ones who directly depend on the resources for their livelihood, either in situ or by harvesting. The secondary users are the ones whose use of a particular resource follows after the direct harvesting or in situ uses. The former would be "more entitled" than the latter in resource management.

Table 2.4	Users of coastal resources in Tanga (Tanzania) (adapted from Gorman, 1995)	
Resource	Primary users	Secondary users
Ocean ecosystem/ seawater	Seaweed farmers, salt boilers, solar salt producers, sea transport workers	Exporters & users of sea transport; tourism operators
Coral reefs	Lime collectors/ burners, house builders, tourism operators, trophy collectors	Builders (cement, limestone)
Fisheries	Fishermen– hand lines, traps, nets (seine & dragnets), dynamite, divers, boat owning fishermen "visiting" fishermen, trawlers Fisherwomen– ach seining, octopus & mollusc collectors, tourism operators (game fishing)	Men and women fish traders, fish processors (fryers, driers, and smokers), and fish dealers for inland market and for export, tourism operators.
Beaches	Fishermen, fisherwomen, households (sanitation needs), tourism operators	Traders, processors
Mangroves	Pole cutters, fishermen, salt boilers, solar salt producers, lime burners, boat builders, house builders, traditional healers, households engaged in crab & other fisheries, mariculture.	Mangrove pole traders, saw millers.
Bare Saline areas	Solar salt producers, brine wells	Salt traders
Rivers	Households, sisal estates, coconut plantations, transport, industries	
Ground Water	Households, farmers, sisal estates, industries.	
Coastal forests & woodlands	Households of salt boilers, lime burners, timber cutters, charcoal makers, boat builders, traditional healers, honey gatherers, hunters	Saw millers, transporters of fuel wood, fish processors
Wildlife	Hunters, tourism operators, trophy collectors, safari companies	

Finally, there is also a school of analysis that stresses not only an attribute of relevant social actors ("local", "producer", "primary user") but singles out outright one of them– the indigenous peoples and local traditional communities– as being in all cases the primary and most important of them all. For Farvar (1989) the most important characteristic of local communities is that they have evolved with the natural resources, and have developed rich and detailed management systems that have stood the test of time. A variety of intruders in the community space (colonial powers and other foreign invaders, the national state and government agencies, missionaries of various denominations, traders and business, national and international corporations, donors and developers of all venues) clamour for attention and pretend to be considered rightful stakeholders. The solutions to the local problems imported by these outsiders have generally not improved the management systems devised by local communities and have at times even destroyed whatever existed and replaced it with tragically ineffective open access regimes. The local communities may or may not wish to accept the claims and/ or enter into partnership relationships with external actors in a variety of syncretic natural resource management systems adapted to the new environmental, social and economic conditions (see Chapter 1). The local communities, however, should always maintain a position of predominance and control vis-à-vis others.

...considering local communities the primary and most relevant social actor... as they have evolved with the natural resources, and have developed rich and detailed management systems that have stood the test of time....

We may agree with Murphree, Ostrom, Gorman or Farvar on a crucial distinction among key relevant social actors on the basis of locality, productive efforts, dependency for livelihood or belonging to an age-old resident or mobile community. We may pick an entirely different criterion, whether or not listed among the ones in Checklist 2.2. Or we may remark that many important criteria– such as locality, productive efforts or dependency for livelihood– tend to converge on the same social actors. In a typical situation, a complex patchwork of claims (often several claims for each relevant actor) interplay with important power differentials within a context of relatively limited opportunities and resources. In all cases, having appreciated a plurality of relevant actors and their related bundles of entitlements and claims– we can ask ourselves a crucial question: in a given, specific and usually complex context, what does "striving for equity" mean? How could the system be rendered the fairest possible? The following statements offer some initial reflections:

- Striving for equity in natural resource management means helping the underprivileged to "develop their own entitlements"[23].

- Striving for equity in natural resource management means recognising entitlements rooted in valid and legitimate grounds (as defined by the relevant society) rather than entitlements rooted in the exercise of one or the other form of power.

- Striving for equity in natural resource management means promoting a fair negotiation of functions, benefits and responsibilities among entitled social actors.

To explore the practical implications of the above we may examine a generic (and by necessity fairly idealised) process by which social actors empower themselves as entitled and responsible resource managers (see Figure 2.1). At every step of that process we will ask ourselves what concrete conditions and inputs may be necessary to enhance equity. (Figure 2.1 is indeed an "idealised" sketch, as real life processes are generally more chaotic, with steps back and forth in place of a linear and smooth progression.)

---

23 This point is stressed by Vithal Rajan (personal communication, 1997).

Figure 2.1 Towards social actors empowered and responsible in natural resource management– a schematic view

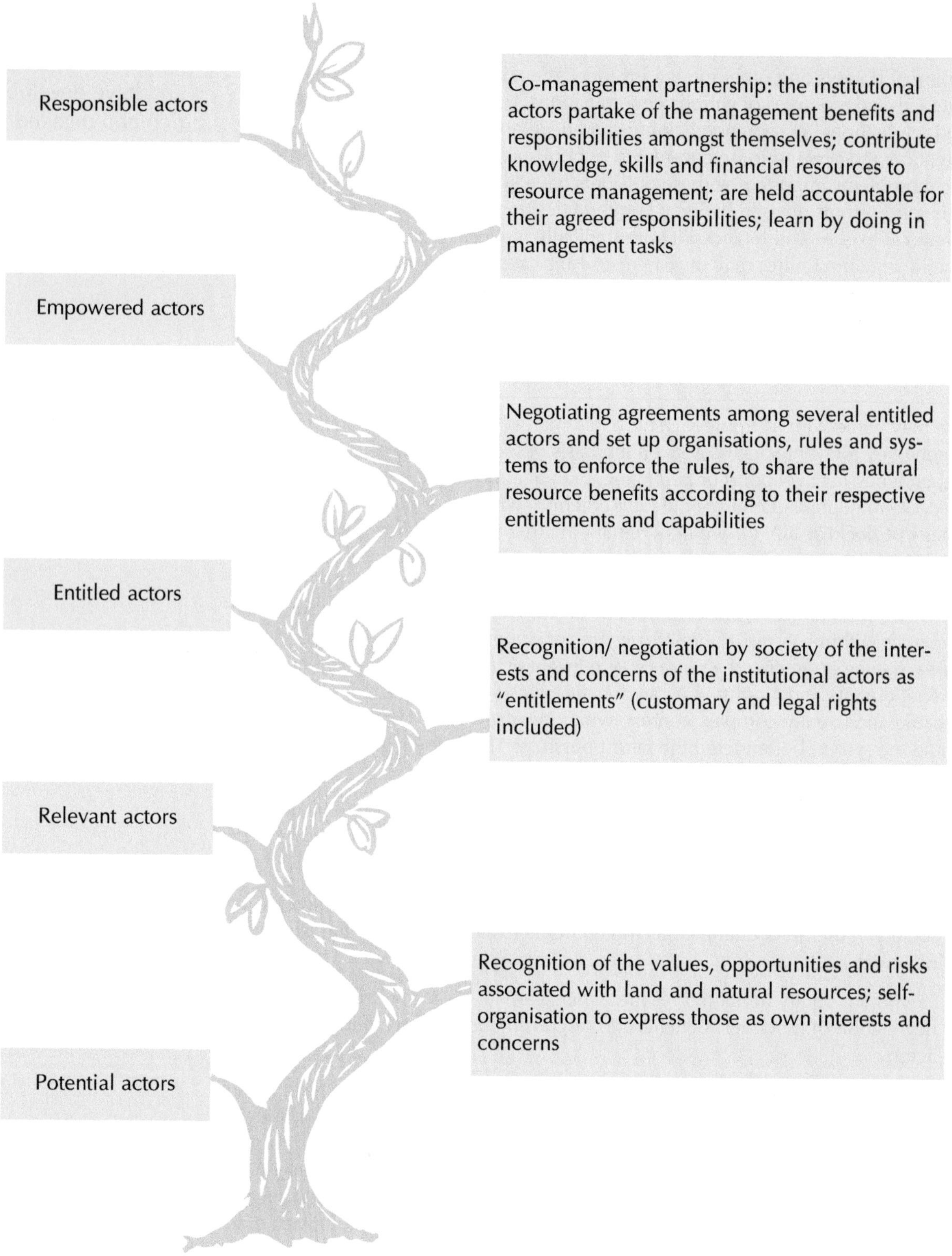

Responsible actors

Co-management partnership: the institutional actors partake of the management benefits and responsibilities amongst themselves; contribute knowledge, skills and financial resources to resource management; are held accountable for their agreed responsibilities; learn by doing in management tasks

Empowered actors

Negotiating agreements among several entitled actors and set up organisations, rules and systems to enforce the rules, to share the natural resource benefits according to their respective entitlements and capabilities

Entitled actors

Recognition/ negotiation by society of the interests and concerns of the institutional actors as "entitlements" (customary and legal rights included)

Relevant actors

Recognition of the values, opportunities and risks associated with land and natural resources; self-organisation to express those as own interests and concerns

Potential actors

We propose that the first step in the process is for social actors to recognise some specific opportunities and risks in a relevant territory or set of natural resources. Opportunities may include all kinds of feasible or profitable utilisation of natural resources, ranging from shifting cultivation over a forested region to indigenous nomadic pastoralism in rangelands; from harvesting and channelling water for irrigation to covering the land with cement to enlarge a landing strip; from gathering medicinal plants and other natural products to pasturing animals in rangelands,

...relevant information [should be made] available to everyone potentially concerned.

and from recreation by spending a few days in wilderness to setting up a habitat preservation area. Risks may include all kinds of damages that may come from the environment– from contracting malaria in the surroundings of a tropical wetland to having agricultural plots destroyed by flooding; from losing a harvest because of pests to being exposed to attacks by wild animals in the surrounding of a protected area. Risks may also include all sorts of negative impacts the environment may suffer as a result of human activities.

Many environmental opportunities and risks are well know by people and acted upon on a daily basis. Others, however, are not known at all, possibly because of lack of specific information or awareness of conditions and consequences. A second equity concern is thus about assuring that the relevant information is available to everyone potentially concerned. If some social actors are not sufficiently informed and aware about the resource management issues, there is little they can contribute or do about them.

Once individuals, groups and organisations recognise for themselves some relevant environmental opportunities and risks, they need to articulate and express those as their own interests and concerns. Thus, a head of household in rural Burkina Faso planning to open up new land to agriculture will express his intention to the local Chef de Terre, and ask for the customary permission. An environment NGO in the United States of America (USA) will call for a meeting of its members, discuss the priority issues among a number of potential topics, and then begin a letter campaign, organise a demonstration, lobby politicians, or do whatever else is appropriate to be heard and obtain results. A national environmental protection agency will set up an investigation on a topic of concern and then develop, publicise and enforce rules on the matter on the basis of the obtained results. A Council of Elders in a nomadic pastoral community in Iran will meet to assess the carrying capacity of their summering and wintering grounds before the season of migration and to take decisions on migratory routes for their flocks. As we have already argued, communities, organisations and individuals become "institutional actors" by expressing their interests and concerns and organising for action. The latter point is particularly important, as social actors may be powerless simply because they are not sufficiently or effectively organised.

...communities, organisations and individuals become "institutional actors" by expressing their interests and concerns and organising for action.

In the above, equity would require that social actors are free to express their views and opinions, as well as free to gather and organise to further their views and interests. Both of these requirements are far from trivial in many countries today. In fact, assembling and organising– a fundamental human right in the UN Charter– can still be treated as a crime. When organising is politically feasible, it may still be difficult because of legal constraints (such as complex procedures, or simple lack of a legally-recognised status for communities and local associations of resource users). Finally, the process of organising may be challenging because of a more prosaic but no less impeding lack of time, financial resources or human skills.

Depending on the context in which the interests and concerns need to be heard, social actors may require more or less extensive preparatory work before being able to effectively convey their claims. Sometimes this includes establishing one's own legal identity (as an accepted association or organisation gathering a constituency that shares some basic NRM interests and concerns, and is willing to act (see Box 2.4). Nearly always, however, this involves discussions and agreements on priorities, objectives and strategy. It may include establishing a representation system (see Box 2.5), joining an existing organisation or even establishing a new one (with membership rules, etc.).

Box 2.4   Social groups organised to manage forests in India
            (adapted from Sarin, 1996)

Among the more complex aspects of the forest protection process is the definition through inter-group negotiations of the "social units of organisation" and of the specific boundaries of the forest area to protect. Due to the scattered settlement pattern of tribal and semi-tribal communities, most villages near the forests do not have compact settlements. Instead, they consist of individual houses scattered next to agricultural landholdings. Most villages have a number of falias (hamlets) named after the particular sub-caste or tribe residing in it. These are not easily identifiable as physical units as they are essentially social units. In addition, the boundaries of the administrative "revenue village" (gram panchayat) do not necessarily overlap with the boundaries of the social units. There is also considerable variation in the amount of forestland within the boundaries of different revenue villages, with little correlation between a village's population and the forest area within its boundaries, despite the fact that the majority of the population continues to have similar levels of dependence on forest produce. In all, physical proximity, extent of dependence and social relations, rather than formal "revenue village" boundaries, have determined which people use which forest area, as well as the composition of the forest protection groups.

The process of organising with others to bring forward one's own interests and concerns requires time, financial resources and human skills that may not be readily available, especially among the underprivileged social actors who may need them the most. A poor, single head of household may be a careful natural resource manager, possess a wealth of knowledge and skills and have solid customary rights over a given set of natural resources. Yet she may have little spare time to take part in meetings, no transport facilities to travel to a gathering place, no literacy to check on background information and little self-confidence to speak in public.

Traditional and long-standing local bodies of various kinds offer important opportunities for local people to be represented vis-à-vis external actors interested in the management of the same territory or set of resources. Today, however, many such local bodies are losing rather than acquiring importance. It is an unfortunate development of recent history that many communities that did possess traditional institutions for resource management have seen them devalued and weakened by modern state policies that do not recognise them, learn from them, nor assign to them any meaningful role.[24] In the words of Baland and Platteau,[25] "...state authorities have an interest in tightly controlling all significant attempts by local communities at organizing themselves, particularly so if these attempts result in the development of large-scale grassroots movements or networks or in the assertion of claims for more authority." In some cases, effective traditional systems of resource management exist and could play a most important role for conservation and development, but their recognition by outsiders may still be limited.[26] In other cases, the traditional organisations exist but are unable or unwilling to represent the variety of interests and concerns of their communities and can be corrupted by outside forces.[27]

...many communties that did possess traditional instittuions for resource management have seen them devalued and weakened by modern state policies that do not recognise them nor assign to them any meaningful role.

Box 2.5   Forms of representation
            (adapted from Borrini, 1994)

- self-representation (face-to-face; people personally express their opinions, discuss, vote, work, offer a material contribution, receive a benefit, etc.; people represent themselves);

- direct representation (people delegate others– relatives, friends, respected members of their community, traditional leaders, leaders of a community-based group– to represent them in all sorts of activities but maintain a direct, face-to-face relationship with their representatives);

- indirect representation (people delegate others– experts, appointees of large associations, non-governmental organisations, parties, elected or other government officials– to represent them in all sorts of activities, but they rarely, if ever, interact with their representatives on a person-to-person basis).

Some may argue that elected political officials and administrators at various levels are the ones to represent local interests and concerns, including concerns regarding natural resource management. There is some truth in this, insofar as freedom of information and the formal procedures of democracy (e.g., periodic elections) are respected, but there are also obvious limitations. For instance, indirect representation systems (see Box 2.5) are rarely appropriate to convey the specific and detailed concerns of small groups of people, and surely cannot deliver the full range of knowledge and skills of local resource users. In general, effective direct representation is crucial to assure the participation of stakeholders who do not enjoy a high social status, and it is thus an essential concern for equity in natural resource management.[28] In many cases, the traditional organisational structures for the management of common property or common pool resources (such as a council of elders) remain the most appropriate to represent local interests. These organisations may need to be identified, recognised,

---

[24]   Bromley and Cernea, 1989.
[25]   Page 379 in Baland and Platteau, 1996.
[26]   In the Bijagos archipelago (Guinea Bissau) the local people have a varied, complex and effective system of natural resource management of enormous value for the Bijagos Biosphere Reserve (IUCN, 1996a; Maretti, 2003). Yet, the communication between the local councils of chiefs and the rest of society (state administrators, economic operators, etc.) is still limited.
[27]   A community in New Guinea faced a choice between fast, lucrative and destructive timber exploitation and slower, a bit less lucrative but sustainable timber exploitation in its own ancestral territory. The elders from the community– in charge of deciding for everyone– unequivocally chose the former option. One of them, interviewed on why they did so, replied "I have old teeth and like to eat tender rice. I like to eat it now." See McCallum and Sekhran, 1997.
[28]   Borrini-Feyerabend, 1998.

understood, supported and empowered to act. Some corrective and support measures could in fact be negotiated with them (for example, to incorporate the representation of missing segments of the community, to take on some self-monitoring and feed-back procedures or to ensure a high level of interaction with their constituencies).

Informed, organised and effectively-represented social actors are just a starting point in the struggle to further one's interests and concerns in NRM. It is only in the political moment of acceptance and recognition by society that those interests and concerns become "entitlements". Some entitlements are legally-sanctioned and uncontested rights, recognised pretty much everywhere in the world (e.g., an owner of a plot can cut grass on her land). Other management entitlements are fuzzily defined and/ or actively challenged. A governmental agency with responsibility about public health matters might need to fight and win a legal battle with industry owners before being able to tighten regulation on polluting discharges in the environment. A community that lived for centuries in a territory now declared protected area might need to struggle at length if it wishes to maintain some form of access to its natural resources. A factory owner dependent on the water discharge from a watershed might have to negotiate with a watershed committee to assure a regular supply to his factory. Justly or unjustly, others in society may not share the subjective perception of one's own entitlements and that recognition might have to be achieved, bargained for, or even "conquered".

Again, some equity considerations are paramount to assure a fair chance to all relevant actors in the sensitive moment of negotiation. A society ridden with discriminatory procedures, for instance, will not be able to assure to all the same chances to be heard and responded to in a positive way. Moreover, only a political arena open to new ideas and offering the concrete possibility to meet and discuss conflicting views and interests allows new key relevant social actors to emerge and their entitlements to be recognised. In other words, a measure of political openness and participatory democracy is needed for new subjects to be socially accepted (e.g., for community representatives to sit on a Park Management Board, or for an association of squatters to manage a water supply and sanitation system in their own neighbourhood).

[Equity demands] a measure of political openness and participatory democracy.

In time, the newly recognised entitlements will be specified, systematised and codified. Stronger or weaker types of entitlements will then correspond to the breadth and strength of the social consensus around them. Within stable systems of reference, entitlements will likely evolve and stabilise into socially-codified norms and/ or legally-codified rights.

Box 2.6   Asymmetrical rights in Joint Forest Management in India
(adapted from Sarin, 1995)

The Joint Forest Management (JFM) programme seeks to develop partnerships between local community institutions (as managers) and state forest departments (as owners) for sustainable management and joint benefit sharing of (usually degraded) public forest lands. In essence, the states Joint Forest Management resolutions assure participating villagers free access to most non-timber forest products and a 25 to 50 % share of poles and timber at final harvesting. In return, the villagers are expected to protect the forest after conforming to the membership and structure specified by the forest department. The forest departments reserve the right to cancel the JFM agreement unilaterally (and, in most cases, even to dissolve the community institution itself). In such a situation, the community has no right to any compensation for its investments of labour, time or capital. If the forest department fails to honour its commitments, the villagers have no reciprocal rights for penal action (except in Haryana where they can at least demand compensation).

On the basis of the entitlements recognised in society, concrete management initiatives can begin. The entitled social actors can identify priorities, develop plans and find among themselves, or acquire from outside, the skills and resources necessary to manage the territory or set of natural resources at stake. It is here that each actor can assume, on the basis of the agreed entitlements and its own capabilities, a specific set of management functions, benefits and responsibilities. With Leach et al. (1997), it is paramount to recognise that, in this essentially political moment of negotiation: "...different groups of actors may give priority to different environmental resources and services, and particular trajectories of landscape change will bring a different distribution of costs and benefits to different groups of people.... Landscape change is a fundamentally political process, involving negotiations and conflicts between actors with different priorities [and] who are differently positioned in relations of power."

In political struggles, equity considerations are again paramount. On the one hand, there should exist places and times for negotiation (negotiation platforms or fora) and some form of logistical organising. A powerful way to maintain an inequitable status quo may be simply never to allow a meeting and organised discussion to happen. If the meetings do happen, however, every participating actor should possess the capability to negotiate. Such capability is the end result of a subtle combination of qualities, which may involve various human skills (e.g., personal assertiveness, clarity and forcefulness of communication, language skills, etc.) but also freedom from fear and freedom from needs which may impose the silence and withdrawal of some actors. In the negotiation process, the use of relatively neutral meeting places, timings that allow everyone to participate and presence of impartial and competent facilitators are generally helpful (see Chapter 6).

A limited space of anarchy (..."absence of fixed governing structures") [promotes] democratic experimentalism, which, in turn, is likely to foster more resilient and stronger societies.

When the management functions are expected to last through time, it is appropriate to institutionalise the social agreement by establishing a multi-stakeholder management body. (The process of negotiation among relevant actors and the types of plans, agreements and organisations that may result from it are explored in detail in Chapters 5 to 9 of this volume). Again, only a socio-political context in which the development of new organisations is allowed in a non-regimented way would permit such events to take place. Such a measure of democratic experimentalism characterises strong societies, in which the citizens and civil subjects in general are accustomed to assuming social responsibilities.[29] A limited space of anarchy (where anarchy is intended in the literal sense of "absence of fixed governing structures") seems thus to promote democratic experimentalism, which, in turn, is likely to foster more resilient and stronger societies.[30] For instance, if a national law establishes that the management board of protected areas in the country must be composed of– let us say– ten elected local officials and university experts, the Boards will never include other concerned and well-informed representatives of the civil society. Important management contributions that may surface on a case-by-case basis will not have a chance to be incorporated...

[Equity demands that] the interests of the weakest actors [be protected by] reliable conflict management, arbitration and legal enforcement procedures and by a fair and effective judiciary system.

Only by assuming responsibilities corresponding to their own socially recognised entitlements and by engaging in a flexible process of learning by doing in management, the relevant actors become effectively and fully empowered. Again, for the sake of equity, flexibility is needed in revising plans and agreements and in re-arranging rules on the basis of lessons from experience (this may allow some partners to contribute in the implementation phases what they might have not been able to contribute earlier on). To balance that flexibility and to protect the interests of the weakest actors, reliable conflict management, arbitration and legal enforcement procedures, and a fair and effective judiciary system, are also paramount.

In Part II of this volume, Checklists 5.3, 5.4 and 5.5 offer some concrete ideas about how to foster equity in natural resource management. Figure 2.2 also offers a sketch of what can be done to increase equity in the various steps of the CM process.

---

[29] An example in point is Switzerland, where federalism and strong devolved powers created a society where social responsibility if fully assumed by citizens. See Dorf and Sabel, 1998 and Scott, 1998.

[30] Borrini-Feyerabend, 2004 (in press).

Figure 2.2 Including equity considerations in the process towards empowered and responsible social actors– a schematic view

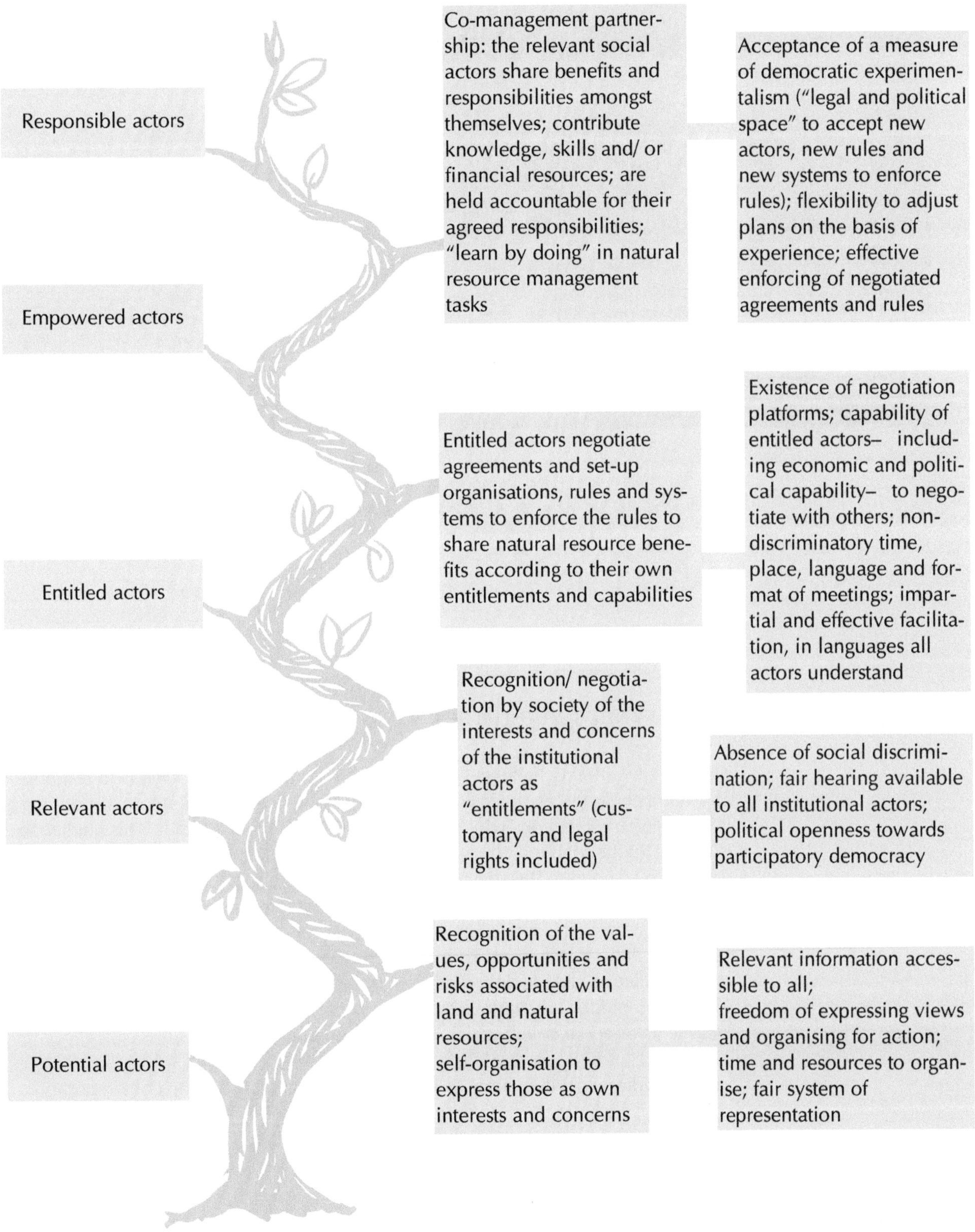

Responsible actors

Empowered actors

Entitled actors

Relevant actors

Potential actors

Co-management partnership: the relevant social actors share benefits and responsibilities amongst themselves; contribute knowledge, skills and/ or financial resources; are held accountable for their agreed responsibilities; "learn by doing" in natural resource management tasks

Acceptance of a measure of democratic experimentalism ("legal and political space" to accept new actors, new rules and new systems to enforce rules); flexibility to adjust plans on the basis of experience; effective enforcing of negotiated agreements and rules

Entitled actors negotiate agreements and set-up organisations, rules and systems to enforce the rules to share natural resource benefits according to their own entitlements and capabilities

Existence of negotiation platforms; capability of entitled actors– including economic and political capability– to negotiate with others; non-discriminatory time, place, language and format of meetings; impartial and effective facilitation, in languages all actors understand

Recognition/ negotiation by society of the interests and concerns of the institutional actors as "entitlements" (customary and legal rights included)

Absence of social discrimination; fair hearing available to all institutional actors; political openness towards participatory democracy

Recognition of the values, opportunities and risks associated with land and natural resources; self-organisation to express those as own interests and concerns

Relevant information accessible to all; freedom of expressing views and organising for action; time and resources to organise; fair system of representation

Chapter 3. CO-MANAGEMENT OF NATURAL RESOURCES

3.1 What's in a name?

There are two main challenges in managing natural resources. One is to respond appropriately to the ecological characteristics of a given environment, preserving its integrity and functions while assuring a flow of benefits from it. This challenge is mostly about content– the what and when of managing natural resources. The other is to respond to the social characteristics of the same environment, dealing in an effective way with the inevitably conflicting interests and concerns of different social actors. This challenge is mostly about process– the who and how of managing natural resources. Throughout history, attempts to respond to the latter social challenge have included many forms of hostile struggle, both open and violent and hidden, via various means of social control. Fortunately, they also include a variety of collaborative, co-management solutions.[1]

In this chapter we will attempt to illustrate and systematise some contemporary collaborative solutions to resource management challenges. Under diverse socio-political and economic circumstances, these span a bewildering array of processes, agreements and organisations, as it will be apparent from the concrete examples we will describe.

---

[1]   And at times, they include a mix of both...

Terminology is not a trivial issue here. There is no doubt that it would be useful to have a common lexicon for phenomena found throughout the world, which in the least would facilitate communicating experiences and lessons learned. But there are pitfalls to avoid. We could use the term "co-management" in a broad and general sense, but lumping too much under the concept may add to a generic "corrupted language" by which some vague and appealing terms are utilised to cover all sorts of practices and behaviours.[2] We could, on the contrary, develop a set of air-tight definitions for similar yet slightly distinct phenomena. But that may complicate communication, without necessarily fitting the complexity of real events. In the last decades, various terms have been employed to describe different levels, stages or areas of application of "co-management situations". A selection of those terms is listed in Table 3.1, given in the chronological order in which they were introduced, beginning with a quote of historical value.

...but air-tight definitions may complicate communication, without necessarily fitting the complexity of real events....

Table 3.1 Concepts and terms used to understand and describe collaboration in managing natural resources

Mutual aid	In the practice of human aid we can retrace the earliest beginning of evolution, we thus find the positive and undoubted origin of our ethical conceptions, and we can affirm that in the ethical progress of man, mutual support– not mutual struggle– has had the leading part. In its wide extension, even at the present time, we also see the best guarantee of a still loftier evolution of our race. (Kropotkin, 1902)
Adaptive management	A guiding principle for the design of the interface between society and biosphere, between community and ecosystem, between household and environment.... The release of human opportunity requires flexible, diverse and redundant regulation, monitoring that leads to corrective action, and experimental probing of the continually changing reality of the external world.... The emphasis is on social learning about the complex adaptive systems of which we are a part. Human institutions are crucial factors in this learning. (Holling, 1978 and others quoted in Röling and Maarleveld, 1999)
Participation	Organised efforts to increase control over resources and regulative institutions in given social situations, on the part of groups and movements of those hitherto excluded from such control. (UNRISD, 1979)
Networking	A number of autonomous ... groups link up to share knowledge, practice solidarity or act jointly and/ or simultaneously in different spaces. Based on moral (as distinct from professional or institutional) motivations, networks are cooperative, not competitive. Communication is of their essence. ... Their raison d'être is not in themselves, but in a job to be done. ... They foster solidarity and a sense of belonging. They expand the sphere of autonomy and freedom. The source of the movement is the same everywhere– people's autonomous power– and so is their most universal goal, survival. (Nerfin, 1986)
Co-management	...a political claim [by local people] to the right to share management power and responsibility with the state... (McCay and Acheson, 1987)
Collaboration	The pooling of appreciation and/ or tangible resources (e.g., information, money, labour) by two or more stakeholders to solve a set of problems neither can solve individually. (Gray, 1989)

---

[2] Majid Rahnema (1992) powerfully warns against this danger, which has plagued terms such as "participation," "aid" and "development" for a long time.

Popular participation	As an end in itself, popular participation is the fundamental right of the people to fully and effectively participate in the determination of the decisions which affect their lives at all levels and at all times. (African Charter for Popular Participation in Development and Transformation, 1990)
Co-management	The sharing of power and responsibility between government and local resource users. (Berkes, George and Preston, 1991)
Community forestry	The control and management of forest resources by the rural people who use them especially for domestic purposes and as an integral part of their farming system. (Gilmour and Fisher, 1991)
Co-management (of protected areas)	The substantial sharing of protected areas management responsibilities and authority among government officials and local people. (West and Brechin, 1991)
Democratisation	The act of subjecting all interests to competition, of institutionalising uncertainly. The decisive step towards democracy is the devolution of power from a group of people to a set of rules. (Przeworski, 1991)
Joint forest management	Collaboration in forest management between agencies with legal authority over state-owned forests and the people who live in and around these forests. (Fisher, 1995)
Environmental partnerships	Voluntary, jointly defined activities and decision-making processes among corporate, non-profit, and agency organisations that aim to improve environmental quality or natural resource utilisation. (Long and Arnold, 1995)
Collaborative management (of protected areas)	A situation in which some or all of the relevant stakeholders are involved in a substantial way in management activities. Specifically, in a collaborative management process the agency with jurisdiction over natural resources develops a partnership with other relevant stakeholders (primarily including local residents and resource users) which specifies and guarantees the respective management functions, rights and responsibilities. (Borrini-Feyerabend, 1996)
Joint protected area management	The management of a protected area and its surrounds with the objective of conserving natural ecosystems and their wildlife, as well as of ensuring the livelihood security of local traditional communities, through legal and institutional mechanisms which ensure an equal partnership between these communities and governmental agencies. (Kothari et al. 1996)
Participation	A process through which stakeholders influence and share control over development initiatives and the decisions and resources that affect them. (World Bank, 1996)
Collaborative management for conservation	A partnership in which government agencies, local communities and resource users, non governmental organisations and other stakeholders negotiate, as appropriate for each context, the authority and responsibility for the management of specific area or set of resources. (IUCN, 1996b)
Co-management	True co-management goes far beyond mere consultation. With co-management, the involvement of indigenous peoples in protected areas becomes a formal partnership, with conservation management authority shared between indigenous peoples and government agencies... or national and international non-governmental organisations. [...] true co-management requires involvement in policy-formulation, planning, management and evaluation. (Stevens, 1997)

Affirmative democracy	In analogy to [the concept of] "affirmative action" prevailing in the USA, in affirmative democracy marginalised social groups are to be given the same capacities and rights as those enjoyed by the groups on the top. (Navarro, 1997)
Collaborative management agreement for a conservation initiative	Representatives of all key stakeholders agree on objectives for the conservation initiative and accept specific roles, rights and responsibilities in its management.... [They] ensure that the trade offs and compensations are clear and that all parties are aware of the commitments made by the others. (Borrini-Feyerabend, 1997)
Patrimonial mediation	Patrimonial refers to all the material and non-material elements that maintain and develop the identity and autonomy of the holder in time and space through adaptation in a changing environment.... The mediation establishes long-term patrimonial objectives, legitimates them by culturally appropriate rituals, elaborates strategies to achieve the objectives and sets up natural resource management organisations. (Weber, 1998)
Stewardship	People taking care of the earth... a range of private and public approaches to create, nurture and enable responsibility in users and owners to manage and protect land and natural resources. (Mitchell and Brown, 1998)
Shared production regimes	Regimes that produce goods or services by utilising inputs from at least two individuals or legal entities which are not part of the same organisation and are not under the control of the same principal. Each party independently decides the level of input to contribute to the shared production process and the overall goal or goals are jointly determined. Responsibility for bearing the costs of inputs is negotiated between the partners as is the share of any eventual profit and no single entity has the right to modify these terms unilaterally. (Vira et al., 1998)
Natural resource co-management	The collaborative and participatory process of regulatory decision-making among representatives of user-groups, government agencies and research institutes. (Jentoft et al., 1998)
Co-management	A system that enables a sharing of decision-making power, responsibility and risk between governments and stakeholders, including but not limited to resource users, environmental interests, experts and wealth generators.... Essentially a form of power sharing... by degrees... through various legal or administrative arrangements... often implying a discussion forum and a negotiation/ mediation process. (NRTEE, 1998).
Pluralism	The recognition of the presence and role of multiple actors and their influence in shaping the performance of both natural systems and man-made institutions. (Ramírez, 1998)
Democratic experimentalism	Citizens in many countries directly participating with government in solving problems of economic development, schooling, policing, the management of complex ecosystems or drug abuse. Central governments of nearly all political colours at times encourage these developments by devolving authority to lower levels and loosening the grip of public bureaucracies on the provision of some services while wholly privatising others. At times they simply tolerate local experimentation by waiving formally, or through inaction, their statutory rights to specify how programmes are administered. (Sabel, 1998)
Platform for collective action	A negotiating and/ or decision-making body (voluntary or statutory) comprising different stakeholders who perceive the same resource management problem, realise their interdependence in solving it, and come together to agree on action strategies for solving the problem. (Steins and Edwards, 1999)

Co-management of natural resources (also participatory, collaborative, joint, mixed, multi-party or round-table management)	A situation in which two or more social actors negotiate, define and guarantee amongst themselves a fair sharing of the management functions, entitlements and responsibilities for a given territory, area or set of natural resources. (Borrini-Feyerabend et al., 2000)
New social partnerships	People and organisations from some combination of public, business and civic constituencies who engage in voluntary, mutually beneficial, innovative relationships to address common societal aims through combining their resources and competencies. (Nelson and Zadek, 2001)
Deliberative democracy	Deliberation is the "careful consideration" of the "discussion of reason for and against". Inclusion is the action of involving others, with an emphasis on previously excluded citizens. Deliberative inclusionary processes enable participants to evaluate and re-evaluate their positions in the light of different perspectives and new evidence. Democracy without citizen deliberation and participation is ultimately an empty and meaningless concept. (Pimbert and Wakeford, 2001b)
A management-centred paradigm	In contrast with a benefit-centred paradigm, this approach to community participation is concerned with transforming the way the forest is managed and seeks to achieve this through a transfer of responsibility with authority to the forest-local communities. This is a power sharing rather than a product-sharing process. (Alden Wily and Mbaya, 2001)
Decentralisation (de-concentration) Privatisation (delegation) Democratic decentralisation (devolution)	Decentralisation is any act in which a central government formally cedes powers to actors at lower levels in a political-administrative and territorial hierarchy. De-concentration involves the transfer of power to lower branches of the central state, such as prefects, administrators or local ministry agents. Privatisation is the transfer to non-state entities, including individuals, corporations, NGOs, etc. Democratic decentralisation is the transfer to authorities representative of and downwardly accountable to local populations. (Ribot, 2002)
Multi-stakeholder processes	Processes that bring together all major stakeholders in new forms of communication and decision-finding (and possibly decision-making),... recognise the importance of equity and accountability... and the democratic principles of transparency and participation. (Hemmati, 2002)
Sound governance	Sound governance is based on the application of UN principles, such as legitimacy and voice (through broad participation and consensus-based decisions), transparency and accountability, performance (including responsiveness to stakeholders, effectiveness and efficiency), fairness (equity and the rule of law) and direction (including strategic vision and the capacity to respond to unique historical, cultural and social complexities). (Institute on Governance, 2002)
Public involvement in governance	Public involvement is generally recognised to have three pillars: public access to information, public participation in decision-making processes and access to justice. As a practical matter, it also implicates the right of free association and free speech. These rights operate synergistically. (Bruch and Filbey, 2002)

In this work we deal mostly with the concept of "co-management", for which we have adopted a broad but factual working definition (see Box 3.1).

Box 3.1   Co-management of Natural Resources

In this volume we employ the term co-management (CM) to describe a partnership by which two or more relevant social actors collectively negotiate, agree upon, guarantee and implement a fair share of management functions, benefits and responsibilities for a particular territory, area or set of natural resources.

Our definition of "co-management" is not specific regarding forms, types or levels of power sharing, and it is more concerned with actual events (shared management functions, benefits and responsibilities) than with stated management objectives. Some believe that it would be more appropriate to use different terms for different formal levels of involvement.[3] It is difficult, however, to identify a sharp demarcation between formal types of participation and actual power sharing in management activities. For instance, a process of active consultation with local stakeholders may result in the full incorporation of their concerns into the management plan of a state-controlled protected area. Or a multi-party body without legal authority may enjoy a high level of social recognition and see its recommendations invariably endorsed by decision makers (see Box 6.12). This is de facto power sharing. Conversely, it is possible that several actors who officially participate in negotiating management decisions (let us say because they hold seats in the decision-making body, they are de jure[4] in charge) end up more often than not in a minority position and are powerless to influence the final decisional outcome. Is the second case necessarily more "co-managed" than the first? There is, however, one situation, in which the formal inclusion of social actors in a decision-making body makes the entire difference. This is when decision—making is stipulated by consensus rather than by vote. A pluralist body in which decisions are made by consensus– rather than by vote– assigns the full value to the meaning of co-management.

> A pluralist body in which decisions are made by consensus–ther than by vote– assigns the full value to the meaning of co-management.

In sum, we understand co-management as a broad concept spanning a variety of ways by which two or more relevant social actors develop and implement a management partnership. We speak about it in a pragmatic, de facto sense, regardless of the de jure condition it corresponds to, ignores or contradicts. Obviously, supportive tenure rights, policies and legislation strengthen collaborative processes and partnerships. Yet, more often than one may think, there is a schism between policy and practice, and practice is ahead of policy in many cases.[5]

---

3   See, for instance, Franks, 1995, for the case of a protected area. Stevens (1997) also discusses this at some length.

4   The distinction between de jure and de facto corresponds to the distinction between what is prescribed by norms and laws and what actually happens in real life.

5   See Part IV of this volume.

...more often than
one may think, there
is a schism between
policy and practice,
and practice is
ahead of policy in
many cases.

Co-management is not a new approach. Partnerships for resource management are as old as human cultures,[6] exist in all countries of the world[7] and concern all types of territories and natural resources. Forests, fisheries and coastal resources, grazing lands and wildlife are included in existing management agreements among various parties.[8] At times the partnership does not regard any specific territory but only a resource that may be temporarily found on a given territory— e.g., water or migratory wildlife.

Management partnerships can be found in state-owned, communally owned, privately owned and mixed-property territories. The scale at which the agreement works may be as large as an entire watershed or as small as a forest patch. The partners may include state and para-statal bodies– such as national governments, ministries, district development committees, state universities and protected area agencies, and private bodies– such as indigenous councils, landowners, communities and interest groups within communities, NGOs and private operators. Usually, different types of partners are involved (e.g., a public agency, several local communities and private operators) but the partners can also be all of the same kind, for instance several landowners or several interest groups within a community. As discussed in Chapter 2, the co-management approach stresses partnerships with communities as well as within communities.

...the co-manage-
ment approach
stresses partnerships
with communities as
well as within
communities.

Some find it useful to distinguish between management partnerships for productive purposes (e.g., agriculture or animal husbandry) and partnerships for conservation (e.g., to preserve the habitat of a given species or manage a protected area). Such distinction, however, is not easily drawn. Whenever the management of natural resources for productive purposes involves some consideration of future and not only present production, it inevitably involves measures for the preservation of the environmental elements that sustain production– e.g., soil, water, vegetation and fodder, biodiversity, or the local climate. Conversely, biodiversity and environmental functions sustain community livelihoods and support many small and big businesses throughout the world. As a matter of fact, it is hardly possible to separate what is done by society for the sake of conservation from what is done for the sake of the economy.

In the following, a variety of concrete examples of co-management are introduced and discussed. A possible distinction between productive and conservation objectives is mentioned, but ultimately left to the judgement of the reader.

---

6   Kropotkin, 1902.
7   For a recent review of principles and practices of partnerships see McNeely, 1995.
8   McCay and Acheson, 1987. Co-management settings for non-renewable resources (e.g., oil and
    mineral deposits) seem to be much less common, although some initiatives may now be promoting them (Mate, 2001).

3.2 Practicing co-management

...in agriculture

A variety of partnerships are in place through-out the world to sustain agricultural production. Some have traditions rooted in the millennia, such as the minga (communal works) of Andean people,[9] the naam gatherings of Sahelian societies[10], the nafir systems of Sudan or the boneh systems still found throughout western and southern Asia (see Box 3.2). The minga, for instance, is a central event in the lives of Andean communities and a main avenue of people's solidarity. It is communal work, decided upon and regulated by the community members themselves during their assembly at the end of each month. Every family sends a member to the minga, which can be called upon to open an irrigation channel, break up some particularly hard soil in common agricultural plot or carry out any other task needed by the community. The minga usually happens once a week, and after work the people eat together or conclude their efforts with a drinking party. If a family does not fulfil its obligations, it is subjected to heavy social pressure. Today, this traditional practice is still very much alive and actually spreading to private land, with people working on privately owned plots on a rotational basis (in this case the minga is called prestamano– "lending a hand").

...[common agricultural work] is a central event in the lives of [rural] communities and a main avenue of people's solidarity.

Even in non-traditional societies farmers, communities, government agencies, researchers and non-governmental organisations collaborate in agricultural production by contributing a variety of inputs and supportive conditions.[11] Increasingly, they also link their production-oriented efforts to forms of care that allow extracting natural resources sustainably, i.e., to maintain productivity in the future. For this, farmers communicate with one another, agree on a common course of action and share the responsibilities for carrying it out.

Box 3.2   The boneh– a co-management system based on crop-sharing
(adapted from Farvar, 1991)

In most of southwest Asia crop sharing is common when the factors of production are owned by different people or groups. For instance, some people own land, others own water, others have seeds and animal traction, and still others can provide labour. If they pool together what they have to produce some crops they will be entitled to a share of the harvest according to their contribution. In this system each partner, including the landlords and the landless peasants, have benefits and responsibilities.

One such crop sharing system, which has been quite common in Iran and neighbouring countries, is the boneh (known also with many other names including haraseh, sahra, jogh, boluk, dang, etc.). A boneh is a production unit including an area of land usually equal to what the water source available will irrigate in one 24-hour period, the water rights to irrigate that land, the peasants assigned to working it, and the animal power needed for ploughing and harvesting. The entire agricultural land of a community is often subdivided into a number of bonehs equal to the number of days in the irrigation

---

9   Sanchez Parga et al., 1984.
10   Pradervand, 1989.
11   Thrupp, 1996.

cycle. The council of Elders of the community roughly coincides with the Council of the Chiefs of the bonehs (Irrigation Council). The turn for irrigation is usually determined by drawing lots. Once a year, prior to the start of the irrigation season, the elders representing all the bonehs get together and decide by drawing lots whose boneh would get to use all the water available to irrigate on the first day, whose on the second, and so on. In this way, the risk of starting on the last day of the irrigation cycle (which would expose the crops to longer periods of drought) is distributed at random ("decided by God"). Within each boneh, a further management system for water distribution usually functions like clockworks.

At the end of the season, the crop is harvested collaboratively, and literally heaped up into the number of shares decided by agreement or tradition. Each owner of a factor of production arrives on the scene and hauls away his or her share of the harvest. These arrangements are often codified and written down in contracts, some of which are still preserved and studied.

Although the various land reform schemes in Iran have in some respects weakened the boneh, this is still the preferred system for irrigation management and the organisation of production in the semi-arid areas of the country. Entrepreneurs from central Iran use it to organise workers, land and irrigation when penetrating new agricultural lands, for example areas irrigated by a new dam.

If [the members of the Landcare Group] decide to take action together, they usually elect a steering committee, which is then asked to investigate local problems, opportunities and available resources in a systematic way.

A telling example of farmer collaboration comes from Australia, where thousands of voluntary groups are currently engaged in what is known as Landcare programme.[12] The programme aims at developing more sustainable systems of land use, counteracting the severe environmental impact brought about by the un-adapted farming practiced of European immigrants in the last centuries. There is no typical Landcare group (they show a remarkable diversity among themselves) but, basically, a Landcare group gathers individuals who come together voluntarily to co-operate in caring for the land. One of the points of strength of Landcare is that such individuals are not only farmers, but also community members at large, environmental activists and government agency staff. A Landcare group may begin with an informal gathering of individuals who end up discussing land management problems. If they decide to take action together, they usually elect a steering committee, which is then asked to investigate local problems, opportunities and available resources in a systematic way. That steering committee may in turn call for a more formal group to take shape, and elect its own executive team.

A Landcare group becomes operational with decisions regarding management boundaries, goals and memberships. The land degradation problems are discussed, the potential resources to solve them investigated, and the relationships with state and governmental assistance agencies and other sources of support developed. Among the routine duties of a group is usually the monitoring of local land status via innovative "land literacy" approaches (community-based action research, farmer-fly-overs, using of living organisms as indicators, listening to interpretative tapes when travelling, or even becoming "hands-on" users of sophisticated techniques and computer programmes for Geographic Information Systems– GIS). Participatory methods (observation walks and drives, mapping, etc.) are used to plan the management of farms and water catchments in an integrated way. In all this, new relationships are established with government extension agents and consultants, who may provide specific technical support. Many groups identify a facilitator (possibly a professional one). If the group's activities require on-going care that cannot be provided by volunteers only, they hire a pro-

---

12 Campbell, 1994a.

fessional co-ordinator. If necessary, the groups apply for funds and other resources from the government and other sources.

The organised groups with worthy projects to implement can also refer themselves to the Landcare Programme itself, which may decide to assign some financial support. The Programme fosters various and non-uniform rules among the Landcare groups, and this has proven one of its winning features. It is too early to have conclusive data on the impact of the Programme for the whole country. Today, however, communities and agencies co-operate to define and tackle land degradation problems and further research and new extension approaches in ways that did not even seem possible only a decade ago.

…in water and watershed management

Perhaps more than any other natural resource, water has been co-managed for centuries, under different cultures and geographical conditions, resulting in the effective utilisation of a most essential input to life and agriculture (see Box 3.3). Throughout the world, there exist innumerable examples of traditional associations for water management, many of whom have been studied extensively to understand their characteristics and functional mechanisms[13], often as part of the study of traditional management practices of common property resources. Some insights from these studies will be reviewed in Part III of this volume.

…water has been co-managed for centuries, under different cultures and geographical conditions.

Box 3.3   Cultural co-management in Bali
            (adapted from Reader, 1990)

The island of Bali enjoys a constant climate, suitable for the continuous production of rice throughout the year. To fulfil this potential the Balinese people have had to cope with two main challenges: adapting to cultivation in their steep, deeply fissured mountain environment and managing water. In fact, although water is available all year around, it is needed in the rice fields only part of the time, such as during planting and growing but not at harvesting and immediately afterwards. The Balinese people have solved the problem of steep terrain by building terraces on the mountain slopes. They have solved the water management problem by setting up an irrigation system that controls the flow of water down the slopes, alternatively flooding and draining fields, and maximising production on every terrace.

An optimal use of the water can be achieved only if the timing of cultivation in different fields is co-ordinated in a rotational cycle. For instance, the fields at the top may be flooded and prepared for planting while the crop is already well-advanced in the middle terraces and already being harvested in the lower ones. Obviously, such a well-timed cycle needs advanced co-operation among all farmers. Since times immemorial, this has been achieved in Bali by local organisations called subak (irrigation societies), comprising all the owners of the landholdings irrigated by the same water source.

An individual water source (tempek) is composed of a dam and system of channels and aqueducts that keep water flowing at optimum speed from the main lakes on the top of the island. Each land unit (tenah) is due to receive precisely the same amount of water from the tempek it depends on, regardless of its owner and position. The technical difficulties of dividing water accurately and regulating the timing of its supply are taken in charge by the subak council, who also collects taxes to finance upkeep and improvements and calls the members to contribute to maintenance and construction works. Each subak has a written constitution (at times written on a palm leaf!), each member casts one vote on matters of policy and election of officials (regardless of the size of land units held)

---

13   Ostrom, 1992; Tang, 1992.

and fines are imposed for infraction of subak rules.

The Balinese people have set the context of the subak in the realm of a transcendent authority— Dewi Sri, the goddess of rice and fertility. Every stage of water division is marked by a ritual ceremony, held in the temples at the top of the water flow and in the shrines interspersed among the rice terraces. The ceremonies are scheduled according to the Balinese calendar (the Balinese year is 210 days, exactly the double of the local cycle of rice growing), and at each ceremony the subak farmers are reminded of the timings and sequence of the water flows. Thus, at each ceremony the co-operative relationship among farmers is strengthened. The religious occasions and the growing cycle of rice match closely, structuring the whole island into a co-ordinated system in which water management, rice production, spiritual life and social reciprocities closely merge.

...the management plan for the river [was the occasion to create] a most fruitful and appreciated experience in local democracy.

Partnerships for water management can play an important role for the sake of local ecosystem health but also for social development. For instance, a "River Parliament" has been created among various bearers of interests and concerns on the management of the river Drôme, in France. France's law declares rivers to be property of the nation, to be managed for the general interest. The problem is that everyone needs to agree on what this interest is, within a complex system of management conditions. For the Drôme, three years of meetings, studies and encounters produced a consensus among all major interested parties. This consensus, spelled out in a document called "The Drôme Sage", is now the management plan for the river, the ground on which a number of contracts mobilise conspicuous national resources, and a most fruitful and appreciated experience in local democracy.[14] French politicians are proud of their experience with the Drôme, and are proposing it as a model for the European Community, on the basis of the European Union (EU) Directive on watershed management.

In Argentina, the Encadenadas lake watershed (south-west of Buenos Aires) has been subjected for decades to a recurrent alternation of floods and droughts that

has accustomed the local residents to natural disasters. Such disasters went side-by-side with social conflicts, as some groups could protect themselves from floods only if others would accept to be subjected to water shortages. Thus conflicting interests stalled decisions or prompted one-sided measures that left many people unsatisfied. In fact, at one time or another, everyone in the Encadenadas area was hit very hard by water management failures. Droughts severely affected agriculture and tourism. Destructive floods became so severe as to make some areas permanently un-inhabitable. The crucial challenge was managing water as a common good for different local administrative units, each with its own socio-geographic peculiarities and ecologic/ economic priorities.

For some time the Argentinean government saw the problem as merely technical, i.e., a problem that could be solved by appropriate technical solutions such as water reservoirs and other

---

¹⁴ Voir Media, 1998.

hydraulic works. It was not as simple as that. In practice, the providers of public service did not even manage to agree on a definition of the problems that satisfied all interest groups (e.g., tourism-dependent businesses, agriculturists, fisher folk, people from upstream and downstream villages, etc.). In addition, some of the hydraulic works they set in place actually ended up aggravating local hardships rather than solving them. It was at this time that a change of attitude began to be felt among the various actors interested in water management. Rather than discussing technical fixes, they turned to discussing rights, responsibilities and equity issues. The management of the whole watershed took centre stage, instead of the usual conflicts to appropriate specific water benefits in specific locations. This change also signalled the emergence of new social actors, viz. local ad-hoc associations, which started acting alongside the state-sponsored technical administrators and the political administrators elected in various municipalities. Thus began a laborious process that eventually established some co-ordinated management plans and set in place a Watershed Management Committee. The richer definition of the water problem and the emergence of organised social actors, capable of co-managing water rights as well as economic compensations and indemnities for water damages, are now widely regarded as crucial steps in both the development of the region and its democratic re-awakening.[15]

> ...a change of attitude began to be felt among the various actors interested in water management. Rather than discussing technical fixes, they turned to discussing rights, responsibilities and equity issues.

...in agricultural research

Not only soil or water can be profitably co-managed, but also agricultural research,[16] for instance on new seed technologies, on irrigation systems and on a variety of management practices. In fact, the participation of peasants– the main users of the research results– in defining research objectives and methods is considered by some among the most promising innovations in modern agriculture.[17]

Box 3.4   Participatory research with women farmers in dry-land agriculture
(adapted from Pimbert, 1991, and Pastapur and Pimbert, 1991)

Joint problem solving, mutual learning and negotiated agreements were at the heart of a participatory research process involving scientists and women farmers cultivating marginal land in Andhra Pradesh, India. Actors involved in this decentralised research jointly established reversals in the conventional roles of scientists and farmers: women farmers took key decisions and scientists acted in a facilitating and support role. This was farmer-led research on insect pest management.

To begin with, major insect pests of pigeon-pea, an important food crop in India, were jointly identified by farmers and scientists who surveyed the crop as they walked through farmers' fields. Women farmers discussed and documented together the characteristics of their pigeon-pea varieties and their local crop management practices. They thus agreed that pest-resistant varieties were an important component of integrated pest management approaches. On the basis of such an indication, the scientists searched for and identified improved pest-resistant pigeon-pea lines that closely matched the characteristics of the farmers' varieties. Small batches of pest resistant pigeon-pea identified by the scientists on research stations were then grown out by farmers along local varieties (landraces) to test their performance in different risk-prone farming situations. The results of these trials were evaluated entirely on the basis of the farmers' own criteria. In fact, the parameters considered by the women went well beyond the scientists' conventional ones, such as "yield" and "pest resistance". The women rated the pigeon-pea lines according to ten agronomic and social criteria, including pest resistance, taste, wood production and

---

[15]   Monachesi and Albaladejo, 1997.
[16]   Pimbert, 1991; Sowerwine et al., 1994; and http://www.prgaprogram.org
[17]   Carmen Aalbers, personal communication, 1997.

quality, fodder value, obtainable market price and the retention of quality during storage. The women farmers' criteria and priorities were elicited in individual and group interviews using ranking methods drawn from Participatory Rural Appraisal approaches.

At all stages of the co-managed research process, women of different ages and wealth, and from different villages, were included in negotiations with scientists and a local non governmental organisation to reach agreements on what to monitor and evaluate, what indicators to use, how and when to collect and analyse data, what data actually meant, how findings should be shared and what follow up was needed. The women sanghams (collectives or community groups) from different villages were regularly involved in discussing and cross-checking the findings, as well as planning each next step in a flexible and adaptive way. The women collectives offered invaluable guidance to the outside scientists as to which research questions and categories of knowledge were most relevant to farmers' needs and priorities and to the local agro-ecological and social contexts.

The participatory research resulted in stunning outcomes:
- One of the improved pigeon-pea lines evaluated by the women farmers was decisively rejected by the farmers because of its bitter taste. However, by the time the women farmers reached this conclusion, the same pigeon-pea variety had just been officially released in the state of Andhra Pradesh on the basis of research station and on-farm trials managed by scientists alone, as part of a conventional transfer of technology approach to agricultural development

- Two other improved pigeon-pea varieties evaluated by the farmers performed well under their conditions and, in some cases, were rated as superior to the local landraces. But despite the advantages of the improved pest resistant pigeon-pea, the women farmers still wanted to retain their landraces and other improved varieties they had tested. They believed that pest attack was lower when they grew a mosaic of mixed varieties than when they grew a single variety. The farmers' insistence on biodiversity as a principle of production in risk-prone environments led the scientist to further explore this pest management option by analysing the pest-suppressant impact of mixing different pigeon-pea lines in various combinations.

The participatory research and jointly agreed procedures were particularly appropriate in supporting diversity as a means of sustainability and food security in the local, risk-prone environments. The co-management of agricultural research by scientists and the largely illiterate women farmers also highlighted the needs for changes in institutions, attitudes and behaviours to allow more people to learn and create knowledge and technologies together, through dialogue, collective inquiry and negotiation of roles, rights and responsibilities.

…in rangeland management

Partnerships among pastoralists and between pastoralists and peasant communities have stood the test of centuries in many environments. In the first case, it is necessary to assure that communities dependent on similar modes of production coexist and do not compete destructively with one another.[18] In the second, as different modes of production draw resources from complementary ecological niches, pastoralists and peasants must find rules for a fair exchange of products and for benefiting from one another (e.g., because of the fertilising of the land by passing animals).[19] In both cases, the need for co-operation and the potential for conflict are high, and entire cultures developed to respond to these challenges.

The hema system, once common in the Islamic world and now sadly rarer, consists of a set of rules for the grazing of herds on a given territory utilised by one

---

[18] Horowitz and Salem-Murdock, 1987; Bassi, 1996.
[19] Franke and Chasin, 1980; Horowitz and Little, 1987.

or more pastoralist communities (e.g., particular tribes or villages).[20] The families may possess hereditary ownership or right of use or have de facto been grazing on the territory for a long time (in other words, the property regime is usually mixed). The hema rules bind all the members of the community and specify areas where animal grazing is prohibited (with the exception of specific periods and drought times, when cutting of grass is allowed as special privileges for needy people); areas where grazing and cutting is permitted except in some seasons; areas where grazing is allowed all year round (but the kind and number of animals permitted to graze are specified); areas reserved for beekeeping; areas reserved to protect forest trees such as juniper, acacia or ghada (these areas are usually held under common property of a village or a tribe). A person committing offence against the hema rules has to pay a fine; repeated offenders receive severe social sanctions.

A most interesting feature of agreements within and among pastoral societies is a propensity towards flexibility through informality, ad-hoc-ness, un-boundness, porosity, impermanence and a continual socio-political negotiation.[21] In other words, pasture access is often granted through alliances and political processes that better serve the interests of the partners when they are open and informal, leaving space for bargaining and re-adjustments. This best responds to the variable ecological and economic conditions that characterise pastoral life

> The hema system... consists of a set of rules for the grazing of herds on a given territory utilised by one or more pastoralist communities....

Box 3.5   Forole, the sacred mountain of the Galbo people
(adapted from Bassi, 2003)

Forole is a sacred mountain just north of the border between Kenya and Ethiopia where the Galbo peoples (a sub-group of the Gabbra) hold the jila galana ceremonies. Most of the Galbo live in Kenya, but they move in pilgrimage to the Forole on occasion of the ceremony. The trees of Forole Mountain are totally protected by the Gabbra and access to the upper part is only allowed to a few people who preside over the ceremony of the sacrifice to the Sacred Python. The lower part of the mountain provides permanent water and is used as reserve grazing area by both the Gabbra and the Borana pastoralists. Sometimes there are tensions over pastoral resources among the two groups, but the Borana fully respect the sacredness of Forole Mountain and the inherent restrictions, indirectly assuring its conservation. This community conserved area is not univocally associated with a single ethnic group and engages local actors in complex economic and symbolic relationships that work quite effectively in maintaining the quality of pasture and the livelihood of people.

Unfortunately, the forces of economic modernisation (e.g., the money-dominated economy, the predominance of market values versus use values) and socio-cultural change (emergence of state power and bureaucracies, urbanisation, loss of value of traditional institutions and systems of reciprocities, propensity towards fixed access rules and regulations in place of flexible, on-going, political negotiations) managed to severely weaken many culture-based partnerships throughout the world,[22] such as the hema and ghada mentioned above. In some places the occupation of crucial land and destruction of traditional natural resource management systems of pastoral communities has resulted in tragedies of huge proportions, as in Ethiopia, where millions of Oromo-Borana people survive today at the mercy of climatic conditions to which earlier they were well able to respond.[23]

---

[20]   Draz, 1985.
[21]   Turner, 1999. See also Box 3.5 in this Chapter.
[22]   Watts, 1983a; Watts, 1983b; Horowitz and Little, 1987.
[23]   Bassi, 2002.

It is a welcome
change that some
national
governments and
international donors
are now
"discovering" the
management
capacities of pastoral
people.

It is a welcome change that some national governments and international donors are now "discovering" the management capacities of pastoral people. Thus in Kenya, the Loita Maasai communities have recently been re-assigned the management rights over the Loita Forest, after a decade of struggles in court and in the field.[24] In Mauritania, a recent law called Code Pastoral recognises the economic and management value of pastoral practices and some projects have promoted the establishment of various types of pastoral and farmers associations. These associations are encouraged and facilitated to enter into agreements with the government and among themselves to improve herds' health and land productivity while preserving the environment from excessive exploitation.[25] And in Iran, pastoral communities, the government and progressive NGOs are experimenting with new forms of support to sustainable use of pastoral resources.[26]

...in forest management

Besides agricultural and grazing lands, forestlands throughout the world have been the objects of multiple interests and seen many conflicts developing around them. Fortunately, they have also been the focus of encouraging types of collaborative solutions. Here below are contemporary examples from three continents.

In the Pacific Northwest region of the United States, the Applegate River watershed is located in Southwest Oregon and northern California. Long the object of intense polarisation and controversy over forest management practices, the Applegate Valley is composed of a patchwork of federal, state, county, and private lands. Tired of the gridlock, a number of the key stakeholders convened in 1992 to form the Applegate Partnership, a group uniting natural resource agencies, industry, conservation associations and local residents towards the goal of ecosystem health, diversity and productivity. This sixty-member group is co-ordinated by a nine-member Board of Directors. The partnership serves in an advisory capacity to relevant resource management agencies and seeks to educate private landowners and provide them with incentives to manage their forestlands in a sustainable fashion. The partnership has no legal authority to make decisions on behalf of participating agencies but, because of its broad representation and shared purpose, it has considerable de facto influence over forest

---

[24] Karanja et al., 2002.

[25] Pye Smith and Borrini-Feyerabend, 1994. For a summary of the achievements of Mauritania's second livestock project see Shanmugaratnam et al., 1993.

[26] See the case example 1.4 in chapter 1 of this volume.

management practices in the Applegate Valley, and has succeeded to improve the whole management climate in the region. In particular, it succeeded to remove from the scene the deeply entrenched animosity and the polarity around the issues that had been so pervasive before. In place of the gridlock, "positive relationships developed between polarised groups, agencies and the community; a common vision was attained."[27]

In India, beginning in the 1970s, the expansion of an informal grassroots forest protection movement eventually triggered the issuing of a national resolution in June 1990. The resolution provided the authority for communities to participate in the management of state forests (no other institutional actor was contemplated in the resolution and the private sectors remained out of its scope). Subsequently, sixteen state governments issued resolutions extending rights and responsibilities to local communities for state forest protection under what is now called the Joint Forest Management (JFM) programme. As part of the programme, forestry department officials and ad-hoc local committees from the villages sited close to the forests develop joint management agreements and micro-plans. Over 10,000 village committees are currently active, representing a significant but still limited percentage of the potential and need in the Indian federation.[28] The Joint Forest Management programme has achieved impressive results in forest conservation, but is limited by local people's lack of secure tenure to the resources they are managing. The state regulations, in fact, fail to address the long-term rights of participating communities.[29]

...forestry department officials and ad-hoc local committees from the villages... develop joint management agreements and micro-plans.

Box 3.6   Conserving their palm groves: the pride of Gaya communities in Niger
(adapted from Price and Gaoh, 2000; and personal communication by Anada Tiega, 2003)

The Gaya region in southwest Niger offers an example of local communities re-appropriating– as well as reinventing and reorganizing– their rights to their surrounding natural resources. About 80 villages with a population of 80,000 reside in the midst of a region of the Sahel blessed with superior conditions for agriculture, including a resource unique in potential and diversity of use: the ron palm (Borassus aethiopum). Benefits derived from the ron palm extend to much of the rural population in Gaya, with distribution of goods and revenues shared between different groups in the society. Thus, women, farmers, herders, fisher folks and artisans all have recognised rights to access to, and use of, the palm.

The palm is of particular interest given a wide range of products harvested from its different parts. In the past it had been overexploited throughout the country to the point that Gaya harboured one of the few standing groves left in the whole country. External support to conserve and develop the potential of the local ecosystems initially focused on "technical" conditions for environmental regeneration, but has since progressively moved to efforts to promote community initiatives for conservation, management of wild resources and establishing basic conditions necessary for sustainable livelihoods. The ron palm has become the central focus for important changes in local forms of association, governance, law and economic organisation. In particular, some community land-use management groups (unités de gestion de terroir) have emerged, enjoying great local specificity and independence in their decision making process. Each group exercises the right to govern common resources as well as financial autonomy. The progressive recognition by government of the groups and their rights has a direct impact on revision and application of land tenure law and legislation on forms of association, as well as on common property and rights and responsibilities in natural resource management. Progressively, the local groups have extended their interests to a variety of other resources, such as wetlands and fisheries. Their success has been so important that one of their wetlands has now been declared a Ramsar site.

---

27   Wondolleck and Yaffe, 1994. See also Box 8.6, in chapter 8 of this volume.
28   Pandey, 1996; Poffenberger, 1996.
29   SPWD, 1992. For a thorough analysis of Joint Forest Management in India see Poffenberger and McGean, 1998.

In Tanzania, local user groups in the Babati district are entrusted with full decision-making power about conservation and resource use in the communal forests close to their villages. The forestry department and the Swedish aid agency worked with the user groups to develop management tools and criteria, but all final decisions were left to them. For their local "communal forests", this is fully in agreement with Tanzanian law. Discussions are being held, however, to extend their management responsibility also to nearby state-owned forests, a fact that falls outside of the scope of the existing legislation.[30] Some pilot experiences are occurring in the south of the Babati district (Duru-Haitemba) where several forests controlled by local communities have been declared Village Forest Reserves. These are gazetted nationally but planning, management, patrolling and enforcement of rules (established as village by-laws) remain with the locals. In this sense, local groups are recognised to have not just some rights and responsibilities in management, but full authority and control over the local resources that they themselves wish to place under protection.[31] A similar situation is found for Mgori Forest, which, however, had a different starting point. Prior to 1995, Mgori Forest was claimed as government land. When it became apparent that the government did not have the means to manage it, it turned for assistance to the local communities. The resulting agreement stipulated that the 44.000-hectare forest would be managed by the five forest-adjacent villages in partnership with their district council. The presence of the district council was not too strong (one field officer only), but the communities soon organised to establish five Village Forest Management Areas, each demarcated and guarded by their village forest guards (totalling more than 100 people) on the basis of village by-laws. Fires, illegal harvesting and clearing for millet production ceased, and the illegal hunting of elephants was also curtailed. The villages have now obtained their Certificates of Village Land and plan to register their Forest Management Areas as common property.[32]

> Fires, illegal harvesting and clearing for millet production ceased, and the illegal hunting of elephants was also curtailed.

Box 3.7 Devolving power: a way to promote management partnerships!
(adapted from Garreau, 2002)

The 1996s law on the devolution of management authority and responsibility to organised local communities that goes under the name of GELOSE (Gestion Locale Sécurisée or local security of resource management) created the conditions for a profound change of approach in natural resource management in Madagascar. Typical "integrated conservation and development projects"– such as the one operated by WWF around the protected areas of Marojejy et Anjanaharibe-Sud– took advantage of this law and offered a new chance to management partnerships in the region.

At the beginning the project accompanied the local communities, as well as the administration of the communes and the sub-districts, in revisiting their history and discussing the future of their land, resources and livelihoods. This patrimonial approach created new ties among the local families and villages, which discovered similarities among their problems and wishes. Local people seemed even to start developing a common identity, despite the mixed ethnicity of the region (a pole of recent immigration). At the same time, the project diffused information on the two main components of the GELOSE law: the devolution of power regarding forests and other common property resources and the clarification and attribution of land tenure rights regarding areas under family cultivation. As time went by, the project ended up playing a role of advisor and intermediary between the communities and the administration and help building the capacities of everyone in the process, including the "mediators" foreseen by the national GELOSE procedures. It also helped the communities to ritualise the long-term manage-

---

[30] Johansson and Westman, 1992. Also: David Gilmour, personal communication, 1996.
[31] Wily and Haule, 1995.
[32] Alden Wily and Mbaya, 2001.

ment objectives, to organise internally (developing structures and rules through traditional agreements called dina) and to develop the necessary simple management plan and terms of reference.

The quality of this process was highly dependent on the pace of activities, which proceeded at the actors' own rhythm. The issues, beginning with forest conservation, slowly became "owned" by the communities and no longer needed to be promoted by outsiders. The communities discovered the complexity of forest management and the ways of sustainable use of forest products as well as soil and water. They themselves ask for all available tools and technical help to fulfil their forest management obligations and guarantee their future. Importantly, the state technical services become their natural partners, both to assist in surveillance and to provide technical solutions to problems. And the state administrations found their role in the coordinating initiatives and defending the established management rules vis-à-vis the external partners. In this light, the management devolution promoted by the GELOSE law seems indeed to have offered a unique occasion for collaboration and partnership among local actors.

...in the management of coastal resources

If examples of participatory management of forests abound, co-management regimes are also becoming frequent for water-based resources.[33] The firths of Scotland,[34] for instance, are marine and coastal wetlands including large estuaries, sea areas and coastal hinterlands– a sort of "arms of the sea", where water changes from salty to fresh and generates a complex mosaic of habitats and species. The firths are also the subject of numerous economic and cultural interests of local communities. In recent years, separate management projects have been set up for each firth, each run by a cross-sectoral, non-statutory partnership called "forum". Individual people have a chance to participate, although the statutory agencies tend to play a predominant role. The voluntary nature of these bodies constitutes both a strength and weakness for them. It is a strength insofar as people generously contribute their time and efforts for something they deeply care for. It is a weakness insofar as the decisions of a non-institutionalised forum may be stalled by a variety of obstacles and vested interests.

Box 3.8 Co-managing the Sian Ka'an Biosphere Reserve
(adapted from Ramsar Convention Bureau, 2000)

In Mexico, an impressive co-management case is under way in the Sian Ka'an Biosphere Reserve, a coastal limestone flat of 628,000 ha located mid-way between Belize and Cancun on the eastern coast of the Yucatan peninsula. There, the land and sea converge gradually into a complex hydrological system of mangrove stands and creeks, salt and freshwater marshes, brackish lagoons and huge shallow bays of varying salinity, sea grass beds, islets and mangrove keys– all protected by a barrier reef growing along the coast. This sensitive ecological system has been under severe threat of irreversible degradation because of unbridled "development" based on forest exploitation, tourism and cattle ranching, and unplanned urbanisation.

In the early 1980s, the state government, headed by a committed governor named Joaquin Coldwell, agreed to take some major immediate measures: ending timber concessions to private companies, establishing community forestry programmes with local ejidos (a Mexican system of communal ownership) and asking that the area be classified as a biosphere reserve. In 1984, the process of developing a management plan for the reserve was started. The state and federal government created a steering com-

---

[33] For an illustrative review, see White et al., 1994.
[34] de Sherbinin, 2000.

mittee to coordinate the work and established a local council including representatives of the fisher folks, coconut growers, cattle owners and peasants besides employees of the municipalities and scientists from the Autonomous University of Mexico. Gradually, forest concessions and cattle growers were asked to leave the area, fishermen organised themselves to control their fishing grounds and a zoning scheme was discussed and adopted. The initiative attracted the attention of national and international people and NGOs, which came together to create an association called the Amigos de Sian Ka'an.

The Association has promoted participatory action research and development initiatives based on the sustainable use of local resources and local environmental knowledge. Land tenure issues also needed to be addressed. The land in the ejidos belongs to the communities but the land in the biosphere reserve was federally owned and the local residents were concerned about their access to resources. The Council proposed the establishment of 90-year concessions for agricultural lots, reversible in case the occupants would not respect the regulations of the biosphere reserve. In a unique experiment, this concept was also applied to the sea. The lobster fishing grounds in the two bays were divided by the fishermen into "fields". Strictly speaking this modality cannot be legalised, but it has already become a "traditional management structure" in Sian Ka'an. Each fisherman cares for his field, devoting efforts to improve the lobster habitat, while their overall organisation carries out the surveillance against poachers.

...local residents survey against dynamite fishing [and] monitor marine biodiversity.

In the coastal area of Tanga (Tanzania), a co-management experiment has been on its way for several years with yearly planning workshops that bring together representatives of villages, government authorities, commercial users of the coastal resources and non-governmental organisations.[35] The workshops are promoted by an IUCN-assisted project, which is also engaged in encouraging villagers to analyse the situation and prospects of their natural resources and plan appropriate management activities for their land and sea territories. This is done with the concurrence and support of the other institutional actors gathered in the yearly workshops. To tackle coastal erosion, some villagers have replanted degraded mangrove areas. To support their fish stock, others are surveying their waters against dynamite fishing. The coastal residents had enjoyed resource abundance for centuries, and the project did not find a trace of traditional systems of coastal resource management in the area. Today, however, local residents not only survey against dynamite fishing, but they monitor directly marine biodiversity (including coral reef health and presence and abundance of fish species), after being specifically trained by the project staff.

In Thailand, the Yadfon Association has been working with 40 small fishing communities in Trang province starting with three villages in 1985, when the organisation was formed. The motivation was not to protect these habitats for the sake of conservation, but to secure the source of local livelihood, threatened by continual declining harvest of fish, squid, crabs, and shellfish. Fishers joined together to stop using destructive gear and practices, such as dynamite fishing and cyanide poisoning, and to restore the mangroves and sea grass beds. They successfully petitioned the local government to ensure regulations within their coastal zone. Following their successful example, in the upstream wetlands the rice farmers established a network to protect the sago palm and nypa palm forests. In all, the villagers are demonstrating their willingness and capacity to manage their coastal resources and are now active to ask the government to formally recognise their role.[36] In Sri Lanka, co-management of natural resources has been promoted by Special Area Management (SAM) processes in 11 coastal sites. These processes

---

[35] Gorman and van Ingen, 1996.
[36] Ferrari, 2003.

sought to involve communities as key managers and are now being evaluated in terms of their capacity to contribute to local livelihood sustainability.[37] Initiatives are also advancing, with different results, in countries as far as Belize,[38] Fiji,[39] Ecuador,[40] Australia (see later under co-management of protected areas) and Mauritania, where the Banc d'Arguin National Park and World Heritage Site is moving towards a co-management setting with the local fishing communities.[41]

Box 3.9   Marine Co-management in Soufriere (Saint Lucia)
(adapted from Renard and Koester, 1995; and Geoghegan et al., 1999)

In the Caribbean island of Saint Lucia, a regional NGO called the Caribbean Natural Resource Institute (CANARI) and the local Department of Fisheries jointly facilitated a laborious conflict resolution process among local fishing communities, hotel owners, dive operators, community institutions and government agencies— for years in bitter confrontation over different management options for their area's coastal resources. The conflict resolution efforts paid off beautifully, as an effective co-management agreement is now in place.

A pluralist coordinating body, named the Soufriere Marine Management Association (SMMA), is composed of representatives of all major actors interested in the management of coastal resources. The Association developed a shared vision of the future of the marine and coastal environment of the Soufriere region, which includes sustainable development, the equitable sharing of its benefits and the fostering of wide social participation in decision-making. The Association is constituted as a "non-profit company" with charitable, developmental and scientific objectives and is assigned the powers of coordinating the implementation of the agreements to manage the Soufriere Marine Management Area, as well as related programmes and financial, technical and human resources.

Zoning is a main component of the agreement. So far, five zones have been identified, including Marine Reserves, Fishing Priority Areas, Multiple Use Areas, Recreational Areas and Yacht Mooring Sites. According to the zoning, different regulations for resource use are established for fishing, diving, yachting and water sports. Complementary programmes include activities in education, public awareness and communication, social and economic development, infrastructure, research and monitoring. The Association has established its own by-laws, with periodicity and arrangements for meetings, conditions for new members (they would have to become signatories to the agreement and be accepted as legitimate stakeholders at an annual general meeting of the Association), conditions for the nomination or election of officers on the board of directors (Chairperson, Deputy Chairperson, Secretary and Treasurer) as well as the duties of these officers, and procedures to constitute advisory committees and other bodies to assist the Board in the implementation of its programmes and the running of its operations.

The co-management setting has enhanced the protection of the marine reserves and thus profited the tourism industry. The fishermen, on the other hand, obtained a guaranteed access to the fishing zones and feel more secure in their livelihood. As a consequence, they actively support the reproduction and maintenance of the fish stock, resulting in environmental and economic benefits for everyone.

---

[37] Senaratna and Milner-Gulland, 2002.
[38] http://www.communityconservation.org/Belize.html
[39] http://www.lmmanetwork.org
[40] See Box 6.12 in Chapter 6.
[41] Heylings, 2002.

...in the management of freshwater wetlands

For the management of freshwater wetlands, typical limited attempts at participatory approaches are supported by conservation and development projects, as in the cases of Djoudj National Park, Senegal and the adjacent Diawling National Park, Mauritania[42]. For neither Park an effective co-management setting is yet in place, but in both a variety of committees and meetings to engage stakeholders in discussions and advice are slowly substituting top-down decision making practices. The local environmental knowledge and the indisputable advantage of local communities in carrying out park surveillance are today recognised by governments and experts alike. With those, the right of the local people to maintain the integrity of their livelihoods (which includes their own forms of resource management and use) is also becoming recognised.

In Mexico, the coastal wetlands of the southern state of Sonora encompass 62,000 ha of high biological diversity located along an important shorebird and migratory bird flyway. Effluents from irrigated agriculture pose the primary threat to the conservation of the wetlands, followed by cattle husbandry, shrimp aquaculture and urbanisation. Among the social actors with primary interests and concerns are the local permanent and seasonal fisher folks and the indigenous residents (Yaquis and Mayos) but also the aquaculturalists, farmers, livestock raisers, hunters, tourists, industrialists and other local residents. Through a series of workshops beginning in 1994 all these groups had the opportunity to work together and provide inputs into a strategic plan prepared together with governmental agencies, academic bodies, NGOs and donors.[43]

In India, Keoladeo National Park[44] (Rajastan) is a natural depression re-designed by local kings (e.g., using small dams) to attract as many birds as possible. Throughout centuries of careful water management, the site became an internationally famous bird sanctuary and began attracting more and more tourists. In order to favour conservation and tourism, however, the Indian government went possibly too far. In 1992 a three-meter wall topped with barbed wire was constructed all around the Park to prevent buffalo grazing and other Park access. These measures were implemented without consultation with the local communities, who saw their historical pattern of access and use suddenly becoming illegal. Years of violent conflict, non-cooperation and passive resistance ensued. Paradoxically, a very expensive scientific study ended up "discovering" that buffalo grazing is essential for the maintenance of the ecological characteristics that attract the birds, something that local people had known and fought for all along! It is with the help of the World Wide Fund for Nature (WWF) that a new atmosphere of dialogue and collaboration is finally developing between the park management and the local communities. A number of agreements have been drawn to regulate fodder collection and access to temples inside the park. Some welfare measures have also been initiated by park authorities and the tourist fees to visit the Park have been increased. The Park authorities report to be willing to allow controlled grazing of weeds inside the Park, sharing of tourist revenues with the local communities and setting up effective joint management schemes. In 2000, however, the situation was still quite unclear and potentially stalled, as national park policy in India was deemed not yet equipped to allow these kinds of formal agreements.

> ... the right of the local people to maintain the integrity of their livelihoods (which includes their own forms of resource management and use) is... being recognised.

> ...a very expensive scientific study ended up "discovering" that buffalo grazing is essential for the maintenance of the ecological characteristics that attract the birds– something that local people had known and fought for all along!

---

[42] Hamerlynck, 1997; ould Bah et al., 2003.

[43] Ramsar Convention Bureau, 2000.

[44] Pimbert and Gujja, 1997; and Biksham Gujja, personal communication, 2000.

Kenya's Lake Naivasha is the only freshwater lake in the otherwise saline lakes in the Great Rift Valley, supporting a rich biodiversity of plants, mammals, birds and amphibians. Over 60,000 people live close to the lake, using its water for drinking water and agricultural production. Human activities on the shores and the untreated water flowing back into the lake threaten the local ecology. Most land around the lake is privately owned and since 1931, the landowners organised themselves in the Lake Naivasha Riparian Association. This association manages the lands around the lake in the way it sees fit, the only constraint being that no permanent structures may be erected. Some years ago, the Association's Environmental Subcommittee, out of a growing concern about the state of the lake and its environs, started a management plan development process. This led to establishing codes of conduct (e.g., for the flower growers, the tourism industry people and the livestock keepers) for the wise use of the lake's water,[45] which prompted the listing of the lake as a Ramsar site.

Box 3.10   Community based river conservation in Mandailing (North Sumatra, Indonesia) (adapted from Ferrari, 2003)

The Lubuk Larangan system has been carried out by the people of Mandailing Natal district (North Sumatra) since the 1980s. The system is used to protect a river, which is entirely forbidden to exploit during the "closed season" that generally lasts a full year. The monitoring for the fishing prohibition is carried out by the community located close to the river and applies to all the people who interact with the river. At the end of the closed season– which usually coincides with the Islamic celebration of the end of the fasting month, Raya Idul Fitri in Bhasa Indonesia language– the prohibition is lifted for a few hours. Everyone can participate in fishing activities in the river after paying a fee which goes to fund community development activities. The occasion generally turns into a community festival.

Before the spread of the Lubuk Larangan system in the 1980s traditional conservation activities applied to rivers and forests were practised by the Mandailing and known as rarangan (prohibition). These were closely interlinked with the traditional land use system, which was governed by the traditional authority. Since Indonesian independence, however, these traditional systems have been replaced by the central government and the local forest prohibitions have been abandoned. One of the major ecological and social problems currently affecting the province of Mandailing Natal is both legal and illegal logging. Various local communities in Mandailing restarted practising river protection in the 1980s in order to raise funds for public needs such as teachers' salaries, building of religious schools, provision of assistance to orphans and the poorest people, community road construction, etc. The fee collected during the fishing festival varies between 3 to 10 million Rupias which goes a long way in meeting community needs. The Lubuk Larangan system has been adopted from a neighbouring province but closely resembles local practise of the past. The district government passed a decree to regulate the Lubuk Larangan system in 1988.

The re-introduction of the Lubuk Larangan has created a spirit of cooperation and solidarity among the local people and has provided valuable economic benefit to the community. More studies need to be done to assess the ecological effects. It is believed, however, that an increase in river biodiversity should be revealed.

---

45   http://www.iucn.org/themes/wetlands/naivasha.html

...large river basins call for a joint jurisdiction regime involving multiple stakeholders at various levels. The co-management path is ridden with difficulties but the costs of not attempting it are even greater.

The management of large scale river basins is determined by the competing claims on water and water-dependent resources by international, national, sub-national and local actors. Such competing claims need to be resolved by a socio-political negotiation and the resulting decisions need to be properly enforced. Indeed, the very complexity of the situation of large river basins calls for a joint jurisdiction regime involving multiple stakeholders at various levels. The co-management path is ridden with difficulties but the costs of not attempting it are even greater. Two typical cases, the ones of Mekong and Okavango,[46] illustrate the attempts at establishing river-wide commissions, involving various countries and tackling issues according to collaborating rather than competing or hostile processes. Given the extent, importance and complexity of the relevant issues, the programmes developed by such River Basin Commissions begin by detailed, and often interminable, socio-ecological surveys. Fortunately, while the surveys are going on, limited attempts at co-managing resources, in particular fisheries, can be pursued with success in particular locations (see Box 3.11).

...in fishery management

Fisheries is a sector where co-management has been practised for a long time with excellent results. In the words of Pinkerton (1989) "The accomplishments of co-management [fishery] regimes in which governments and users have shared power and responsibilities in enhancement of long-range stock recovery planning and habitat protection are especially notable in producing superior and more efficient management". In Europe, one of the earliest arrangements to involve devolution of central government powers and the formal sharing of fishery management jurisdiction with fishermen is the Lofoten Cod-fishery Co-management. This arrangement evolved as a solution of last resort to serious and protracted conflicts among fishermen crowded in the same, exceptionally rich cod migration routes. On the basis of the Lofoten Act, approved in Norway in the 1890s, the co-management arrangement became possible, and indeed succeeded in bringing peace where the Norwegian state had not been able to. As soon as the fishermen assumed responsibility to manage the fishery, they developed their own committees in charge of developing rules (fishing time, type of gear, space allocated, inspections, etc.). Those rules, upon adjustments on a "learning by doing" mode, have been effective for more than a century.[47]

The maritime tradition of Japan never included the idea that the sea could be an open access environment.

In Japan, the offshore, distant fisheries and deep-water resources are managed in much the same way as other countries, by granting licenses to commercial companies. The inshore fisheries, however, have a long history of collective marine tenure arrangements, comparable to the one of land commons in Europe, with records that at times go back nearly a thousand years.[48] The current co-management system assigns regulatory authority at national and regional levels and decision-making power mostly at the local level.[49] This arrangement was designed to formalise traditional fishing rights, which in the past were in the hands of village guilds. Interestingly, the maritime tradition of Japan never included the idea that the sea could be an open access environment.[50] The rights are vested now in local fisheries co-operative associations, with membership based on residency and a period of apprenticeship in the fishery.

---

[46] The Permanent Okavango River Basin Commission (OKACOM) was established in 1994, while the Mekong River Commission (MRC) was established already in the 1950s.

[47] Jentoft, 1989.

[48] Ruddle and Akimichi, 1984, quoted in Weinstein, 1998.

[49] Lim, Matsuda and Shigemi, 1995.

[50] See the summary of the Japanese fishery case in NRTEE, 1998.

The members of a co-operative obtain their own individual rights of use, which are not transferable.[51] The co-operative associations own the local coastal waters but need to apply to the government for fishing licences, which they then distribute among their members. The national government establishes the total allowable catch for the offshore and coastal fishing areas, and the local co-operatives sub-divide the quota among the fishermen. In addition, and in co-operation with other local authorities and partners, the co-operatives set up regulations, special projects, management plans, commercial ventures, purchase of supplies, and so on.

Rio Grande da Buba[52] is a brackish estuary with very productive fisheries, a high density of marine and terrestrial mammals and a wide range of bird life in the south-western coast of Guinea Bissau. Since the early 1990s the IUCN has facilitated there the development of co-management arrangements between local villages and government agencies for the sustainable use of fisheries. The local fishermen were assisted to organise and set up among themselves a credit scheme based on traditional customs, which was remarkably successful. At the same time, government-assisted research was underway to identify sustainable levels of fishery exploitations. When it became clear that barracudas were being over-exploited, the local communities and government agencies agreed on promulgating and enforcing limitations on the number of boats and the use of fine meshed nets during reproduction time. These limitations have been overall very well respected. In the meantime, the IUCN was supporting the commercialisation of fish through women's co-operatives, which met astounding commercial success. Prior to the conflict that unfortunately engulfed the country in 1998 there were more than 30 organised groups of fishermen and women fish-sellers in Rio Grande da Buba. They had managed to stabilise their fishery catch while greatly increasing the benefits for their own communities. All the above was accompanied by repeated requests for training and social support by villagers, the result of successful village-driven development efforts. At the time of this writing some relatively peaceful if not stable political conditions have returned to the country and the fishermen organisations are active as ever, demonstrating a remarkable sustainability and resilience, and the capacity to survive even the most erratic socio-political conditions.

When it became clear that barracudas were being over-exploited, the local communities and government agencies agreed on promulgating and enforcing limitations on the number of boats and use of fine meshed nets during reproduction time.

---

[51] Weinstein, 1998.
[52] de Sherbinin, 2000.

Box 3.11   Fishery co-management in the Mekong– Khong district (southern Lao PDR) (adapted from Baird, 1999)

Between 1993 and 1998, 63 villages in Khong district, Champasak province, southern Lao People's Democratic Republic (PDR) established co-management regulations to sustainably manage and conserve inland aquatic resources, including fisheries in the Mekong River, streams, backwater wetlands, and rice paddy fields. Local government endorsed these regulations, but the villages themselves choose what regulations to adopt based on local conditions and community consensus. The same communities are now empowered to alter regulations in response to changing circumstances.

Up until the 1950s and early 1960s fisheries practices in Khong were largely traditional. Fishing was conducted almost entirely for subsistence purposes, with the exception of a small amount of barter trade for certain high quality preserved fish, and the resources were managed as common property. Over the last few decades there have been many changes in aquatic resource management patterns in Khong district, and in Laos as a whole. The human population of Khong has increased rapidly. Lines and nets made of nylon, including mono and multi-filament gillnets, have become extremely common. As fish now fetches higher prices in the market and people are becoming accustomed to consumer goods, subsistence fishing has turned into market fishing.

The Lao PDR is supporting co-management with the assistance of some specific projects. Communities generally learn about this from neighbouring villages, friends and relatives, or from government officials. If their leaders are interested, they write a short letter to the Khong district authority, who later come to visit and assist in the process of developing a co-management plan (see also Boxes 5.10, 6.10 and 9.21). The plan included detailed regulations, such as fisheries conservation zones (partial or total), bans on stream blocking, on using lights at night, on chasing fish into nets, on destroying flooded forests and forests at the edges of the river, on using frog hooks and traps, on catching juveniles, and so on. It is generally up to the village headmen to assure that regulations are implemented. Most communities rely on a mixed strategy that includes enforcement of regulations and awareness raising, which are both important, especially at initial stages of implementation.

The aquatic resource co-management programme in Khong has been very successful. It has enhanced village solidarity, increased natural resource management capacity and increases the fish and frog stocks and catches. It demonstrated to be a most important option for equitably managing natural resources in the region.

...in mountain environments

Mountain environments present unique difficulties for the development of co-management settings. The relevant territories are often large, sparsely populated and comprise difficult terrains, sometimes including barriers that separate entire cultures and countries. And yet, remarkable examples of co-managed natural resources in mountain environments do exist. In the Annapurna Conservation Area– an internationally renowned high mountain environment in Nepal– a large-scale attempt at integrating conservation and local development has been promoted and supported for a decade by the King Mahendra Nature Conservation Trust.[53] Local, regional and national organisations discuss on an on-going basis the specific management decisions to be taken at various levels (including decisions over distribution of tourism revenues). The main aim is to involve all the relevant parties in management, so that their interests, concerns

---

[53] King Mahendra Trust, 1994.

and capacities are fully taken into account. Several committees participate in developing specific agreements, and dedicated agents called lami (matchmakers) facilitate the process.

A similar co-management experience is also pursued, albeit with different mechanisms and results, in the buffer zones of some National Parks in Nepal.[54] This builds upon several years of experience and positive results in community forestry initiatives in the country, another example of co-management involving governmental agencies and local communities.[55] In Pakistan, the Mountain Areas Conservancy Project is engaging local communities, concerned government departments and various conservation agencies such as IUCN, WWF, the Aga Khan Rural Support Programme and the Himalayan Wildlife Foundation. One of its aims is the development of community conservancies. A conservancy has a territory (usually a watershed), various conservation committees and a valley conservation plan and fund. The pluralist watershed conservation committees are organised into clusters and apex bodies at each level.[56]

In Scotland, the Cairngorms Area is an important element of the natural heritage– probably the largest integral area of high and wild ground in the United Kingdom. The Area is managed by a Partnership Board composed of 20 members in representation of a wide range of social actors with relevant interests and concerns. In turn, the Board calls together the even larger spectrum of concerned individuals, groups, agencies and organisations that need to agree and co-ordinate action if any measure of conservation and sustainable development is to take place. This is done in meetings and conferences, privately and in public, and via many community-outreach activities. Through such extended consultations, the Board has developed a conservation and sustainable development strategy.[57] Zoning is a major means of composing different interests and concerns in the strategy, and several projects have been identified in different zones.

A similar pluralist management setting is sought but far from being achieved for the Mont Blanc region, a foremost scenic and biodiversity icon in Europe. This charismatic mountain environment, shared among Italy, France and Switzerland, is home to 30 municipalities with important common cultural characteristics developed through centuries of human and economic exchanges. On paper, a Trans-boundary Conference for the Mont Blanc and an ambitious joint programme have been set up, but in practice only the elected politicians of the three countries seem to have a voice in the management of the area, downplaying environmental concerns, responding only too well to economic imperatives and derailing any attempt at genuine participatory conservation attempts.[58] Currently, an umbrella NGO is actively organising national and international meetings among social actors concerned with the future of the mountain, its people and culture, and demanding an active role in deciding about it.

...dedicated agents called lami (matchmakers) facilitate the process of developing specific agreements.

Zoning is a major means of composing different interests and concerns in the strategy, and several projects have been identified in different zones.

---

54   Kettel, 1996a and 1996b.
55   Gilmour and Fisher, 1991; Hobley, 1993.
56   Pathak et al., 2003.
57   Cairngorms Partnership, 1996.
58   Chatelain and Ehringhaus, 2002.

Box 3.12   Ambondrombe (Madagascar): caring together for a sacred mountain
          (adapted from Rabetaliana and Schachenmann, 2000)

Ambondrombe is a sacred mountain and historic site on the border between Betsileo and Tanala lands, towards the southern end of the Malagasy eastern escarpment between Ranomafana and Andringitra National Parks. Still relatively intact, dense tropical forest covers its flanks, giving way to rare cloud forests at the summit. At lower elevation to the East, the forest dwelling Tanala cultivate mainly bananas and robusta coffee. At lower elevation to the West the undulating savannah gives way to the manicured farms of irrigated rice, tobacco, maize, potato and fruit trees of the Betsileo agriculturists. In the last century, the Ambondrombe Mountain and surrounding lands were also inhabited by several generations of Betsileo royal families. These families called in some Merina people, who brought in their handicraft and agricultural skills. The Merina's cultural influence was absorbed rather then fought by local people, and its impact is still evident today in local architecture, handicrafts, legend, folklore and taboos. For both the Tanala and Bestileo peoples, the mountain forest offers rich natural resources, abundant water, relatively fertile soils, wood for building and cooking, natural fibres, medicinal plants and a vast variety of bush food for hunting and gathering, It is only too reasonable that they both claim the mountain forest as part of their ancestral inheritance and favour settlements of their own people at the edges of this forest corridor. More claims are also coming from new migrants and stakeholders (scientific, commercial and tourism) as Ambondrombe constitutes the only intact biodiversity bridge left between north and south along the eastern Malagasy escarpment.

How can the complex interests and conflicts at play be effectively managed to conserve this unique natural and cultural jewel of Madagascar? The exceptional self-help spirit of local elders and leaders around Ambondrombe is showing the way. A community-based natural and cultural resource management programme has started with voluntary forest guards organised by a committee of village elders. The elders are accustomed to protecting the forest against illegal migrants and settlers and to make sure that the use of local resources is done in a sustainable way according to customary laws (dina).

The programme is taking advantage of a state-approved system of natural resource management called GELOSE (Gestion Locale Sécurisée, or local security of resource management) in which they work with various national and international, governmental and non-governmental partners (see also Box 3.7 in this Chapter). The Water and Forests Service assists in land use and fire control and management. An NGO is helping with reforestation for timber and firewood, training local farmers in plantation management, sawing and semi-industrial charcoal production with improved mobile kilns. Another NGO assists in agricultural diversification and intensification, e.g., the restoration of silk worm production for the weaving of traditional garments (lambas) and in agroforestry approaches. Local consultants assist with a comprehensive ecotourism strategy, involving the descendants of the Betsileo royal family, custodians of cultural and sacred sites in the area.

The stakes are high and the challenge is impressive. In the course of the negotiations the poor face the rich; the local visions, aspirations, actions and taboos stand up to global perspectives, interests and influences; the demands of traditional subsistence livelihoods clash with the ones of modern economy; and the local governance system based on customary law needs to deal with the rules and inflexibility of a modern nation state. Fortunately, all the stakeholders involved have expressed a common aim: developing and applying self-help approaches to preserve the natural and cultural diversity and identity of the unique Ambondrombe "lifescape". The work is on-going.

…in managing migratory wildlife

Co-management arrangements do not necessarily refer to a specific territory or area of sea. Such is the case for agreements on the management of migratory wildlife, which refer to specific animal species, for instance the Beluga whales found in the coastal and estuarine areas of the Eastern Canadian Arctic. This species of whales has been managed for years through agreements between Fisheries and Oceans Canada and various communities and organisations of the Inuit indigenous nation. Under the agreements, female whales are protected, there is a sanctuary area where calves can grow undisturbed, and hunting rules are established and respected[59].

Similarly, a large herd of porcupine caribou, ranging across two Canadian territories and the state of Alaska, is managed as a result of an international agreement between the governments of the USA and Canada.[60] The herd is of major economic and cultural importance to a number of Alaskan and Canadian indigenous communities. This is true not only because the caribou meat is an essential component of their diet. Hunting, preparing the meat and sharing the harvest are the building blocks of their cultures. The agreement between the USA and Canada provides for the constitution of the International Porcupine Caribou Board, in charge of developing a management plan for the herd and its habitat. In Canada, a similar "national" Board exists, including members from the Gwich'in Tribal Council, the Council for Yukon Indians, the Inuvialuit Game Council, the Yukon Territorial Government, the Government of Canada and the Government of the Northwest Territories. Every year, management plan updates and reports are agreed upon and distributed among the various interested groups within Canada, and across the border.

Possibly the best known example of co-management of migratory wildlife is the CAMPFIRE initiative in Zimbabwe.[61] The initiative– described also in case example 1.3 in chapter 1 of this volume– has succeeded in establishing many specific partnerships among local communities, district authorities, the national government, some national NGOs, research institutions and business operators. The "producer communities" involved live right in the midst of the habitat of wildlife (including the large animals prized by trophy hunters), and directly sustain the relevant opportunity costs and direct damages. Occasionally they also actively improve the habitat of wildlife, for instance by digging water pits for the elephants in case of severe droughts. On the basis of a specific Act of the national government, the district authorities are in charge of wildlife management. The national NGOs and research institutions provide technical and organisational help to the producer communities and district authorities. The business operators organise the flow of tourists and hunters that inject financial resources into the system and provide a return to the producer communities and the district administrations. The initiative has obtained positive results for both conservation

Co-management arrangements do not necessarily refer to a specific territory or sea area. Such is the case for agreements on the management of migratory wildlife, which refer to specific animal species....

---

59 Drolet et al., 1987.
60 Porcupine Caribou Management Board, 1995. See also Table 8.1 in Chapter 8.
61 Jones and Murphree, 2001.

Even limited levels
of authority and
responsibility seem
to make a significant
difference.

objectives and the local economy and livelihoods. At the time of this writing, big game hunting seems to remain the only economic initiative strained but not substantially affected by the current socio-political crisis in the country. Big game hunting remains popular, allowing a relatively stable source of income to the wildlife-dependent communities.

The CAMPFIRE initiative has been so successful that it has been replicated under similar models in Botswana, Zambia, Mozambique, Namibia, Tanzania, and has inspired practice in many other African countries. The devolution of management authority and responsibility to local communities, however, has been more or less effective depending on a country-by-country basis. In Namibia the communities that joint together to form conservancies (see Box 3.13) have substantial decision-making power. The 51 communities in the surroundings of Tanzania's Selous Game Reserve– one of Africa's oldest and largest protected areas– on the other hand, have much less power. They are assigned rights and responsibilities over the wildlife that penetrates in their territories in a rather paternalistic way.[62] And yet, even such limited levels of authority and responsibility seem to make a significant difference. There appear to be a reduction in poaching between the Serengeti and Selous by a factor of 10, attributable to the fact that only in the surroundings of Selous the local communities benefit from the wildlife that moves out of the park into their adjacent lands.[63]

Box 3.13   Private and community conservancies in Namibia:
co-managing land for game farming and wildlife-related livelihoods
(adapted from Jones, 2003)

Namibia has about 75% of its wildlife outside formal state-run protected areas. Private farms developed a multi-million euro industry based on consumptive and non-consumptive uses of wildlife. But individual farm units are not large enough for successful game farming, as game requires large areas where to take opportunistic advantage of pasture growth and water supply in arid and unpredictable environments. Mobility and flexibility are the keys to survival. Private farmers soon realised the advantages of pooling their land and resources to manage wildlife collectively and established "conservancies" with common operating rules, management plans and criteria for distribution of income derived from wildlife. There are now at least 24 conservancies on private land in Namibia (there were only 12 in 1998) covering an area of close to four million hectares. Efficiency of scale means that their returns are more than twice those of individual wildlife ranches.

Namibian communities have followed suit. There are now also 15 "community conservancies" in Namibia, managing another four million hectares of land with more than 200,000 wild animals, including endangered black rhino, endemic species such as Hartmann's mountain zebra, and large parts of Namibia's elephant population. Important habitats managed by community conservancies include the western escarpment of the central plateau, which is a major centre of endemism, seasonal and permanent wetlands; northern broad-leafed woodlands; and west flowing rivers which form linear oases in the Namib Desert. Several community conservancies have set some of their land aside as core wildlife and tourism areas within broader land use plans and wildlife has been re-introduced to at least three such conservancies. Torra[64], a community conservancy with more than 350,000 ha in north western Namibia, has one up-market tourism lodge generating about €50,000 annually. Trophy hunting is worth nearly €18,000 annually and a recent sale of Springbok raised

---

[62]   Baldus et al., 2003.

[63]   R.K. Bagine, Chief Scientist of Kenya Wildlife Service, personal communication, 2003.

[64]   Torra is the first and most economically successful community conservancy in Namibia. Other conservancies are less fortunate in terms of tourism potential and the lack of sustainable income may constitute a problem for their long-term viability.

€13,000. The size of the conservancy means that it could certainly develop two more lodges without causing environmental damage or spoiling the wilderness experience for tourists. This would more than double the existing income, making considerably more money available for the 120 households once the operating costs of about €18,000 have been covered.

...in managing protected areas

Protected areas of various IUCN categories– from national parks to protected landscapes– are increasingly managed by partnerships involving governmental and non-governmental actors.[65] The 2003 World Parks Congress in Durban (South Africa) endorsed recommendations that identify and acknowledge several governance types for protected areas (PAs), including co-management and community management (community conserved areas). The openness to a diversity of institutional arrangements was recognised as a determinant of strengthening the management and expanding the coverage of the world's protected areas, addressing gaps in national PA systems, improving connectivity at the landscape and seascape level, enhancing public support for conservation, increasing the flexibility and responsiveness of PA systems, improving their sustainability and strengthening the relationship between people and nature. It was also endorsed that the IUCN PA category system (based on key management objectives) was to be integrated with a new dimension for "governance type" and strengthened with reference to cultural management objectives (more attention to be given to the crucial ties between biological and cultural diversity). As major as they appear, these statements do not signal a change in orientation but, rather, the full legitimisation of processes underway for several years, which were already recognised at the World Parks Congress in Caracas (1993) and at the Seville International Conference of 1995.[66] The Caracas Congress stressed the importance of "conservation partnerships"[67] and the Seville Conference emphasised that the biosphere reserves are to be managed with the active involvement of local authorities, NGOs and economic operators, in addition to local communities, scientists and conservation professionals.[68]

An interesting example of a biosphere reserve engaged to transform the participation theory into practice is the Sierra Nevada de Santa Marta (Colombia), the highest coastal mountain range in the world (it raises to 5,775 meters just 42 kilometres from the Caribbean coast). There, the Fundación Pro-Sierra Nevada de Santa Marta conceived and tirelessly supported a collaborative process to develop a strategy for the preservation of biodiversity and the sustainable use of natural resources. Innumerable meetings have been held among various institutional actors– including representatives of thirteen municipalities, two national parks, the indigenous inhabitants of the territory, the business sector (heavily dependent on the Sierra as a "water factory"), as well as the army and even some guerrilla groups and paramilitary factions. Despite the foreseeable spectrum of opinions and interests among stakeholders, some common concerns could be identified and a large number of potential initiatives were consolidated

The 2003 World Parks Congress endorsed recommendations that identify and acknowledge several governance types for protected areas, including co-management and community management (community conserved areas).

---

65 See, for instance, West and Brechin, 1991; Barzetti, 1993; Amend and Amend, 1995; Sarkar et al., 1995; IUCN, 1996b; Borrini-Feyerabend, 1996. For recent reviews of case examples of co-managed protected areas and community conserved areas, see two recent special issues of Policy Matters, the journal of IUCN/ CEESP, No. 10 on Co-management and Sustainable Livelihoods and No. 12 on Community Empowerment for Conservation http://www.iucn.org/themes/ceesp/publications/publications.htm

66 UNESCO, 1995.

67 McNeely, 1995.

68 This statement was needed. A survey of biosphere reserves concluded in 1995 that they had made little progress in involving communities in decision making. The study stated that collaborative action was slow to develop, alternative lifestyles were not taking hold, biological scientists were remaining in the drivers' seat and local participation was not given the attention it deserved (IUCN, 1995).

... management
agreements can be
signed between the
landowners and the
Park Authority and
are considered to be
legally binding
contracts.

into a Sustainable Development Plan for the whole bioregion.[69] This Plan is the expression of a major social agreement developed under extremely difficult socio-political conditions. The implementation of the plan is understandably constrained by the political instability of the area, but the process has been very positive overall.

In some parts of the world, the participatory approach to protected area management has been for some time the rule rather than the exception. In Western Europe, for instance, the interests of local people are central to the stated objectives of protected areas ("...the well-being of those who live and work in the National Parks must always be a first consideration..."[70]), privately owned plots are commonly included in the protected territory, and local administrators are largely involved in management activities. This is not surprising, as the landscapes of Europe are the product of a long history of interaction between people and the land. In fact, biodiversity values are often found in association with traditional land uses (such as pastoral farming systems) and the most appreciated landscapes are those that combine natural and cultural features. For such "cultural landscapes", as aptly described by Phillips (1996):

"...the real protected area managers are not the park rangers but the farmers and the foresters who live there and make use of the land in a traditional way, as well as some branches of regional or local government in democratic representation of local residents. Day to day conservation is undertaken in partnership with a range of stakeholders in the public, private and voluntary sectors. In this sense, collaborative management has been widely practised in Europe for many years".

An example in point is the North York Moors National Park (United Kingdom), which includes land settled and farmed for millennia.[71] The landscape encompasses large areas of semi-natural vegetation– such as ancient woodlands– interspersed with grazing areas, hedgerows, farmland and some small towns and villages. The relationship between the park and the local people is so close that the Park Management Plan is included as part of the general plan of Town and Country Development, prepared with the extensive involvement of the public. In fact, most of the land in North York Moors is under private ownership (a factor common to many protected areas in Europe) and the management plan is therefore dependent on the co-operation of the landowners. Management agreements can be signed between the landowners and the Park Authority and are considered to be legally binding contracts. The agreements are entirely voluntary, although the Park Authority can provide financial incentives and compensations in return for agreed works or environmentally sound farming practices. Land use changes can be controlled in part by the Park Authority, but farming activities generally remain outside these controls. The formal structural arrangement for co-management involves regular meetings, various forms of consultation, local input to the management plan and the representation of the local community on the Management Board. The Park Director, however, believes that the attitude of both management and the local parties is the most important ingredient of this very effective collaboration.[72]

The Park Director
believes that the
attitude of both
management and the
local parties is the
most important
ingredient of effec-
tive collaboration.

In France, the Parcs Naturels Régionaux[73] (PNRs, Regional Natural Parks) fully

---

69 Fundación pro Sierra Nevada de Santa Marta, 1997.
70 Harmon, 1991.
71 Statham, 1994.
72 Wilson, A., 2003.
73 Allali-Puz, Béchaux and Jenkins, 2003.

demonstrate the power of a new approach, citizen-based and citizen-controlled, to establishing and managing protected areas. For each of the 38 existing PNRs in the country (covering 11% of the national territory), the state retains its role of evaluator and supervisor but all other decisions, from boundaries to management objectives, are taken by local social actors. Such decisions are collected into "the Charter" of each Park, a voluntary contract among all the relevant parties. In other words, the citizens get together (usually through their elected representatives but also because of the impulse of NGOs and others) and decide that they want to manage their land, protect their natural and cultural patrimony and experiment

with the best way of doing it. Together, they generate a vision, transcribe it into the Charter, and identify a variety of initiatives, partnerships and new and innovative agreements to take the Charter to action and awaken the natural, cultural and economic potential of the land. They themselves originate the request to the government that their land is declared a Regional Natural Park, which is a stamp of environmental quality. The state delivers the denomination on the basis of certain criteria and withdraws it if and when the criteria are no longer respected. A typical PNR is managed by a mixed body gathering elected officials at various levels and socio-professional representatives. This body works in on-going, close consultation with the civil society at large, organised in commissions, committees, etc. The adherence to the PNR is totally voluntary (a municipality can "keep itself out" of a PNR even if entirely surrounded by it) and the territory of the Park is entirely accessible.

The citizens generate a vision, transcribe it into the Charter, and identify a variety of initiatives, partnerships and innovative agreements to take the Charter to action and awaken the natural, cultural and economic potential of the land.

Box 3.14   Tayna Gorilla Reserve (Democratic Republic of Congo)
(adapted from Nelson and Gami, 2003)

The Tayna Gorilla Reserve located in North Kivu, DRC was created in 1999 through collaboration between conservation agencies and two traditional leaders of the Batangi and Bamate people. The Statutes for this "Community-based Reserve" of 800 sq km constitute a formal agreement between the customary landholders, government and NGOs. Local people directly participate in the management of this protected area, whose goals includes both the conservation of biodiversity and the promotion of rural development. In this region of ongoing armed conflict, the Tayna forest guards are unarmed, and repressive protection measures are not employed by them. Communities have been directly involved in the development of the Reserve's management plan, including to establish a forest zoning scheme and to address the long-term development of the protected area. The Reserve programme recognises that customary use of the local resources will continue as part of the long-term management and conservation of the forest habitat. Key dilemmas faced by this initiative are the degree to which unauthorised use by outsiders can be prevented during periods of political instability, and how to include the local Pygmy population, which so far has been marginalised in the process of establishing this initiative.

...community-selected and certified local users can extract a limited quantity of specific resources (e.g., vines, honey, medicinal plants) from the National Park.

Unlike in Western Europe, in most countries of the developing South the forms of participatory management of protected areas now in place has evolved as a sort of "last resort" measure. Many have been promoted to palliate the scarcity of management funds, to deal with situation of high political uncertainty (see Box 3.14), or to mend long standing conflicts.[74] The latter was the case, for instance, for Bwindi Impenetrable National Park, one of the most famous and valuable national parks in Uganda, including as the habitat of the rare mountain gorilla. At the establishment of the Park the conflicts between local residents and park authorities were so severe that "spontaneous fires" in the park became a common phenomenon. Local people even refused to help when a ranger died in the area.[75] This was entirely understandable, as the local communities had been suddenly deprived of access to forest products needed for their own physical and social survival (forest foods, honey, medicinal herbs, poles, vines necessary to build their tools, etc.). Fortunately, a number of studies ascertained the conditions for sustainable, non-damaging use of some Park resources and a project supported by the Cooperative for Assistance and Relief Everywhere (CARE) facilitated the development of co-management agreements between the Uganda Wildlife Authority and the local communities on the border of the Park.[76] The agreements guarantee that a number of community-selected and certified local users can extract a limited quantity of specific resources (e.g., vines, honey, medicinal plants) from the National Park. In exchange, the communities agree to comply with rules and restrictions and assist in conserving the habitat as a whole. The "spontaneous fires" have greatly diminished and the relationship between the Park authorities and the local communities has substantially improved.

Co-management is also embraced in other National Parks in Uganda. In Ruwenzori, agreements were developed to specify in detail what types of rules and limits are to be followed for the collection of specific types of resources in the park area (e.g., for mushrooms, medicinal plants, honey, etc.).[77] Similarly, agreements are being signed between the Park agency and local parishes for Mt. Elgon National Park and Kibali National Park, assigning some surveillance responsibility to local groups, which, in turn, are allowed to gather natural resources that can be extracted in a sustainable way (e.g., bamboo shoots). Between 1996 and 1998 a number of agreements were developed and tested in both Mt Elgon[78] and Kibale.[79] Kibale entered into eight agreements, involving 29% of surrounding parishes. Of these, three agreements were for harvesting wild coffee in the park by people in Mbale, Kabirizi and Nyakarongo parishes (each parish consists of about 10 villages), one agreement allowed extraction of multiple resources such as papyrus, craft materials, medicinal plants, grass for thatching and access to crater lakes for fishing at Nyabweya, and four agreements allowed placement of bee-hives inside the Park. Meanwhile Mount Elgon entered into three agreements that provide access to a wide range of subsistence resources, such as firewood, and dozens more were developed later. As a whole, Mount Elgon is attempting to engage about 20% of its surrounding parishes (over 10,000 households) in collaborative resource management agreements. The Ugandan experience has been financially and technically supported by several foreign donors and international NGOs.

---

[74] See, for instance, West and Brechin, 1991; Adams and McShane, 1992; De Marconi, 1995; Ghimire and Pimbert, 1997; and Kothari et al. 1997. For an illustrative review of conflicts around protected areas and ways to attempt managing them, see Lewis, 1997.

[75] Philip Franks, personal communication, 1995.

[76] Wild and Mutebi, 1996.

[77] Penny Scott, personal communication, 1996.

[78] Scott, 1996.

[79] Chhetri et al., 2003.

Many co-management initiatives for protected areas in the South begin timidly, as if the government agencies were afraid to lose power if the experiments went too far. Most often, the local institutional actors are invited to participate only in an advisory way. For instance, this was the case in Jamaica, where an Advisory Committee including representatives of different interests and concerns was established during the setting up phases of the Blue Mountains National Park.[80] In India, the debate on the possibility of Joint Protected Area Management (JPAM) is very lively and pilot initiatives are being promoted in selected protected areas,[81] but their importance is much less than the one of the Joint Forest Management Programme. Even in the Ugandan cases described above, much is still to be done to assure the true and effective engagement of local actors. The agreements satisfy some of the needs of local communities and give them a new status and a voice that may grow with time, but the Uganda Wildlife Authority still retains full management authority. When "participatory planning" is limited to "consulting" local actors, it cannot and does not affect the substance of accepted management narratives and related action.[82] Some ask whether the experience is not more an attempt to shed responsibilities than to devolve rights.[83]

The partnership approach to managing protected areas is likely to have to expand under the current socio-political and economic conditions. Several countries are under pressure to restructure their internal budgets, and reluctant to invest scarce resources in government-run conservation. Sharing the burden among various entities, public as well as private, or even transferring control of territories to communities or private owners are becoming increasingly appealing options. Even governments that expect major tourist revenues out of the conservation investments are concerned that local social support is essential to guarantee the conditions for tourism to prosper. Meanwhile, the growing reality of private engagement in conservation is becoming better known and recognised and, in the wake of the fifth World Parks Congress of 2003, a wide constituency is building up around the recognition of the conservation importance of community conserved areas and co-managed protected areas. As part of this, a major phenomenon can be singled out: land restitution claims by displaced indigenous and local communities are acquiring legitimacy and sprouting innovative solutions.[84] And, after years of hostile relationships, indigenous peoples and local communities and national conservation agencies are beginning to work together to establish and manage new protected areas.[85]

...land restitution claims by displaced indigenous and local communities are acquiring legitimacy and sprouting innovative solutions.

80 Northrup and Green, 1993.
81 See Kothari et al., 1996. As an example, in Kaila Devi Sanctuary (western India) local pastoralists have access to pasture in the sanctuary's territory in return for help in monitoring against illegal grazing and mining (Kothari, 1995). Several action research studies have been carried out on the possibility of developing joint management agreements in a number of protected areas (Kothari and IIPA Team, 1997).
82 Risby et al., 2002.
83 Blomley and Namara, 2003.
84 See Box 4.3 in Chapter 4. On 14 October 2003, the Constitutional Court of South Africa ruled that indigenous peoples had both communal land ownership and mineral rights over their territory. Laws that tried to dispossess them are to be considered "racial discrimination." The decision is that indigenous people who own land under their own unwritten law have the right to have this upheld in spite of the legal systems subsequently imposed by the state. This ruling has important implications also for other countries, such as Botswana, which operate under the same "Roman-Dutch" legal system.
85 See examples described in Boxes 3.16, 4.4, 4.9, 4.10, 7.10 and 8.5.

Land Trusts are a key force in land protection in the USA and Canada.[86] Basically, they involve a partnership among an environmentally oriented NGO, some local authorities, state authorities (when relevant) and a number of local landowners. The NGO, typically staffed by volunteers and endowed with a tiny budget, mobilises to respond on a timely manner to special conservation opportunities or risks. It contacts a number of landowners in adjacent lands and convinces them to agree to some management practices, sign a conservation easement and/ or donate their land for conservation purposes. The landowners are motivated by conservation values and positive social pressure but also by the tax advantages provided by local authorities and/ or the state to those who enter into such a partnership.

...there are now over 1,200 Land Trusts in the USA (a third of them in New England) and many are also found in the Atlantic coast of Canada.

At times, the agreement is simply a verbal statement between the landowner and the NGO, with technical assistance sometimes provided to the landowner. It may include restrictions to certain types of land development, assurance of keeping the land under appropriate use (e.g., forestry or agriculture) or assurance of using specific management practices (e.g., integrated pest management or run-off control devices). In other cases, full management plans are agreed upon by the landowners and the NGO or a conservation easement (deed restriction) is signed. The latter formally prohibits "in perpetuity" certain land uses (e.g., infrastructure developments and buildings) and allows only others (e.g., traditional agriculture). In other words, land ownership is retained with restriction of uses. For an easement to be effective, a specific legislation needs to be developed and approved, usually to provide tax incentives to the signatories of the easement. An extreme form of Land Trust is the one in which the landowners donate their property to the NGO, which assumes the responsibility to manage it. There are now over 1,200 Land Trusts in the USA (a third of them in New England) and many are also found in the Atlantic coast of Canada. The basic outcome is more land dedicated to conservation while people enjoy their property rights but also save in terms of taxes.

Conservation partnerships with the private sector are not limited to the North America continent. In South Africa, for instance, the National Parks Trust has negotiated an agreement with a private group, the Conservation Corporation, for the management of the Ngala Game Reserve. This led to the establishment of the first "Contract Reserve" between Kruger National Park and a private enterprise. Signed in 1992, the agreement foresees that the Conservation Corporation has exclusive rights for operating tourist activities over 14,000 hectares of Kruger National Park. The Corporation pays dues to the Park, which uses them for wildlife management, research, educational programmes and community-based projects in areas bordering the protected environment.[87] This is an example of a quite extreme partnership, basically the passing on of management authority to a private institutional actor in exchange for economic benefits to be re-invested in conservation.

Another private arrangement is found in Belize. There, the Community Baboon Sanctuary was formed in 1985 to protect one of the few healthy black howler monkey populations still existing in the world. Unlike other wildlife management projects, the sanctuary is a voluntary, grassroots conservation programme depending on the co-operation of private landowners within active farm communities. Nearly all the landowners in the eighteen-square mile sanctuary along the Belize

---

[86] Mitchell and Brown, 1998.
[87] Conservation Corporation Ltd., undated.

River signed voluntary conservation pledges to make their farming practices compatible with the preservation of the habitat of the black howler monkey. Each landowner pledged to follow an individual conservation plan, receiving only modest financial support from the World Wildlife Fund and the Zoological Society of Milwaukee County.

...promoted by conservation and development projects

The so-called Integrated Conservation and Development Projects (ICDPs) grappled for years with the complexity of issues at stakes and the multiplicity of actors involved in pursuing joint conservation and development goals. Recently, the contractual approach has become a fairly commonplace response to such complexities.[88] In this approach, more or less formal contracts spell out the rights and responsibilities of various parties (e.g., donors, local authorities, local communities, natural resource user groups) for the management of a territory or set of natural resources. Typically, a contract assigns to a local community the responsibility to carry out certain management tasks and/ or prevent certain destructive practices and unsustainable uses. In exchange, the community receives an assurance of access to certain natural resources and benefits and/ or it is provided with external aid in various forms (see Box 3.15)

Box 3.15   The contractual approach to manage forest resources in Mali
(adapted from Aalbers, 1997)

In Mali's Kita district, the local forest reserves used to be heavily exploited by firewood merchants with the tacit consent of forestry officers and authorities. In contrast, local residents– dependent on the forests for firewood, timber, game and other non-wood products– were subjected to fines and imprisonment if they entered the forest even to gather for their livelihood needs. They were denied access to the forests that belonged to their ancestors from times immemorial. Obviously, strong hostile relations developed between the villagers and the forestry officers. From the early 1990s, that hostility has given way to new forms of collaboration as a direct result of an experimental project supported by the International Labour Organisation (ILO). The project, with joint development, conservation and social organising objectives, focused on elaborating new contractual arrangements for wood supply and forest management.

After completion of a forestry and socio-economic study, the project began by hiring some local villagers to carry out forest improvement works, including regeneration, scarification, and the building of firebreaks and access roads. The collaboration was stipulated in labour contracts and the work was remunerated with carts and donkeys, so that the villagers could more easily transport wood to the villages or to the town of Kita. This equipment, together with the experience gained in performing the forestry improvement works, enabled the villagers to undertake further contracts. The new contracts were more specific and sophisticated, and through them the villagers agreed to comply with forest management rules in exchange for a direct share of profits from the sale of wood. The villagers received training on methods of cutting and species to be preserved, and the amount of wood authorised for harvest remained a fraction of the regenerative capacity of the forests concerned. The latter Contracts for Wood Supply and Forest Management were institutionalised in 1991 by an Interim National Government sensitive to the needs of rural populations. This took place despite the opposition of forestry officers at regional and district levels, who did not readily accept either a partnership with the villagers or the obligations this entailed (loss of power, financial gain, etc).

The contractual forest exploitation is closely linked to the establishment of a wood distribution network

---

88   For a review of experience with integrated conservation and development projects that recommends the contractual approach, see: Larson, Freudenberger and Wyckoff-Baird, 1997. See also Agersnap and Funder, 2001.

organised according to principles defined by the villagers and the state. Contractual exploitation, in fact, competes with uncontrolled and illicit exploitation. A revised taxation system now gives preference to wood derived from contractual exploitation. Together with tight controls at the entrance to the town of Kita, this is providing an incentive to contractual exploitation. A system of tax rebates– to establish funds for forest improvement and maintenance works, and for village investments– is under consideration by the Government. A share of the rebates would be received at the local level.

Entrusting villagers with forest management and exploitation has increased their sense of responsibility for the forest resources within their village lands. Through their own organisation (which now includes a federation uniting about thirty five villages), villagers currently survey their local forests and require that merchants pay for the resources they gather, rather than getting them for free. Moreover, the role of the forestry officers has been redefined as advisory, rather than enforcement or executive. All this had positive consequences on the villagers' own sense of dignity. The acceptance of the contractual approach at the national level, as well as its integration into the country's forestry legislation, generated great interests in rural populations outside Kita district. Rural people throughout the country are impatient to become involved in controlled contractual exploitation.

In general, many ICDPs have now adopted a methodology that includes an in-depth stakeholder analysis early on into operations, stakeholder workshops to involve various partners in the design and implementation of initiatives and conflict mediation support. Setting up various kinds of pluralist workshops and committees has proven useful in various circumstances. For instance, CARE has helped set up a pluralist task force in the process of demarcating the boundaries of the Pa-Kluay community territory (a Karen community in northern Thailand), the local forest, the Doi Inthanond National Park and three neighbouring communities.[89] The Task Force included several villagers from the local communities, staff of the forest department and staff of the national park. The demarcation was carried out with the satisfaction of everyone involved with the help of both in-forest surveys and analysis of existing maps of the area.

…with indigenous peoples

In the last decades, many indigenous peoples have negotiated agreements with national governments for the management of their ancestral territories. In Australia, the Great Barrier Reef Marine Park (a major source of revenue to the country– more than one thousand million Australian dollars per year[90]) is managed by a specific Authority with hundreds of staff and a budget larger than the national budgets of some small countries. In the last decade or so, the Authority has substantially developed its position vis-à-vis local interests and concerns in the management of the Park. In the beginning, they used to only consult the stakeholders (including the Aboriginal People and people whose livelihood depends on Park resources). Then they started calling for workshops among local stakeholders to agree on specific management decisions (e.g., zoning arrangements). Now, some stakeholders (e.g., representatives of the Aboriginal People from the area) sit permanently in the Management Board of the Authority itself. This latter development happened after a ruling by the Australian High Court repealed the concept of terra nullius (no-man's land) held true at the time of the colonial conquest of Australia, and began the complex process of recognising the tenure rights of the Aboriginal People.[91] The development also built upon the positive experiences of co-management regimes established elsewhere in the

…the Australian High Court repealed the concept of terra nullius (no-man's land) held true at the time of the colonial conquest of Australia, and began the complex process of recognising the tenure rights of the Aboriginal People.

---

89 Prasittiboon, 1997.
90 GBRMPA, 1994.
91 This ruling, which recognises that a native title existed under British common law, is known as the Mabo Decision.

country (e.g., in Gurig, Coburg and Kakadu National Parks[92]) and on the positive experience of the Authority itself in its interaction with local institutional actors. The trend appears to be from informal to formal mechanisms, from advisory to power-sharing roles, from a management focus to a policy and planning focus.[93]

In Canada there exist several Joint Management Boards, on which both representatives of government agencies and indigenous peoples sit.[94] Such Boards deal with a full range of management matters, from long-term strategic planning to daily operations. The Boards, established by legislation, have formalised the right of indigenous stakeholders to participate in management. Numerous umbrella agreements have obtained legislative backing,[95] and under those agreements several communities have, in turn, prepared their own co-management plans (only some of those plans, however, take into account the interests of non-indigenous stakeholders[96]). Despite this, a recent review reports only a few bright spots (see Box 3.16) and not a few problems with regards to the establishment and management of national parks in aboriginal land in Canada, especially regarding the Government's "duty of consultation" with the owners of aboriginal title.[97] The Supreme Court of Canada has not offered a clear direction on this, stating that the nature and scope of such consultation may "vary with the circumstances".

...the trend appears to be from informal to formal mechanisms, from advisory to power-sharing roles, from a management focus to a policy and planning focus.

Box 3.16 Gwaii Haanas: the bright spot among Canada's co-managed Parks (adapted from Gladu, 2003)

In the Haida language, gwaii haanas means "islands of wonder and beauty." The Gwaii Haanas National Park Reserve, located within the Queen Charlotte Islands off the coast of British Columbia, was established in 1986 under an agreement between Parks Canada and the Council of the Haida Nation. The Haida themselves initiated the process, after their land and culture started to disappear due to heavy logging in their traditional territories. Through alliances with conservation organisations, the Haida people drew international attention to the spectacular beauty and diversity of their homeland and the need to protect it. The dual Park-Reserve status stems from the land ownership dispute. Both the government of Canada and the Haida claim ownership of the land. Fortunately, both sides have been able to put aside their differences regarding ownership and promote instead their common interests and goals. The Haida intent is to protect the area from environmental harm and degradation and continue traditional resource uses. The federal government's intent is to protect the area as a natural cultural environment as part of the national protected area system. Such objectives are perfectly compatible, leading to a relationship based on respect, reciprocity, empowerment and effective cooperation. In fact, Gwaii Haanas is now governed by a joint Management Board, made up of two Haida representatives and two Parks Canada representatives, working by consensus. This may slow down

---

[92] See Table 4.3 in Chapter 4; Hill and Press, 1994; and Smyth, 2001. For Australia as a whole an impressive and far-sighted development now sees Indigenous Protected Areas, declared and run by the Aboriginal People, recognised and supported as part of the national protected area system. See Chester and Marshall, 2003.

[93] Weaver, 1991.

[94] East, 1991.

[95] For instance: the James Bay and Northern Quebec Agreement of 1975; the Inuivialuit Agreement of 1984 in the western Arctic; the Nunavut Agreement of 1993 in the eastern Arctic; the Yukon First Nation Settlement Agreement of 1995 and the Nis'gaa agreement of 1996 in northern British Colombia. Some non-aboriginal groups failed to be recognised as legitimate parties in the agreements (Fikret Berkes, personal communication, 1996).

[96] In the early agreements, the Management Boards included nearly exclusively representatives of government agencies and aboriginal peoples, and some of the latter fought to exclude from the agreements other stakeholders, such as sport hunters (Fikret Berkes, personal communication, 1996). In some later agreements, the Boards include non-aboriginal, non-governmental stakeholders as well (Stephan Fuller, personal communication, 1996).

[97] Gladu, 2003.

some decisions but assures that they are all well thought out and widely accepted. The connections between land and culture are vital for the Haida, who are dependent on the natural resources for livelihood (through fishing, hunting and trapping) and also for medicines and the expression of their cultural identity through art. Five heritage sites within the borders of Gwaii Haanas are of particular high value to the Haida and are carefully protected. All this has been recognised and supported by Parks Canada. Consultation during the establishment and management of the protected area was adequate, and the process was not rushed (it took five years to come to an agreement). The establishment of the Park has promoted a shift in the local economy from logging to tourism. Employment opportunities have also been created by the Park itself (more than 50% of Park staff is Haida people). The only remaining challenge is to acknowledge the Haida presence, rights and participation in the management of the boundary waters of Gwaii Haanas. To the Haida, there is no separation of land and sea. Parks Canada, on the other hand, is promoting a new federal legislation that could disrupt the Haida Nation's ability to move freely between the land and the sea by introducing different levels of protection for various areas and restricting the fishing rights in some of those areas.

...the process... managed to legitimise the traditional ownership rights of the indigenous peoples, in the absence of other legal avenues for the registration of customary claims.

Several inspiring examples of management collaborations between indigenous peoples and national conservation agencies exist in Latin America, some of which are described elsewhere in this volume.[98] In Asia co-management is accepted in principle in the Philippines and is being put into practice in the buffer zone of the National Park of Ratanikiri in Cambodia and in the Annapurna Sanctuary in Nepal.[99]

In Papua New Guinea "wildlife management areas" are a special type of protected area initiated by local communities on their customary territories and only later formalised by official government legislation.[100] An example in point is the Bagiai Wildlife Management Area, declared in the Bagiai Island in 1976. The area occupies slightly more than half of the island and was declared under protection because the local people had become concerned about the decrease in wildlife, the over-fishing and the clearing of vegetation. The management rules for the area nearly entirely prohibit the use of firearms, large nets and lamps to attract fish at night, and ban fishing altogether in certain seasons. The central crater in the island is declared a sacred area, which cannot even be visited. The indigenous communities developed all these rules and boundaries and the government participated only in the sense that it approved and codified them and had them printed in the National Gazette. Not only did the process succeed in improving the resource status in the area, but also managed to legitimise the traditional ownership rights of the indigenous peoples in the absence of other legal avenues for the registration of customary claims.

For cases such as the last one, in which the participation of the national authority is rather "hands-off" and limited to a policy decision, the terms "community-based management" or "indigenous management" are also appropriately used in place of "co-management".[101] Hopefully, however, these examples of direct management by indigenous peoples remain examples of co-management as well. This is the case if they still associate in management a multiplicity of institutional actors within the local communities and societies.

---

[98] See Boxes 4.4 and 4.10 in Chapter 4. as well as Parques Nacionales de Colombia, 1999; Winer, 2001; Aburto and Stotz, 2003; Luque, 2003; Oviedo, 2003; Winer, 2003; Zuluaga et al., 2003.

[99] See Colchester and Erni, 1999; Pathak et al., 2003; and Ferrari, 2003.

[100] Fauna Protection and Control Act of New Zealand, 1966.

[101] Stevens, 1997.

3.3 The characteristics of co-management systems

From the examples described above, we can draw some general understanding and identify characteristics pertaining to co-management approaches.

- Co-management capitalises on multiplicity and diversity. Different social actors possess different capacities and comparative advantages in management, and a partnership stresses and builds upon their complementary roles. Different social actors, however, may also possess contrasting interests and concerns. The challenge is to create a situation in which the pay-offs for everyone involved are greater for collaboration than for competition.

- Co-management is usually multi-party but also multi-level and multi-disciplinary. Processes, agreements and institutions are inclusive rather than exclusive, they attempt to include all the bearers of interests and concerns who wish to participate. Yet, inclusiveness has to be balanced by the requirement to contain the transaction costs of the process (information provision, individual consultations, large facilitated meetings, translation costs, time and skills to negotiate, etc.).

- Co-management is based upon a negotiated, joint decision-making approach and some degree of power-sharing and fair distribution of benefits among all institutional actors. While the type and extent of power-sharing and benefit distribution varies from situation to situation, all entitled actors receive some benefits from their involvement. This fact alone may uplift the least powerful stakeholders, redressing power imbalances in society and fostering social justice.

- Co-management strives to assure all relevant actors of the chance and capacity to express concerns and take part in decisions on the basis of entitlements recognised by society. In short, co-management attempts to achieve more equitable management. Yet, equity does not mean equality and different grounds for entitlement need to result in different roles in resource management.

- Co-management stands on the principle of linking management rights and responsibilities. In the words of Murphree (1996b): "Authority and responsibility are conceptually linked. When they are de-linked and assigned to different institutional actors, both are eroded".

- Collaborative management stands on the concept of common good, the trust that it is possible to follow a course of action that harmonises different interests while responding, at least to some extent, to all of them. An inclusive, collaborative approach to the identification of institutional actors and negotiation of management agreements is a necessary condition for the common good to be identified and achieved.

- Co-management is part of a broad social development towards more direct and collaborative democracy. In it, the civil society– organised in forms and ways that respond to variable conditions– assumes increasingly important roles and responsibilities.

Co-management is based upon a negotiated, joint decision-making approach and some degree of power-sharing and fair distribution of benefits among all institutional actors.

Effective co-management depends on quality of public opinion... and strives to recognise cultural differences while building upon some underlying common interests.

- Effective co-management depends on quality of public opinion. This means that people understand the consequences of their choices (risks and opportunities) and are willing to pay the price for those. Both an excellent flow of relevant information and transparency in the management process are essential for this. Yet, different people hold true different values, opinions and wishes even on the same basis of "factual" information. Co-management strives to recognise such cultural differences while building upon some underlying common interests.

- Co-management initiatives can take on a large variety of shapes and forms

Co-management initiatives can take on a large variety of shapes and forms and need to be tailored to fit the unique needs and opportunities of each context.

and need to be tailored to fit the unique needs and opportunities of each context. Approaches to stakeholder participation in different environments have to be sensitive to their specific historical, cultural and socio-political contexts and cannot be appreciated outside of such contexts. CM regimes may present very different characteristics from place to place.

- Co-management builds upon what exists, in particular local, traditional institutions for resource management. It usually begins with an analysis of existing management systems, including institutional problems and opportunities. The next step is to strengthen what can be strengthened, also drawing from the creativity and inventiveness of new management partners. In taking advantage of the capacities and practices of new actors, co-management may play an important role in socio-cultural innovation.

- Co-management is a process requiring on-going review and improvement, rather than the strict application of a set of established rules. Its most important result is not a management plan but a management partnership, capable of responding to varying needs in an effective and flexible way. As in the case of the Great Barrier Reef Marine Park Authority,[102] intervening changes in legal, political, socio-economic and ecological factors induce consequent modifications to the institutional setting and/ or practice of conservation. In addition, a process of "learning by doing" generally leads towards a better recognition of specific needs, and new opportunities to involve institutional actors.

In other cases it may not be wise to have people express openly their opinions and concerns when they could expose themselves to violent repression and persecution.

Potential advantages for natural resource management exist in all types of arrangements, but so do potential problems. For instance, when authority is fully in the hands of a local body which has broken loose from traditional social controls, this may be co-opted by powerful individuals for their own interests, which may win over the interests of both conservation and the national and local communities. Conversely, when control is fully in the hands of a public agency, local rights, knowledge and skills in resource management may go unrecognised. In some cases, there can even be a decline in biodiversity as a result of the removal of people from a given territory.[103]

Is co-management thus a panacea? Should it be attempted and pursued in all possible circumstances? Indeed, it is not and it should not be pursued in all circumstances. If the social actors with relevant interests and concerns are not effectively organised, capable of conveying their positions and willing to develop an agreement, the time and resources invested in a collaborative process may be fully wasted. In other cases it may simply not be wise to have people express openly their opinions and concerns when they could expose themselves to violent repression and persecution. In addition, mistrust among the social actors (at times amply justified by lack of transparency and good faith) can stall negotiations seemingly forever (see Box 3.17). As a matter of fact it seems appropriate to close this chapter, which listed many relatively successful examples of co-management settings, with an example of failed agreement and persistent conflicts. Co-management is not easy and indeed requires a constellation of circumstances to be taken to fruition.[104]

Box 3.17   Contested reefs in the Miskito Coast of Nicaragua: no co-management in sight!
(adapted from Nietschmann, 1997)

The Miskito people, living on the north-east shore of Nicaragua, are the indigenous owners of one of the largest and least disturbed tracts of coral reef in the near shore Caribbean. The Miskito Shelf contains large expanses of coral patch and bank reefs, large beds of sea grasses and several coastal lagoons and associated wetlands, habitat of rare species such as the manatee and a small coastal-marine dolphin. For a long time, the Miskito control of their reef and shoreline has been a contested matter. Their opponents included foreign powers and commercial fishing businesses (one can count eleven wars against invaders since the early 1970s). More recently, they also included the Sandinista government (at the time of Contra-led insurgencies), resource pirates and drug dealers, and US-supported conservationists attempting to establish a biosphere reserve in the area. With whatever means they could master, the Miskito have consistently opposed the resource

---

[102]   For another example of variation of management regime, see Bertrand and Weber, 1995.
[103]   Ghimire and Pimbert, 1997; Brown and Wyckoff-Baird, 1994.
[104]   On this, see also Chapter 4 and Part IV of this volume.

management schemes proposed from outside their communities. What they wish is to establish their own indigenous coral reef management system based on customary rights and responsibilities, including regulation of fish catch, number of allowed fisherfolk and access to fishing areas. They also need concrete help to defend themselves against the large-scale exploitation of their marine resources by outsiders.

In 1991, twenty-three coastal Miskito communities, the Nicaraguan Ministry of Natural Resources and an international conservation NGO formally agreed to establish the largest Latin American coastal marine protected area, including the Miskito's Reefs. The agreement included provisions for Nicaragua to recognise the Miskito ownership of their ancestral land, lagoons and sea territories, and to assist in protecting them against resource piracy, industrial fishing and drug trafficking. The indigenous communities would manage the protected area with some technical assistance from outside, and receive financial assistance to carry out a number of conservation and development projects.

The Nicaraguan government administration includes people interested in donor funding and tourist revenues (and thus in favour of resource conservation), but also others accustomed to receiving income from the sale of fishing permits and payoffs by resource pirates and drug traffickers. As a result of internal power struggles, the government soon retreated from the initial agreement and attempted to open up to commercial fishing a large corridor that cut in two the original area to be managed. It also declared protected territory an inland area including five communities that had not yet entered the discussions on agreement. As not uncommon in the developing South, the government ministries of Nicaragua had little financial means, poor disposal of technical capacities, and overlapping and conflicting internal authorities (different ministries and branches responsible for conservation, commercial fishing, fishing permits, law enforcement and regional governance). In addition, they were used to planning for short-term goals only and showing an omnipresent desire to control the natural resources from far away offices. It is not surprising that the interests of the Miskito people found themselves in contradiction with those of the government.

In 1992, a local Miskito NGO was created to protect the local interests in management. The name of the NGO is Mikupia, meaning "Miskito heart". Despite meagre means, Mikupia managed to foster environmental discussions and organising in several communities. But new and powerful actors soon entered the scene. As soon as the provisional protected area was declared, a number of conservation and development NGOs from the North received some major funding to assist in the management and further their own goals– such as the conservation of local biodiversity but also more prosaic conservation of their own organisations and jobs. About 10% of the financial resources made available by the donors went to the Miskito communities and Mikupia. The remaining 90%– in the name of "community-based development"– was disbursed to US-based non-governmental organisations (with the consent of both the US donors and some branches of the Nicaraguan government). A new biosphere reserve management plan was soon prepared, with no mentioning of the provisions agreed upon in the initial plan– in particular the measures to confront piracy, industrial fishing and drug trafficking, and the conservation and development projects to be carried out by the local communities. On the contrary, the funds meant for those projects were spent to support the operations of the Northern NGO that considered itself the decision-maker on behalf of the communities and developed the management plan according to its own analysis and understanding.

The Miskito communities eventually learned the truth and realised that the foreign NGOs were more inclined to blame them for resource depletion than to support them in obtaining their resource rights. They banned the NGO from their land, and denounced it to the US donor. An investigation from the US donor was carried out, but did not acknowledge any wrongdoing on the part of the NGO. This prompted the Miskito communities to ban also the US donor from their region.

Despite these heated conflicts, the US donor decided to invest in the contested project and assigned management responsibility to other international NGOs, again without consultation or agreement with the Miskito people or their local NGO. On their part, the Miskito Reef communities created their own Miskito Community Protected Territory, and are now busy fighting drug trafficking and resource piracy in their area, and mapping their reefs and marine resource. The "colonialist conservationists" are still banned from their territories and no co-management agreement is in sight.

Part II. TOWARDS EFFECTIVE
PROCESSES

Chapter 4. A POINT OF DEPARTURE...

4.1   What is to be managed? Who is to be involved?

The basic point of departure for co-management (CM) is a situation in which several social actors– bearing different interests, concerns and capacities for the management of a given territory or set of natural resources– not yet found, or possibly not even explored, the possibility of joining their forces and agreeing on a way to do it together. These actors may comprise indigenous and local communities, local authorities, government agencies and representatives at different levels, NGOs, associations, individuals with special interests and private companies and businesses of various kinds. In recent decades, the number of social actors interested in managing natural resources has increased as a result of widespread socio-political change, including governments' decentralisation processes, the privatisation of previously state-controlled initiatives, the emergence of new democratic institutions, and the proliferation of NGOs, associations and business companies. Many such "new actors" perceive environmental or social problems and opportunities and believe that they can adequately respond to those if they are allowed to participate in management decisions and actions.

Box 4.1   What type of decentralisation?
            (adapted from Ribot, 2002 and Alcorn et al., 2003)

The term "decentralisation" describes an act by which a central government formally cedes power to actors and institutions at lower levels in a political-administrative and territorial hierarchy. If those are local branches of the central state (e.g., prefects, or local administration and technical ministries) the process is referred to as "administrative decentralisation" or "de-concentration". If those are private bodies such as individuals, corporations or NGOs, the process is called "privatisation" or "delegation". If those are local authorities downwardly accountable to local people, the process is called "democratic decentralisation" or "devolution".

The powers that can be transferred are: legislative (elaboration of rules), executive (implementing and enforcing decisions) and judicial. These powers and the financial resources to implement actions are rarely transferred together in integrated packages or ways that create positive synergies, a fact that complicates the process and often creates conflicts.

Extremely rare are the territories or natural resources not under some form of management (de jure or de facto), even if not outright "visible" or discernible by non-local people. Usually, one or a few social actors have access to the resources and can take management decisions. Others are excluded and may sometimes feel (and be) damaged, deprived of their rights, unjustly treated and unsatisfied. They also may be attempting, overtly or covertly, to gain access to natural resources and their benefits, engendering acute or chronic conflict situations. In other cases, the control over natural resources is shared among some organisations, groups or individuals, but the rules and conditions of this sharing are unclear or have fallen in disrespect. Or the management activities are simply ineffective, and are themselves a cause of ecological and economic damages. In some extreme cases it may even be that control on the part of any one actor is utterly limited and that the resources are in an "open access" state, with no one willing or capable of exercising management authority. In all the cases just mentioned, the need to attempt more effective and collaborative solutions is likely to become, sooner or later, evident.

Yes but… where to begin? In an ideal case, all relevant social actors would together take the initiative to meet, decide what to do and share fairly among themselves the relevant management rights and responsibilities. They would aim at a negotiated agreement and would have all the necessary means and capacities at their disposal, including professional help and time to negotiate. Unfortunately, this ideal case is far from common. A more typical situation sees only one or a few social actors holding most of the authority and the means to set a partnership process in motion. A co-management process is thus strongly dependent on the initiative of the most powerful parties, a good reason to explain why the phenomenon is not yet as widespread as it could be. This notwithstanding, the variety of "prime movers" and practical occasions to initiate a co-management process is impressive. These comprise responses to ecological and socio-economic crises (including natural disasters and conflicts over resources, such as legal battles and violent clashes), the emergence of new legislation and favourable socio-political changes (e.g., attempts to promote more equitable and democratic societies), new conservation or development initiatives (especially internationally-assisted projects) and, last but not least, the dedication and commitment of some exceptional individuals.

A typical situation sees only one or a few social actors holding most of the authority and means to set a partnership process in motion.

In India, it was deforestation and the loss of local control over forest resources that prompted villagers to organise sit-ins in the state forestry directors' offices until their grievances were heard and at least some solutions were found.[1] In Argentina, a destructive succession of floods and droughts made everyone aware of the need for co-operation in managing local water resources.[2] In Canada, co-management agreements marked the end of decades of legal conflicts opposing the federal government and the representative of Indigenous Nations. In Ecuador, a major natural disaster ushered a wave of cooperation, solidarity and joint initiatives (see Box 4.2). In many island states, the growth of tourism and its impact on local livelihoods generated social conflicts that eventually provided the impetus for CM processes (see Box 3.9 in Chapter 3).

Box 4.2   A natural disaster gives birth to solidarity, partnerships and participatory democracy in the Andes
(adapted from Rodas, 2002)

In the municipality of Paute (Ecuador), much has changed in less than a decade. It all started after an event that disrupted everyone's life: the "disaster of the Josephina". In the Spring of 1993, a landslide from the hill of Tamuga dammed the rivers Cuenca and Jadan. The natural dam resisted for some time, but eventually broke down and flooded a huge area, including several villages and the town of Paute. The residents of the town– originally not a particularly cooperative population– ended up sharing the same plastic tents and precarious uphill quarters for months. They had to live together, organise themselves for basic necessities, talk and listen to one another. Later, they had to clean up the town from the tons of mud that invaded it and rebuild all that had been destroyed. From this long and humiliating but also empowering experience, a new sense of communality and solidarity was born.

They begun with an organisation called Paute Construye, which started rebuilding the damaged or destroyed homes with a totally new conception of community involvement in all stages– from the definition of who should be helped on the basis of local "scale of need" (defined and established by the people themselves), to the local drawing of construction plans (all houses being different and designed according to the needs of the families to live there), to the cooperation between families and new organisations of local artisans in the construction of the houses themselves. A women's network was created, which is still active ten years later with training, various types of production and credit initiatives. The peasants from the driest rural areas got together and built one of the most ambitious irrigation and water supply efforts in the region. The artisans created new associations and improved their skills, a new cooperative credit scheme was set up (now serving 11 municipalities and having more than 10,000 members) and several community buildings were collectively designed and constructed. Currently, a five year development plan has been developed and approved for the Municipality of Paute. The Plan is simple but extraordinary, as it is centred on common visions of the relevant people about what they want their municipality, and their single parishes, to become. The visions were developed in local community workshops and, from those visions, specific areas of intervention were drawn and for each of those a number of specific projects, many of whom are now in operation.

The process that developed the plan was as important as the product. The participation of all actors, and the local communities in particular, has been its true heart. Support was provided by the Church, a local NGO called CECCA (Centro de Educación y Capacitación del Campesinado del Azuay) and the municipal authorities. Innumerable meetings and workshops took place in forty-three villages and urban quarters of the seven parishes in the municipality, as well as many encounters with the main agricultural employers (production of flowers for the foreign markets) and the national, regional and district institutions. Early in 1999, as a consequence of all these meetings but also because of contingent social rebel-

---

[1]   Madhu Sarin, personal communication, 1997.
[2]   See the example of Encadenadas Lakes, in Argentina, described in Section 3.2 under "water and watershed management".

lion against corruption, the process gave birth to the Municipal Development Committee, a local parliament with representatives of 27 organisations. The development plan has been the result of the work of this committee, with ideas from workshops at the grassroots being sent to the committee, which commented upon them and sent them back to the grassroots, which commented and sent them back again for final approval, in an iterative process. The committee has also established some local expert commissions to assess specific issues or problems. Once the decisions are taken, an Executive Committee has the responsibility of carrying them out. The Executive Committee is composed of four delegates from the Municipal Development Committee and four representatives of the municipality, headed by the Mayor.

Not everything is well in Paute. Many peasant families still survive on smallholdings in harsh environments, health and social problems are serious, migration from the area is still high, environmental problems with roots in the last fifty years of unplanned "development" are very severe. With respect to other municipalities, however, Paute shows a tremendous difference in terms of local organizing, solidarity, achievements and hope. Surely, this is because of the presence of generous and genial individuals that motivated and supported the participatory process. Most likely, however, this is also because of the shock– and aftershocks– of the disaster of the Josephina.

In Zimbabwe, the CAMPFIRE operation owed its existence to a new piece of legislation assigning wildlife management power to "deserving" districts,[3] and its subsequent success to the economic profitability of the sector and to the fact that many operations were self-directed and motivated.[4] In Madagascar, the GELOSE law, providing for the transfer of management rights and responsibility of common pool natural resources to local communities under specified conditions, ushered a series of impressive social processes and NRM regulations. In the United States, the 1964 Wilderness Act, the 1969 National Environmental Policy Act, the 1972 Endangered Species Act, and the 1976 National Forest Management Act all contained provisions for public input into agency decision-making. And yet, they stressed public participation in an individual and nationalistic sense rather than in a collective or community-based sense and did not generate much dialogue or discussion. The factor that prompted the enormous popularity currently enjoyed by collaborative stewardship of forests– by 1997, 90% of US forests were managed through some co-management structure– was, in fact, the success of a few concrete examples of collaborative regimes.[5]

In Mali, an ILO project prompted the conditions for a new share of benefits and responsibilities between the government and the local villages in forest management.[6] In Cameroon, an initiative for the rehabilitation of the Waza Logone flood plain identified the need for collective management institutions and assisted the local society to express them.[7] In Australia, informal discussions among local farmers are at the roots of the impressive and widespread Landcare co-management programme.[8] And all over Africa co-management agreements have been developed to attempt providing a solution to the many conflicts opposing local communities and authorities in charge of enforcing protected area regulations.[9]

---

[3]   In turn, this was the result of the work of some exceptional individuals (Child, 2003). See also case example 1.3 in Chapter 1 of this volume.

[4]   Child, 2003.

[5]   Wilson, R.K., 2003.

[6]   See Box 3.15 in Chapter 3.

[7]   de Noray, 2002.

[8]   See a brief description of the Landcare initiatives in Section 3.2 of this volume.

[9]   Numerous examples are illustrated in this volume. See, for instance, Boxes 3.6, 3.7, 3.13, 4.3, 5.5, 5.9, 5.12, 5.14, 6.11, 6.17, 7.11, 7.15, 9.5, 9.8, 9.17, 9.22.

The case of Miraflor (Nicaragua) is an uncommon example of the opposite situation. There a cooperative of small-scale farmers successfully struggled to have their land declared under a protected status (protected landscape under IUCN Category V)[10] and co-managed with the environment ministry. This demand for officially-sanctioned constraints was a conscious attempt to make the land less attractive to resourceful landowners who had started buying it up, and to avoid the health and environmental problems the farmers had experienced elsewhere under large scale production approaches.[11] The farmers offered the environment ministry their commitment to a livelihood based on small-scale, organic farming and their support to rehabilitate the local cloud forest patches. In exchange, they obtained legal and management support to remain in control of their land and some financial support from external donors.

Box 4.3   Balancing the powers in Makuleke land (South Africa):
a co-management framework solves conflicts over land ownership and use
(adapted from Steenkamp, 2002)

In 1969, the Makuleke community of the Limpopo province was forcibly removed from a tract of land in the northeastern-most corner of South Africa. Their land was incorporated into the Kruger National Park (KNP) and the community relocated some 70 km towards the south. Close to thirty years later, ownership of the land was returned to them by way of a co-management agreement with the South African National Parks (SANP). This settlement was negotiated under the auspices of the land reform programme launched by South Africa's first post-apartheid government.

Land ownership gave the Makuleke substantial bargaining might and the settlement fundamentally changed the balance of power between the two parties. The agreement made it possible for the Makuleke to pro-actively pursue their interests in the land relative to those of the SANP and the state. It also created a secure framework for the longer-term conservation of the Makuleke Region's exceptional biodiversity.

A lack of conflict around management issues is often indicative of the prevalence of an oppressive relationship. In this instance, the open conflicts that emerged as part of the redressing of rights after the fall of the apartheid regime were successfully settled as part of the co-management process. The implementation of the agreement did not immediately "solve" the controversies, but all tensions were ultimately dealt with within the framework of the agreement. With the resource base secured, the ultimate success of the "Makuleke model" will depend on the Makuleke leadership's ability to ensure the rational and equitable distribution of the benefits of conservation to all sections of their community.

Energetic and dedicated individuals are found in nearly all situations where a management partnership successfully developed.

At the roots of effective co-management are often some visionary and dedicated individuals. Some of them work hard for a long time to prepare the conditions for local NRM agreements. Others suddenly change the scene by introducing new incentives. In the region of Menabé, in Madagascar, Mady Abdoulanzis managed to awaken a relatively sleepy, depressed and dis-organised civil society by calling it to decide what to do with a sizeable sum of money. Mady was a Member of Parliament and in the early 1990s he had been offered, according to a national law, some resources to help in the "economic development" of his constituency. Many other MPs spent those resources enriching their friends and personal supporters. Mady called the social actors in the region ("les forces vives de la société") to meet, analyse together the situation and decide how to invest the

---

[10]   IUCN/ WCPA, 1994.
[11]   Munk Ravnborg, 2003.

resources for the best environmental and social returns. This led to the significant engagement of many people and, over the years, the Comité Régional de Développement (CRD) du Menabé became a model of civic engagement and participatory decision-making for the whole country and the true "development and regulations engine" in the region. As Mady used to say, the strength of the CRD was that, despite no legal mandate, it had all the legitimacy one could desire!

Energetic and enthusiastic individuals are invariably found in nearly all situations where a management partnership successfully developed. These people may be local residents, project staff and consultants, or government and NGO personnel. Community leaders may take the initiative to meet with governments to claim specific rights and solve specific conflicts and problems. NGOs and research professionals may seek alliances to promote the conservation of a territory in management limbo or of a species in jeopardy. The staff in charge of a protected area may call for local actors to discuss common issues and concerns and reach some agreements for the benefits of both the territory and the surrounding communities.[12] Such dedicated individuals usually prompt the creation of a local team to find the needed resources and to set the co-management process in motion (more on this later).

Some distinctions should be made among the impressive variety of "potential beginnings" for a management partnership. Co-management is, overall, a political process. The aim of many of its promoters is a more equitable management of natural resources. But the aim may also be the co-option of others, and the gaining of unfair advantages over established entitlements. As briefly discussed in Chapter 1 of this book, colonialism and the emergence of nation states and private property have progressively weakened and disempowered the traditional, community-based institutions in charge of common property resources in many countries. From such a starting point, a co-management regime may offer new chances to local institutions– e.g., village committees and community user groups– to regain lost influence and positively affect the environment and society. Some indigenous peoples are also using co-management agreements as a way of securing their entitlements over their ancestral lands (this has been the case for some time in Canada, Australia and now in various countries in South America, see Box 4.4). From different starting points, however– for instance where traditional structures are still effectively in charge of indigenous domains– a move towards shared management responsibility with the government and other actors should be carefully evaluated (see Section 4.4 in this Chapter).

Some indigenous peoples are using co-management agreements as a way of securing their entitlements over their ancestral lands.

---

12   It may seem paradoxical that government staff initiates a process to relinquish some of their powers. Indeed, this is still the exception rather than the rule, but conservation professionals are increasingly aware of the benefits to be expected from co-management agreements. Many are willing to go well beyond the call of duty to improve the long-term chances of the protected areas they are entrusted with.

Box 4.4   Securing land tenure and rights through a co-management agreement:
the Alto Fragua—Indiwasi National Park (Colombia)
(adapted from Oviedo, 2003 and Zuluaga et al., 2003)

The Alto Fragua-Indiwasi National Park was created in February 2002, after negotiations involving the Colombian government, the Association of Indigenous Ingano Councils and the Amazon Conservation Team, an environmental NGO focusing on projects to assist the Ingano and other indigenous peoples in the Amazon basin. The Park is located on the piedmont of the Colombian Amazon on the headwaters of the Fragua River. Inventories conducted by Colombia's von Humboldt Institute determined that the site is part of a region harbouring the highest biodiversity in the country and is also one of the top hotspots of the world. The protection of the site will assure the conservation of various tropical Andean ecosystems, including the highly endangered humid sub-Andean forests, some endemic species such as the spectacled bear (Tremarctos ornatus) and sacred sites of unique cultural value.

Under the terms of the decree that created the Park, the Ingano peoples are the key actors in charge of its design and management. The area– whose name means House of the Sun in the Ingano language– is a sacred place for the indigenous communities. This is one of the reasons why traditional authorities have insisted that the area's management should be entrusted to them. Although several protected areas of Colombia share management responsibilities with indigenous and local communities, this is the first one where the indigenous people is fully in charge. This has been possible thanks to Colombia's legislation that recognises traditional authorities (Asociaciones de cabildos) as legal subjects with faculty to develop their own development plans, including environmental management provisions.

The creation of the Park has been a long dream of the Ingano communities of the Amazon Piedmont, for whom it naturally fits their Plan of Life (Plan de Vida), i.e., a broad, long-term vision for the entirety of their territory and the region. The creation of Alto Fragua-Indiwasi National Park, with the Ingano as principal actors in the design and management of the site, represents an important historic precedent for all the indigenous peoples of Colombia and elsewhere, and an example to follow.

There is no simple way of distinguishing between a co-management process that leads to increased social justice and more sustainable use of natural resources, and one that may "sell-out" existing entitlements or resources. The unique set of entitlements recognised at a given time over a body of natural resources is a socio-cultural construct, a product of a negotiation in a given historical and socio-political context, which can only be appreciated in its light. It is clear, however, that important power differentials among the relevant social actors do not create a positive and constructive climate. And it is clear that some basic political and social conditions (e.g., freedom to express needs and concerns, freedom to organise, confidence in the respect of laws and agreements, some democratic experimentation allowed in society) need to be present for the process to develop. When these conditions are unclear, a co-management process can be complex, long, arduous and even distressing and confused. Rather than a smooth operation, one should expect surprises, conflicts, the emergence of contradictory information and the need to retrace one's own steps.[13] And yet, with good will and political support, a co-management process can also be smooth and rewarding…

Given the need to cope with social complexity and the dependence on political feasibility, we would venture to state that effective co-management regimes are the expression of "mature societies". Mature societies can be defined as societies whose institutions enjoy a widespread sense of legitimacy, whose collective rules are generally respected and whose internal socio-political structuring is vibrant

---

[13]   For a case of co-management derailed in mid-course in the Republic of Congo, see Box 9.25.

and complex. Many examples are found among traditional societies, and some also among modern societies. The opposite are societies that combine utmost centralisation of decisions, feeble respect of rules and the repression of free social structuring.[14] Indeed, mature societies tend to reject the myth of unique and objective solutions to manage natural resources. They instead realise that there exists a multiplicity of suitable options compatible with both traditional and scientific knowledge systems and capable of meeting the needs of conservation and development… as well as a multitude of negative or disastrous options. The relevant parties in the co-management process analyse and choose among such options in the light of their multiple interests, concerns, capacities and entitlements. They generally seek to define and foster both effectiveness and equity in the management of natural resources but, in so doing, they also bear upon some of the most important aspects of social life– such as human and economic development, citizen participation and culture.

In a generic situation in which one or more social actors are concerned enough to be willing to work towards a management partnership, they usually begin by the following steps:

- identify the management unit and main social actors with interests, concerns and capacities to manage it (at times referred to as "relevant social actors")

- re-assess together the need and feasibility of co-management in the specific context and for the specific unit;

- if co-management is found to be needed and feasible, identify the human and financial resources available to support the process;

- establish a "Start-up Team" to promote and facilitate the process up to the setting up of the multi-party negotiating forum.

The above are not always undertaken in a conscious fashion or in the order mentioned. Sooner or later, however, an analysis of the relevant management unit and actors and of the needs, feasibility and resources available is done for all CM processes. These steps will now be explored in more detail.

The natural resource management unit

At the very beginning of the CM process, the territory or resources to be managed should be identified, at least in a preliminary way. This is very important and less straightforward than it may appear. A natural resource management (NRM) unit needs to make ecological sense, i.e., it should comprise the essential elements of an ecosystem, allowing the coherent planning and implementation of needed initiatives (sustainable use, protection, restoration, etc.). The natural limits of an ecosystem, however, are often hard to define, and even more so when we try to comprise into a "unit" all the key factors impinging upon the ecosystem. For instance, a coral reef can be affected by the detritus and pollution brought to the sea by a river. Should the relevant NRM unit comprise only the reef or also the river basins opening into it? If we wish to conserve the reef, it is apparent that we need to act at the level of the river basins– a fact that significantly enlarges the scope of management.

In addition, a management unit needs also to make economic sense, which can

Effective co-management regimes are the expression of "mature societies"… [which] renounce the myth of unique and objective solutions to manage natural resources [and] realise that there exists a multiplicity of suitable options….

The definition of NRM unit brings us to face the complexity of socio-ecological systems.

---

14   Examples are the so-called "weak states" or societies dominated by a few private interest groups. See http://www.yale.edu/leitner/pdf/PEW-Way.pdf

best be illustrated by another example. Let us say that most of the benefits of protecting a given watershed are enjoyed by the inhabitants of a plain, while the costs are felt by the inhabitants of the upper watershed alone. For the sake of management effectiveness, but also of equity and sustainability, the inhabitants of the plain should be involved in bearing some of the management costs and the inhabitants of the upper watershed should be receiving some of the relevant benefits. In this sense the whole river basin would be a more appropriate management unit than the upper watershed or the plain alone. Thus, if we wish to make sure that a NRM unit is ecologically and economic coherent, we often see it grow in size. This is not necessarily a problem, but the larger the size the more numerous the social actors that will ask/ need to be involved. In the example of the reef, we may see the relevant communities multiply, as well as the affected municipalities, some of which may be centrally interested in the reef management and others very limitedly so. In addition, besides fishing and tourism operators, we will see the agricultural and industry sectors becoming hotly involved. In other words, the definition of NRM unit brings us to face the complexity of socio-ecological systems while the "solution of the problem" necessarily involves a compromise among competing requirements.

In traditional societies there is generally a remarkable coincidence between a distinct body of natural resources and a social unit ("local community") closely related to those resources. Many villages have been created to take advantage of the water and forest products related to a patch of forest or a mountain system, or to the fishery resources of a coral reef. Many nomadic tribes coincide with the management of specific wintering and summering (or wet season and dry season) pasture grounds and the migration routes in between. Specific social groups or tribes have been, through generations, the caretakers and users of a given spring, animal species or portion of a river. In fact, in traditional societies natural resource management and social organisation are closely intertwined (see Box 4.5). As communities manage and conserve natural resources they ensure other needs, such as food production, dwelling, income and security, and they exercise and continuously re-build their identity and culture– all of which instil and strengthen their social interdependence. In more than one way, thus, the territories, areas and natural resources under the care of a traditional community identify a management unit in a rather straightforward and natural way.

… in traditional societies there is generally a remarkable coincidence between a distinct body of natural resources and the social unit ("local community") managing them… the territories, areas and natural resources under the care of a local community identify a management unit.

This does not mean that at community level all is simple. Overlaps between the territories under the care of different communities, in particular nomadic and sedentary communities, do exist. They present particular challenges today, in the context of diminishing resources for livelihoods and larger numbers of people. Boundary issues between sedentary communities may also be thorny, as it may be the management of water and wildlife, not usually confined to the territory of any one community. Ideally, issues related to broader problems and opportunities would define a higher management level where the representatives of the communities and other relevant actors can meet and agree on common decisions. In this sense, an effective management structure would comprise a series of nested NR management units (for instance several micro-catchment units managed by different communities, nested within a river basin watershed, itself part of a larger island ecosystem).

Besides linkages among management levels, the key challenge in nested systems is about the effective interaction between traditional and "modern" authorities. Most governments are organised in a compartmentalised manner, with separate line agencies handling different issues and objectives at different levels, and administrative responsibilities that do not reflect ecological or socio-cultural boundaries. Because of this, communication and collaboration between communities and governmental agencies at one or more of the nested levels may not be easy. The fact remains, however, that territories and resources traditionally managed by different communities offer a natural way to subdivide an environment into viable management units, and that nested management bodies offer to national governments ingenious ways to benefit from existing capacities and resources.

Box 4.5   "Natural" geographic units in aboriginal management systems (adapted from Weinstein, 1998)

The aboriginal fisheries of coastal British Columbia (BC, Canada) were differently organised than the contemporary fisheries that derive from European fishing traditions. The geographic scale was very different, as were the rules for who had access. The details of the organisation varied among different cultural groups. Some groups used formal, quasi-legal arrangements to limit and transfer rights of access to resources. Other groups controlled access more informally by limiting the distribution of critical knowledge about the territory and its resources.

For the Nisga'a and the Gitksan, the lands and adjacent coastal and riparian areas were divided into territories. These territories belonged to house groups, or wilp, whose membership was defined by matrilineal descent rules. Typically, the boundaries of a territory radiated from a reach of the coast or river shore up mountain slopes, framing a salmon stream in between. Each house had exclusive ownership rights to their territory and its resources. The separation of land into controlled territories was the basis for the traditional management system for fisheries and for other natural resources.

In general, contiguous territories, consisting of a drainage area or a coastal inlet and its tributary drainages, were recognised as belonging to specific tribal groups. These territories might be considered the geographic units for the aboriginal management systems. The tribal groupings were made up of kinship units, which often resided in one large dwelling, housing about 50 people. These house groups were the coastal societies' economic unit. The house groups held recognised tenure to designated areas and resources within the tribal territories. A group's economy was based on the resources within the area to which they held rights. The specifics of management varied among the different cultural groups, but all coastal BC groups appear to have had two institutions in common: 1) territorial resource harvesting rights held by residential corporate kinship groups, and 2) an obligation for the leaders of these groups to publicly demonstrate adequate resource husbanding through the ceremonial re-distribution of harvested products.

A rather safe option for identifying a NRM unit may be to start from a relatively small and clearly delimited geographical territory or set of resources, selected as preliminary. Alternatively, one can start from a recognised social unit and its management territory. When such a unit is fairly small, the actors who negotiate the co-management agreements are likely to be the same ones later called to implement the related activities, a characteristic often conducive to good management. In addition, smaller units are easier to manage than larger ones. In fact, many professionals would maintain that the best management level is the lowest possible one with the sufficient capacity to take decisions and authority to implement them. This criterion, which goes under the name of "subsidiarity", derives from various religious and cultural traditions, including Catholic social teachings, and is now included in European Community Law.[15] The subsidiarity principle is also commonly applied in traditional resource management systems. One example is nomadic pastoral societies, where the management of rangelands, their rehabilitation and the resolution of disputes and conflicts are handled at the level of the camp, clan, subtribe and tribe, as appropriate, in that order. Another example is the traditional management of water in a karez system, where the neighbourhood, the boneh and the village are responsible for the hourly and daily management of the distribution, once the allocation of shares and turns has been made at the level of the whole water source. As a matter of fact, subsidiarity often prompts the recognition of the existence and capacities of local communities as environmental managers.

Box 4.6   Conservation of the Asiatic Cheetah in Iran– defining the management "ring"

Once widespread in South, Central and West Asia, the Asiatic Cheetah became a highly endangered species in the second half of the twentieth century, confined only to the peri-desert regions of Iran. A joint project of the Global Environment Facility, the United Nations Development Programme (UNDP) and the Department of the Environment in Iran sought to respond by following a co-management strategy for its conservation. The basic analysis of the social situation was carried out in 2003 by IUCN's Commission on Environmental, Economic and Social Policy (CEESP), backed by the Iranian Centre for Sustainable Development (CENESTA). The survey found that the same rangeland areas where the prey species of the Asiatic Cheetah (including gazelles, mountain sheep and ibex) normally live are shared by both nomadic pastoral communities, such as the Sangsari Tribe and local villages and other communities of sheep and camel pastoralists, and that the local communities were just as upset as anyone about the disappearing wildlife. In a workshop gathering all the contacted local community groups, they saw themselves as the stewards of their natural heritage, and identified the causes and consequences of the wildlife loss. They pointed at the widespread ownership of heavy firearms and at urban hunters, who at times come accompanied by cold storage trucks, ready to kill large numbers of wildlife indiscriminately and make commercial use of it.

Initially the Department of the Environment in Iran was considering a protection programme based on five specific protected areas. These had been established over the past three decades and were supposed to serve as relatively "secure" areas for cheetah. In reality neither cheetah nor local communities pay much attention to the boundaries of these areas. Cheetah, in particular, is a highly mobile species, often going up tens and even hundreds of kilometres in search of prey and mate.

A co-management Start Up Team (see Section 4.3 in this Chapter) was set up consisting mostly of staff

---

15   Treaty on European Union (Maastricht Treaty).

from CENESTA with experience in co-management and linkages with the relevant communities. The Team also included a professional from the Government's Organisation for Nomadic Peoples Affairs. The Start-up Team proceeded to identify the stakeholder groups, in particular the local communities with a role and interest in the issue. They were all contacted and asked to contribute to the analysis. It was this enlarged Set-up Team that, after long discussions, realised that the NRM unit for the Cheetah and its associated prey and habitat was a "ring" around the central desert in Iran, some 1500 kilometres across.

The "ring" covers the territory of eight official protected areas and the interstitial spaces among them, thus including the land and resources utilised by the nomadic and sedentary herders and their traditional institutions of management. The best way to assure the protection of the wildlife throughout the "ring" is through encouraging local communities to create and manage "Community Conserved Areas" (CCAs). These could be set up by alliances among these communities and formally backed up by the government. In this scheme, all CCAs and all official protected areas would constitute management "sub-units" of the same overall habitat of the Cheetah."

Figure 4.1   A ring around the Central Desert as a possible "management unit" for the Asiatic Cheetah in Iran– a schematic diagram including the official protected areas (numbered areas) and the migration routes of the Sangsari nomadic pastoral tribe (large arrows).

In the USA, the Center for Watershed Protection[16] carried out a study among watershed practitioners from a wide cross-section of disciplines (planners, municipal officials, consultants, scientists, and others) and found that most plans failed to adequately protect their watersheds. A chief reason was that they were drawn up on too large a scale– 50 square miles or more. Too many sub-watersheds and their individual problems had to be consolidated, and the focus of the plans became blurred. As the number of relevant social actors proliferated, responsibility for implementing the plans became diffused. In short, the planning process appeared too large and complicated, with a typical municipality or county in charge of 10 to 50 sub-watersheds. Based on such analysis of first-generation watershed plans, the Center proposed a dozen elements that every plan should incorporate. Chief among them, the plan was to be developed around the sub-watershed unit– defined as having a drainage area between 2 to 15 square miles. Due to their size, many such sub-watersheds were entirely contained within a single political jurisdiction, which helped to establish a clear regulatory authority. Sub-watershed mapping, monitoring, and other study tasks could be completed relatively quickly (6 to 12 months) and the entire management plan could be completed within a year. A division into management sub-units can also be prompted by the existence of different ecological requirements. The area of Mount Cameroon National Park, for example, has been sub-divided into different units for the purpose of rationally managing different species (e.g., Prunus africanus) and sub-ecosystems.[17]

Box 4.7   By splitting the area into five, problems in one corner of the bay will not hamper progress elsewhere...
The experience of Limingalahti Bay (Finland)
(adapted from: Kovanen, 1997)

Around the Gulf of Bothnia, one of the continent's youngest landscapes is still emerging from the waters. The vast 116 km Liminganlahti bay, one of Finland's finest wetlands, is undergoing a process called isostatic uplift wherein its post-glacial bedrock is rising to its original level. Almost one third of the bay is less than 1 metre deep, with the coastline moving forward at 18 metres a year or 1.5 Km per century. The exceptional natural wealth of Liminganlahti bay is reflected in the presence of a particularly rich and diverse wildlife, including 250 bird species and flora that include 20 species endemic to the Baltic. Centuries of traditional human activity have maintained the shore meadows, vital for many birds and rare plants, as open grasslands. This went against their natural tendency, which was to succeed into forests. Four townships and several settlements ring the bay with privately owned farmland. Under ancient law and custom, the newly risen lands are collectively owned by the landowners bordering them.

A recent increase in waterfowl hunting, fishing and tourism has required an integrated approach to the different land uses as well as an extensive consultation process to reconcile site conservation needs with the socio-economic needs of the local community and interest groups. The Liminganlahti LIFE project, approved in 1995, is run by a partnership among the Finnish Environment Ministry's regional office, the five municipalities which govern Liminganlahti and its island of Hailuoto, two NGOs (WWF and Birdlife), two scientific institutes, several local schools and the regional council for the district concerned. Such a large cross section of local society in the project steering committee allows for it to air and solve many of the conflicts. But further, the project has embraced a bottom up approach and divided the bay, its shores and its islands into five sub-regions. Each sub-region has established a working

---

16 EPA, 1997.
17 Mambo Okenye, personal communication, 1999. See also box 7 in Borrini-Feyerabend et al., 2000.

group, with an 18-month mandate to allow for meetings to bring together the relevant authorities, conservationists, landowners, hunters, farmers, fisher folk, etc. Using the knowledge already acquired on the ecology of the area, each working group is given the task to draft a plan for its sustainable use, i.e., to find a consensus on practical ways to combine nature conservation with the livelihoods and pastimes of the local population. By splitting the area into five, it was considered that problems in one corner of the bay should not hamper progress elsewhere! In this sense, the management "units" have been designed with effectiveness and efficiency of work in mind.

The sub-regional plans are expected to be later merged into a general plan, including some strict nature reserves within it. The general plan will represent the nearest thing to the consensus of all citizens and interest groups affected, and will be integrated into the official land use plans of the local municipalities. The initial sub-regional meetings have been lively, with attendance often higher than expected. People with very different backgrounds and agendas, many of them not used to formal meetings or policy debate, voiced their wishes and concerns. The very fact that all interest groups are being heard by the authorities (the hunters, in particular, claim they were previously ignored) is seen as a sign of positive change.

In general, the management unit should be large enough to accommodate an ecosystem or habitat, and small enough to accommodate a social unit in charge. A coherent socio-ecological topography is fundamental for management sustainability and the identification of the "units" and "sub-units" to be managed is a crucial decision, which bears upon all the subsequent co-management steps. As eloquently expressed by Murphree (1977b):

"The institutional requirements of a local natural resource management regime include social cohesion, locally sanctioned authority and co-operation and compliance reliant primarily on peer pressure. This implies a tightly knit interactive social unit spatially located to permit this. However, while social topography suggests "small-scale" regimes, ecological considerations tend to mandate "large-scale" regimes. This may arise from ecosystem considerations or when key resources are widely dispersed or mobile, as in the case of elephant and buffalo. Economic considerations may also dictate "large-scale" regimes where market factors require that several ownership units manage and tender their resources collectively. There is no inherent reason why social and ecological topographies cannot be harmonised, although this requires context-specific institutional engineering through negotiation. Often this will involve nested systems of collective enterprise between proprietary units. Built upward in this fashion such larger ecosystem units of management have a built-in incentive to spread, even beyond national borders. Dissonance arises when larger ecosystem regimes are imposed rather than endogenous. Such impositions in the form of ecologically-determined project domains often force together social units which have not negotiated between each other. Worse still, they could cut through existing social units. In so doing they would concentrate on ecological sustainability at the cost of ignoring the institutional sustainability on which it depends."

A coherent socio-ecological topography is fundamental for management sustainability. The identification of the "units" and "sub-units" to be managed is a crucial decision, which bears upon all the subsequent co-management steps.

The relevant social actors

Once a tentative management unit is identified, a second step in the co-management process is to compile a preliminary list of the agencies, organisations, groups and individuals possessing interests and concerns relative to it. These are usually referred to as "relevant social actors" or "stakeholders" (see Chapter 2). At this stage, the purpose is not to conduct a detailed analysis of these actors (see Chapter 5), but simply to identify them. Checklists 4.1 and 4.2 offer a number of questions that may assist in the task.

Checklist 4.1   A snapshot of the interests and concerns at stake

● Affected groups. Are there communities, groups or individuals actually or potentially affected by the management decisions? Who lives and works in or around the territory at stake? Are there historic occupants (e.g., indigenous communities or regular transients and nomadic user groups) and other traditional resource users with customary rights of ownership or usufruct? Are there recent migrants? Non resident users of resources? Absentee landlords? Major secondary users of local resources (e.g., buyers of products, tourists)? Are the territories or resources currently being accessed and used? By whom specifically? Are people of different gender, age, class or economic power differently affected and concerned? Are there businesses and industries potentially impinged upon by the NRM decisions? How many employees (national and international) live in the area because of such projects? Are these people active in natural resource management?

● Concerned groups. Are there communities, groups or individuals with specific concerns about management decisions? Are there government agencies with a specific mandate to manage all or part of the relevant resources? Is anyone officially responsible for them? Which government sectors and ministry departments share some such responsibility? Are there local associations or NGOs dealing with natural resources? Are there research, development or conservation projects in the area? Are there local authorities or local and national politicians with a specific stake in territory or resources? Are there national and/ or international bodies involved because of specific laws or treaties?

● Dependent groups. Are there communities, groups or individuals dependent on the resources at stake? Is their dependency a matter of livelihood or economic advantage? Are these resources replaceable by others, possibly in less ecologically valuable or fragile areas?

● Groups with claims. Are there communities, groups or individuals upholding claims, including customary rights and legal jurisdiction over the territory, area or resources at stake? Are there communities with ancestral and/ or other types of acquired rights? Are indigenous peoples involved? Are tribal minorities involved? Are various government sectors and ministry departments involved? Are there national and/ or international bodies involved because of specific laws or treaties? In general, who are the social actors with recognised entitlements and the ones with unrecognised claims on the territory or resources at stake?

● Impacting groups. Are there communities, groups or individuals whose activities impact on the territory and its resources? In addition to those of local users, are there activities that take place outside the territory and that impact on its resources and their sustainability?

● Special circumstances. Are there seasonal/ geographical variations in resource use patterns and interests of the users? Are resource uses geographically and seasonally stable (e.g., are there seasonal migration patterns)? Are there major events or trends currently affecting local communities and other social actors (e.g., development initiatives, land reforms, migration, important phenomena of population mobility or natural growth or decline)?

Table 2.1 in Chapter 2 provides a list of 18 different relevant social actors identified for Rajaji National Park, in Northern India, only on the basis of their own stated interests and concerns. From that example one can easily appreciate the variety of intertwining issues at play for a given territory. It is true that the stakeholders identified for Rajaji could be further subsumed under broader categories, such as the following four: residents of local communities, government agencies with official mandates (including park authorities), NGOs and research/ training institutions. Yet, it would soon be apparent that conflicts of interest and concerns are as common within such categories as they are among them.

An important area in which the initial promoters of a co-management process may play a role is the identification and recognition of those social actors who not only have interests and concerns at stake, but also capacities and comparative advantages to offer for resource management. Some of them may be individuals or local groups already involved in managing natural resources, such as a user group in charge of a community forest patch, a fisherfolks association that established rules for a given fishing area, a committee in charge of a water source or a council of elders protecting a sacred grove. The following checklist offers some examples of questions to identify social actors with capacities to offer for the management of natural resources. Obviously, social actors with specific interests and concerns and social actors with specific capacities and comparative advantages often overlap.

Checklist 4.2   A snapshot of the capacities and comparative advantages at stake

● Managers and users. Who is currently managing the territory or resources? With what results? Who used to manage those in the past? With what results? Who has access to the land, area or resources at stake? Who is using the natural resources at present– whether permanently, seasonally, occasionally or temporarily? In what ways? Has this changed over time?

● Holders of knowledge and skills. Who are the people or groups most knowledgeable about, and capable of dealing with the territory or natural resources? Are there examples of valuable "local knowledge and skills" for the management at stake?

● Neighbours. Are there communities or individuals living in close proximity with the resources and thus able to monitor and survey them with relative ease and comparative advantage?

● Traditional authorities. Who are the main traditional authorities in the area at stake? Are there respected institutions, to which people recur in a variety of needs and circumstances? Are there agencies and organisations capable of offering human resources, technical capacities and financial resources to the management cause?

● National authorities. Which local or national authorities have the mandate to develop and implement rules, policies, legislation and accompanying measures for the benefit of the territory or resources at stake?

● Well trusted individuals. Are there groups or individuals trusted by the majorities of the relevant social actors and possessing convening power, and/ or negotiation and conflict management skills?

● Potential investors. Are there local and non-local groups and individuals who may wish to invest human or financial resources in developing a more ecologically and socially sound situation in the local context?

• Special circumstances. Are there people who can convey lessons from examples of similar territories and resources managed with good results in relatively similar social contexts? Are there projects that may be willing to provide technical or financial help? Are there NGOs and associations that may provide some form of assistance?

By identifying not only the main actors possessing interests and concerns but also the ones possessing specific capacities and comparative advantages for the management of the territory or resources at stake, one can enrich the preliminary list of key relevant social actors and begin to explore the potential management roles they could assume (see Table 4.1, below).

Table 4.1   Relevant social actors in Kikori watershed (Papua New Guinea) (adapted from Regis, 1997)

Relevant social actor	Main interests and concerns	Main capacities and comparative advantages
Government	Revenue maximisation	Setting of policies and rules
Local Communities	Development and cash income; social & physical infrastructure	Living close to the natural resources, surveillance ability, knowledge of the resources
Local Land Owner Companies & Incorporated Land Groups	Business opportunities; capturing maximum rent and benefits from developers	Legal authority over some land
Chevron New Guinea & Partners	"Bottom line" (petrodollars)	Financial means
Local NGOs	Social development, awareness building, community empowerment, protection of forests	Staff time and (limited) resources that could be dedicated to the sustainable management of the watershed
WWF	Protecting biodiversity	Technical support, financial means, capacity to attract national and international attention
World Bank	"Independently certified community-based forestry and sustainable development projects"	Financial resources, technical staff, international visibility
Collins Pine company	Marketing "green timber"	Can provide economic opportunities for the sustainable use of timber
Kikori Pacific company	Local "green timber" operation	Local sustainable management capacities
Logging Companies	Quick profits through export of unprocessed logs	Financial resources

The preliminary identification of key relevant actors should be quite inclusive and detailed. More parties may mean more controversies and discussions, but excluding some of them may, in the long run, be even more costly. Factions and divisions rarely disappear spontaneously and, as they surface, they may direct their energies against the co-management process itself. In some cases, however, the outright exclusion of one key actor from the negotiation forum appears to be the necessary condition for all the others to be able to work together effectively, or even to work at all. This was the case for the Galapagos Marine Reserve, where the participatory process that set up both the legislation and the practice of the local co-management regime decided to eliminate from the area and from the overall management discussion the industrial fishing sector, whose goals and practices were deemed incompatible with the conservation goals of the reserve. The artisan fishermen and tourist operators participate in the management discussions, but the industrial fishermen are de facto and de jure excluded.[18] The decision has been fiercely opposed, and the industrial fishermen have kept both contravening the law, and fighting it in court. The last court case was for the alleged anti-constitutionality of the measure of exclusion, but the Supreme Court of Ecuador, in 2001, rejected nearly unanimously such a denunciation. The exclusion of industrial fishermen from the management of the marine reserve is now thoroughly legal.

The promoters of co-management should ask themselves whether the identified relevant social actors represent all major concerns at stake. In particular, does anyone speak for conserving local biodiversity, using resources in a sustainable way and preserving environmental functions? In many traditional societies this was the responsibility of the elders and chiefs, but cultural change has sometimes eroded these responsibilities.[19] In a number of countries, conservation and sustainable use are government statutory responsibilities, mandated to specific agencies.[20] When this is not the case, or when there is an ample gulf between stated responsibilities and actual performance, non-governmental organisations, conservation groups or even charismatic individuals may take upon themselves the defence of sustainability.

> Does anyone effectively represent the interests of future generations?

Once the process promoters have identified the preliminary "relevant social actors" they may find out whether they are clear about their interests and concerns in the NRM unit, whether they are organised to communicate and promote them and whether they are willing to take on NRM responsibilities. Often, this is not the case. Some may not be willing to invest time and resources. Others may be willing but disorganised. Still others, willing to participate in management, might not have been identified as relevant actors. Basically, the "list" should be kept open and expected to change. The important point is that the promoters do not miss the social actors that obviously possess major and distinct interests, rights, concerns, capacities and comparative advantages in natural resource management– and especially the local communities.

What to do when an identified relevant actor (let us say a community in the vicinity of a forest) includes a variety of different interests, concerns and capacities vis-à-vis the natural resources? Should one or several actors be invited to participate in the management negotiation process? There is no simple answer to this ques-

---

[18] Heylings and Bravo, 2001; Bravo and Heylings, 2002.

[19] A telling example can be found in McCallum and Sekhran, 1997.

[20] In the case illustrated in Table 4.1 sustainability is stated as the main interest of an involved NGO (WWF). In Table 2.1 of Chapter 2, sustainability (expressed as "wildlife conservation") is the concern of the state agency in charge of park management (this is a relatively special case, however, as it involves a protected area).

tion. The CM promoters may wish to explore the pros and cons of different solutions with the most directly concerned people and groups while assisting them to organise (see Chapter 5). For instance, a united community has more weight at the discussion table than several people who cannot agree on a common position. And yet, many communities may be willing to speak as one voice on certain occasions and as many on others. In other words, the people who find themselves united as "one relevant actor" for some decisions may need to split and regroup for another one. This phenomenon, at times referred to as "multi-cultural character" of stakeholders[21] should be acknowledged and recognised as normal. Allowing it to be accommodated in co-management settings would prevent the forced lumping of contrasting interests– a subtle but recognised problem of representative democracies.

Many communities may be willing to speak as one voice on certain occasions and as many on others.

Another fundamental dilemma: are "interests and concerns" and the willingness to participate sufficient for a social actor to claim a management role? Shouldn't the promoters also ask: "Who are the social actors entitled to manage the unit(s) at stake?" They certainly should. And yet, the understanding of what constitutes a legitimate entitlement is an evolving socio-political phenomenon, best approached in a participatory way. The CM promoters could begin by asking the potential relevant social actors whether they consider that they have a fair claim to participate in the management of natural resources and, if so, on what grounds. In this way, they will obtain a list of factors and characteristics that at least some people recognise as legitimate "roots of entitlements" in the local context. Some examples of such factors and characteristics are listed in Checklist 2.2 in Chapter 2.

4.2   Is co-management needed? Is co-management feasible?

Collaborative approaches to natural resource management capitalise on two main lessons. The first is that there exist a variety of interests and concerns at stake for any given set of natural resources, and what meets conservation objectives and benefits one social actor, may harm another. The owners of tourist businesses may be well served by a hunting ban, but the local hunters club may find it totally inappropriate. The forest agency personnel may wish to restrict forest uses until timber can be felled and provide revenues to the district's coffers, but the local residents may need timber on an on-going basis for their own domestic uses. The water resources utilised by the families living closer to a river may be interesting also for the peasants owning plots far from it, who may wish to gain their equitable water share. Even relatively homogeneous units (e.g., a local "community") include among themselves a variety of interests and concerns and, as just men-

---

[21]   Otchet, 2000.

tioned, may wish to speak as one voice certain times and as many voices at others. Indeed, accepting the existence and legitimacy of a multiplicity of voices and interests in resource management is a fundamental tenet of the co-management approach.

The second lesson is that different social actors possess different and often complementary capacities and comparative advantages to optimally manage a set of natural resources. For instance, important regulatory and coordination faculties are usually with public bodies, often at the national or district level, but local knowledge and surveillance power most often stay with local communities. In the words of Kothari:[22]

"Communities lack the resources to tackle threats or ecological issues at a regional scale, and in many places have lost their traditional ethos and institutions; government agencies lack the necessary micro-knowledge, on-the-spot human power, or even often the necessary mandate when other agencies overrule them. With rare exceptions, neither local communities nor governmental agencies are able to face on their own the onslaught of commercial forces, or able to check the destruction caused by some of their own members".

Thus, both agency staff and local residents can broaden their perspectives and join forces to become stronger and more effective natural resource managers. Management partnerships can provide some protection against ineptitude and corruption (at times associated with agency management) and the parochialism and other shortcomings sometimes associated with local communities and other stakeholders. Examples of complementary capacities include entrepreneurial power (e.g., to set up a tourism initiative), unique technical capacity (e.g., understanding and acting upon the crucial conditions for the conservation of a species), business sense (e.g., for keeping accounts straight) and convening capacity (e.g., to obtain that all relevant actors sit together and begin discussions). All of the above are rarely found in one social actor alone!

Different social actors possess different, and often complementary, management capacities and comparative advantages.

Is it thus always appropriate to pursue a management partnership? Is it sufficient that different social actors exist, with capacities to offer and interests and concerns to convey? Not really. In some situations the promoters need to use their best judgement before embarking in a process that may be unacceptably long or destined to failure under the prevailing conditions. For instance, when the basic conditions for freedom of speech and personal safety are missing, a "partnership" loses its meaning and attempting it may actually endanger people. When a seemingly endless "search for consensus" is utilised by some parties as a way to stall

---

[22] Kothari, 1995.

There are situations of entrenched powers in which a confrontational strategy is more appropriate than a collaborative one. In such cases, promoting CM would mean supporting an illusory "social pacifier", which may waste time and energy that can be used to muster a more useful opposition stand.

decisions, others may be rightly compelled to abandon the game. And when rapid decisions and action are required, e.g., to block the very fast ecological deterioration of an area, it may be better to act unilaterally than to achieve a broad consensus on how to protect... a devastated territory. Most importantly, there are situations of entrenched powers in which a confrontational strategy is more appropriate than a collaborative one. In such cases, promoting CM would mean supporting an illusory "social pacifier", which may waste time and energy that can be used to muster a more useful opposition stand. In general, the decision to pursue a CM process is both technical and political, and should thus be based on an analysis of technical and political needs.

It has been proposed[23] that there exist situations in which a management partnership is clearly needed, namely:

- when the active commitment and collaboration of various social actors is essential for the sustainable management of the natural resources; and
- when the access to the natural resources is essential for the livelihood security and cultural survival of one or more social actors.

In these cases, two fundamental values– environmental sustainability and livelihood security– need to be pursued together if they are to be pursued at all. Other conditions that would recommend embarking upon a CM process may be relevant from the perspective of particular social actors. For instance, from the point of view of government agencies possessing legal jurisdiction over a territory, area or resources at stake, it may be very appropriate to pursue partnership agreements and prevent wasteful conflicts when one or more of the following conditions apply:

- local actors have historically enjoyed customary/ legal rights over the territory or resources;
- local livelihoods are strongly affected by NRM decisions;
- the decisions to be taken are complex and controversial (e.g., different values need to be harmonised or there is disagreement on the distribution of entitlements over the land or resources);
- the current NRM system has failed to produce the desired results and meet the needs of the local actors;
- the relevant actors are ready to collaborate and request to do so;
- there is ample time to negotiate.

On the contrary, it may be inappropriate or not yet appropriate to embark on an entirely new CM process when very rapid decisions are needed (emergency situations).

From the point of view of local communities who have customarily enjoyed full access to the relevant territory, area or resources, it may be appropriate to pursue a NRM partnership when:

- powerful non-local actors are forcing their way into the territory or extracting resources with no respect for traditional customary rules and rights (in this case a partnership agreement with the state government or some NGO or research organisation may help assure some protection and respect for customary practices);

---

23 Borrini-Feyerabend, 1996.

- customary practices are falling into disarray and an open access status has ensued with resources being extracted in unsustainable ways.
- the state is willing to provide legal recognition to the customary rights as part of the co-management agreement.

It may instead be not advisable to enter into a NRM partnership when:

- in so doing the local communities would be renouncing a customary status of unique rights with no comparable advantage in exchange;
- the political environment does not secure the safety of all negotiating parties.

A mild version of participatory management, involving the consultation of key relevant actors and the seeking of a broad social consensus on management practices can be maintained to be an essential component of any successful management setting. A strong version of CM, implying the inclusion of various social actors in a management board endowed with authority and responsibility, may or may not be appropriate according to the specific conditions at stake. In general, a management partnership offers benefits and has costs. Some examples of such benefits and costs[24] are summarised in Checklist 4.3 and 4.4.

Checklist 4.3 Co-management of natural resources: potential benefits

- the effective sharing of management responsibilities among all the parties involved in the agreement lessens the burden of any one party in charge;

- CM produces negotiated specific benefits for all parties involved (this point has major ethical implications, as some negotiated benefits may be crucial for the survival of some local communities and/ or to compensate for losses incurred[25] or for the survival of wildlife species);

- alliances between governmental agencies and local social actors tend to fend off resource exploitation from non-local interests, which often represent the main threat to conservation and sustainable resource use;[26]

- CM promotes more effective management as a consequence of harnessing the capacities[27] and comparative advantages of various social actors (e.g., local knowledge and skills for monitoring the status of natural resources, proximity for surveying the protected area's borders, maintenance of natural resource uses that are beneficial to the local ecology);[28]

- CM reduces enforcement expenditures because of agreed, voluntary compliance;

- CM enhances the capacity for resource management among all parties involved (as a consequence of enhanced communication, dialogue and shared experience);

---

[24] Lists adapted from Borrini-Feyerabend, 1996.

[25] In countries of the South, more emphasis may be placed on tangible benefits such as access to natural resources for food and income, while in industrialised societies local residents may stress their active choice in the type of land uses they wish for an area.

[26] For instance, in Sariska Tiger Reserve (western India) villagers and local forest officials have fought together against mining interests (Kothari et al., 1996).

[27] See, for instance, Gadgil et al., 1993; Ruddle, 1994; and Poffenberger, 1997. See also the dedicated journals Indigenous Knowledge and Development Monitor, published by CIRAN in the Netherlands and Etnoecologica, published in three languages by the Centro de Ecología, Mexico.

[28] In Keoladeo National Park (India) buffalo grazing is an essential practice for the conservation of the local ecosystem and species, yet the PA management initially banned the grazing, which resulted in violent clashes with local herders and residents (Kothari et al., 1996). In the Royal Bardia National Park (Nepal) ecological management relies on human disturbance in the form of grass cutting, which is currently "permitted" for a ten day period each year. All throughout Europe, the ecological conditions of many rural or Alpine environments are dependent on the permanence on them of local populations, engaged in cattle rearing and forest and water management.

- CM enhances the trust between state agencies and relevant actors, shared "ownership" of the conservation process, and strong commitment to implement decisions taken together;

- CM promotes a sense of security and stability (of policies, priorities, tenure...) leading to increased confidence in investments, long-term perspective and enhanced sustainability of negotiated management;[29]

- CM promotes understanding and knowledge among all concerned about the views and positions of others, preventing or minimising conflicts and disputes due to miscommunication;

- CM promotes the public awareness of conservation issues and the integration of conservation and sustainable use efforts within social, economic and cultural initiatives;

- CM contributes towards participatory democracy in society (by promoting social communication, conflict prevention and resolution, and the development of rules, policies and laws via the direct involvement of citizens and interest groups).

Checklist 4.4   Co-management of natural resources: potential costs and obstacles

- early and substantial investments of time, financial resources and human resources (high "transaction costs") in both the preparation of the partnership and negotiation of agreements. This is a serious issue, as the time requirement may be unaffordable for short-term projects and/ or the financial requirements may be unaffordable for some relevant actors. The human resources need to include professionals with uncommon skills (e.g., capable of carrying out a fair stakeholder analysis, supporting the organizing of the relevant actors, facilitating participatory processes and the negotiation of agreements, etc.) who may not be easily available.

- potential opposition by the parties required to share authority, substantially change their livelihood systems[30] or forego current advantages and benefits (the commitment of most parties in the CM process is a crucial condition for success);

- explicit conflicts among relevant social actors with different power bases, which, in the absence of protection measures, may bring about negative outcomes for the weaker ones;

- chances of negotiation stalls when a co-management agreement cannot be achieved without compromising in a substantial way the interests and concerns of some parties (e.g., some key conservation or development goals);

- poor sustainability of the negotiated agreements because of underestimated problems or new intervening factors (e.g., changes in the economic conditions that make a management option viable and profitable,[31] changes of political administration, emergence of new relevant social actors, violent unrest, etc.).

Ultimately, a judgement should be made as to whether the expected benefits are likely to justify the human and financial resources to be invested in the co-management process, i.e., as to whether co-management is indeed needed. If so, this

---

[29] For instance, co-management has a great role to play in so-called "peace parks" in trans-boundary situations (Sandwith et al., 2001).

[30] This may be the case also for local communities. In South Africa, local communities will oppose the establishment of protected areas if no benefits are made available to them (Koch, 1994).

[31] As expressed by Baland and Platteau (1996, page 351) "...even well conceived schemes of co-management become seriously stressed as market opportunities expand and cause an intensive commercial exploitation of certain natural resources." For instance, in Narayan Srovar Sanctuary (Western India) villagers welcomed the de-notification of the reserve to make way for a cement factory, since they got no income from the forest and are expecting jobs from the factory (Kothari et al., 1996).

information should be combined with the results of a feasibility analysis to decide whether a co-management process should be initiated.

The feasibility analysis

A co-management feasibility analysis begins by a broad assessment of the existing management system,[32] structure and practices, the recognised entitlements and the unrecognised claims for the territory or resources at stake. Together with the list of preliminarily identified relevant actors, this offers a picture of the power system and relationships at stake. The promoters of the CM process should examine this in the light of the legal, political, institutional, economic and socio-cultural characteristics of the context at stake. Some feasibility questions useful in such an analysis are listed in Checklist 4.5. These questions do not spell out all the conditions that need to be met for co-management to be successful. They offer, however, an idea of the potential obstacles and difficulties that may be encountered in any specific context.

Checklist 4.5   Investigating the co-management feasibility in a specific context

Is the process legally feasible?
Who has the mandate to control the land and resources? Can a pluralist approach be accommodated within the existing customary/ legal frameworks? Examine traditional, customary law and modern laws, regulations, permits....

Is the process politically feasible?
What is the history of land management and resource use in the territory or area at stake? Examine current political will and stability, the capacity to enforce decisions, the confidence in the participatory process, the presence of phenomena such as corruption and intimidation.... Are there relevant actors with strong interests to maintain the status quo? If some actors are better served by the absence rather than the presence of co-management agreements (for instance they currently enjoy undue benefits and/ or have others bear substantial costs in their place) they have no incentive to enter into a process of negotiation and may attempt to block it or sabotage it from the outside. This is sometimes expressed as the presence of actors with strong "better alternatives to a negotiated solution" (BATNAs)– a powerful feasibility obstacle to co-management.

Is the process institutionally feasible?
Is there a chance of building a pluralistic management institution for the territory, area or natural resources? Examine inter-institutional relations and their possible conflicts, existing examples of multiparty resource management organisations and rules, the capacity of social actors to organise themselves and to identify representatives to convey their interests and concerns....

Is the process economically feasible?
Are there economic opportunities and alternatives to the current, possibly inefficient exploitation of natural resources? Examine local opportunities to reconcile the conservation of nature with the satisfaction of economic needs, examine the extent of poverty in the region, the availability of capital for local investments....

Is the process socio-culturally feasible?
Are or were there traditional systems of natural resource management in the context at stake? What are (or were) their main features and strengths? Are those still valid today? Are the traditional NRM systems

---

32 This should involve not only an analysis of the de jure conditions (the existing legal entitlements) but also of the de facto conditions, i.e., the management roles actually taken up by various people and institutions. You may wish to answer questions such as: who takes decisions? Who knows about those decisions? Who is accountable to whom? Who plans? Who advises? Who has access to the resources? Who benefits from the resources? Who evaluates whether NRM activities need to change?

still in use? Regardless of the answer, why? Who is keeping them alive? What is specifically sustaining or demeaning them? If they are not being used any more, does anyone have a living memory of the systems (for instance, are there elders who practiced them and still remember "how it was done")? Examine the current population status, population dynamics and structure, the main socio-cultural changes under way. Examine social and cultural diversity amongst the relevant social actors and the history of group relations among them. Examine factors affecting opportunities for social communication, including:

- language diversity
- varying degrees of access to information
- different attitudes, for example with regard to speaking in public or defending personal advantages
- traditional and modern media currently used in the particular context

An important question is also, "For all main relevant actors, what are the best alternatives to a negotiated agreement (BATNA)?" If some of them are better served by the absence rather than the presence of co-management agreements (e.g., if they enjoy undue benefits and/ or have others bear substantial management costs, so that their BATNA is the maintenance of the existing situation[33]) they will have no incentive to enter into the process of negotiation and they may attempt to block it or sabotage it from outside. This can be a crucial feasibility obstacle in any environment.

It is important to understand whether some social actors with vested interests in the status quo may stall the process of change. In such cases the feasibility of co-management is severely reduced and outright opposition to the CM process can be expected. Some special incentives, cajoling or even law enforcement and coercive measures may be needed before all actors agree to negotiate. Outsiders, however, should carefully investigate the local situation before assuming that a group is blocking negotiations to maintain an unfair advantage. A social actor may rightly feel better protected by a firm and uncompromising stand than by entering into a negotiation as the weakest among several parties.

What can be done when the desired feasibility conditions are not in place, or the BATNAs[34] of several social actors are very attractive? One strategy is to proceed towards the partnership and, in parallel, attempt to modify the conditions and enhance the collaboration incentives of all relevant actors. For instance, limited pilot agreements may be developed while changes in the relevant policies and legislation are being discussed. People and institutions may be offered training programmes and seminars to familiarise themselves with the partnership approach. A public debate on management issues may be stimulated, enhancing the social status and prestige of whoever will act to solve current problems. When obstacles and bottlenecks are clear, the relevant actors in favour of the co-management process may also meet to identify, discuss and implement initiatives to remove them.

Another strategy in the face of strong odds is simply to give up the particular site, and concentrate resources and efforts on territories with better chances of developing successful management partnerships. This is the recommendation surfacing from a failed integrated conservation and development project in Papua New Guinea. The project focused on an area important for biodiversity, but already targeted by a powerful logging operation, which had established linkages with the local communities and aroused vested interests. The project did not manage to reverse any of that, and wasted lots of time and resources in the process. Another lesson learned is that timing may be crucial. If external conservationists wish to

---

[33] LeBaron et al. 1995.
[34] This term is defined in Checklist 4.5.

promote sustainable development initiatives, they may need an early entry with local communities and the careful building of rapport and trust.[35]

A summary of the results of a feasibility analysis carried out prior to the inception of a co-management process is reported in Table 4.2.

Table 4.2 Developing a co-management setting in the Sierra Tarahumara (Mexico): are the necessary conditions in place?
(adapted from Cordova y Vazquez, 1998)

In a feasibility study of collaborative management for the sierra Tahumanara, a list of important conditions were compared with the local socio-economic situation and consequently assessed. Five of the main conditions were found to be strongly satisfied (+++), three moderately satisfied (++) and two weakly satisfied (+).Three conditions were found to be variable relatively to the specific interest group. The study concluded that a collaborative management regime would be feasible in the region.

Conditions	Assessment
1. There exist several problems to discuss, several ideas about how to solve them, and several interest groups involved. No interest groups can solve the problems alone.	+++
2. Collaboration is convenient for all parties as they all have common interests and concerns and are inter-dependent.	+++
3. The interest groups are willing to collaborate with external bodies.	++
4. The institutional and legal context is favourable to involving several interest groups in decision making and the development of agreements	+++
5. The moment is favourable: the issues have been already extensively debated and there is time to take decisions.	++ +++
6. There are local capacities to develop a negotiated decision: information and prior experiences are available.	+++
7. There are local capacities to develop a negotiated decision: the interest groups are intrinsically homogeneous, internally cohesive, can easily identify a representative, have functional mechanisms to take their own decisions, and have experience in taking decisions.	+ ++ variable scoring
8. There is a power balance around the decision-making table. The arena will be fair.	+

4.3 Gathering resources and creating a Start-up Team

As part of exploring feasibility, a most important question the co-management promoters ask themselves is: "What human and financial resources can we count on?" Fortunately or unfortunately, in fact, promoting a co-management process is

---

35 McCallum and Sekhran, 1997.

all but routine work, and needs especially dedicated resources. The process demands energy, passion, willingness, creativity, sacrifice, continuity... and it needs at least one and possibly more "champions"– dedicated individuals for whom work is a matter of personal satisfaction and pride more than a job or a duty. As stressed by professionals with direct field experience, the development of co-management regimes has much more to do with informal than with formal relationships.[36] For instance, it depends crucially on the capacity of some individuals to communicate with others on a personal basis, and elicit their confidence, trust and support. In addition to the uncommon human qualities of the process promoters, specific capacities and technical support may also be required for a variety of tasks– from mediating conflicts to understanding ecosystem functioning, from social organising to setting up economic enterprises. The co-management promoters need to be able to recognise when such forms of technical support are needed, and where they can be accessed.

Financial support to a CM process is very useful to sustain social communication activities, carry out specific studies or provide professional assistance to the negotiation process and to understand all the issues at stake. Conservation and development projects have played a useful role here, providing funds for events, professional facilitators for meetings and helping to overcome the "culture of distrust" that often inhibits positive relationships between governments and local groups.[37] Yet, co-management should not be made to depend on large influxes of financial resources. It may even suffice to have the commitment of some individuals to change a situation of "business as usual" and promote dialogue and agreements

in place of hostility, and interest groups may provide in kind resources as necessary. Indeed, a sudden influx of major external resources may create more problems than solutions and there are cases of co-management that have been thwarted and broken down by financial inflows provided in inappropriate amounts and with strings attached.[38]

As soon as the need and feasibility have been assessed and the necessary human and financial resources have been set aside, it is advisable to create a co-management "Start-up Team", to be in charge of preparing and launching the whole process.[39] A Start-up Team (at times also called initiation committee, launch com-

---

[36] Daniel Ngantou, personal communication, 1999. See also Nguinguiri, 2003.
[37] Freudenberger, 1996.
[38] Sarin, 2003.
[39] National Civic League, undated.

mittee, pilot team, etc.)[40] is a small group of individuals dedicated to preparing and launching the co-management process. The group may play the main facilitating role in the process, or it may decide to use the services of a third party to facilitate the negotiation of the CM agreement. The number of Team members is generally fewer than ten, in extreme cases even one only,[41] with occasional help from others. Often, the Team is composed of volunteers. At times it includes some paid professionals, especially when a project or other externally supported initiatives are involved. It is important that the people in the Start-up Team have a high personal motivation but that they are also socially recognised as credible and trustworthy. In most cases this amounts to a strong recommendation to involve local people in the Start-up Team, and sometimes to even compose it of local people only. In addition, the team should be "diverse", i.e., it should include people with whom all the relevant actors expected to take a role in the management process are able to identify, relate and communicate. In other words, all social actors concerned with the management at stake should trust and be able to relate easily with at least one person in the Start-up Team, even if they do not feel represented by him/ her.

An interesting example of a Start-up Team, called Grupo Nucleo, facilitated the process that brought about the co-management setting for the Galapagos Marine Reserve in Ecuador. In 1997 none of the institutional or legal frameworks that support this setting today were yet in place. The local Grupo Nucleo, including individuals close to the fishing and tourist sector as well as to the local research and conservation bodies, first gathered local interests and concerns in view of the upcoming special law of Galapagos. On the momentum created by such a law, it then facilitated a broad social agreement on a new cooperative, consensus-based institutional setting. For the Galapagos Marine Reserve, all the achievements of today have roots in the numerous meetings and tireless organising promoted by the Grupo Nucleo and supported by a far-sighted project from 1997 to 1999.[42]

A good Start-up Team is active, efficient, multi-disciplinary, transparent in all its activities and determined to launch but not to lead or dominate the co-management process. In fact, its role and responsibility are limited to only one phase of the process, namely the one in which the partnership is prepared and rooted in the local context (see Figure 4.2). After that, the social actors themselves need to take charge.

Already at this stage we are facing one of the main characteristics of a co-management process: the iterative mode of work. Nearly every step in co-management is susceptible to subsequent adjustments and re-elaboration, but particularly so the initial steps. These include the preliminary identification of the territory or resources to be managed and of the "relevant social actors" to take an active role in that. These definitions are among the most delicate and controversial in the whole process and thus, inevitably, they are a first approximation of what will be agreed upon by the relevant partners. They even present some circular dilemma. For instance, the management boundaries should be established by the partners involved. But then, the "partners" are themselves determined by their own inter-

Key criteria to identify the members of a Start-up Team:
- diversity
- credibility
- personal motivation
- excellent capacity to communicate.

One of the main characteristics of a co-management process is the iterative mode of work. Nearly every step in co-management is susceptible to subsequent adjustments and re-elaboration, but particularly so the initial steps.

---

40 In French, terms that are used are Comité de Pilotage or Noyau Dur, in Spanish Grupo Nucleo or Comité de Lanzamiento.

41 In the Nta-ali forest (Cameroon) a co-management process was single-handedly promoted by a key forest official, native of the local community and member of the local elite. His capacity to mediate between the culture of the governmental agencies and the local culture, and the support provided by a dedicated project allowed him to win the confidence of all major relevant social actors. See Box 1 in Borrini-Feyerabend et al., 2000.

42 Heylings and Bravo, 2001. In some way this Grupo Nucleo was already a co-management platform, as it promoted a number of initiatives and events with direct management results. On the other, however, it was only a Start-up Team, as it has now been disbanded and a legal pluralist decision-making system has taken its place.

There is no "right process" to develop a "right management partnership" but the quality of the process is extremely important, as a partnership is generally as strong, or as weak, as the process that generated it.

ests, concerns and capacities vis-à-vis the area to be managed! As mentioned, it may be wise to start out with a relatively small geographic area and its primary actors (e.g., the ones with longest tenure status, specific government mandate, highest dependence and highest capacities and comparative advantages vis-à-vis the territory or resources at stake), but then such actors should review the definition of the management unit(s) and the list of recognised relevant actors. And so on.

There is no recipe for developing a management partnership. While extremely valuable lessons have been learned in different cases throughout the world– and some such lessons are the very heart of this book– in every new situation the partners themselves need to decide on the most appropriate process to follow. In other words, there is no "right process" to develop a "right management partnership" but the quality of the process is extremely important, as a partnership is generally as strong, or as weak, as the process that generated it.

In general, three phases in the co-management process can be broadly identified:

1. organising for the partnership;

2. negotiating the co-management agreements and organisations;

3. implementing and reviewing the agreements and organisations (learning by doing).

These phases are schematically illustrated[43] in Figure 4.2 and will be further described in Chapters 5 and 6 of Part II and in Chapter 9 of Part III of this volume.

| Box 4.8 | The co-management conveners |
| | (adapted from Ramírez, 1998) |

Any group or organisation seeking to convene other relevant actors should first analyze its own role and objectives, and its relationship with those actors it seeks to invite. The questions to ask are: are we in a position to convene? What are the constraints of our organisation? Do we have the legitimacy, power and urgency required to bring the parties together? In the words of Gray (1989) "The convener may or may not be an actor in the issue or problem situation. The role of the convener is to identify and bring all the legitimate actors to the table. Thus conveners require convening power, i.e., the ability to induce social actors to participate. Convening power may derive from holding a formal office, from a long-standing trusted reputation with the relevant local actors, or from experience and reputation as an unbiased expert on the problem. The conveners' tasks are distinct from those of a third-party mediator, although at times one person can assume both roles." The decisions made by the convenor are biased by the convenor's understanding of the nature of the issue, the boundaries of the issue, and the criteria to select the relevant actor that appear to be legitimate. These are always approximate decisions and become more accurate through a cyclical adjustment process. Another question to ask is to what extent is the convenor able to transform itself during the process.

---

[43] Modified from Borrini-Feyerabend, 1996.

Figure 4.2 Phases of a collaborative management process

Phase III: implementing and reviewing the agreement ("learning by doing")

- implement and enforce the agreements, organisations and rules (including management plans for the natural resources)
- if necessary, clarify the entitlements and responsibilities of the relevant social actors
- collect data to monitor progress and impact (as in the follow up protocol)
- as appropriate, experiment with innovation (e.g., as a result of new information, refinement of technical solutions and/ or a wider-scale application of activities)
- organise review meetings at regular intervals to evaluate the results obtained and lessons learned; as necessary, modify activities and/ or develop new management agreements

Phase II: developing the agreement

- hold the first meeting of relevant social actors on the negotiation procedures
- hold one or several meetings to review the socio-ecological situation and its trends, and agree on a long-term, common vision for the area at stake
- hold a ceremony to ritualise the agreed common vision
- hold meetings to identify a strategy towards the long-term vision
- hold meetings to negotiate specific agreements (e.g., management plans, contracts, memoranda of understanding) for each component of the strategy; support the mediation of conflicts, as needed; clarify zoning arrangements and specific functions, rights and responsibilities of the relevant actors; agree on a follow-up protocol)
- hold meetings to agree on all the elements of the partnership institution (e.g., principles, rules, organisations in charge of implementing, enforcing and reviewing the agreements)
- legitimise and publicise the co-management institution

Phase I: preparing for the partnership

- gather information and tools (e.g., maps) on the ecological and socio-economic issues and problems at stake
- launch and maintain a social communication campaign on the need for co-management and the process expected to bring it about
- contact the relevant social actors, facilitate their appraisal exercises and continue the ecological and socio-economic analysis in a participatory way
- as necessary, help the relevant social actors to develop an internal consensus on their management interests, concerns and capacities, to organise themselves and to identify representatives
- propose a set of procedures for the negotiation phase and, in particular, for the first meeting of relevant social actors

a point of departure...

- identify the preliminary management unit and main relevant social actors
- assess the need and feasibility of a co-management setting
- assess the available human and financial resources
- create a Start-up Team

4.4 The special case of indigenous peoples: can co-management help them assert their rights to land and natural resources?

Indigenous peoples are self-identified human groups characterised by peculiar socio-political systems, languages, cultures, values and beliefs, by a close relationship with the land and natural resources in their territory, and often by historical continuity with pre-colonial societies.

The imposition of external values, technologies and livelihood systems has been a main feature of colonisation, imperialism and unequal relationships with traditional and indigenous peoples. Today's new ideas and concepts, such as sustainable use or co-management of natural resources are easily perceived as a new version of such imposition. However sincere the intention of co-management promoters may be, it is a fact that indigenous control over territories and resources has been and continues to be systematically diminished, not least because of conservation aims (in particular to incorporate territories into official protected areas). Thus, while some indigenous peoples and traditional communities may be willing to

enter into management partnerships with other social actors, others understandably remain reluctant to any type of external influence on their livelihoods and environments. They prefer to hold to their ancestral land rights and management systems without interfacing or compromising with other systems (see Box 4.9). This may be a decision in view of cultural survival, especially where traditional knowledge systems are already fragile because of strong external influences, but local resistance to decisions and forms of "development" defined from outside has often been beneficial also to conservation.

Box 4.9   Mayan resistance in Totonicapán:
           a gentle reverberating echo in the volcanic altiplano
           (adapted from Gramajo, 1997)

Invasions on the ancestral lands of the K'iché in the volcanic Sierra Madre ranges of Totonicapán were for territorial domination in the pre-Hispanic and colonial eras. More recent invasions have come in the form of the "Green Revolution": agricultural reforms and rural development projects over the last three decades, which have manipulated use and access to natural resources. Rather than alleviating poverty, however, most interventions benefited the rich and created dependency on modern technology, unaffordable by most peasants. Indiscriminate logging, inappropriate agricultural technologies, "improved" seeds and inadequate water resource management generated pollution, diminished endogenous flora and agricultural biodiversity, and created serious socio-economic impacts and health problems for the native Mayans (95% of the local population). Projects that tried to identify local needs, aspirations and potential ended up reflecting more the opinions of external planners than of local people. "Local participation" has been usually sought only after the design of the project was done and established.

The Mayan culture keeps alive its ancestral resource knowledge and social structures through an oral tradition rich in topographic vocabulary, and a world vision focusing on the value of nature, specific ceremonies, social solidarity and consultation with the community elders. A recent welcome trend has been towards re-evaluating indigenous resource management practices in communally owned forests. There has also been a strong, if not always successful, show of resistance to the unsustainable exploitation and degradation of natural resources by outsiders (loggers, entrepreneurs and transport companies that succeeded in gaining concessions). In one particular region the local people, jointly with the reforestation committee and the municipality, reached an agreement to prohibit governmental and non-governmental agencies from developing projects in communally-owned forests. One Elder declared: "...the government wanted to impose on us a project to create a market for our wood. If we would had allowed it, we would have nothing today. We do not think in the government's way, for we believe that the mountains can give us all we need, but all in measure. We take just what we need, and no one from our community makes a business out of wood or timber." Another community imposed grave sanctions against a park ranger who abused his authority for personal benefit, destroying the oldest and largest tree in the forest, which was sacred to the people. In another case, a mayor was imprisoned for authorising logging concessions without community approval. Since then, no mayor has dared to authorise any logging concession.

As only recently fully acknowledged and described, biological and cultural diversity are strongly linked, as are their alarming losses currently experienced in the world.[44] By preserving cultural integrity, the conditions for maintaining a specific type of interaction with the environment and natural resources are also maintained. The interests of indigenous peoples and conservationists may thus broadly coincide and management partnerships may play a vital role to promote both the survival of cultural diversity and the safeguard of biological environments.

In the light of the above, are indigenous peoples "social actors" on the same level as all others, such as a private firm or a governmental agency? Many would stress that they are not. Indigenous peoples hold ancestral rights to the environments where they have lived and worked for centuries if not millennia.[45] They usually do not possess the economic strength and legal backing enjoyed by modern entrepreneurs and affluent people. And, importantly, many of them have lifestyles with limited impact upon the land (the very reason why, in their midst, there is still much worth conserving and managing sustainably) and are bearers of valu-

---

44   Posey, 1996; Maffi, Oviedo and Larsen, 2000.
45   Price-Cohen, 1998.

able and unique local knowledge and skills. In other words, they are both a comparatively weaker and more benign and useful social actor.

The Convention on Biological Diversity stresses that: "special consideration [should be] given to the indigenous and local communities embodying traditional lifestyles relevant for the conservation and sustainable use of biological diversity".[46] Such special considerations should involve not only respecting the cultural identity of indigenous and traditional peoples, but also ensuring mechanisms that guarantee fair communication and consultation processes, continuity and/ or revitalisation of their traditional lifestyles (as deemed appropriate by the traditional societies) and the active education and enrichment of non-indigenous partners concerning traditional values, knowledge and practices.

In practical terms, a Start-up Team should make sure that the rights, needs and capacities of traditional communities are duly respected and recognised. It should also veer to avoid their "acculturation", which may be one of the most insidious dangers of co-management for an indigenous community. Many aspects of the participatory management model proceed from a mainstream logic and value system that, in the attempt of accommodating multiple interests, may overshadow or uproot the fundamental tenets of a traditional society. For example, practices such as assigning economic value to natural resources or promoting gender equality in natural resource management may be perceived as appropriate to most social actors but objectionable and destructive to some traditional communities. These different views should be handled with respect. To this end, the Start-up Team has to be well informed about the values, beliefs, lifestyles and management systems of the indigenous and traditional partners, and aware of the benefits of local cultural cohesion. A Start-up Team is a herald of an opportunity to review and improve resource management practices, not an active promoter of social restructuring and cultural change. It may assist different groups within a society to develop their own views on the issues at stake, but the ultimate decisions about how to handle issues of internal consensus and representation belong to the peoples themselves.

In the last decades, many indigenous communities have agreed on various forms of co-management settings for protected areas. In Australia,[47] relatively strong co-management arrangements for protected areas have been developed following the passing of legislation that recognised aboriginal rights to land and natural resources. In 1981, Gurig National Park became the first jointly managed National Park in Australia and since then further co-management arrangements have been developed for other parks in various Territories, according to several "models" (see Table 4.3). Joint management represents a trade-off between the rights and interests of traditional owners and the rights and interests of government conservation agencies and the wider Australian community. In some arrangements developed subsequent to the Gurig model, the trade-off involves the transfer of land ownership to Aboriginal People in exchange for continuity into the foreseeable future of the national park status and shared responsibility for park management. The transfer of ownership back to Aboriginal People is thus conditional on their support (through leases or other legal mechanisms) for the continuation of the National Park. The land occupied by a Park is simultaneously returned to aboriginal ownership and leased back to a government conservation agency under a co-management board and with the agreement of an arbitration process in case of disputes.

...a Start-up Team should make sure that the rights, needs and capacities of traditional communities are duly respected and recognised. It should also veer to avoid their "acculturation"....

...the ultimate decisions about how to handle issues of internal consensus and representation belong to the peoples themselves.

---

[46] Convention on Biological Diversity, Article 8j.
[47] Smyth, 2001.

Table 4.3	Four co-management "models" in Australia (adapted from Smyth, 2001)		
Gurig model	Uluru model	Queensland model	Witjira model
Aboriginal ownership	Aboriginal ownership	Aboriginal ownership	Ownership of land remains with the government
Equal representation of traditional owners and government representatives on management board	Aboriginal majority on management board	No guarantee of Aboriginal majority on management board	Aboriginal majority on management board
No lease-back to government Agency	Lease-back to government agency for long period	Lease-back to government agency in perpetuity	Lease of the national park to traditional owners
Annual fee to traditional owners (for the use of land as a National Park)	Annual fee to traditional owners, community council or board	No annual fee paid	
Example: Gurig National Park	Examples: Uluru-Kata Tjuta, Kakadu, Nitmiluk, Booderee and Mutawintji National Parks	Examples: none finalised; the model is currently under review...	Example: Witjira National Park

A further, more recent form of protected area established voluntarily on existing aboriginal-owned land– the Indigenous Protected Area model– presents a challenge to all co-management models, as it is more advanced in terms of self-determination of the aboriginal owners, and self-management practices (see Box 4.10).

Box 4.10	The new Indigenous Protected Area model (Australia) (adapted from Smyth, 2001)

Since 1998, Indigenous Protected Areas (IPAs) have become officially recognised and promoted in Australia as part of the national protected area system.[48] It was in fact realised that some aboriginal landholders were prepared to "protect" their land and part of the Australia National Reserve System in return for government funds and, if required, other types of management assistance. The first IPA was formally proclaimed in August 1998 over an aboriginal owned property called Nantawarrina in the northern Flinders Ranges of South Australia. Several more IPAs were proclaimed in other states during 1999.

IPAs can be established as formal conservation agreements under state or territory legislation, or under Indigenous Law. Aboriginal land owners there have a variety of legal mechanisms to control activities on their land, including local government by-laws and privacy laws. The declaration of IPAs is the first occasion in Australia whereby aboriginal land owners voluntarily accepted a protected area status over their land. Because the process is voluntary, and fully prompted and promoted by them, Aboriginal People choose the level of government involvement, the level of visitor access (if any) and the extent of development to meet their needs. In return for government assistance, aboriginal owners of IPAs are

---

[48] http://www.ea.gov.au/indigenous/ipa/index.html

required to develop a management plan and to make a commitment to manage their land (and/ or waters and resources) with the goal of conserving its biodiversity values.

IPAs are attractive to some aboriginal land owners because they bring management resources without the loss of autonomy associated with co-management regimes (see Table 4.3). IPAs also provide public recognition of the natural and cultural values of aboriginal land, and of the capacity of the Aboriginal People to protect and nurture those values. IPAs are attractive to government conservation agencies because they effectively add to the nation's conservation estate without the need to acquire the land, and without the cost of establishing all the infrastructure, staffing, housing etc of a conventional national park. Overall, IPAs can be seen as a particularly strong example of Community Conserved Area (strong insofar as the decision making power is entirely in the hands of the Aboriginal People and the government has understood and legalised that).[49]

In other world regions, such as Latin America and the Caribbean, the experimentation with co-responsibility in PA management between the civil society and the state has also been gaining significant strength and recognition. A recent review identified 79 distinct experiences in Central America[50] with an important variety of management types taking advantage of the relative state of flux and openness of the relevant legislations and policies, although the difficulties and potential failures faced by many of these experiences should not be underestimated.[51] Experiences in the Andean region also offer a number of inspiring examples, including areas voluntarily subjected to a conservation regime by indigenous and local communities with the explicit intent of obtaining a legal recognition of their customary land tenure rights, and assurance from governments that the land will be protected and not destined to a variety of forms of exploitation.[52] In a climate of tenure insecurity, lack of confidence in state institutions and policies, and after a long history of abuse of indigenous and community rights, people are searching for all possible instruments to secure long-term access to natural resources. Under present circumstances in a number of Latin American countries a protected area regime can offer them such security, besides also attracting funding, support, visibility, and income from tourism to the concerned areas. When this proves true, community benefits related to the establishment of a co-management agreement can be substantial.

---

49 Borrini-Feyerabend et al., 2004 (in press).
50 Solis Riviera et al., 2003.
51 Kaimowitz, Faune and Mendoza, 2003. See also Box 3.17 in Chapter 3.
52 Oviedo, 2003. See also Boxes 4.4 and 4.10, in this Chapter.

Box 4.11   The Kaa-ya Iya National Park in Bolivia:
            ensuring territorial recognition for the Guaraní Izoceño people
            (adapted from Winer, 2001 and Winer, 2003)

The Kaa-ya Iya National Park (83.4 million hectares) is the largest in Bolivia and contains the world's largest area of dry tropical forest under legal protection. Its most unique characteristic, however, is that the park was created in response to demands for territorial recognition by the Guaraní Izoceño people. This is the first park in the Americas declared on the basis of a demand by an indigenous people and the only park in the Americas where an indigenous people's organisation (CABI– Capitanía del Alto y Bajo Izozog) has primary administrative responsibility. In fact, the Park's Management Committee comprises staff of the Ministry of Sustainable Development and Planning and representatives of CABI, the Wildlife Conservation Society (WCS, a foreign NGO), local municipalities, a community group of Chiquitanos, the Ayoreo Community of Santa Teresita and the group of women of the Izozog indigenous communities. The indigenous representatives are the majority in the Committee, which participates in the definition of policies for the management of the Park.

By Bolivian law, the "Capitanías" are indigenous municipalities that own and administer the land under their jurisdiction. In 1993, the new Agrarian Reform Law first recognised Bolivia as a multiethnic and multicultural country. This law allowed for the existence of community land ownership and legalised the creation of indigenous territories (Territorio Comunitario de Origen– TCO). It was not until these provisions on legal land titling were implemented in the Kaa-ya Iya area that CABI and the indigenous communities could become fully involved in management of the Park, and that many conservation problems started to be effectively addressed. CABI is the long-standing political authority structure of the Guaraní people of the Izozog. It has contributed significantly to the social mobilisation that ushered the national decentralisation reforms. For the indigenous communities represented in CABI, legal recognition of their TCO was the primary condition for any meaningful conservation commitment for their lands

Having established the park has only partially fulfilled the historic objective of re-claiming land upheld by CABI. Currently, 1.9 million hectares bordering the park and straddling the river are titled in their favour and the rest has being gazetted as park territory. CABI would have preferred that all 5.3 million hectares (the 1.9 m. ha. land settlement and the Park's 3.4 m. ha.) were titled in their favour. The park's creation, on the other hand, was a realistic political compromise on all sides. It served to halt the rapid expanse of the agro-industrial sector, fanning out inexorably from its base in Santa Cruz de la Sierra (Bolivia's second largest city), and ensured that traditional lands were not to be clear-cut for farming. CABI has also been able to capitalise on its internal cohesion to pressure the hydro-carbon industry into making significant compensatory payments to them for the impact of that portion of the 32 inch-diameter gas pipeline with a total length of 3,146 kilometres that runs through their indigenous territory and the park. Such compensatory payments, totalling $3.7 million, and the activities that came in with the hydro-carbon industry, ensured CABI's ability to invest significant funds in the running of the park. This strengthened their standing as effective co-management partners. In addition, the hydro-carbon funds were crucial to supporting the indigenous organisations themselves, promoting rural development and accelerating the process of titling indigenous lands. Co-management would have taken hold in Bolivia without these funds, but would not have developed so rapidly, or garnered as much enthusiasm from the governmental agency in charge.

Chapter 5. ORGANISING FOR THE PARTNERSHIP

5.1 Gathering relevant information and tools and promoting social communication

The process will be iterative– as the social actors get involved, they bring about refinements and improvements in defining, understanding, deciding and taking action– but a good beginning positively affects all future outcomes.

The organising phase of the partnership is the realm of the Start-up Team, which prepares and facilitates the work of the relevant social actors. This is a critical moment in the process. On the one hand, the initiators and Start-up Team are usually self-appointed and have thus limited legitimacy to take decisions. On the other, they need to deal with several substantive issues, even if only in a preliminary way. The manner in which they shape the space and style of discussions, the language they use (for instance, what they introduce as "problems", "opportunities", "resources", etc.) and, most of all, their preliminary identification of the territory and resources at stake and of the social actors to participate in the negotiation are the cornerstones of the co-management process. To be sure, the process will be iterative– as the social actors get involved, they bring about refinements and improvements in defining, understanding, deciding and taking action– but a good beginning positively affects all future outcomes.

The members of the Start-up Team are usually well aware of the issues, problems and opportunities that concern various social actors about a territory, area or set of resources. They have reviewed them during the CM need and feasibility analyses, but they should refrain from discussing technical questions or the best ways to solve problems or respond to opportunities, as this is not their role. In the organising phase of the CM process, the Start-up Team prepares for, and enables, the relevant social actors to do that themselves.

Gathering information and tools

The Start-up Team may begin by gathering and listing available data and information on the "management unit" at stake. This includes historical data and reports (trend data and records of exceptional events are particularly useful), ecological and anthropological studies, maps (including old maps), copies of property and usufruct records, etc. Among such documents, an ecological analysis of the territory and natural resources would be particularly useful as it could describe their ecological value, the threats they sustain, the impacts of current activities and the current trends in biological diversity and performance of ecological functions. Even when such an analysis is available, there are benefits to be gained from revisiting it in a participatory way, with the input of local people as well as expert professionals.[1] Other useful studies could deal with specific resources, such as water, mineral ore, or migratory wildlife; with the local economy and its potential in the light of national policies (trends in volume and prices of key agricultural and natural resource outputs, including timber and wildlife products; trends in productive activities, such as tourism; etc.) or with population dynamics, such as reviews of human fertility, mortality, morbidity and migration in the concerned territory. All such analyses should be considered background material on which to ground substantial discussions and not "final statements", as they need to be validated by all management partners in the light of other information and a shared vision of the desired future.

Besides gathering various information and documents, the Start-up Team may prepare a short summary report of the issues at stake, to be offered to the relevant social actors at the beginning of the negotiation process. The report could review the particular NRM context from various perspectives (historical, social, legal, political, institutional) but the Start-up Team should refrain from stating the positions of various parties. If there are controversies, the report may mention them, and simply say what they are about. Preparing such a preliminary report is not always appropriate. It should be avoided when it is likely that the social actors may be intimidated or upset by it.

Not only the report, but also the maps and other relevant data and information should be made available to all relevant actors, particularly to local communities who may otherwise be deprived of the information they contain. In fact, the Start-up Team may wish to constitute a small reference library at the disposal of all participants in the negotiations. The availability of such information may be a novelty for some social actors, and the Team should be aware that the effective use of information needs previous experience and adapting time and is, in itself, an empowering experience.[2] Even more empowering, as a matter of fact, is the generation of information. Mapping of ancestral territories, in particular, is a key

...the relevant social actors organise themselves by preparing maps, documents and reports and by describing features, uses and entitlements of land and natural resources as seen, known and recognised by them.

---

[1] Long term residents and resource users may be of great help in an ecological analysis. An interesting view of how to identify priorities in biodiversity conservation within a socio-political context is found in Vane-Wright, 1996.

[2] Information is rarely, if ever, neutral, and confers power to the holder. For instance, legislation can be selectively enforced by the few who know the details. Market values in the cities, unknown to the producers, may be many times as high as the prices paid for the same product in the countryside. The environment now heralded as "pristine" may have been inhabited for centuries, a fact that conservationists may prefer not to expose. And so on.

instrument currently used by local communities to re-vindicate land and resource rights[3] and to illustrate existing systems of natural resource management (see Box 5.1). The Start-up Team usually begins by gathering existing information and using it to promote social communication, but it can also encourage the generation of new information, which the social actors themselves substantiate according to their own knowledge and experience (see Section 5.2). Indeed, a most empowering moment in the preparatory phase is when the social actors organise themselves by preparing maps, documents and reports, and by describing features, uses and entitlements of land and natural resources as seen, known and recognised by them.

Box 5.1   Participatory mapping in the Brazilian Amazon
(adapted from Viana and Freire, 2001)

A growing number of experiences in land use planning include participatory mapping of community land and resources assisted by NGOs. The Institute of Forest and Agriculture Certification and Management (IMAFLORA), a non-governmental organisation based in Piracicaba (Brazil), has facilitated a number of such initiatives.

The Tapajós National Forest is located in Central Amazon, near Santarém, along the Tapajós River. 18 riverine communities, including some descendants of last century's cabano's movement, live within the National Forest and have a history of conflicts with IBAMA, the federal agency in charge of managing the forest. From 1995 onwards, these communities have been engaged in a planning process that included the participatory mapping of land and resources. The maps were validated in a public assembly, with the participation of all communities, IBAMA and observers from various institutions. The maps showed that the community ancestral rights extended over an area larger than what had been previously claimed by the communities themselves. Unfortunately, their detailed claims have not been recognised by IBAMA, which produced its own maps without local participation. Nevertheless, the community mapping process has been useful, as it helped developing a zoning plan (the Management Plan of the Tapajós National Forest), "empowering" local leaders and community members and setting the stage for the creation of a pluralist Board of Directors (Grupo Gestor) for the National Forest.

The Municipality of Boa Vista do Ramos, located along the Amazon River near Manaus, comprises 43

---

3   See, for instance, Colchester and Erni, 1999, and the examples collected in Section 5.2 later in this Chapter.

communities. In 1998-99 these communities were involved in participatory land use planning exercises that included the selection and training of local "environmental defence agents" in mapping techniques and sustainable development concepts. The Municipality of Boa Vista do Ramos was very interested in the participatory mapping process as a tool for inter-agency planning and as a means to bring rules to land tenure and promote economic development based on sustainable natural resource use. The product of the participatory mapping was made available to all agencies of the municipal government and incorporated into a geographic information system. Atlases have later been developed and used in local schools, in a municipal land tenure programme and to plan for community initiatives.

A key lesson that emerges from these cases is that participatory mapping is an effective method to promote land tenure regularisation, to value local knowledge and to strengthen cultural identity. It was found important that different groups (formal and informal, divided by gender, age, religion and origin) were asked to draw the landscape and the resource uses, that maps were used to discuss a variety of issues (e.g., health, transportation, education) and that great care was taken in the process of "restituting information", through special tools (cartilhas) prepared for each particular stakeholder group.

As for biophysical and ecological information, the collection and analysis of social information begins with the work of the Start-up Team but needs to be refined through a discussion of the recognised entitlements and unrecognised claims by the relevant actors themselves. This is a sensitive task, and it must be carried out in a participatory and iterative way. As mentioned in Chapter 2, the assessment of the relative "weight" of different entitlements brings the management partners to distinguish between "primary" and "secondary" actors (and even lesser important ones) who may consequently receive different social recognition and benefits in management. The gathering and validation of the information necessary to assess the relevant entitlements (for instance: "How old is the history of occupation and resource use of a community in an area?"; "Is a particular exploitation permit still valid?"; "Who is paying the opportunity costs of conservation activities?") have major political implications. For equity's sake, the people and groups with a limited capacity to represent and assert themselves should be assisted to organise and gather the necessary information in support of their claims.

Several participatory management initiatives have commissioned substantial background ecological and social research prior to the negotiating phase. For instance, in the Muthurajawela Marsh and Lagoon Area of Sri Lanka, detailed environmental impact assessments of proposed activities, flora and fauna studies, socio-economic assessments of local communities, and other such factors were studied as part of the participatory exercise to develop a management plan for the area.[4] In the case of Mt. Elgon National Park, in Uganda, comprehensive studies on human use of natural resources and their impacts on the ecosystem preceded the negotiation of participatory management agreements between Uganda National Parks and local parishes.[5]

The information base for the CM negotiation process can been strengthened by a growing confidence in community knowledge, moving away from an exclusive dependence on formal and "scientific" information provided by professionals from outside the community or even the country concerned. It is important, however, that such local knowledge is recognised beyond the rhetoric. Some large scale

[4] Avanti Jayatilake, personal communication, 1997; see also Decosse and Jayawickrama, 1996.
[5] Scott, 1998. The same has been true for other national parks experimenting with co-management processes in Uganda, in particular for the pioneering Bwindi Impenetrable National Park.

programmes implemented by state governments and involving impressive multi-million budgets– such as the Eco-development Programme in India or the Parks and People Project in Nepal– affirm that local, community-based knowledge should be respected and utilised, but it is not clear how they actually translate this recognition into practice. The greatest use of local knowledge is usually found in the case of community-initiated or NGO-initiated natural resource management initiatives, for instance among the Kuna peoples of Panama, the Chipko movement in the Indian Himalaya, or the forest protection committees of Rajasthan in western India, all of which are built around traditional knowledge and practices about forests and biodiversity. It is also important that community knowledge is compared and discussed vis-à-vis other forms of knowledge. For instance, local knowledge about endangered species appeared to clash in an important way with information collected by the Great Barrier Reef Marine Park Authority, in Australia. The local Aboriginal peoples were reported to believe that the manatees are sea marsupials ("the small ones are capable of finding refuge in the body of the mother"), and much more numerous than marine scientists found them to be.[6]

Box 5.2   Examples of People's Biodiversity Registers
(adapted from Gadgil, 1996; Palmer et al., 1991)

In India, an innovative strategy of documenting local community knowledge and benefiting from its use has been devised during the last decade. Some groups and networks involved in environment, health, agriculture, and traditional science and technology prepared a simple guide/ format called the People's (or Community) Biodiversity Register. With the help of community-based organisations, they tested it in several villages, assisting villagers to record detailed information on their relationship with their biological surroundings, both in text and visual form.

The Indian Ministry of Environment and Forests (MoEF) was asked to assist in spreading the guide/ format widely, including by publishing it in regional languages, and providing the Register a legal status so that it could be used in disputes over intellectual property rights. After the MoEF's lukewarm response, however, some NGOs translated the guide/ format on their own and used various versions of it in several states of India. They agreed with communities never to publish information that is sensitive or that the communities do not want publicised.

In a similar effort, on the other side of the globe, high school students of Costa Rica's Talamanca coast have documented villagers' knowledge about forests and wildlife, as well as indigenous history and knowledge about the environment. In the process, they developed a deeper understanding of their own cultural roots, and an appreciation for the practices of the indigenous BriBri and Cabecar peoples.

Co-management approaches are uniquely suited to promote complementarity between traditional and modern knowledge systems[7], in particular during social communication events and participatory action research. In this light, a particular concern regards the safeguard of the intellectual property rights of local communities. To this aim, models of conduct have been developed and detailed guidelines for researchers working with local communities have recently been published.[8]

---

6   Graeme Kelleher, personal communication, 1995.
7   On this, see also Chapter 1 of this volume.
8   Laird, 2002.

Social communication

The heart of a co-management process is the negotiation among the representatives of various interest groups on concrete decisions, such as a management plan and one or more complementary initiatives. Negotiations, however, are not meaningful if they happen in an "information vacuum", with only a few people aware and concerned about what is being discussed and what consequences the decisions will entail. On the contrary, the interest groups that participate in the negotiation need to be well informed, knowledgeable and aware of issues and reciprocal concerns– all of which can be achieved by well-designed social communication efforts.

But there is more. Successful social communication can help not only to better understand the partners' perspectives and learn from different knowledge bases. They also yield new perspectives, synergistic innovations and innovative breakthroughs.[9] All too often, decisions are taken "based on limited consideration of a limited number of options, or skewed by biases in cognition– limitations in human judgement that are similar to optical illusions".[10] Well-designed communication efforts may not completely eliminate these problems but can reduce them considerably. In the words of Wheatley (1992): "Innovation arises from ongoing circles of exchange, where information is not just accumulated or stored, but created. Knowledge is generated anew from connections that weren't there before."

> Negotiations are not meaningful if they happen in an "information vacuum", with only a few people aware and concerned about what is being discussed and what consequences the decisions will entail.

Box 5.3   Informal contacts between actors are important!
(adapted from Lavigne Delville, 2000)

In development and conservation initiatives the communication strategy is rarely taken as seriously as it deserves to be. The external agencies cultivate the illusion of local mechanisms assuring perfect social communication. It is instead part of the responsibility of outside agents to assure that information and dialogue arrive to distant households and are not confined to the individuals holding positions of power and local privilege. The habit of holding only few and formal field meetings with local elite and decision-makers may make an outside agency completely blind with respect to what is really happening. It is instead essential to have "free time" to discuss issues informally, in a direct relationship between a variety of local and non-local actors.

Building upon the work of Röling (1994) we may see a few key tasks to be accomplished by social communication in natural resource management:

- making things visible (i.e., clarifying and raising awareness on natural and social phenomena);

- fostering policy understanding and acceptance;

- preparing for, and supporting, the negotiation process.

We use here the term "social communication" in the preparatory phase of a co-management process to describe the on-going dialogue and information flow between the Start-up Team and the interest groups, and among the interest groups themselves. This can be prompted by the Start-up Team through a specific event (e.g., a public party, a community meeting, a fair, a travelling theatre piece), but

---

[9]   Ramírez, 1997.
[10] Lee, 1993.

needs also to include an on-going component, such as regular meetings or a newsletter and a well identified focal point for information (a bulletin board, a phone number, a designated person) where questions and suggestions can be posted or heard and needs can be reported through time.

While the planning and negotiation process will typically rely on meetings and similar events, the facilitators of CM processes must recognise that there will always be people and groups who remain unwilling or unable to participate in such events. It is therefore advisable to remain aware of the limitations of "meetings", and to design and use additional means of social communication that promote the on-going information and, as much as possible, the inclusion and participation of all relevant social actors.

Box 5.4 Social communication for co-management
(adapted from Borrini-Feyerabend et al., 2000)

Communication may be personal (one-to-one), inter-personal (among a few individuals) and social (when it involves groups, such as a local community). Social communication is about providing the conditions for interactive learning and informed decision making in society, i.e., fostering the sharing of information and the discussion of problems, opportunities and alternative options for action. It is a complex undertaking, including a variety of avenues, from personal (one-to-one dialogues) to interpersonal (group meetings) to social (e.g., via the use of mass media such as the radio, TV or Internet).

Interactive learning is crucial for co-management initiatives, as these seek to overcome the logic of top-down expert authority and prescribed behaviour. Whenever there is a gap or a conflict between what is legal (prescribed) and what is legitimate (emerging from social consensus) efforts at merely transferring information, awareness or skills are likely to be in vain. Only interactive learning, built on the direct confrontation and dialogue among different views (thinking, discussing and acting together), can overcome the gap or help in managing the conflict. A few points to consider:

● "Communication occurs when people have something in common." (Fuglesang, 1982). If we wish to communicate with people we need to understand the language(s) by which they describe their own reality, including fundamental beliefs, values and concepts (such as time, space, matter).

● Effective communication processes and tools do not discriminate against the weaker and less influential in society (e.g., people who do not feel confident enough to attend meetings, who are not literate, who live far from main centres, etc.). In this sense, audiovisual presentations, such as picture stories and community radio programmes or "broad participation events", such as street theatre, may be less discriminatory than the printed media.

● Any information conveyed should be truthful, fair and reasonably complete. Information depends on context, and decisions are conditioned by the perception of available alternatives. Fairness in communication is thus a complex phenomenon, depending on completeness of information as much as on strict adherence of information to "facts".

● Any awareness raising initiative (e.g., a travelling theatre piece) should be respectful of local cultural traits and norms. Difficult subjects could and should be raised, but cultural features and beliefs should be treated with respect and not made to appear inadequate or ridiculous.

● Any training initiative should be offered with an eye to its social implications. Training a few individuals in crucial new skills for local production systems can originate important power changes and imbalances, and should be done to enhance not only available skills but also social equity in the relevant context.

● Most importantly, social communication initiatives should include plenty of occasions for dialogue and discussion, and the opportunity for everyone to express their own views, to ask questions and to dissent. This, in fact, represents the main difference between social communication and conventional information, education and training initiatives. While in the latter information flows from the sender to the receiver of messages, in the former information flows in all directions and collective knowledge, awareness and skills are actually generated as part of that very flow and exchange (e.g., by social dialogue and debate).

In the CM preparatory phase, social communication promotes an open debate and critical understanding of issues, including content questions, such as: "Do we have any problem regarding our natural resources?"; "Are there opportunities we should seize?"; "What could be done about them?". There are also process questions, such as: "What is co-management?"; "Is it needed here?"; "If so, how do we develop it?". In other words, one would need to start with a discussion on existing environment and development problems and opportunities, and move, at a comfortable and unhurried pace, towards what capacities exist to do something about those, and what roles different actors may wish to play.

It is useful to have a good "name" for the co-management process being promoted and a good description (words, images, definition of problems, etc.) of the ecological and social issues to be tackled. Those are an important visit card for the Start-up Team and need to be culturally valid and broadly understood and accepted in the context at stake, even if they may last only a limited time (any good process ends up developing, though dialogue and discussions, its own and unique "accepted common language"). The Start-up Team may wish to test and adopt some terms or phrase in the local language, which would hopefully be perceived as meaningful, appealing and inspiring (e.g., "Let's manage the forest together!", "Solidarity between people and the land", "Save our wetlands!", "The Parliament of the Silver River", "People and the Sea", "Designing our life",[11] etc.). The local name of the CM process is usually important for local acceptance and success. The terms and phrases should not be trite or resemble party slogans; on the contrary, they should convey the spirit of non-partisan collaboration, solidarity, working together for the common good. It is also important to avoid "picking a good name" from the top of the head of a few professionals. Instead, the name should ideally evolve in informal conversations with members of local communities and various relevant social actors. Possible problems and inadequacies with the translation of the names and descriptions in various local languages should also be given careful consideration.

...the "name" of the CM process should ideally evolve in informal conversations with members of local communities and various relevant social actors....

---

11   The latter "Desegnando la vida" was utilised in the Paute community (Ecuador), described in Box 4.2.

Box 5.5   First and most important step: accompanying a new perception of problems, actors,
           resources and opportunities within the local communities
           (adapted from Garreau, 2002)

The Andapa valley, in Madagascar, comprises a plain delimited by the mountain ranges of Marojejy
and Anjanaharibe-Sud, covered by high and low altitude forests of great biodiversity value. The valley,
excellent for growing rice, started being inhabited at the beginning of the XX century, after some colons
established there the cultivation of vanilla beans. The fertile land and the opportunities provided by the
production of vanilla, and later also coffee and rice, attracted thousands of poor peoples from the surrounding regions. The enormous growth of the resident population went hand in hand with uncontrolled deforestation. In the last forty years, the local population tripled and many continued to use
slash and burn practices (tavy) to grow pluvial rice. The relative proportion between forest and people
passed from 1 hectare per person to 1 hectare per 10 persons. Local land prices soared.

A ten-year integrated conservation and development project started being implemented in 1993 by
WWF around the protected areas of Marojejy et Anjanaharibe-Sud. The project begun by controlling
access to the protected areas, carrying out some "environmental education" and diffusing alternative
production techniques (irrigated rice versus the tavy, houses made of bricks rather than wood, beekeeping rather than collection of wild honey). In 1996, however, a new law on the devolution of resource
management rights to local communities (the so-called GELOSE law) allowed to change the approach
and to offer a new and better chance to the local communities and the local environment.

The project understood that what local communities lacked the most was information on their own situation. It thus invited local peoples and, later on, local authorities, to re-read their own history and to
examine their future in the light of the conditions of their natural resources– their common patrimony.
This created new ties among the families and communities that were discovering similarities of problems across the region, and strengthened the local identity, which had been precarious given the various ethnic and geographic origins of most residents. As part of social communication initiatives, information was conveyed on the new GELOSE law, which foresaw the possibility of assigning to the local
communities the management responsibility for their own forests, to give them security of tenure over
the cultivated land and to acquire specific management capacities. As the new opportunities got understood, the communities started changing their perspective of the situation and the project could also
change its own role.

Initially the project was a main partner of the state in controlling infraction to the rules that excluded
people from the protected areas, it diffused new technologies and promoted rural credit... all with the
type of patron-client relationships that this implies. After the broad change of attitude, however, the
communities started seeing the betterment of their lives as depending on the management conditions of
their environment, for which they could now be in charge. Change became their own priority and they
began demanding help to organise and learn how to use their resources in more effective and sustainable ways. The project could then adopt a new role, providing advice and acting as intermediary
between the communities and the government.

One of the early objectives of social communication is to inform the public at
large about the relevance of management concepts and practices for the local
context. But people should be more than "informed". They should appropriate
for themselves what management is all about, and transform it as they see fit. In
other words, social communication initiatives should be much more open and
dialogue-oriented than conventional information or education initiatives. They
should not merely aim at "passing a message about an issue" but at promoting
its critical understanding and appropriation in society. In line with this, the most

important result sought by a genuine co-management initiative is not for people to behave in tune with what some experts– including the experts in the Start-up Team– believe is right for them, but for people to think, find agreements and act together on their own accord.

One aspect of the politics of information is that information moves among the dominant sectors of society, or between them and the less privileged, but rarely it is allowed to flow among the less privileged themselves. In fact, lack of information and lack of control over the means and avenues of information is one of the ways by which marginalisation is created and maintained. And even when information passes from one local community to another, it is often mediated by outsiders (government agents, NGOs, commercial media houses, etc.). Simultaneous to this is the fact that the traditional means of communication amongst rural communities across regions (e.g., pilgrimages, local traders, wandering minstrels and jostlers) are disappearing, with the commercial aspects of such contacts becoming dominant over the informal exchanges they used to represent and convey.

Fortunately, some participatory natural resource management initiatives have themselves revived people-to-people contacts. Communities are encouraged to visit other communities where innovative resource management initiatives are going on, and other are supported to do so by NGOs or, more rarely, by government agencies. In Columbia, horizontal campesino to campesino (farmer to farmer) communication has enormous potential, especially in matters such as protection or revival of native seed diversity.[12] Traditional healers have also been supported to meet and exchange their knowledge and skills as a way to promote the survival of their unique bio-cultural heritage.[13] Indigenous peoples in many parts of the world, and in particular in South and North America, are coming together more and more frequently to learn from each other and to jointly respond to challenges from outsiders. In India, the time-honoured tradition of pilgrimage (yatras) is also being revived. In 1995, a major such journey of communication and exploration involved tens of local community representatives, conservationists, officials and academics who travelled for thousands of kilometres through eighteen national parks and sanctuaries, initiating dialogues with communities and government officials along the way, examining local problems and raising awareness of possible solutions.[14]

Such contacts and communication are also a powerful way of keeping the oral tradition alive. In the past, intra- and inter-generational communication was largely oral, and this continues to be the case with many indigenous and rural communities. The written form cannot possibly convey the richness, depth, and lasting impression of the oral form. Leopold Sedar Senghor, ex-president of Senegal, urged anthropologists to tape and photograph what the shamans, street performers, and old people of Africa had to tell and show; he said that they were "the final keepers of a long human history, entrusted only to their voices... and when they die, it will be as if for you, for your civilisation, all the libraries were to be burned". Much of those "unwritten books" contain precious resource management information and, as documentation always reduces and misrepresents to some extent, community-to-community contacts are necessary to keep that oral tradition alive.

The most important result sought by a genuine co-management initiative is not for people to behave in tune with what some experts– including the experts in the Start-up Team– believe is right for them, but for people to think, find agreements and act together on their own accord.

In many participatory management initiatives people-to-people contacts are being revived.

---

12 Ramírez, 1998.
13 Zuluaga and Diaz, 1999; Zuluaga, 2000.
14 Kothari, 1995.

A great diversity of tools and techniques can be used in social communication efforts, from informal face-to-face dialogues to global electronic conferences where most participants never physically meet. No one tool is likely to be appropriate for all occasions, even within the same socio-cultural and ecological setting. Community meetings, posters, maps, drawings, poetry, debates, films and photos, radio, the print media, street theatre and other folk media… the tools are as diverse as the situations in which they have to be employed, and should be adapted to them. In Cameroon, a conservation and development initiative supported by the German Technical Cooperation Agency (GTZ) in a tropical forest environment organised a series of visits to local communities, mostly inhabited by illiterate people. Their communication efforts centred on the use of particular tool– a paper canvas of about 2.5 meter width, with a series of drawings in a specific sequence. The images were exposed one after the other during the community meetings and a facilitator helped the people to reflect on their environment, discuss on the trends they perceived about it, identify possible solutions, identify the need for a facilitated dialogue/ negotiation among all the interested actors and brainstorm about who could do what (e.g., who could play a facilitator role among contrasting needs and concerns). These meetings were very useful for people to understand that the project staff was a "distinct actor" with respect to the government or the park conservation staff, and could play a role as mediator among various actors and concerns.[15]

In Congo Brazzaville, a similar project encountered tremendous local opposition until a person of local tribal affiliation understood the issue at stake and agreed to visit the local communities and initiate a series of open discussions.[16] In that case, until the local people accepted the carriers of information, the invitation to dialogue fell on deaf ears. The carrier was the message! Again in the Congo, some cassette tapes were prepared containing both music and information about conservation and development issues. The cassettes were sold at market places and distributed among the drivers of the taxi-brousse (the only means of local transportation), where people could listen to them and possibly start discussing options while sharing a ride….

…until the local people accepted the carriers of information, the invitation to dialogue fell on deaf ears. The carrier was the message!

Songs, drama, dance, storytelling, and other cultural forms are used to great effect all over South America. These moments of social communication are not separated from normal life but merged with it. Traditional forms of mutually supporting labour, such as the minga of the Andean region, are energised by songs and special foods, and followed by a gathering where people eat, drink and celebrate

---

15 Karin Augustat, personal communication, 1999; and Augustat, 1999.
16 Chatelain et al., 2004.

together. In Ecuador, federations of local communities built a major irrigation system, planted a million trees, and carried out soil conservation measures on slopes, through such a system.[17] In this sense, informal social communication activities such as joint mapping and surveying of the natural resources to be managed, involving a variety of social actors (and especially the ones not formally recognised!) can help develop confidence and trust on the Start-up Team. Dialogues, mutual learning exercises and the participation in common events are some of the most useful tools in this respect.

5.2 Engaging the partners in participatory action research

Quite naturally, social communication events may merge into participatory action research, i.e., specific inquiries by which local and outside actors join forces to understand the current situation and respond to its problems and opportunities. Conventional research on natural resource management is an activity carried out by experts (usually outside experts), which involves local actors only as informants or labour. Local people are asked to provide information, but are not let to elaborate on the context or meaning of such information, and even less allowed to shape questions, define problems or test solutions. This is unfortunate, as local people are depository of knowledge and insights critical for management decisions. As a concrete example, most natural resource management projects do not have provisions for historical research (including oral history of local communities). A Navajo teacher eloquently brings out the importance of such an understanding:

"Ethnic history is like a bow and arrow. The farther back you pull the bowstring, the farther the arrow flies. The same is true with historical vision: the farther back you look, the farther you can see into the future. If you pull the bowstring back only a little, the arrow only goes forward a short way. The same with history. If you only look back a short distance, your vision into the future is equally short."

Participatory action research[18] (PAR) is based on the involvement of local and non-local partners in a joint learning process. It has an orientation towards the felt needs of local people and institutions and locally-generated initiatives. It values and respects local history and institutional memory. And it has a focus on action, rather than on the collection of mere data and information. The results of research are meant to feed directly into planning and concrete activities and a minimum time gap is expected between data collection, analysis and feed-back. Last but not least, PAR exhibits a strong focus on process, with an equal concern for both final results and the process that leads to them, a built-in communication strategy and the redefinition of the role of non-local professionals, evaluated not so much for "what they know" but for "how useful they are" to local people and communities.

---

[17] Kleymeyer, 1996.
[18] Fals Borda and Rahman, 1991; Barton et al., 1997; Castellanet and Jordan, 2002; CGIR, 2003.

Participatory action research (PAR) has a focus on action, rather than on the collection of mere data and information; its results are meant to feed directly into planning and concrete activities....

Collaborative management efforts throughout the world have involved a variety of social actors in both baseline research and analysis, often generating a synergy between traditional and modern knowledge and tools (e.g., between visual tools such as maps, pictures, films and diagrams, and oral tools, such as open meetings, traditional media and rural radio). For instance, people of eastern Panama, threatened by logging, ranching, and a proposed highway, combined community-generated maps with government maps, aerial photographs, and the Global Positioning System (GPS) to show the extent of local natural resource use. When used in lobbying and campaigns, their composite maps proved extremely effective in convincing the government of the need for rethinking development in the area.[19] In Indonesia, WWF helped villagers with similar mapping exercises, used to ascertain, clearly and factually, the customary rights of local communities in the territories declared part of Kayan Mentarang National Park. This was an essential step towards developing fairer zoning plans based on customary regulations (adat) and a legal co-management structure for the park.[20] In Bolivia, the people of Tiwanaku joined efforts with external scientists to understand the local irrigation problems and ended up reviving ancient farm beds and interlacing canals.[21] Such a revival of local, traditional knowledge for water harvesting, used in conjunction with modern engineering science, has been happening also in some parts of India, with remarkable results.[22] The methods and tools of participatory action research are usually close to the community livelihood experience and thus generally effective and well accepted. A telling example are the "family portraits",[23] which examine and describe in detail the production systems and copying strategies of typical families in a given context. Another example is the focus group discussion of stakeholders rights, responsibilities and revenues vis-à-vis the resources.[24]

Box 5.6 Participatory land and resource mapping as an empowering, capacity building process
(adapted from Poole, 1997)

A number of methods for land use and occupancy studies evolved in the 1970s in the Canadian north, amidst the Inuit organisations in Arctic Quebec (Nunavik) and the Northwest Territories (Nunavut). These included the development of local maps (with supporting text) resulting from community-based research involving interviews with elders and expert hunters and fishers. Each interview led to a personal or family "map biography". Using traditional cartographical methods, these maps were then assembled to produce a comprehensive geographic statement about areas and resources traditionally used. These, in turn, were first used to negotiate land settlements, and later to develop resource inventories, management plans, environmental impact studies, etc.

The Ye'kuana communities of Venezuela have been inspired by the Inuit experience, and received the support of Canadian and other organisations to replicate it in their own environment. In fact, they adopted participatory mapping as a strategy to both demonstrate evidence of historical occupancy and evidence of capacity to manage resources. The process began in the early 1990s and was based on an ingenious demarcation method, adapted to their immense and densely forested environment. The com-

---

19 Lynch and Talbott, 1995.
20 Eghenter and Labo, 2003.
21 Kleymeyer, 1996.
22 CSE, 1997.
23 Bocoum et al., 2003.
24 Tache and Irwin, 2003.

munity members cut trails from the villages to strategic entry points to the Ye'kuana territory. Once they reached those points, they marked them by opening up circles of 20 or more 30 m. diameter, which could be visible from above. Intervening boundary markers were either rivers or straight lines. The work was accomplished by several teams, each comprising thirty men and women, which covered agreed border segments in about 2 months each. A light aircraft was then used to locate the circles and geo-code their positions with a GPS system. In Ottawa, 3 versions of the resulting map were subsequently produced: 3,000 copies of the basic map for distribution to each Ye'kuana, several glossy enlargements for national officials, and about fifty work maps with all place names deleted save those of the communities.

In a subsequent phase, the work maps were used by the communities to assign Ye'kuana names to streams and places and identify their traditional resources and the places that are special for spiritual reasons. This kind of mapping is about what people do as much as what they know. The Ye'kuana affirm that knowledge in the form of named places and resources indicates regular use of the land which is tantamount to ownership. This employs an argument that has been used elsewhere in its reverse mode: to deny indigenous ownership of resources. When used by mining interests during the Nunavut negotiations, this argument held that Inuit do not qualify for land ownership on the grounds that they lack the technical capacity to identify the presence of mineral resources, or to mine them: they couldn't own them because they couldn't know them. The mineral companies would qualify for ownership by virtue of their capacity both to know where minerals are and to exploit these resources. Following this, the Grand Council of the Crees demonstrated the importance of using the land and being able to prove that use in their case against a major hydro project. The Cree disputed the claim that the land to be flooded was unoccupied by showing heavily documented evidence of their intensive and extensive land-based activities.

The Ye'kuana were made aware of this and communities planned to maintain the boundary circles they had created, for instance by establishing a camp and garden nearby. This demarcation strategy, to show evidence of use at strategic entry points by cutting a manga, was also used by the Awa, in the early 1980s, in demarcating the Awa Ethnic Forest Reserve in Ecuador. The final phase of the mapping project foresees the development of a long-term environmental protection and sustainable plan, designed to feature in negotiations as evidence of the local capacity to manage such a large territory. Elements of the plan and map include issues of conservation, inventories, domestication of plant varieties, location of protected habitats and renewable energy resources, potential new village/ camp sites and location and control of tourism.

Conscious of having to defend a territory that amounts to 10,000 ha. per person, the Ye'kuana are taking steps to convince both the public and officialdom that they are best qualified to look after it. When a project coordinator, Simeon Jimenez, had his seven minutes on Venezuelan national television, he used them to reassure viewers about Ye'kuana intentions. He referred to pressure from intrusions of garimpeiro (gold-miners from Brazil), he cited incursions of Colombian narco-guerrillas across the Orinoco and proposed that the public think of the Ye'kuana as guardians of the national forest patrimony, acting on their behalf. Their strategy is around the proposition that they are the people best qualified, by tradition, knowledge, intentions and capacity, to look after their traditional territory.

In summary, the expanded interests and activities precipitated by the initial demarcation phase served two purposes: to reinforce the Ye'kuana case for legal recognition of their lands and to address present social and economic issues confronting the communities. Quite apart from mapping, the project is being used as a medium for exploring new ways to utilise the traditional resource base. These are seen to have survival value and would probably continue even if the Ye'kuana case for their land was eventually to fail. In fact, the maps are useful, but equally useful is the way that the mapping process has provided opportunities for communities and individuals to become directly engaged in generating the case for their land, to a depth that would not be possible if their case was conducted by proxy, and to gradually assume command of the process. In addition, the local technical capacities generated went beyond expectations and, as the mapping proceeded, community members took advantage of new contacts and information sources to pursue various lines of inquiry and development of local interest, such as the possibility of mini-hydro and solar fruit dryers, a pilot project in ecotourism and other ways to address the local economic opportunities and social problems.

Importantly, the process promoted new inter-community relations, drawing together communities that had remained out of contact for over thirty years and renewing their solidarity. This is reflected in the composition of the project maps. Although communities accepted local responsibilities for demarcation, and agreed amongst themselves the border between different community territories, there was no placing of community boundaries on any of the project maps. This collective approach implies an obligation to ensure contributions from all communities. The process also promoted some local strategy to protect traditional knowledge. Tactics ranged from the "just don't tell anyone" method to community-based mechanisms for gathering and consolidating knowledge and advising individuals on how to recognise and treat overtures from bio-prospectors. The methods require a high degree of local cohesion, access to external information and means to disseminate local information. The Ye'kuana have also started a systematic collection of local plant uses and are gathering the information needed to identify and anticipate bio-prospectors. Ultimately, they are developing a way of conserving traditional ecological knowledge in the most effective way possible: by using it.

Several villagers in Maharashtra (India) have initiated "study circles" (abhyas gats) on various subjects (e.g., forest-based rights), in which interested people come together to discuss and invite outside experts to participate– but only on an equal level.[25] These initiatives help in keeping the people well-informed and aid in participatory research on matters of importance to the village. In the villages of Mendha-Lekha and Saigata these events brought powerfully to light the long-term damages of commercial exploitation of forests– even when seen in the light of the immediate economic gains of forest exploitation. Through similar interactions the villagers have been able to solve complicated issues such as conflicts involving illegal extraction of resources and encroachments (while forest officials are still struggling with such issues in near-by areas). In Jardhargaon village, information from both within and outside, garnered by the Save the Seeds Movement (beej bachao andolan) and the forest protection committee (van suraksha samiti) was crucial in initiating the switch back to traditional seeds and agro-practices.

Unfortunately the local open discussion of basic information on natural resource management is still more the exception than the rule throughout India. Too often, people are not even aware of developmental or other schemes and plans envisaged for their areas. Ideally, government officials and outside experts would bring in the larger perspectives not so easily perceived by the villagers given their limited experiences and access to outside information. In turn, they could learn from the detailed site-specific information that only the local people have. Together, local people and outsiders could make the best of their combined knowledge and skills.[26]

The essential outcome of the preparatory phase in co-management processes are well-informed actors, willing to engage themselves, assume an active role in management and negotiate a fair share of the related benefits and responsibilities. For this, the members of the Start-up Team may wish to organise specific meetings with the identified parties, or at least with the "primary stakeholders" among

25   Neema Pathak, personal communication, 1998; Hiralal and Tare, 2001; http://www.freedominfo.org/case/mkss/mkss.htm
26   Pathak and Gour-Broome, 2001.

them. The members of the Team who feel most trusted by the relevant people meet with individuals deemed to be representatives of each of the parties and discuss with them the possibility of their participation in a co-management process. This is not a straightforward task. Even when social communication initiatives have aroused their attention, the parties may not be clear about their management interests, concerns and capacities and/ or not be internally organised to promote them[27]. At times, even getting together to discuss issues is a controversial matter, and the Start-up Team has to devise special mechanisms to ensure that a group is allowed to contribute. In Pakistan, for instance, women in rural areas are rarely allowed to meet with people from outside their village, and basically never with men from outside their families. The staff of a FAO project devised an interesting way to overcome this restriction and assign to local women their role as "separate actors" in natural resource management. They had local women and men discussing together a variety of issues by partitioning a room with a curtain and asking people of different gender to take place in separate compartments.[28] People were thus in no direct contact but could express their views and hear one another.

Whenever possible, a useful setting for an initial contact between the Start-up Team and one of the "relevant actors" is a joint visit to the NRM unit(s) at stake. On the spot, issues and problems can be discussed with the help of participatory appraisal exercises such as transect walks, interviews with spontaneous groups and key informants, land use mapping, historical mapping, etc. In these, a basic aim of the Start-up Team may be to elicit views on the major problems the people would like to solve, and the major opportunities they would like to see exploited. These views should be later refined and possibly brought into the negotiation process.

Interestingly, these field visits may be important to dispel incorrect beliefs prior to the negotiation meetings, as it happened some years ago in Albania. During the designation process for a Ramsar site, a few prominent academics representing national conservation NGOs kept lobbying the authorities and consultants for a very strict, no hunting and no local use management regime because of what they described to be a "huge recent rise in the population of the settlements around the site". They stated that many people were moving into the area from northern Albania and that this was going to cause an unsustainable destructive pressure on the lagoon. As evidence, they showed pictures of new houses being built in the settlements around the lagoon. And yet, during a participatory public consultation exercise, immigration and emigration mobility maps were drawn by the residents of those settlements and it emerged that in 11 out of the 12 villages around the site immigration had actually been decreasing in the last decade, and the new houses were being built by and for local residents only. This was confirmed by further analyses and took the wind out of the sails of the conservation lobbyists. A more appropriate and relaxed conservation regime, including limited hunting zones, emerged in the final management plan. Without the participatory consultation and the mapping exercise, there would probably have been a complete hunting ban imposed on the whole area and the management plan of the Ramsar site would have been deeply unpopular and likely ineffective.[29]

Care should be taken to ensure that the views of the individuals preliminarily identified by the Start-up Team as possible representative of one of the parties are not automatically interpreted as the "views of that party" on problems and oppor-

…even when social communication initiatives have aroused their attention, the "relevant actors" may not be clear about their management interests, concerns and capacities and/ or not be internally organised to promote them….

---

27 Some authors suggest that intra-group processes are just as critical and inter-group negotiations. In other words, negotiation within organisations is bound to influence negotiations between organisations (Pruitt and Carnevale, 1993).

28 Marilee Kane, personal communication, 1999.

29 Andrew Inglis, personal communication, 2000.

... [the social actors] need to decide for themselves if and on what grounds they wish to claim any management entitlement... and to clarify what type of entitlement they claim.

tunities. The next step should, in fact, be meetings and discussions with more people expected to share the same interests and concerns of the ones initially contacted. In other words, if early contacts were held with a fisherman leader, the later meetings may be held with various fishermen associations. If they were held with a forester or a park ranger only, the later meetings may be with staff from various government agencies. If they were held with a traditional chief or the local teacher, the later meetings may include the community at large. In such larger gatherings and in informal consultations, the NRM issues and problems identified thus far can be introduced and discussed, and thereby validated, made more specific, or entirely re-interpreted. The goal of these meetings is for the relevant social actors to identify and clarify their own NRM interests, concerns and capacities, as well as to decide for themselves if and on what grounds they wish to claim any management entitlement (examples of such grounds were described in chapter 2 as the "roots of entitlements"). In addition, they may also clarify what type of entitlement they claim. For instance, are they interested in drafting and approving a management plan, including setting up resource use regulations and zoning? Are they interested in taking-on management jobs? In drafting policy changes on the basis of the management results? Or simply in achieving the legalisation of some forms of access to, and use of, natural resources?

The separate meetings in the organising phase offer an occasion for the Start-up Team to deepen and refine the preliminary situation analysis and stakeholder analysis with the help of the social actors themselves. Each one actor, in fact, can be asked to discuss about other actors, and about their relative rights and responsibilities to participate in managing the territory, area or natural resources at stake. This can be prompted by some simple questions, such as the ones of Checklist 5.1.

Checklist 5.1   Questions and ranking exercises to engage the relevant social actors in the CM process (including a participative/ iterative stakeholder analysis)

Questions for each "relevant actor"

- Do you care about [name X, the specific territory, area or natural resources at stake]?

- Why? What does it represent for you? Why is it important?

- Do you have any specific worry about what is happening or may happen to X?

- Who is managing X?

- Are you at all involved?

- Do you have any special knowledge or capacity to manage X?

- Should you be involved in managing it?

- If yes, would you wish to take an advisory role? A decision-making role? An executive role?

- Would you wish to have a share in the benefits deriving from the natural resources?

- If you wish to take on a management role and receive NRM benefits, do you believe you are entitled to it? If yes, why (on what grounds)?

- In light of the above, what management responsibilities are you ready to take on?

- Besides yourselves, who are the main social actors (e.g., agencies, groups, entities, individuals) who can contribute to and should receive benefits from the management of X?

- Why, in your view, are they entitled? On what grounds?

- What do they have to offer? Specifically, could they contribute to developing the situation analysis, taking decisions, advising decision makers, planning, implementing activities, monitoring and reviewing results or to any other useful activity?

- What management responsibilities could be confided to them?

- What benefits should they receive in compensation for what they would offer?

- If some management decisions need to be taken, who among all the actors you identified should sit in a "committee" in charge of taking decisions?

- Who should be advising that committee?

- Who should take part in implementing the decisions?

Ranking exercises (comparing the various actors, including the respondent)

- Between actors A and B, who is "more entitled" to take management decisions?

- Why?

- Between actors A and B, who is "more entitled" to assume management responsibilities?

- Why?

- Between actors A and B, who is more "more entitled" to receive benefits from the territory or natural resources?

- Why?

These discussions will provide an overview of the main NRM stakes in the specific context, and inform the Start-up Team of controversies likely to surface during the negotiation phase. On the basis of both the collected perceptions of the relevant actors and the legally recognised claims in the territory at stake, the Start-up Team can draw a preliminary broad picture of who are the "primary" actors, the ones that must be engaged in the subsequent management negotiation. Ultimately, their total number is also a consideration. Too many social actors would complicate and slow down the process. Too few may end up leaving out key players.[30] It should be clear, however, where and how the groups and individuals who believe to be "legitimate actors" can claim such a status and argue their case on the basis of explicit "grounds".

Not all societies or groups within a society recognise all management claims from all social actors. They may recognise some but not others. They may recognise claims only in combinations with others (e.g., dependency for survival + long-term relationship with the resources + uses based on traditional knowledge). Some social actors may recognise their respective claims, but other actors may deny them. In some cases, the participatory stakeholder analysis does not present any problem. In others, it may trigger latent conflicts. For some parties the recognition of any claim of other social actors poses an insurmountable obstacle. For instance, a set of natural resources may be sacred to a traditional community and considered by them non-negotiable. Or a government agency may go by the books and not be willing to recognise any interest or concern besides its own government mandate. Or some conservation NGOs may chose civil disobedience

No one will be compelled to relinquish authority or renounce acquired rights, but all can profit from solutions that are satisfactory or acceptable to everyone.

---

30 Ostrom, 1997.

rather than accepting government decisions that affect the survival of a given species. If this is the case, the Start-up Team may need to dedicate much energy to open up a social debate on the basic principles and advantages of co-management. Among those, it may stress that all relevant actors are expected to both contribute and benefit from resource management and that agreements can be developed in an "experimental" way, according to adaptive management principles. No one will be compelled to relinquish authority or renounce acquired rights, but all can profit from solutions that are satisfactory and acceptable to everyone.

Even before the relevant actors meet, the Start-up Team may be confronted by a variety of old and new natural resource conflicts. The analysis of such conflicts is quite relevant in view of future management agreements and the Start-up Team may wish to engage in it with the active participation of social actors themselves. Care must be taken not to rekindle or exacerbate controversies but simply to clarify issues.[31]

5.3   Assisting local communities to organise

Community organising to manage natural resources is a natural occurrence, at the heart of human livelihoods in all cultures. Today, however, new actors, from state agencies to private entrepreneurs and corporations, have taken centre stage for it. Policies and practices that subtract authority and responsibilities from local communities have been promoted now for several centuries– from the enclosure of the commons to the imposition of "development" initiatives on a huge scale, from colonial systems to disruptive agricultural advice and related credits, from school curricula that devalue local customs to the daily brainwashing of advertisements. All this may explain why so many communities, today, are less than well organised to manage their natural resources and may need new efforts or even external support to re-gain the necessary capabilities. To be sure, all social actors to be involved in co-management processes need to organise for it. But local communities are likely to be the ones most in need of re-empowering themselves for the task.

Kothari (2000) reports that several Indian villages gained new social respect and became politically stronger by organising around the restoration and sound management of their natural resources. Jardhargaon is a typical village in the Himalayan foothills of Tehri Garhwal district, Uttar Pradesh. About twenty years ago, faced with serious shortages of fuel, fodder and water, residents took charge of the protection and management of the slopes above their village. Today, their regenerated forests are providing them with their basic needs. These forests now harbour significant wildlife and biodiversity, and professional botanists have shown them to be amongst the most diverse in this region. Jardhargaon's farmers are also getting increasingly disillusioned about the short-term lures of chemical-

---

31   A number of ideas and options for action to deal with conflicts will be discussed in Chapter 6, Section 6.4. A special case, which needs particular attention, is the one of traditional and indigenous communities, discussed in Section 4.4 of Chapter 4.

intensive farming, and are switching back to some traditional practices and reviving their traditional seed diversity. Some of them, through traditional journeys on foots (padayatras) to the remote villages of their region, have collected several hundred varieties of seeds lost elsewhere (up to 250 varieties of rice, 170 varieties of beans, and many others). The village is also maintaining its own equitable system of irrigation, with specific individuals (koolwalas) appointed by the residents to look over the traditional water sharing patterns, ensure that no-one misuses or over-uses the water and maintain the channels in good operating conditions. Jardhargaon has also fought off attempts by outside forces to start mining on some of its slopes.

Similarly, Mendha is a small Gond tribal village in Gadchiroli district (Maharashtra). The early interaction with government officials has meant for them only exploitation and extortion. The forests in the vicinity of the village were taken over and access to villagers was restricted while the government was extracting commercial timber, gave permission to the paper industry to harvest bamboo and awarded contracts to outsiders to gather non-wood forest produce. In the 1970s, Mendha's villagers participated in the massive and successful tribal movement against the Bhopalpatnam-Ichhampalli dams, which would have submerged their homes and forests. Subsequently, with the help of a local NGO called Vrikshamitra, the villagers organised under the motto Dilli Bambai hamari sarkar, hamare gaon mein ham hein sarkar ("our representatives form the government in Delhi and Bombay, but we are the government in our village"). They formed a Village Forest Protection Committee to manage the surrounding forests, and forced a stop to commercial destructive practices by both locals and outsiders (including the government and the local paper mill). Since then, the village has explored various avenues for generating employment, and has ensured year-round jobs for all residents. Today the village assembly (gram sabha) is so strong that no programme, with or without government backing, can be implemented without being first discussed and approved by the villagers... Biogas production, fishing, irrigated agriculture, sustainable forest production and handicrafts are common activities. Indeed, the study circles initiatives described earlier in this chapter produced, in Mendha, remarkable results.

Today, the village assembly (gram sabha) is so strong that no programme, with or without government backing, can be implemented without being first discussed and approved by the villagers....

Box 5.7 Community organising: a powerful NRM tool in Mongolia
(adapted from Schmidt et al., 2002)

From unmemorable times, Mongolia's nomadic herders have been the managers of the natural resources at the basis of their livelihoods– the very resources upon which the country's economy still depends today. Their traditional practices were based on common property of pasture and mobility as a key management strategy. Those, however, have been altered over the decades of centrally-planned economy and during more recent socio-economic changes, resulting in unsustainable practices (increased numbers of herding households, changes in herd structure, lack of proper grassland manage-ment, indiscriminate cutting of shrubs and trees for fuel wood). These practices, as well as changes in climate, appear to be at the roots of the current processes of land degradation and desertification throughout the country. To face both ecological and economic problems, some Mongolian communi-ties in the Gobi and the Altai Tavan Bogd areas, bordering China, are re-organising themselves. They formed Nukhurluls (support groups) attempting to combine the benefits of both traditional and modern learning. In the Nukhurluls, for instance, the community initiatives are typically led by young couples (in fact, mostly young women) but in the background remains the support of the community elders, who keep sharing their wisdom and knowledge rooted in community history and traditional resource management practices. Unlike with previous socialist collectives, the new community organisations and initiatives are all on a voluntary basis. Their current thrust is to increase the community capacities, diversify its sources of livelihood, add value to its products and assert its natural resource rights. As right holders, they can negotiate and agree with other stakeholders on rules and mechanisms for the man-agement of natural resources and protected areas.

Some external technical cooperation agencies have played an important role in this, facilitating the analysis of problems and opportunities within the communities, promoting an exchange of experience among them, supporting linkages between communities and private and public sector organisations and civil society as a whole, and fostering consensus as the basis of co-management decisions. Different local co-management models are now emerging. Park facilities, such as visitor centres, are co-managed. Local communities assign member families to patrol certain valleys, and "Volunteer Rangers" are authorised by the park. The vigilance of local communities who have a strong sense of stewardship over local resources helps to control poaching and illegal trade, for example of falcons. Tourism deci-sions and related income are shared between park authorities and local communities. Importantly, self-organizing of community groups is occurring also in the absence of project support and contracts for transferring natural resource rights to local communities are currently being discussed between gover-nors and community organisations in several districts. Those concern medicinal plants, wildlife and community-based tourism.

A working group including representatives of local governments, communities, research organisations and policy makers has also been established to develop appropriate concepts for community-based nat-ural resource management in the whole of Mongolia. The group is examining issues of transfer of resource rights and management responsibility to local community institutions, long-term custodian-ship, ecological and economic viability of resource uses, capacity building of organisations, and devel-oping policies in support of all of the above. The Nukhurluls, strong of the experience of several years of work, are taking community organizing into a new era by forming district-wide associations and exploring legal and structural aspects of establishing an overall apex institution. This genuine grassroots organizing is playing an increasingly important role in rural development and sustainable natural resource management in Mongolia.

Unfortunately, the experience of Jardhargaon and Medha, the Mongolian commu-nities described in Box 5.7 or the Iranian nomads described in the Case Example 1.3 in Chapter 1, are the exception rather than the rule in much of the rural areas of the world. Local communities, groups of natural resource users, and especially disadvantaged groups such as women or ethnic and religious minorities, are rarely capable of defending their interests and concerns with competence and forcefulness through avenues and systems too often defined and controlled by outsiders. To be sure, however, if they wish to participate effectively in negotiation processes, they need to do so. In other words, they need to "organise themselves." What does it mean? Three main components of a generic organising process (not necessarily in the given order) may be particularly important and will be discussed here:

- acquiring specific capacities (e.g., to attend meetings, to negotiate, to be recognised as a legal entity, to survey natural resources, to monitor biological diversity, etc.);

- developing an internal agreement on their own values, interests and concerns about the territory or natural resources at stake; and

- appointing a representative to convey such "internal agreement" to the negotiation forum.

In all these components, some external support may play an important role, and the Start-up Team is well placed to assist in the process. To begin with, however, it is important to respect the cultural differences at play. "Organising" is a different concept for different peoples and situations (see Box 5.8) and particularly so when done through traditional procedures (e.g., via extensive rounds of community consultations). In the mid-nineties, an IUCN-supported project in East Africa learned this at its own cost. It assumed that the presence of two local Maasai in the round of discussions leading to an agreement over the Ngorongoro management plan was equivalent to the participation and consent of their whole community. It was not! A wave of protests followed the approval of the plan, which was in fact rejected by the Maasai communities. More than the specific content of the plan, the Maasai protested about the lack of respect during the negotiations. The specific requirements (e.g., time and communication support) needed to gain their collective consensus and approval had not even been foreseen, let alone provided.

Of course, if indigenous peoples have reservations about the ways of other social actors, other social actors have reservations about the ways of indigenous peoples. In this sense, questions and dilemmas sometimes arise regarding democratic procedures and the respect of human rights (gender equity, age equity) within different cultural settings. In some societies "… people do not have opinions because… it would be offensive towards village elders if they had."[32] These dilemmas are sensitive and should be approached in a case-by-case manner.

> "Organising" is a different concept for different peoples and situations.

Box 5.8   Organising of the Maya, between tradition and modernity
(adapted from Gramajo, 1997)

The current local organisation and representation mechanisms in the rural Altiplano of Guatemala are fairly complex. They include: the Communal Sessions (i.e., village-level discussion and decision-making forum); the Council of Elders (whose decisions on regional and natural resource issues uphold the cultural integrity of the community and are final); the Community Leaders (including Mayan professionals from diverse sectors); the Auxiliary Municipality (which bridges community interests with state institu-

---

[32] Engberg-Pedersen, 1995.

tions, holds significant responsibility in natural resource issues, and is highly accountable to the locals); and the Local Protection Committees, dedicated to conservation. In the Communal Sessions, community officials are elected, projects are approved and conflicts are resolved. No one in the community makes individual decisions on issues that are within the competence of the Communal Sessions. The resistance of the Maya K'iché has been one of principle and integrity, validated by experience. Gradually, Totonicapán is consciously reaffirming its autonomy and proven ancestral practices.

Acquiring specific capacities

We understand the term "capacities" as to encompass the attitudes, knowledge, skills, resources and social recognition that allow a social actor to take part meaningfully in the CM process. This covers an ample variety of issues and themes, from the trivial to the lofty. If a group lacks the resources to travel to a meeting, or lacks a good translation of the discussions into its own language, it would do it little good to have been identified as a "legitimate actor" or to possess unique local knowledge of the natural resources at stake. Vice versa, if the group does not master the basic conditions for conservation of the natural resources, no amount of rhetorical skills in meetings will compensate for the fallacies of their misunderstanding.

> "Capacity" encompasses different kinds of attitudes, knowledge, skills, institutional settings and resources [all of which] allows a social actor to take part meaningfully in the CM process.

In general, external support can help, but "local motivation", an attitude that cannot be provided from outside, appears to be an essential condition for success. A good example of this is provided by the village of Som Thom, in Cambodia, which responded in an exceptional way to the opportunity of a local UNDP initiative. The village demonstrated great willingness and motivation to develop a management plan for the village forest, developed the plan and was soon thereafter granted forest management rights. In contrast, other villages in the same province of Ratanakiri demonstrated far less motivation and failed to acquire similar rights. Likely, the motivation of Som Thom was a function of community solidarity and the willingness to act together, while most other villages had adopted more individualistic livelihoods approaches, perceived by them as "more modern". Som Thom could also benefit from the energy and activism of a powerful local leader. Interestingly, a difference in attitude (motivation and willingness to act) proved essential for both effective NRM and the acquisition of NR rights.[33]

A variety of social actors, including governmental agencies, benefit from or even require support to build their capacity towards more participatory forms of natural resource management. This may comprise changes in their structure, organisational culture, attitudes, skills and work programmes. In Nepal, bold pronouncements of "handing over forests to village user groups", with forest officials working as extension agents rather than control and command agents, remained for a long time mere statements on paper. The agency staff needed re-orientation towards understanding people's needs and rights, appreciating their knowledge and practices, and grasping the social complexities of community rules.[34] A thorough analysis in the conflict-ridden Rajaji National Park, in northern India, realised a similar type of shortcoming and tackled it directly with capacity-building programmes for agency staff.[35] In Australia, when the Barrier Reef Marine Park Authority looked for key actors with whom to discuss the management plan of the park, they found that conservation groups had already formed their umbrella organisations but the tourist operators had not. The Authority called for a major

---

[33] McCaul, 2000.
[34] Chhetri and Pandey, 1992.
[35] Rathore, 1997.

conference of tourist operators and supported them to form an association.[36]

Regarding the capacities of local communities, many NRM projects have specific initiatives developed as part of their field operations. In Sri Lanka, for instance, a project supported the development of Community-Based Organisations (CBOs) for natural resource management and development purposes. Soon, however, it recognised that the CBOs were not entirely able to carry on their agreed tasks. Specific initiatives were then set up to train the members of the CBOs to gain a more in depth understanding of environmental phenomena, to collect relevant information, to keep systematic records and books, to write proposals and reports, to handle their own field projects, and so on.[37]

Box 5.9   What makes an organisation capable of participating in co-management? The answer of CANARI
(adapted from Krishnarayan et al., 2002)

From its experience in capacity-building for participatory natural resource management in the insular Caribbean, the Caribbean Natural Resources Institute (CANARI) developed a framework for understanding and assessing organisational capacities. The framework includes the following elements:

● World view: a coherent frame of reference that the organisation or group uses to interpret the environment in which it operates and define its place within it. This includes a vision and mission for the organisation, providing a rationale for all other aspects of capacity;

● Culture: a way of doing things that enables the organisation or group to achieve its objectives, and believe it can be effective and have an impact;

● Structure: a clear definition of roles, functions, lines of communication and mechanisms for accountability;

● Adaptive strategies: practices and policies that enable an organisation to adapt and respond to changes in its operating environment;

● Skills: needed knowledge, abilities and competencies;

● Material resources: needed technology, finance and equipment;

● Linkages: an ability to develop and manage relationships with individuals, groups and organisations in pursuit of the organisation vision and mission.

In the experience of CANARI it is the collective sum of these elements that constitutes capacity and that can be rather simply assessed to determine the extent to which the organisation is able to participate meaningfully in management processes and institutions.

Several conservation programmes limit their capacity-building role to "environmental education", often interpreted as "teaching" people about the value of the environment and natural resources around them. This is a limited and limiting interpretation. Understanding the broad ecological picture of one's own environment is indeed important, but equally so is the awareness of the various forces at play (including markets, policies and laws), and the rebuilding, where it has been lost, of the ability to value and manage natural resources on one's own terms. Some "capacity-building" initiatives have taken this path. In Iran, local Baluch and Kurd communities have been assisted to evaluate the problems and

---

36 Graeme Kelleher, personal communication, 1995.
37 Jayatilake et al., 1998.

The first "capacity" they were supported to develop was the capacity to think collectively and develop an internal consensus on what needed to be done. After that, the communities identified their "capacity needs" as they arose....

opportunities of their environment on the basis of their traditional knowledge and skills, decide what they can do and implement what they have decided.[38] The first "capacity" they were supported to develop was thus the capacity to think collectively and develop an internal consensus on what needed to be done. After that, the communities identified their "capacity needs" as they arose (for instance the need to control a few pest species without chemical pesticides, the need to keep clear and detailed financial accountings, the need to develop a project proposal). Because the capacity needs had been identified by them, they had a strong motivation to acquire the relevant knowledge and skills. They asked for what they needed and the supporting NGO responded positively.

As the Start-up Team assists the social actors to organise, it may face a variety of requests for assistance. Certain types of assistance are generally non problematic for the promoters of a co-management process (e.g., financing meetings to select a representative, or travel costs to allow the representative to participate in the negotiations). Other types, however (e.g., supporting the establishment and legal recognition of a new association), imply more continuous and onerous commitments and may take on a political connotation that not all Start-up Teams are ready to embrace.

The Start-up Team should keep in mind that support may be needed for all actors to understand what co-management is and entails. In this sense, orientation sessions, time for questions and answers and exchange visits to sites where CM is already in operation are extremely valuable. As participatory management initiatives become more common throughout the world, local expertise is developed, recognised and better utilised. This is especially true for the countries of the South, where field-based networking, exchange of experience and mutual support amongst actors involved in co-management initiatives have proven powerful avenues for building local capacities and achieving environmental and social results (see Box 5.10). A relatively costly but powerful option is to organise exchange visits between communities, at least one of whom has taken interesting and possibly unusual action for natural resource management. This has proven enormously effective not only to increase the knowledge of the relevant communities, but also to improve their attitudes.[39] As a matter of fact, local/ national and regional networks have scaled up impressively the capacity of civil society to affect their broader social context and, in particular, to influence national policy for the management of natural resources.[40]

---

[38] This was part of a UNICEF-supported project implemented by the NGO CENESTA.

[39] Chatelain et al., 2004.

[40] Konaté, 2003.

Box 5.10   Collective Learning on Collaborative Management of Natural Resources in
the Congo Basin
(adapted and updated from Nguinguiri, 2000)

Since the 1980s, several countries of the Congo Basin have experimented with co-management (CM) approaches towards the sustainable management of their natural resources. Their main challenge has been "how to do it?". GTZ, the IUCN Regional Office for Central Africa and the IUCN/ CEESP Collaborative Management Working Group have been working together to provide answers to the question. Since 1998, they supported a partnership among relevant field initiatives in the region, which called themselves Learning Sites (sites d'apprentissage). Ten such sites agreed to become involved in a joint process of "learning by doing".

At the beginning of the initiative, the personnel from the Learning Sites were not enthusiastic. They just saw a further demand of time and efforts placed upon them. Through time, however, they realised that they were acquiring a variety of capacities (information, skills, tools and methods, new ideas and various forms of specific support) that helped them clarify their work strategy and improve their performance. After the first meeting of the network of Learning Sites and the first technical assistance missions, the perception of the members in the network became overwhelming positive. After the first two years, the participants in the initiative demanded its continuation. After the completion of the fourth year, they promoted further joint initiatives, this time focusing on basic training for natural resource management and involving all key professional schools in the region.

Regular meetings among social actors from the Learning Sites have been the key steps in the group learning process. Each meeting was dedicated to a specific CM topic, such as "negotiation processes", "conflict management", "monitoring and evaluation", "social communication", etc. A typical meeting started with the Sites presenting their experiences on the specific topic, followed by group discussion to identify common problems and explore possible solutions. The presence of resource persons helped to fill the gaps and illustrate relevant methods and tools. The meetings usually included a field visit and some joint planning sessions, through which the participants acted as consultants for each other. Through these regular meetings, a relatively stable network of CM practitioners developed a common language to discuss co-management issues and a "regional vision" of what CM entails– a vision re-discussed and pursued in practice in each Learning Site.

The achievements of the initiative include:
- better understanding of key process steps of CM;
- better and more widespread knowledge about it (also through the diffusion of dedicated publications);
- broadly improved attitudes (more confidence of practitioners in the CM process, enhanced mutual trust and willingness to dialogue among local stakeholders, aroused interest among key actors and institutions in the region);
- greatly enhanced skills among the members in the network (for instance in terms of stakeholder analysis, social communication, facilitation of negotiation, participatory evaluation); and
- concrete field results, such as effective negotiation processes, multi-party agreements and new pluralist management organisations.

It is highly desirable that similar initiatives are repeated in the future, hopefully with improvements deriving from the lessons learned in the Congo Basin. For instance, while the Congo Basin network was nearly exclusively constituted of project staff and government officials, it would have been more effective to include more representatives of local actors, and especially of local communities.

In summary, "capacity-building" initiatives in co-management processes can support social actors to:

- understand what co-management entails and how a social actor can organise to participate;

- master knowledge and information about the natural resources at stake, including knowledge of existing environmental problems, needs, constraints and opportunities (comprising the costs and benefits of various management options), and assess relevant change;[41]

- become a socially recognised (legitimate) actor (this may imply taking on a legal identity);

- deal effectively with agenda of meetings, records, accountings, financial reports, proposals, etc.;

- communicate clearly with other social actors, listen to them with an open and respectful attitude and think afresh, including about new management options on the basis of various points of view;

- participate in preparatory and NRM negotiation meetings through covering the costs of travel and accommodation.

Two last considerations. First, the capacity building process is inevitably time-consuming and effective results may take years to unfold, a fact that clashes against the shorter time spans of usual "projects". Second, while external support is often important to stimulate new capacities and action, care should be taken that such support, for instance to attend meetings and training sessions, does not become an "end in itself". Too many meetings are attended by people interested only in the payment of honoraria and generous "per-diems" offered by international organisations eager to show that people "participate" in their initiatives.[42] In some cases, such people may be nevertheless exposed to debates and new knowledge, and benefit despite their lack of care. More often, however, the meetings whose participants are not specifically motivated to attend are shallow and ineffective. In the long run they may even prove counterproductive, as they "take the space" that could be productively occupied by other types of discussion platforms and organisations.

Developing an internal agreement on their own values, interests and concerns about the territory or natural resources at stake

A social actor has a "place" at a negotiation table insofar as it presents the coherent point of view of a cohesive unit or group. In Chapter 4 we discussed an exception to this rule, i.e., the so-called "multi-cultural character" of stakeholders (meaning that a social actor may speak at times with one voice but, at other times, may need to split into different points of view). In general, however, any social actor willing to participate in a negotiation table needs to form its opinion on the values, interests and concerns to take forward and on the desired outcomes of items in the agenda of the negotiation. For this, it needs to organise internally, with mechanisms to exchange ideas and arrive at a common position. Ideally, this will be a consensus position, implying a well-informed constituency and, as necessary, a rich internal debate. More commonly, this will be a majority or an expert position, with one form or another of voting or expressing a preference. Traditional decision-making systems may rely on either of the above. For instance,

...a social actor may speak at times with one voice but, at other times, may need to split into different points of view....

---

41   On this, see especially Sections 5.1 and 5.2 of this Chapter.
42   The World Bank has often been singled out in this respect.

the internal organising of the Maya K'iché in Guatemala relies heavily on collective consensus, indirectly informed by the ancestral values preserved by the community elders (see Box 5.8). The Anishinabe Ojibwa in Canada, on the other hand, keep their elders in direct and full control of decisions on the use of natural resources.[43] Traditional communities in Laos value both community consensus and leadership experience (see Box 5.11).

Box 5.11 Community internal consensus on fishing rules prior to the co-management workshop found essential in Lao PDR
(adapted from Baird, 1999)

In Khong district, in the southern province of Lao PDR (see Box 3.11), the communities interested in the aquatic resources of the Mekong usually learn about the possibility of setting up a co-management scheme from neighbouring villages, friends and relatives, or from government officials. If their leaders are in agreement, they write a short letter to their district authorities, who later come to visit and assist in the process of developing a co-management plan. The communities are never pressured into establishing management regulations. They are only assisted upon request.

The process begins with the village and its leaders asking for the relevant government permission. During the time in which the permission is being sought, extension workers remain in contact with the community and provide information and advice on the process to come. They also collect information on what village leaders expect to achieve and encourage them to consult with their community.

The leaders call their fellow villagers to meetings and explain the kinds of regulations previously established by other villages in Khong and how the implementation and enforcement of those regulations have worked out. On the basis of those experiences, they then draft a list of regulations that the community can agree to respect. Such advance discussions are important, because villagers feel more comfortable if the regulations are discussed and debated within the community before any outsider is involved. The villagers need ample time to carefully consider the implications of establishing particular rules. In this sense, co-management is not as much about regulations being established as it is about the communication and collaboration process through which such regulations are identified and agreed upon. Usually about a month or more is allowed after the extension workers visit a village before a formal co-management workshop is organised in a community.

Unfortunately it is not uncommon that the position of a "social actor" is determined not by a well informed internal consensus but by the opinion of one or more persons in power within the group. In some cases, the opinions expressed in the name of the group may even be contrary to its best interests (see Box 5.12).

Box 5.12 The elusive nature of the "fishing sector" in Galapagos
(adapted from Heylings and Bravo, 2001)

The Special Law of Galapagos stipulates that artisan fishermen are to be represented in the Management Board of the reserve. In turn, all individual bona-fide fishermen need to be "organised", i.e., registered as a Cooperative. After the promulgation of the Law, a moratorium was established for the registration of new fishermen, with the intention of identifying and legitimising the existing members of the sector, together with their entitlements to the resource. This was to strengthen their sense of common identity, responsibility and ownership of the marine resources. Paradoxically, the announcement of the formal process of registration gave rise to an uncontrolled increase in the number of mem-

---

[43] Peckett, 1996.

bers registered in the Cooperatives. The number of registered members nearly doubled between 1998 and 2000, reflecting an influx of both new migrants from outside and of opportunistic islanders previously unconnected with fisheries. This was the consequence of particular concurrent factors, such as the reopening of the extremely lucrative sea cucumber fishery, but also of the poor dialogue within the fishing sector and the dominance of the views of people with vested interests.

A traditional fishing community with a strong sense of property rights over the local resources would have used the registration process to legitimise and protect their acquired custodian and ownership rights. The Galapagos fishing Cooperatives, however, were young, weak, and several of their leaders vulnerable to corruption and political interests. New members– many of whom with no local fishing background but plenty of political and economic influence– were registered without proper procedure. Such newly registered members were not part of the process that had defined the common vision for managing the Marine Reserve and their interests focused on privileged access to lucrative resources rather than on an integrated system of sustainable fisheries. This led to profound divisions within the fishing sector and has had a destabilizing effect on the leadership of the different Cooperatives.

Since 1999, different agreements were reached between the fishing sector and the relevant authorities as to how to rectify this situation, but none succeeded. Fortunately, in February 2001, at the last negotiation of the Participatory Management Board on the annual fisheries calendar, a consensus was reached on the fact that the management of fisheries was dependent on "a system of closed access". A large group of legitimate fishermen are committed to this. The challenge is now dealing with those who consider to have acquired some "rights" in the recent registration frenzy and marginalise those among the fishermen leaders who still put personal advantage above the collective advantage of their sector.

Another common occurrence are political representatives elected by a fairly large electoral college being requested to "represent" their constituency for very specific management decisions, which chiefly concern only a minority of people in their college. The risk, in those cases, is that the interests of such minorities are not fairly represented. For instance, in the United Kingdom the politicians who represent urban zones (who in Europe usually outnumber those representing rural zones) are the dominant voice with regard to protected area issues.[44] The people living in and/ or next to protected areas find it hard to get their voice heard and their rights, needs and aspirations taken into account, despite being the people most directly and powerfully affected. The process is deeply frustrating for many of them.

Urban people need protected areas as recreation space. Tourism companies depend on growing numbers of visitors and are a powerful lobby. The media tend to concentrate on issues that affect large numbers of people and thus, when reporting on protected areas, they side with urban interests. It is only too understandable that politicians cater to the same interests and pay much less attention to the views of smaller rural communities. Yet, this can become a serious obstacle to good protected area management, as the concerns of the local communities may never get properly discussed or solved. For example, the statutory bodies in charge of national and regional protected areas in Italy include, as representatives of the interested local communities, the majors of the municipalities that comprise such communities within their administrative territories. Not uncommonly, these are large urban municipalities, the interests of whose residents may end up prevailing. Even in the case of innovative forms of protected area governance, such as the Parcs Naturels Régionaux of France (see Box 7.10 in Chapter 7), the

---

44 Inglis, 2002.

politicians elected in large electoral colleges are considered fair representatives of local interests. This may or may not be true.

The above considerations touch the nerve centre of the difference between participatory and representative democracy. Ideally, a social actor willing to participate in co-management should develop an internal debate and a consensus position with regard to the specific NRM issues at stake. Elected professional politicians, however, rarely engage their constituencies in the analysis of specific issues, e.g., what is needed to manage a territory or body of natural resource. More often they simply assume management responsibilities– i.e., they take and enforce decisions– even when they hardly master the relevant implications and subtleties.[45] Such failures in internal organising are one of the least analysed and most insidious problems in co-management, which ultimately corrupt and spoil its meaning and value. In a nutshell, "participatory management needs participatory roots!", i.e., some measure of effective dialogue, discussion of issues and participatory democracy internal to all relevant social actors.

In a nutshell: "participatory management needs participatory roots!" i.e., some measure of participatory democracy internal to the relevant social actors.

Appointing a representative to convey the "internal agreement" to the negotiation forum

The social actors who wish to take part in the negotiation process need to identify and appoint one or more individuals to represent them vis-à-vis other actors (see also Box 2.5 in Chapter 2). For some (e.g., an established government agency, a cohesive traditional community, a well organised modern municipality), this may require little effort. For others (e.g., a heterogeneous community or a resource user group some of whose members may be in internal competition), this may require a major investment in time and resources and the Start-up Team may be requested, again, to provide support.

In some cases a split between the NRM opinions and views of community members and those of the people officially in charge of representing them becomes apparent. For instance, a resource management committee was established in the 1990s to act as liaison between the Djawling National Park (located at the delta of the Senegal river, in Mauritania) and the local administrative authorities. The committee was staffed with the "intellectuals" of the area, namely the local teachers who had left their villages many years before for teacher training. Having lost contact with the local ecosystem and having being imbued with a concept of "development" as something measured in cubic metres of concrete, these people were visceral against the national park. Instead of the park, they supported the construction of a dam, despite the fact that such a dam would entirely destroy their delta ecosystem and traditional landscape. In contrast, most local villagers, who made a living from the resources of the delta, could see the logic of what the park management was trying to do to maintain the integrity of the ecosystem, and agreed with it.[46]

The Iranian NGO CENESTA, which promotes community-based sustainable livelihood initiatives, devised a simple and ingenious way to help communities to identify who should take on a role on behalf of the whole community (e.g., a representative for a given forum, a project animator, etc.). They call for a general meeting in which people are encouraged to brainstorm on the main qualities and characteristics of an ideal person to take on the requested role. Views are

---

[45] Bebbington, 1998.
[46] Hamerlynck, 1997.

… a simple and
ingenious way to
help communities to
identify who should
take on a role on
behalf of the whole
community….

elicited, listed, discussed and agreed upon through open discussion. On the basis of the list of criteria thereby produced (including, for instance, factors such as "knowledge of the local NRM situation", "personal commitment to the wellbeing of the community", "honesty", "negotiation skills", "maturity and stature to represent the community", or even "having lots of children and needing a job") the group is later invited to list, discuss and prioritise the names of "individuals who fit the criteria" and could effectively play the requested role. In this way, the community is freed from having to choose the most obvious persons, such as the ones who usually deal with government officials, the relatives of the chief, etc.

Learning from the experience of CENESTA, it should be stressed that the criteria to identify a representative need to be genuinely identified by the community or interest group, and not by the Start-up Team, and that the decision should be taken in a congenial atmosphere, free from rush and coercion. Time is also needed to gauge various factors, and the community or group, ideally, would have time to discuss in detail the pros and cons of various options on its own. An alternative to this method is the voting system, open or secret. Usually, this is framed by the obliged choice among self-appointed candidates, and the group does not have the time to openly discuss the pros and cons of different choices. The choice of representatives of a rather large community of people can be the fruit of delicate compromises and needs to pay attention to a variety of considerations, including respect for gender, ethnic and tribal differences (see, for instance, Box 5.13, as well as Box 2.4 in Chapter 2).

Box 5.13   Twelve clans of a tribe need twelve representatives… not ten and not fifteen!

In the 1980s, a project supported by UNDP was engaged in the promotion of sustainable livelihoods among numerous communities in the Darfur region of Sudan. As part of the initiatives supported by the project, the Beni Helba tribe of Baqqara (cattle herding) pastoralists needed to be represented in a decision making body for the purpose of a tribal ceremony. Since a history of interventions from the government had weakened the tribal system of governance, the tribe at first decided to convene a representative from each of the forty communities into which many of the tribespeople had settled. Once convened, this group was named "The Committee of the Forty" and was clearly at odds with the normal organisation of the tribe which consisted of twelve clans.

As if by magic, as soon as the Committee of the Forty met, it became clear to everyone that it would not work. They decided to select from among themselves a small group of twelve representatives to handle the work of deciding, planning and organising the events more efficiently, and, lo and behold, each of the twelve representatives happened to be from one of the twelve clans of the Beni Helba tribe! Things went very smoothly from then on until the tribal chief, who was a bit dishonest, convinced them that if a group of twelve could work better than forty, then a still smaller number would do even better. No sooner had he appointed a few of his cronies to handle the considerable money that had been collected from the whole tribe, than the money disappeared. This caused a great uprising against him, and the Grand Council of Elders of the whole tribe met with a single agenda item– to start impeachment procedures for the chief. Only when the existing chief made a public apology and promised to never indulge in such behaviour again, and restored the Committee of the Twelve, did the Grand Council of Elders agree to forgive him and restore him to his chiefdom. All went smoothly afterwards!

In general, identifying a representative involves finding an effective compromise between two interpretations of what "participation" entail. As mentioned above, representative democracy sees people's participation as mediated by political leaders, usually professional politicians (in the best of cases locally elected and in touch with their constituencies; in the worst, imposed by party politics and detached from local sentiments and aspirations). Participatory democracy stresses the direct involvement of communities and individuals through their active roles in a variety of social duties. In this latter sense, representation is a more complex process, and each act of representing a group is backed by prior discussions, collective analyses, and even referendum-based decisions. The specific person assigned the representation role is also more likely to rotate though time. Some professional politicians are actually endorsing this mode of operation in their work.

The Start-up Team should be supportive but "hands off" with regard to the choice of representatives of each social actor. Before representatives are admitted at the table of negotiation, however, it should make sure of a few points. Is each representative actually an agreed spokesperson for the group he or she is representing? Can this be independently verified? Also, what reporting mechanisms are in place to ensure that the local communities or other represented social actors will receive comprehensive information on the participatory management processes and decisions? If the CM process is done in isolation from the grassroots, the result may be their disaffection or even their opposition to the decisions taken in their name. A genuine participatory process accommodates the grassroots involvement in the discussions through their representatives, but also allows enough time for the information to flow among the relevant peoples and to be internally discussed before decisions are taken. This can and should be explicitly monitored in the co-management process.

A genuine participatory process accommodates the grassroots involvement in the discussions through their representatives, but also allows enough time for the information to flow among the relevant peoples and to be internally discussed before decisions are taken.

5.4 Preparing for the negotiation meetings: procedures, rules, logistics and equity considerations

Once the key relevant actors are organised to take part in the negotiation, the CM process is quite advanced. The next task for the Start-up Team is to identify a preliminary set of procedures and rules about how the negotiation should be held– an advice charged with cultural and political implications. The task also involves the organisation of the logistics for the meetings.

Procedures, rules and logistics

Traditional societies have arrays of procedures for negotiating agreements, such as discussions of facts among community elders or in larger gathering in the occasion of a religious festivity or a market fair. Many of those procedures are convivial, simple, effective and inexpensive. A Start-up Team in tune with the relevant social actors will know about the existence of such procedures, and eventually agree on linking the natural resource management negotiation with appropriate, culturally-specific institutions and events (see Box 5.14).

Box 5.14 Traditional jirga as a model for "roundtable" meetings
(adapted from Halle, 2002; G.N. Jamy, personal communication, 1997)

In the northwest province of Sarhad, Pakistan, at the border with Afghanistan, China and Russia, a new participatory process has been reaffirming the old tradition of Jirga for nearly a decade. Jirga is the customary tribunal system of the Pathan people, where a community gathers in an open space before its elders to discuss important matters and resolve conflicts. Applying this method to discussing environmental issues gave birth to cross-sectoral "roundtable" consultations on issues of environmental sustainability in Sarhad.[47] In a roundtable the representatives of various social actors– including government sectors, NGOs, media, women's groups, academics, and the private sector– sit together to discuss issues of economy, environment and development. There is no permanent Chair, and no special recognition of power positions. Facilitation is on a rotational basis, usually carried out by one of the participants. The roundtables have the important recognition of the government, which "notifies" the expected participants to attend the gathering, but, at least at the beginning, they encountered some major resistance. The resistance was due to their non-hierarchical process and was only partially mitigated by the fact that the model was related to the local tradition (the model is also similar to the model of roundtable consultations practiced in Canada).

Sarhad is a tribal area where the Pathan people continue to practice customary law, conserving a strong sense of collective decision-making. Consultation is the basis of Pathan society. Many Pathan people function through a non-monetary economy and harvest the same resources on a rotation system. The province encompasses barren mountains that, because of various causes, have suffered heavy deforestation. There is little agriculture and industry, with activities principally based on live-

---

[47] To fit local customs more appropriately those could have been called "roundrug" discussions.

stock rearing. Land ownership is in the hands of a few, and the small landholders are usually pastoralists. The literacy level is low, except among the non-Pathan Pakistanis. Sarhad is unique in that it has the largest refugee population in the world (more than 40% of the residents of Peshawar are actually Afghan refugees), a fact that exercises a strong influence on the economy, business and transport sectors. The official language is English, with Urdu and many others spoken.

The initial roundtable gatherings took place in the mid nineties and were held every 3-4 months, each including 40-45 members, some of whom in charge of bridging ideas from and to villages and grassroots communities. Special efforts were made to recruit educated women to communicate with village women who, by custom, do not talk to men who do not belong to their families. The groups generated ideas, discussed issues, made recommendations, and reached consensus on strategies for action, on which they reported back at the following meeting. Written inputs were submitted to the roundtable members in the meeting interim periods. Overall, the roundtable process proved inexpensive, as the costs incurred were only the venue and travel/ accommodation for the participants. Round tables usually took place in the capital city of Peshawar, with rotating venues.

A key to trust-building in the Jirgas on environment was the fact that meetings did not to start by tacking controversial issues, but rather with discussing positive topics, such as exploring what is involved in a conservation strategy. One of the most productive effects of the round tables is that they led to changes of attitude among government officials. In the presence of the press and NGOs, the government had to make concrete efforts to take on a protagonist role, and, as a direct result of trust-building, it invited to meetings some of the social actors and sectors that were formerly excluded from decisions. The visibility promoted transparency, as decisions could no longer be taken behind closed doors. This is particularly significant for Pakistan, where the communication gap between government and civil society tends to be large. In the Jirga meetings people began to see that relevant actors are not necessarily juxtaposed in their aims, that decisions need not to be taken in isolation, and that, gradually, civil society can affect governance issues. Concurrently, the NGO sector was also gaining strength. At the end of each session, the participants made an assessment of the proceedings. The collected assessments were reviewed at the beginning of each year, for an inventory of lessons learned to refine the process.

In the mid-1990s, two of the 22 districts in Sarhad had roundtable processes in place to discuss their district strategies. In 1996, six specific roundtables were initiated, all with environment and conservation as an underlying theme, but each with a distinct focus: Environmental Education; Industries; Agriculture; Urban Environment; NGOs; and Communications. Later, a roundtable on Cultural Heritage and Sustainable Tourism was added, as well as 2 specific ones for the Chitral Conservation Strategy and the Abbottabad Conservation Strategy. In 2002, the roundtables are a broadly accepted norm of public decision-making in Sarhad and have also being adopted in Balochistan and Northern Areas provinces. Some topics, such as Forestry, have proven extremely difficult to handle, as the Forest Department, with some support from the military government, resented what it perceived as a threat to its authority. After a long delay due to such resistance, the Forestry roundtable has been only recently notified in Sarhad. The roundtables on Industries and on Agriculture, on the other hand, have been particularly active, while the ones on Environmental Education, Communications and the Cultural Heritage exist but appear dormant. An important lesson from the experience of the roundtables is that they require a clearly defined role to fulfil– best if including a realistic policy agenda. The issue of leadership and support is also critical as the roundtables are rarely self-propelled and need some on going facilitation and incentives. In all, however, roundtables have proven to be a useful and creative vehicle. They reinforced the concept of participatory decision-making, even though their policy influence remains somehow limited.

In some cases convivial gatherings may not be sufficient for negotiating a fair and sustainable NRM agreement. This is especially true when the relevant actors do not share the same cultural backgrounds, values, attitudes and habits. A handshake equivalent to a sacred pact for some may just be a pleasant discussion of possibilities for someone else. Some people may not speak the same language, both literally and metaphorically, in the sense that the meaning of terms and concepts may need a careful "translation" between them. There may also be large power gaps or unsettled conflicts among the social actors, so that people may not feel comfortable or even safe, to volunteer their views and expose their interests and concerns.

In such cases, the Start-up Team would better take a pro-active role and propose a schedule of meetings, some rules and procedures for participation, and some professional support to facilitate the negotiation. The relevant actors could well discuss and modify such proposed rules and procedures but it is important that an entity trusted by all parties takes the initiative to plan in detail at least the first meeting among the relevant actors. To begin with, an agreement should be obtained on the participants, agenda, place, date, hour, working language, languages in which translation will be available, logistics and facilities necessary for the meeting that will launch the CM process (see Checklist 5.2). The Start-up Team is best placed to propose such procedures and obtain an agreement upon them.

Checklist 5.2 Clarifying the procedures and logistics for the negotiation meetings

● Who will need to be present at the negotiation meetings? (Who are the main relevant actors in NRM in our specific context? Have all been contacted? Have we missed anyone so far? Can new participants "volunteer" to attend? What are the procedures for new "relevant actors" to be accepted?)

● The representation shall be formal (written affidavit) or accepted also in informal ways? (The appropriateness of a written affidavit should be gauged according to the context, including the relative number of literate versus non literate people in the communities.)

● What percentage of the total relevant actors has to be present to declare the meeting valid? (Consider possible coalitions of social actors who may wish to boycott meetings.)

● What language(s) shall we speak? Is there a need for interpreters? (This is a fundamental issue to assure a fair and equitable negotiation.)

● What are the aims of the CM process, as identified by the Start-up Team? Are those well known by the relevant actors? Will those be recalled, discussed and finalised in the first negotiation meeting?

● Who is the convener of the first meeting? How are invitations transmitted? How far in advance of the meeting itself?

● Has the preliminary agenda of the first meeting been transmitted to the relevant actors? Will it be recalled, discussed and finalised during the first meeting? By whom?

● Who will act as Chair of the first meeting? Is there a need for one (or more) facilitator(s)? Could the facilitator be a local person, or should we call for a professional from outside? Is a Chair needed at all, i.e., could the meeting simply be managed by a facilitator?

● Where shall they meet and, at least approximately, when? (Consider seasonal changes in workload of rural communities.)

- Approximately, how many times are the actors expected to meet during the negotiation phase? (This should be communicated during the first meeting)

- How shall people be seated in plenary meetings? (Round arrangements, with or without tables, are generally preferable.) Will observers be allowed? What is the maximum number of people allowed in the main meeting room?

- Are facilities available for smaller meetings of working groups, close to the main meeting room?

- What toilet facilities are available? Are those in good working conditions?

- Are refreshments to be served? Meals? Drinks? If not, can those be found near by the meeting venue? Where will drinking water be made available?

- What is the total budget available to support the negotiation phase? Who provides those resources? When and how will the providers be acknowledged?

- On which basis shall travel costs be reimbursed? If people cannot afford to advance the travel costs, how can such costs be disbursed in advance? Who handles the money?

- Is there a need for chairs, tables, rugs and mats, lamps, boards, paper, cards, felt pens, sticking tape, soft boards, pins, projectors, microphones, standing tables and/ or other materials to support discussions and presentations? Will everyone feel comfortable using those means for presentations? If not, how can cultural sensitivities be accommodated?

- Are special requirements catered for? For instance, for vegetarians, for Ramadan observers, for people needing to stop work for prayers, for people with handicaps, for women in need of someone to care for small children?

- Who is responsible for the smooth functioning of the logistics (e.g., send a reminder to the agreed participants, get the premises opened, cleaned, make sure that light is available if the meeting will last after sunset, etc.)?

All relevant actors should be informed in advance about the proposed agenda for the first of a series of meetings and receive an invitation for their chosen representative to participate in it. The note will make reference to the name and process description already adopted during the social communication events. The goal of the meetings to come may be set quite high, for example a series of meetings "..to understand the main challenges to our natural resources in the next twenty years, and prepare together to face them" or be simple and specific, such as "...to decide together the best fishing rules for the part of the river comprised between village A and village B". It should be specified that substantive issues of relevance to the social actors will be discussed and the main points of the proposed procedures, logistics and rules should be included. Whenever possible, the conveners should be a respected local authority or a governmental agency with local presence and legitimacy, although the Start-up Team could also play that role.

The rules of a negotiation process are cultural rules. This cannot be stressed enough. But, modern societies always include a multiplicity of cultures. How can the process be fair if it risks being culturally alien or imposing for some of its participants? A possible answer is "by embracing cultural pluralism". Cultural pluralism basically sees human beings as cultural beings. Their cultural diversity is recognised and appreciated and their dialogue encouraged. Cultural minorities are protected against conscious or unconscious discrimination and allowed to

Cultural pluralism implies an on-going– and very demanding– "political judgement" exercise.

carry out their life differently from others within a range of permissible diversity that is, for each society, historically determined. Between assimilation and laissez-faire, this third way of cultural pluralism implies an on-going– and very demanding– political judgement" exercise. For instance, an important step of such political judgement involves devising a set of preliminary rules for the negotiation process. The Start-up Team is in charge of that, and should propose such preliminary rules to the relevant actors during their first negotiation meeting. Checklist 5.3 presents an example of a set of rules, which may be appropriate in some situations and quite inappropriate in others, and which should be discussed, revised and eventually approved by all actors involved in the negotiation.

Checklist 5.3 Example of rules for the negotiation process

- all identified relevant actors are invited to the negotiation meetings and participate via formal representatives;

- participation is voluntary but whoever does not come is taken as not being interested in taking part in decisions; however, if more than 40% of the relevant actors are not present for a meeting, the meeting will be adjourned;

- language should always be respectful (people should refrain from insults and verbal abuse) and disrespectful individuals shall not be recognised as legitimate representatives;

- everyone agrees not to interrupt people who are speaking but also no one is allowed to speak about a specific point for more than 3 minutes (or 5 minutes or...);

- everyone agrees on talking only on the basis of personal experience and/ or concrete, verifiable facts;

- everyone agrees about not putting forth the opinions of people who are not attending the meetings (and are not represented officially);

- consensus is to be reached on all decisions and voting should be resorted to in most exceptional cases only;

- "observers" are welcome to attend all negotiation meetings;

- a facilitator will always be present to moderate the discussion and ensure its fairness, but he/ she will never discuss or take side on substantive issues;

- meetings will never last more than 4 hours; evening meetings will always end before or at 10:00 p.m.

Equity considerations

The tasks of the Start-up Team are not only of a practical nature. Indeed, the Team is also the prime guarantor of fairness and equity throughout the CM process. For that, it is never too early to carry out a specific reflection on equity, and on how it can be fostered. The results of such a reflection can be made explicit and incorporated into the rules and procedures of the negotiation.

What does "equity" mean in a co-management process? The question has been examined in some detail in Chapter 2.3. As it was discussed, specific answers depend on specific contexts but, in general, equity can be sought by:

- promoting the recognition of entitlements held by unprivileged groups;

- promoting the recognition of entitlements rooted in valid and legitimate grounds (as defined by the relevant society) versus entitlements rooted in the exercise of some form of power (see Checklist 2.3 in chapter 2);

● promoting a fair share of management functions, benefits and responsibilities among the entitled actors, and a fair negotiation process to decide about it.

Checklists 5.4 and 5.5 offer some concrete examples of how to go about that.

Checklist 5.4   Promoting equity in co-management: some examples and ideas
(adapted from Borrini-Feyerabend et al., 2000)

● disseminating information on the environmental values, opportunities and risks of relevance for all social actors;

● disseminating information on various natural resource management options;

● ensuring freedom of expressing views and organising for action;

● providing support to the social actors, and in particular the weakest actors, to organise (e.g., to build their own capacities, to develop and internal agreement on NRM issues, to develop a fair system of representation);

● promoting a fair setting (forum, platform) to negotiate management functions, rights, benefits and responsibilities; this should be non-discriminatory, follow agreed procedures and be assisted by an impartial and competent facilitator;

● helping the social actors, and in particular the weakest actors, to participate in the negotiation process (e.g., by supporting them to travel, by offering translation service, by providing training in negotiation and conflict management techniques);

● allowing a fair hearing to the "grounds for entitlement" and views put forth by every actor;

● utilising a variety of forms of participation (consultation, advice, technical committees, etc.) to reach the broadest possible mutual satisfaction of all relevant actors;

● utilising a variety of flexible NRM mechanisms (zoning, detailed rules of use, etc.) to accommodate the interests and concerns of different actors;

● promoting a tight proportionality between the management entitlements and responsibilities and the benefits and costs assigned to each relevant actor;

● adopting deliberations by consensus (coupled with fair negotiation rules) among the key relevant actors;

● keeping an open door to new actors who may identify themselves as the discussion develops, and offer to contribute;

● supporting participatory action research, adaptive management and a fair measure of democratic experimentalism (learning by doing), allowing to adjust NRM plans, agreements, organisations and rules on the basis of concrete experience;

● assuring that the negotiated co-management plans, agreements and rules are fairly and effectively enforced.

Checklist 5.5 Evaluating the outcome of a settlement on the basis of its fairness
(from Susskind and Cruikshank, 1987)

● Was the process open to public scrutiny?

● Were all the groups who wanted to participate given an adequate chance to do so?

● Were all parties given access to the technical information they needed?

● Was everyone given an opportunity to express his or her views?

● Were the people involved accountable to the constituencies they ostensibly represented?

● Was there a means whereby a due process complaint could have been heard at the conclusion of the negotiations?

It is also useful to consider that co-management processes can expose the disadvantaged groups to the risks of manipulation and control by the more powerful ones. As a matter of fact, the more advantaged in societies are also likely to be the people best capable of exploiting participatory approaches and participatory management systems. This can only be counteracted by some form of affirmative action, i.e., special support for marginalised groups. In order to promote more just outcomes, the politics at work should be discussed openly. Some steps can be taken to help place the vulnerability of the disadvantaged groups at the centre of concerns (see Checklist 5.6).

Checklist 5.6 Some ideas for truly "levelling the playing field"
(adapted from Edmunds and Wollengberg, 2002)

● inform participants fully about to whom conveners and facilitators are accountable;

● give disadvantaged groups the options of not participating in negotiations (avoid being more "visible" to powerful stakeholders);

● create possibilities far disadvantaged groups to use alliances with more powerful groups in negotiations;

● acknowledge the right of disadvantaged groups to identify "non-negotiable" topics, or items they view as inappropriate for discussion in the negotiations;

● acknowledge that not each group may wish to support fully and unconditionally the agreements to be developed. Encourage stakeholders to express their doubts about impending agreements. View a "consensus" too easily reached as a possible way to mask differences in perspective and discount the input of disadvantaged groups;

● assess the likelihood that external events require revisions in agreements and make provisions for disadvantaged groups to be involved in those revisions;

● approach negotiations as one strategy among several that disadvantaged groups may pursue simultaneously, and in particular help them identify alterative strategies in case the good will of other actors may not last;

- assess the legitimacy of processes, decisions and agreements in terms of the role and implications for disadvantaged groups; for each group participating in negotiations analyze the reasons far participation or non-participation, how groups are represented, and the history of relationships among groups;

- view negotiations as a long-term, iterative process and be ready to monitor impacts and adjust strategies to assist disadvantaged groups accordingly.

Conspicuous differences in privilege and power are quite common between social actors, for instance between governmental agencies and local communities. But local communities are also ridden with internal inequities, based on caste, class, gender, ethnic origin, age groups, etc. These inequities can be significant deterrents to participatory management of natural resources and conservation of the environment as they are of any other democratic process. There are many examples where local communities have tackled this problem on their own, but there are probably many more cases where this has not happened (the inability of lower caste families to secure their own land and the many cases of political and economic discrimination about women are typical examples). Unfortunately, conservation initiatives can exacerbate such inequities[48] and it is only too rare that they may attempt to redress them. Some unusual examples are described in Boxes 5.15 and 5.16.

Box 5.15   Strengthening social actors before the negotiation process: the case of the Baka People in the Dja reserve (Cameroon)

The Dja Game Reserve is situated in the heart of the dense humid forests of Southern Cameroon. It is part of the world network of biosphere reserves and has been declared a World Heritage Site. The management of this reserve affects and concerns several social actors, including the Bantu and Baka residents, the timber exploiting companies, the Ministry of Environment and Forests, and the local administration.

The Baka are pygmies. They are a hunter and gatherer society characterised by nomadic customs. Under the influence of the government settlement policy, some Baka communities have been compelled to settle down in villages located in proximity of Bantu villages. This unprecedented co-existence has perturbed the organisation of the Baka society and modified their customary relations with the Bantu. The settled Baka found themselves obliged to abide by the norms regulating the social relations of the Bantu. Thus, the Baka were deprived of their traditional rights to land and natural resources: the Bantu recognised for them only the right of subsistence. As a matter of fact, the Bantu have a prejudicial image of the Baka. For them, the Baka are inferior people.

It is in such a context that the project Conservation and Sustainable Use of the Biodiversity of the Dja Reserve, financed by the Dutch Cooperation Agency and implemented by the IUCN, decided to promote a co-management process. For that, it appeared necessary to ensure that the Baka would be able to sit at the negotiation table, and that the Bantu would recognise them as a social actor with valid resource entitlements. To this purpose, activities were designed to address both the Bantu and Baka communities. Regarding the Baka, the project facilitated the recognition of the Baka chiefdom by the government administration, the rightful remuneration for Baka work by the Bantu employers, the government's attribution of community forests to the Baka, the self-reliance of the Baka women in the

---

48   Sarin et al.,1998; Raju, 1998.

acquisition of their cooking salt, etc.

At the beginning, the support of the project was geared towards the internal sharing of information and discussion among the Baka themselves about their entitlements and about what they recognised to be the entitlements of the Bantu. As a second step, opportunities for discussion were provided also between the Baka and Bantu communities. The two ethnic groups recognised to be interdependent for a number of reasons, including the practice of barter, which makes them fully complementary with respect to several needs, and the custom of blood pacts, which binds some Baka clans and Bantu families.

The project stood on the ground of this interdependence to promote a dialogue on issues hitherto considered taboo and to bring the Bantu to accept to lose certain prerogatives by ensuring just remuneration to the Baka and by recognising their chieftaincy and their rights to have access to community forests. In this way the project succeeded in bringing both the Baka and Bantu to agree on the daily wages for the Baka who work in the fields of the Bantu. This agreement has been legitimised in a ceremony in 1988, during which the Baka and Bantu delegates embraced each other– a truly remarkable feat in the local context! Unfortunately, the severe scaling down of the operation of the Dja Project in 1999 has all but interrupted the efforts towards the co-management process in the area.

Box 5.16 Towards more gender and equity sensitive representation in local Joint Forest Management organisations
(adapted from Sarin et al., 1998)

Joint Forest Management (JFM) in India represents a radical departure from the tradition of centralised forest management. In less than a decade some remarkable results have been achieved: 16 states have issued JFM orders; large numbers of forest officers, NGOs and village men and women are experimenting with new approaches and relationships; and between one to two million hectares of degraded forests are regenerating under local care. The participatory management institutions in JFM play a mediating role between the forest department and its general body membership. To be able to play this role in a gender and equity sensitive manner, the local institution should be able to articulate and represent the interests of all user sub-groups of a forest area in the partnership agreement.

All state JFM orders, except those of Gujarat and the draft JFM rules of Haryana, use the household as the basic unit of membership for the local institutions. The initial JFM orders prescribed eligibility of only one "representative" per household as a general body member. This automatically denied the majority of women, and some marginalised men acutely dependent on forests, the right to participate in JFM on their own behalf. The rule prevented them from gaining an institutional identity and direct access to all the tangible and intangible resources and benefits available through the new participatory management institutions being promoted. This is so because the one representative is invariably the man who is socially and culturally perceived to be the "head" of the household. Only exceptions are all-women households or households of widows without adult sons.

In order to make JFM more gender and equity sensitive, several changes were suggested in the existing JFM framework and especially in the membership norms of the participatory management institutions. For example, it was proposed that each household be represented by at least two persons, one being male and the other female, and that all states make the presence of 30 to 50 percent women mandatory for completing the quorum for JFM institution meetings. In addition to these proposals, several practical strategies have been being tried out to increase the influence of forest-dependent women and men. For example, gender-separate meetings have been organised, Some women organisations and some local associations and coalitions based on people-to-people processes have been promoted. More women staff are employed in Forest Departments. And some new silvicultural practices, responsive to gender and class-differentiated survival needs, have been developed.

Chapter 6. NEGOTIATING THE CO-MANAGEMENT AGREEMENT AND ORGANISATION

6.1 Agreeing on the rules and procedures of negotiation

Negotiating among social actors is the heart of the co-management process. It is wise to invest as much energy as possible in it, as the co-management agreements and organisations are generally as good as the process that generated them. Typically, the social actors involved in the negotiation face two main challenges. The first one is process-related and concerns "communication" in its richest sense. How can a partnership be developed among people who, besides having different interests and concerns, often do not share the same values, attitudes, capacities, ways of working, reference systems and languages– in a word, people who belong to different "cultures"? This implies overcoming serious communication difficulties, both verbal (co-management meetings have been known to need to accommodate five or more languages!) and non-verbal. And yet, communication difficulties are not insurmountable, and plenty of examples exist of collaborative agreements among groups that, at the beginning, appeared very distant or even incompatible (see Box 6.1). The secret, if one is there, seems to be a combination of determination, time, resources and an encouraging social environment.

> **Box 6.1** Bicultural co-management in New Zealand
> (adapted from Taiepa et al., 1996)
>
> Collaboration between Maori and Pakeha (non-Maori, predominantly of European origin) is a fundamental constitutional requirement of the Treaty of Waitangi. A number of initiatives to involve Maori and Pakeha in co-management have emerged on the west coast of the North Island. Their principles embrace both traditional ecological knowledge and relationships with nature (expressed in Maori tradition as kaitiakitanga) and modern scientific understanding of interconnectedness and interdependence (expressed through the concept of ecosystem, concerns for the conservation of biodiversity and assumption of stewardship responsibilities). The agreements developed under these arrangements recognise the mana (a fundamental Maori concept meaning influence, prestige, power, authority and control) of each iwi (tribe) and give effect to their status as a Treaty partner and traditional kaitiaki (environmental guardians ensuring the mauri or life force) of their resources. The agreements also recognise the responsibilities of statutory agencies that have specialised knowledge in the areas of interest.
>
> One of the innovative steps of these agreements is that they had their first meetings in the local marae (the courtyard in front of the Maori meeting house). These marae-based gatherings, open to the whole community, helped to create a basis for mutual understanding, trust and dialogue. The kawa (traditional protocols followed by each iwi) have much to contribute to the development of effective NRM agreements, starting from putting to use the tradition of dynamic debate and decision making by consensus, and the building of a common spirit through the sharing of meals and spiritual invocations. For instance, such discussions have taken place regarding the traditional harvest of the titi bird, which is locally very important, both as food and for local cultural practices. A joint research project on titi ecology and the impact of its harvesting practices has been developed, including "cultural safety" rules. The contract foresees that Maori people guide the research in consultation with a university research team. The data gathered will be published, but with a delay clause, so that the Maori could meet and formulate their collective view on the research and specific responses, if need be.

The second main challenge is more related to the products of the co-management partnership than to its process. Is it possible for a partnership to distribute the benefits and responsibilities of natural resource management in an efficient and equitable manner, starting from a situation that, quite likely, is neither efficient nor equitable? As described in Chapter 2.1, the starting point of a co-management process may even be an existing conflict, as for the Galapagos Marine Reserve (Ecuador) or the Makuleke land (South Africa). To move from an acute conflict to a peaceful and just situation is a challenge indeed. The learning-by-doing experiences throughout the world summarised in this volume do not provide a recipe for solution, but nevertheless offer several insights. Importantly, for instance, the fairness of the process by which an agreement is developed has lots to do with the quality of its results and overall impact. Some authors refer to this as "procedural justice".[1]

The fairness of the process by which the agreement is developed has lots to do with its quality.

No matter whether the relevant social actors identified by the Start-up Team are many or few, whether they are formally or informally organised, whether they share interests and concerns or are opposed by strongly contrasting positions and values, they need to meet and discuss issues of common concern. The basic ingredients of the negotiation phase are thus:

● the social actors themselves (hopefully well-informed and organised, as described in Chapter 5);

● an agreed place and time where they can discuss (a discussion forum or

---

[1] Pruitt and Carnevale, 1993.

platform);

- some rules and procedures for those discussions (at least suggested); and

- some competent support to facilitate the communication, assist in the negotiation and mediate conflicts, as necessary.

Every negotiation process is unique and needs to respond to the specific conditions and needs at hand. Nevertheless, some broadly similar steps are taken by many processes of negotiation for the management of natural resources. These, which can be taken to represent some "process milestones", include:

- a long-term shared vision (ecological and social) for the NRM unit(s) at stake;

- an agreed strategy to approach such a vision, based on a common understanding of the issues and obstacles that currently prevent the realisation of that vision;

- a specific agreement on how to implement the strategy (usually including a co-management plan for the natural resources at stake and complementary accords, as necessary, to address relevant socio-economic issues, cultural issues, etc.);

- a pluralist organisation set up to implement the strategy and review it, as necessary, on an on-going basis.

Box 6.2   Setting up a partnership to manage a watershed in the USA
(adapted from EPA, 1997)

No one entity alone can solve all the management issues in a given watershed. That is why it is essential to pull together a management partnership. Ideally, this will represent the key interests in the watershed, will be of manageable size and will create many synergies. In the USA such partnerships are common. Some are loosely structured, while others are quite formal. Some are open, while others are closed, meaning they do not allow anyone else to join besides its founding members. Regardless of how they are structured, making partnerships work is challenging and takes commitment. Common tasks that partnerships face include: selecting a leader, ensuring that all the right people are involved, and moving beyond any hostility that may exist among members. A group able to develop its esprit de corps can be very effective indeed.

Partners can include any group that has an interest in the watershed. They may be conservation groups, local elected officials, chambers of commerce, environmental education organisations, local military bases, farm groups, students, senior citizens groups, religious organisations, financial groups, credit unions and land developers, among others. The important thing is to include all the key interest groups so that the partnership can tap into their strengths, increase its credibility, reduce duplication of effort, and make optimal use of limited funds.

To get past the "forming and storming stages," some groups that formed for the management of specific watersheds set their own ground rules. Examples: one group has decided that individuals can complain for only a certain amount of time, after which they must move on; some groups have decided to say that issues that are too divisive will simply... not be discussed! Essential ingredients for effective partnerships include: focusing on common interests, respecting each participant's view point, thanking each other, being willing to learn about others' needs and positions, and building trust.

Experienced watershed co-managers say that one-on-one contact is most effective in eliciting support.

Further, building partnerships takes time and commitment, and once built they need to be nurtured. However, their benefits are clear, as they lead to wider acceptance and quicker implementation of all sorts of initiatives.

The first procedural meeting

The first step of a multi-party negotiation process is an initial collective contact, a gathering or workshop where the social actors meet in a rather formal way. As mentioned in Chapter 5, one of the fundamental tasks of the Start-up Team is the good organisation of this first meeting. Attention should be paid to the venue (a "neutral" forum such as a school building, a community market or a theatre is preferable to a forum that some could see as partisan– such as a church or government office), to the timing (which should be convenient for people with normal working schedules and should strive to accommodate also particular groups, such as women responsible for cooking for their families) and to the seating arrangement (a circular arrangement without hierarchical dispositions, on the ground or around a table, on rugs, mats, or chairs, is usually appropriate). The agenda should be made available to the relevant actors in advance, to allow them time to discuss their views internally.

Procedural questions are usually easier to deal with than substantive questions....

At the beginning, the convenor greets the participants and the members of the Start-up Team introduce themselves and recapitulate the work thus far. It is important to be transparent on who has facilitated and financially supported the Team's work and why. In turn, the representatives of the social actors introduce themselves and explain how their groups have internally organised and identified their representatives. The Start-up Team may then wish to recall and clarify what the CM process is set up to achieve. This is relatively easy when the meeting of the parties refers to a specific mandate, but more elusive when the parties face incomplete or unclear legislation, policy and competencies. Also, the more complex the natural resource unit to be managed, the more vague the situation may be. For instance, some biosphere reserves set up a forum of concerned parties with the mandate of "coordinating", "providing impulse" and "watching over" their evolving situation. If such a forum would pretend to take decisions it would be seen as a sort of "parallel government", which would be politically unacceptable.[2] And yet, a forum of concerned parties may build up its own legitimacy to such an extent that its proposals get to be invariably accepted by the political

...a first meeting in a calm and productive atmosphere is important to establish good working relationships and for the participants to start "owning" the CM process.

---

2   Juan Rita Larrucea, personal communication, 1996.

authorities. With or without an explicit mandate for decision-making, an effective stakeholder forum can influence local land use plans and NRM regulations, the concession of permits, the sharing of costs, benefits and revenues and the orientation of research. In some cases, it can even be asked to develop the technical proposals to be later decided upon,[3] indeed an extremely important way of affecting decisions!

In a first procedural meeting the members of the Start-up Team or a facilitator (if one is present) can illustrate a proposed set of procedures and rules for the negotiation phase (see some examples in Chapter 5, Checklists 5.2 and 5.3) as well as a proposed schedule of meetings. The discussion can then be opened until a broad accord is achieved. In this context, the participants can be invited to state a commitment to fairness and equity in the process. All of them (and especially the professional experts!) can also be invited to agree to a mature, non-paternalist and non-ethnocentric attitude, and to acknowledge the legitimacy of values, interests and opinions different from their own. A skilled facilitator[4] Lay succeed in getting this point included as part of the basic rules for discussion.

At the moment of agreeing upon who shall attend the next meeting, some people may object to the very presence of others and attempt to exclude them. The facilitator can help diffuse these potential disruptive objections by assuring that an inclusive approach at the discussion table does not mean that everyone will equally share in entitlements and responsibilities for natural resource management. It will be the task of all representatives together to identify everyone's role and weight in terms of substantive issues and decisions. Some people may also push to discuss substantive issues well before the procedures and rules are agreed upon. A skilled facilitator will not allow this to happen. He/ she can remind the participants that substantive agenda items will be discussed in future meetings, as the rules need to be agreed upon before the discussion can go ahead in an effective way. A productive and friendly first meeting is an important foothold for the subsequent ones, in which specific and often sensitive problems, needs, resources and opportunities will be identified and discussed.

...the negotiation process will need to make sure that enough flexibility is embedded in the final agreement, so that it can adapt and respond to change.

The facilitator may also remind the participants that for every unit of natural resources there exist a multiplicity of good and poor management options (the terms good and poor referring to the wide range of goals and objectives to be defined by the process), and that conflicts of interest among the social actors are inevitable but, in most cases, manageable. The concerned parties do not even have to agree on the same goals or priorities, provided they can reach a practical compromise. Importantly, in the light of the complexity of ecological and social systems, the best approach is generally one of adaptive management (learning-by-doing). This means that the decisions taken at the negotiation forum should be strictly adhered to until they produce some measurable results, after which they will be revisited and evaluated. On the basis of the evaluation and other intervening change, the decisions could then be adjusted or changed. As a matter of fact, even a satisfactory NRM solution does not remain valid forever, as the surrounding ecological, economic and social conditions do change and management rules and practices need to change in response to them– something everyone has to be prepared for. Flexibility can be embedded in the final agreement through specific monitoring and evaluation procedures (sometimes called "a follow-up protocol") that allow the agreement to adapt and respond to change.

---

[3]   See Box 6.13 in this Chapter.

[4]   Here and in the rest of the Chapter we will use the term "facilitator" with the understanding that the role may be played by one or more external professionals or others, including the members of the Start-up Team.

After the first procedural meeting, there are various possible courses of action, depending on the level of engagement that is being sought. It may be that the first meeting is followed by extensive public consultations lasting several months (this was the case for the Great Barrier Reef Marine Park in Australia[5]). It may be that only two main parties are going to be involved (e.g., an agency in charge of a protected area and a local community) and that substantive matters can be agreed upon in a series of workshops (this was the case for several National Parks in Uganda[6]). Or it may be that months or even years of negotiations are about to begin among a variety of parties (this was the case for the Galapagos Marine Reserve in Ecuador[7] and for the Soufriere Marine Management Area in Saint Lucia[8]). In most situations, if the relevant actors are expected and willing to take an active role in management, a series of meetings and workshops is planned ahead, often beginning with the development of a common vision of the desired future.

The role of the facilitator

Negotiation processes have to be firmly anchored in the culture and mores of the actors concerned. Many traditional societies know extremely well how to negotiate in convivial manners as part of normal life and do not need external facilitators, who may actually complicate rather than ease up matters. In other cases, the members of the Start-up Team are sufficiently various and broadly respected to be able to facilitate themselves the co-management process. An external facilitator may be essential, however, when there are strong power imbalances, unresolved conflicts or communication problems among the concerned parties, when the parties belong to very different "cultural" backgrounds or when there is lack of clarity regarding local authorities and rules. Many societies are today characterised by multiple and competing decision-making systems and actors (e.g., customary systems and legal systems, traditional leaders, state administrators, agency personnel, project advisors) and people can "shop around" among institutions until they obtain the decision favourable to them.[9] These are situations in which positive and lasting agreements are unlikely to generate spontaneously and some external facilitation and the provision of a clear system of reference and rules may be crucial.

One of the key tasks of the process facilitator– whoever is playing that role– is making sure that all the relevant actors express their concerns, that no one dominates the meetings and that the discussion is adequately structured and proceeds towards the shared objectives. The facilitator can also assist in managing conflicts, usually by helping people to move from apparently irreconcilable claims and positions (for instance "we want a road across the forest" and "we want to eliminate access to the forest") into the fundamental interests of the parties[10] ("we want access to the zone north of the forest because it is an important market for one of our major products" and "we want to maintain a viable habitat for this animal species"). This is actually best done when the parties have taken the time to express, listen to and reflect upon their fundamental interests, and have articulated a long-term common vision (see Section 6.2).

---

5 GBRMPA, 1994.
6 Chhetri et al., 2003.
7 Heylings and Bravo, 2001.
8 Geoghegan et al., 1999; Pierre-Nathoniel, 2003.
9 Egeimi et al., 2003.
10 Lewis, 1997.

Checklist 6.1 Qualities and tasks of a good facilitator/ mediator for a co-management process

A process facilitator should be:

● recognised as independent;

● respected by all those involved in the negotiation;

● capable of relating with everyone in the negotiation;

● extremely able to listen;

● calm, insightful and capable of posing the key questions (for example, on the root causes of the various problems and the feasibility of the options put forward);

● capable of eliciting the best out of the participants and helping them to see a different future for themselves and their communities.

Tasks of a process facilitator:

● helping the Start-up Team and the relevant actors to identify and agree upon the rules and procedures of the negotiation meetings;

● being responsible for the logistics of the meetings (e.g., selection of venue, agenda, seating arrangements, translation services, discussion tools, transportation arrangements, etc.);

● ensuring that the process takes place in accordance with the agreed rules (ensuring a comfortable situation in the meetings) and that everyone has a fair chance to participate;

● checking out that the representatives of the social actors truly represent them (e.g., they are not merely self-appointed);

● helping the group to be conscious of itself and of its goals, mission and opportunities;

● refusing to state his/ her opinion on substantive issues and never deciding for the group on substantive matters;

● promoting the best possible communication among social actors, e.g., by re-phrasing points, asking questions, suggesting the exploration of key ideas in depth;

● helping the group to broaden the range of its options and open up to constructive attitudes, for example encouraging and assisting the group members to:

  ▶ talk to each other directly, if this was impossible before;

  ▶ take time to listen to and respect the positions of other groups;

  ▶ raise new points of doubt and self-doubt;

  ▶ clarify and enhance their own perception of the situation and opinions of other participants;

  ▶ bring new information to the attention of everyone;

  ▶ discover points of agreement that promise to be sustainable and deal with them before other contentious subjects.

The facilitator is also called to prevent the process from being unduly determined and run by "partisan politics". Party positions are often rigid stands made for the sake of visibility, and clever politicians are more capable of arousing divisive tendencies than collaboration and agreements on common concerns.

Indeed, this is a sensitive issue. Professional politicians may see the negotiation of an agreement over natural resource management as an excellent opportunity to exploit for their own partisan or private interests. This, for instance, was a recurrent problem in the early stages of the local agreements between park authorities and local communities in Mt. Elgon (Uganda)[11] where some local politicians saw the negotiation forum as an electoral platform. Because of problems like this, some bodies tend to exclude professional politicians from representation roles in the CM process.[12] This is an intriguing and controversial suggestion, hard to achieve in practice. As a matter of fact, many legally-sanctioned CM bodies, such as the pluralist management boards of protected areas in Europe, recognise as representatives of "local communities" only elected political representatives, such as the mayors of the main relevant municipalities.

Fairness, conflicts and power differentials

Politicians or not, it is logical to expect that the parties will be using all sorts of means to advance their interests in the negotiation process. This is inevitable and, given the existing power differentials among people usually engaged at the same forum for negotiation, it seems to present a major and possibly insurmountable obstacle to fairness in negotiation. As aptly expressed by Edmunds and Wollenberg:[13]

"…a truly level playing field is impossible to achieve. Power differences persist, if in no other way than through historical relationships among stakeholders. Rather than assuming that neutral conditions can ever be achieved, we need to assume that we can only work towards this ideal. We need to be vigilantly alert to and deal explicitly with power differences. Instead of assuming we have eliminated or temporarily neutralised political differences within negotiations, practitioners need to acknowledge power relations in negotiations and work actively to increase the decision-making power of disadvantaged groups. […] a more politically sensitive approach to negotiations can yield better benefits for disadvantaged groups."

Indeed, power differentials are a serious obstacle to fairness, but they should be seen in the light of what is happening all over the world outside the enhanced visibility of a pluralist negotiation forum. The existence of an open negotiation platform, the agreement on rules and procedures and the presence of a competent external facilitator are important steps towards guaranteeing at least a measure of fairness in the negotiation even when strong power differentials exist. An experienced facilitator can help the parties take the best advantage of the openness and visibility of the process, making sure that correct behaviour is acknowledged and incorrect behaviour discouraged. The aim is to develop agreements that are as equitable as possible and that do not leave any major social actors out of the picture, humiliated, exploited or treated unfairly. Equitable agreements are desirable per se, and some maintain they may have better chances of remaining valid through time.[14]

One of the important elements to agree upon in advance is what to do in case of

The existence of an open negotiation platform, the agreement on rules and procedures and the presence of a competent external facilitator may be important steps towards guaranteeing at least a measure of fairness in the negotiation process, even when strong power differentials exist among the parties.

---

[11] Penny Scott, personal communication, 1996.

[12] This is the case for the Junta de Manejo Participativo of the Galapagos Marine Reserve.

[13] Edmunds and Wollenberg, 2002.

[14] In the words of Phillips, for instance, "An iron rule" is that "no protected area can succeed for long in the teeth of local opposition." (Borrini-Feyerabend et al., 2002). Others, however, stress that injustice can be sustained for the sake of conservation with remarkable robustness (Brockington, 2003).

serious conflict among the parties, such as blockages in the negotiation, different interpretation of agreements or seemingly unsolvable procedural disagreements. The facilitator may stress that internal consensus-seeking procedures are the first and most promising option. Basically this involves the thorough discussion of the issues and reasons for the parties to uphold their positions, as well as the exploration of any nook and cranny for agreement and compromise. If this is not sufficient to resolve the dispute, a number of possible advisors (individuals or bodies), arbiters and judicial resolution systems can be called to help. Ideally, those would be identified well before disputes arise, as part of a hierarchy of dispute resolution mechanisms agreed upon early in the process.

The facilitator should be well aware of local customs, cultural peculiarities and relevant experiences and institutions, in particular customary ways and institutions capable of managing conflicts, and which could be called in to help in difficult circumstances. Box 6.4 cautions against attempting to understand conflict resolution processes without a sophisticated degree of cultural sensitivity. In Nepal, the Forest Department took nearly two decades to discover that the village-based Panchayats provided more effective and respected forms of conflict resolution among forest users than the western-style law enforcement introduced in the 1970s.[15] In Canada, it has been found that conflicts between the Inuit people and the government biologists could only be resolved through extensive community-based communication efforts and mutual respect. Only if that was present, modern technology could help. A major dispute over the size of a Kaminuriak caribou herd, for instance, was resolved through the use and analysis of videotapes, but this was achieved only when everyone had learned to listen and ensured to the others the full respect of their dignity and a fair share in the final decisions.[16]

Box 6.3   Conflict management– Chinese style
(adapted from Cao and Zhang, 1997)

In China, it is said that management of the forest can never take place without conflicts, both within and among communities. Intra-village conflicts usually take place over the sharing of forest products among members of the same family. Excess want and unfair allocation are the main reasons for the conflicts. The conflict is usually settled within the family with the village committee as mediator. Inter-village conflicts usually have a long history, at times traced to the very first local settlements. Most disputes are about boundaries of control areas, resulting from the changing patterns of village settlements and immigration.

Mr. Li, a former headman of Dongda village, in the Yunnan province (south-central China), explained the way in which Chinese villages deal with conflicts: "Solving inter-village conflicts involves the participation of local government officials. When two villages debate on the ownership of a certain patch of forest land, the neighbouring committees come in for a debate and the local government is requested to send its representative. The discussion is held alternatively in each of the villages– one day in one and the following day in the other. During the discussion, the host village provides food and accommodation for the visiting village committee. The hot debate is always after the meal, not during the meal. Each side presents all the documents and materials supporting their case, even from the pre-Communist period, and the conflict-solving process takes at the most three days. In case the conflict cannot be settled by the discussion, the local government gives a final judgment and ends the conflict."

---

15   Don Gilmour, personal communication, 1996.

16   Snowden, Kusagak and MacLoed, 1984.

Box 6.4   Conflict management– Iranian style

An American anthropologist was doing his doctoral research on conflict resolution in the "bazaar" of Tehran. After several months of work, he was exceeding frustrated and wrote a letter to his thesis advisor. " I've now been preparing to observe this process for 6 months. I've learned the language and have put myself in positions of trust. I've been present at various occasions in meetings where a conflict is expected to be resolved. I turn on my tape recorder, and wait endlessly. These people just keep drinking tea and talking about everything in the world except the issue that is the cause of the conflict to be resolved! Please tell me, Professor, how can I make them talk about the conflict to be resolved, so that I can collect the data I need for my thesis? Help!"

The advisor wrote him that he had just missed the most beautiful way in which they traditionally resolve conflicts: being hospitable and friendly, drinking tea and conversing about all the other things in the world that are not conductive to conflict, until the problem goes away![17]

6.2   Developing and "ritualising" a common vision of the desired future

At the beginning of the substantive negotiations, after the partners have agreed on the rules and procedures to guide the process, one or more meetings can be devoted to establishing a base of common interests and concerns among all the relevant actors. In such meetings, the participants are encouraged to discuss their long-term wishes for the NRM unit(s) at stake, i.e.,the kind of environment, natural resources and living conditions they would like, ideally, to leave to their children and grandchildren. The time frame is usually set to twenty or more years from the present, so that people can free themselves, if at all possible, from pressing needs and current controversies. This is a crucial moment in the development of a co-management setting, as it is the first time in which different values and views come to face one another openly and publicly. One of the most powerful confrontations is likely to take place between "local" perspectives and values, often practical, hard-headed and locally wise, and more "general" and abstract perspectives and values, including scientific and ecological views, biodiversity conservation values and the "development" concerns of national governments and private sector interests.

Acknowledging the existence of such differences, the facilitator can nevertheless help the participants to develop a consensus on a common vision of a desired future, with specific descriptions– as visual and concrete as possible– of the ecological and socio-economic situation in the NRM unit(s). This can be done through visioning exercises, scenario-building or simply through dialogues and broad discussion sessions.[18] Visioning exercises are commonly done in many environments and they can be more or less comfortable for the people involved according to local customs and to the homogeneity of participants. In Ghana, a visioning exercise done at the district level proved that local people– ranging from traditional chiefs to bank officials, from small farmers to transport operators,

---

[17]   John Bennett, personal communication, 1971.

[18]   For a simple guidance to visioning exercises see Borrini-Feyerabend et al. (2000). Many resources are also available in the Internet, for instance at: http://www.sustainable.org/creating/vision.html

from local government authorities to charcoal producers– succeeded to achieve a fairly harmonious outcome. Different people could indeed harmonise their goals and develop a new willingness to work together. This required some work, however, as the original visions of different actors were not entirely compatible. For instance, some actors saw a future centred on industrial development for the district, while others wanted to maintain its agricultural vocation and stressed environmental sustainability. Eventually, a compromise was developed. Interestingly, it was not a minimum common denominator compromise but a specific and meaningful vision agreed by all (see Box 6.5).

Box 6.5 A Vision for Wenchi district (Ghana) as developed by the participants in a multi-stakeholder workshop
(from Borrini-Feyerabend, 2000)

Twenty years from now Wenchi is an exceptionally rich district, including a large, well-planned and functional town. Its economy is based on modern, mechanised, irrigated and biologically sound agriculture, with diversified production for both the export market (cashew, yam, palm oil) and the domestic market (grains, vegetables, legumes, palm oil). Livestock production is centred on stall-fed animals producing manure to fertilise the land, and small poultry farms. Revenues also come from the mining of stone and gold (with great care to prevent environmental damage), some industrial production (e.g., a brick and tile factory making use of a local clay deposit, a textile factory, a soap factory making use of palm oil products) as well as from handicrafts (e.g., pottery) and other tourism activities (there are several hotels in Wenchi, and even an airport).

Agricultural and industrial activities are based on a well-planned zoning of the district and a consciously sought-out diversification of the economy. The Bai dam near Benda is providing the electricity supply for many small processing facilities and some larger ones (cassava chips, cashew and vegetables).

Agriculture and local food sufficiency are sustained by:
● secured access to land of small farmers on equitable leasing and sharecropping systems;

● a vibrant market system, well linked with Ghaneian and foreign buyers, making use of standard weights and measures in the whole district (today not yet available!) and allowing full and free circulation of products and people;

● an excellent road network and telecommunication system, providing farmers with timely information and connection to local and distant markets;

● superb agricultural advice (the Wenchi Farm Institute has evolved into an Agricultural University), including advice on how to grow crops organically and conduct farm-based experimental trials;

● community credit schemes to assist both agriculture and industry;

● great care to protect environmental resources such as soil fertility (e.g., intercropping, crop rotation, use of compost, legumes, farm manure) sustained by long term land leases;

● full literacy of farmers;

● community organisations sharing irrigation facilities, transport vehicles, storage facilities and farming and processing machineries.

The whole Wenchi district is a beautiful mosaic of well-planned farmland, forest patches sustaining a variety of local plants and animals, and human settlements. More than forty forest patches of sacred groves remain undisturbed since times immemorial. The river banks are lined with vegetation and particularly beautiful river sites, including waterfalls, are renowned as tourist attractions. The actual increase in forest extension in the district in the last twenty years has brought about an improved rainfall pattern.

Natural resource management is regulated by the District Assembly. Local by-laws (e.g., for the protection of sacred groves, the collection of non-timber forest products, the collection of poles, the creation of windbreaks, the protection of water bodies, the prevention of bush fires) are proclaimed and enforced by local relevant institutions, which include representatives of traditional leaders, farmers, elected representatives and the government. Private and community-owned tree plantations are scattered all over the district, and trees are also found in most farms. Bush fires are a very rare occurrence caused by lightning, no longer intentionally lit by hunting parties or farmers (slash and burn methods).

Services in health, education, electricity, drinking water, sanitation, markets, etc., are available in all district villages. Everywhere children have access to good primary education and infant and maternal deaths are rare. As a consequence, people have no need to move to town, and enjoy being farmers and living in the countryside. The population of the district is relatively stable, and couples plan their family with the help of safe and effective methods.

The services are sustained by a tax system locally collected and managed by the District Assembly. Decentralisation policies have been in place for many years and have developed effective and transparent form of local government.

Private houses are well built, with effective ventilation systems and often surrounded by gardens. Most cooking stoves make use of liquid pressured gas, which has freed the district from destructive charcoal-production practices. The district hosts many schools and colleges, producing a skilled labour force. Due to improvements in food availability, hygiene, housing and health care, diseases such as malaria, polio and Guinea worm are a memory of the past, while measles, bilharzia and diarrhoeal diseases have become very rare. A health insurance scheme is available in the district.

A distinctive feature of the district is the unique disposition of its people to collaborate. Individuals are ready to work together and many productive follow-up are carried out by community-based organisations (CBOs). This is rooted in the cultural traditions of the various ethnic groups inhabiting the district, such as the nnoboa work solidarity schemes. There are even special events such as an annual festival that has become an occasion for participatory democracy, when people engage together in a variety of planning and organising activities. Other festive celebrations are often held in the communities scattered throughout the district.

People are sensitive towards avoiding all sorts of discrimination (e.g., public structures are accessible to disabled people; women and men have equal access to higher education; relationships among different ethnic groups are cordial). People are generally healthy, wealthy, well educated, satisfied, free to speak their mind and practice the religion of their choice. There is safe and adequate food supply for all. People enjoy a peaceful and good life.

A visioning exercise should not be taken lightly. If done with appropriate preparation and care it is a powerful moment in the life of a community and should be respected as such. Unfortunately, many projects and donor agencies promote visioning as just "another step" in a rapid appraisal exercise, raising hopes and expectations and later failing to respond to them.[19] This is a dangerous pitfall. External actors should refrain from promoting participatory visioning and planning exercises if they do not have the intention of helping the community carry them through, at least in part.

---

19 An example is the donor agency that promoted the visioning illustrated in Box 6.5 but failed to respond to the raised expectations.

In North America, community visioning and scenario building exercises have been practiced for decades with inspiring success. One early example among many is the one of the city of Corvallis in Oregon.[20] A complex visioning process was started there in the late 1980s and involved developing a profile of the community, articulating a statement of community values, analysing major trends affecting the community, preparing alternative scenarios of the future and, on the basis of the results of the prior exercises, developing a final vision statement. Local citizens were involved at every juncture through special "focus groups" (including some of children only), neighbourhood meetings and community-wide forums to examine the alternative scenarios. The final result was compiled in a colourful, tabloid-style vision statement with a feedback form inviting citizen comments, and was mailed to literally every household in the community. The document mailed to everyone included a large, bird's-eye view illustration of the territory, with highlights for foreseen new initiatives. The process lasted well longer than a year but resulted in a vibrant vision that sprouted new activities and initiatives and served as pioneer for many other communities in Oregon.

The social consensus on a vision of a desired future is extremely important for the negotiation of effective co-management plans and agreements. If conflicts and disagreements will surface during the negotiation process, the facilitator will be able to bring everyone back to the vision they developed together. For this, it is useful to record the agreed common vision on a large sheet of paper (or other appropriate support) and pin it on a visible surface at the site of the negotiation. It is also good to transform the vision into a charter of principles or other appropriate form of social contract. In many cases it is also appropriate to develop a drawing, portrait or tri-dimensional map of the vision.[21] When different stakeholders develop their own drawings and show it to one another, they often discover previously unappreciated commonalities.[22] Last but not least, it is important that people feel free to describe their vision in the local language, as local languages are very rich and in translation may lose part of the meaning that a common vision needs to convey (see Box 6.6).

Box 6.6   A vision for Moloka'i (USA)
(from a personal communication by Tarita Holms, 2003)

This is the transcript of the result of a long process in Moloka'i:

"Moloka'i is the last Hawaiian island. We who live here choose not to be strangers in our own land. The value of aloha 'aina and malama'aina (love and care for the land) guide our stewardship of Moloka'i's natural resources, which nourish our families both physically and spiritually. We live by our

---

[20]   Ames, 1997.

[21]   Lightfoot et al., 2002.

[22]   An example from the fishery sector in Chile can be found in www.isglink.org

kupuna's (elders) historic legacy of pule o'o (powerful prayer). We honour our island's Hawaiian cultural heritage, no matter what our ethnicity, and what culture is practiced in our everyday lives. Our true wealth is measured by the extent of our generosity.

● We envision strong 'ohana (families) who steadfastly preserve, protect and perpetuate these core Hawaiian values.

● We envision a wise and caring community that takes pride in its resourcefulness, self-sufficiency and resilience, and is firmly in charge of Moloka'i' s resources and destiny.

● We envision a Moloka' that leaves for its children a visible legacy: an island momona (abundant) with natural and cultural resources, people who kokua (help) and look after one another, and a community that strives to build an even better future on the pa'a (firm) foundation left to us by those whose iwi (bones) guard our land."

As there can be many visions of the desired future for any given environment, the act of choosing one takes on a strong political value. For instance, the Gulf of Fonseca (Honduras) is a Ramsar site. The Bay of Algesiras (Spain) is a biosphere reserve established under UNESCO's Man and the Biosphere (MAB) programme. Such international labels are social and legal sanctions to a vision of a future dedicated to conservation and sustainable development, in the respective cases centred upon artisan fishing and ecotourism. Currently, there are attempts to revisit those visions– attempts that are not getting by unnoticed. The destruction of coastal mangroves for industrial shrimp farming in the gulf of Fonseca (Honduras) and the starting up of oil prospecting in the Bay of Algesiras (Spain) both approved by the relevant authorities but in contrast with what the same authorities had earlier espoused, generated open popular protests in 2002 and 2003. As a matter of fact, an agreed vision of the future, and especially a vision with international recognition and visibility, has good chances of being internalised and defended by the local people. This is beginning to be recognised by communities all over the world. Setting an environment under some form of national and international protection or restriction constitutes an important strategic move to assure a community vision of its desired future. In chapter 4 we discussed the examples of Miraflor (Nicaragua), Alto Fragua-Indiwasi (Colombia) and Kaa-ya Iya (Bolivia).[23]

Box 6.7   Involve the stakeholders and pursue a common vision!
(adapted from Tylor and Woodruff, 1997)

Consultations with relevant social actors were essential in developing a proposal for a marine protected area within the Great Australian Bight. The proposed site includes fishing areas important to the South Australian fishing industry. By involving the affected users and, in particular, the regional fishing industry, Environment Australia managed to develop a credible proposal for a marine protected area, which now enjoys reasonable public support. Valuable lessons were learned in the process. Here are the most important:

● there are benefits in entering the negotiation process without pre-determined outcomes;

● the boundaries of the proposed protected area, as well as the proposed management intentions, need to be negotiated with the relevant resource users;

● a shared vision and common agreement must be rigorously pursued; however,

---

[23] Munk Ravnborg, 2003; Zuluaga et al., 2003; Winer, 2001; Winer, 2003.

● the risks of compromising conservation objectives because of the involvement of resource users are potentially significant.

An agreement is legitimised when it is accepted and recognised as binding not only by the social actors who developed it, but also by society as a whole. The process by which such legitimisation is achieved, however, is different according to the importance of the agreement. A simple local rule is easily accepted and easily undone. A common vision of the desired future of an entire community, instead, is a sort of constitutional agreement. In many cultures this calls for a strong ritual, respected and acknowledged by the whole society. Such a ritual helps raise the common vision to the spiritual and symbolic level, making it valid in the long term and particularly difficult to disavow.

A common vision of the desired future of an entire community… is a sort of constitutional agreement. In many cultures this calls for a strong ritual….

The choice of the appropriate type of ritual is a culturally specific act, concerning the moral, spiritual and often religious values of the social actors at stake. Traditional practices are often at the heart of such ceremonies. When non-traditional actors and/ or governmental representatives are involved, however, it is advisable that they also produce and sign a written document. In this case, the ceremony held to ritualise the vision could include both a traditional ritual and a modern ritual. The latter could be the public reading, signing and celebration of a document, such as a charter of principles for natural resource management and development approaches in the territory at stake.

The common vision of a desired future is a most appropriate type of agreement to ritualise. If such a vision is ritualised, in fact, it will be regarded as intangible and sacrosanct. As such, it will be possible to use it as a common ground where all social actors can reconcile the controversies and conflicts that may present themselves in the course of negotiations. It cannot be said, on the other hand, when it is best to hold the ritual ceremony. In certain cases, the ceremony precedes the negotiation of specific plans and agreements. In others, the ritual comes only after the agreements, as some partners need to see that something concrete can come out of their vision before committing the time and social capital necessary to celebrate it with a strong ritual.

Box 6.8	Fusing the traditional and the modern to ritualise a co-management vision (Republic of Congo)

(from a personal communication by Jean Claude Nuinguiri, 2000 and Borrini-Feyerabend et al., 2000)

The Conkouati—Douli National Park is situated in the coastal region of the Republic of Congo and characterised by a diversity of ecosystems (savannah, forest, lake, lagoon, etc.). From 1994 to 1999, the IUCN supported a co-management process that offered to a variety of local stakeholders an opportunity to develop a common vision for the future of their natural resources. On the basis of such vision, they agreed on the basic elements of a management system (particularly a zoning arrangement and some species-specific rules) and to institute a multi-stakeholder management authority– le Comité de Gestion des Ressources Naturelles de Conkouati– COGEREN.

The vision of the future was facilitated and developed through a series of meetings between stakeholders and was legitimised and ritualised during a major ceremony that took place on 8 May, 1999. The ceremony merged aspects from traditional village rituals and administrative and political ceremonies.

On the one hand, there were prepared speeches, a chart to be signed, banners, tee-shirts with slogans, a cameraman filming the event for the national television and all the usual paraphernalia of modern events. On the other, there were songs during which spirits were invoked, oaths taken by the local traditional land authorities (fumu si or chefs de terre) and dances performed– the same dances usually exhibited during the supplication of spirits for the fertility of women and natural resources (cianga). In other words, there was a fusion of rituals: a modern ritual dominated by the signature of the charter on the management of natural resources and a traditional ritual characterised by fertility cults offered to the clan spirits.

The fused ritual was not organised immediately after agreeing on the long-term vision, but nearly a couple of years later, after the zoning of the national park's land and the pluralist management authority had been agreed upon. There were at least three reasons for this:

- Essentially, a vision is an anticipation on time. The local stakeholders did not have the habit of projecting or speculating on future events. The visioning exercise was totally unfamiliar to them and they did not feel particularly confident after having it done.

- The vision appeared to people as an abstraction, dangerously similar to the promises of the political parties, which the local populations consider with considerable scepticism.

- The most important ritual in prior years– the hand washing ceremony of the political class in June 1991– has not been respected despite its "sacred" value: the armed conflicts that brought the country to mourn many deaths were evidence enough of the violation and transgression of oaths.

By organising the ritual only after the specific agreements had been achieved, the co-management facilitators departed from abstract considerations and founded it on concrete and transparent engagements, a fact which re-assured the local stakeholders.

6.3   Developing a strategy to approach the common vision

Once a shared vision of the desired future has been agreed upon and, possibly, ritualised, the social actors may wish to compare it with the current ecological, social and economic situation and trends, and thus identify issues and obstacles that currently prevent the realisation of that vision and need to be addressed. This is done in one or more subsequent meetings, where the discussion can start on the basis of a short report illustrated by the Start-up Team (possibly submitted in advance to all social actors), taking care that the report does not define the limits of the discussion. Some of the parties in the discussion, for instance government agencies and conservation NGOs, may also have specific information and analyses to offer to the attention of the others. It is particularly important to review reliable data on issues perceived by the parties as "urgent problems" in NRM. Other good starting points are participatory exercises, such as historical mapping of the management unit at stake, discussion of desirable and undesirable trends with the participation of local elders, or a transect walk. A facilitator can accompany these exercises and pose the crucial questions: "what are the main points of difference between the situation as it is and the situation as we would like to be, i.e.,our shared vision? Is society moving towards or away from our vision? What are the key problems and obstacles blocking progress towards it? What opportunities, resources and assets can we rely on?" A realistic discussion of these points may

What are the key problems and obstacles blocking progress towards our vision? What opportunities, resources and assets can we rely on? What tangible results could constitute the "building blocks" of our vision?

take some time, and result in agreed lists of problems and opportunities. It is then the time to focus attention on a short- to medium-term strategy to achieve the common vision. "What needs to change for us to attain our vision?" What would be the main components (dimensions of work, key performance areas) of an effective strategy towards it? What tangible results could constitute its "building blocks"?"

A variety of methods and tools can be utilised to facilitate the development of an agreed strategy. Some groups rely on a free-flowing discussion on issues and opportunities in a non-committal form (i.e., anyone can launch ideas without being committed to agree on them later on). If this moment is truly open and visionary, it can actually free people from the sectoral positions they may be entrenched in. Others are more systematic, examining problems and opportunities in depth, and comparing different options for action. Some relevant methods and tools are briefly described in Checklist 6.2.

Checklist 6.2 Methods and tools to identify the components and objectives of a common strategy
(adapted from Borrini-Feyerabend,1996; Goethert and Hamdi,1988)

Brainstorming and structured brainstorming. A basic technique employed to gather the views and perceptions of a group of people. Ideas are offered freewheeling after the facilitator puts forth an open-ended and somewhat provocative question, such as "What are the main obstacles that forbid us to live in the ideal community we visualised for our children?" or "What needs to change for us to attain our vision?" Opening statements and questions should be general and non-leading, i.e., should not stress or overemphasise a point of view that could bias the participants. It should be clear that brainstorming is a free and non-committal way of exploring ideas, i.e., no one commits himself or herself to something by suggesting it in a brainstorming session. At times people offer ideas orally, one after another, and the facilitator writes or illustrates the ideas up on a board. The grouping and refining of ideas is then done by general discussion.

If the participants in the exercise are all literate it is also possible to utilise a structured brainstorming exercise. In this case the facilitator asks a question and leaves time for people to think about their own answers and write them down in large letters on colour cards (there should be one idea per card, represented by a few words). Each participant then presents her/ his ideas to the rest of the group. After each idea card is illustrated, it is pinned up on the wall and the whole group decides where it should be set, to cluster it with related ideas. The final result is a series of "clusters of cards", each dealing with a main issue. Each cluster is usually later assigned to a sub-group, which examines it in depth and synthesises from it a composite answer.

Analysing strengths, weaknesses, opportunities and limitations (SWOL). SWOL[24] is a powerful tool for a group to assess an issue of concern, in particular a project, organisation or public service, and to identify opportunities for improving it. Basically, it is a group brainstorming on the positive factors (strengths), the negative factors (weaknesses), the possible improvements (opportunities) and the constraints (limitations) related to the initiative or entity at stake. Usually the results of the brainstorming are listed on a four-column matrix, drafted on flipcharts pinned on a board or wall.

Participants may have widely different opinions or express statements that are mutually contradictory. In such cases, the facilitator can ask further questions to deepen the arguments, but a consensus among the group members is not necessary. Contrasting views and alternative options can be listed on the same

---

[24] Sometimes called SWOT (T for threats).

column in the matrix. It may be useful, however, to gather more information on the controversial issues once the meeting is over– information that will be communicated to the whole group in the next meeting).

Situation analysis and problem analysis. Depending on the questions posed to the group, a strategic component may be expressed in different forms (e.g., "managing the watershed in a sustainable way" or "stopping soil erosion in the watershed"). In all cases, the situation, issue or problem needs to be clarified and analysed by the social actors with the help of the facilitator.

"Clarifying" means obtaining a coherent common understanding of the situation, issue or problem at the present moment. In particular, does everyone agree on what are the major "problems" to face? If people disagree on what a problem actually is, the facilitator may propose that a problem is "an effective blockage towards the achievement of the common vision of our desired future". If the main components of the strategy end up being described in a concise and effective manner, it is a good idea to have them written up on a large sheet of paper and posted on the wall on the premises of the meeting, possibly next to the description of the agreed vision of the desired future. An experienced facilitator takes also care of encouraging the group to be as specific as possible. For instance, instead of "lack of money" the problem may be better described as "scarce capital to invest and lack of entrepreneurial activities that could generate local income".

"Analysing" means setting the situation/ issues/ problems within a meaningful context of root causes and consequences, in particular with respect to the vision of the ideal future agreed upon by everyone. Such an analysis is vital to directing energy and resources in an effective way. Can everyone see the same causes and consequences for a given issue or problem? A good analysis is comprehensive and invests several dimensions of a given context, but can be completed in a reasonable amount of time and, most importantly, is understood by everyone.

Graphic conceptual framework. Graphic conceptual frameworks are tools to systematise and communicate a situation or problem analysis. They basically consist of a schematic illustration of the relationships between an issue or problem, the phenomena contributing to creating and maintaining it, and the consequences arising from its existence. A usual form is a set of text boxes, with arrows representing causal relationships among them. Another form is a sketched drawing of a tree. On the trunk of the tree is written the name of the problem, at the roots are its causes and at the tip of the branches the effects (see the drawing on the side, produced in Yemen). Ideally, a conceptual framework is coherent and comprehensive, for instance able to accommodate the potentially multi-sectoral nature of problems, but also simple. If possible, it includes some consideration of the time dimension (history, seasonality, processes of social and environmental change, etc.).

Whatever the methods employed, the collective thinking of the group about what needs to change and what needs to happen must be developed and expressed. The discussion should continue until everyone is satisfied or at least "can live with" the collective results. Importantly, the analysis underlying the results should be written down and possibly accompanied by graphs, pictures or other graphic support that would make communication easier. At this broad level of planning it is important to make sure that everyone has understood the key points of agreement but it is unwise to enter into very precise details. For instance, in the last decades so-called logical framework analyses have been used too early in planning processes and in mechanical, uninspiring ways to the impatience of scores of workshop participants. Often, they produced apparently precise results (e.g., indicators and targets for third level objectives) that did not stand any wind of reality. Effective strategic approaches achieve a balance between specificity (e.g., what do we seek to achieve? What needs to change for that to be achieved? How can we track progress?) and the need to remain open to the inevitable changes and adjustments that reality always demands. If that balance is kept in mind, logical framework analyses and other analytic tools can indeed help. An example of a broad strategic agreement is reported in Table 6.1.

Table 6.1   A strategy to reach the shared vision of Wenchi district (Ghana), developed by a multi-stakeholder workshop
(adapted from Borrini-Feyerabend, 2000)

After agreeing on a shared vision of the desired future (see Box 6.5), the stakeholders of Wenchi district compared it with the lists of key district problems and resources (elements of strength) they had also identified. They asked themselves: what crucial change is necessary to achieve our vision? Six main areas of needed strategic change were identified and sub-groups were formed to work on each area. Each sub-group identified the specific objectives for the strategic component, but also who were to be the key actors, what they were to accomplish (activities) and with what means. The six identified areas of needed strategic change were the following:

Six main areas of strategic change	Objectives to be pursued within each strategic area
Productivity of the local farming systems	Increase productivity (crops and animals) in environmentally-sound ways by: ● improving land leasing contracts; ● promoting farmer-to-farmer agricultural extension services; ● promoting the growing of non-traditional crops; ● promoting agro-forestry techniques.

Management of the district's natural resources	Manage the forests, waterways and wildlife of the district in a sound way by: ● preventing and controlling bush fires; ● banning indiscriminate hunting; ● regulating charcoal production; ● restoring degraded habitats; ● conserving the variety of plants and animal species in the district.
Capacity of local communities and institutions	Support various local actors to enhance their own capacities to manage natural resources and/ or assist others to manage. In particular: ● improve the capacity of people, CBOs and communities to utilise natural resources in a sustainable way; ● improve the capacity of extension officers to serve the needs of farmers; ● improve the capacity of the administration to provided needed social services and assist communities.
Local access to funds and credit	Assist small farmers to access credit via: ● reduced interest rate of loans (which will promote higher repayment rates); ● strengthened funding of rural banks.
Better markets and more private enterprises in the district	Develop a coherent market policy for the district by: ● promoting strong and democratic farm trade organisations; ● establishing effective market centres; ● providing easier access to credit from financial institutions; ● attracting investors by developing foreign exchange revenues.
Enhanced cultural identity and social exchanges and improved governance in the district	Harmonise the efforts of the Local Chiefs and the Central Government towards: ● addressing problems associated with the land tenure system; ● peacefully resolving conflicts of interest; ● ensuring religious and cultural tolerance; ● using cultural celebrations for recreation and relaxation; ● building the capacity of CBOs and social organisations to make them functional, committed, democratic and effective; ● encouraging the creation of new NGOs; ● supervising the activities of the CARE project; ● identifying developmental constraints, needed support to vulnerable groups and ways to influence policy decisions to facilitate community growth and prosperity.

As shown in the example of Table 6.1, some of the components of a strategy deal directly with natural resources (e.g., through management plans for specific forests, a water body, or wildlife throughout the district) whereas others bear upon it in indirect and complementary ways, such as via interventions for economic development, capacity building, governance and culture. Indeed, it would be neither effective nor wise to conceive a strategy to improve the status of the environment and natural resources in isolation from the socio-economic reality that embeds them. In particular, coordinated interventions in several sectors are crucial to allow an equitable distribution of the social costs and benefits of sound

A strategy "links"
the management of
a specific set of
natural resources to
the surrounding
environmental,
socio-economic,
institutional and
cultural landscape.

natural resource management. In this sense, a strategy is a broad, interdisciplinary and multi-level setting of intents and main ways to attain them. The management of a specific set of natural resources (e.g., a given watershed or forest) may be its key concern, but a strategy "links" that to the surrounding environmental, socio-economic, institutional and cultural landscape, and grounds it as part of local and regional land use plans. Obviously, the group negotiating the NRM management agreement needs to be conscious of the institutional setting in which it is nested and identify ways to connect with other social actors and institutions at various levels. This is essential for all those bodies and authorities whose decisions will bear upon the plans and agreements to be discussed by the specific group of stakeholders.

A strategic agreement does not need to enter into the details of everything that is to happen but needs to specify:

● the key areas or problems to be tackled (i.e., the components of the strategy); and

● the broadly desirable outcomes (objectives) for each such component.

● the main ways chosen to attain them.

If the discussion proceeds well and the key components of a strategy are agreed upon by the relevant social actors, the facilitator may challenge the group to go a step forward, i.e.,to understand and evaluate the relationships among the components of the strategy, watching for the possible synergies or oppositions among the identified objectives and checking for its overall coherence.

In this sense, the relationship between territories and resources dedicated to conservation and their neighbouring farming systems ought to be considered in particular detail. There are more than a few examples of protected areas dedicated to ecosystem and species conservation surrounded by agricultural areas where ecologically-destructive practices are promoted and subsidised. One example is the Park of the W of Niger, in West Africa. Park W is a World Heritage Area and a refuge of savannah wildlife shared by Benin, Burkina Faso and Niger. In Benin and Burkina Faso the planting of cotton, heavily dependent on pesticides, is subsidised up to the physical border of the protected area. The pesticides have a deleterious effect on pollinators and pollute the waters flowing into the park. Further, the cotton cultivation exhausts the soil and new lands are needed after a few crop cycles. Last but not least, small and landless producers often end up impoverished and destitute, as the cash-dominated crop enriches moneylenders and larger land owners. Many peasants in the periphery of the park have no alternative but trying to find some land by encroaching into the protected area. In this light, the government promotion of conservation side by side with cotton production is inherently non-sustainable and needs to be mended through a broader strategic approach, more at the level of the regional landscape than at the level of a specific body of resources.[25]

While the shared vision begins to be articulated and made specific, one or more people may distinguish themselves for the extent and quality of their engagement in the process, for their charisma and their capacity to focus the energy of the group. This is sometimes referred to as "leadership quality". The facilitator may wish to assign to them the responsibility of some important task, while nourishing their capacity to elicit the support and concurrence of others rather than the tendency "to advance alone" shown by some such very valuable persons (see Box 6.9).

Box 6.9   Leaders in the Napa Valley Watershed (California, USA)
(adapted from EPA, 1997)

Leadership is a critical factor in managing a watershed. Watersheds can be large or small, urban or rural, degraded or pristine. They can have resources of local or national importance, and can have little or great development pressure on them. Government may be trusted and relied upon, or distrusted and feared. As watersheds can differ so much, so can their leaders. A leader can be a farmer, a rancher, a coal miner, a member of a non-profit organisation or of a local council, a government staff person, a tribal leader, a federal agent. Leadership can also come in the form of a group or entity, such as a local board, state agency, or the federal government. Essentially, leaders are individuals or groups who strongly care about the watershed and its future.

Leaders tend to reflect the values of the local community and know what works there. They generally are good communicators, have the ability to bring about change and set things in motion, and are committed to making their (or a group's) vision a reality. They also tend to know how to engage, respect, and empower others and are able to find new or leverage existing resources. Because leadership is so important, many seek to encourage and nurture it. Some states offer grants to budding watershed associations. Several non-profit organisations maintain lists of watershed leaders who are willing to talk to others about their success. Other groups offer training and leadership workshops. Focusing on improving environmental conditions and developing inclusive common goals, rather than simply implementing policies and regulations, tends to be vital for the success of the common efforts.

The process facilitators should also be aware that specific factors and forces may encourage or oblige some of the actors to drop out of the negotiation exercise. Powerful groups, for example, may be inclined to use their political and economic influence to seek desired results outside of the agreed process. Weaker actors may find themselves progressively marginalised, or may at some point lose confidence in the ability of the process to deliver a fair outcome. Facilitators should be consistently vigilant to such occurrences, they should look out for signs of possible exclusion, and use all available means, including mass media and other forms of public scrutiny, to encourage all actors to remain faithful to the process.

The multi-stakeholder meetings have several types of results. If all goes well they manage to achieve important agreements on substance, such as a shared vision and strategy for the environment or resources at stake. They also, however, establish an on-going space for common discussion, where people get to know each other and hopefully learn to respect the views of others and build some mutual trust. A measure of mutual trust is essential in any form of co-management despite or actually, because of, the different interests and positions of the different parties.

A measure of mutual trust is essential in any form of co-management despite or actually, because of, the different interests and positions of the different parties.

---

[25]   Bennet, 1998; Beresford and Phillips, 2000.

Box 6.10 Mutual trust built on the respect for local knowledge and practices: the experience
          of Tanga (Tanzania)
          (from a personal communication by Rodney Salm, 1997)

Trust-building between government officials, local villagers and project personnel was, from the very beginning, identified as a project priority in the Tanga Coastal Zone Conservation and Development initiative, in Tanzania. A history of patronising attitudes toward villagers and poor government relations had created a deep sense of alienation and distrust between villagers and government officials. How could they work together for the management of the coastal resources?

The environmental problems were also serious. Dynamite fishing in coral reefs by commercial groups had greatly depleted the local fish supply, destroying the breeding grounds. Because of uncontrolled mangrove cutting, the area was also suffering from beach erosion. Since natural resources had always been abundant, the local communities had not developed new management rules to cope with changing conditions. Following the recent depletions, their normal fishing activities amounted to resource over-harvesting. The villagers blamed the government for not enforcing dynamiting regulations in the area. The government blamed the villagers for being wasteful in resource use. Lacking effective NGOs or other major potential partners, the only two actors interested in finding a solution were the villagers and government officials.

It is in this context that an Irish-funded and IUCN-managed conservation initiative intervened in the early 1990s. The initiative started with a three-year phase meant to build the conditions for a partnership, beginning with some measure of trust and willingness to dialogue between the parties. During this phase, communication efforts were crucial. Participatory appraisal exercises were facilitated in every village to analyse problems in natural resource use. The government officials who participated in these meetings were soon impressed by the extensive knowledge of the villagers, in sharp contrast with their prior stereotypes.

After some time, government extension workers took on the role of facilitators of assessment exercises and providers of technical advice. In turn, villagers became capable of doing their basic action plans, they carried out their own cause and effect analysis, identified objectives, drew timetables and selected and monitored progress indicators. To verify the extent of reef damages, villagers helped fisheries officers collect biodiversity information and review the results in a rapid survey. The villagers also set up specific committees to discuss topical issues, all reporting to the village assembly.

As a result of the trust-building and co-management efforts between government and local communities, in the space of a few years dynamite fishing has decreased tenfold in the area, and the coral reefs are being revitalised. Under Tanzania's recent decentralising efforts, government officials are seeing the advantages of greater involvement of village committees in management actions.

6.4   Negotiating and legitimising the co-management agreement and organisation

Progressing from the vision to the strategy, matters become a bit more explicit, but not yet enough.... The identified strategic objectives are generally still broad (e.g., "to manage the forest on top of the hills in a sustainable manner") and need to be transformed into agreed work plans that answer specific questions such as "What exactly shall be done? Who shall do it? By when? Where? How? With what financial means and human resources? To what specific aims? What indicators will be used to measure progress?". This is the moment when everything becomes concrete, a multiplicity of options and choices becomes apparent to everyone, different points of view abound, and conflicts surface in all their power and complexity. The parties in the negotiation have to find an agreement that answers these questions for each one of the strategic objectives, or at the very least for the ones that are of high priority. In addition, they have to identify or create a body to remain in charge of implementing, reviewing and modifying the agreement, as necessary through time.

The discussion will likely focus on a management plan and organisation for the territory or resources at stake, but a variety of complementary accords and initiatives will need to be associated with it to make the plan viable and acceptable to all. These may span new by-laws and policies, changes in local taxation systems, improved services, contracts assigning exclusive rights, training and research projects, as well as investments in a variety of initiatives, from productive activities to conservation measures and communication infrastructures. In other words, the agreement will cover a "package" including a management plan for the natural resources at stake as well as various complementary accords. The accords– which can be seen as conservation incentives or compensations for relevant losses– create a concrete link between the interests of the parties and the interest of conservation. The negotiation meetings are in charge of conceiving such a package agreement and figuring out the conditions for its setting into operation. In this sense, an enormous challenge emerges if the management plan demands important changes in the livelihood system of one or more parties. The complementary accords may need to identify nothing less than alternate means of livelihood for a potentially large group of people, a daunting task indeed!

For each dimension of the strategy the actors need to consider the various options for action to reach the agreed objectives and, among them, select the one best suited to the conditions and needs of the context and to the capacities available among the parties. The discussion may involve examining the experiences and lessons learned in other natural resource management situations, assessing competencies, requirements, procedures and regulations, and refining options through extensive bargaining and compromising. Complex problems require complex and detailed solutions, and everyone should contribute. For this type of discussion small groups work better than large ones, and a dedicated committee or working group may be formed for each component of the strategy, making sure that it includes representatives of the actors most directly affected by the issues under discussion.

Since different avenues and options bring different costs and benefits to different social actors, some such actors are likely to have strong interests and concerns attached to one course of action versus another. How can they all reach a consensus or at least a broad accord among themselves? The tools already used to arrive at the long-term vision and strategy (e.g., brainstorming, problem analysis, conceptual frameworks) can help again, but other methods and tools can also be useful, such as the ones described in Checklist 6.3. In some cases the comparison of alternative options vis-à-vis a number of criteria identified by the parties in the negotiation can be delegated to an external resource person or group, for example an NGO, a research group or a consulting firm, which will present its results in a

...everything becomes concrete, a multiplicity of options and choices becomes apparent to everyone, different points of view abound, and conflicts surface in all their power and complexity.

...the agreement covers a "package" including a management plan for the natural resources at stake as well as various complementary accords. The accords– which can be seen as conservation incentives or compensations for relevant losses– create a concrete link between the interests of the parties and the interest of conservation....

meeting and possibly facilitate the agreement over a compromise solution.[26] At times the representatives of some parties in the negotiation need to report to their constituencies and consult with them before advancing discussions on a topic and possibly agreeing on a consensus position. At other times it may be necessary to call in expert advice or find out new information (market trends, costs of technologies, etc.). These are some of the reasons why a long time and several planning meetings may be necessary before a full agreement is reached.

Checklist 6.3 Methods and tools to agree on a course of action
(modified from Borrini-Feyerabend, 1996)

● Breaking down large issues into smaller or sectoral ones. A strategic objective that is too broad and complex is difficult to treat. A way of overcoming a related impasse is to break it down into smaller sub-objectives and to assign those for discussion to sub-groups and task forces. Moments of common discussions and an overall strategic view, however, should be maintained.

● Stimulating the explicit discussion of the hypotheses and assumptions underlying the proposed activities. Why it is thought that a certain action will lead to a desired outcome? Taking a natural resource management plan as an example, the expected results of implementing the plan should be made explicit (e.g., by specifying the expected change in biological and environmental indicators) and the ecological plausibility of achieving those values should be addressed. The results to be expected from socio-cultural or economic interventions should also be made explicit, for example by identifying expected change in social or economic indicators. The plausibility of the assumptions should be examined in the light of the lessons learned from similar interventions in the past or in other places.

● Calling upon expert opinion on controversial issues. If disagreements among the social actors exist over matters of fact, it may be useful to call upon the service of expert professionals (such as a biologist to explain the characteristics of a viable habitat, a hydrologist to estimate how much water can be extracted from a source in a sustainable way, a community elder to recall instances of local extreme weather, and so on). This is not to say that expert opinion should be followed, nor that, indeed, different experts may not disagree. On the contrary. But expert opinions (especially when free from economic and political conditioning) can be helpful to elucidate a controversial discussion.

● Providing effective conflict mediation. Conflict mediation focuses on the fact that an agreement that satisfies every party is likely to be more long-lasting and more satisfactory than win-lose results. In the

---

26 Tom Nesbitt, personal communication, 2001.

long run, compromise may be the best way to serve everyone's interests, especially when overt conflict is replaced by the stability and predictability of a mutually agreeable solution. An effective mediator brings the conflicting parties to agree upon a compromise solution with the help of several expedients.

One expedient is to provide space and time for everyone concerned to clearly explain their views and positions: what they want and why. They should not be interrupted except for points of clarification. Another expedient is to recall the common vision of the desired future (coming back to the present from the future). If all relevant actors have agreed upon, and perhaps even ritualised, a common vision of the desired future, it is difficult for anyone of them to abandon the negotiation table. The mediator can explain the disagreements as a matter of different paths to reach the same goal. If this is clear, then such paths can be compared with respect to various criteria (see below).

● Comparing alternative options vis-à-vis a number of criteria. Alternative paths, positions and options can be examined with respect to various criteria, such as effectiveness; feasibility; cost in human, material and financial resources; expected benefits and impacts (in particular impacts in terms of environment and social equity, and contribution to social needs, such as community identity and solidarity); sustainability; and so on. The open comparison of alternative options is a very useful tool to help a group decide on selecting one option over many. The discussion can be easily summarised on a board, with alternative options listed in columns and criteria in rows. First the group agrees on the criteria. Second, for all the criteria chosen by the group, the alternative options are assessed and "scored". The matrix is compiled to offer a broad comparative view of options and scores. Importantly, scores should not be assigned from the top of the head, but only after a discussion of concrete issues. For example, regarding feasibility, who is ready to take on the major responsibility for each alternative option? In what time frame? With what material and financial resources? Regarding the impact, what are the expected environmental but also the social, cultural and economic consequences of the proposed options? To what degree of certainty are those foreseen? Are there options expected to have a positive impact on most or all of the components of the strategy to reach the agreed vision? Are there options expected to have a negative impact on some components of the overall strategy, regardless of the positive impact they are expected to have on the one being examined?

Agreements, disagreements, consensus and compromise

The ideal method of deliberating in a co-management negotiation is the consensus. Deliberations by consensus are based on the informed, conscious, voluntary and active development of an agreement among various parties, which often benefit from facilitation and conflict resolution support. Contrary to what is commonly believed, consensus does not mean that everyone is entirely and totally satisfied by the decision collectively taken, but that no one feels strong enough to block the wishes of everyone else over a point of disagreement.

Given the multiple perspectives involved and the importance of perceptions and values in forging agreements, deliberations by consensus are commonly developed through incremental compromise, accommodation and inventiveness. Working by consensus also implies collective responsibilities for the parties involved, as the agreement brings at least some benefits and some response to the concerns of every one of them. Decision-making by consensus has been the traditional way of reaching an agreement over a common decision for local communities all over the world, and still is a superb path for co-management regimes today (see Boxes 6.11 and 6.13).

> Deliberations by consensus are based on the informed, conscious, voluntary and active development of an agreement among various parties.

Box 6.11 Consensus decision-making for acquatic resource co-management in Khong district (Lao PDR)
(adapted from Baird, 1999)

The most important official step in establishing government-recognised co-management regulations of village fisheries in Khong district are one-day workshops (see also Boxes 3.11, 5.11 and 9.11). All the adult members of the community are requested to attend such workshops (usually one or two members of each household participate). Government and project officials also attend, as well as the village headmen of neighbouring communities. Government officials generally arrive in the village the day prior to the workshop, to advise on the necessary arrangements. Since villages initiate the co-management process, the government of Khong feels strongly that communities also need to control the workshop proceedings. Government and project guests act mainly as observers and facilitators and not as active participants. Officials are concerned that problems could arise if villages become overly dependent on government support, leading to a lack of village initiative. They want villagers to own the process.

The village headman chairs the co-management workshops, and opens the proceedings by explaining its objectives and how the agenda will unfold. After short presentations by the government and project officials on the experiences of other villages, the village headman presents the draft of the co-management regulations developed by the community. The community is then divided up into two gender groups for open discussions regarding the draft regulations. Apart from considering the regulations to be endorsed, the groups are required to consider what sanctions (level of punishment) should be mandated for those who break the regulations. Villagers are free to make recommendations regarding management strategies, but they are not allowed to advocate regulations that either conflict with already established national laws, result in increased degradation to natural resources, or cause serious conflicts between or within communities. The district officials are there to ensure that such problems do not arise.

There is no time limit for the villagers to discuss the proposed regulations, but discussions generally last between one and two hours, depending on how much preparation has been conducted prior to the workshop, and the level of internal controversy regarding the management strategies being considered. The discussions, which are not attended by government officials or other guests of the workshop, are generally spirited and lively, and broad villager participation is the norm. Most villagers in Khong possess a great deal of traditional knowledge regarding aquatic natural resources and can easily converse on detailed and specific aspects of management. When group discussions have ended, the men and women rejoin government officials and other guests in the main meeting area, which is generally the village school or the main hall of the village Buddhist temple. Representatives of each of the two discussion groups present their respective conclusions, including recommendations regarding management regulations proposed by the village, and additional regulations which were not considered in the original draft of the management plan. Men generally concentrate on management issues related to large bodies of water and large and valuable fish species. Women tend to focus on issues related to small water bodies and aquatic-life in streams, ponds and rice paddy fields. This gender-related divergence of special interest helps to balance and broaden the final content of management plans. After the group presentations, all the participants debate the regulations to adopt. If the recommendations of the women differ from those of the men, or if one or both groups have ideas that conflict with those of the original proposal, discussions continue until consensus is reached. While Lao villages are not without conflict, they are typically governed by consensus. If disagreements cannot be resolved, the government representative generally recommends that the issue be deferred until later, so as to allow time for resolving any differences that remain. Nobody has ever suggested that a vote be taken to determine whether a regulation should be adopted!

Once a community has agreed upon a set of regulations, the host village headman asks the headmen from neighbouring villages to comment on the appropriateness of individual regulations. Although guest chiefs rarely object to the decisions of the host community, they sometimes suggest improvements and provide new perspectives. If suggested changes are justified, the host village adjusts its regulations in order to maintain good relations with its neighbours, which is an important cultural norm. However, if the request is considered unreasonable, villagers from the host community have no qualms about refuting ideas. Government officials sometimes act as mediator. When a final set of regulations has been agreed upon and recorded by villagers, the regulations are read back to all the participants one last time. Any errors in recording regulations are corrected as they are read out. Before the village headman closes the workshop, the district chief endorses the decisions of the community. Government support for community-based management is important to villagers, and is certainly a major factor in successful co-management, as the signed plan is officially recognised as "village law". Four copies of each plan are made. One copy remains with the village, one is filed by district officers in Khong, one is given to the provincial officers, and one is kept by the supporting project.

Deliberations by consensus are facilitated by the use of flexible instruments, such as the zoning of the territory or area to be managed and/ or the specification of multiple uses and detailed conditions of resource use (such as by type, time, season, users and technology). Zoning basically involves subdividing a territory or area into sub-areas subjected to different objectives, conditions and rules. Multiple uses refer to one or more resources in the same area and the relevant rules that balance their utilisation by various stakeholders. Multiple use arrangements are striking when involving people engaged in different types of livelihoods in the same territories, such as pastoralists and sedentary agriculturalists or fisherfolk. While there are plenty of opportunities for controversy, there are also for synergy and mutual benefits. Finally, an important flexible instrument in NRM are rules detailing the conditions of resource use. Examples include quantities of resources that can be harvested, level of maturity, time of day or season, legitimate users, and extraction and processing technologies that can and cannot be employed. Specifying the zoning of an area, its allowed multiple uses of resources and the detailed conditions of such uses greatly enhances the spectrum of options available to the negotiation partners. Overall, it enhances the flexibility of an NRM plan and the chances of its fitting the needs and capabilities of a given social environment.

As a matter of fact, zoning is one of the most common mechanisms utilised in natural resource management to develop a broad consensus on objectives and regulations. At times, a specific zoning proposal is prepared by some resource management professionals and later submitted to the various stakeholders for their comments and desired changes. This, for instance, happened for the Cairngorm Partnership[27] in Scotland and for the Great Barrier Reef Marine Park, in Australia. For the latter, legislation mandates "public participation" in management and the Authority in charge carried out extensive inquiries with stakeholders prior to developing a draft zoning plan. The draft was then supposed to go to the public for at least one month, but the Authority extended this period to three months to ensure a larger feedback, and organised several specific workshops where the draft plan was discussed in detail.[28] In other cases, the parties prepare their own separate zoning proposals and those are later confronted and merged towards a viable compromise, at times with some external facilitation and support. This was the case for the management plan of the Conkouati-Douli National Park, in the Republic of Congo.[29] The most typical example where sub-areas are designated and regulated is a biosphere reserve, with its "core", "buffer" and "transition"

> Deliberations by consensus are facilitated by the use of instruments– such as zoning and the specification of detailed conditions of resource use (e.g., type, time, season, users and technology... which enhance the flexibility of an NRM plan and the chances of its fitting the needs and capabilities of a given social environment.

27 Cainrgorms Partnership, 1996
28 Graeme Kelleher, personal communication, 1995.
29 Chatelain et al., 2004.

zones. One of the characteristics of zoning is that it is usually impossible to develop it if not "on the ground", and thus it requires that various social actors spend time together in the field and in meetings, and that they discuss very concrete issues, a fact that can do wonders to develop more transparent and collaborative relationships. This was proven, for instance, for the Galapagos Marine Reserve.[30] Mapping techniques of various sophistication (from hand mapping to electronic GIS systems) can be of great help in developing a zoning system (see Box 6.12).

Box 6.12   Zoning as a product of a participatory GIS in the Amazons
(adapted from Saragoussi et al., 2002)

Jaú National Park is the largest National Park in Brazil. Located in the Amazon region, it is managed through an agreement comprising an environment NGO called Fundação Vitória Amazônica (FVA) and IBAMA, the Brazilian agency responsible for environmental issues. The NGO took upon itself to integrate in the management decisions the park residents (locally known as caboclos or riberenos), greatly knowledgeable about natural resources but generally illiterate and unaccustomed to deal with modern "management plans" as understood by the authorities in charge. To accomplish the task, the NGO opted for the use of a sophisticated Geographical Information System (GIS) in a fully participatory way.

Work began by digitalising a database. This included physical features of landscape (vegetation cover, soil types, geology, etc.) from secondary data provided by the government. It also included social and economic characteristics of the park resident population, such as natural resource uses, demographic and migration indicators, life history and family relationships– all from primary data collected especially for the database. The information from the residents was collected through participatory assessment exercises and in meetings where concepts such as "planning", "zoning" and "sustainable use" were also discussed at length. The information on the use of natural resources was incorporated into the maps by using small flags (for instance, flags that depicted vegetal fibres, game animals, fish, turtles etc.). These maps were then discussed in workshops among park dwellers, researchers, local decision-makers, and FVA and IBAMA technicians. Ultimately, the maps were the key to delimit the special use zone, where extractive activities are now fully allowed. The remainder of the park was considered primitive zone, except a small area indicated by the dwellers as recuperation zone. Each zone has its own rules of access and use. Currently, the FVA and the local communities are developing further zoning details, allowing for clearer day-to-day use decisions. In all, participatory GIS demonstrated to be a very useful tool, which allowed the integration of information from several sources and the promotion of the engagement of different social actors.

A plethora of instruments such as leases, concessions, use permits, licenses, quotas, collector identity cards, certificates and customary rules can be utilised to regulate access.

Other flexible instruments that facilitate the development of consensus decisions regulate the access to natural resource and the sharing of benefits and rights assigned to the relevant social actors. Rather than "yes or no" answers to access problems, a plethora of instruments such as leases, concessions, use permits, licenses, quotas, collector's identity cards, certificates and customary rules can be utilised to regulate access. In particular, access to resources can be assigned to specific groups only and on conditions of the use of certain types of technology and not others. An important example is provided by the Parc National du Banc d'Arguin (PNBA) in Mauritania. PNBA is engaged in some mild form of co-management in which the government staff developed a package of agreements with the representatives of the park's residents– local people known with the name of Imraguen (fishermen). The Imraguen are allowed to reside within the park boundaries and to fish in its marine portion, but only if they do so with artisan fishing equipment and sail boats, without the use of a motor. In addition, they agreed on a number of fishing restrictions, including the ban on fishing sharks, in exchange

---

[30]   Pippa Heylings, personal communication, 2001.

for some development benefits. It is extremely important that the Imraguen remain in the park, as they represent the most powerful social defence and provide a wide-spread and effective form of surveillance against the motorised fishermen who surround the park's boundaries and could easily help themselves with the park's resources.[31]

Similarly, one of the first agreements between Uganda Wildlife Authority (then Uganda National Parks) and the local communities living around Bwindi Impenetrable

National Park was about the collection of medicinal plants and lianas from the park. It was agreed that these products, essential for local livelihoods, would be collected only by specialised individuals, selected by the communities and acting on the communities' behalf. The authorised collectors had a quantity limitation, received some training and carried with themselves a special identity card. In this way, some of the many and profound conflicts that opposed the local communities and the park agency could be solved.

Box 6.13   Consensus in a co-management board: a key incentive towards effective agreements for the Galapagos Marine Reserve
(adapted from Heylings and Bravo, 2001)

Located approximately 1,500 km from the Ecuadorian mainland, the volcanic Galapagos Islands contain remarkable terrestrial and marine ecosystems and became, some years ago, the focus of complex and violent multi-stakeholder conflicts. The rapid economic and demographic change, the presence of unregulated industrial fishing, the appearance of high-value fisheries for Asian markets, the state-imposed policy and regulations and the general non-compliance with the management plan of the Marine Reserve were all factors fuelling those conflicts. In 1998, in response to national and international concern about the threats facing them, Ecuador passed innovative legislation through a Special Law that, amongst other measures, introduced the control of migration to the islands, created one of the largest marine reserves in the world (some 130,000 km2), prohibited industrial fishing and established institutions for co-management of the reserve. The creation of the Galapagos Marine Reserve was the fruit of a local exhaustive participatory planning process, which took two years (74 meetings of the multi-stakeholder planning group called the "Grupo Núcleo", 2 fisheries summit meetings and 3 community workshops) and produced a consensus management plan. The implementation of this plan, through a legally based participatory management regime, has been in progress now for several years.

The Galapagos co-management institution essentially consists of a tree-pole arrangement (see Figure 6.1) uniting a local Participatory Management Board (PMB), an Inter-institutional Management Authority (IMA) and the Galapagos National Park (GNP). The Participatory Management Board is made up of the primary local stakeholders whilst the IMA comprises representatives of Ministers and local stakeholders. In the PMB, the members introduce specific management proposals (e.g., concerning regulations of fisheries and tourism) which are analysed, negotiated and eventually agreed upon by consensus. The consensus-based proposals are channelled for approval to the IMA and then to the GNP, for

---

31   Pierre Campredon, personal communication, 2002.

implementation and control. Proposals that have reached a consensus in the PMB carry an important social weight at the IMA level. If no consensus is reached in the PMB, the different stakeholder positions are submitted to the IMA, where the decision is left in the hands of a majority of mainland ministerial officials. Statistics are compelling. Basically one hundred percent of consensus-based technical proposals developed by the PMB (which, incidentally, managed to secure excellent conservation results) are approved without modification by the IMA. Clearly, the fact that consensus proposals are invariably approved creates a very strong incentive for local stakeholders to develop and agree upon viable technical arrangements in the PMB.

Figure 6.1 Schematic description of the co-management setting for the Galapagos Marine Reserve

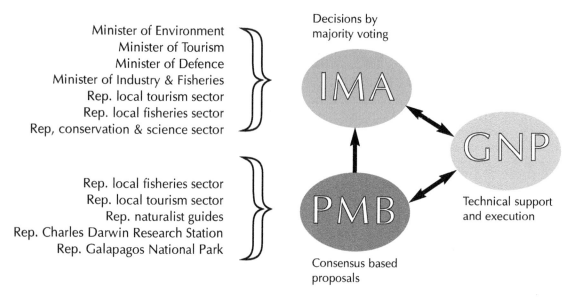

Minister of Environment
Minister of Tourism
Minister of Defence
Minister of Industry & Fisheries
Rep. local tourism sector
Rep. local fisheries sector
Rep, conservation & science sector

Rep. local fisheries sector
Rep. local tourism sector
Rep. naturalist guides
Rep. Charles Darwin Research Station
Rep. Galapagos National Park

Decisions by majority voting

IMA

GNP

PMB

Technical support and execution

Consensus based proposals

If the negotiating parties identify a management option that is particularly interesting but demands major costs and sacrifices from one or a few of the relevant social actors, all the partners could figure out how to compensate the losers for everyone's benefit. This could involve the provision of specific incentives and clauses in the plans and agreements. The very actors who would be compensated may advance suggestions about the incentives that they would like to receive, which could then be discussed by everyone (costs, feasibility, assurance of benefits to be obtained, etc.). Among the incentive mechanisms intended to benefit a whole community rather than specific individuals are Community Investment Funds.

Among the incentive mechanisms intended to benefit a whole community are Community Investment Funds.

A case encountered rather frequently is the one of communities with customary entitlement to a set of natural resources (say a forest, rangeland or a fishing area) but who have been deprived of their customary rights, or who are not wealthy enough or organised enough to invest the means and human resources necessary to manage it productively or to defend its own acquired rights. As a consequence, the natural resources may be falling into an open-access status, and may be used in an exploitative fashion by all sorts of other entitled and un-entitled actors. In other situations the local resources may be well managed, but the community may badly need funds for sustainable development initiatives. In such cases it is most useful to establish a productive partnership among the community as a whole (which may contribute natural resources such as land, water, access to a fishing area), some community members (who may contribute their labour) and other partners who may bring in the missing factors of production (such as seeds, water, boats, engines and nets, a tourism business, etc.). The productive partnership is set to work (e.g., the community land is laboured by community members with a tractor, water and seeds provided by an external party; the community fishery zones are exploited by local fisherfolk with a boat provided from outside) and the benefits are divided among the production partners, one of which is the community in its entirety. The community share of such benefits (and, at times, also the share corresponding to an initial "factor of production" donated from outside, such as pumps for irrigation water, boats for fishing, tractors for ploughing fields or vehicles for transport) can be utilised to set up a Community Investment Fund.

The rules to manage a Community Investment Fund need to be devised by the members of the specific community, who may also set up a managing committee. In general, the fund is not loaned nor replenished by payments. It is instead invested in productive activities, which generate a suitable wealth for the community and income for those directly involved in its operations. This tends to make a Community Investment Fund grow rather than shrink under the effect of inflation and missed repayments. At the end of each production cycle the fund can be partially or totally re-invested for community-based productive initiatives, with or without partnerships with other groups or individuals. Community Investment Funds for sustainable development have important and natural applications in the field of co-management, both as an approach that promotes and strengthens collaboration in society and as a co-management institution in its own right, with internalised incentives for using natural resources in a sustainable way. They are also, however, critically dependent on the viability of the related productive initiatives.

In Iran, Community Investment Funds are called sanduqs and have roots in ancient traditions of communal solidarity, also supported by Islam. Sanduqs are now being utilised as part of agreements for natural resource management, for instance in the Hable Rood watershed, east of Teheran, and in the Qashqai territories (see Case Example 1.4 in Chapter 1). The management partnerships involve local communities, several departments of the Ministry of Agriculture, the Department of the Environment and a national NGO. The sanduq resources are being utilised to boost organic production of fruits, vegetables and cereals and to restore the viability of pastoral livelihoods as well as to promote local community-based trade.

...many NRM conflict situations are related to the perception of a violent exercise of power by one party over others.

Managing conflicts

Conflicts in natural resource management can be latent or manifest and generally exist when different parties believe that their aspirations cannot be simultaneously achieved. Conflicts may be rooted in structural power imbalances among the parties or in a power vacuum, in ambiguous land and resource tenure regimes or in rapidly changing environmental and socio-economic conditions. A perceived or real scarcity of natural resources to meet survival needs is one of the most serious causes of conflicts in NRM, but less tangible issues, such as dignity and recognition, physical access to territories, and unresolved historical events can also be involved. Today, new ecological and conservation dimensions have been added to the more usual moral, political and economic issues at the roots of conflicts over natural resources.[32]

---

[32] Gadgil and Guha, 1995.

In the last centuries, more and more conflicts have been generated by the impossibility of ensuring survival or cultural continuity within newly imposed legal systems and market conditions. The forced breaking down of traditional institutions and community entitlements rendered authority unclear. The imposition of new values and modes of NRM without the consent of the most directly affected people was bound to generate conflicts. As a matter of fact, many NRM conflict situations are related to the perception of a violent or excessive exercise of power by one party over others. Box 6.14 and Checklists 6.3 and 6.4 include a number of considerations useful in conflict-management processes.

Box 6.14   Common themes and considerations in conflict management
(adapted from Fisher, 1996)

● Power imbalances. There are often serious disparities among the parties in terms of access to technical, administrative, economic and organisational resources. Authoritarian local government leaders, major commercial or political interests and, in some places, the presence of a strong military or other armed group, can severely constrain the dialogue and choice in resolving conflicts. A general rule is that unequal power leads to unequal agreements. The perceived legitimacy of the conflict resolution process can obscure these dynamics but forced accommodations, cooptation, or "coercive harmony" results in agreements that are often neither fair nor enforceable.

● Diversity of interests within any one social actor. There are obvious distinctions among the interests of local communities, conservationists, developers and the state, but distinctions also exist within these groups. "Communities" in Southeast Asia, for instance, may consist of mixed caste, clan, ethnic and economic groups, and may include migrants or squatters with little official recognition. Another example: jurisdictional disputes between line agencies within a national government are often the centrepiece of controversy over resource management. Thus, what is being portrayed as "the position" of a given social actor, may actually be the position of a special subgroup, with little force and representational quality.

● The role of the Start-up Team and facilitator. The Start-up Team and facilitator wield considerable authority, and can introduce serious biases in defining the domain of discourse, the relevant actors and the negotiation methods and atmosphere. In particular it is often the case that the facilitator role is played by an "insider partial" rather than an "outsider neutral". This is not a problem a priori– a community leader or a concerned public official may be very capable of assuring participation, fairness and trust– but it can become a serious problem if they misuse their position.

● The influence of culture. The importance of values and cultural norms in creating, maintaining and solving conflicts is often underestimated. Traditional forms of dispute resolution, such as those practised in rural Indonesia, emphasise communal inclusiveness and the role of respected elders as arbitrators, in sharp contrast to the Western model of rationalist dialogue facilitated by a neutral third-party. Indigenous conflict resolution techniques can provide effective local mechanisms for dealing with community-level disputes. At the same time, the complex nature of modern common property conflicts– involving larger ecological units, multiple communities and ethnic groups, sophisticated technical aspects, market forces and various institutional jurisdictions– has little precursor in traditional systems.

Checklist 6.4   Ideas for managing conflict

The following ideas[33] have proven their effectiveness in some settings but, indeed, each case is unique and the mediator in the negotiation will have to consult extensively and use her or his best judgement to provide the most effective conditions for reaching an agreement:

● Start with small issues that are easily settled

If there are different issues at stake and some are easier to solve than others, starting from those and reaching some satisfactory agreements will help the participants develop a sense of mutual trust and confidence in the process, encouraging them to tackle more thorny issues.

● Promote personal relationships between the parties in conflict

Interaction at the personal level even in mundane activities such as travelling together, eating together, sharing the same housing among people who enjoy the respect, credibility and authority of their relevant groups are useful to smooth the way towards effective listening and dialogue.

● Involve all stakeholders when the parties directly in conflict are about to break up dialogue

A conflict among some of the negotiating parties may be so serious that one or more of them may chose to withdraw from the negotiation meeting. Among the rules to be set up ahead it is useful to include that withdrawal from discussion is certainly a possibility, but all parties engage themselves to do so only after clearly explaining their problem(s) and seeing if those problem(s) can be addressed with the help of the larger group of stakeholders. This may require separate meetings among each conflicting party and the stakeholder groups.

● Offer transparency and potential extensive information/ publicity about the controversy

Some conflicts are rooted in chronic situations of privilege and corruption that could not stand the light of day if openly recognised and assessed. Visibility and the presence of independent parties may break such deadlocks. In this sense, transparent negotiation processes and the potential or actual ample publicity about a controversy may be in themselves effective to change the status quo.

● Do not gloss over major past injustices and losses; rather, recognise them and promote their fair and respectful "closure"

A process of conflict management should not be an excuse to make a blank slate over past injustices and major losses, often sustained by the weakest parties. Processes of "truth and reconciliation" are not only more equitable than glossing over a painful and often violent past– they are the only way to bring a sense of closure to them, and the willingness to build up a different future.

● Provide occasions to vent frustrations and discharge negative energy prior to the time of negotiation

In many cases, even when no major injustices and irreplaceable losses have been felt, people have the need to "vent" their frustrations. Some local debates, possibly with the presence of the mediator and other external actors, can provide a way to channel the accumulated negative energy and aggressiveness. Often, people need to be heard and recognised before moving on.[34]

● Promote the taking of unilateral action that inspires trust in the other parties

At times a deep seated distrust of the intention of the other parties acts as a stumbling block for dialogue and meaningful negotiation. In such cases it may be helpful for some parties to break the deadlock by announcing and carrying out some friendly unilateral innovation that encounters the favour of the others.

● Show examples of similar conflicts successfully solved and, if at all possible, have the parties visit such examples

Often a possible solution to conflicts exists but the parties do not manage to see it because they are stuck in their long-term grievances and positions. Translating their case into a different setting may produce a refreshing change of perspective and inspire the parties to act.

---

[33] Some of these are also discussed in Lewis, 1997.
[34] Chatelain et al., 2004.

The conflicts opposing the parties are often a complex combination of social elements intertwined with all sorts of NRM problems. In such cases the negotiation may need to address the various aspects of "local peace" and can take several months if not years to get to a satisfactory conclusion. The issues at stake need to be explored thoroughly and external mediators are crucially useful, as also may be a variety of tools and external inputs.[35] For instance, some social conflicts have been resolved by external inputs that helped to enhance the security and productivity of natural resource use (see Box 6.15).

Box 6.15   Enhanced productive use of natural resources helps solving conflicts between pastoralists and agriculturalists in Itoh (Cameroon)
(adapted from Nguemdjiom, 2003)

Successful conflict resolution linked with conservation benefits and the generation of local wealth took place around the Itoh community grazing area, at the border of the high altitude mountain forest of Kilum, in north-west Cameroon. The grazing area is exploited by both Mbororo pastoralists, who settled in the area about 30 years ago, and by local agriculturalists of a different ethnic origin. For years, the area has been the theatre of bitter confrontations among these people, while the forest was not spared deforestation and encroachments that lowered its water retention capacity and endangered biodiversity. Fortunately, with some appropriate financial and technical help, the situation has now been entirely transformed. Fencing with live sticks has been created around the pasture area to prevent both cattle encroachment into the cultivated fields and the unilateral extension of fields into pasture, as well as stables and paddocks for the animals. The pasture has been improved with the planting of new types of forage and deforestation reversed by the planting of over 30,000 multi-purpose trees. A safer water supply has also been set up for both humans and livestock and very many training initiatives implemented.

The combined impact of these (project-based) interventions has been dramatic. Local wealth and capacities has been created, human and animal health have greatly improved, the Kilum's biodiversity is much better protected and water is reliably available to all. Peaceful coexistence and new bounds of collaboration and mutual exchange have ensued among the previously conflicting social groups.[36]

Despite best efforts, a working group may not arrive at an agreement on any one given option for a strategy component because of a variety of contingent reasons (see some relevant considerations in Box 6.14). In this case, a possibility is to present all the retained alternatives to the larger group and ask for advice. The assembly may again examine and compare alternative options vis-à-vis a number of specific criteria but also with respect to the actions retained for the other components of the strategy. Examining at once all the strategy's components may reveal, for instance, that the "losers" in one of the dimensions are the "winners" in another one. Or the discussion may advance with the help of proposals for cross-component compensations and incentives.

Taking the process to a productive close

The final aim of the negotiation phase is a broadly shared agreement on what needs to happen for each component of the agreed strategy, including specific aims, actors, means, activities and a follow-up protocol.[37] As mentioned, this is likely to include specific co-management plans for the relevant unit(s) of natural

---

[35] Ramírez, 2002; Egeimi et al., 2003.

[36] Unpublished information from André Nguemdjiom, UNDP Cameroon, 2003.

[37] This includes results anticipated, progress indicators that will be monitored, individuals and organisations in charge of collecting and communicating data, specific plans for evaluation reviews, etc.

resources, but also complementary accords rendering viable the building blocks of the common vision of the desired future. The co-management plans specify a share of functions, benefits and responsibilities for the various parties and are usually co-signed by them (see Chapter 7 for more details). The complementary accords are approved as appropriate (they may include project implementation contracts, letters of intent, municipal by-laws, the endorsement of traditional authorities, etc.). The more actors and the more important the resources involved, the more advisable it is for the plans and agreements to be made binding (such as formal or legal contracts). The signatories should be those individuals who are directly assigned responsibility in the plans and agreement (and not the authorities who may represent them!).

> The final aim of the negotiation phase is a broadly shared agreement on what needs to happen.

Box 6.16   The process we followed in Takiéta: developing a co-management setting for a Forest Reserve in Niger
(adapted from Amadou et al., 2003)

Takiéta Forest Reserve is located in the agro-pastoral zone of the department of Zinder, Niger, at the heart of a Sahelian environment with scarce and highly variable rainfall. The reserve represents the largest non-cultivated area in the region and is a crucial silvo-pastoral resource in a zone where land is otherwise entirely occupied by agricultural fields (it is rare to find even a few square metres of idle land). Created in the 1950s and, theoretically, owned, managed and protected by the state government, Takiéta Forest Reserve soon became subject to uncontrolled and destructive exploitation by local people and outsiders, with unchecked and rapidly expanding agricultural clearance taking place both at the boundaries of the forest and within the forest itself. Pressure on the dwindling and degraded pastoral resources within the reserve progressively increased as sedentary communities diversified into livestock production, which brought them into increased competition with transhumant pastoral groups. Despite its degraded state, the reserve continued to play a strategic role in local production systems, but was also threatened by an influential local "de-reservation" lobby that aimed to convert what was a de facto common property resource (because of local community traditions and the absence of management/ presence of state agents) into private land.

The Takiéta Joint Forest Management Project was set up in 1995 to promote a process towards the sustainable, decentralised co-management of the reserve. It was implemented by SOS Sahel UK. In 2003, with the project terminated and its objectives fully achieved, it is interesting to review the key steps in the process (see also Figure 6.2). These included:

Stakeholder identification. Clear identification of the natural resources at stake and their limits, and identification of all direct and indirect actors affecting and affected by the management decisions (e.g., local communities subdivided according to their main interests, transhumant groups, government agencies, etc.).

Information, analysis and discussion at the individual "actor" level. This involved an analysis by each group of the natural resources at stake and the role they play in their system of production. It covered historical NRM strategies/ roles; the current situation; decentralisation, including stakes and perspectives for local management; and changing roles and relations.

Information sharing among all the actors. The collated and unmodified information from the different groups was shared among all the actors, exposing each of them to the analysis made by others.

A series of stakeholder workshops. Three workshops were held, where 180-200 representatives debated subjects as varied as: the situation, their joint interest and commitment to doing something about it and how it should be done. Collective decisions were formalised as written recommendations from the workshops.

Election of delegates to a Local Management Structure (LMS). This was carried out internally within each stakeholder group, according to criteria and modalities agreed in the stakeholder workshops.

Preliminary meetings of all the delegates to the LMS. These meetings served to allow delegates to get to know one another, share information about the resources to be managed, retrace the process leading to the creation of the LMS, discuss and reach agreement on the LMS structure and proposed function, determine internal "roles and relationships" as well as rules and regulations, define what "management" means to the LMS and the people it represents, elect an Executive Committee from amongst the delegates, and formally present the members of the LMS Executive Committee to the local and regional administrative and traditional authorities, which had also been present at stakeholder workshops. The meetings thus included:

● planning and programming activities;

● sharing experiences with other LMS (inter-structure exchange);

● finalising the internal rules and regulations for the structure and presenting them to the relevant communities for their comments and ratification.

Further LMS meetings concerning the natural resources and how to manage them. At this juncture, information regarding the natural resources and their potential, including an inventory and base maps, was collected, analysed and shared; all known users were listed and uses analysed. On the basis of all this, an analysis of the resources and their trends was developed; actual and potential conflicts were examined; a vision of the desired future for the resources was developed; and basic rules of good governance were progressively drafted. Options for improving the resources over time were explored. A proposed management document was drafted.

Establishing institutional relations and communication systems. Links were established between the LMS and the authorities, government services and other partners, including pastoral associations from Nigeria.

Official recognition of the status of the association. The LMS was formally recognised by the state as the "Association Kou Tayani", i.e., it acquired legal recognition.

Stakeholder review workshop. The proposed management document was presented to all stakeholders for review, discussion and final amendments.

Official submission to local regional authorities. The management document was presented to the local regional authorities asking for a legal recognition of the association's right to implement their management plan.

Autonomous management. For six months, autonomous management by the LMS went on before the closure of the support project.

Participatory evaluation of the project. A participatory evaluation of the project including both process and results was conducted.

Project closure… and continuation of the management process!

Figure 6.2   Schematic view of the composition of the Local Management Structure for Takiéta Forest Reserve (Niger) (19 elected and 3 non-elected members in all).

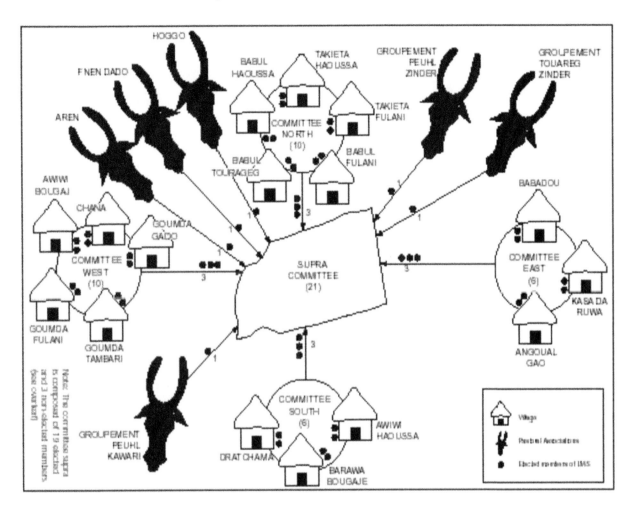

It is recommendable that, in the sharing of management functions, rights and responsibilities, the social actors take to full use their comparative advantages and capacities. For instance, government niger agencies can contribute a variety of technical and administrative functions, ensure that legal and policy frameworks are respected, enforced and protected against negative interferences with the agreement (e.g., by external encroachers). In addition, government agencies are well positioned to provide economic incentives and financial support, to process and diffuse information[38] and to make sure that initiatives in various sectors (e.g., natural resource management, agriculture, fishery, forestry, education, training, health and credit schemes) are effectively harmonised. As the impact of economic forces on CM agreements is considerable, market forces may need to be tamed for the benefit of conservation. This is another role government partners can take on. Non-governmental actors can provide specialised knowledge and skills on both the ecological and socio-economic environment (ranging from the responsibility of monitoring biodiversity to the responsibility of assuring a steady flow of tourist income to the natural resource area). Most of all, NGOs often have a unique power of convening actors from various parts of society. In the case of local residents, providing surveillance for fire and other natural risks and preventing

---

38   Baland and Platteau, 1996.

resource use by unauthorised people are responsibilities of great comparative advantage. Para-wardens and para-scouts can be appointed among the local residents with, at times, the power to arrest violators of CM agreements.[39] Local traditional resource knowledge may also be applied to the regeneration of biological diversity.

Ultimately, the effectiveness of an "agreement package" depends on a number of factors, including the capacity of the relevant social actors to take on the agreed functions and responsibilities and to absorb the agreed benefits. In this sense, it has been found that well-organised social actors are more capable of taking advantage of incentives, and especially so when the incentives are provided through time and distributed equitably.[40] Another important feature of successful agreements is their expected capacity of providing benefits on the long-term (see Table 6.2)

Table 6.2   Benefit sharing: a company-community agreement in Cameroon
(adapted from Laird and Lisinge, 1998)

In Cameroon, the company Plantecam Medicam and the villages of Mapanja and Bokwongo signed an agreement for the sourcing of Prunus africana bark– the Agreement for Sustainable Management of the Species and Production of Prunus africana. The agreement outlines general benefits for the village and promotes the sustainable management of Prunus africana in the forest. Examples of benefits resulting from the agreement include:

Actor	Short term benefit: monetary	Long term benefit: monetary
Villages	Set fees for supplies of bark	Resources for Village Development Fund and the Union Fund
Gov. of Cameroon	Increased tax revenues	On-going tax revenues from a sustainable industry
Actor	Short term benefit: non-monetary	Long term benefit: non-monetary
Villages	Training; capacity-and institution-building; infrastructure and equipment	Increased capacity to share in benefits from the exploitation of Prunus africana; improved institutions and infrastructure, such as water projects
Plantecam Medicam		Assured supply of Prunus africana bark
Gov. of Cameroon	Reduced illegal exploitation	Reduced illegal exploitation

Ultimately, even a good negotiation process cannot guarantee a faultless output. On the contrary, one should expect that pluralist management is bound to be affected by a certain amount of incoherence and uncertainty, especially when voting and majority rule are taken as decision-making method in place of consensus. For some, this is to be expected from all types of democratic decision-making, which can hardly be called "rational":[41]

---

39   KWS and Mbeere County Council, 1996
40   McNeely, 1988.
41   Navarro, 1997.

"...democracy calls for a particular form of suspension of belief: the certainty that one outcome is best for all, rational. Decisions by numbers or by rules do not have prima facie rationality. The everyday life of democratic politics is not a spectacle that inspires awe: an endless squabble among petty ambitions, rhetoric designed to hide and mislead, shady connections between power and money, laws that make no pretence of justice, policies that reinforce privilege. This experience is particularly painful for people who had to idealise democracy in the struggle against authoritarian oppression, people for whom democracy was the paradise forbidden. When paradise turns into everyday life, disenchantment sets in."[42]

And yet, despite a strong chance of disenchantment, collective decision-making carries with itself a liberating power. On the one hand, the dialogue and transparency are bound to reduce malpractices and corrupted deals. On the other, the knowledge of the rules of the game is a powerful de-mystifier. It creates, little by little, a political culture of informed and active citizens, it reduces the chances of populism and demagogy. Participatory decision-making is not a guarantee for intelligent or successful decisions. But it brings about decisions that are "owned" and can become part of the knowledge of the ones who made them.

Once an agreement (e.g., a consensus over a management plan and a given sharing of rights and responsibilities) is reached, it should be recorded in terms clear and comprehensible to all and in both official and local languages. The agreement may not be written on stone, but it should certainly be written on paper (various copies should be kept by various parties) and publicised as widely as possible within the relevant communities and among the relevant actors. As mentioned below, it is also good to underline its importance by means of a specific event or ceremony. As far as possible, the signatories should be people directly taking on management responsibilities (e.g., the Head of a village, the President of a fisherfolk cooperative or the District Chief Administrator)– not distant authorities who have little to do with the agreement. The parties should commit themselves in public (see an example in Box 6.8), and the agreement should be given ample visibility, e.g., a copy of the agreement could be posted in local communities as well as in the premises of an agency in charge of the natural resource area, if applicable.

A good agreement includes provisions for how to deal with exceptional situations (e.g., who should take responsibility for what in case of acute ecological stress or social crisis). It also makes clear what results are expected and how those are to be monitored and evaluated. Following such evaluation, certain provisions of the management plan may also be reviewed and modified. Some forms of complementary accords, such as a memorandum of understanding, are also usually flexible and allow for revisions. Other forms, such as contracts among legally-recognised parties and involving substantial economic and financial resources, are less easily modified. Even less so are agreements formalised as a local by-law or enshrined in legislation. While, as discussed earlier in this Chapter, it is useful to have flexibility embedded in an agreement, it has also been observed that co-management agreements incorporated in legislation– including in "weak" legislation that calls for voluntary compliance– are stronger and tend to be better respected than the others.[43]

> Participatory decision-making is not a guarantee for intelligent or successful decisions. But it brings about decisions that are "owned" and can become part of the knowledge of the ones who made them.

---

42   Przeworski, 1991, quoted in Navarro, 1997.
43   Graeme Kelleher, personal communication, 1995.

Box 6.17   Developing an integrated, participatory development plan in Richtersveld
            (South Africa)
            (adapted from Turner et al., 2002)

The process that sustained the integrated development plans in Richtersveld resulted in a strong public commitment to conservation objectives, and in the identification of various conservancy initiatives by the communities themselves, initiatives that amount to community owned and managed protected areas. The process was built around intensive, repeated rounds of information sharing, awareness raising and consultation. In addition to public meetings in each of the four towns in the area, letters were written to all Richtersveld residents to explain the process and to brief them on progress. Besides broad consultations with the general public, a range of more focused consultations took place with key players, such as SANP (South African National Parks) and the mining industries that are active in the area. Local capacity to conduct public meetings and manage conflict was also strengthened and the process had a unifying and empowering effect on the local communities, who are now able to express clearly their priorities and commitments.

The core planning process, built around these consultations, went through to the following steps:

● agreeing on a development vision for the Richtersveld;

● identifying development priorities;

● filtering the vision and the priorities through a situational analysis of the area, which helped to assess how much was feasible;

● devising development strategies;

● adjusting these strategies in the light of the Land Development Objectives also drafted as part of the public process;

● preparing the integrated development plan through a series of drafts, including an initial Working Plan, submitted to the provincial government for review;

● following initial approval of the plan, sending it for approval to provincial government.

As the co-management plan and the complementary accords require on-going monitoring, evaluation, experimenting and learning, the process of negotiating and implementing the agreement is never "finished". A pluralist organisation usually needs to remain in charge of reviewing the agreement(s) on an on-going basis (more on this in Chapter 8). The composition of such an organisation may be very similar to the one of the negotiation platform, i.e., include the representatives of the parties that developed the agreement in the first place and "continue" the negotiation platform on a more stable basis. The parties may also identify or set up several CM organisations for the same NRM unit(s), for instance an advisory body, a body to originate technical proposals, an executive secretariat, a decision-making board.

Regardless of the type of organisations developed though the negotiation process, it may be useful that the social actors involved in it engage in reflection on what constitutes "good governance", and on whether they are actually developing such a system for the natural resources of their concern.[44] It can be argued that, if good governance principles are upheld, the CM organisational setting will be stronger and rendered more sustainable.[45] It is also likely that the very process of a pluralist negotiation enhances the chances of every participant to understand what governance is all about and how to attempt to improve upon it. Table 6.3 provides an overall view of principles and conditions of good governance derived from the work of the United Nations.

Table 6.3	Five Principles of Good Governance (modified from UNDP, 1999; UNDP, 2002; Abrams et al., 2003)	
The Five Principles	The United Nations Principles on which the five principles are based	Primary indicators of good governance in co-management settings
1. Legitimacy and Voice	Participation: All men and women should have a voice in decision-making, either directly or through legitimate intermediate institutions that represent their intention. Such broad participation is built on freedom of association and speech, as well as capacities to participate constructively. Consensus orientation: Good governance mediates differing interests to reach a broad consensus on what is in the best interest of the group and, where possible, on policies and procedures.	Views are freely expressed, with no discrimination related to gender, ethnicity, social class, etc. Dialogue is active and consensus is often achieved. There is a measure of trust among stakeholders. Agreed rules are respected because they are "owned" by people and not solely because of fear of repression.
2. Accountability	Accountability: Decision-makers in government, the private sector and civil society organisations are accountable to the public, as well as to institutional stakeholders. This accountability differs depending on the organisations and whether the decision is internal or external. Transparency: Transparency is built on the free flow of information. Processes, institutions and information are directly accessible to those concerned with them, and enough information is provided to understand and monitor them.	All management partners possess adequate knowledge, and quality of knowledge, about what is at stake in decision-making, who is responsible for what and how responsibilities can be rendered accountable. The avenues to demand accountability are accessible to all. Accountability is not limited to verbal exchanges but linked to concrete and appropriate rewards and sanctions.

---

44 This exercise could be proposed and assisted by the process facilitator.
45 Abrams et al., 2003.

3. Performance	Responsiveness: Institutions and processes try to serve all stakeholders. Effectiveness and efficiency: Processes and institutions produce results that meet needs while making the best use of resources.	A competent administration is in place, assessed through management effectiveness mechanisms. Institutional and human capacity is available to assume management responsibilities, as appropriate. The management regime is robust and resilient, i.e., able to overcome a variety of threats/ obstacles and come out strengthened from the experiences.
4. Fairness	Equity: All men and women have opportunities to improve or maintain their well being. Rule of Law: Legal frameworks should be fair and enforced impartially, particularly as they regard human rights.	Conservation is undertaken with decency and dignity, without humiliating or harming people. The governing mechanisms (e.g., laws, policies, conflict resolution forums, funding opportunities, etc.) distribute equitably the costs and benefits deriving from conservation. Public service promotions are merit-based. Laws and regulations are applied consistently through time Fair avenues for conflict management are available as is, eventually, non discriminatory recourse to justice
5. Direction	Strategic vision: Leaders and the public have a broad and long-term perspective on good governance and human development, along with a sense of what is needed for such development. There is also an understanding of the historical, cultural and social complexities in which that perspective is grounded.	Effective leadership draws from customary and innovative ideas and processes and provides a model of good conduct, being consistent in what it is said and done.

The end of the negotiation process (or at least of its first round) is usually marked by a meeting in which the results of the participatory process are made known to the relevant communities and the public at large. The meeting is usually held in the presence of authorities with more extensive powers than those who participated in the negotiations, thus providing an ostensible political endorsement of the outcomes of the process. The relevant actors review the common vision of the desired future, the components of a strategy designed to move from the present situation to the common vision, the co-management plan for the natural resources, the agreements set up for each component of the strategy and the organisations and rules developed to accompany everything through. For any major component of the strategy (e.g., the NRM plan or other key initiatives or projects), someone should be appointed as "responsible" for communication and carrying out the follow-up protocol (including results anticipated, progress indicators to be monitored, individuals and organisations in charge, etc.).

This meeting is an excellent opportunity to acknowledge the work of the negotiating parties as well as the co-management convener, Start-up Team and facilitator(s) and, in general, to celebrate the new hope generated for the entire community. At the meeting, the key actors can also publicly vow to respect and "collectively guarantee" the co-management package, which is described and discussed as openly as possible.

The co-management agreement and the pluralist organisations possibly identified or established to implement and review it should be confirmed and celebrated, but not ritualised to render them sacrosanct, as it might have been the case for the common vision of the desired future agreed upon by all relevant actors. On the contrary, the plans, agreements and organisations are to be monitored, evaluated and modified in an on-going way, according to their performance, results and eventual impacts. Trial and error, experimentation and even some slightly erratic management adjustments may be quite healthy, as NRM decisions need to be made regularly, and demand the on-going participation of the relevant social actors. This is not to mean, however, that an agreement can be changed at will by the unilateral decision of some parties. Unfortunately, many powerful stakeholders are the most reluctant to enter into the negotiation process because they "fear that the local communities will not respect the agreements" but later on they are the ones who actually break the agreements and fail to deliver.[46] For some, this potential lack of robustness of the agreements vis-à-vis the most powerful stakeholders is the most insidious problem of co-management.[47] Where is the guarantee that the agreement will be respected and that the organisation set in place by the process will remain recognised through time? A crucial question indeed!

...the key actors can also publicly vow to respect and "collectively guarantee" the co-management plans and agreements.

---

46 Chatelain et al., 2004.
47 Peter Schachenmann, personal communication, 2000.

Part III. TOWARDS EFFECTIVE INSTITUTIONS

Chapter 7. CO-MANAGEMENT AGREEMENTS

There is no standard co-management agreement, as each must be tailored to its specific subject context and scale, and negotiated with the relevant actors.[1] In particular, different types of agreements exist at the local, national and international level.

...each co-management agreement must be tailored to its specific subject, context and scale, and negotiated with the relevant actors.

At the local and national levels, agreements may involve local communities, indigenous peoples' organisations and private enterprises as well as state, provincial and territorial authorities, government agencies, research and educational institutions, international agencies and development cooperation agencies. International agreements may be multilateral or bilateral and be related to a general convention or specific ad hoc situations. Here is a non exhaustive list of the many forms that agreements can take:

● ad hoc and non legalised pacts (e.g., via traditional ceremonies, public declarations, public handshakes, etc.) among various parties interested in managing a given body of natural resources;

● written bylaws or customary rules concerning natural resource management, developed cooperatively by local governing bodies, such as village or local councils;

---

[1]   Borrini-Feyerabend, 1996; Lawrence, 1996.

- management plans for a body of natural resources, such as a local woodland, forest, pasture, fishing area;

- legislative protection and regulation of sustainable use rights as framework within which to develop NR management plans;

- agreed provision of NR management assistance from government to resource users (e.g., a memorandum of understanding);

- agreed settlements of NR conflict among various parties, from government to resource users;

- legal contracts between two or more parties regulating the costs and benefits of NR use;

- project-based agreements between donors and recipient communities and relevant authorities, which may include operations of community investment funds and revolving funds with a link to sound environmental management;

- conditional licenses issued by public sector agencies following negotiation with actors and interest groups on resource extraction and management;

- memoranda of understanding between local communities and protected area agencies;

- formal and informal agreements among local actors and public or private sector agencies and organisations, specifying their entitlements, rights and duties, and providing incentives to encourage local integrated conservation and development activities;

- contracts between different levels of government (e.g., federal, state, local, indigenous) or between various government agencies within a level (e.g., a forestry department and a national park agency);

- international treaties and conventions concerning biodiversity and environmental issues.

Some of the components of a co-management agreement deal directly with natural resources and are usually referred to as "co-management plans". Others bear upon natural resources in more indirect and complementary ways, such as through interventions for economic development, health, education, social organising, governance, culture, etc. Indeed, it would not be effective nor wise, nor even feasible to conceive a co-management approach to improve the status of an environment or a body of natural resources in isolation from the socio-economic reality in which they are embedded. Coordinated interventions in several sectors are important to allow for an equitable distribution of the social costs and benefits of sound natural resource management. In this sense, a co-management approach is a broad, interdisciplinary and multi-level setting of intents. Even if the management of a well defined set of natural resources is at its heart, the strategy "links" it to the surrounding environmental, socio-economic, institutional and cultural landscape, and grounds it as part of local and regional land use plans. In practice, this means that a co-management agreement is often developed as a package, including a co-management plan for the natural resources at stake as well as one or more complementary accords addressing relevant socio-economic and cultural issues. Such complementary accords are crucially important, as they make the management plan acceptable to all parties and thus ensure its sustainability. Natural resource management agreements are constantly being negotiated

It would not be effective nor wise, nor even feasible to conceive a co-management approach to improve the status of an environment or a body of natural resources in isolation from the socio-economic reality in which they are embedded.

A co-management agreement is often developed as a package, including a co-management plan for the natural resources at stake as well as one or more complementary accords addressing relevant socio-economic and cultural issues.

throughout the world. Whilst some agreements are reached after complex and lengthy negotiations involving lawyers and mediators, others are simply made by farmers or nomads shaking hands under a baobab tree or in the village hall. Several specific examples of ad hoc covenants, customary treaties and legally-sanctioned resource management agreements are presented throughout this chapter and in Table 8.1 of Chapter 8.

7.1   Customary and non-notarised agreements

...many unspoken agreements [are] embedded in local culture, history, social systems and cultural practices, such as reciprocity and solidarity.

Indigenous peoples and rural communities negotiate and enforce a wide spectrum of norms (customary law and practice) and procedures (for law making, conflict management, dispute settlement) to govern the use of natural resources. Such norms and procedures are often unique to a given culture or local society and developed as that culture evolved over many generations in a particular environment. Indigenous knowledge is the foundation of such customary or ethnic[2] governance systems, and its evolution through experimentation and innovation is the basis of local decision making in natural resource management. Examples include the customary land tenure systems of Papua New Guinea, which specify the conditions under which forests and forest products can be harvested, used, collected or hunted; the migration patterns of the Oromo Borana communities of Ethiopia, carefully responding to ever changing climatic and political conditions[3]; and the customary harvest restrictions (sasi) practiced by communities living in the Molucca islands of Indonesia and in the Pacific islands to ensure sustainable use of marine species.[4]

There exist many unspoken agreements embedded in local culture, history, social systems and cultural practices such as reciprocity and solidarity. Indeed, most indigenous management agreements spring from, and are shaped by, cosmologies that recognise linkages between human and environmental health, local dietary and medicinal sources and spiritual well-being, and livelihoods and natural resource management practices (see Box 7.1). There is a close association between a cosmovision, or how the relationship between people and nature in its widest sense is perceived, and customary resource management systems and agreements.[5]

Box 7.1   Holistic relationships between indigenous culture and land determine customary management agreements for indigenous agriculture in the Peruvian Andes (adapted from Fernandez and Vasquez, cited in IUCN, 1997)

Andean culture perceives "nature" as if it were a living and highly sensitive being, capable of responding positively when handled well, but also of responding furiously when mistreated. The Andean women and men see the flora, fauna, soil, and water as parts of a whole also including their children:

---

2   Bassi, 2003.
3   Bassi, 1996.
4   Zerner, 1991.
5   Haverkort and Hiemstra, 1999; Posey, 1999.

"We are part of the earth". This relationship does not imply immobility but rather continuous transformation and domestication of the environment, not for the unilateral benefit of humankind but for the reciprocal benefit of nature and society.

Andean culture is agro-centric since the prime concern of the society is to assure adequate and sufficient food, and to produce raw materials for processing. Agro-centrism means that the social organisation, science, art, philosophy, religion, perceptual frameworks, language, and technology (including natural resource management agreements) are all functions of the farming activities. The Andean society seeks an integral relationship with its medium, as reflected in the careful organisation of space and the eagerness to create beauty that benefits nature and society. For example, the construction of irrigation systems benefits society as it allows an increase in production. At the same time, it benefits nature in the sense that it allows greater total biomass production, i.e., a greater quantity of life in the environment.

For the technician, a plot is no more than a medium for production. For the campesino it is at the same time the source of food, a meeting place and a sacred place where rituals are carried out.

The customary management agreements of indigenous farmers, fishers, pastoralists and hunters-gatherers generally value the diversity of available ecological zones and allocate resource use in ways that are conscious of the spatial, distributional and ecological consequences on the landscape-wide mosaic (see Box 7.2). Agreements can include rules for allocation of resources within a community and/ or between communities and be mediated by a variety of cultural processes. Even marriage may reinforce a desired management agreement. For example, Tukanoan fishing communities in the rich waters of the upper Amazon are responsible for distributing fish to other Tukanoan communities with fewer fishery resources. Marriage rules require out-marriage between resource-rich and resource-poor villages, thus supporting this custom of solidarity, equity and reciprocity.[6]

Box 7.2   Indigenous peoples' "social agreements" on natural resource management
(adapted from Matowanyika, 1997; Durning, 1992; Shanley and Galvao, 1999;
Zoundjihekpon and Dossou-Glehouenou, 1999; Richards, 1999; Kabuye, 1999)

Customary rules to manage plant and animal species
Traditional management and knowledge systems include regimes to sustainably harvest and process materials from individual species. For example, Ficus natalensis and F. thonningii bark harvesting in Buganda (Kenya) involves elaborate protocols, including the tying of banana leaves to the de-barked tree, followed by the application of cow-dung to protect the tree. In Shona country, rural Zimbabwe, the many totems of the residents of Kagore are all linked to animals. In Shona society the individual has a special relationship with a totem animal. One injunction is that meat of the totem animal should not be eaten. Both types of rules reduce pressure on certain species.

Customary rules for fisheries and water management
In the South Pacific, ritual restrictions based on area, season, and species prevent overfishing. Religious events often open and close fishing seasons. Canadian Pacific tribes believe salmon spirits give their bodies to humans for food but punish those who waste fish, catch more than they can use, or disrupt aquatic habitats.

---

6   Alcorn, 1999.

For coastal peoples in Benin and the Ivory Coast, the great fishing period (May to October) is initiated by an opening rite over the "Aby" lagoon, sometimes carried out simultaneously in the different areas. It is the priest of the spirit called Assohon who opens the fishing in May and closes it in October. Sacred catfish of Sapia are sheltered by the Dransi river which is formally forbidden to fisherfolk. Together with sacred crocodiles from Gbanhui, all the aquatic species are covered by food prohibitions to the villagers. During the day dedicated to sacred and venerated crocodiles, it is forbidden to go to the Yonyongo river.

The customary management agreements of the fisherfolk of Jambudip (India) help coordinate the complex variables of seabed topography, seawater conditions and sequences of tide with fish behaviour, to ensure both successful catches and the safety of fisherfolk at sea. In their selection of the appropriate seabed over which to conduct their activities, these fisherfolk are like the agriculturists who tend to classify the soil according to its relative fertility and the types of crops grown. The "soil" of the seabed is classified by its capacity to support the net poles and by its fertility regarding the types and quantity of fish in the waters above it. Such management agreements and practices have helped to conserve a considerable amount of marine diversity.

Several water bodies (village tanks, ponds, rivers and others) are attributed sacred qualities in India and are protected against over-fishing or over-extraction of any other resource available. Some of them exist within the bounds of sacred groves. Management agreements based in spiritual beliefs help preserve the water bodies, allowing for the underwater forms of life, even at the micro-level, to flourish undisturbed. The only surviving population of Trionyx nigricans, the large freshwater turtle, is found in Chittagong (Bangladesh) in a sacred pond dedicated to a Muslim Saint.

Customary management of forests

Integral to traditional forest management agreements is the use of elaborate taboos, myths, folklore, and other culturally-controlled systems that bring coherence and shared community values to resource use and management. In the Eastern Amazon, for example, hunters who are greedy, or do not heed the wishes of the giant cobra, giant sloth, and the curupira, will become lost, or otherwise suffer some punishment. These creatures require respect for the forest, and what might be called "sustainable" approaches to the harvesting of game and plants.

Interdicts, totems, and sacred forbidden species and areas based on religious beliefs, and implemented by religious chiefs, are widely used throughout West Africa to control the use and management of forests and resources. For example, in Benin the panther is venerated by the Houegbonou clan, who can neither kill nor eat it. The Houedas people adore, protect and breed pythons. Fon and Torris people identify monkeys with twins, which leads to the protection of some monkey habitat. Milicia excelsa (iroko) is a sacred tree, protected and revered throughout West and Central Africa. On the western edge of the Gola Forest Reserve– the largest element in a complex of four surviving areas of high rain forest on the Sierra Leonean side of the border with Liberia– villagers have a taboo against bringing the wood of Musanga cecropiodes into the village for use as fuelwood.

In general, indigenous peoples and traditional communities have developed, and continue to follow, rules and regulations that govern their use of and relationship to natural resources. Sometimes formalised and codified, often informal and seldom written, these rules and regulations define collective behaviour, and provide a valuable basis for co-management arrangements that may also involve non-local partners. Within the diversity of customary systems around the world, a few common characteristics of such "internal agreements" seem to emerge:

● land, water and biotic resources are assigned livelihood values but also symbolic and religious significance: they contribute to determine the cultural identity of a group;

- rights and responsibilities are usually collectively held;

- individual, heritable rights in land (and wetlands) can be accommodated, but most such rights are either rights of use subject to a superior group right; rights to particular resources (such as tree or animal species); or rights to harvest a particular cultivated spot;

- land tenure, resource tenure and access rights are not necessarily the same, and one parcel of land or area of water is often subjected to a variety of rights held by different persons and groups;

- traditional rights over land, waters and natural resources are rarely recorded in maps or written documents; generally, orders and "ownership marks" make use of natural features and mutual understandings that are more significant to the community of users than to outsiders;

- limits are frequently set on the exploitation of resources, often on the basis of seasonal regulations, and some areas and resources can be placed completely off limits (e.g., sacred groves);

- little conceptual or practical separation exists between resource use and conservation.

Whilst indigenous and local governance of natural resources respond to many of the needs of local peoples, the diverse concerns of different groups within communities are often differently accommodated. Indeed, in all societies (indigenous or not) various types of co-management agreements may be more or less fair and capable of accommodating the specific interests of different social actors (see Box 7.3).

Box 7.3   The type of resource management agreement depends on who has the right to speak! An example from the Solomon Islands
(adapted from Adams, 1996)

Resource management agreements must be located in their cultural context. In the Solomon islands customary law has a profound influence on the capacity to participate in decision making. Land and marine tenure systems define the rights and entitlements to speak about and for resources. Individual legal titles to specific marine or land areas do not exist. It is membership in corporate, kinship based clans or butubutus that defines a person's relationship to resources. Although resources are claimed and controlled by the butubutu as a collective, there are clear distinctions between the power to speak about resources (and frame the resource management agreements) and the rights to merely use them. Rights and entitlements are unevenly distributed within and among communities, and are coming under increasing pressure from new commercial forces.

In the Solomons, women have inherently weak negotiating positions in traditional community institutions and decision making processes. They are often uninformed about resource management issues and do not participate in public debate and in the framing of resource management agreements. By custom it is male relatives who speak on behalf of a woman landholder. However, customary law does not oblige them to consult with the women. "In decision making processes, a male relation's vote is seen as equivalent to her choice".

Where women do find the confidence to talk as a group against the decisions made by men, it is likely they will be ignored. When the Tobakokorapa Association took the decision to designate an area used by women as protected, Michi women expressed their dissatisfaction at a general meeting. They were overruled by the older men and were told they would get "used to" the idea.

Gender bias is thus expressed not just in community structures but, more fundamentally, in intra-community power relationships and in the type of resource management agreements negotiated between members of the community.

Informal resource management agreements are constantly negotiated among a variety of parties. For example, the arrangements to establish a livestock corridor through a farmers' field in semi-arid northern Senegal are usually the product of informal discussions at the village mosque.[7] Such ad hoc agreements have no formal legal status and are not enforced by the government. Conflicts between two or more parties are informally arbitrated by respected authorities such as the village chief, a village council, or a wise elder.

Informal resource management agreements are constantly negotiated among a variety of parties.

Among indigenous peoples, resource management agreements are usually enforced through social sanctions according to customary law, with decision-making in the hands of local institutions. The recognition of such agreements by governmental agencies can foster very effective co-management systems (see Box 7.4). In Rajasthan (western India), self-initiated forest protection committees even levy fines on offenders (the amount often depending on the ability of the offender to pay) besides imposing social sanctions, a practice that is informally condoned by official agencies.[8]

Box 7.4   Village law and co-management of aquatic resources in Khong district (Lao PDR) (adapted from Baird, 1999)

The aquatic resource co-management system in Khong district is part of the existing administrative structure of Lao villages. No attempts were made to establish new levels of bureaucracy at the village level, although certain villages have established their own informal or ad hoc working groups to deal with particular issues. Regulation, implementation and enforcement are left up to the community. From a legal perspective, Khong district administrators consider that the aquatic resource co-management regulations of villages fit well into what is known as "village law" (kot labiap ban). The legal system of Lao PDR allows villages to make certain regulations regarding local issues, provided that they do not conflict with national laws or the constitution. In the recent past, village regulations were rarely utilised to deal with natural resource management issues (except for some security issues, or the tying up or releasing of water buffaloes). Now, Khong district officials believe that the village law system accommodates well for aquatic resource co-management not only within a village but even among villages. A

---

7   Freudenberger and Freudenberger, 1993.
8   Kothari et al., 2000.

fundamental issue with regards to any aquatic resource co-management programme relates to boundaries of management jurisdiction between villages. For several years no major conflicts between villages with regards to boundaries and aquatic resources have been reported. There seems to be a great potential for utilising village law for dealing with other natural resource management issues as well.

The village structure is the foundation of ethnic lowland Lao society. Villages are self-sustaining communities relatively unconnected with larger political and social units, have very limited social and economic stratification and possess a strong sense of social equality, cooperation and mutual dependence. Currently, disparities in wealth and power within villages are growing, but villagers are still able to speak with one voice when dealing with outsiders, a fact that positively influences the outcome of co-management regulations. There appear to be three interlocked and mutually reinforcing elements maintaining Lao village cooperation and solidarity: (1) a village ideology of mutuality, (2) successful events of cooperation, and (3) shallow socio-economic stratification.

Informal resource management agreements are also increasingly being negotiated between local communities and rural development and conservation projects. Covenants, memoranda of understanding, project and research agreements such as the ones described in Box 7.5 rarely have a legal standing. Yet such non-notarised written agreements can be effective in formalising the roles, rights and responsibilities of the rural communities and external agencies involved.

**Box 7.5   The Protocol for the Community Biodiversity Development and Conservation
Programme**
(adapted from CBDC Programme, 1994)

The Community Biodiversity Development and Conservation (CBDC) Programme is an inter-regional initiative developed by agricultural non-governmental organisations in Africa, Asia and Latin America, in cooperation with northern partners. Its purpose is to strengthen the ongoing work of farming communities in conserving and enhancing the agricultural biodiversity that is vital to their livelihoods and food security. The CBDC programme is also a unique attempt to establish a working relationship between farmer communities and institutional systems of innovation (national agricultural research systems and universities).

The CBDC's Programme Protocol was adopted in Barcelona in 1994 and spells out the agreements which CBDC partners have reached with one another. It was developed to guide relations concerning intellectual property, rights and responsibilities in relation to genetic resources, information, funds, technologies, methodologies and systems. The partners recognise that one particularly difficult element to this programme is the relationship between institutional and farmer/ community innovation systems. All partners believe that farmers, and humanity at large, are best served through the full and free exchange of plant genetic resources unfettered by the constraints imposed by intellectual property or other monopolistic market practices. Partner NGOs do not wish to cooperate with institutions (public or private) that impose or facilitate intellectual property control over plant genetic resources.

The Protocol assumes that the partners have mutual trust, confidence and are willing to cooperate, and that a highly-legalistic document is not necessary. It also recognises that other partners at the regional, national and community level may not know all their colleagues and, therefore, basic working relations should be spelled out adequately. In addition, the Protocol recognises that there is an imbalance in the ability of partners to access genetic resources, information and financial resources. The occasional and sometimes long standing tension between the community and institutional system, and a history of mutual misunderstanding, should be taken into account. For these reasons, the Protocol operates on the assumption that decisions are taken "bottom up" (from the community to the global level) and that the authority will rest, as far as possible, at the community level.

The Protocol is divided into two operational parts: the first addresses issues of intellectual integrity intended to assure that germplasm, information, funds, technologies, methodologies and systems, and the rights and responsibilities that go with them, will be respected. The second section addresses issues of institutional integrity intended to protect and promote the interests of the partners. The Protocol is seen as an evolutionary document that is modified and adapted as partners learn how to work with one another at the local, national, regional and global levels.

To date there exist few examples of written agreements between communities and researchers. Despite the international calls for the requirement of prior informed consent, respect and local control over the use of knowledge and resources, the examples offered by the Awa in Ecuador (Box 7.6) and the Soufriere Marine Management Area in Saint Lucia (see Box 3.9 in Chapter 3) are the exception rather than the rule. The development of such research and benefit sharing agreements illustrate the importance, and the difficulty, of intercultural dialogue in a co-management process. Any agreement– verbal or written– will take shape in the context of existing customary norms and the Four Directions Council (an organisation of North American indigenous peoples) has warned about the risks inherent in broad and all-encompassing regulations:[9]

"Indigenous peoples possess their own locally-specific systems of jurisprudence with respect to the classification of different types of knowledge, proper procedures for acquiring and sharing knowledge, and the rights and responsibilities related to possessing knowledge, all of which are embedded in each culture and its language.... Any attempt to devise uniform guidelines for the recognition and protection of indigenous peoples' knowledge runs the risk of collapsing this rich jurisprudential diversity into a single "model" that will not fit the values, conceptions, or laws of any indigenous society...".

Box 7.6   The Awa Federation and research agreements (Ecuador)
            (adapted from Laird, 2002)

The Awa Federation is a legal institution that administers 101,000 hectares held under communal title by the Awa Peoples in Ecuador, makes collective decisions regarding land use, and works on the development of socio-economic infrastructure. The Awa acquired legal recognition of communal title to their land in 1995. Prior to this time, they were considered "wards of the state", and their territory was a "forest reserve" of the communal settlement of the Awa people. Since 1995 the Awa have demarcated their territory by planting a 50 meter wide border with fruit trees, and patrolling and securing their boundaries. Due to the botanical and ethno-botanical wealth of the Awa and their lands, a number of research institutions have begun collaboration with the Awa. In 1993, the Convenio– Reglamentos para la Realización de Estudios Científicos en el Territorio de la Federación Awa– was developed to set terms for research relationships. The Convenio includes the following provisions:

● all scientists must ask for written permission to carry out studies. The written request for permission must include a description of objectives, size, and composition of research party, length of research programme, species or object of study, and the manner in which this research will benefit the Awa community;

● the request for permission must be given with a minimum of two months' notice (widely dispersed

---
9   Four Directions Council, 1996 quoted in Laird, 2002.

communities only meet four time a year for four days);

- more than five people to a research group is prohibited;

- more than one group of scientists are prohibited from entering at the same time (this and the preceding provisions are intended to minimise the cultural impact of the research process);

- local guides and informants must accompany all scientists;

- the collection of animals, insects, or plants for commercial purposes is prohibited;

- only 3 specimens of each species are to be collected– one each for the research group, the Awa federation, and the Tobar Donoso Project in Quito (in 1995 this provision was modified to allow for the collection of more than just 3 specimens);

- the removal of any object from Awa territory not approved by the Federation is prohibited (the main concerns are cultural artefacts and property, including stone mortars found in the forest and believed to be possessions of the ancestors);

- scientists must dispose of their own garbage;

- the prices established by the Awa Federation for their services are as follows: each member of each scientific group must contribute to the Federation 1,000 sucres in order to enter Awa territory; guides and informants receive 700 sucres per day, cooks, cleaners, and other workers receive 500 sucres per day; members of scientific groups from Ecuadorean universities or institutions pay 500 sucres per day to enter Awa territory;

- gifts or distribution of money outside of the established regulations are not allowed;

- scientists who do not respect these rules or Awa organisations and cultures will be expelled immediately from their territories;

- the Awa Federation must receive acknowledgement in relevant publications.

The collection of specimens in Awa territory requires two tiers of permission: first the researcher must secure permission from the Awa, and secondly, they must obtain permission from the Ecuadorian government.

7.2   Formal legal agreements

Legally recognised agreements can be stipulated at local, national or international levels, but the difference between these types of agreements is often blurred. For example, a natural resource management agreement may be codified in national law but signed locally. Conversely, local agreements may influence national level processes and legislation for resource management. And international treaties may deeply affect national policies and local resource management regimes.

There has been a trend in some countries (e.g., Australia, USA, and Ecuador) towards increased use of conservation agreements over private land. Examples are the land use and conservation easements now numbering in the thousands in the USA (see Box 7.7). Such agreements address the protection of species, ecological communities, habitats or potential habitats and are usually legally binding on the contracting parties and successors in title. The parties include one or more landowners and the relevant government authorities, often with the facilitation of

Legal agreements are stipulated at local, national or international levels.

Co-management
agreements over
private lands.

an environment-concerned NGO. The agreements are effective until terminated or revoked, may be registered and can be amended if so provided in the agreement or in legislation. In general, where an area is under a conservation easement, the authority of the landowner is affected in accordance with the terms of the covenant or the regulations corresponding to the management plan for the area.[10]

Box 7.7   Conservation easements in the USA
(Brent Mitchell, personal communication, 2003)

The fastest growing tool for conservation in the Americas is the easement, or deed restriction, which prohibits certain land uses and allows others. Easements are especially popular among private landowners, and particularly useful in working landscapes, allowing traditional land uses such as farming or forestry while prohibiting future conversion in use, e.g., for industrial or residential development.

Easements are based on a concept that rights to land are plural and divisible; that is, rights to farm, cut wood, build a house, mine material, etc., are "bundled" into the idea of land ownership. From that concept springs the idea that a landowner may not only sell or transfer all his or her rights to land, but that these rights may be separated, and one or more may be transferred while the others are retained. Thus a farmer might voluntarily transfer development rights to his land but continue farming. He therefore protects his land from future land conversion, continues farming, and may reap benefits from the (technically) decreased land value (lower property taxes, for example).

While securing conservation "in perpetuity", an easement allows a landowner to retain ownership and rights to uses deemed appropriate to the land.   Landowners may thus benefit materially by donating land or a restriction (e.g., tax relief), but it is to be stressed that the most common motivation for the easements is a sense of responsibility for the land and the resources, and a concern about what may happen to them in the future. Because of that, the present landowners restrict the choices that future landowners might take. Easements are attached to the deed (legal title to the property) and future landowners are bound by the conservation restriction. In most cases, and always in the US, easements are legally binding in perpetuity, i.e., forever.

Benefits to conservation include: easements are permanent; they cost less than acquiring all rights to the land; and they encourage maintaining traditional land uses. Presently, a very large number of conservation easements are protecting working forest land from future development. There is some on-going cost however. The transferred rights do not simply disappear; they must be held by someone else, often a non-profit land trust or corresponding government authority. The receiving entity has a legal obligation to monitor and enforce easement violations.

Though easements have been legally possible for a long time, they have been applied in large scale in the US only in the last 30 years or so. Their use reflects a trend toward voluntary, less-than-absolute land conservation strategies, and has been aided by the development of various tax and policy incentives. Easement legislation has recently been passed in most Canadian provinces, accompanied by national efforts to create more incentives for landowners to grant them. Similarly, model easements and/or precedents have been established in several Latin American countries in the past five years.

Other examples of co-management agreements over private lands include the contracts that establish discrete areas for community management of natural resources on land that is privately owned. Under such contracts the village persuades individuals and households to cede some of their land for communal or

[10] Sutherland, 1996; Farrier, 1995.

group management. The land may include woodlots, orchards, springs and valued hunting or plant collecting grounds that need special protection. The Upper Guinea Resource management agreements are an example of such private land cession relationships (see Box 7.8).

Box 7.8   Les ententes: resource management agreements in Upper Guinea
(adapted from Diallo, 1995)

In Upper Guinea, private land cession agreements are known as ententes. The entente is a written contract of cession which is translated into French and local languages and certified by a government notary. Copies are made for all the parties to the agreement, and for the government authorities. These cession agreements are not transfers of ownership, but long term leases with stated terms ranging between 20 and 30 years. For example, the agreement between Elhadji Amadou Diallo, Maamadou Orz Diallo and the villagers of Tzankoy in the Fouta Djallon in Upper Guinea, which became official on 3 February 1994, stipulates the following:

● the proprietors make the plot of land available to the village for reforestation;

● trees will be planted at the head of the spring of Diaberehoun;

● the proprietors have no rights to the trees planted;

● the trees belong to the entire village;

● the proprietors have the right to plant and exploit individually fruit trees in the zone;

● other villagers do not have the right to plant trees in this area;

● the clauses contained in this agreement cannot be modified, added to, or subtracted unless an agreement is reached between the two parties in presence of a qualified authority.

The contractual approach is becoming commonplace in conservation and development initiatives....

The so-called "contractual approach" is becoming common place in conservation and development initiatives. A recent review has highlighted the growing use of local conventions and contracts throughout the Sahelian region of francophone Africa.[11] This is partly because the contractual approach offers the flexibility required for the implementation of both integrated conservation and development initiatives[12] and agreements that need to change in content and scope as relationships between social actors evolve and as natural resources are regenerated or better managed over time. For example, gender and equity concerns are increasingly reflected in agreements on natural resource management (Box 7.9).

Box 7.9   Gender supportive articles in the local contract/ convention of N'Dour N'Dour (Senegal)
(adapted from Gueye and Tall, 2004)

Article 2   Women have priority use over lowland rice paddies.

Article 3   Each resident woman in the village has the right to a plot of land in the valley.

Article 4   Each woman has the right to share part of her land with her husband or a close relative living in the village.

Article 5   Any person who leaves the village to live elsewhere no longer has rights of access and control over land. All his/ her rights to land are automatically ceded back to the village community.

Article 6   In case of the death of a woman, either her daughter in law or/ and daughter resident in the village will inherit the plots of land.

In France, co-management agreements for regional parks and protected areas include natural resource management plans as well as complementary accords or contracts with state authorities and the private sector involved in broader socio-economic development (see Box 7.10).

Box 7.10   Co-management of protected areas and landscapes through negotiated territorial charters in France
(adapted from Finger-Stitch and Ghimire, 1997; Allali-Puz et al., 2003)

In 1965, just one year after the creation of the first national park in France, the government adopted also a further, more flexible approach to protected area management than the Parc National model. Based on the German approach to landscape management, the French concept of Parc Naturel Régional aimed to conserve fragile environments and regenerate rural economies and to offer relaxing spaces for urban populations. The Parc Naturel Régional was and still is the embodiment of an innovative policy that seeks to build the future by combining natural, cultural and human assets within a given territory.

In the Parcs Naturels Régionaux, all conservation and development activities are regulated by the charter of the park. This is a contract endorsed and signed by the local authorities and the private and public partners who have a stake in the future of the area defined by the park. The charter is based on a participatory planning and implementation process towards local sustainable development, but it also provides for the respect of other national and international programmes, acting as a useful mechanism for policy coherence at a number of levels and across various sectors. With the signing of the charter,

---

[11]   Tall and Guèye, 2003; see also Box 3.15 in Chapter 3.

[12]   A review of experience with integrated conservation and development projects that recommends the contractual approach is available in Larson et al., 1997.

the local authorities and other partners agree to respect and follow the rules and agreements they have themselves developed and laid out in a democratically negotiated contract. Success chiefly depends on the inclusion and participation of all actors dependent on the relevant territory for livelihoods and culture.

Agreements over the management of protected areas have been tried out to lessen conflicts between people and park authorities and reduce pressure on the government staff responsible for managing large parks (See Boxes 7.11 and 7.12).

Box 7.11   Gurig National Park (Australia)
            (adapted from Smyth, 2001)

For thousands of years, the Cobourg Peninsula and its surrounding sea formed the traditional lands of four Aboriginal clans. In 1924, the peninsula became North Australia's first Flora and Fauna Reserve. During the 1950s, all the remaining Aboriginal traditional owners were removed to a government settlement on nearby Croker Island. In 1981, the establishment of Gurig National Park was agreed to by the Northern Territory Government and the Aboriginal traditional owners, to resolve a pending land claim under the Aboriginal Land Rights Act of the Northern Territory (NT). Rather than proceeding with the claim, the traditional owners consented to the establishment of the National Park in return for regaining title to their traditional lands. The key features of the joint management of Gurig National Park are:

- the declaration of the park under its own legislation— The Cobourg Peninsula Land and Sanctuary Act 1981 (NT);

- the vesting of the land in a Land Trust on behalf of the traditional owners;

- the establishment of a Board of Management comprising 8 members, of whom 4 are traditional owners and 4 are representatives of the Northern Territory Government; the Board is chaired by one of the traditional owner members who also has a casting vote;

- the payment of an annual fee by the Government to traditional owners for use of their land as a National Park; the fee was set at 20,000 Australian Dollars in 1981 and increased annually by a percentage equal to the percentage increase in the average male wage in Darwin;

- the placement of the responsibility for day to day management with the Conservation Commission of the Northern Territory (now the Parks and Wildlife Commission);

- the recognition of the rights of traditional owners to use and occupy the park.

The Cobourg Peninsula Land and Sanctuary Act 1981 (NT) sets out the respective functions of the Board and the Conservation Commission of the Northern Territory. The functions of the Board are:

- to prepare the management plans;

- to protect and enforce the rights of the traditional owners to use and occupy the park;

- to determine, in accordance with the plan of management, the rights of access to parts of the sanctuary by persons who are not traditional owners;

- to ensure adequate protection of sites of spiritual or other significance in the Aboriginal tradition;

- to make by-laws with respect to the management of the park; and

- to carry out other functions as imposed on the Board by the plan of management.

The functions of the Commission are to act on behalf of and subject to the direction of the Board in:

- the preparation of the management plans; and

- the control and management of the park.

The Act also states that where differences of opinion arise between the Board and the Commission with respect to the preparations of plans of management or the control and management of the park, the matter shall be resolved by a resolution of the Board. The plan contains many practical details relating to the exercise of the rights and interests of traditional owners over the park, including:

- the location of Aboriginal residential areas;

- the recognition of traditional hunting and fishing;

- a commitment to train and employ Aboriginal people as rangers and in other capacities on the park (subject to budgetary constraints).

In 1996, the Cobourg Peninsula Land and Sanctuary Act 1981 (NT) was amended to extend the powers of the Board to include supervision of the management of the adjacent Cobourg Marine Park, which includes customary marine clan estates of the traditional owners. In summary, the joint management arrangements for Gurig National Park provide the Aboriginal people with secure tenure over their traditional lands, as well as nominal control over policy and planning matters via their voting majority on the board. The Northern Territory Government, through its representation on the Board and through the operations of the Parks and Wildlife Commission, maintains a strong role in determining the management of the park. It is significant that these arrangements do not require the traditional owners to lease their lands to the government.

Co-management of protected areas have been tried out to lessen conflicts between people and park authorities.

The actual subject matter of protected area management agreements can vary considerably. An example of such diversity can be seen in the agreements reached between conservation agencies and communities neighbouring protected areas in South Africa. Twelve protected area management agencies have developed innovative agreements with local neighbours to cover issues of access and use of different types of protected resources as well as benefit sharing arrangements.[13] Examples include:

1. Land use agreements. The 1620 sq km Richtersveld National Park is leased from the Nama for a period of 30 years with rights to graze an agreed number of livestock and to controlled harvest of natural products. The lease payments are paid into a Trust appointed by the community to manage the funds.

2. Revenue sharing. Twenty percent of the gross revenue for a reserve in Kwa Zulu Natal is allocated to a neighbouring Tribal Authority and fifty per cent of the revenue generated by the protected area is passed on to the Tribal Authority in Lebowa.

3. Fuelwood collection rights. In KaNgwane, people from the neighbouring communities are allowed to remove one head-load of fuelwood per week. The wood has to be from fallen trees or from areas shortly scheduled for burning as part of the range management programme. People from more distant villages may collect fuelwood only for ceremonial purposes, provided they have received the permission of the local Tribal Authority.

4. Rights to harvest medicinal plants. Tribal herbalists or Inyangas are permitted to collect plants or plant parts in Bophuthtswana and KaNgwane National Parks.

---

[13] Anderson, 1995.

Box 7.12   Forest use agreement between Mount Elgon National Park and the people of
Ulukusi Parish (Uganda)
(adapted from Wild and Mutebi, 1996)

The Forest Use Agreement between Mount Elgon National Park and the People of Ulukusi Parish, Uganda is a good example of an agreement designed after a careful investigation into the types of resource use and the spectrum of resource users. The agreement begins with an area description in which the buffer zone between Ulukusi Parish (comprised of nine villages, of which four border on the park) and Mount Elgon National Park is divided into three contiguous zones, of which the third is located within the outer rim of the park limit. The communities bordering the park are essentially involved in agriculture, but many seek additional livelihood sources from the forest, such as collecting bamboo shoots and stems, bee-keeping and sawing wood timber. The next section declares the general management objectives of the agreement, of which the first is the integration of community's use needs with the conservation objectives of the park. The agreement is explicit in its aim to gain people's acceptance of the national park and the respect for its boundaries through a constructive working relationship.

The third section of the agreement touches upon the mode of representation of the community and the park in the form of a committee. The Kitsatsa Forest Use Committee is composed of forty representatives from the bordering communities (each of the 9 villages elect 4 to represent their interests), in addition two specialist groups (the herbalists and the pitsawers) each get to elect two members to the committee. The agreement designates the Regional Council Chairman, its Secretary for Women, the Parish Chief, the Mount Elgon National Park Boundary Ranger and a parish-based extension worker as co-opted members of the Kitsatsa Forest Use Committee. Five sub-committees have been named, formed by villagers located on each of the five trails leading from the parish to the park. These sub-committees are responsible for the day-to-day monitoring of compliance to the agreement and are accountable to the Kitsatsa Committee.

The fourth section divides the management and enforcement tasks between the four villages, and along the five trails. Four use categories are distinguished:

1. forest uses open to all people of Ulukusi and for which no prior permission from the committee is required;
2. forest uses which are open to all people of Ulukusi but for which prior permission is required from the sub-committees or the committee on a case by case basis;
3. forest uses which are restricted to a limited and registered number of people only; and
4. forest uses on which there is a total ban.

These use categories are applied for the three management zones that have been identified in the park territory, in which the type of use, the user group and the time period and resource allocation are specified. This is clearly derived from a detailed inventory of resource uses, in their spatial and temporal variability. There is also mention of Cultural Sites in the innermost sector of the park (Zone III), such as Pina, a sacred site to which villagers may have access for religious rituals.

A fifth section of the agreement defines the mechanisms for monitoring and control of forest use. The sub-committees located along trails leading to the park are responsible for monitoring activities and denouncing abuses. The law-enforcement and policing functions are left to the warden in charge and the park rangers, particularly in the case of smoking bamboo shoots through fire. Sanctions, however, are decided by the Kitsatsa Committee, and justice is administered through a graduated system. Fines are defined for first and second offenders, while third offenders are sent to court in the justice system of the state of Uganda. Leases and charges for bee-keeping and bamboo collecting are also fixed and levied by the committee. There is an explicit difference between insiders and outsiders, as outsiders are charged higher rates for access to the resource. Additional linkage activities are also contemplated in the sixth and seventh section of the agreement, in which the Kitsatsa Committee serves as an intermediary or nested institution to link to other community development initiatives.

International legal agreements focus on the management of natural resources of great value for residents of neighbouring countries. Large free roaming herds of animals or fish that regularly migrate across international boundaries between two countries may be the subject of such bilateral management agreements (see Box 7.13). The subject of agreements can also be water or air (e.g., in pollution prevention agreements).

Box 7.13   The Agreement between the Government of Canada and the Government of the United States of America on the conservation of the porcupine caribou herd
(adapted from Government of Canada and Government of the USA, 1987)

This international agreement acknowledges that there are various human uses of caribou herds, that for generations peoples of Yukon Territory and the Northwest Territories in Canada and rural residents of the state of Alaska in the United States of America have customarily and traditionally harvested porcupine caribou to meet their nutritional, cultural and other essential needs, and that these peoples will continue to do so in the future. The agreement starts from the premise that local people should participate in the conservation of the porcupine caribou and its habitat.

The main objectives of the legal agreement signed by both countries in 1987 are:

● to conserve the porcupine caribou herd and its habitat through international cooperation and coordination so that the risk of irreversible damage or long term adverse effects as a result of use of caribou or its habitat is minimised;

● to ensure opportunities for customary and traditional uses of the porcupine caribou herds by rural residents and indigenous peoples while prohibiting the commercial sale of their meat.

Under this type of agreement the parties are asked to establish an advisory board known as the International Porcupine Caribou Board. The Board's main function is to seek information from management agencies, local communities, users of porcupine caribou herds, scientific bodies and other interested and to make recommendations on all aspects of the conservation of the porcupine caribou herds and their habitat that require international coordination.

Whether formal or informal, simple or comprehensive, detailed or principle setting– different agreements are shaped by the social and ecological context in which they are negotiated. An important aim of these negotiations is clarity of meaning and purpose, which should be reflected in the contents of the co-management agreement. This is important to avoid ambiguities and divergent interpretations and on-going conflict during the phase of implementation of agreements, and learning by doing.

7.3 The components of a co-management agreement

A co-management agreement usually specifies:

- the agreement's purpose, the parties in the agreement and the relevant territory, area or natural resources;
- benefits and responsibilities assigned to the parties to the agreement;
- means of protecting the investment each party makes in the agreement;
- means of resolving disputes;
- specification of the duration of the agreement;
- schedules and procedures for review, reporting, monitoring and evaluation;
- confidentiality and other special clauses.

We review below primarily written and legal CM agreements, providing a general checklist for their usual components. No attempt is made to describe the diversity of non-written agreements rooted in customary law and indigenous institutions, which indeed are as varied and rich as human cultures.

... non-written agreements rooted in customary law and indigenous institutions are as varied and rich as human cultures....

Title

The title of the agreement or process usually includes a reference to the management of resources or territory at stake and specifies whether it is a contract, a memorandum of understanding or otherwise.

Preamble and statement of purpose

A preamble is the opening statement to an agreement, and it may describe its history, principal characteristics, and the principles on which it is based. It can

A preamble can identify the principles and rationale which will guide the implementation of the agreement.

refer to the institutional actors (stakeholders) interested in the natural and cultural resource management and commit the parties to cooperation, coordination, mutual recognition, trust and respect. It may acknowledge the importance of appropriate resource management to those stakeholders and wider communities. It might refer to the rights of relevant stakeholders under local, state, national or international law, to the values of the particular resources that are the subject of the agreement, and to the relevant authorities that authorise the agreement or render it legally binding and enforceable. Ideally, a common vision would have been achieved and ritualised among the parties for the territories or resources at stake. If so, the preamble should make explicit reference to it (see Chapter 5), and should enunciate clear, realistic and measurable objectives. A preamble is not just an issue of symbolic importance because it can identify the principles and rationale that will guide the implementation of the agreement, and thus assist in its interpretation.

Definitions

All parties to the agreement and those abiding by it need to understand the meaning of the terms used within it. A definition section assists with this.

Defining territory, area or set of resources at stake is relatively easy in those countries where a tenure system is recognised. The real property description may be used, and it may be helpful to attach a map. If the agreement refers to works in a specific part of the land (e.g., "clear the south paddock of weeds"), such areas should also be clearly described and/ or marked on a map. In marine and coastal areas, the agreement should recognise the difficulty inherent in defining maritime boundaries; in the absence of physical demarcation, these will be expressed by a distance from shore, or by depth, or with respect to landmarks on shore.

If the agreement is to have legal validity, it is important that the parties have the legal power to enter into such an agreement.

With respect to the parties, if these are simply individuals ("real persons" in legal terms) and the agreement amounts to a common law contract, things are relatively simple. However, each party should check carefully that the others do have the legal right to contract with respect to the land (for example, a manager or member of the family of a registered owner may need to demonstrate power of attorney; it is never wise simply to take someone's word that they have such rights). Careful checks may be needed in the case of a company, consortium or community customary rightholders.

In the case of indigenous communities, deciding who is the appropriate "party" with whom to enter a legal agreement is often a complex issue, legally, politically and culturally. Clan or tribal relationships, intra-community politics, land claims, relationships between councils of elders and members of modern governing structures, tribal members who live elsewhere, gender issues, and tensions between "traditional" owners and people more recently arrived can all cloud the picture. A wrong choice of "appropriate party" can not only result in serious legal complications, it can also cause grave offence and lead to breakdown in communications with the community or indigenous group.

If the agreement is to have legal validity, it is important that the parties have the legal power to enter into such an agreement. Further, if the agreement incorporates works to or on land, or financial transactions relating to these, it is equally important that the land itself be defined. Some caution, however, should be exercised about not imposing definitions of land and resources that are incompatible with customary governance and management systems, which are usually quite complex (see Box 7.14).

Box 7.14 Substantial flexibility in NRM agreements is needed to accommodate the complexity of customary governance and management systems

In customary governance systems, land and resource tenure are normally ascribed to several actors at the same time. These may include households, extended families, villages, lineages, clans, etc. Usually, customary land use patterns recognise overlapping claims on the same territory, connected to collective identities of different importance and defining different types of rights. In addition, mobile indigenous peoples traditionally manage land in migration patterns that are changeable according to climate and other variable circumstances. The definition of their territories and migration routes needs to accommodate for "porous" and changing borders and requires a less-than-sharp definition of the area to which the management agreements ultimately apply. Such complex governance and management systems require substantial flexibility in developing NRM agreements.

Scope of authority of the parties in the agreement

The parties in the agreement include all relevant actors and are usually identified in the preamble of the co-management agreement. The scope of the authority of parties to the agreement should be clearly defined. It may be broad or narrow.

In defining the scope of authority, the agreement should clearly enunciate the distribution of power, taking into account pre-existing legal mandates. In many instances, co-management agreements do not actually change these existing mandates, but they provide a new mechanism for the co-ordination of existing management functions, while filling the voids and empowering civil society actors (see Box 7.15).

Box 7.15 An inclusive management body with consultative power developed for Retezat National Park (Romania)
(adapted from Stanciu, 2001)

A small area of outstanding beauty and biodiversity– 100 square kilometres of untouched forest and alpine areas within the Retezat Massif– was declared national park in 1935. The area around the park is rich in natural and cultural reserves and the local people are engaged in traditional agriculture. Romanian and foreign visitors come mostly in the summer to this remote area. The Retezat National Park Management Authority (PMA) was established in November 1999 with the main role of setting up the park management infrastructure. Early in 2000, the park area was enlarged and a stakeholder analysis was undertaken. In 2001, a Consultative Council with representatives from main concerned actors was established. The Council comprises representatives of twenty-five relevant social actors, including eight local communities, forest districts, NGOs, mountain rescue teams, school inspectorates, local scientific bodies and county level institutes. All were identified and included in the Consultative Council as landowners, administrators, representatives of the natural resource users and/ or social actors whose activities may impact the park or be affected by the park. The Consultative Council holds two meetings per year to express opinions on park management activities and develop solutions to problems jointly with the PMA. All important management decisions are to be made only after consulting the Council and, if necessary, also the public at large.

The general covenants of an agreement specify the rights and obligations of the parties with respect to several relevant areas, and are often compiled into a coherent management plan. Legislation may specify, or parties may agree on, whether the agreement should bind the land or waters which is the subject of the agreement. Where land owners are involved, this may affect the commercial value of the property depending on the impact of the agreement and its financial terms. The covenants may include:

Key institutional issues in NR management

- aims and objectives of management;

- land and resource tenure systems;

- intellectual property rights and other rights of the relevant parties;

- decision making authority, including legitimate members and functioning rules of a participatory management organisation;

- public consultation and participation procedures;

- provision of legal, scientific, technical or other advice and information;

- agreed procedures for planning and environmental and social impact assessment;

- codes of practice for implementing and monitoring policies (including intra-governmental, corporate, NGO and personal commitments);

- procedures for involving indigenous peoples, disfavoured gender and minorities in NR management and for integrating traditional and scientific research and knowledge, e.g., through participatory management institutions;

- zoning and land-use controls, including issues related to residence, heritage, culture, hunting, commerce, conservation, pollution control, etc.;

- systems of surveillance and enforcement of rules, consequences of infringement; and,

- links with other management agreements at various levels (See Box 7.16).

Box 7.16   Detailed co-management agreements developed for sylvo-pastoral zones in southern Mali
(adapted from Hilhorst and Coulibaly, 1999)

Sylvo-pastoral areas in southern Mali include non-arable lands and long term fallow. These woodlands are common pool resources used for grazing and supply of firewood, timber, fruits and other forest products. Degradation of these resources prompted six villages to unite and develop a more sustainable management system. With the help of the district extension services and an agricultural research institute, the villagers developed a Local Convention– a co-management agreement made possible under Mali's new forest law.

The Local Convention starts by stating its main aim as reinforcing respect for regulations developed by the Village Councils and expresses hope that the official village forestry legislation will also adhere to this objective. It then deals with various natural resources such as firewood, timber, fruits and pastures.

The Convention lists all trees that are to be protected. Trees for timber may be cut only with permission from the village chief. Planting timber trees is encouraged. Regarding firewood, a woman may not cut more than three carts full of "green" firewood per season. Use of improved stoves is an obligation. Extra taxes are proposed for commercial firewood cutting and charcoal production. These are additional taxes paid to the Forestry Department. Non residents pay more than residents. The start of the harvesting season for Néré and Karité trees is also fixed. Sanctions are proposed for non-compliance with regulations, and proceeds from confiscations, fines and firewood taxes are to be divided among the village co-management bodies (Siwaa). Ultimately, such proceeds are to be used for financing reforestation, the installation of anti-erosion structures and the Siwaa's operating expenses. The villagers also proposed that the Siwaa is charged with the supervision of the Local Convention.

The elaboration of the Local Convention has been the major activity of the Siwaas. The six villages took two years to reach an agreement among themselves. The document they compiled was then sent to the Forestry Department, which took another two years to deliver comments and approval.

Conservation and resource use issues
- biodiversity management including wildlife and flora protection, ecosystem maintenance, monitoring and surveys, species reintroduction, habitat protection and restoration (revegetation, rehabilitation, weed control);
- maintenance of geological processes;
- soil use and rehabilitation;
- river and water management;
- animal control and fencing, wildlife corridors, buffer zones;
- disease control;
- fire control;
- cultural and heritage management (site protection, interpretation);
- tourism management (including interpretation, visitor experience, codes of conduct regarding photographs, drugs, feeding wild animals, etc.);
- waste disposal;
- identification of threats and recovery processes;
- allowed harvest times and quantities for specific plant and animal species;
- sustainable agricultural practices;
- farming and other income generating activities;
- marketing arrangements for local produce, products and services;
- rules and procedures for mining, quarrying and fossicking;
- utilities and communications infrastructure;
- roads and access corridors; and,
- military access.

Issues concerning communications, capacity building, research and evaluation
- description of specific social communication avenues and initiatives;

- description of ad hoc training and continuing education initiatives;

- description of rules to be adopted in local research;

- a follow-up protocol for monitoring; and,

- plans for internal and external evaluation.

Financial issues

- financial planning, programme funding, compensation for lost income from conservation activities, taxation benefits and other incentives (including rate relief, payments, education, health, housing services, information, etc.), protection of investments (see Box 7.17);

- land swaps, offset and debt-for-nature arrangements;

- affirmative action employment policies for local residents including equity in income earning ventures;

- support to local employment and commercial initiatives;

- interest payments, royalties and bounty payments; and,

- cost allocation for co-management meetings and processes.

Other issues dealt with in the general covenants may include: linked negotiations, amendment procedures, agreed schedules of meetings, protection of local customary practices and traditional approaches to resource management, etc.

Box 7.17   Protecting the investment

As co-management agreements often involve considerable investment of time, money and other resources, the parties who wish to protect their investment to the greatest legal extent possible attempt to ensure that the other parties are bound to keep the agreement.

Many agreements are common law contracts. In this case, each party needs to check them carefully and be satisfied that the contract offers an acceptable level of assurance. Less commonly, the agreement itself may be enshrined in an Act of Parliament. An interesting example of this kind is being tried out in Lebanon, where three new national parks have been created and local NGOs have been given responsibility for the running of each park. A separate act has been created for each park. Each act is brief, and sets out the responsibilities of the parties, along with broad term administrative arrangements.

In the most common form of "one—on-one" agreement, the government provides resources in return for some action by the landholder. It is therefore the government agency which has the greater interest in protecting its investment, since it will hand over the money, equipment, etc. at a specific time, while the actions of the landholder may be ongoing. Possible mechanisms for protecting the investment include:

- setting out a timetable for works, with a schedule of payments related to achievement of agreed milestones;

- penalty clauses, including "payback" provisions (with or without interest) if the landholder fails to display "stewardship", undoes or fails to maintain the agreed works, or acts contrary to the agreement at some time in the future;

- a monitoring programme, with "payback" or "make good" provisions.

Inclusions of this kind need to be handled carefully. They can appear unfair, the ability to enforce them will decrease over time, and the government agency needs to weigh up the likely effectiveness of any such provisions against the negative impression they may create.

Protecting the government's investment can be even more difficult if the land is sold in the future. The most effective way to do this is to register the agreement on the title as a form of covenant, easement or other legal protection which runs with the title of the land (i.e., all future owners are bound by the terms). Some forms of agreement lend themselves to this, while others do not. Some jurisdictions may be reluctant to register such agreements as constraints on title.

An alternative is the use of a novation of deed on transfer as part of the cooperative management agreement itself. In essence, a novation means that the landholder agrees to sell the land only to a purchaser who agrees in turn to be bound by the terms of the original agreement. If the purchaser breaks the agreement, the original owner may be liable. Novations are unlikely to be enforceable after the first couple of property transactions.

Landholders also seek to protect their "investment", i.e., the natural resource/ conservation values or the land they have managed, in this way. Many wish to protect the land "forever" or at least for their children. In this regard, registration of some form of covenant on title is the most effective mechanism. Even this, however, cannot provide absolute certainty, as governments can (and do) revoke protective covenants if they wish to use the land for other purposes (e.g., transmission corridor for public utility).

Duration
Co-management agreements may be temporary or permanent. The general covenants may also specify amendment and termination procedures, if any.

Agreements may be:

- effectively unrelated to the passage of time (e.g., an agreement about the purchase of a capital item– "if you contribute labour to dig the well, the government will contribute the pumping equipment and the pump will become community property to all effects"). Agreements of this kind relate to specific events which occur at some point in time and are not repeated;

- obviously time limited– e.g., an agreement about restricted access to certain resources until a recovery threshold has been reached. When the threshold is reached, the agreement comes to an end;

- applicable over an extended time– e.g., an agreement that requires ongoing maintenance of certain agreed responsibilities: i.e., "the community will have access to limited harvesting of vines in the protected forest and biodiversity monitoring reports will be delivered each month to the rangers' office". As the requirement for maintenance cannot be effectively enforced indefinitely, it is usually good to set a realistic time limit; and,

- open ended (in this case, the agreement is meant to apply "for all time"– e.g., "the state will support the freeholding of a land lease and declare the land a wildlife refuge, and the landowner will promise to protect and preserve the values of the wetland areas for all time"). While the landholder may agree to protect the heritage values of the forest in perpetuity in return for certain considerations from the government, agreements of this kind can be very difficult to

Agreements may be:
- unrelated to the passage of time;
- time limited;
- applicable over an extended time;
- open ended.

enforce over an extended time, even with agreed penalty provisions, unless registered on title.

Agreements of the last kind mentioned above are often requested by landholders in the North, who seek to protect the land permanently without giving up title to it (see Box 7.7). There is also a growing demand for this kind of agreement from citizens mistrustful of the real degree of protection offered by natural resource management schemes operated by governments. Increasingly, people with a strong conservation or sustainable development ethic are seeking to protect land through private ownership and some kind of covenant on title. If government views this trend in a positive light and is prepared to assist with appropriate legal mechanisms, a good deal of valuable conservation can be achieved at minimal cost to the taxpayer.

At any rate, all parties should be clear over what period of time the agreement applies and what are its main implications. The duration should be specified in the agreement. It may also be appropriate to specify what happens after the agreement expires.

Powers and responsibilities of co-management organisations

This section of the agreement deals with co-management organisations and specify the scope of their authority and their specific functions and responsibilities. It may deal with issues such as the regularity of meetings, express commitments to co-operation and goodwill, etc. Co-management organisations tend to complement the work of government resource management agencies rather than replace them. Some commentators have suggested that funding for co-management organisations should be sufficient to support independent secretariats or joint resource centres. This may be particularly necessary where traditional knowledge is not articulated in the professional language used by resource managers, or where the scientific research on which management plans are based has not incorporated traditional knowledge.[14] Co-management organisations are described at some length in Chapter 8 of this volume.

Dispute resolution and amendment procedures

Disputes may arise in co-management situations concerning competing access to resources, restrictions on their use, etc. In several jurisdictions, such conflicts are resolved by the courts, which are also often guided by specific recommendations on how competing claims to resources might best be resolved (see Box 7.18).

---

[14]   Canada Royal Commission on Aboriginal Peoples, 1996.

Box 7.18   Canadians set priority criteria for resolving disputes about resource management
            (adapted from Sparrow versus Canadian Court of Law, 1990)

Canadian case law suggests that conflict resolution over natural resource use should follow the principles of priority for conservation and the public interest, with reasonable and objective regulation being acceptable, followed by priority for subsistence or indigenous/ customary users. The interests of recreational and commercial users follow with lowest priority. For example, as aboriginal and treaty rights have Constitutional protection, in the decision of Sparrow versus Canadian Court of Law it was established that fisheries regulations do not extinguish aboriginal peoples' customary rights to fish unless a clear and plain intent to do so is manifest in the legislation. The court noted that government regulation that impinges on aboriginal rights must be shown to be justified, and that the court shall determine whether the regulation is reasonable, whether it imposes undue hardship, and whether the limitation denies the holders of the right their preferred means of enforcing their right. The court held that when assessing government justifications for interfering with aboriginal peoples rights, court priorities should be: 1) conservation, 2) subsistence needs, and 3) commercial and recreational fishers' rights.

Although disputes over legal contracts can be resolved in court, it is highly desirable to build into a co-management agreement a non-court dispute resolution mechanism trusted by all parties. This may include:

● time limits for resolving disputes directly among the parties, or for responding to requests, notices, etc.;

● a requirement that parties attempt informal dispute resolution before having recourse to the courts;

● identification of an agreed independent mediator or arbiter and the circumstances in which the services of this person or body shall be required, and whether their decision shall be final;

● whether the parties shall be legally represented in arbitration; and,

● circumstances in which either party shall simply have the right to terminate the agreement.

The level of detail adopted will depend on:

● the extent to which the parties feel they can trust each other;

● how much is at stake; and,

● how much the parties wish to avoid the courts if the agreement does break down.

The procedures set by the agreement should be culturally appropriate and the parties must ensure that suitably skilled people will be available to implement them. It is also important to remember that the agreements are about the management of natural resources and should not be overloaded it with dispute resolution and/ or penalty clauses.

Disputes are often a symptom of more deep-seated problems and deficiencies in the management regime. If they are frequent, the agreement is probably not working in some fundamental way. Even without active disputes, circumstances change, people change and knowledge grows– either party may wish to change the agreement at some time in the future. A mechanism for this should be foreseen as part of the original agreement, so that:

- amendment is possible with the minimum of expense and complication;

- the risk of acrimonious debate is minimised; and,

- procedures are fair and equitable, and respect the interests of all parties.

Individuals involved in the original negotiations may feel a strong sense of ownership of an agreement in its original form. Any request for amendment may be seen as a threat or an implication of failure or inadequacy. A request to change an agreement, however, should be seen simply as evidence that the world changes, not as a reason for frustration or recriminations. Building amendment procedures into the original agreement may help everyone to accept and understand that agreements are designed to meet the circumstances of a particular time in history and unlikely to remain appropriate forever.

In the case of natural resource management, the path to needed amendments is smoothed if the parties agree beforehand on some form of monitoring, designed to be at least partly independent of the parties or their aspirations for the treaty. This might mean that the monitoring is done by an independent body, or a team where parties are equally represented, or that it consists of objective measurements that are recorded by mechanical devices. If the monitoring reveals that an agreed threshold has been passed notwithstanding that the treaty conditions were scrupulously observed, it will be difficult to argue that a change is not needed.

It is crucial, however, that agreements are never changed unilaterally. Any agreement that can be changed unilaterally is not a co-management agreement by definition, since the parties are not equal in a matter of fundamental importance. There is little point in negotiating an agreement in good faith if one party can later change it at will. The rights of the parties in this respect should be fully protected by law. At the very least, the need for all parties to agree to any amendments should be clearly stated in the agreement itself.

Information, communication and confidentiality clauses

Information and communication issues can have considerable significance for many parties, and are a major element of a well designed agreement. In particular, information that affects the status and operation of the treaty needs to be treated with care and an agreed balance of transparency and discretion. The kind of information involved might include:

- any proposed legislative or policy changes;

- any proposed tenure changes;

- financial balance sheets showing receipts and expenditures;

- development initiatives;

- budget proposals;

- public opinion polls;

- visitor figures;

- intentions to review the operation of the agreement itself;

- number and recipients of hunting permits issued;

Building amendment procedures into the original agreement may help everyone to accept and understand that agreements can only meet the circumstances of a particular time in history.

Information and communication issues can have considerable significance for many parties, and are a major element of a well designed agreement.

- numbers of animals taken, trees felled, etc.;

- noticeable changes in size or distribution of animal populations;

- breaches of the agreement, or law breaking by others (e.g., poaching); and,

- effects of traditional management practices (e.g., burning, swidden agriculture).

In general, the constituencies of all the parties in the agreement (and not just their representatives who participated in the negotiation process) need to be informed about the agreement as a whole. What is it about and why was it thought necessary? This will be especially important if the terms of the agreement may lead to conflict with other users of the area. Sufficient funds will need to be set aside to inform all the parties and the public at large.[15]

There should be clarity within the agreement on who, when and how will set up and maintain a communication flow with all the parties and with local communities in particular. Implementation arrangements for positive provisions also need to be clear. For example it should be specified who will receive the tourism benefits, who is allowed to tap water from a given source, who is allowed to collect medicinal plants from the wild. And it should be specified when, where and how often; who will monitor outcomes; whether a monitoring protocol is to be followed; and what specific mechanism should be used to alert the parties if problems arise.

If agreed management practices include traditional practices, and/ or people returning to live on their ancestral land, it may be important to include also a strategy for communicating and explaining these decisions to the general public. In Richtersveld National Park in South Africa, for example, the park land is leased from the Nama people, who retain rights to graze livestock and to harvest natural products in a controlled way.[16] This needs to be clearly explained to the public at large.

Indigenous people may also wish to have general cultural education initiatives included as part of the deal (e.g., interpretive signs inside a park explaining cultural history, use of particular plants, spiritual significance of landscape features). For indigenous people and other communities and societies emerging from a history of oppression, it may also be important to have such history acknowledged publicly, either in the agreement itself or in explanatory material associated with it. A government party not prepared to be understanding and transparent about this may not get very far in the agreement process.

For indigenous people emerging from a history of oppression, it may also be important to have this history acknowledged publicly, either in the agreement itself or in explanatory material associated with it.

Notwithstanding the above, one or more parties may wish to keep at least some of the agreement confidential. Although it is generally better to make the whole document public and easily accessible, the parties may wish to respect their mutual concerns. In some cases, landholders seek a confidentiality clause in the contract because they do not wish to be known that they are dealing with a conservation agency in a community where there is little sympathy for conservation. Or they may not wish others to know they are accepting financial assistance. Some people simply wish to keep their affairs private and will not enter an agreement unless confidentiality is guaranteed.

Confidentiality may be a particular issue when dealing with indigenous peoples,

---

[15] Farley, 1997.
[16] Anderson, 1995.

in relation to cultural and spiritual information as well as intellectual property rights over knowledge on the uses of plants, animals and micro-organisms. If, for example, part of what an indigenous community seeks from the agreement is assistance in recording the cultural knowledge of its elders, the government agency may need to accept that the information gathered at its expense will remain the property of the indigenous community, who may not even wish to allow it access. Government parties need to be sensitive and flexible about requests for confidentiality that relate to culturally sensitive information. A useful compromise might be to specify that no communication material will be publicly released until the indigenous community signs off on it.

> Government parties need to be sensitive and flexible about requests for confidentiality that relate to culturally sensitive information.

While confidentiality issues are important, the money or other assistance provided by a government agency comes ultimately from the public purse and there is a valid argument that its application should be transparent– perhaps especially when being applied to individual private landholders. As a matter of fact, many countries have Freedom of Information provisions that apply to these cases and need to be respected.

Specific clauses

In relation to the benefits and undertakings, more detailed clauses may outline who will do or provide what, and how. Examples of what different parties may ask for or provide vary according to context and the institutional actor's relationship with the resources.

7.4   Recognition of efforts and commitment

Special forms of public recognition can be stipulated as part of a management agreement. Government agencies are often surprised by how important this is to individuals and communities, and how much people are prepared to do for little more than social recognition. Recognition may take the form of an attractive sign for the front of the property identifying it as a Wildlife Refuge, sustainable farm, or other "special place", preferably identifying the resident community or landowner by name. Recognition of this kind costs little and can have excellent spin-offs for conservation. Government agencies can address communities with a known pride in their history and citizens who are influential within their community for this kind of public recognition. Once a few signs go up in a district, the local acceptance level increases, the co-management concept gets talked about, and new parties ask to join in. Other forms of recognition may include a press release, presentation of an award, or hosting of a public ceremony in the relevant space. The added status that comes with this kind of public recognition is important in rural communities, and a significant incentive for others to join in the efforts. In Victoria, for example, the Land for Wildlife Scheme ran a feature on Landline, the rural programme on the national Australian television network in early 1995. In the weeks following the screening, interstate inquiries averaged one per day.[17]

> Government agencies are often surprised by... how much people are prepared to do for little more than social recognition.

---

[17]   Vicki Pattemore, personal communication, 2003.

Moral support for existing efforts

This is closely allied to public recognition, but is often less tangible. It may require no more than an enthusiastic government officer who offers to explain ecological processes and lend books, or a community leader convincing government agencies of the importance of a community conserved area for regional conservation. Very often, individuals and communities ask for flora and fauna surveys to be done of their land. They may not want to do anything specific with such inventories, but they greatly appreciate "knowing what's there", especially if they can walk around with the botanist and learn the scientific names of trees, or help the zoologist check the mammal traps. The increased understanding and appreciation of the land which is gained, along with the moral support of the professionals doing the survey (whose very presence affirms their existing conservation efforts) is all some communities and landholders need to continue practising their stewardship– or to step up their efforts. This recognition is actually crucial for communities and landowners whose land and resources are included in government-established protected areas.

"A legacy for future generations"

Landholders already committed to good stewardship will often seek some form of guarantee that the conservation values they have worked to protect will be protected "for all time". This can be difficult to achieve, for reasons that will be discussed further below.

Material contributions

Communities and landowners committed to good stewardship may not have the financial or other resources to do what is needed. They may seek material (e.g., seedlings for planting, stones for terracing) or cash contributions (e.g., tied to the purchase of equipment, fences, etc.) to support their conservation work. Weed control, replanting, demarcation of land, compensation for community guards and prevention of human-wildlife conflicts are often in need of specific material or cash contributions.

Tax concessions

One of the most commonly sought inclusions in a co-management agreement with private landowners is some form of tax or rate concession or rebate (local government tax). Such a rebate provides recognition that the landowner is managing responsibly and possibly foregoing some material gain in the process. It also relieves him or her of some financial burden without the need for the government to make actual cash payments. Tax concessions are widely used to encourage protection of the environment in many countries (See Box 7.7 in this Chapter).

Technical advice

This is frequently sought by indigenous and local communities and private landholders. It may range from the very specific (e.g.: "What should we plant here?" "Where should we place the pig traps?") to a full scale plan of management for the land. A request to prepare a management plan offers boundless opportunities for improved management on a cooperative basis. It is crucial, however, that the preparation of the plan involves the relevant parties at every stage. Training is frequently sought by individuals and communities, and some form of capacity build-

One of the most commonly sought inclusions in a co-management agreement with private landowners is some form of tax or rate concession or rebate.

ing for all parties involved should be a routine component of any co-management agreement.

Strategic advice

This is something of a variant on the above. An example will serve to illustrate. An aboriginal community which sought a co-management agreement in New Zealand was concerned at the level of visitation by commercial tours and individual tourists to a waterfall on their traditional land. They did not want to keep people out, but they wanted the site respected. They did not want rubbish left behind or damage done to roads or forests, and they wanted some benefit for the community (since the visitors were simply driving into their traditional lands without so much as asking permission). The government agency agreed to discuss a strategic plan for dealing with tourism. One idea discussed was charging commercial tours access for entry in return for a roster system which guaranteed they would be the only visitors at the falls at a specified time.

Trade-offs

These are sought when one of the parties in the agreement wants to do, or has already done, something which one or more of the other parties would not normally support. For example, a farmer whose operations have over the years (and perhaps unknowingly) encroached onto a national park may seek to have that part of the park excised in return for transfer to the government of another part of the property. This can often be mutually beneficial. In a real example in north Queensland (Australia), a landholder was prepared to hand over to the Crown a large area of forested land in return for excision of a small area of flat land. The flat land had been cleared many years previously and planted to sugar cane every year since. Its conservation value was zero. The forested land was very steep and of no value for agriculture, but was biologically important.

Obviously, arrangements of this kind represent something of a tightrope for a government agency with natural resource management responsibilities. They should not be allowed to become the means for excusing landholders from breaking the law providing they "make it up" afterwards. Nor should they be allowed to be seen as an invitation for others to break the law and be rewarded for doing so.

Support (or the withholding of opposition)

This item has some overlap with the item above. Some parties may seek to have another party (often a governmental agency) offer support (e.g., by a letter) to assist them in negotiating with another agency. For that, they may be ready to make some important concessions. For example, a letter from a protected area authority to the local government authority might say "On behalf of agency X, I support the proposal to build a car park and boardwalk to allow tourists to view the swamp forest at Laguna Grande in the land customarily owned by the Y community." The Y community may then agree to support the maintenance of the swamp in it original extension and conditions. More active support may also be requested, such as assisting the community in face-to-face negotiations.

As a variation, it may be routine practice for the department which administers land tenure to seek comment from a conservation agency when, for example, a leaseholder is seeking to buy land or extend the terms of a lease. In some cases, the conservation agency may have legal power of veto over the dealing. The landowner may seek an assurance that the agency will not oppose the sale in return for some agreed management action, or trade-off.

This kind of landowner benefit contains significant risks for the government agency agreeing to it, which must be very careful to ensure it is not acting illegally, or contrary to government policy, or promising something it cannot deliver. In most cases, it is sensible to involve a "third party" department or agency at an early stage, even if only informally, to avoid unexpected and undesirable outcomes.

Indigenous peoples and local communities tend to hold an inclusive view of the world, and thus of what needs to be comprised in a resource management agreement. Government negotiators need to be prepared to adopt an inclusive approach that respects and accepts indigenous rights and aspirations.[18] As the BCCTF suggested: "There should be no unilateral restriction by any party on the scope of negotiations."[19]

7.5   Crucial issues for indigenous peoples and local communities

Who owns the land?

Perhaps the most fundamental matter for agreement and acknowledgement in co-management documents is the relationship of the indigenous peoples and local communities to the land in question. All other inclusions, and how they are dealt with, will flow from the extent to which ownership of the land, including customary ownership, is acknowledged in writing and in the law.

One of the most important benefits sought by indigenous peoples and local communities in a co-management agreement is an acknowledgement of their custom-

---

[18]   Farley, 1997.
[19]   British Columbia Claims Task Force, 1991.

One of the most important benefits sought by indigenous and local communities in a co-management agreement is an acknowledgement of their customary ownership and rights or affiliation with the land and resources at stake.

ary ownership and rights or affiliation with the land and resources at stake. While this certainly has moral force, its power as a negotiating lever is greatly overtaken in Western societies when the recognition is translated into legal ownership. In Australia, the USA and Canada, the indigenous peoples that managed to obtain a legal title to their land found out that governments and industry that previously dismissed their claims came to actively seek negotiation. The extent of "ownership" often marks the watershed between the role of supplicant and peer for the indigenous or local party in the negotiation process.

If ownership or affiliation is acknowledged with an indigenous people or local community, the question of who will be the formal party to the treaty must be confronted. This may be a council of elders, a corporation, a community council or other representative body. If the land has been successfully claimed by a group or body under an established legal mechanism, the decision is much easier. If this situation does not apply, however, this should not be used as an excuse for not embarking on negotiations. Government negotiators will simply need to work closely and cautiously with the indigenous people or community and assist them to identify the most appropriate formal representative of the right holders.

Who else is involved?

A key matter for early determination is who should be involved in the agreement. This can be a vexed question. Inclusion of new parties and their interests is often opposed by the original parties ("primary stakeholders") who may see such additions as a means of "outnumbering" them, and who may feel anyway that other parties do not have legitimate rights to be involved. While the latter may well be true, inclusion of some new legitimate parties in negotiations– and inclusion of their interests in the agreement– may prevent a good deal of troubles.

For protected areas or wilderness such parties frequently are recreational users, including powerful hunting lobbies. Recreational users, however, have achieved variable results in their efforts to be involved in co-management agreement negotiations in protected areas, e.g., in Alaska and Canada.[20]

Where resource use is part of the agreement, or the land involved is resource-rich, existing or prospective mining, logging or grazing interests need to be carefully considered. In Australia and Canada, it is common for indigenous peoples and mining companies (with or without government support) to enter into formal agreements over resource use before work begins. Such agreements commonly concentrate on financial compensation, rehabilitation, ongoing access, and the conduct of operations in ways, and in places, that respect the spiritual values of the land. In Bolivia, an agreement between a gas and oil company and indigenous peoples provided the essential conditions for a major co-management agreement for the country (see Box 7.19).

Box 7.19   Co-management of protected areas, the oil and gas industry and indigenous empowerment– the experience of Bolivia's Kaa Iya del Gran Chaco (Bolivia) (adapted from Winer, 2003)

The National Park Kaa-Iya del Gran Chaco was established in September 1995 in Southern Bolivia. This park of 3.4 million hectares is the largest in Bolivia and contains the world's largest area of dry

[20] Sneed, 1997.

tropical forest under legal protection. Its most unique characteristic, however, is that the park was created in response to demands for territorial recognition by the Guaraní Izoceño people. This is the first park in the Americas declared on the basis of a demand by indigenous people and assigning to an indigenous people's organisation a primary administrative responsibility. The co-administration agreement that set up the park is a model document that creates new opportunities for both indigenous peoples and the under-staffed and under-funded national conservation authorities. Having established the park has only partially fulfilled the historic objective of re-claiming their own customary land upheld by CABI (Capitanóa de Alto y Bajo Izozog), the traditional representative structure of the Guaranó Izoceóo. Currently, besides what is gazetted as park territory, another 1.9 million hectares bordering the park and straddling the river are being titled in their favour.

How was this possible? CABI was able to capitalise on its internal cohesion to pressure the hydro-carbon industry into making significant compensatory payments to them for the impact of that portion of the 32" diameter, 3,146 Kilometres gas pipeline that runs through their indigenous territory and the park. Such compensatory payments, totalling $3.7 million, and the activities that came in with the hydro-carbon industry, ensured CABI's ability to invest significant funds in the running of the park. This obviously strengthened their standing as effective co-management partners. In addition, the hydro-carbon funds were crucial to support the indigenous organisations themselves, promote rural development and accelerate the process of titling indigenous lands. Co-management would have taken hold in Bolivia without these funds, but would not have developed so rapidly, or garnered as much enthusiasm from the government agency in charge.

The Wildlife Conservation Society (WCS) has been the principal broker supporting the negotiations for the park, the indigenous territory, the park's management plan and its administrative structures. It had the vision of a successful co-management agreement and the wisdom to know that this would take years of on-going support. In the 1.9 million hectare indigenous territory adjacent to the park, WCS has also worked closely with CABI since 1991, fostering the full appreciation of the links between wildlife (a crucial element of Izoceño cultural heritage) and the management decisions in their habitats.

Financial outcomes

Many conservation agreements refer to land and resources that belong, or belonged to, an indigenous party or a local community or one or more private landowners. On this basis it is agreed that there should be some financial compensation for their loss, and/ or that the land should return an ongoing income to its customary or legal owners. Agreed financial outcomes may take the form of:

- rental paid by the government (for instance, Aboriginal peoples in Kakadu, Nitmiluk, Booderee and Mutawintji National Parks, in Australia,[21] lease their land to the government for an independently-determined market value return);

- proportion of income or profits (for instance, the Anangu people receive 25% of entrance and other fees at Uluru-Kata Tjuta National Park in Australia;[22] in 1994, this arrangement returned them 600,000 Australian Dollars from entrance fees alone; in South Africa, where the revenue from entrance fees may be considerable, from 10 to 15% of revenue[23] is allocated to neighbouring tribal authorities in various provinces and homelands– a type of arrangement often used also in agreements with mining companies;

- guaranteed employment (this is a very common provision for protected areas throughout the world, but it may benefit only a small proportion of the community);

[21] See Table 4.3 in Chapter 4.
[22] De Lacy and Lawson, 1997.
[23] Anderson, 1995.

● financial compensation, either on-going or once-off, used where government acquires the land and/ or the desired use is considered incompatible with ongoing indigenous use or ownership.

The latter type of arrangement is envisaged, for example, by the Native Title Act 1993 (Commonwealth) of Australia, which provides for acquisition (with compensation) of native title rights, and regional agreements by which the Aboriginal people agree to yield their native title rights in return for agreed compensation. This kind of agreement modifies in a most important way the rights of indigenous peoples and should be subjected to very careful consideration and strict provisions for prior informed consent. In 2004[24] the Programme of Work on Protected Areas of the Convention on Biological Diversity actually ruled out forcible expropriation and resettlement of indigenous peoples for the purpose of establishing new protected areas, and upheld the principles of prior informed consent.

Resource extraction companies frequently seek to negotiate one-off compensation arrangements, or compensation that is ongoing but unrelated to profits (e.g., providing schools, housing, vehicles). Arrangements of this kind need to be approached with great caution, as they can be superficially attractive (greatly needed benefits, expected to arrive quickly) but are often unfair and inequitable in the long term, especially if the resource extraction operation destroys natural resources on which the people depend for their subsistence. Also, often promises are forgotten soon after they have been made. The Finima community on Bonny island (Nigeria) learned this the hard way, as they ended up reaping all sort of misfortunes and social and environmental costs for their initial consent to establish a liquefying gas plant in their midst.[25]

The agreement should be very clear on what financial outcomes is to flow to which parties, for how long and in what circumstances. What happens in the case of ongoing compensation tied to profits, for example, if the operation makes a loss? How can the local community know if there really is a loss, or how much the profits really are? Any conditions and obligations should be clearly spelt out, be verifiable, and be understood by all parties.

As well as setting out who gets what funds, the agreement should specify who decides how funds available for the management of the natural resources are to be spent. Generally speaking, this decision should be taken by the co-management organisation, but in some cases a proportion of the funds may be directed to another body that decides how to spend it within broad guidelines. In any case, it is important that the government party is not paternalistic and does not attempt to take control of this aspect. Avoiding long transfer lines for the funds destined to local communities is equally important. Long transfer lines, the "safeguarding" of bank documents by state agencies and the deposit of money on state accounts, which often lasts much longer than anticipated, can hamper the community access to, and decision on, the use of financial resources.

Governance of protected areas

A number of authors have pointed out that basing conservation on a "protected area" model is proper of a western understanding of nature, wildlife and wilderness, which is foreign to many indigenous peoples.[26] It is important for governments to remember this in negotiating treaties over land considered to have

Resource extraction companies frequently seek to negotiate one-off compensation arrangements, or compensation that is ongoing but unrelated to profits…. Arrangements of this kind need to be approached with great caution, as they can be superficially attractive but are often unfair and inequitable in the long term, especially if the resource extraction operation destroys natural resources on which the people depend for their subsistence.

---

24   See http://www.biodiv.org/decisions/default.aspx?m=COP-07&id=7765&lg=0
25   Wittenberg, 2004.
26   Anderson, 1995; Dwyer, 1994; Ghimire and Pimbert, 1997.

high conservation values. Indigenous peoples will value the land and wish to protect it, but their ways of doing so and their priorities may be different from those of government agencies.[27]

Yet, over half of protected areas in the world (and much more than that in some regions) have been created in areas inhabited by indigenous and local communities. Many of these communities still live there, or maintain close interests and relations to those areas and resources. In addition, a sizeable part of the remaining biodiversity in the world– in forests, rangelands, mountain environments, wetlands, freshwater bodies and coastal and marine environments, including mangroves, coral reefs and sea grass beds– exists in areas inhabited by indigenous peoples or areas held as "commons" by local communities outside of official protected areas. Fortunately, despite the lack of incentives and even the presence of disincentives, many such indigenous peoples and local communities are still engaged in various types of management efforts. Some of those efforts have an outright orientation towards the production and sustainable use of one or more natural resources. Others aim at fully conserving an area for its spiritual, cultural or aesthetic values. In general, community rules privilege livelihood sustainability, risk-aversion, flexibility, social reciprocities and use-values.[28] Within such broad terms, relatively strictly protected elements of the land– such as sacred groves or areas with well-regulated access and use– can still be found in many inhabited territories.[29] A typical resulting landscape is a mosaic pattern of resource units under different use regimes and regulations, including conserved areas and resources of relatively limited size.[30]

community rules privilege livelihood sustainability, risk-aversion, flexibility, social reciprocities and use-values.

For most indigenous peoples and local communities, protecting the land means living on it, close to it, and with it– still a difficult concept to accept for many national parks staff, foresters and rangeland managers. Frequently it will also mean some form of subsistence on the land or its natural resources, and some degree of ecosystem manipulation.[31] Negotiations on land management therefore need to be conducted with care, sensitivity and open minds, and as few preconceived ideas as possible. It is important to arrive at "mutually acceptable planning and management objectives,"[32] agreeing on the objectives of management before the mechanisms are discussed. Often the mechanisms will involve a combination of traditional and "modern" land management practices, and much can be learned and achieved in an atmosphere of good will. Although people and park conflicts still endure throughout the world, community conserved areas and resources are being increasingly recognised as very important for conservation. Community engagement in the conservation of official protected areas is also being increasingly appreciated, as theory and practice move from the old perception of PAs as "islands" of conservation to the more current perception of PAs as integral elements of a landscape/ seascape in which multiple management objectives effectively co-exist.[33]

For most indigenous peoples and local communities, protecting the land means living on it, close to it and with it.

27 A draft synthesis of regional studies prepared in the eve of the Vth World Parks Congress is available at: http://www.iucn.org/themes/ceesp/Wkg_grp/TILCEPA/community.htm#synthesis. See also Borrini-Feyerabend et al., 2004 (in press).
28 In contrast, state-established protected areas generally privilege stability, legal authority and market values (e.g., mega-fauna species).
29 A typical example is the landscape of the Karen villages found in Ob Long National Park, in Thailand. While alarmed park authorities point at the plots of land where the communities practice swidden agriculture, the villagers point at the areas they strictly conserve as sacred or actively protect from forest fires, and stress that they use only about 10% of the land in the park, as shown in the maps they have prepared.
30 In contrast, state-established protected areas generally privilege large scale gazetted environments surrounded by un-regulated territories.
31 Pimbert and Pretty, 1998; Pimbert and Toledo, 1994.
32 Sneed, 1997.
33 See McNeely and Pitt, 1985; Ghimire and Pimbert, 1997; Gadgil, 1998; Borrini-Feyerabend et al., 2002; Phillips, 2003; the Accord, Action Plan and Recommendations developed by the Vth World Parks Congress, 2003 (http://www.iucn.org/themes/wcpa/wpc2003); the CBD Programme of Work on Protected Areas (http://www. biodiv.org/programmes/cross-cutting/protected/wopo.asp) and Borrini-Feyerabend et al., 2004 (in press).

Some co-management agreements formally recognise the importance of community engagement in conservation and, in particular, provide support to Community Conserved Areas (CCAs) and Co-managed Protected Areas (CMPAs).[34] The most direct way to support a CCA is to attribute a clear legal status to communities and entrust them with the authority and responsibility to conserve their land and resources, in continuity with established patterns and structures. This is currently done in places as diverse as Senegal, Colombia, and Australia.[35] For CMPAs, specific agreements need to be developed to clarify the rights and responsibilities of each party in the agreement. It is also important to agree on how the decisions are to be implemented and enforced. If, for example, the parties agree that a certain threatened species will not be hunted until an indicator of its population passes a particular threshold, there should be overt agreement over who deals with offenders who break this rule. The procedures for enforcement need to be workable, and understood by all. While enforcement should to be done sensitively, failure to do it at all may cast doubt on the credibility of the agreement as a whole and the likelihood that other aspects of it will be adhered to. These questions apply equally (though with somewhat different problems) to offences by those affiliated with the parties to the agreement, and to offences by outsiders.

> Some co-management agreements formally recognise the importance of community engagement in conservation and provide support to Community Conserved Areas (CCAs).

Hunting, fishing and human-wildlife conflicts

The right to use and dispose of resources is likely to be one of the more controversial aspects of any co-management agreement. The concept of hunting and fishing in protected areas, in particular, is anathema to many conservationists, especially when modern rather than "traditional" weaponry and techniques are used. The cultural significance of the hunting itself and its political symbolism as an act of self determination are resented by conservationists as well as other parties in society. The problems often arise as the national economy relies on tourists being able to see wildlife at close range in protected areas. During the phases of negotiation it will be important to establish agreed management objectives, enforcement procedures and social communication strategies, in particular to convey to the public at large the special significance of hunting and fishing for the indigenous and local communities. Ultimately, however, traditional hunting and fishing is likely to receive public sympathy (and government support) only if it can be done in ways that do not endanger species and ecosystems, or the safety of other users of the area. In some cases, the parties to the agreement have set up a special body to preside over such sensitive issues (e.g., the Mackay Council of Elders decides on the issue of permits to traditional owners for taking marine

---

[34] A review of related issues and options for action can be found in Borrini-Feyerabend et al., 2004 (in press).
[35] See the special issue of Policy Matters (No.12) on Community Empowerment for Conservation, 2003.

species in a part of Australia's Great Barrier Reef Marine Park). At times, the mechanisms for regulating hunting or fishing are developed with minimal government guidance, but the practice is submitted to some form of joint or independent monitoring.

The existence of customary hunting practices should not detract attention from the fact that sport hunting is often practiced by foreign tourists, in elite conditions and environments. In West Africa, for instance, many hunting concessions are established in territories just adjacent to protected areas. Local communities bear the cost of not being able to hunt, fish, farm, graze animals or even legally collect water inside the protected areas dedicated to supporting wildlife. This same wildlife, however, ends up feeding lucrative sport hunting and tourism businesses exploited by local and foreign elites in their strategically located concessions.

An increasing number of agreements, starting from the CAMPFIRE examples of the late 1980s, deal today with a fair community share of the benefits deriving from wildlife, including from hunting, fishing and tourism. These have provided some communities with much needed influxes of financial resources, but problems have not been lacking. Depending on where infrastructure and tourism investments are made and the ways in which benefits are allocated, there may be large discrepancies among communities in adjacent territories, and within communities.[36] Also, there may be artificial separations between wildlife management and management of other types of natural resources (e.g., water, pasture, trees), and governments may maintain a paternalistic attitude, remaining reluctant to devolve effective wildlife management authority and rights, and requiring that community members be "trained to the purpose", while other partners, including tourism operators, are not.[37]

Apart from native animals for hunting, other resources considered in a co-management agreement may include rules and procedures for the use of fuelwood, vegetation for thatching, medicinal plants, canes and vines for basket weaving, wildlife as a source of protein-rich food (as distinct from the cultural needs of hunting as an activity), feral animals (e.g., wild pigs), carcasses from culling programmes, grass and other vegetation for grazing livestock, and even intellectual property rights (e.g., collecting a plant for personal medicinal use is quite different from providing sampling and explaining its use to a pharmaceutical company; if the company decides to market the active ingredient, the question of who owns both the plants and the knowledge becomes important).

Underlying all these issues is the question of who owns the resources and the land. Do indigenous peoples and local communities have the right, for instance, to claim ownership of forests, waters, wildlife and/ or mineral resources, and therefore decide on their use(s)? If the government retains ownership and wishes to sell them, will the indigenous party or local community have rights of veto, rights to impose conditions, or the right to expect a portion of the proceeds? The "rights to negotiate" are also likely to be an important aspect of any co-management agreement. These rights allow indigenous parties, local communities and other actors to negotiate directly with a resource extraction company over conditions and compensation payments. The recommendations on indigenous peoples that were adopted in 2003 at the 5th World Parks Congress address future co-management agreements that involve indigenous peoples in protected areas and wildlife management (Box 7.20).

> ...local communities bear the cost of not being able to hunt, fish, farm, graze animals or even legally collect water inside the protected areas dedicated to supporting wildlife. This same wildlife may end up feeding lucrative industries exploited by local and foreign elites....

---

36 Kothari et al., 2000; Long, 2004.
37 Borrini-Feyerabend and Sandwith, 2003; Long, 2004; Mainspeizer, 2004.

Box 7.20   The 5th World Parks Congress recommendations on indigenous peoples and protected areas– extracts with special relevance for co-management agreements (see http://www.iucn.org/themes/wcpa/wpc2003/english/outputs/recommendations.htm)

The following recommendations were addressed in Sept. 2003 to governments, inter-governmental organisations, NGOs, local communities and civil society, and were to be implemented in partnership with the freely chosen representatives of indigenous peoples. Several of them were later incorporated in the Programme of Work on Protected Areas of the Convention on Biological Diversity (Feb. 2004):

- Ensure that existing and future protected areas respect the rights of indigenous peoples.

- Cease all involuntary resettlement and expulsions of indigenous peoples from their lands in connection with protected areas, as well as involuntary sedentarisation of mobile indigenous peoples.

- Ensure that the establishment of protected areas is based on the free, prior informed consent of indigenous peoples, and of prior social, economic, cultural and environmental impact assessment, undertaken with the full participation of indigenous peoples.

- Recognise the value and importance of protected areas established by indigenous peoples as a sound basis for securing and extending national protected areas networks.

- Provide support and funding to indigenous peoples for community conserved, co-managed and indigenous-owned and -managed protected areas.

- Establish and enforce appropriate laws and policies to protect the intellectual property of indigenous peoples with regards to their traditional knowledge, innovation systems and cultural and biological resources, and to penalise all biopiracy activities.

- Enact laws and policies that recognise and guarantee indigenous peoples' rights over their ancestral lands and waters.

- Establish participatory mechanisms for the restitution of indigenous peoples' lands, territories and resources that have been taken over by protected areas without their free, prior informed consent, and for providing prompt and fair compensation, agreed upon in a transparent and culturally appropriate manner.

- Ensure respect for indigenous peoples' decision-making authority and support their local, sustainable management and conservation of natural resources in protected areas, recognising the central role of traditional authorities, institutions and representative organisations, as appropriate.

- Require protected area managers to actively support indigenous peoples' initiatives aimed at revitalising and applying, as appropriate, traditional knowledge and practices for land, water, and natural resource management within protected areas.

- Ensure open and transparent processes and genuine negotiation with indigenous peoples in relation to any plan to establish or expand protected area systems, so that their lands, waters and natural resources are preserved and decisions affecting them are taken in mutually agreed terms.

- Ensure that protected areas are geared towards poverty alleviation and improve the living standards of the communities around and within the parks through effective and agreeable benefit sharing mechanisms.

- Encourage international conservation agencies and organisations to adopt clear policies on indigenous peoples and conservation and establish mechanisms for the redress of grievances.

Training and employment

A better economic lot for members of the indigenous and local communities is usually a key concern of one or more parties in the agreement. While this may be achieved through financial compensation, communities also often seek guaranteed employment clauses. Employment and trade or professional skills offer a more powerful road to self respect and self determination than mere financial security. In fact, having a large bank account but no work or profession is seen by some communities as counter-productive as it can reinforce a welfare mentality.

Wherever possible, financial benefits should be associated with guaranteed training and identified prospects for advancement, to reduce the risk that the outcome will be a small number of people in low paid menial jobs. This is especially important if the agreement is structured round a resource extraction operation that will come to an end in the short or medium term– leaving the people with no further prospects of employment.

Guaranteed access to the relevant territory, area of natural resources

Many agreements need to incorporate clauses about NR access for all parties. These may specify:

- any places where either party agrees not to enter (e.g., a site of spiritual significance may be off limits for government staff, who may in turn seek to limit access to an ecologically sensitive area undergoing rehabilitation);

- the positive rights of access of each party (e.g., a government agency may seek to retain rights of access for fire fighting purposes across indigenous lands from which other non-indigenous people may be effectively excluded; similarly, it may be important for indigenous people to have ongoing access for ceremonial or traditional purposes to areas where other park users are constrained from entering);

All parties may wish to exercise a degree of control over commercial activities such as tourism....

- constraints on access for the general community, and information on who will control such access. If the agreement effectively acknowledges the land as being under indigenous ownership and/ or management, then it may be appropriate for the indigenous owners to exercise control over access directly. This may involve nothing more than the need to obtain a permit to cross the land. Even if no charge is levied, the system allows the traditional owners to be aware of who is on their land and how many visits they are receiving. In the case of an agreement over a national park, or similar area, direct control may continue to be exercised by park staff, but only after agreement with the treaty partner on such matters as entrance fees, camping sites, permit conditions, etc.;

- constraints on access for commercial purposes (e.g., tourism, mining, bioprospecting).

All parties may wish to exercise a degree of control over commercial activities such as tourism. In some cases, such activities will simply be inappropriate and the treaty should make clear that they will not be allowed. Otherwise, the agreement should address a number of practical questions, such as:

- Will tourist access numbers be limited?

- If yes, how? To what threshold?

- Who will decide? Will parties have powers of veto?

- Who will issue permits?

- What conditions and fees will be attached to tourist access?

- Who will collect and guard the fees?

- Who will monitor tourist use and enforce the relevant rules and conditions?

- Will indigenous or local guides be compulsory?

- Will accreditation of the guides be required, which may include a requirement for cross cultural training?

- What commercial activities will be permitted?

- Under what circumstances the parties will be allowed to directly engage in commercial activities with the tourists?

7.6   Crucial issues for government agencies

In broad terms, what government agencies should seek from co-management agreements is to further their legislated objectives and policy aims. The relevant "benefits" should be for the land, the natural resources, "conservation", "sustainable development" or other similar goals rather than for the agency itself or its individual staff. But specific agreements may also, of course, benefit the agency directly by saving it money, staff time or other resources, or by helping to spread its "message" and/ or perpetuate itself as a "legitimate organisation". In the sense just described, crucial aspects of the agreement include:

Good management– stewardship

Good management of the land ensures the conservation of species and ecosystems and the sustainable use of natural resources. A government agency may use financial incentives or other rewards to encourage landholders to agree to:

- limit clearing;

- stock pasture at sustainable levels;

- keep livestock out of forests or away from stream banks (e.g., by paying for fencing);

- rotate use of areas for grazing or agriculture;

- use sound productive methods and inputs (e.g., no chemical pesticides and genetically modified organisms);

- limit the number of visitors allowed on the land.

Protection of scenic views

Siting of a house or road may be negotiated to limit the visual impact on an otherwise natural scenic view (as well as the impact on conservation values). Communities and landholders may be willing to paint existing structures in camouflage colours for the cost of the paint.

Access

Access for management purposes or for the public to visit a notable feature may be negotiated with the relevant customary or legal owners. A community or landholder may agree to allow access across a relevant property that is essential for, say, fire control, if the fire authority does a little annual maintenance on the road. In north Queensland (Australia), several landowners agreed to guarantee public walking access across their property to a popular waterfall in return for assistance in closing an unofficial vehicular track and some minor construction to define the walking route more clearly.

Protection of local cultural heritage

On the ancestral lands of indigenous peoples, significant locations of rock art, cave paintings and other important indigenous cultural sites often occur on community or private land. The relevant communities and landholders may be enthusiastic about protecting these, but may need advice or financial assistance. A responsible government agency will include the relevant indigenous groups, communities and landowners in planning and negotiating an action strategy. The agreement will likely include access arrangements for traditional custodians or access regulated by law or custom.

The relevant communities and landowners may be enthusiastic about protecting indigenous cultural sites (rock art, cave paintings) but may need advice or financial assistance.

Rehabilitation of degraded areas

The government agency needs to be confident that:

● the agreed work will get done;

● the reforestation initiatives will be followed up (e.g., communities and landholders may undertake planting of seedlings with volunteer help only, but later they might lose interest in regular watering or weeding; careful choice of species and sites can minimise the need for follow up care, and automated watering systems can be a wise investment);

● appropriate species of local origin will be used;

● chemicals pest control will be avoided.

For an effective outcome, the government agency or a reliable contractor will need to be closely involved in the planning and execution of this component of a co-management agreement. Some form of ongoing monitoring is desirable.

Diffusing the conservation message

Signs, media events, presentations and other communication avenues that acknowledge the efforts of various local parties at conserving natural resources help to diffuse awareness and relevant information in a positive way. Many social communication methods and tools can be used, especially with tourists or other visitors. If a governmental agency is assisting a community or private landowner to site, design or build a car park, boardwalk or walking track, for example, it should include in the agreement the provision of interpretive material. Small posters and signs can explain forest ecology, conservation issues or indigenous history effectively and unobtrusively. The community or landowner may also be pleased to have a small shelter or pergola built to house educative material, or may agree to maintain and display a small herbarium or insect collection.

Control of weeds and pests

This is another area where a governmental agency can reap significant benefits from co-management agreements, but will need to be closely involved in design, training and monitoring to ensure that:

- traps or chemicals are avoided and, if needed for subsistence livelihoods, trapped animals (including feral) are treated humanely;

- non-target species are not affected;

- there is no risk to human safety or health;

- equipment is looked after, and returned in sound condition if that is part of the deal;

- follow up action is taken as necessary (the initial investment may be wasted if this is not done).

Fire and flood management

Fire management is a genuine and often emotional issue, and will require careful explanation and negotiation, not only with the particular communities and landowners, but with neighbours, conservation groups and other relevant government bodies. "Natural" fire management regimes, which include the intentional setting of fire when required for the maintenance of a specific habitat, and their effects on ecosystems are often not well understood. The risks to human life, property and conservation values may be enormous if something goes wrong. The chances of bad publicity and irretrievable damage to the reputation and credibility of a governmental agency are also very high (as is the risk to its budget if damage leads to compensation claims!).

Inclusion of fire management in co-management agreements therefore requires great caution. A "safe" inclusion might be no more than purchase or loan of fire fighting equipment. Any inclusion of fire manipulation or prescribed (controlled) burns in the agreement should specify the involvement of qualified professional fire management or control experts. This may include both biologists and professional fire fighters. A wise government agency might also seek to specify what will happen in the event of a managed fire (lit under the terms of the agreement) going out of control– though this will be no protection if negligence is involved, and may not help in the case of a public liability suit.

The management of flooding and water regimes also needs to be approached with caution. Along the Murray River and its tributaries (Australia), where irrigation farming is widespread and flooding regimes tightly controlled, landholders are now being encouraged to allow regular flooding of river red gum forests which is essential for forest ecology. This offers considerable scope for co-management agreements.

Fire management is a genuine and often emotional issue, and will require careful explanation and negotiation, not only with the particular communities and landowners, but with neighbours, conservation groups and other relevant government bodies.

Avoiding damage

A co-management agreement based on this concept is a little different from the others, and is often more closely akin to a straight commercial transaction. The basic discourse (from the government agency's perspective) is "I will agree that you are entitled to benefit X, if you promise to do (or not to do) Y". In this case, Y will be an activity which would improve (or damage) the values of the area. It may be planting, maintaining and caring for desirable species, or conversely, clearing, building a structure, subdividing, burning, starting up a tourist operation, diverting a watercourse, mining, quarrying or any number of other activities.

In some cases, it will be possible to negotiate a change of location, or way of doing Y which minimises the damage. In some cases, the agency (assuming it does not have the legal powers to stop Y) will need to find a powerful incentive. Often this will be simply money, and may (if the landholders are willing and the agency wealthy enough) lead to voluntary acquisition of the land by the government.

When this is not possible, the government agency may need to find an alternative which provides the same outcome as Y. In this respect, it is important to establish in negotiations what the actual desired outcome is (which is not always immediately clear). A landholder seeking to subdivide his or her land, for example, may want to provide a house site for each of her or his grown children. Negotiations with the local government authority may suggest ways of providing for multiple occupancy of a given plot without subdivision. A community may wish free access to a water resource inside a protected area. A new water point outside the border may give it exactly what it wants without any need to compromise on access.

In dealing with the above kind of co-management agreements, the agency is often "on the back foot", as it is likely to be entering negotiations after a community or landholder has already made the decision to do Y; presumably, it has also no legal means to prevent Y. It will need to be very creative, and use its most skilled negotiators. It will also need to be pragmatic, and realistic about what can be achieved. Preventing Y may be the preferred outcome, but minimising the damage is better than nothing.

Bringing it all together in a management plan

Where a complex mixture of management regimes and initiatives is proposed by various parties at various times, it may be desirable to prepare a comprehensive co-management plan. The plan can set out agreed objectives and strategies and a detailed work schedule. It is to be signed off by the parties and it is the heart of the overall agreement.

In some cases it may be possible to make the plan a legal instrument in its own right. A statutory management plan will need to have the strong support of all parties, as it will be legally binding on the social community at large, not just the parties, and will be much more difficult to revoke than a contract under common law. The positive side of this is that such a plan represents a more secure and long term form of protection for the land than a simple contract, and especially so when the latter does not run with title.

> A statutory management plan will need to have the strong support of all parties, as it will be legally binding on the social community at large, not just the parties, and will be much more difficult to revoke than a contract under common law.

Chapter 8. CO-MANAGEMENT ORGANISATIONS

Socio-economic development and the management of natural resources require experimenting and learning on an on-going basis. As a matter of fact, the process of negotiating and implementing the co-management agreements is never "finished", and some "body" or organisation needs to remain in charge of executing, monitoring and reviewing such agreements through time. Such organisation may be very similar to the negotiation platform among the parties that developed the agreements in the first place and, in fact, it may just continue that negotiation space on a more stable basis. Importantly, as the negotiation platform was pluralist and included various parties, so should be the co-management organisation.

Organisational forms vary among regions and depending on whether initiatives are self-mobilised or externally catalysed. Their composition depends on the range of institutional actors interested in the given natural and cultural resources. Their powers span from full management authority to consultative status. And their structure and rules of the game include a very large range of possibilities and may even vary through time.

8.1 Types and characteristics of co-management organsations

The co-management organisations may be of different types (e.g., a board, a council, a formal or informal association, a fund) and span different levels of authority and responsibility. They all, however, share at least two characteristics: they include at least two parties (and often many more), and they deal with the management of a given area, territory or body of natural resources. The key types of co-management organisations include:

- decision-making bodies– which are fully responsible for the management of a given territory, area or set of resources (examples may be a co-management board in charge of a state forest or protected area, or a trust in charge of managing an area jointly owned by several people; see Boxes 6.16, 7.11, 8.3 and 8.6);

- advisory bodies– which are responsible for advising decision-makers, e.g., by developing technical proposals, playing a brokering role, etc. (examples may be a committee in charge of developing a consensus over resource use thresholds and a fishing calendar or a high-level task force in charge of overseeing negotiations and managing conflicts; see Boxes 6.13, 7.15 and 8.1);

- mixed bodies– which hold a combination of responsibilities, such as partial management responsibility and partial advisory responsibility (an example may be an advisory or management committee responsible for advising on park management issues but fully in charge of decisions pertaining to the natural resources in its buffer zone; see Box 8.2);

- executive bodies– which are responsible for interpreting and implementing decisions within a broad framework provided by others (an example may be a local co-management committee in charge of applying a national legislation in a specific local context; see Box 8.4).

> *The key types of co-management organisations include decision-making bodies, advisory bodies mixed bodies and executive bodies....*

Box 8.1 A co-management organisation with a high-level "brokering" role
(adapted from British Columbia Claims Task Force, 1991)

The British Columbia Claims Task Force (BCCTF), whose 1991 Report on appropriate processes for developing treaties represents an impressive cooperative agreement in its own right, comprised three indigenous representatives (selected by indigenous peoples), two federal representatives and two state government representatives. All the recommendations of the Task Force were accepted by government, including the establishment of a British Columbia Treaty Commission (in 1992). The Commission was set up to be an "impartial body which will facilitate and monitor treaty negotiations".[1] It includes two Commissioners nominated by the First Nations Summit and one each by the governments of Canada and British Columbia, respectively. A Chief Commissioner is nominated by all parties. The Commission does not negotiate treaties but coordinates the process, acts as an "honest broker" and provides dispute resolution services. It also allocates government funds provided for the treaty process.

---

[1]   British Columbia Treaty Commission Act,1995

Functions

The functions of a co-management organisation at the local level usually relate to analysing situations, appraising different types of interventions, making strategic decisions, developing plans and agreements, implementing, monitoring and evaluating activities and adjusting them on the basis of lessons learned. Co-management organisations at regional, national and international levels, on the other hand, are more concerned with enabling conditions, scaling-up concerns and institutional learning. The authority and terms of reference may be specified in legislation or in participatory management agreements, and the members of the organisations may be paid or voluntary.

Co-management organisations can be further distinguished on the basis of:

- legal status and form (e.g., board, council, authority, association, trust, company, etc.);

- functions, responsibilities and legal powers to carry them out (including decision making powers, enforcement provisions and assets owned);

- composition, including the proportional representation of the parties who nominate or elect the chair and other key members, decide what is their terms of office and in what circumstances their appointments can be terminated;

- to whom the chair and key members (e.g., the bureau) report and what are the meetings' schedules and reporting arrangements;

- funding received and by whom;

- whether members are paid, voluntary or need to pay to be members;

- whether a secretariat or some technical staff is available to work for the organisation;

- confidentiality or transparency of meetings and decision-making procedures;

- quality of the relationship between members and the "constituency" they represent (depending also on the constituency internal organising and representation procedures).

Box 8.2   An innovative co-management organisation for Waza National Park (Cameroon)
(adapted from Borrini-Feyerabend et al., 2000)

The Waza National Park, situated in the Extreme North province of Cameroon, was created some decades ago. Following the national legislation, the residents of the villages situated inside the park's territory were forcibly relocated outside, right at the park's borders (actually all communities were relocated except one, which possibly had important connections in high places...). The relocated communities never resigned themselves to the decision, in particular regarding the prohibition of collecting natural resources necessary for their own livelihood. Throughout the years they continued to claim fishing rights on the ponds excavated and managed by their ancestors inside the park, the right of harvesting certain plant products (for instance gum Arabic) from within the park, the right to take their animals to graze inside the park in times of drought, etc. The ensuing conflicts between communities and park management brought the Waza Logone project, implemented by the IUCN and financed by the Dutch Development Agency, to initiate a co-management process to secure the natural resources of the park via agreements among the different stakeholders.

The process of negotiating among stakeholders brought about the establishment of a multi-stakeholder management structure, with the aim of approving the conventions that would regulate the management of the park and the natural resources at its periphery. Noticeably, the definition of the mandate of the structure encountered the strong reluctance of the park conservation service. After months spent in search of a suitable compromise, the parties agreed on a "double mandate": a consulting role regarding the management of the park (whose mandate stays with the conservation service), and a full management role regarding the zone at the periphery of the park. With this double role in mind, the structure was named the Consultative/ Management Committee of the Waza National Park and its Periphery.

The Consultative/ Management Committee of the Waza National Park and its Periphery was legalised by the Minister of Environment and Forests of Cameroon with a decision pertaining to its internal organisation and functioning rules. The structure includes members possessing full rights and members with consultative powers only.

The members with full (voting) rights are:
● 4 representatives from the Park Conservation Service;

● 1 representative from the Provincial Delegation of Environment and Forests;

● 3 representatives of the Central Service of the Environment and Forests Ministry;

● 5 representatives of the men from the settled communities in the park's periphery;

● 5 representatives of the women from the settled communities in the park's periphery;

● 2 representatives of cattle-rearing nomads (a man and a woman) and 1 representative of transhumant cattle-rearing people interested in the pasture of Waza National Park and the surrounding plain;

● 2 representatives of youths (a man and a woman) from the settled communities in the park's periphery.

The members with consultative powers only are:
● the mayors of the interested rural municipalities (Waza, Zina, Petté);

● the head authorities of the relevant districts (Waza, Zina, Ngodeni, Fadaré, Kossa);

● a representative of the Scientific Council for Waza National Park;

● three representatives of the Waza Logone project;

● a representative of the Management Committee of the Waza-Logone Plain (another multi-party management structure in the same province, also promoted by the Waza Logone project).

Deciding about the institutional arrangement that best suits the co-management situation (i.e., what type of organisation, composition, rules, functions, powers, responsibilities) is invariably an iterative process. To some extent, institutional arrangements arise from the reality on the ground (i.e., what is to be managed? How much is there to be shared?). On the other hand, the degree of flexibility the parties have about institutional arrangements (which includes the legal framework for decision making) determines what can reasonably be included in the agreement and the type of co-management organisation that can be developed. Examples of substantially

Deciding about the institutional arrangement that best suits the co-management situation... is an iterative process.

different types of co-management organisations are given in Box 8.1, Box 8.2 and Box 8.3 and several more are listed in Table 8.1 along with a selection of their aims, functions and powers. Noticeably, several organisations with different functions, powers and responsibilities may be needed for a particular area and act in complementary ways (see, for instance, Box 6.12, on the sophisticated co-management setting for the Galapagos Marine Reserve).

Box 8.3   An organisation created to co-manage woodlands in Scotland
(adapted from Jeanrenaud and Jeanrenaud, 1996)

Self—mobilised groups in Scotland have developed community-based organisations specifically to coordinate and implement woodland management on a wide area. In Assynt, for instance, the local farmers (called crofters) established in 1992 the Assynt Crofters' Trust, with some 130 members spread across 13 townships. The trust raised the money for the purchase of the former North Lochinver Estate by public subscription, grants and loans from public bodies. The members elected directors to the trust's board on a township basis, and the trust was then run by an executive company chairman and various officers. Since then, the trust has developed the potential of the estate, including through a native woodlands programme.

Nested co-management institutions can develop different agreements at different levels of detail within the same co-management scheme.

Nested co-management institutions can develop different agreements at different levels of detail within the same co-management scheme. In Sweden for example, the institutional framework for the management of freshwater fisheries is made up of a nested set of institutions at different organisational levels that combine government bodies and fishing associations (see Box 8.4). In Canada, the Yukon Umbrella Final Agreement created two levels of wildlife co-management boards: a Fish and Wildlife Management Board for the Yukon as a whole, and separate Renewable Resource Councils in each Yukon First Nation's traditional territory. The Board is the primary instrument for fish and wildlife management in the Yukon as a whole, and the Councils are the main bodies responsible for developing agreements on, and implementing, local renewable resource management. The structures include approximately equal numbers of government and Inuvialuit representatives, except in a few specified cases. Similar institutional arrangements are foreseen in many other comprehensive agreements on wildlife management that have been negotiated throughout the Canadian North.[2] Wide-ranging co-management responsibilities are usually assigned to co-management boards and extensive self-regulatory responsibilities devolved to aboriginal organisations. The complementary activities of these nested co-management organisations work towards the conservation of resources through processes that determine how much of the total allowable harvest is allocated among aboriginal peoples and other users. One of their salient characteristics is the flexible and creative use of legal and economic instruments while striving for open negotiation processes and conflict resolution.

Box 8.4   Fishing associations and the co-management of freshwater ecosystems in Sweden
(adapted from Olsson and Folke, 2001)

Local fishing associations are common in Sweden. These associations, which in many respects resemble common-property systems, manage many of Sweden's vast number of lakes, rivers and streams. National laws introduced in the 1980s and 1990s make it possible for freshwater associations not only to manage lakes and rivers but also watersheds. Fishing associations have the right to make decisions

---

2   Nesbitt, 1997.

concerning fishing and fish conservation. The national government, however, is still in charge of broader decisions, such as instituting bans on certain fishing methods or granting permission for stocking fish and shellfish.

A detailed study of the management of the Lake Racken watershed has highlighted the key role of local fishing associations in sustaining crayfish populations and the larger ecosystem. The institutional framework for the management of crayfish populations is made up of a nested set of institutions at different organisational levels. Rules for the management of crayfish are both informal and formal, and are developed by both the local fishing associations and the government. Much of the learning by doing for the co-management of fisheries, however, is carried out by the local fishing associations, whose members develop site-specific ecological knowledge as well as adaptive organisations and rules.

Some co-management organisations are created as interim measures during the resolution of title claims over natural and cultural resources. For example in Canada, representatives of Inuit and Haida communities were called in to participate in processed around the management of two National Parks while their territorial claims were being resolved. Both processes ended up establishing co-management agreements.[3] Similarly, in the South Moresby/ Gwaii Haanas National Park Reserve, co-management structures were initially created as an interim dispute resolution mechanism. Nine Inuit representatives participate today in the management of the Auyuittuq National Park Reserve on Baffin Island, with three Parks Canada staff acting as advisors. The committee advises on general park management, including wildlife harvesting and interpretation programmes, and is reported to have reduced local conflicts over the area. Under the Sub-agreement on Impact and Benefits of the Nunavut Final Agreement, issues such as employment and economic benefits, zoning, and new committees are also examined.

Some co-management organisations are created as interim measures.

Composition

As mentioned, a co management organisation is necessarily multiparty, i.e., it includes at least two, and often many more, social actors. These actors may represent broadly similar or different interests (see Box 8.5).

Box 8.5	Representation of stakeholders in co-management organisations: two examples from India

(adapted from Agarwal and Narain, 1989; Agarwal and Saigal,1996)

"Similar" actors in charge: the example of Seed village. Seed village near Udaipur in the state of Rajasthan is registered under a unique law known as the Rajastan Gramdian Act 1971, which gives executive and legal powers to the gram sabha (village council). The entire adult population from 100 households is directly represented in the gram sabha. The gram sabha elects the karyapalika (the executive), as well as the adhyaksh (chairperson) for a definite period. The executive committee, which is made up of unpaid representatives from all sections of the community, cannot take decisions unless a resolution to that effect has been taken by the gram sabha, which meets at least once every month. Seed's gram sabha has formed six committees to oversee different types of work in the village: crop loans, forest and nursery development, water resource management, legal problems and disputes, development programmes and finances. The gram sabha has full control over the use of land within the village boundary. In managing this territory, it also has the power to judge, penalise and prosecute. The gram sabha has also devised rules for protection of the village common lands by dividing them into two categories: one where both grazing and leaf collection is banned, and the other where grazing is

---

3   Commission on Aboriginal Peoples, 1996.

permitted but leaf collection or harming trees is banned. This local management organisation also has jurisdiction over trees in private lands, where cutting is allowed only for domestic reasons but not for sale.

"Different" actors in charge: the example of Joint Forest Management. Forest Protection Committees (FPCs), whose members are drawn from the local communities dependent on forest resources, were first set up in the 1970s and 1980s in the states of West Bengal, Gujarat and Haryana. The National Forest Policy (1998) and the circular regarding community involvement in forestry issued by the Government of India, emphasised the increasing importance of Joint Forest Management between state agencies and local communities. For the FPCs, the important issues include adopting and implementing regulations for community collection and allocation of fuel wood, minor forest products, grazing access, labour for forestry activities, sharing the proceeds from timber and polewood harvests, and managing intra-and inter-village conflicts. The presence of primary and secondary stakeholders in the CM bodies manifests itself in the differing priorities each stakeholder group assigns to forest management as well as the form and degree of benefit sharing. For example, in most areas JFM is used as a strategy to regenerate degraded forests and improve survival in plantations; in other words, for meeting the objectives of the Forest Department, which often do not coincide with the needs and interests of forest-dependent villagers.

The capacity of a social actor– a public or private agency, a group, an organisation or an individual– to become a member of a co-management organisation depends on the social status of that actor, i.e., on the acceptance by the other members of the organisation (and by society at large) of its claims to participate in management. In other words, it depends on its recognised entitlements (see Section 2.2 of this volume). Legal issues, including customary or legal tenure, jurisdiction and authority also need to be addressed. For example, if lands are held under leasehold, the written consent of the relevant owners, tenants, occupiers and security holders (such as mortgagees) may be required in the development of a co-management institution. Some jurisdictions and legislation may require that organisations are formally incorporated as legal persons before they can take part in a management body. In other cases, the government has to recognise the validity of customary laws and allow for management authority and responsibility to be taken up not in individual but in collective ways (see Box 8.6)

Box 8.6   The Dayak people co-manage the Kayan Mentarang National Park: a first in Indonesia!
(adapted from Ferrari, 2003)

The Kayan Mentarang National Park (KMNP) situated in the interior of East Kalimantan (Indonesian Borneo) lies at the border with Sarawak to the west and Sabah to the north. With its gazetted 1.4 million ha, it is the largest protected area of rainforest in Borneo and one of the largest in Southeast Asia. The history of the natural landscape of the park is intertwined with the history of its people. About 16,000 Dayak people live inside or in close proximity of the park. These are still communities largely regulated by customary law, or adat, in the conduct of their daily affairs and the management of natural resources in their customary territory (wilayah adat). The chief (kepala adat) and council (lembaga adat) administer the customary law. All elected officials at village level and prominent leaders of the community are members of the customary council, which declare traditional forest areas with protection status or strict management regime. These are referred to as "lands whose access is restricted or limited" (tana ulen). Such lands cover primary forest rich in natural resources such as rattan (Calamus sp.), sang leaves

(Licuala sp.), hardwood for construction (e.g., Dipterocarpus sp., Shorea sp., Quercus sp.) and fish and game, all of which have high use value for the local community.

In 1980 the area was established as Nature Reserve, under a strict protection status that allowed no human activity. Later on, a study that included community mapping exercises showed the Dayak communities rightful claims to the land and its resources. This study basically recommended a change of status from Nature Reserve to National Park, where traditional activities are allowed. A WWF project identified as primary the problem of lack of tenure security, which had effectively transformed the Dayak's forest into an "open access forest", where the state could decide to allocate exploitation rights or establish a conservation area without their prior consent. The Dayak communities had very little power to defend the forest or secure their economic livelihoods against logging companies, mining exploration, or outside collectors of forest products. Under these circumstances, the project decided to give priority to activities that would lead to the recognition of adat claims and adat rights, so that indigenous communities could continue to use and manage forest resources in the conservation area. From 1996 to 2000, the project engaged in the assessment of the use and availability of forest resources with economic value, in workshops for

the recognition of forest under traditional customary management (tana ulen), in participatory planning for zoning recommendations and the redrawing of the external boundaries of the park, in the drafting of adat or customary regulations for the management of the national park, and in the strengthening of local organisations.

The Alliance of the Indigenous People of Kayan Mentarang National Park (FoMMA) was formally established on October 2000 by the leaders of the ten customary lands of the park. This was to create a forum for conveying the aspirations of the indigenous communities and debating issues concerning the management of natural resources in the customary lands of the KMNP. The Alliance is concerned with guaranteeing protection of the forest and the sustainable use of natural resources in the ten customary lands of the NP area, as well as with the protection of the rights of indigenous people and their economic prosperity in and around the park. The Alliance now legally represents the concerned indigenous people in the Policy Board (Dewan Penentu Kebijakan), a new organisation set up to preside over the park's management. The Policy Board includes representatives of the central government (Agency for Forest Protection and Nature Conservation), the provincial and district governments and the Alliance. The operating principles of the board emphasise the importance of coordination, competence, shared responsibilities, and equal partnership among all stakeholders. The board was formally established in April 2002 with a decree of the Ministry of Forestry, which also spelled out that the park was to be managed through collaborative management– a first in Indonesia!

Still in other cases, it is the country as a whole that must go through a process of testing various approaches on the basis of diverse views of what is possible and desirable. In this sense, co-management institutions emerge as a way of solving problems and signalling the acquired maturity of the natural resource management debate (see Box 8.7).

Box 8.7   Major institutional change in the management of national forests in western USA
             (adapted from Wilson, R.K., 2003)

The vast majority of protected areas in the United States lie within the national system of public lands and resources. National forests differ from other forms of public lands insofar as the original rationale for their retention within the public domain includes the continuation of natural resource development for commercial purposes, as well as ecological preservation, scientific research, and endangered species protection (this is in line with the 1960 Multiple Use and Sustained Yield Act).

For the first one hundred years after independence, the dominant attitudes toward public lands and resources was characterised by a process of land acquisition (colonial westward expansion), followed by settlement (the transfer of the public domain into private ownership), and relatively unfettered commercial development. By the close of the 19th century, however, the social and ecological costs of these laissez-faire policies were taking their toll in the form of deforestation, soil erosion, large-scale forest fires, loss of native species, and a host of urban social and economic problems. Progressive ideals were a response to this state of crisis. In general terms, progressives argued that only the federal government could provide the objectivity, rationality and expertise needed to properly regulate, manage and provide for the public good. By preventing the wasteful practices of those seeking short-term economic gain, the vast natural resources in the United States would not be squandered, but last for generations, managed according to scientific principles by a corps of highly trained and "unbiased" state officials.

Despite this policy of centralised management authority, local residents remained economically dependent on these new national forests and, in practice continued to exercise varying levels of influence over management decisions. Public participation in the management process was formalised in the 1960s and 1970s with the passage of a series of new federal environmental laws, which emphasised the need for public hearings and stressed public participation in an individual and nationalistic sense rather than in a collective or community-based sense. Avenues for "participation" were in fact designed to allow individuals to express their personal views or interests, rather than groups and communities to express collective concerns. Rather than facilitating dialogue and open discussion, public hearings tended to be linear presentations of information from federal officials to a public audience.

In the 1990s, regional socio-economic shifts created increasing tensions in many western rural communities over public land use issues. Soon it became clear that the existing institutional structure for integrating public input into forest management processes was insufficient and tended to exacerbate local disputes and alienate federal officials from community residents rather than to create an atmosphere of collaboration. In those years, on the other hand, a number of "real" partnerships– such as the Quincy Library Group in California, the Applegate Partnership in Oregon and the Ponderosa Pine Forest Partnership in Colorado– began to emerge and provided concrete examples of what might be achieved through collaboration. These different types of partnerships provided a forum where local residents and federal managers could work together to solve common problems. On the basis of their results, interest in community-based approaches proliferated rapidly across western USA. By 1997, over 90% of national forests in the United States was said to be engaged in some form of collaborative stewardship as part of their management strategy.

Scope of authority

While there may not be a stand-alone body with permanent premises, staff, budget, etc., some kind of joint organisational forum is essential if a natural resource or territory is to be managed by more than one party. Such joint "bodies" often vary in their decision-making powers. The weakest form of organisation is simply an advisory body to the "real" decision-maker (which may be by mandate a governmental agency). In such cases, the body may have strong moral force but little real power. Some indigenous parties and organised sectors of civil society are increasingly unlikely to accept this model, given the existence of other types of organisations that can better represent their rights (see Box 8.8). Others, however, consider that advisory bodies with strong legitimacy– and especially advisory bodies in charge of developing technical proposals and arrangements– often end up strongly affecting or determining decisions despite their lack of legal mandate (see Box 6.13).

Box 8.8   Co-management organisations with different decision making powers: examples from Australia
(adapted from De Lacy and Lawson, 1997)

"Token" co-management organisations. Under Queensland's Aboriginal Land Act 1991 successfully claimed national parks are leased back to government and managed by a board of management. Under s.5.20(3) "The Aboriginal people particularly concerned with the National Park land are to be represented on the Board of Management." No mention is made of who else will be on the board, how many, or what the proportional representation of those Aboriginal people shall be. In practice, anyway, the board has few real powers. Its principal function is to "cooperate" with the chief executive of the government in the preparation and revision of a management plan. Under the Nature Conservation Act 1992, to which the parks remain subject, real power remains in the hands of the chief executive. Management plans do not have statutory force, unless specifically determined under a separate regulation. Very few national parks have been successfully claimed under this act and Aboriginal people generally express little confidence in it. Progress has been inordinately slow.

Equitable and effective co-management organisations. At Uluru and Kakadu National Parks, similar claims, leases and board of management arrangements also apply. In these cases, however, the lease is for a limited term (five years) subject to renewal, and provides guaranteed financial compensation. The Kakadu Board of Management, for example, comprises 14 individuals, 10 of whom are Aboriginal people nominated by traditional owners. The board is responsible for preparing a management plan (which is subtly but significantly different from "cooperating in its preparation") and making day-to-day management decisions. In practice, the traditional owners are a powerful force in the management of both parks, which are run according to both national parks law and indigenous law. Management arrangements for these parks are genuinely cooperative.

Size and level of operations

Co-management organisations can be large or small, simple or highly complex, single or multiple, and thus operate at various scales and levels. An example of a complex institutional structure for the management of a World Heritage site is given in Box 8.9. The size and level of operation of this joint management body clearly contrasts with the smaller scale village level institutions described in Box 8.4.

Box 8.9   A co-management organisation working on a large scale in Australia's Wet Tropics World Heritage Area
(adapted from Pattemore, 2000)

In the Wet Tropics of north-eastern Australia, a complex institutional structure has been developed with the intention of achieving some community involvement in the management of the World Heritage Area (WHA), as well as a balance between the perspectives of Commonwealth and state governments. A great deal of attention was paid to the process of setting up the participatory management institutions because of serious conflicts– between the Commonwealth and state governments, and within the north Queensland community– over the listing of the area and the compulsory cessation of logging under a Commonwealth regulation. The participatory management scheme responsible for the implementation of the Wet Tropics Management Inter-governmental Agreement is complex and multilayered. Its main components are:

The Wet Tropics Ministerial Council. As the ultimate decision making body, the Council includes two Commonwealth ministers. The portfolios represented by these ministers change from time to time, but always includes the Commonwealth minister responsible for the environment. Other ministers, such as those representing Aboriginal and Torres Strait Islander Affairs and State Tourism may be invited to attend as "observers" from time to time.

Under the Act, the Ministerial Council's responsibilities are:
- approving the budget;
- nominating the chairperson of the board (see below);
- recommending for approval the final management plans to the state Governor in Council.

The Wet Tropics Management Authority. The WTM Authority consists of a board, an executive director and staff. The staff and executive director are state government officers employed under Queensland public service laws. The board consists of five part-time members who are private citizens. The executive director is a non-voting member of the board. The voting members are appointed under Queensland law on the nomination of the Commonwealth (two), the state of Queensland (two) and the Ministerial Council (the Chair of the Board). While the Wet Tropics World Heritage Protection and Management Act 1993 requires only that board members not be public servants, and have experience or qualifications in a field relevant to the Wet Tropics WHA, the Commonwealth is obliged under the Wet Tropics of Queensland World Heritage Conservation Act 1994 to make at least one of its nominees an Aboriginal person.

The Authority is advised by two statutory committees: a Scientific Advisory Committee, and a Community Consultative Committee (CCC). While these committees have functions specified under the act, they do not have decision making powers. Initially the members on the CCC were chosen by the Ministerial Council. After proclamation of the act, appointment of the committees became the WTM Authority's responsibility. There is now a formal policy and written procedures for selecting committee members. Public notices call for expressions of interest, and the policy requires the authority to choose members who provide a range of skills and interests, and are spread geographically across the entire area. Preference is given to nominees who can demonstrate the support of a community group. Where a particularly contentious issue is to be discussed at a board meeting, the authority may also hold community meetings with key stakeholder representatives from the conservation sector, tourism industry, indigenous groups or World Heritage Area landholders and neighbours. The meetings are chaired by a board member, who canvasses views on issues to be considered by the Wet Tropics Board. Each board meeting is attended by government officials representing the four Ministerial Council portfolios. The officials attend as observers and have no statutory role but are nonetheless very influential.

Co-management organisations can also be distinguished on the basis of the scale on which they operate to improve natural resource management and local livelihoods. Three levels of operation appear most important:

1. The local level. The focus at this level is on primary actors. Co-management organisations are usually engaged in situation analysis, appraisal of different types of interventions, making strategic decisions, developing plans and agree-

ments, and implementing, monitoring and evaluating activities. Time and resources may need to be invested in participatory processes, dialogues to elicit multiple perspectives, group learning processes, conflict resolution and the active engagement of underprivileged actors (e.g., women, the poor).[4] The full and effective involvement of primary actors in a co-management organisation at the local level makes the whole difference between token participation/ consultation and real co-operative decision making and power sharing.

2. The district or regional level. The focus at this level is on providing the enabling conditions for co-management of natural resources to happen at the local level over wide areas. Co-management organisations may be set up to identify and promote needed conditions and forms of support, to encourage and promote local action, to mediate conflicts, to strengthen networks, and to facilitate exchanges and joint learning. Typical activities include the federation and coordination of local initiatives and the building and strengthening of local organisations to involve more local actors in the management of natural resources.

3. The national and international level. The focus at this level is on legislation, policy and institutional transformation. Co-management organisations operating on a very large scale usually include as major actors governmental agencies, large NGOs, donor agencies and representatives of first nation peoples. Their key challenge is to ensure the broad conditions and incentives necessary to establish flexible, innovative and transparent management practices. More specifically, they should refrain from imposing "participation" from above through standardised structures that may inhibit, rather than facilitate, co-management at the local level.

Ideally, co-management organisations operate at these three interrelated levels to secure local livelihoods and sustain natural resources.

> Ideally, co-management organisations operate at local, regional and national/ international levels in an interrelated way.

8.2 Examples of co-management agreements and organisations

In Table 8.1 we have collected and compared a number of co-management agreements and organisations. The cases span international, national and local examples.

---

4   Pimbert and Pretty, 1995.

Table 8.1	Examples of co-management agreements and organisations	
Name of, and parties to the agreement	CM organisation(s) (bodies in charge of decision making, advice, enforcing rules, etc.)	Selected aims and main clauses of the agreement, resource(s) to be managed, functions and powers of the CM organisations...
A. International CM agreements and organisations		
Agreement between the Government of Canada and the Government of the United States of America on the Conservation of the Porcupine Caribou Herd (1987)	International Porcupine Caribou Board: 8 members (4 US, 4 Canada)	Objectives: • to conserve Porcupine Caribou herd and its habitat • to further the objectives of the agreement; • to facilitate coordination, communication and cooperation between the parties and develop an International Conservation Plan; • to collect, share and provide advice and recommendations to the parties concerning herd monitoring, harvest limits and data, habitat conservation; • to ensure opportunities for customary and traditional uses of the herd and participatory management.
Agreement on the recognition of Kgalagadi Trans-frontier Park between the government of the Republic of Botswana and the Government of the Republic of South Africa (1999)[5]	Kgalagadi Trans-frontier Park Foundation– composed of 8 persons in representation of the 4 high level officials in each country— with the general aim of sharing ideas, developing proposals, providing general guidance and facilitating the joint management of Kgalagadi Trans-frontier Park	Objectives: • to monitor the implementation of the management plan; • to advise about the plan; • to foster cooperation and integration of activities; • to receive and distribute funds.
Protocol of cooperation on the conservation of the Caspian Sea between the Government of Iran and the Soviet Union (1973)[6]	Joint Commission on Environmental Protection of the Caspian Sea: five members including high-level experts from Iran and from the Soviet Union, with a co-chair from each side.	Objectives: • monitoring of pollution of the Caspian Sea; • assessment of risks and damage to biodiversity, including 400 endemic species, such as the Caspian seal, 5 endemic species of sturgeon producing the world's highest quality caviar, and the migratory bird species associated with several wetland areas; • recommending decisions for impact prevention and abatement; • carrying out joint research projects on the environmental aspects of the Caspian Sea.
B. National CM agreements and organisations		
James Bay and Northern Quebec Agreement (1975) between the Government of Canada and	Hunting, Fishing and Trapping Coordinating Committee: composed of government representatives and aboriginal parties in equal numbers and	Agreement: • aboriginal people to have exclusive harvest rights of aquatic species and furbearers on specified lands and to have priority subsistence harvesting rights on other lands within specified harvest level; • guaranteed minimum income for fur hunters;

---

5   Sandwith et al., 2001.

6   Protocol signed between the Department of the Environment, Iran and the Ministry of Agriculture and Water Resources of the Soviet Union in 1973. The Protocol was in force until the breakdown of the Soviet Union in the early 1990s, and is considered to have played a major role in maintaining a relatively high environmental quality in the Caspian.

Indian First Nations	in charge of reviewing, managing, supervising the co-management regime (advisory capacity)	• local community landholding corporations to manage exclusive harvesting rights; • authority to set harvest level in some specific areas; • aboriginal parties pay own costs of participation from agreement compensation fund.
Memorandum of Understanding for the Joint Management of Selected Forests[7] Agreement between Kenya Wildlife Service (KWS) and the Forestry Department (FD) in the Ministry of Environment and Natural Resources	Joint Steering Committee to oversee implementation of joint management plans KWS and FD to nominate representatives to Committee	Key clauses: The agreement is established on a 25-year term, with joint review and updating every 5 years. It foresees joint objectives, plans and initiatives, including: • patrols, training, fencing, extension work, fire plans; • surveys and research; • controlled and rational use of forest products; • development and maintenance of facilities and infrastructure for minimum impact tourism and recreation, including conservation education facilities (such as nature trails); • joint definition of areas of value; • erecting and maintaining wildlife barriers; • protecting tree plantations and ecological balance; • revenue collection and use.
Inuvialuit Final Agreement on the Wildlife and Environmental Management Regime between the Government of Canada and Indian First Nations	• Hunters and Trappers Committee: advise the Inuvialuit game council on local issues, including wildlife requirements and quotas, issue harvesting bylaws, collect harvest data, contribute to community conservation plans and assist other committees; • Inuvialuit Game Council (IGC): 13 representatives from 6 hunters and trappers committees and chair, appoints Inuvialuit members to advisory bodies, advises governments and assigns hunting areas and quotas, represents Inuvialuit internationally; • Fisheries Joint Management Committee: 5 members: 2 IGC, 2 Federal Government; 1 independent chair. The committee determines harvest levels, reviews fishing data, registers fishers, allocates quotas, advises governments; • Wildlife Management Advisory Council: 7 members: 2 IGC, 2 North West Territories (NWT) Government, 1 Federal Government, NWT Chair: advises on wildlife management, advises Ministers, IGC, Environmental Screening Committee, Environmental Impact Review Board: determines harvest quotas, and advises on international issues, prepares wildlife conservation and management plan for western Arctic region; • Environmental Impact Review Board: determines harvest quotas, and advises on international issues, prepares wildlife conservation and management plan for western Arctic region; • Wildlife Management Advisory Council (North Slope): 5 members: 2 IGC, 1 Yukon Government, 1 Federal Environment Representative, Yukon Government Chair: wildlife conservation and management plan, protected area planning and management; • Environmental Impact Screening Committee: 7 members: 3 Government, 3 IGC, Government chair: examines development proposals, refers significant project to review board or elsewhere; • Environmental Impact Review Board: 7 members: Federal chair, 3 IGC, 3 Federal Government: conducts public reviews of development proposals referred by screening committee; • Joint Secretariat: serves all committees except North Slope; • Inuvialuit Regional Corporation.	

---

[7] KWS and FD, 1991.

Wadden Sea Agreement: the Sea and Coastal Fisheries Policy in the Netherlands[8]	The members comprise the nature conservation groups, producer organisation of the cockle fisherfolk, research bodies, community representatives and government representatives	Agreement: • 26% of the Wadden Sea closed for fishing; • in years of food shortage, 60 % of cockle and mussel stocks reserved for birds and a quota is set for fisherfolk; • reduction of the fishing fleet from 36 to 22 vessels and decision to equip boats with a "black box" (a computer registering all fishing position and activity); • producer organisations have right to sanction and fine any fisher breaking the agreed rules.
Porcupine Caribou Management Agreement (1985) between rural residents and the Government of Canada	Porcupine Caribou Management Board 8 members: 1 Government of Canada, 2 Yukon, 2 Council of Yukon, 1 North West Territories, 1 Dene/ Metis, 1 IGC	Objectives: • make recommendations on herd and habitat conservation and management, and annual allowable harvest; • develop native users' guidelines and training; • promote research and data collection; • carry out land use planning and land management; • identify sensitive habitat areas; • agree on rules and procedures, rights of native users, prohibition on commercial harvest; • spread information.
	C. Local CM agreements and organisations	
Fishery management agreements in Lake Aheme, Benin[9]	National and regional government organisations, National Fishery Service, Akaja and Xha fishermen and other lake stakeholders (priests, women organisations, village representatives)	Agreement: • design new governing institutions for the lake; • create new co-management body for the lake that involves representatives from government; • ban some Akaja and Xha practices.
Oyster fishing agreement on wild beds in Cowes Harbor, Isle of Wight (UK)[10]	Cowes Harbour Commissioners and oyster fisherman company	Basic agreement: Fishermen's long term access to wild oyster beds guaranteed, and fisheries management rules developed.
Memorandum of Understanding establishing a Joint Land Use Regulatory Programme and Minimum Development Guidelines between the Quinault Indian Nation and Jefferson and Grays Harbor Counties[11]	Quinault Indian Nation and Jefferson and Grays Harbor Counties Land Use Advisory Board, comprising 2 Quinault Indian appointees, 1 Jefferson County, 1 Grays Harbor County (Canada	Agreement: • commitment to consultation and cooperation with planning, zoning and other land use and development controls; • geographic area subject to agreement with comprehensive plans and agreed minimum development guidelines; • development and land use permits; • review process, amendments, jurisdiction; • county owned lands located on the reservation; • technical assistance; • joint statement of goals and policies to guide the parties.

8   Steins, 1997a.
9   Maarleveld and Dangbegnon, 1999.
10   Steins and Edwards, 1998.
11   Quinault Indian Nation and Jefferson and Grays Harbor Counties, 1993.

Informal agreement on management of marine resources in Killary Harbor, Connemara, Ireland[12]	Department of the Marine and local mussel farming cooperative and fishermen association	Agreement: ● keep the fishing grounds free from rafts and long-lines; ● grant membership to local people only, making it impossible for non-locals and large investors to get mussel farming licences.
Memorandum of Understanding Regarding the Control of Aboriginal Cultural Material in Kakadu National Park[13]	Director, National Parks and Wildlife, Northern Land Council, Australia and representatives of Aboriginal groups	Main components of agreement: Responsibilities of parties concerning park management, Aboriginal interests, register of Aboriginal cultural material, protocol of access to register, photographs, recordings, no publication without consent, approval processes for research permits and commercial filming, storage areas, repatriation of cultural material, other protocols, no transfer of authority, native title not affected, amendment procedures.
Joint management agreements under Hazara Protected Forests (Community Participation) Rules 1996, Pakistan[14]	Government of the North-West Frontier Province Forest Department, and Fathebandi local community Joint Forest Management Committee comprising village representatives and Forestry, Fisheries and Wildlife Department staff Audit committee comprising up to 5 beneficiaries of agreements	Objectives: ● to develop and ensure smooth implementation of the Joint Forest Management Plan, Plan of Operation and Land Use Plan; ● to ensure beneficiaries receive and share equitably benefits under the plan; ● to ensure effective forest protection activities, prevent trespassing, encroachment, illegal grazing and tree cutting, fires or other damage or prohibited acts. Responsibilities: ● conflict resolution; ● producing witnesses for court hearings concerning forest prosecutions as required; ● setting up meetings and agendas; Agreement to be reviewed after 5 years or as required.
Draft Forest Use Agreement between Uganda National Parks, represented by Mt. Elgon National Park (MENP), and the People of Ulukusi Parish, represented by the Kitsatsa Forest Use Committee of Ulukusi Parish, Uganda[15]	Parish Committee and Uganda Wildlife Authority: 4 representatives for each of 9 villages to represent interests in firewood, bamboo, honey, vegetable/mushroom; 2 elected herbalists; 2 elected pitsawers; co-opted chair, secretary for women, parish chief, ranger boundary MENP, parish-based extension worker	Objectives: ● to meet use and conservation needs; ● to promote acceptance of park; ● to allow swift regeneration of encroached area; ● to protect forested zone; ● to protect the area from hunting and grazing; ● to ensure local responsibility for monitoring and control of forest-use access; ● to reduce local dependence on some resources.

12 Steins, 1997b.
13 National Parks and Wildlife (Australia) and Northern Land Council, 1995.
14 North-West Frontier Province, 1996.
15 Uganda National Parks and Kitsatsa Forest Use Committee of Ulukusi Parish, undated.

Resolution establishing forest protection committees in West Bengal[16]	West Bengal Forest Department and local Panchayat (village council) Executive Committee of forest committee includes Panchayat member, village head, up to 6 beneficiaries, Beat Officer	Objectives: • maintain register of beneficiaries; • hold annual general meetings and keep minutes; • ensure protection of forests, smooth forestry works and harvests; • prevent trespass, encroachment, grazing, fire, theft, etc. • distribution of sale proceeds; • monitor the enjoyment of use rights; • Forest Department to provide investments, harvesting assistance, monitor implementation of plan, provide legal advice, other technical assistance as required.
Agreement between Government of Congo and villages in and around the Conkouati-Douli National Park[17]	COGEREN– Committee for the management of natural resources, 7 government, 18 village and 2 NGO representatives	Objectives: • frame local management policies and monitor management agreement; • evolve specific agreements for the protection of threatened species and harvest quotas; • develop and enforce rules and sanctions.
Co-management agreement for Lake Racken Watershed, Sweden[18]	Fishing Associations and representatives from government agencies	Agreement: • local management rules: minimum crayfish catch size changed from 9 to 10 cm, harvest time changed from two consecutive days in early August to two widely separated days at the beginning and end of the month, precautionary rules on the use of fishing gear, boats and other equipment, and number of traps per household restricted to 15; • embed local practices (above) in a larger institutional framework set by the government: Swedish Codes of Statutes that a) provide regulations for controlling the mink population and b) place restrictions on stocking and ban certain fishing methods.
Tatshenshini Alsek agreement between Champagne and Aishihik First Nations and Province of British Columbia, Canada[19]	Tatshenshini Alsek Park Management Board: 2 representatives from British Columbia, one of whom is the District Parks Manager and 2 representatives from the Champagne and Aishihik First Nations	Agreement: Aboriginal people will continue to harvest the resources of the lands and waters of the park for food, social and ceremonial purposes using either traditional or contemporary methods to exercise that entitlement. Objectives: • minimise interference to natural processes and provide for the protection of fish and wildlife; • identify commercial, economic training and employment opportunities for aboriginal people in the park; • establish a regional centre for training in the protection, conservation and presentation of cultural

---

[16] Government of West Bengal, 1989.
[17] Taty et al., 2003; Chatelain et al., 2004.
[18] Olsson and Folke, 2001.
[19] Champagne and Aishihik First Nations and British Columbia, 1996.

		and natural heritage as provided for under the World Heritage Convention; • carry out a joint annual evaluation of the agreement to ensure that objectives continue to be met.
Memorandum of Understanding between Mbeere County Council and Kenya Wildlife Service for the Management of Mbeere National Reserve[20]	Joint management plan for reserve and adjacent community advisory committee: 3 Kenya Wildlife Service, 3 Council, District Commissioner, Mbeere ex-officio member	Objectives: • improve flora, fauna and tourism management; • implement community-based wildlife management programme; • ensure equitable distribution of revenues and other opportunities from tourism; • maintain integrity of the reserve and its ecosystem; • provide appropriate visitor facilities; • encourage efficient and effective administration; • including through rational zoning system; • implement community based wildlife conservation and equitable distribution of revenue; • support sustainable exploitation of wildlife resources and generation of revenue for reserve management and local development; • support conservation education and research; • support protection and preservation of special areas; • minimise risks from wildlife to human life, crops, livestock and property. Agreement: This is a 20-year agreement subject to extension, with joint 5-yearly review, amendments to be mutually approved and management plan to be updated 5-yearly; policy measures including research, infrastructure planning, patrols and protection including resource sharing, termination, preference for local employees.
Agreement to Manage the Soufriere Marine Management Area, Saint Lucia.	Soufriere Marine Management Association, a not—for-profit company with an equal number of government agencies and community organisations serving as members and directors of the company. Makes use of the provisions of the Fisheries Act to establish a Local Fisheries Management Area and to declare the Association as the Local Fisheries Management Authority.	Objectives: • to conserve the natural resource base of the Soufriere region; • to enhance the equitable economic, social and cultural benefits generated from the sustainable use of the coastal and marine resources of the Soufriere region, at the local and national levels; • to manage the conflicts that may occur among uses and users of natural resources in Soufriere. Main provisions: • zoning; • regulations of resource use; • social and economic development programmes; • user fees collected and used for management; • joint decision-making by institutional members of the association; • individual agencies retain their management authority • a broad-based Stakeholder Committee acts as advisory body.

[20] KWS and Mbeere County Council, 1996.

Chapter 9. LEARNING BY DOING IN CO-MANAGEMENT INSTITUTIONS

*In a context...
[of continuous and
pervasive change
adaptive manage-
ment is the only
sensible approach.*

Social actors involved in the co-management of natural resources typically act as innovators, trying out in practice novel technical and institutional solutions to problems, which often demand a re-adjustment of their habitual ways of working. This adds to the always present need to deal with the complex, uncertain, and rapidly changing characteristics of environment and society. It is well known that the environment is currently responding to a variety of influences– from climate change to overexploitation and pollution– which alter its natural features, rhythms and cycles. Equally pervasively, socio-cultural and economic change has been sweeping across the planet. Today, even remote rural livelihoods are undergoing dynamic change, and all human communities increasingly express differentiated and evolving needs. In this context, adaptive management[1] is the only sensible approach. Adaptive management emphasises on-going learning through iterative processes and fitting solutions to specific contexts. It is based on systematic experimentation and careful analysis of feedback to policies and management interventions. Possibly more than any other regime, a co-management regime ought to follow its tenets, and the more the co-management actors will invest in joint learning processes, the more their collaboration will be relevant and effective. "Learning by doing" is thus an integral part of each stage of the co-manage-

---

[1]   Holling, 1978; Gunderson et al., 1995; Taylor, 1998; Gunderson and Holling, 2002.

ment process, but it is truly the heart of the matter in the third phase– the one of implementation of the agreements.

Three broad themes run through the considerations, examples and lessons presented in this Chapter:

- Institutional and organisational learning for adaptive co-management benefits from being rooted in indigenous and local knowledge, skills and institutions, and from using local indicators to track and respond to environmental and social changes.[2]

- Co-management organisations ought to challenge themselves: they have to become learning-oriented at their core. Learning-oriented organisations encourage experimentation, questioning and the abandonment of stereotypes; develop skills in recording, applying and disseminating lessons; build relationships based on mutual respect; and foster a non-threatening environment where people learn from one another.

- Facilitating and encouraging individual and collective learning for co-management requires action at various levels, including not only the local but also the national and international institutional contexts. There is where the hard limitations on the spread, scaling up and mainstreaming of the co-management process very often lie.[3]

> Co-management organisations ought to challenge themselves: they have to become learning-oriented at their core.

> ...an agreement is often as strong, or as weak, as the process that generated and sustained it.

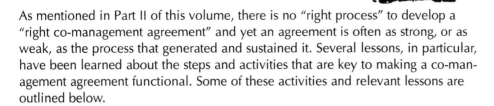

9.1   Making the agreement functional

As mentioned in Part II of this volume, there is no "right process" to develop a "right co-management agreement" and yet an agreement is often as strong, or as weak, as the process that generated and sustained it. Several lessons, in particular, have been learned about the steps and activities that are key to making a co-management agreement functional. Some of these activities and relevant lessons are outlined below.

Providing fair support for the parties to join the agreement

The provision of resources for effective and equitable participation in negotiations and implementing agreements is an important requirement for the agreements to be functional. The support provided to the participation of the Maori people in decisions and implementation of natural resource management is an inspiring example of how governments can "level the playing field" by facilitating more equitable access to expertise, financial resources and spaces where dialogue and negotiation are possible (see Box 9.1). Similar types of assistance to support the fulfilment of co-management agreements have proven essential for the success of other large scale initiatives such as the Landcare and Rivercare programmes in Australia (see Box 9.2).

> ...resources for equitable participation in negotiations and implementing agreements [are] important.

Box 9.1	"Levelling the playing field" for the Maori to participate…. (adapted from Crengle, 1997)

The Resource Management Law Reform (RMLR) undertaken by New Zealand has been remarkable for

---

[2]   See, for instance, the resilience network web site: http://www.resalliance.org/
[3]   This theme is mostly explored in part IV of this volume.

the provision of a range of alternate mechanisms for Maori participation. This process has been effective through being responsive to Maori cultural preferences, particularly with respect to using oral communication and time frames appropriate for decision making by consensus. Mechanisms included:

- an intensive set of hui (meetings) held in the marae (customary community meeting places);

- covering of the personal and travel costs of participants for the hui;

- an open-door policy, sensitive to tribal time frames, enabling submissions to be accepted and incorporated in the review at any time;

- provision of a free phone service for recording of oral submissions;

- comprehensive funding and human resource assistance to tribal organisations for the preparation of written submissions.

Formal structural arrangements for advocating Maori interests have been crucially important for successfully integrating those interests in all aspects of the reform. The government established a core group of four people responsible for coordinating the RMLR process and facilitating two way communication between Maori and the review team.

The RMLR consultation on natural resource management issues has been the largest and most comprehensive process for Maori participation in the formulation of policy and law ever carried out by the New Zealand government. It elicited an exceptional response from the Maori, which further emphasised the interrelationship between the integrity of natural resources and the social, cultural, economic, physical and spiritual well being of Maori communities. It also raised to an unprecedented level the Maori's expectations for the integration of their priorities in resource management agreements, and strengthened their commitment to implement the agreements and to make them work.

Box 9.2   Financial support from the government helps implement co-management
           agreements in Australia
           (adapted from Campbell, 1994b, including case studies by Siepen, 1994)

In Australia, co-management programmes foresee government assistance for community-based management such as the Landcare, Rivercare and Coastcare programmes. The Natural Resources Management (Financial Assistance) Act 1992 (Cwlth), administered by the Australian Department of Primary Industries and Energy, provides for inter-governmental agreements regarding natural resource management, with the primary aim of achieving "efficient, sustainable and equitable management of natural resources, consistent with the principles of ecologically sustainable development". Its other objectives are:

- to promote community, industry and governmental partnership in the management of natural resources;

- to assist in establishing institutional arrangements to develop and implement policies, programmes and practices that will encourage sustainable use of natural resources;

- to assist in enhancing the long term productivity of natural resources;

- to assist in developing approaches to help resolve conflicts over access to natural resources.

The Act deals with agreements with states regarding the provision of financial assistance for natural resource management projects, as well as agreements with other persons, including associations, authorities or other organisations, whether incorporated or not. The Act also establishes a Natural Resources Management Fund and a National Landcare Advisory Committee.

In 1997, the Australian Federal Parliament created a Reserve Fund for the Natural Heritage Trust of Australia. Its main source of financial resources (A$ 1.1 billion) was the partial privatisation of one of Australia's major telephone companies. The Reserve Fund is intended to "conserve, repair and replenish Australia's natural capital infrastructure" by supporting initiatives on the environment, sustainable agriculture and natural resource management. Some of these initiatives are part of the Landcare, Rivercare and Coastcare programmes.

Recognising and building upon local resources, technologies and natural resource management systems

Many successful co-management settings rely on local resources and informal innovation systems. Local technologies are improved to intensify the use of natural resources. In this way sustainable and relatively inexpensive solutions can be found by communities engaged in identifying their needs, designing and testing new technologies and/ or adapting existing technologies to the local conditions. The potential for intensification of internal resource use without reliance on external inputs is enormous. In India (see Box 9.26) the co-managed Public Distribution System allowed women farmers to achieve greater self reliance and reduced dependency on outside supplies of food, pesticides, fertilisers and seeds by enriching and diversifying their farming systems with locally available resources. Similarly, when co-management bodies encourage local communities to engage in the planning, implementation and maintenance phases of projects designed to meet health, housing, sanitation, water needs and revenue generating activities, the results are often more sustainable and effective than those imposed by outside professionals and external agencies.

...a great diversity of local knowledge, skills and institutions can be effectively employed....

Local natural resource management systems are naturally tuned to the needs of local people and often possess a substantial capacity to adapt to dynamic social and ecological circumstances. While many of these systems have been more or less forcibly replaced by others (e.g., market—oriented production under private or state property, conservation managed by state agencies), there remains a great diversity of local knowledge, skills and institutions that can still be effectively employed. Local management systems are closely linked with local livelihoods, and often rooted in cultural practices and religion and spiritual beliefs. Sacred groves, for example, are clusters of forest vegetation preserved for religious purposes. They may honour a deity, provide a sanctuary for the burial ground of venerable peoples, or protect from contamination a place where rituals can be performed; some derive their sacred character from the springs of water they protect, from the medicinal and ritual properties of their plants, or from the wild animals they support.[4] Such sacred groves are common throughout southern and south eastern Asia, Africa, the Pacific islands and Latin America.[5] If sacred groves are extremely rich in biodiversity, they are generally limited in size. By contrast, the pastoral landscapes of mobile indigenous peoples offer examples of traditional management systems of large dimensions and complexity.

Co-management is an effective way to build upon what people already have, know and do to secure their identity, culture, livelihoods and the diversity of natural resources on which they depend.

Co-management is an effective way to build upon what people already have, know and do to secure their identity, culture, livelihoods and the diversity of natural resources on which they depend.[6] Neglecting this may engender human and environmental disasters of large proportions (see Box 9.3).

---

[4]   Chandrakanth and Romm, 1991.
[5]   Shengji, 1991; Ntiamo-Baidu et al., 1992; Gadgil, 1998; Pathak, 2003; Nelson and Gami, 2003; Oviedo, 2003.
[6]   Pimbert and Pretty, 1998; Borrini-Feyerabend et al., 2004 (in press).

Box 9.3 The making of unsustainable livelihoods: eroding the community-conserved
landscape of the Oromo-Borana (Ethiopia)
(adapted from Tache, 2000a; Tache, 2000b; Bassi, 2002)

The whole ethnic territory of the Borana, in Ethiopia, can be considered a community (ethnic) conserved area. The territory has been managed for centuries through rules that assured the sustainable use
of renewable natural resource. Some specific provisions embedded in culture assured bio-diversity conservation per se and the sound management of natural resources was promoted through norms of inclu-
sion/ exclusion designed for all pastoral activities and known as seera marraa bisanii—"the law of grass
and water". The Borana "law of grass" shares the basic principles of most East African pastoral groups.
It differentiates between dry season pastures (with permanent water points) and wet season pastures
(with good grass, but only accessible during rains), imposing the maximisation of use of wet-season pasture whenever possible (during rains), to minimise pressure on the most intensely utilised rangelands
served by permanent water points. The "law of water" is instead peculiar to the Borana and their environment, which is characterised by the presence of numerous well complexes (the tulaa wells being the
most famous among them). This law is extremely articulated, regulating in various ways the social and
economic investment necessary to develop traditional wells and water points, access and maintenance.
Through the normal cycle of well excavation and collapse, over-exploited dry season areas are abandoned and new ones are developed.

The juniper forests found in Borana lands have a special role, which is common to many East African
forests used by pastoralists. Being too humid, they are not suitable for permanent pastoral settlement.
Some open patches, however, contain excellent pasture and the forest also provides permanent springs.
For centuries such forests have never been permanently inhabited but reserved as dry-season pasture.
They had a crucial function as last refuge for grazing in case of drought, reserve for medical and ritual
plants and overall symbolic and ecological meaning. They were not subject to special management
provisions besides the very strict prohibition to start fires inside them, but were an integral and essential
part of the survival system of the Borana.

The environmentally sound management of natural resources in Borana land assured the conservation
of a unique biodiversity patrimony (including 43 species of wild mammals, 283 species of birds and
many unique plants and habitats) until the 1970s, despite the establishment of some small towns close
to the main forests already at the beginning of the 20th Century. From the 1970s onwards, however, the
Borana environment was confronted with major changes in land use. The government limited movement within the ethnic territory and promoted agriculture, facts that deeply affected the Borana natural
resource management system. The situation dramatically collapsed after the change of government in
1991. Political representation of the Borana within the local government became utterly marginal and
policies that could only be described as "actively destructive" of their livelihoods were implemented.
The United Nations High Commissioner for Refugees (UNHCR) facilitated the resettlement of people in
Boranaland who were not actually from the area (the great majority of them being neither Borana nor
Oromo speaking), multiplying the number of permanent settlements in the region. The resettled villages
were assisted through international aid and agriculture was promoted as their livelihood strategy.
Among the newcomers were also some non-Oromo pastoral groups that managed to manipulate international aid and gained political support. They obtained large tracts of Eastern Borana territory, which
were annexed to "their" region, including critical pastoral areas of the Borana. More land resources
were lost by the Borana in the process of "economic liberalisation". Large ranches were acquired by
international investors and extensive portions of land around the towns, located in their critical dry-season pastures, were assigned to town dwellers for small-holding cultivation. The majority of the town
dwellers are neither Borana nor Oromo. A high inflow of migrant Muslim Oromo was also allowed,
and those undertook extensive farming, especially in the Liiban area.

The local government has been acting as if common property land is no-man's land, to be assigned to whoever is claiming it. Indeed customary common property and community conserved areas are not currently recognised in Ethiopia. This process of land alienation has been affecting the most productive lands and the crucial ecosystem patches. The Borana have been squeezed into the driest pockets, bound to become overgrazed. Scarce rain during the last decade produced devastating effects and acute livestock destitution. The only possible survival strategy for the Borana has been to engage in farming in the remaining least suitable places, hoping for a harvest next year. Thus, the amount of land put under cultivation and alienated to the pastoral mode of production dramatically increased, as a sort of chain reaction. The patches of biodiversity in forests got exploited for a variety of commercial purposes, with no regard to sustainability. But, as everyone should have known, the traditional land of the Borana is not suitable for agriculture due to both low and irregular rainfall. Since 1998, the Borana and millions of other pastoralists and agro-pastoralists survive in Ethiopia on the brink of starvation, often entirely dependent on food donations from abroad. Neglect and active tampering with traditional resource management systems created a pattern of unsustainable livelihoods for an entire people and are effectively destroying most of the unique biodiversity harboured in the area.

Many successful co-management institutions are rooted in, and built upon, existing customary and local organisations and rules. Local organisations are crucial for the conservation and sustainable use of natural resources. As Michael Cernea has put it "...resource degradation in the developing countries, while incorrectly attributed to "common property systems", actually originates in the dissolution of local level institutional arrangements whose very purpose was to give rise to resource use patterns that were sustainable."[7]. Local groups have a comparatively easier time enforcing rules and providing social incentives and penalties for the effective conservation and use of natural resources. Successful initiatives run by local and/ or traditional institutions include watershed protection and reforestation, wildlife management schemes, processing plants for natural products derived from the wild, and many forms of community conserved areas.[8]

> Many successful co-management organisations are built on customary and local organisations and rules.

Box 9.4 Restoring the traditional tribal organisation– the first step towards managing a Community Conserved Area
(adapted and updated from Farvar, 2003; see also Field example 1.3 in Chapter 1)

The Kuhi– one of about 20 Sub-tribes of the Shish Bayli Tribe of the Qashqai nomadic pastoralists of Iran– are currently engaged in participatory action research about their own "sustainable livelihoods" and the conservation of biodiversity in their landscape. Their action-research refers to a resource management unit comprising their summering and wintering grounds and their associated migration routes in between. As part of this, the Kuhi held several workshops and their first concern was to involve the whole community. One of the major problems identified was the breakdown of the traditional organisational strength of the tribes. They analysed their governance situation in some depth and decided to re-create their autonomous organisation, building upon traditional patters but ensuring that those would be able to respond to modern challenges, including notions of participatory democracy. Extended negotiations led to the establishment of the "Council for Sustainable Livelihoods of the Kuhi Migratory Pastoralists" and its associated Community Investment Fund, which is now pursuing initiatives in each of the 5 categories of problems/ needs identified by the Sub-tribe. Such initiatives include support to animal raising, marketing and quality-control for highly priced gabbeh rugs produced by women, health care access, capturing of solar energy for various uses, access to legal support, and access to educational books and videos. The initiative that excited them the most, however, is about restoring natural resources to their common property care and control.

---

[7] Cernea, 1993.
[8] Kothari et al., 1998; Haverkort et al., 2003; Borrini-Feyerabend et al., 2004 (in press). See also Boxes 1.3; 3.3; 3.5; 3.6; 3.10; 3.11; 9.4 and 9.20.

tres in length, shared between the Kuhi and the Kolahli Sub-tribes. This has been a community conserved wetland from time immemorial. The Kuhi know all too well that they obtain many "ecosystem
benefits" from this wetland, including water reserves, reeds for handicrafts, fodder for animals, fish,
medicinal plants, micro-climate control, and wildlife. In a controversial plan, the government had earmarked part of the area to be divided up among households for agricultural use and had diverted part
of the water of the wetland for irrigation. The newly constituted Council, on the other hand, believes it
is better to preserve this area as a "qorukh" or "hema"– to be conserved by the community. It thus submitted a petition to the relevant governmental authorities to formally declare the wetland and the surrounding rangelands as a Community Conserved Area (CCA), with use rights being regulated by the
Sub-tribe elders. The petition is being reviewed by the government and it is hoped it will be accepted
under a larger co-management accord by which the respective areas of authority and responsibility of
the government and the community will be agreed to mutual satisfaction. In terms of IUCN categories,
the overall CCA could be considered as a protected area of category V (landscape management objective), with the wetland as a portion under category II (ecosystem management objective). The Council
of Elders has managed to register itself as a legal entity– a unique occurrence in Iran for an indigenous
social organisation. Action recently taken by the Council includes a successful redressing of recent
invasions of its customary rangelands through court action.

This initiative is showing important ways in which nomadic livelihoods can fully reconcile with conser-
vation. The initiative is supported by the Centre for Sustainable Development (CENESTA, a national
NGO in Iran), the Organisation for Nomadic Peoples Affairs (ONPA, a government institution), the
International Institute for Environment and Development (IIED), IUCN/ CEESP's Working Group on
Sustainable Livelihoods, FAO (interested, among other things, in coping strategies of nomadic pastoralists in the face of drought), and WAMIP (World Alliance of Mobile Indigenous Peoples). The GEF
(Global Environment Facility) implemented by UNDP has expressed interest in learning from the experi-
ence of the project for policy advocacy, and the Christensen Fund said it will support its extension and
replication in other tribes and countries as a strategy for both conservation and cultural survival.

Conservationists
should seriously
consider ways to
legitimise and
strengthen
customary and
traditional
organisations for
natural resource
management.

Customary and traditional organisations have many points of strength. For example, they know more than anyone else how to identify the members of user
groups or community; how to assist in conflict management and administer sanctions for rule infringement at the local level; and how to develop rules for
resource management based on local knowledge of ecological dynamics.[9] In an
age of increasing globalisation, however, their political standing is often in peril.
Conservationists should seriously consider ways to legitimise and strengthen such
organisations, as managing natural resources requires the capacity to develop and
enforce appropriate rules in the local context. As discussed in Chapter 1 of this
volume, successful co-management organisations often combine formal arrangements, which may be initiated and supported by the state or other external agents,
side by side with other arrangements of older, customary origin.

Letting the agreement specify the co-management organisation, and not
vice versa

If the agreement foresees the establishment of an advisory or management body,
such as a local conservation council or an extended natural resource management board, specifications of who is to be represented, what is the mandate, what
are the tasks, etc. should be reached in the planning phases. It is important, however, that a body entrusted with specific tasks is set up towards the end and not at
the very beginning of the process of developing the agreement. In fact, it is

---

9   Cousins, 1995.

through dialogue and negotiation that the most useful information and appropriate guiding principles are often discovered. For instance, it was through a few years of discussion of issues and policy development among the key relevant parties that the sophisticated and effective structure now in charge of the Galapagos Marine Reserve was designed and developed in practice (see Box 6.13). Similarly, in the Republic of Congo, the Conkouati management board could be envisaged only after a lengthy process of discussion and negotiation had started bearing fruits (see Box 9.5).

Box 9.5   From social communication to negotiation, to establishing a management body– the co-management path in Conkouati (Republic of Congo)
(adapted from Taty et al., 2003; Chatelain et al., 2004)

In the mid-nineties, the IUCN assisted in the development of a co-management setting for Conkouati National Park, in the Republic of Congo– a "difficult" and conflict-ridden site where other agencies had refused to work. Indeed, an enormous amount of energy had to be invested in social communication processes before the project could even properly start. Through time, however, the communication efforts generated some timidly positive perceptions of the social actors with respect to one another. This eventually developed into a concrete dialogue, and the park managers and local residents started envisaging that they could become "partners", they could work together for mutually beneficial initiatives.

The facilitation process focused on the local natural patrimony of Conkouati, and promoted negotiations on the basis of the common interests to maintain it for everyone's benefit. The parties figured out that they were obliged to find solutions together– not as police and robbers but as social actors sharing an interest to maintain the abundance of natural resources in the area. At the beginning, their proposals were widely different, but the project staff brought everyone to discuss the pros and cons of each perspective and managed to obtain an agreement around a charter of principles, progressively refined and accepted by all. It was only after this that a co-management organisation, the Comité de Gestion des Ressources Naturelles de Conkouati (COGEREN) was formally established, and took on the task of refining the charter further, establishing a zoning system and developing a number of specific accords for the three local most endangered species (manatees, marine turtles and bamboos). COGEREN includes representatives of the local communities, the state administration, the NGOs locally active in environment and development issues and some locally elected officials. The legitimisation of the organisation actually took place with the signing of an official Co-management Charter by the national and local government authorities, which was accompanied by rituals through which the local traditional authorities also engaged themselves publicly.

It is important to ascertain that any collaborative management body is created at the appropriate level, i.e., that it gathers representatives of stakeholders who can put into practice the agreement that has been developed. For instance, a management board at the level of the district may not be appropriate if the resources to be managed affect only one or two specific communities and businesses. It may be more useful to create instead an ad-hoc committee with direct representation of the social groups most directly affected. In other occasions, umbrella bodies may be needed to facilitate coordination between local resource users and relevant government departments. In Uganda, one such organisation links the 22 "Forest Societies" established in each of the 22 parishes bordering Bwindi National Park.[10] Each one of the societies,[11] however, is autonomously organised and decides its own work objectives.

...a management board at the level of the district may not be appropriate if the resources to be managed affect only one or two specific communities and businesses.

---

[10]   Wild and Mutebi, 1996.

[11]   The name "Forest Society" derives from the first one that was set up, called Ekibiina Kya'beihamba-Omuruka gwa Mpungu or Forest Society of the Mpungu Parish.

Fostering relatively small, diverse, committed and accountable co-management bodies

Several characteristics of effective co-management organisations have been identified on the basis of field experience. Some were drawn in the context of particular sectors but they are reasonably valid for other areas of natural resource co-management, in different ecological and economic settings. These characteristics include:

Manageable size
There is a greater chance of success (and an easier ride) with a single-tenure area of moderate size and a relatively limited number of management issues and parties to the agreement. If the area is large, the issues are complex and interlocking and many actors are involved, progress may be exceedingly slow, and frustrations and setbacks may set in. The more complex the situation, the greater the need for support from government or well-organised federations of actors. A non-supportive government bureaucracy is a very substantial handicap.[12]

Diverse and committed membership of the management body
The diversity of members in the management body is a precious asset for learning by doing. Through dialogue and deliberation, resource users, government staff, planners, local authorities, business people and scientists can identify problems and questions, explore alternatives and adjust decisions and actions, as necessary. Ideally the membership of the co-management body would include representatives from a variety of disciplines and backgrounds, connected with a range of community sectors and well conscious of the duties and functions of governing bodies, and their responsibilities as members. They should also be prepared, ultimately, to set aside their personal and sectoral interests and make decisions in the best interests of all parties and the environment. The most effective members of co-management bodies are usually "fearless", but also strategic. If necessary, they stand up to individuals and institutions accustomed to exercising power (senior public servants and politicians, for example), but are also capable of exercising good judgement about which battles are winnable and what to do about those that are not.

The most effective members of co-management bodies are usually "fearless", but also strategic.

The members of the co-management body need to elect a good chairperson, capable of welding the group into a united team with a clear vision. And the CM body should be adequately resourced. People work better, and are more respected by their community, if they are seen to be valued and compensated. High fees or salaries, however, tend to attract criticism, especially in rural communities. To prevent this, the members of the CM bodies should be chosen in a most transparent way. Membership should balance the need to represent all key sectors and geographical areas (and sometimes ethnic groups) adequately against the need to keep numbers small enough for efficient functioning.

---

12 Ghai and Vivian, 1992; Finger-Stitch and Finger, 2003; Tall and Guèye, 2003; Fakih et al., 2003; Pimbert, 2004.

Clear responsibility and reporting lines
The lines of reporting in co-management bodies should be clear, and staff should not have multiple masters. A fearless decision-making body prepared to do battle with government can place a government-employed chief executive in an impossible position by ordering her or him to carry out provocative or confrontational initiatives. At worst, this can paralyse the organisation and alienate the community. The government-preferred model, of having the chief executive as the chair of the board (and/ or the board dominated by government officers) may avoid the problem of conflicting reporting lines, but is rarely accepted by the community as a model of true participatory management. The co-management governing body and the chief executive should understand the dividing line between governance and management, and respect it. Ideally, however, the governing body should strongly back its chief executive and should thus be involved in choosing him or her.

Accountable procedures
Good co-management organisations should be accountable to all its members. In most circumstances, however, they are requested to be accountable only to the government of the relevant countries. Often, in fact, a co-management body is legally answerable to a ministerial department, which may also fund it, partially or totally. This may represent a moral tightrope for such organisations, and those involved must be prepared to walk it and remain accountable to both the government and the other partners in the agreement, including the local communities. In particular, the organisation's budget, policies, decisions and decision-making process should be open to public scrutiny, i.e., they should be accessible and transparent.

A CM organisation is generally set up with the ultimate objectives of managing natural resources. Accountability should be mostly related to this goal, although some members– and communities in particular– may be trying to hold it accountable for aspirations beyond its charter. For instance, an organisation set up to protect the natural heritage values of an area is not primarily responsible for the economic welfare of the surrounding communities. While both ends can often be jointly served, the CM body may sometimes be obliged to make decisions that are not primarily for economic advancement, or even contrary to it. If such a decision causes community distress, it is up to all the concerned parties to weigh all factors and make a final decision in the best interests of the community as a whole, not to the CM body to compromise its agreed responsibilities. Alternatively, another co-management structure with a more comprehensive mandate may be set up to focus on both conservation and livelihoods in the same context.

The organisation's budget, policies, decisions and decision-making process should be open to public scrutiny, and should be accessible and transparent.

Open dialogue with a broad range of interest groups should be provided whenever possible. The CM body needs to inform the wider community about what it is doing by whatever means best suit local circumstances– newsletters, broadcasts, visits, public meetings, workshops, etc. The CM body also needs to listen hard, and have both formal and informal means of feeding public opinion back into its operations. Community meetings and attitude surveys carried out at regular intervals can be invaluable to focus community relations and mutual learning efforts, as well as to generally target weak areas of operation. Indigenous peoples, nomadic peoples and local communities– including their weaker, discriminated groups– should be actively informed and encouraged to have a say.

...it is important that the process is not entrapped in some rigid and bureaucratic enforcement system ...[as] co-management feeds on passion and creativity... and on the ability to manage human relations in informal and convivial manners.

The co-management plan for the natural resources and the accords that complement it as part of the same agreement need to be implemented as soon as possible after the public celebration of the conclusion of negotiations. The organisations and rules agreed upon by all relevant actors also need to be set up and enforced in a timely manner. This allows the partners to capitalise on the momentum of the negotiation phase. A committee and/ or specific individual should be in charge and be made accountable for each component of the strategy, co-management plan or main activity, reporting to the relevant actors (and/ or to the organisations set in place by them) on the on-going progress. Compliance with the agreements and rules is essential to the effectiveness of the whole CM process. If some actors disobey the rules or do not accomplish what they agreed to do, others are soon likely to follow suit. To prevent this, the co-management agreements need to specify who is responsible for enforcement, as well as by what means and what regular checks they are to be carried out. Indeed the entitlements and responsibilities of relevant actors need to be clear for all the parties involved.

In this sense, accountability is crucial– the people who took on responsibilities need to publicly respond about them. And yet, it is also important that the process is not entrapped in some rigid and bureaucratic enforcement system. Co-management feeds on the passion and creativity of the groups and individuals involved, and on their ability to manage human relations in informal and convivial manners.[13] Flexibility and good human relations may go a long way in solving even complex and thorny controversies. Celebrating small successes along the way can be an effective way of keeping actors together and maintaining a constructive group dynamic (see Box 9.6).

Box 9.6   Build on small successes
(adapted from EPA, 1997)

Small successes fuel future, larger ones. It is important, according to watershed practitioners, to start small and demonstrate success before working on a larger scale. For this reason, demonstration projects are often a popular choice in watershed work. In some states, small victories have been instrumental in prompting the implementation of a state-wide watershed approach. One of the first agreed actions in the Upper Arkansas Watershed Council (Colorado, USA) was a Citizen's Water Law Seminar. In the West, the Prior Appropriation law– based on the idea that water can be privately owned– has evolved into a complex and often mystifying tangle of rules. Additionally, water quality, in-stream flows, and recreation issues had complicated the understanding of water law.

Many of the local community leaders (county commissioners, planning and zoning boards, etc.), several of whom are new to Colorado, admitted to little understanding of the law, yet recognized its importance in their work. The council agreed that it did not matter which side of a water issue anyone represents– agriculture, development, environmental, recreation– the law is the law, and the more citizens who understand the water law, the better. In brief, the seminar was held and was a wonderful success. It was planned in three months, was low-budget, gave the council strong local credibility, and provided an early success upon which to tackle tougher issues. Commitment to the watershed is key, and a small group's passion for its improvement can catch fire. Practitioners also say over and over that it's important to "celebrate success" as it occurs.

---

[13] Nguinguiri, 2003.

Publicising the agreement until it is widely known

Once an agreement (e.g., a consensus over a management plan and an agreed sharing of rights and responsibilities) is reached, it should not be written in stone, but it should certainly be written on paper and publicised as widely as possible within the relevant communities and among the relevant stakeholders. The agreement should be explained in plain terms (clear and comprehensible to all) and in the local language(s), or also in the local language(s) when government officials tend to speak only a national language. If appropriate and feasible, oral and informal forms of communication, including popular theatre, use of audio-visual materials, presentations at traditional gatherings and other media, can be used as very effective complements.

The importance of the agreement should be underlined by means of a specific event or ceremony. As far as possible, the signatories should be people directly taking on management responsibilities (e.g., the local village chief and the local park warden) and not relatively unconcerned and distant authorities. The parties should commit themselves in public and the agreement should be given ample visibility (e.g., a copy of the agreement could be posted in local communities as well as in the premises of the agency in charge of managing the natural resources). Special steps such as the ones taken in Bwindi National Park may be needed to widely publicise and scale up the participatory management agreement (see Box 9.7).

Once an agreement is reached, it should not be written in stone, but it should certainly be written on paper and publicized as widely as possible within the relevant communities and among the relevant stakeholders.

Box 9.7   Signing and publicising a collaborative management agreement in Bwindi Impenetrable National Park (Uganda)
(adapted from Wild and Mutebi, 1996)

In 1992, the staff of Bwindi Impenetrable National Park and the representatives of the residents of the civil parishes adjoining the park began a process of planning and evaluating resource use. The main output of the parish workshops, follow up work and participatory research were memoranda of understanding between the communities and the park authorities, which documented decisions taken in the meetings as "multiple use plans". These were not legally binding documents, but set out the intent and responsibility of each party.

The agreements, in Rukiga and English, were reviewed by each one of the Forest Societies established in the parishes. A ceremony was held in the occasion of the signing of the agreements by the parties. The Director of Uganda National Parks and several park rangers were present, along with members of the Forest Societies such as community leaders, nominated resource users, women representatives, local chiefs and religious leaders.

Harvesting forest resources under these agreements began at Bwindi Impenetrable in late 1994 and involved at first only three of the twenty-two parishes bordering the park. To spread interest and compliance about the agreements, a new cadre of Community Conservation Rangers was established by the park to improve communication and discuss the agreements with each community leadership institution, resource users (e.g., herbalists, basket makers, beekeepers) and interested community members. Publicising the agreement in this way proved not only key to making it functional but was also essential for extending similar agreements to other parishes. Negotiating the memoranda of understanding initially took 15-20 days per parish, spread over a period of 6 to 10 months. The negotiation process for the remaining 17 parishes, however, was considerably faster.

It should be clear that adjustments to the co-management agreements may take place during their implementation, and review times should be scheduled in advance. Some forms of agreement, such as a memorandum of understanding, are quite flexible and allow for regular revisions. Other forms, such as contracts among legally-recognised parties, are less so. The latter are usually required when the agreement foresees some important packages of economic or financial incentives for one or more parties in the agreement. The agreement can also be formalised as a local by-law. It is useful that the agreement includes provisions for dealing with exceptional situations (e.g., how to modify rights and responsibilities in case of acute ecological stress or social crisis).

Dealing fairly with conflicting interpretations of the agreement

During the implementation of activities, conflicting interpretations of the co-management agreement may arise. For formal, contract-type agreements, contract law and environmental public law should include procedures for dealing with conflicts. In cases of conflicts between indigenous peoples and the state or other sectors of society, International Human Rights Law and some UN bodies can provide some guidance.[14] For the less formal agreements it is important to foresee in advance who will assist the parties to clarify entitlements and responsibilities and to mediate in the event of conflicts. The Canadian Royal Commission on Aboriginal Peoples, for example, reports about a conflict over fish management which led to First Nation representatives on a participatory management board being outvoted and resigning.[15] In May 1994, a majority of the members of the Sturgeon Lake Co-management Committee in north-western Ontario voted to create a total sanctuary on all the valley spawning grounds. At the same time the committee, which included tourist outfitters and local hunters and anglers among its members, accused the aboriginal people of damaging fish stocks and habitat and voted to review the legal status of all aboriginal fishing in sanctuaries. It was at this point that the representatives of the local Saugeen First Nation resigned– in protest– from the committee.

Conflicts of interpretation during the implementation phase may be the inevitable result of a co-management process and may depend on the extent to which the relevant government agencies are committed to participatory management, as well as on the political strengths of the relevant social actors. In this sense, the Canadian Royal Commission on Aboriginal Peoples has suggested that if government agencies are to be represented on co-management boards, they should sit as technical advisors and be non-voting, especially where co-management is based on notions of power-sharing.[16] In Australia, the Law Reform Commission recommended in 1986 to uphold the following as priorities for access to natural resources: 1) conservation measures and other identifiable overriding interests such as safety, rights of innocent passage, shelter and safety at sea; 2) traditional hunting and fishing; and 3) commercial and recreational hunting and fishing. The commission recommended that, as a matter of principle, traditional hunting and fishing by the Aboriginal People should take priority over non-traditional activities, including commercial and recreational activities, where the traditional activities are carried on for subsistence purposes. On the basis of this principle the precise allocation of resources is now a matter for the appropriate licensing and management authorities acting in consultation with the Aboriginal People and other user groups.[17]

[14] See Box 9.8 in this Chapter. See also Box 10.14 in Chapter 10.
[15] Canada Royal Commission on Aboriginal Peoples, 1996.
[16] Canada Royal Commission on Aboriginal Peoples, 1996.
[17] Law Reform Commission, 1986.

Box 9.8 The International Covenant on Civil and Political Rights and the UN Commission on Human Rights
(adapted from Posey, 1996)

International environmental and human rights law accord special recognition to the relationship between indigenous peoples and their customary territories. The UN Commission on Human Rights' Committee on the Elimination of Racial Discrimination, for example, adopted a general recommendation concerning indigenous peoples in August 1997. The committee called on the states Parties to the International Covenant to:

- recognise and respect indigenous peoples' distinct cultures, languages and way of life as an enrichment of the state's cultural identity and to promote its preservation;

- ensure the absence of all forms of discrimination;

- provide indigenous peoples with conditions allowing for a sustainable economic and social development compatible with their cultural characteristics;

- ensure that indigenous people have equal rights to participate in public life and that no decisions directly relating to their rights and interests are taken without their informed consent;

- ensure that indigenous communities can exercise their rights to practice and revitalise their cultural traditions and customs and to preserve and practice their languages;

- recognise and protect customary territories and resources, and either return them or compensate for their loss, if indigenous peoples have been dispossessed of those territories.

The UN-adopted International Covenant of Civil and Political Rights has also been called on to elaborate the international human rights standards concerning indigenous peoples and the environment. Article 27 of the Covenant has often provided a basis for communications to the Human Rights Committee about states' violations of rights. Article 27 provides that members of ethnic, religious or linguistic minorities shall not be denied the right to enjoy their own culture, to profess and practise their own religion, or to use their own language in community with other members of their group.

The committee has agreed that the exercise of the cultural rights protected under Article 27 may manifest itself in many ways, including a particular way of life associated with the use of lands and resources, especially for indigenous peoples. The enjoyment of those rights require positive legal measures of protection and measures to ensure the effective participation of members of minority communities in decisions that affect them. In the Kitok versus Sweden case, the Human Rights Committee found that although the regulation of an economic activity is usually an internal state matter, where that activity is an essential element in the culture of an ethnic community, it may be protected by Article 27. But individual rights to culture also need to be assessed in the context of the community's rights, and reasonable and objective restrictions on individual rights so as to preserve community rights may be found to be legitimate.

The committee has expressed the view that the right to enjoy culture needs to be assessed in context, and need not be confined to traditional practices. The use of modern technology, for example, does not deny a given practice the status of continuing traditional culture. It has also suggested that economic activities that have only a limited impact on cultural rights, and which were engaged-in after consultations, may also not violate Article 27.

Ensuring compliance and effective enforcement of the agreement

Monitoring of compliance should be done on a regular basis and, in case of violations of the agreement, enforcing mechanisms need to be applied. This is a crucial aspect for a co-management agreement to remain effective: if some parties can go by without complying to the rules, others are likely to follow suit. "Who enforces" is also very important. It is usually government that has the power and legitimacy to ensure compliance through coercive enforcement. And yet, effective enforcement mechanisms can also be organised and implemented by local communities and organised groups (see some examples in Boxes 9.9, 9.10 and 9.11), at least when the delinquent forces are not overpowering.[18] Enforcing rules, however, is always a delicate task. The natural resource management scheme may involve high stakes for parties that are in the best position to apprehend violations but have no legal basis to do so. If local residents take the enforcement completely "into their hands", for instance if they attempt to arrest people who came to cut timber or shoot wildlife, they risk becoming involved in violent clashes and facing legal prosecution afterwards.

Box 9.9   Enforcing co-management agreements in coastal areas: an example from the Philippines
(adapted from Zerner, 1991)

A community marine resource management programme was initiated in 1984 in fishing communities of the Visayas islands of the Philippines. The co-management programme was designed to promote conservation and sustainable use of coral reefs and associated fisheries through community based efforts to stop over-fishing and destructive fishing techniques using dynamite and cyanide.

Local fishers helped design and implement the reserve and sanctuary systems at all levels. Working with community organisers, they earmarked the portions of the reef to be governed as a reserve, or more strictly protected sanctuaries, and they physically laid the marker buoys themselves. Local communities also formulated regulations prohibiting fishing, the anchoring of motorised boats, and the collection of giant clams within sanctuaries. Within the larger and less restrictive reserve areas, they prohibited dynamite fishing and the use of small mesh gear. These guidelines were subsequently recognised by the government.

Enforcement of the sanctuary rules is also carried out by the communities. Young local men formed groups known as Guardians of the Sea to confront and chase away violators (local and outsiders), sometimes with the help of the Philippine police forces. The Guardians of the Sea also initiate public hearings for local perpetrators who are tried and punished according to an indigenous system of public justice.

Box 9.10   Local enforcement of forest management rules in India
(adapted from Bahuguna, 1992)

In the Indian state of Madhya Pradesh forest protection committees have developed different types of local rules as indicated by the following remarks of villagers: "It was resolved by the committees that all those areas where the trees are marked with red paints along the boundary are closed for grazing and hence all of us unanimously resolve not to take our cattle for grazing in these areas, nor allow the villagers of other villages to do so. We shall keep our cattle at home and all cases of violation would be reported to the forest officer."

For the protection of trees "it was unanimously resolved that we shall not girdle any tree nor allow others to do so. We shall have some strict watch over illegal cutting of trees." For goats "it is resolved that

---

[18] Unfortunately in several cases the delinquent people– poachers and illegal fisherfolk who vie for the international market– can afford vehicles, fuel and weapons out of reach for the local communities and resource users. If the resources are available, however, the local enforcing crews can greatly profit from technology such as binoculars with electronic cameras, radio transmitters, and the like (Will Maheia, personal communication, 2004).

all those villagers who are having goats with them must sell them within a period of 3 days, otherwise action will be taken." As for firewood, "no villager would carry the fuel wood head load for sale outside the village. The defaulters will be charged 51 Rupees per head load."

In some cases, social fines have been imposed not only on villagers but also on forest guards, and in others, communities have taken action on social issues, punishing for anti-social drinking and abuse. In Madhya Pradesh, the benefits have included improvements in fuelwood, grass and crop yields; reduced poaching of elephants and other animals; changed relations between forest officials and local people; and the creation of democratic local organisations.

Box 9.11 Enforcing regulation and awareness raising: two faces of the same coin (Adapted from Baird, 1999)

In the Khong region of Laos, it is generally up to the village headmen to assure that fishing regulations are respected by all (see also Boxes 3.11, 5.11 and 6.11). Most communities rely on a mixed strategy that includes enforcement of regulations and awareness raising, which are both important, especially at initial stages of implementation. The pattern has been that villages hand out a few warnings and fines in the first year in which they implement the new regulation, and in so doing they let everybody know that the village is serious about it. By the second year, they find that much less regulation enforcement is required. By then, locals are familiar with the regulations, and have come to clearly understand why they have been adopted.

When necessary, villagers are effective enforcers of regulations. They are also pragmatic people. Seeing is believing, and they tend to feel more positive about co-management regulations if they begin to see positive results. Fortunately, increases in fish stocks and catches often occur after even just a year of implementation of regulations. There appears to be an association between villages that have done an outstanding job with implementing their plans, and relatively remote villages with a high level of community spirit and solidarity. In other words, solidarity at the village level indirectly benefits community-based natural resource management. When solidarity increases as a result of co-management, there are also other spin-off benefits in terms of community development. Another important factor linked to the success of the co-management system in Khong relates to the good working relationships with district authorities.

9.2 "Learning by doing" through monitoring and evaluation

It is rare that the management plans and complementary accords are perfect in the form in which they were first agreed and do not require adjustments along the way. In view of this, the partnership should start with a basic agreement, but also foresee some reviews at specific times during implementation, to develop and adjust the details. As a matter of fact, the adaptive management approach implies that much of the learning takes place during the implementation phase. Even when the initial plans are very well thought out, there is a need to review them as they are implemented in practice. Too often, organisations wait until there is a crisis to undertake reviews, but monitoring, evaluation and adaptation are more effective when they are part of the normal life of organisations and institutions. In this way, "crises" are replaced by on-going learning and adjustments.

...."monitoring" is the regular recording and analysis of selected information on a given phenomenon or activity.

Monitoring and reviews should be inclusive of multiple perspectives and as participatory as possible. The relevant parties may learn by gathering the data specified in the follow-up protocol (see Chapter 6) but also other information, not even mentioned there. Such data and information should be documented and analysed, to understand in detail the factors that have an impact on the natural resources and resident communities. And this should be done in the sense of both positive and negative impacts and influences or benefits accruing to them. These factors should be brought to the attention of the responsible CM organisations in the monitoring, evaluation and review meetings.

Throughout implementation, meetings should be held to evaluate the results and impacts of the co-management agreements. If the activities and the financial and human commitments are substantial, the evaluation should be both internal (carried out by the key relevant actors) and external (carried out by independent experts), and the results of those evaluations should be compared and analysed together. Various participatory methods can be used to support both the internal and external evaluations, including methods already familiar to the actors who participated in the other phases of the CM process.

...."evaluation" is the measuring of progress with respect to some original objectives, assessing whether they have been attained and/ or whether they are still pertinent.

In the evaluation exercises, the evaluators assess whether the co-management agreements succeeded in progressing towards the short-term environmental and social objectives the parties agreed upon as well as the longer-term vision and goals subscribed by all of them. For this, they use result and impact indicators. Examples of result indicator are the existence of a zoning plan subscribed by all parties (if one of the objectives was to set up such a plan) and the number of infractions to the plan identified in one year of operations. Environmental impact indicators may be the viable presence of a species within a defined territory, or the trend of the water level in a village's well. Social impact indicators may include the nutritional status of children in the local communities, the engagement of women and minorities in decision-making about NRM, the improvement in average household income or the change (increase or decrease) in local conflicts over natural resources. The evaluators examine these indicators and also whether the hypotheses and assumptions on which the agreement was designed remain correct or whether the context conditions have changed.

The evaluators may also assess whether the process that developed the agreement has been appropriate and is still on the right track. For this, they need to use process indicators. An example of a process indicator is the fairness of negotiation, which may be measured by some objective information (were all the parties informed on time? Treated with dignity? Asked to present their views? Listened to carefully?), but also by the perception of participants. Interestingly, some process indicators are also indicators of social impact. For instance, the process may succeed in informing and engaging in

NRM some parties that were not involved before. This is a process result that, in itself, also constitutes a positive social impact.

On the basis of discussions of process, results and impacts, the parties decide whether the co-management agreements have to be modified and, if so, what modifications are needed and who should carry them out. If necessary, the process reverts to a phase of negotiation– although generally at a faster pace than the first time (see Figure 4.2 in Chapter 4). It is also useful to have an emergency plan for situations in which fast intervention is needed.

A co-management setting can thus be monitored and evaluated with respect to its own process (how did it develop? How is it run?), the expected results of that process (e.g., emergence of new organised parties, CM agreements, a co-management body) and the impacts of such results. This is far from a simple matter, requiring the use of both quantitative and qualitative tools, participatory methods and often also the presence of external evaluators. It is neither simple nor immediate to maintain a clear distinction between the co-management process and its results, and the consequences (impacts) of such results. The complexity and demanding nature of the task may be responsible for the frequently inadequate understanding of co-management as a whole. In the rare cases in which co-management settings are evaluated, in fact, this is done by external professionals who tend to concentrate on short term results and involve the local organisations only as informants (see Box 9.12). A more balanced picture could be obtained by investigating process, results and impacts, as well as the links among them, with the active involvement of all parties that played an active role in the process itself. If an "independent" perspective is also required, the results thus generated could be compared and combined with those of an external evaluation.[19]

> A more balanced picture could be obtained by investigating process, results and impacts, as well as the links among them, with the active involvement of all parties that played an active role in the process itself.

Box 9.12   Learning from poor practice in participatory monitoring and evaluation

Too little attention has been given to regular monitoring of participatory management initiatives, including in efforts that appear to be the most promising or successful. Only in the 1990s did some donors begin to insist on such processes. For instance, the Biodiversity Conservation Network, involved in various biodiversity-based enterprises in South and South-east Asia, began at that time to integrate detailed monitoring procedures.[20] In Nepal, it conducted some baseline research in the buffer zones of Chitwan and Bardia National Parks, where the Parks and People Project was being launched. Subsequent monitoring showed that there had been an increase in some wildlife populations, including the rhinoceros and the tiger. Under this project, the protected area warden was supposed to carry out monitoring with the help of staff, and submit monthly reports to the Department of National Parks and Wildlife Conservation. An independent assessment of the project, however, later stated that monitoring and evaluation had been rather weak.[21]

Even where monitoring has been happening, it has rarely been participatory, with outsiders usually conducting it. For instance, the World Bank's main monitoring mechanism of the projects it funds are "missions" that primarily involve expert consultants and its own staff. Rarely are the affected or beneficiary populations involved except as respondents.

Classical donor practice has been to fly in foreign experts, or hire expensive national consultants.[22] In

---

[19] An example of a participatory evaluation of a co-management setting that produced an external report but also prompted the beginning of an on-going local evaluation process is described in Box 9.18 later in this Chapter.

[20] Bhatt, 1998.

[21] Bhatt, 1998.

[22] Chambers, 1993; Chambers, 1996.

some cases, however, this is beginning to change. In Pakistan, under a project entitled "Maintaining Biodiversity with Rural Community Development", promoted by the Aga Khan Rural Support Programme and IUCN, villagers have been trained to carry out wildlife surveys and monitoring exercises, and are now conducting yearly evaluations of the conservation and development plans they have elaborated.[23]

Regular monitoring and evaluation of both the process and results of the co-management initiatives is needed to assess and fill gaps in design and implementation, and to gauge whether progress is being made and is likely to remain sustainable. For both, essential ingredients are baseline data and adequate resources to sustain the collection and analysis of information through time (see Box 9.13).

Box 9.13   McKenzie Watershed Council– action at the sub-watershed level in Oregon (USA) (from EPA, 1997)

Over 200,000 residents of Lane County, Oregon, depend on the McKenzie River watershed for their drinking water. They also use the river for fishing, rafting, and other recreational activities. Agricultural and other industrial users rely on the river to supply them with large amounts of high quality water for their operations. Economic development in the McKenzie watershed and other types of pressures have in recent years threatened the capacity of the river to sustain the quality of its water.

A partnership of two local governments led to the creation of the McKenzie Watershed Council. Lane County and the Eugene Water & Electric Board acted as conveners to organise, seek start-up funds, and provide early support and direction. The council's mission statement reads: "To foster better stewardship of the McKenzie river watershed resources, deal with issues in advance of resource degradation and ensure sustainable health, functions, and uses." The 20-member council was formed in 1993 and is made up of private citizens, public interest groups, locally elected officials, representatives of state government, as well as representatives of the Bureau of Land Management, Army Corps of Engineers, and the U.S. Forest Service. The Environmental Protection Agency (EPA) provided start-up funds and the BPA (Bonneville Power Administration) and other bodies contributed funds for completing the action plans and public outreach.

The council adopted a work programme that focused on four topics: water quality, fish and wildlife habitat, recreation, and human habitat. It adopted action plans for all four topics and implemented several of the prescribed actions, beginning with three key programmes: watershed-wide water quality monitoring, citizen water quality monitoring, and restoration and enhancement projects.

Watershed-wide Water Quality Monitoring Programme. Under the leadership of a local utility (the Eugene Water & Electric Board), the council worked with a team of technical advisors to put into place a coordinated approach to long-term water quality monitoring. The Oregon Department of Environmental Quality conducts the monitoring at seven stations in the watershed, as well as providing part of the funding. Other funding comes from council's partners Eugene Water & Electric Board, Army Corps of Engineers, Bureau of Land Management, and U.S. Forest Service. Since its inception in November 1995, the monitoring programme has expanded co-operation among the council, the Oregon Department of Environmental Quality and technical advisors from both public and private sectors.

Citizen Monitoring Programme. A partnership with RARE (Resource Assistance to Rural Environments, part of the President's Americorps Programme) has been critical to the success of the McKenzie Watershed Council's Citizen Monitoring Programme. This volunteer programme engages students

---

[23]   See http://srdis.ciesin.org/cases/Pakistan-Paper.html and http://www.iucn.org/places/pakistan/macp.htm

throughout the watershed in the evaluation and monitoring of water quality parameters, and has been a very effective outreach tool. Starting with a grant from the state in 1995, the programme now involves over 200 students from six schools, who monitor five sites on a weekly basis. RARE workers have been involved from the beginning– from designing the pilot programme to training students and working with them on a weekly basis to do the sampling over the last two years.

Monitoring should be carried out at an appropriate frequency and the measured data and collected information should be made accessible to the relevant actors and the general public. The indicators should be identified on a case-by-case basis, although some examples of indicators for the different phases of a co-management process[24] may provide useful ideas. Some such examples are noted below.

Assessing the preparatory phase

The preparatory phase is the foundation of the co-management process and the interested actors (in particular the initiators, supporters and members of the Start-up Team) should assess whether its key expected results– which may already include some positive social impact– have been achieved. Checklist 9.1 includes indicators that may be useful to assess the preparatory phase.

Checklist 9.1 Examples of process and result indicators to assess the CM preparatory phase

- a shared understanding of the NRM unit(s) to be managed, identified on the basis of ecological and social considerations;

- available lists of relevant parties to include in negotiation, and preliminary analysis of their respective entitlements, claims and power differentials and of the NRM conflicts, both existing and potential, among them;

- information and tools (e.g., maps) on the main ecological and social issues at stake in the identified NRM unit(s) gathered and made available to all parties;

- understanding of the key political and social factors and institutions that determine resource access and use;

- a "name" and a description of the co-management process that are culturally valid and broadly understood and accepted in the context at stake;

- social communication initiatives that opened and maintain two-way communication channels between the Start-up Team and the relevant actors, and foster a broad discussion of NRM issues in society;

- the parties reasonably well-informed, organised (e.g., they have identified their own representatives and key interests at stake in the management of natural resources) and willing to negotiate a co-management agreement;

- enhanced local confidence of the parties in being able to manage natural resources;

- social emergence of previously unorganised or marginalised groups.

Assessing the negotiation phase

The negotiation phase is the heart of the process and its effectiveness and fairness set out a standard to be expected and observed by all parties. Examples of

---

[24] See Chapter 4 and Figure 4.2 in particular.

indicators to assess the negotiation phase, which may again already include some social impact indicators, are listed in Checklist 9.2.

Checklist 9.2 Examples of process and result indicators to assess the CM negotiation phase

- knowledge and understanding of the relevant actors about the CM process itself;

- existence of mechanisms for exchange and dissemination of NRM information as well as regular meetings to debate and negotiate co-management agreements;

- use of informal media and means, in order to involve and consult those who are unwilling or unable to participate in formal processes such as meetings and workshops;

- actors' ease and fairness of access to communication and negotiation meetings (can all the parties attend the meetings? Are some actors discriminated against?);

- availability of competent facilitators to assist during meetings, mediate conflicts and help relevant actors to communicate among themselves and effectively negotiate agreements;

- active participation of the relevant actors in the development of a common vision and the negotiation of co-management agreements (presence at meetings, effective expression and arguing about their own interests and concerns, willingness to assume responsibilities, etc.);

- existence of a broad common vision among all parties about the desired future of the territory and resources to be managed;

- effectiveness and fairness of the negotiation process as perceived by the relevant parties;

- existence of co-management agreements (either oral or written, formal or informal) providing the parties with a clear understanding of their respective NRM functions, entitlements and responsibilities;

- existence of a clear plan and set of procedures for the monitoring and evaluation of the agreement (follow-up plan);

- existence of CM organisations (with executive, advisory, decision making or mixed roles and with enough resources to carry out their required tasks) expressing a plurality of NRM entitlements in the context at stake;

- quantity and quality of knowledge of the parties about the relevant CM actors; the agreed plans, the rules, the organisations and the roles they are expected to play;

- improved social relationships and trust among the parties participating in the negotiation.

Assessing the implementation phase

During the negotiation phase, follow-up protocols are usually prepared for the co-management agreements to be implemented, and individuals are identified to apply them. The protocols should make explicit the results and impacts each activity is expected to obtain and what indicators will be used to assess them. Thus, with respect to the preceding phases the indicators of interest are now changed. It is now time not only to asses the process of co-management and its immediate results, but also the results and impacts of the agreement it produced, translated into activities on the ground and rules followed by peoples. For this, indicators need to be agreed upon regarding the status and quality of the natural resources in the NRM units and the socio-economic conditions the agreements have specifically set out to influence. Such environmental and socio-economic indicators are unique for each agreement as they refer to its specific objectives.

The co-management process and on-going results, however, remains important and should keep being be monitored. Some such indicators, however, are poorly distinguishable from result and impact indicators (see Checklist 9.3).

Checklist 9.3 Examples of process and result indicators to assess the CM implementation phase (some may also describe results and impacts of the management agreement)

- availability of adequate resources to carry out monitoring and evaluation initiatives;

- availability of competent personnel to clarify entitlements and responsibilities and mediate in the event of conflicts among the relevant actors during implementation of the plans and agreements;

- adherence and compliance of the parties with their agreed entitlements and responsibilities;

- perception of the parties that they are learning through the implementation process, and maintenance of a constructive attitude in solving problems;

- satisfaction of the parties about the way in which the co-management agreements and organisations are working;

- fair distribution among the parties of the actual benefits and costs of the agreements;

- decrease in frequency and seriousness of conflicts among the parties now bound to the agreements;

- long-term commitment of the parties demonstrated by initiatives to promote political and policy changes that facilitate implementing the co-management agreements.

While the co-management agreement is being implemented, the area in which it is enforced may grow in size (e.g., when new communities wish to sign on to the same agreement) and/ or new actors (e.g., a federation of village associations) arrive on the scene. In addition, the people having access to the natural resources generally develop a heightened sense of responsibility and legitimacy of their role. This encourages the parties to refine NRM rules and apply more efficient and complex technical solutions. In such cases the organisations in charge of natural resource management may have to experiment– judiciously– with innovation. Judicious innovation, a key component of learning by doing, is facilitated by flexible management plans and budgets. Expansion in application, appropriation, enhanced fitting of the context through complex rules and judicious innovation are all important signals that the agreement is being "institutionalised" in society. They can be considered as CM indicators for both process and impact.

Expansion, appropriation, enhanced fitting and complexity and judicious innovation are all important signals that the agreement is being "institutionalised" in society.

In order to learn by doing it is important to collect data and information, but even more so to maintain a constructive attitude. If mistakes are regarded as opportunities for learning and if people are rewarded for identifying problems and promoting innovative solutions, learning-by-doing is strongly encouraged. On the other hand, it is important that innovations, and in particular innovations regarding NRM rules that were agreed upon by all parties, are never introduced without proper analysis and authorisation.

Assessing the co-management results

Appropriate indicators allow the relevant actors to assess whether the management objectives have been achieved (what results were obtained) and the degree to which the cooperation of various parties contributed to such achievements. A main management objective is the conservation and sustainable use of natural resources. Another frequent aim is support to the livelihoods of local communities without undermining ecological functions and biological diversity and with due attention to empowering, and not disempowering, the communities themselves. Some basic recommendations around the choice of indicators for monitoring and evaluation purposes are collected in Checklist 9.4.

Checklist 9.4   Characteristics of effective indicators

For both assessing process and results of co-management it is important to select indicators that are:

- significant– i.e., reflect changes or aspects of importance at meaningful spatial and temporal scales;

- sensitive, i.e., change proportionately in response to actual changes in the condition or item being measured;

- measurable, i.e., capable of being recorded and analysed in quantitative or qualitative terms;

- precise, i.e., measured in the same way by all people;

- simple and at low cost, i.e., they should involve simple measurement procedures and be cost-effective in terms of data collection, analysis and interpretation;

- practical, i.e., it should be possible to measure them and analyse the measurement results in a timely fashion;

- comparable, i.e., defined in a way that allows them to be compared to and combined with other indicators (e.g., percent achievement of a standard).

Appropriate and relevant indicators are not easily identified. Many of the difficulties in assessing co-management may actually stem from the scarce fitting and significance of the indicators selected to monitor its process and results. In the initial phases, indicators related to the capacity of the parties and institutions are appropriate and should be studied in detail. This should include the performance of local organisations, the quality of the initial appraisals, the fairness of the negotiations, the knowledge, attitudes and skills of the parties and their respective contributions. Subsequently, during the management and implementation phase, the actual achievement of the management objectives should be investigated, as well as their repercussions on local productivity, livelihood security and well being. While the agreements are consolidated and expanded, the ecological indicators to assess the trends in the status and health of the natural resources should kept being followed, but also equity, poverty reduction, income generation, diversification of livelihoods and lateral networking should be studied along. Finally when the agreements are scaled-up and external support is withdrawn, long term results and impacts such as local empowerment, performance of CM institutions, economic and ecological sustainability of the CM agreement, performance of external support institutions and linkages developed between CM organisations and external parties could be studied.

Box 9.14   A good indicator of environmental impact: percent nutrient reduction for each bay tributary in Chesapeake Bay!
(adapted from EPA, 1997)

In the 1970s, it became increasingly obvious that the Chesapeake Bay was degraded. Bay grasses had

---

died back to a fraction of their historical coverage, large parts of the bay were devoid of oxygen, the water was murky, and some species of fish and shellfish had dramatically declined. By the early 1980s, a scientific consensus emerged that nutrients– both nitrogen and phosphorus– were the primary pollution problem, to which all the bay's 64,000 square mile watershed contributed. In 1983, the first Chesapeake Bay Agreement was signed expressing a vision of a regional approach "to improve and protect water quality and living resources of the Chesapeake Bay estuarine system." The partners in the agreement included the Governors of Maryland, Virginia, and Pennsylvania, the district of Columbia, the Chesapeake Bay Commission (representing the legislative bodies of those states), and the United States' Environmental Protection Agency (EPA).

In 1987, the second Chesapeake Bay Agreement was signed, with a view to "…achieving by the year 2000 at least a 40 percent reduction of nitrogen and phosphorus entering the main stem of the Chesapeake Bay. The strategy should be based on point source loads and on non-point loads in an average rainfall year." This objective is specific, quantified and can be allocated to particular political jurisdictions or river basins. It can be communicated to and understood by the general public, elected officials and others, and progress towards it can be assessed by a very clear measurement: the percent nutrient reduction for each tributary to the bay. Generally, this was perceived as fair and flexible, as each jurisdiction was free to develop its own strategy to meet that goal, based on local land uses, existing programmes, and resources. The objective thus enjoyed the support of the leaders of the relevant states and the EPA, as well as the broad support of local governments, the public, and an array of interest groups.

Evaluations generally compare events and conditions before and after the co-management setting was set up. An example is given in Table 9.1.

Table 9.1   Soil and water conservation in southern Zimbabwe: farmers' perceptions of the old and new management approaches (process and results)
(adapted from Hagmann and Murwira, 1996)

The impact of co-managed research and development programmes on soil and water conservation in southern Zimbabwe was assessed by participating farmers. Their evaluation highlights important features of successful approaches to implement and coordinate soil and water conservation activities.

Old approach	New approach (participatory management)
● forcible methods were used;	● everyone to benefit as all are free to attend meetings now; there is dialogue;
● only few people could benefit (e.g., literate farmers);	● process is well explained (teaching by example);
● intercropping was forbidden;	● farmers are the drivers now;
● failed to convincingly address Soil and Water Conservation (SWC);	● intercropping is encouraged to boost yields;
	● farmers are being treated as partners and equals;
● we were told to do things without questioning;	● no discrimination against poor or rich, educated or uneducated;
	● we are given a choice of options;
● the usefulness of conservation works was never explained;	● they pay attention to us and find time to find solutions to farmers problems;
● no dialogue between farmers and extension agents;	● we are being encouraged to try out new things;

• little cooperation among farmers;	• it helps farmers to work co-operatively;
• extension agents treated our fields as theirs.	• farmers practice SWC with enough knowledge of why they do it;
	• we are learning from others through exchange visits and sharing;
	• farmers develop the ability to encourage each other in farm activities;
	• large numbers of people are mobilised;
	• the approach brings about desirable SWC techniques through participation;
	• farmers are free to ask advice;
	• development has been brought to the area;
	• the conservation of trees, soil and water is now very effective.

Checklist 9.5 Is co-management "successful"? Does it have a positive social impact?
(adapted from Pretty, 1995)

The following checklist may be used to monitor and assess the social impact of a co-management process. Did co-management:

• provide a framework for cooperative action?

• Facilitate and promote forums to develop effective compromises?

• Help organise people to generate and use their own knowledge and research to advocate their own rights?

• Mediate for more equitable access to resources?

• Help secure sustainability in natural resource management?

• Organise labour resources?

• Mobilise the local economic resources to effectively manage natural resources (credit, savings, marketing)?

• Assist some groups to gain new access to productive resources?

• Provide social infrastructure at the village level?

• Provide a link between rural people and external agencies involved in R&D and natural resource management?

• Influence policy institutions that affect it in turn?

• Improve access of rural populations to information?

• Improve information flow from the local context to governments and NGOs?

Importantly, the evaluations should allow for the identification of both expected outcomes (see Box 9.15) and unexpected outcomes (see Box 9.16)

Box 9.15　Monitoring and evaluation of the participatory management agreement in Bwindi National Park (Uganda)
(adapted from Wild and Mutebi, 1996)

Five types of monitoring have been carried out in and with parishes that signed agreements with Uganda National Parks (UNP):

1. Monitoring illegal activities. Park patrol records and data on community assistance in controlling illegal activity were used for monitoring purposes. Initial indications were positive. Over the first two years in which beekeeping was allowed within the park no fires broke out in the relevant areas. Prior to that, fires occurred each dry season. Information from rangers indicated that some beekeepers were using the pretext of checking their hives to set snares. Park wardens held meetings with the beekeeper societies, which warned and fined the responsible individuals.

2. Monitoring utilised species. Depending upon their vulnerability, utilised species were monitored at three levels: by the users themselves, by UNP and by the Institute of Tropical Forest Conservation of Mbarara University.

3. Monitoring secondary ecological impacts. Two secondary effects of utilisation were checked: the impact on species that depend on their direct use and the indirect impact because of the presence of users in the forest. The interactions between users and gorillas have been of most concern.

4. Monitoring user presence. User presence was recorded during each harvesting event and results were compared with tourist and ranger presence levels.

5. Monitoring community attitudes. Park/ community relationships were monitored through "ground relationship graphs" that map changing attitudes between the community and forest managers over the years and the reasons for those changes. This tool consistently recorded not only any deterioration in relationships with increased attempts at law enforcement, but also improvements due to conservation education, permissions to community institutions to judge park infringements, the expectation of being allowed to use multiple resources, agricultural support, etc.

Box 9.16　Watching for unintended and unexpected consequences...
(adapted from Gilmour and Fisher, 1991)

Monitoring and evaluation of community forestry activities are frequently limited to "measuring progress", or checking "project goal attainment". Very little concern is placed on looking for "unintended" or "unanticipated" consequences, such as accidentally making some segment of the population poorer... Further, attention is rarely placed on questioning the appropriateness of project goals themselves. Given the great uncertainty about the social processes involved in community forestry, we suggest that it is vitally important to look for unintended consequences and to carry out fundamental evaluations of project goals and impacts in the light of analysis of the actual effects of project activities. Identifying and understanding "unintended consequences" requires emphasis on social, economic and political processes by direct observation and analysis. Quantitative economic analysis is not, in itself, an adequate tool.

Who evaluates success?

Besides "what to measure" at different moments in the co-management process and especially after the implementation of the co-management agreements, another important question is "according to whom?" Monitoring and evaluation of issues, problems and progress on an ongoing basis is a management function that needs the support of all the partners that generated the co-management agreement. In this light, it is important to understand and include local criteria and categories in the ongoing monitoring and evaluation. Indigenous systems offer many quantitative, qualitative and process oriented indicators that can be effectively utilised (see Table 9.2).

Table 9.2	Indicators to monitor the implementation of participatory management agreements as suggested by indigenous systems of knowledge (adapted from Matowanyika, 1997)	
Objectives	Indicators	Examples in Kagore (Zimbabwe)
stewardship of natural resources	• strength of local institutions • maintenance of natural resource flows	• frequency of village assemblies • role of svikiro (traditional chief) in village assemblies • fruit and water harvests from specific sites
respect for the land	• effectiveness of indigenous regulations • extent of vegetation cover	• number of water points protected • use of local species in reforestation and surface afforested
ecological enhancement	• maintenance of sacred sites • enforcement of indigenous regulations	• quality of environment in the sacred sites • frequency of standing of specific tree species e.g., Syzgium
slope protection	• extent of vegetation cover • extent of gully erosion	• maintenance of terraces by local residents • rehabilitation of specific sites in Kagore

Different indicators are likely to be utilised by women and men, poor and rich, young and old, long time residents and recent migrants. For instance, indicators used to evaluate the performance and impacts of co-management are likely to differ according to the individual's degree of dependence on the natural resources. A woman head of household may be impressed by being able to collect abundant thatching grass and gum Arabic from a protected area. A national policy maker may be guided by the number of elephants residing in the same area, or by the trend in yearly collected tourist fees. The monitoring and evaluation phase in co-management needs to sensitively explore and build upon such different perspectives of what is relevant and important.

Some professionals suggest combining at least three types of indicators in a single process:[25]

● indigenous or experiential indicators used by rural people and reflecting experience-based changes in environmental or socio-economic conditions; these are site-specific and reflect the diverse needs and expectations of community members;

● technical or scientific indicators that are universal, disciplinary and quantitative enough to allow for comparisons between locations and across time;

25 GTZ, 1997.

- indicators that can help relate scientific knowledge and methods to local peoples' experiences.

Different social actors may have different views of what constitutes a positive impact as well as different criteria of evaluation. It is important to include such plural views, indicative of how co-management contributes to:

- community empowerment in planning, implementing, and assessing results;

- resolving conflicts;

- fostering cooperation with government and outside organisations;

- regenerating or maintaining the health of natural resources; and

- sustaining local livelihoods and equity.

In extreme cases, what some may see as progress, others may even see as a problem. As when developing the management plan, some form of facilitated negotiation may be needed to reach consensus on the overall learning objectives, indicators and end-uses of results of the evaluation. Again, as for the management plan, all willing relevant actors should be involved. The members of local communities, in particular, should not be confined to role of information providers or data gatherers. Participatory monitoring and evaluation methods and approaches can allow them to express and analyse their realities on the basis of their own criteria and knowledge of environmental and social processes. Many of these methods involve visualisation, oral testimonies and ecological and natural resource assessment techniques familiar and/ or accessible to local people.[26]

...some form of facilitated negotiation may be needed to reach consensus on the overall learning objectives, indicators and end-uses of results of the evaluation.

Box 9.17   Government foresters comment on the success of resource management institutions in Tanzania
(adapted from Wily, 1997)

In Tanzania local communities were made responsible by government for the management of Duru-Haitemba and Mgori forests. Commenting on the characteristics of the successful co-management village institutions, the foresters described how and what they had gained in the process. They said that it liberated them from the exhaustion and failure of trying to protect miombo woodlands under pressure, with inadequate resources and in conflict with local communities. The local government foresters said that, for the first time in their long career, they were in a position to provide what they can best give– technical advice. District forestry staff have been asked by villagers to advice on issues that they have not been in a position to advise upon before, including mediating roles in disputes or problems which the actors themselves have found difficult to resolve, such as inter-village boundary disputes. The Mgori Forest liaison officer frequently refers to the work of the CM institutions as "conservation, not reservation".

Box 9.18   Evaluating the elements of strength of the participatory management of Galapagos Marine Reserve
(adapted from Borrini-Feyerabend and Farvar, 2001)

The Galapagos Marine Reserve (GMR) has been under a co-management regime since 1999, when the new management plan ushered by the innovative Special Law for Galapagos entered into operation. In

---

26 Abbot and Guijt, 1998; Guijt, 1998; Pimbert and Wakeford, 2001a; Pimbert and Wakeford, 2001b; Pimbert and Wakeford, 2002; PLA Notes, 1998.

the summer of 2001, a participatory evaluation of the co-management setting (see Figure 6.1 in Chapter 6) engaged the local Junta de Manejo Participativo (JMP, the Co-management Council), representatives of all the relevant sectors in the three main inhabited islands of the Galapagos archipelago, and numerous individuals with significant concerns and responsibilities. The evaluation was meant to be "formative" (setting goals and indicators of progress) as well as "summative" (assessing progress towards those goals) and involved both a participatory aspect and an external component (the external evaluators produced their own report but also took advantage of the results of the participatory evaluation they facilitated).

The evaluators identified several elements of weakness and made recommendations to address them. They also stated, however, that the Galapagos Marine Reserve offers a most significant example of institutionalised co-management, which demonstrated resilience and the capacity to achieve consensus positions on important management decisions. In fact, the system managed to overcome various types of disputes, including legal attacks at the higher level in society, local instances of violence, political sabotage and numerous changes in sector leadership. Remarkably, it also allowed the reaching of a consensus over a zoning plan that freed from extractive use 18% of the archipelago coastline (the most depleted areas). Among the characteristics identified as contributing to these successes were the following:

- Strong and clear legal back-up (Special Law of Galapagos of 1998; Management Plan of 1999; Official Regulations of 2000; decision of the Constitutional Supreme Jury of 2001).

- Composite, well-thought-out system with a co-management body (JMP) in charge of elaborating technical proposals by consensus, and another co-management body– the Autoridad Inter-institucional de Manejo (AIM) in charge of casting decisions about such proposals by vote. Importantly, proposals that obtained the consensus of all members of the JMP were consistently approved by the AIM (basically 100% of such proposals were approved). This is a strong embedded incentive towards achieving consensus and avoiding stalling (if the JMP does not reach a consensus, the AIM decides on its own accord).

- Design of the system through a participatory process (the local Start-up Team called Grupo Nucleo worked for a couple of years to draft the Special Law of Galapagos and the GMR Management Plan). This strengthened its legitimacy in the early and most difficult years.

- The favouring of local Galapagos residents in both the JMP and the AIM, a fact that promotes accountability and enhances management effectiveness.

- The choice of the members of the co-management bodies on the basis of their technical competence and not as elected politicians, not even in the case of the Ministry representatives in the AIM. In principle, this set the system remarkably aside from direct political influence, which would not be the case if elected representatives would sit at the negotiation table (indirect influence is another matter).

- The support of a co-management secretariat (Coordinator, Facilitator and Secretary) that provided for several years the indispensable impulse and technical coaching for the development of the new management setting; the secretariat was financed by a WWF project.

- The institutional support provided by the Galapagos National Park, which formally adheres to the participatory approach and houses the technical secretariat for the JMP. This provides an element of equilibrium and stability in the whole CM system, linking in an effective way the development of technical proposals, the decisions regarding their enforcement, and the capacity and effectiveness of the enforcement itself.

- The provision of a regular forum for exchanging views and assuring inter-sectoral dialogue among the key partners, as well as the promotion of joint initiatives among sectors, such as joint biological monitoring by the Galapagos National Park (GNP), the Charles Darwin Research Station (CDRS) and the fishing folks.

9.3   Promoting effective and sustainable co-management institutions

There is, today, a considerable body of experiences in developing agreements and new organisational forms for the co-management of natural resources (forests, wetlands, rangelands, protected areas, species, watersheds, etc.). The lessons learnt from such schemes that have been in operation for several years provide useful insights into the characteristics of successful co-management institutions and how these can be nurtured. This does not mean that all is clear and that there are no more uncertainties about the roles and features of effective co-management institutions in a fast changing world. Far from it! As we have discussed, there are even multiple perspectives on what constitutes successful co-management. And yet, it seems that some advice can be offered towards enhancing the effectiveness and sustainability of the agreements, organisations, rules and culture-based patterns of understanding and action that constitute a "co-management institution".

> Together, CM agreements, organisations, rules and culture-based patterns of understanding and action constitute a "co-management institution".

Developing goodwill among the parties

As the British Columbia Claims Task Force[27] has said, co-management agreements are about rights to land, sea and resources, and the real solutions to the problems they set out to solve lie in a broad based reconciliation, both legal and political. Whatever type of agreement, there is one essential element that all must contain. That is goodwill, i.e., trust, mutual respect and integrity. If that element is not present, developing a co-management agreement becomes extremely hard. There is little point in even commencing negotiations towards functional agreements unless the parties are prepared to:

- respect one another;

- develop even a very broad shared vision of the desired feature for the resources at stake;

- act honestly, in particular by following through and delivering what they have agreed upon.

Mutual goodwill is particularly at stake after the agreement has been signed, when issues associated with co-existence and cooperation in the face of different world-views have to be confronted on a daily basis. Distrust or lack of understanding of the motives and rationale for a conservation agency by local people may be an ongoing problem. Similarly, a paternalistic and distrusting attitude on the part of government staff may be "felt" by people and may suffocate any desire for cooperation. Social communications initiatives during implementation can be helpful to clarify and possibly diffuse conflict. Good faith and commitment to the co-management agreement need to be demonstrated by all parties.

Maintaining flexibility and fostering social experimentation

Co-management is achieved through a cyclical process of dialogue, action, and reflection. An important characteristic of successful co-management is thus to

---

27   British Columbia Claims Task Force, 1991.

value and support such a process without focusing entirely on the results it should achieve. The "process" approach is based on the assumption that when several institutional actors are at stake they need time to get to know their respective needs and capacities. The learning process involves acting together, creating knowledge, and developing an active institution through trial and error. Such a process must be flexible, and responsive to highly differentiated needs and site-specific conditions. Every farm or forest patch has its own signature. No one can predict how ecological conditions and needs will evolve over time. Co-management bodies must "learn by doing", building upon the motivation, confidence and rapport amongst all the parties involved.

An approach based on social experimentation treats error as a source of information to adapt procedures (see Box 9.19). Indicators are developed from those most important to key actors, in particular the local communities, and, rather than pursuing absolute and fixed targets, the actors find occasions to celebrate the milestones they reach along the way. Innovative learning methods promote group demonstrations, village level workshops, and community-to-community visits and extension to achieve effective multiplication of sustainable natural resource management technologies. Co-management schemes based on such a "process approach" must be pursued for realistic lengths of time before evaluating results in terms of social development and sustainable natural resource management. Some of the positive trends and results generated in this way (e.g., local confidence in being able to manage natural resources, social emergence of previously marginalised groups) may be even more important than their concrete, short term, ecological results.

Box 9.19 Learning by doing in co-managing aquatic resources in Khong district (Lao PDR) (adapted from Baird, 1999)

Because formal aquatic resource co-management planning is unfamiliar to the villagers who established the new co-management plans (see also Boxes 3.11, 5.11, 6.11 and 9.11), it is generally necessary for them to adjust regulations after having tried them out. This is an important part of adaptive management and a great way to increase local capacities. Lessons are invariably learnt as time passes, and experiences generally indicate whether regulations should be softened or hardened. Village headmen have the right to change regulations, but they are supposed to organise community-wide meetings and receive everyone's prior approval before alterations are actually made to the plan. They are also supposed to notify the district officials in Khong. Experience indicates that while village headmen almost always seek a mandate from their fellow villagers before instituting changes, they rarely inform the district. They just inform them when the officers pass by. The officers in Khong are mostly concerned that villages do not establish regulations that discriminate against other villages. For instance, they have a policy that villages are not allowed to restrict outsider-fishing activities unless they are willing to enforce the same restrictions on themselves. However, if a village bans a fishing method in their area of jurisdiction, outsiders are expected to abide by the ban in the same way as local fisherfolk. The "non-discriminatory regulation" policy of the district helps to maintain good relationships between villages.

While many of the lessons learnt from the co-management experience in Khong are applicable to other parts of Laos and the region, unique conditions in different areas will require inventive approaches to meet local needs. Common property regimes can break down in crisis, but experience in Khong indicates that they can also be strengthened in response to resource management crisis. The aquatic resource co-management programme in Khong has been very successful. It has enhanced village solidarity, increased natural resource management capacity and increased the fish and frog stocks and catches. Provided that co-management systems remain flexible and can adapt to social and institutional circumstances unique to particular areas, it will continue to be a most important option for equitably managing natural resources in the region.

Allowing the management partnership to mature

The implementation phase can provide inspiring examples of maturation and evolution of the management partnership. At the beginning the emphasis may be on basic resource protection combined with the exercise of some rights of access by specified parties. This may be followed by an increased sense of legitimacy and responsibility on the part of the people exercising such access, and, little by little, the development of more appropriate rules and/ or more complex manipulation and technologies for the sustainable extraction and use of resources. A telling example is the changing attitudes and priorities of villagers after they took over the management of their miombo woodlands in Tanzania (see Box 9.20).

Box 9.20   Villagers regenerate miombo woodlands in Tanzania
            (adapted from Wily, 1997)

In a situation of severe degradation of the forest cover, two Tanzanian communities have pioneered the challenge of achieving sustained, effective control of the use of the forest resource in a very cost-effective way. This was made possible because the government of Tanzania gave them appropriate rights and access to benefits, allowing them to assume their responsibilities as forest managers.

Each one of the villages maintains a Village Forest Committee, the composition of which has steadily shifted from village leaders to ordinary villagers. This local level democratisation has both arisen from, and led to, a growing need for accountability as practical management and controls get under way. As the months pass, more, rather than fewer, villagers become effectively involved in the commitment to conserve and manage the forest. An interesting feature of this process is that whilst villagers cited virtually all uses from timber to grazing as "indispensable" before they were granted control over the woodlands, the same leaders and ordinary villagers swiftly argued for discontinuation of any use that they considered damaging once it was known that the forest was "theirs". As one villager observed when asked why the village was so intensely serious in its forest conservation effort: "Of course we stopped the encroachment and charcoal burning when we were given the forest to look after for ourselves! Now it is ours, we only have ourselves to blame if the forest gets used up. That is why you find us serious."

While the co-management agreement gets fine tuned, the area in which it applies may expand (new parishes or communities may join the agreement) so that the process may move in at least two dimensions– towards more complex accords and towards larger areas of application.[28] This may also be accompanied by the development of new associations among the parties in the agreement, or new nesting institutions (e.g., a federation of fisherfolk associations). Flexible management budgets are very conducive to this maturation through "learning by doing" as they can provide the support necessary for organisations to get on their feet.

---

[28] Mark Poffenberger, personal communication, 1996. Complex agreements may include micro-zoning (mosaic plans), multiple time horizons, adoption of new technologies, etc.

The co-management agreement may expand as the process moves towards more complex management agreements and larger areas of application.

In addition, it is often in the implementation phase that the need for specific policy and legal change to support effective co-management of natural resources becomes well recognised.[29] These changes need to be pursued, as appropriate, by the management partnership (different stakeholders may be able to use different channels to achieve the desired changes). By such processes, several de facto management partnerships may also become de jure, i.e., legalised by government authority. The same Tanzanian villages described in Box 9.20 began to manage their forests by preventing activities they had declared illegal, issuing a limited number of permits for sustainable uses, patrolling the forest, rehabilitating springs, etc., only on the basis of the support they had secured from the local district

council. It soon became clear to them, however, that they needed more formal legal backing if their rules were to be taken seriously by all. Each village was therefore assisted to rephrase their management plans and rules as Village By-Laws. These were then formally approved under the District Authorities Act in 1995. Now each village is the legal authority and manager of that part of the Duru-Haitemba forest specified in the relevant Village By-Law as falling under its jurisdiction.[30]

Promoting people-centred organisational cultures

The quality and depth of a co-management process is dependent on the willingness of the parties to work together. Governmental agencies, in particular, should be willing to trust people– their knowledge, their culture-based organisations, their understanding of their own rights, their capacities to assume responsibilities and innovate. A solid commitment to "people-centeredness" and a philosophy of reversals from top-down management decisions are key features of enabling organisations and an indicator of their engagement in learning by doing.

Both empirical experience and theory suggest that "organisational culture"– i.e., the combination of the individual opinions, shared knowledge, values and norms of the members of an organisation– is the most fundamental level at which transformation needs to take place.[31] Structures and work patterns may be reformed within organisations to enable co-management, but if their "organisational culture" is left untouched, the changes may remain superficial and ultimately without effect.

For natural resource management bureaucracies in particular, narratives and

---

29 The legal and political conditions for successful co-management of natural resources are further discussed in part IV of this volume.
30 Wily, 1997.
31 Bainbridge et al., 2000; Pimbert, 2004; Wright, 1994.

perspectives about people-environment interactions are the central element of their organisational culture. They give rise to, and legitimate, particular procedures, policies, technologies and professional practices that either deny or encourage diversity and participation in natural resource management. For example, an emphasis on relatively "stable" ecosystems feeds into the development of policies and "scientific" practices for conservation controlled by professionals and distant organisations. Conversely, notions of uncertainty, spatial variability and complex non-equilibrium ecological dynamics tend to emphasise flexibility, mobility and adaptive resource management in which local people are central actors.[32]

Simplified and a-historical perspectives perpetuated by the powerful have been a persistent feature of environmental policies and interventions. Neo-Malthusian narratives have been used by bureaucracies to blame people for environmental degradation and justify imposing on them massive packages of standard interventions. To "prevent further deterioration", official policies and bureaucracies have consistently defined local misuse of resources as the principal cause of destruction and excluded people from the management of natural resources.[33] All too often, "by depicting resource users (the local ones) as wild, destructive (or illiterate, uneducated, backward or non-innovative), state resource management agencies think they can justify their use of militaristic environmental protection".[34]

Simplified and a-historical perspectives perpetuated by the powerful have been a persistent feature of environmental policies and interventions.

Such policy (or crisis) narratives are usually robust, hard to challenge and slow to change. They play a key role in policy and project level decision making. They structure options, define relevant data and exclude other views within bureaucracies and professional circles. And yet, recent research has debunked several orthodox views on people-environment interactions (Box 9.21). Effective and inclusive co-management bodies are usually characterised by people-centred organisational cultures that embrace this new knowledge about people-environment interactions. People-centred organisational cultures typically emphasise the importance of social and ecological knowledge, flexible institutions and adaptive organisations for co-management.

Box 9.21   Debunking myths on people-environment interactions
(adapted from Bainbridge et al., 2000; Pimbert, 2004)

Recent research has fundamentally questioned many of the environmental crisis narratives and received wisdoms on the supposed destructiveness of rural people on the environment. A combination of historical analysis, social anthropology, participatory methods to understand local resource users' knowledge and perspectives, and insights from non-equilibrium ecology has challenged some of the environmental knowledge taken for granted by government bureaucracies and donors:

● Contrary to neo-Malthusian, assumptions, population increase may not necessarily mean more environmental degradation and less biological diversity. More people can mean more care for the environment as shown by research in Sierra Leone[35] and Kenya.[36]

● Historical research in West Africa has shown dominant deforestation estimates to be vastly exaggerated. Many of the vegetation forms that ecologists and policy makers have used to indicate forest loss, such as forest patches in savannah, are, according to the knowledge of local resource users and

---

[32] Pimbert, 2004.

[33] Beliefs are often the product of powerful discourse rather than facts. Sundberg (2004) illustrates this with regard to poor migrants in Guatemala, who are invariably considered "the primary cause of deforestation in the reserve, to the exclusion of other actors such as powerful cattle ranchers, loggers, and oil companies...".

[34] Peluso, 1996.

[35] Kandeh and Richards, 1996.

[36] Tiffen et al., 1994.

historical evidence, the results of landscape enrichment by people.[37]

● Many assumed "pristine" wetlands, grasslands, forests and other biodiversity-rich environments in Latin America, the Pacific Islands, Africa, Australia and Asia have been proved to be human modified and enriched landscapes.[38]

● New perspectives in ecology have challenged conventional views of dry lands in Africa as stable ecosystems subject to decline and desertification once carrying capacity is exceeded. Rangelands are resilient and less prone to degradation and desertification than once thought. The new findings concord with the knowledge of many local herders and emphasise how rangelands are subject to high levels of spatial and temporal variability, and ecological dynamics are characterised by sudden transitions rather than slow and predictable change.[39]

● In the insular Caribbean, field research has shown that increases in the level of poverty and unemployment of a coastal community do not automatically lead to increased resource use and degradation, as often assumed.[40]

Promoting participatory approaches and learning attitudes at various levels

Participatory methods [help in] breaking down the conventional distinctions between diagnosis, planning, implementation and evaluation, setting a fluid and flexible process of decision making and action.

Successful co-management organisations enable the people living closest to the resources to identify, exchange and analyse information, understand the issues at stake, negotiate solutions and develop an agenda for action. Their success hinges on a commitment to understand multiple perspectives within communities and among various actors and on sufficient time and space to negotiate workable partnerships with one another. Several families of methods and approaches are of help throughout this, basically revolving around participatory action research (PAR) and participatory learning and action (PLA). When introduced by facilitators in a sensitive and respectful manner, these methods enable people to truly "take part" in understanding issues and making decisions over natural resources and the other issues that affect their lives. The methods also contribute to breaking down the conventional distinctions between diagnosis, planning, implementation and evaluation, setting a fluid and flexible process of decision making and action. They help to identify new skills in the community and to generate local confidence to articulate solutions and take action.

Some co-management processes may wish to move beyond the empowerment process at the local level.

A learning approach implies that people are able to discuss alternatives and choices and develop their own process of appraisal, prioritisation, and decision-making based on locally developed indicators. This is particularly important at the community level, too often by-passed by analyses and decisions. As described in Part II of this volume, an enabling approach involves external support but in a way that complements and does not replace internal capabilities, knowledge and resources. In this sense, co-management processes have still much to do to promote learning attitudes at all levels. The empowerment process at the local level is crucially important and a foundation for any other type of participatory processes and learning, but it can even be envisaged to move beyond that, into institutional development and "lateral learning" (see Table 9.3 for a typology of practices).

---

37 Fairhead and Leach, 1996.
38 Nabham et al., 1982; Pimbert and Pretty, 1995; Saberwal, 1996; Posey, 1999.
39 Sullivan and Homewood, 2004.
40 CANARI, 2003.

Table 9.3	Participatory methodologies and approaches: the spectrum of current practice in co-management (adapted from Shah, 1996; Pimbert and Pretty, 1995)
Mere labelling	Participatory methods used only as a label to make proposals and rhetoric attractive to donors
Participatory methods for staff training	Participatory methods primarily used for one shot training of staff members. No commitment is demonstrated to use methods for field action, no effective skills are available.
Participatory methods for appraisal	Participatory methods are used at the appraisal stage to obtain a list of local priorities for action. Lack of skills, commitment and resources prevent the continuation of the approach for programme management and local organisational development.
Participatory methods for project management	Participatory methods are used to develop an effective sequence of programme implementation and management but are not linked with institution development aspects. The use of methods is sustained as long as funding is available but tapers off on withdrawal of resources in absence of effective local organisations.
Participatory methods for local institutional and organisational development	Participatory methods are used effectively for programme management and local institutional development, which shows short and long term impact. The process, however, may not be accompanied by corresponding changes in support organisations at larger scales (e.g., in learning environment, structures, disbursement procedures and evaluation mechanisms). This may lead to decaying of effectiveness of organisational efforts over time.
Participatory methods for organisational change and "lateral learning"	Participatory methods used as part of a strategy of organisational growth and learning, as well as local institution development. The strategy involves appraisal, planning, negotiation, bargaining and conflict resolution as well as lateral expansion of resource use organisations through peasant to peasant (village to village), herder to herder (tribe to tribe), and institution to institution mechanisms.

Indeed, the institutionalisation of participatory processes may proceed by pursuing negotiation, organisational change and lateral learning at various levels:[41]

The local/ micro level
The more enabling co-management organisations encourage the expansion of participation from one activity, such as appraisal, to the empowering involvement of primary actors and local communities throughout the whole co-management process. In this sense, "participation" involves setting priorities (e.g., what should be conserved, by when and how? Who decides where work should be done?); controlling implementation (whose project is it?); controlling funding (how are funds distributed and to whom? Who benefits?); reporting progress to authorities or donors (whose format counts?); developing institutions (whose power counts?). Co-management organisations may thus encourage a shift in the quality and type of participation, towards learning processes that allow the parties to reflect on their experience and develop knowledge together. Successful participatory learning initiatives often combine specific methodologies, such as PRA/ PLA, with

---

[41] For a more general account of the scaling up and institutionalisation of participatory processes, see Blackburn and Holland, 1998; Bainbridge et al., 2000; Pimbert, 2004.

other methods of participatory learning that are deliberately empowering.[42] For example, they link learning with creating or strengthening local organisations that act in self reliant ways.

From the local/ micro-level to a larger geographical scale
Successful co-management organisations encourage a scaling up of operations to include larger numbers of communities and territories/ resources in the management of natural resources. Once successful local experiences are in place, they can grow through a number of avenues including provision of resources, strengthening of networks, provision of mutual support in conflict resolution, etc. Some most effective learning processes are based in networks of field initiatives and engage the relevant field staff (governmental agencies and projects), local community members, local authorities and other relevant parties. The learning that takes place in such initiatives is directed by the learners and usually encompasses a wide range of skills and experiences (e.g., analytical skills, communication skills, capacity to facilitate and participate in meetings)[43] towards effective co-management. A good example is described in Box 5.10 of Chapter 5.

Co-management organisations have at times achieved larger scale impact by supporting groups who have had successful experiences in one situation to spread their knowledge, innovations and experience to other areas. Exchanges, mutual visits, joint initiatives and information flows lead to lateral spread of participatory approaches over wider geographical areas and offered opportunities to influence policies at various levels. The work of the Aga Khan Rural Support Programme in Gujarat (India) offers an example of this type of scaling up of a participatory approach to natural resource management (see Box 9.22).

> *Successful co-management organisations encourage a scaling up of operations to include larger numbers of communities and places in the management of natural resources.*

Box 9.22   Co-management of natural resources in Gujarat (India): village to village extension (adapted from Shah and Kaul Shah, 1994)

The Aga Khan Rural Support Programme (AKRSP) is an NGO working with village communities in Gujarat to catalyse and promote community participation in natural resource management. AKRSP focuses on promoting village organisations and institutions to implement the villagers' own resource conservation plans. This approach has shown that programmes managed by local bodies result in higher investment by farmers in soil, water and nutrient conservation. Local villagers trained as para-professionals were able to create demand for their services of planning, management and monitoring.

Following this, the participatory process spread widely to neighbouring villages and watersheds. Agricultural productivity increased by 30% to 100% over a two to three year period. Soil loss was reduced, and out-migration slowed. Many households diversified into animal husbandry and horticulture. The local para-professionals and co-management organisations became confident enough to help promote similar activities in neighbouring areas and village level institutions.

The creation of a sustainable network of local institutions by AKRSP in the area depended to a great extent on its ability to provide training and programme support to such bodies to emerge as viable, small-scale commercial entities. The size of AKRSP and its initial operations in 40 villages enabled it to hire a good quality multi disciplinary team, which could provide support to village institutions in a diverse range of functional areas. By virtue of the size of its operations, AKRSP was able to mobilise and attract support from many external agencies, including the Indian government.

---

42   Freire, 1970; Freire, 1985; ActionAid, 2001; Archer and Newman, 2003.
43   Absalom et al., 1995.

Similarly, the scaling up and institutionalising of the Community Integrated Pest Management (CIPM) programme in Indonesia has been remarkable. Through its emphasis on farmer-to-farmer training, action research, policy dialogue and other participatory processes, CIPM has truly transformed the livelihoods of peasants by improving income security, food supply, public health and re-invigorating rural civil society. It has also strengthened social assets by supporting farmers' efforts to build associations and networks, giving them a stronger voice and improved means of collective action and mutual aid (see Box 9.23).

Box 9.23   Community Integrated Pest Management in Indonesia
(adapted from Fakih et al., 2003)

Integrated Pest Management (IPM) emerged in Indonesia in the late 1980s as a reaction to the environmental and social consequences of the Green Revolution model of agriculture. A cooperative programme between the United Nations Food and Agriculture Organisation (FAO) and the Indonesian Government had centred on Farmer Field Schools (FFS), which are schools without walls. The FFS aimed to make farmers experts in their own fields, enabling them to replace their reliance on external inputs, such as pesticides, with endogenous skills, knowledge and resources. Over one million rice paddy farmers and local resource users participated, and are still today involved, in this national programme.

Over time, the emphasis of the programme shifted towards community organisation, community planning and management of IPM, and became known as Community IPM (CIPM). Agro-ecosystem analysis and methods for group dynamics were initially used to enhance farmers' ecological literacy as it related to plant-insect ecology. Farmer IPM trainers and researcher/ scientists learned facilitation and presentation skills and how to make basic experimental designs to analyse and quantify ecological phenomena. Then, the principles of FFS slowly extended from rice to the management of natural resources, from IPM to plant breeding and participatory water management, and from technical domains to broader engagement with policy issues, advocacy, and local governance.

The beneficial environmental impacts of the programme include significantly reduced pesticide use, increased biological and genetic diversity, and a more holistic approach by farmers to maintaining the complex ecological balance of rice agro-ecosystems. Learning to analyse policy, deal with high-level decision-makers in government and produce a newspaper with a print run of 10,000 has been key in enabling farmers and other natural resource users to become organisers, planners, advocates, and policy activists. The empowering dynamic led to a variety of campaign strategies, including a national IPM farmers' congress and the development of a charter for peasant rights. Such activities, together with the strengthened voice of farmers brought about by the Community IPM process overall, created an upsurge of support for a national peasant movement in Indonesia.

Transforming bureaucracies at the institutional scale
Organisations that operate at a large scale and wish to enhance participation in natural resource management have to focus on more than local communities and the micro-level. Possibly, in fact, one of their key challenges is to change themselves. Such organisations, which generally include representatives of national governments, large NGOs and donor agencies, tend to adopt standardised procedures that, no matter how sophisticated, do not adjust well to fine-grained local ecological and social characteristics. Together with the professional attitudes and behaviour usually associated with top-down, expert prescriptions, such standardised procedures are likely to inhibit the flexible, innovative practices needed for the co-management of natural resources to flourish in diverse local contexts.[44]

Institutional transformation and professional re-orientation are often needed.

---

[44]   Chambers, 1993; Borrini-Feyerabend, 1996; Chambers, 1996.

Institutional transformation and professional re-orientation of the kind described in Checklist 9.6 are often needed.

Checklist 9.6 Towards successful co-management organisations: some operational and policy implications of going large-scale
(adapted from Absalom et al., 1995; Shah, Kaul Shah and Pimbert, 1998)

Governments, large NGOs and donors that are effective in the co-management of natural resources typically encourage several types of internal organisational change, as described below:

● Commitment to process

Top managers/ decision makers of government departments and large NGOs commit themselves to a long-term process going "beyond projects" (cycles of 10 years or more are much more appropriate than 2-year projects).

● Organisational culture

The organisational culture provides opportunities to enable learning from experiences and mistakes, and is flexible enough to allow experimentation. Donor funding is flexible and more dependent on open-ended, event-focused targets than on fixed schedules.

● Management styles

There is a transition from management styles based on hierarchy, inhibited communications, command and obedience relationships to more organic styles that encourage lateral communication, collegial authority and flexible roles and procedures. The organisations encourage employees to be participatory in their work with each other, and not just during "field visits".

● Organisational structure

Efforts are on-going at transforming compartmentalised and hierarchical organisations into flatter structures that are multi functional and evolve organically. Innovative mechanisms may include the establishment and funding of small self managed teams within organisations, endowed with the freedom to experiment, motivate and learn from mistakes. Professionals are encouraged to work as "intrapreneurs" (entrepreneurs within organisations) and pilot innovations.

● Quality of support professionals

Co-management of natural resources requires a high degree of professional support in the initial phases until local institutions develop/ re-activate indigenous and local management systems. The need to respond flexibly and provide support in a wide range of areas requires dynamic and committed professionals. Efforts are made to attract and reward excellent professionals in the initial phases of the process in order to be effective in the long run. Donors invest early-on to build the capacity of these professionals and their field collaborators.

● Incentives/ rewards

Incentives and rewards encourage staff to be honest, work in the field with communities, stay on as staff, and encourage joint action between governmental institutions and communities.

● Organisational procedures

Organisational and programme management procedures enable linking of participatory learning and action with programme management and implementation (e.g., through the decentralisation of funds management). They seek to build participatory learning and action from the start of the programme cycle. Co-management processes are piloted on a small-scale and implemented mainly through local organisations.

● Outward Linkages

Priority is given to developing effective linkages (e.g., training exchanges, joint initiatives, on-going information flows) with partner organisations. This is meant to help partners (including donors) to better understand all phases of the participatory processes. Linkages are developed on principles of mutual respect, integrity and trust among partners.

Scaling up and institutionalising co-management approaches offer great opportunities to expand people's participation in natural resource management but also present considerable policy and operational challenges. In particular, few experts and specialised agencies have the will, experience or skills necessary to work in a participatory mode. Support measures may be needed to deal with the insecurity often associated with their changing roles. When this is lacking, one can even see the rapid demise of inspiring co-management (see Box 9.24).

Box 9.24 How to spoil conservation: an effective co-management setting clashes against misunderstanding and the repressive approach
(adapted from Taty et al., 2003; Chatelain et al., 2004)

The Conkouati-Douli National Park (Congo Brazzaville) offers a important example of how an effective management partnership can be developed even while facing some of the most challenging conditions in the world. The co-management organisation it formally established is the Comité de Gestion des Ressources Naturelles de Conkouati (COGEREN), which includes representatives of the local communities, the state administration, the NGOs locally active in environment and development issues and some locally elected officials. The legitimisation of this co-management body was accomplished through the signing of a Co-management Charter by national and local authorities and by a number of social rituals by which the local chiefs became publicly engaged. After this, a zoning plan was developed, as well as a management plan for the park, prepared on the basis of the zoning plan and progressively including three special agreements on the species most highly endangered in the area: the manatees, the marine turtles and rattan. These agreements were prepared cooperatively with all the parties engaged in the COGEREN and spelled out some important hopes for a voluntary code of conduct in the area.

Unfortunately, the achievements in Conkouati– arresting and powerful as they have been– remained vulnerable. After the IUCN project that nourished the development of COGEREN came to an end, COGEREN managed to survive well, continuing and even expanding activities for a couple of years, with a small but crucial support from the Netherlands Committee for the IUCN. All work grounded to a halt, however, when a new Conservateur (park manager) and a new conservation advisor from a foreign NGO[45] came into the area. Instead of valuing the advantages of the situation they found in place, they chose to follow a more conventional and dated "protectionist" and "repressive" approach. In spite of the existing official engagements, they did not respect the authority of COGEREN, prevented both the official signature and the application of the special agreements on the manatees, the marine turtles and rattan, and re-focused park management efforts on the armed repression of poaching. The wisdom of involving in conservation a poorly-paid armed militia in a country just out of a civil war was all to be seen. Far from eliminating poaching, this "repression" appears to have increased it. The armed forces have simply become a new layer in the system, taxing each poached animal that gets out of the park, and thus encouraging the poachers to hunt more than before. As a matter of fact, a sort of alliance is said to have been established between the armed police and the poachers (who are not members of the local communities and come from outside the park) with the first becoming the taxing protectors of the second: a great result indeed! Understandably, the sudden change of approach has angered and disheartened the communities engaged in the COGEREN, and new clashes and conflicts have been recorded. It would be unforgivable if the local communities were made to lose interest altogether after the long process that managed to involve them sincerely and effectively in conservation.

---

45 The Wildlife Conservation Society (WCS).

Encouraging "champions" with enabling attitudes and values

Promoting co-management is particularly problematic where there is little support from government or because of prevailing negative attitudes and negative historical legacies. In such contexts, the role of innovative, charismatic or dynamic individuals is often crucial. These "champions of change" can be found at any level of society– within local or national government, NGOs, local communities and, not least, among resource users. And yet, perhaps more than the existence of champions per se, it is the attitudinal and value orientation of the champions in co-management organisations that really makes the difference.

For example, many features of normal professional attitudes and behaviour– such as dominant and superior attitudes, authoritarian relationships, gender and upper-to-upper biases, failures to honour aroused expectations, rushing, and being "extractive" in terms of resources and information– are surely not conducive to co-management. Examples are the attitude of "we know what's best for them" of officials and powerful actors, the opposite feeling of awe and subservience amongst some community members and weaker actors, the mutual distrust and ill-will built upon a history of conflicts, and the behaviours that perpetuate mystifying symbols of power and authority. As respectful, learning-oriented attitudes are increasingly seen as crucial, abandoning routines (un-learning patterns) and engaging in personal reorientation and organisational learning are increasingly appreciated. In this sense, co-management organisations can encourage their members to:

- interact in a participatory and non dominating way;
- develop a self-critical attitude, recognising that they are continually learning and welcoming rigorous peer review;
- be explicit about whether they are eliciting information or/ and resources for external use, or are promoting community action and devolution of decision making power over the use of natural resources– a distinction that should be made clear and documented;
- make commitments to value fairly the contributions made by all partners (South, North, local, external);
- recognise the need for a diversity of views and approaches, and respect them;
- identify, in partnership with communities, relevant rights and appropriate forms of compensation when eliciting information and resources for external use;
- ensure that credit and compensation are given as they are due;
- strive towards a process of empowerment of women, marginalised people and weaker people in society.

The challenge of unfreezing and/ or shifting attitudes and the working style of bureaucracies (government, donors, large NGOs) demands examining the relationships between working structures and staff attitudes and behaviour, which are often mutually reinforcing. Bureaucratic structures exert pressures on their staff to act and behave in certain ways. In turn, the behaviour and attitudes of staff shape the organisational cultures and influence the way bureaucracies operate, both internally and with their "clients" and "beneficiaries". Organisational change needs to combine training for individual change with structural transformation– a process through which the organisation examines and re-shapes its programmes

More than the existence of champions per se, it is the attitudinal and value orientation of the champions in co-management organisations that really makes the difference.

Bureaucratic structures exert pressures on their staff to act and behave in certain ways. In turn, the behaviour and attitudes of staff shape the organisational cultures and influence the way bureaucracies operate, both internally and with their "clients" and "beneficiaries".

and procedures. The scaling up of co-management implies nothing less than fundamental changes in the operational procedures of bureaucracies, their reward and incentive systems, their organisational culture, their career patterns, and their use of time, space and resources.[46]

Ensuring transparency in the distribution of benefits

Ensuring transparency in the distribution of the natural resource management benefits is an important factor to promote and maintain the good will of the co-management parties. A simple and successful example of "transparency in practice" comes from the early days of the CAMPFIRE programme, in Zimbabwe (see Box 9.25).

Box 9.25 Learning transparency from Mahenye Ward (Zimbabwe)
(adapted from Jones, 2003)

In Mahenye and some other CAMPFIRE areas of Zimbabwe, village meetings are held when the Ward Wildlife Committee gives a statement of accounts for the year and decisions are taken on how to spend the next year's income from wildlife and tourism. When the income is distributed, each head of household individually collects the cash. If it was decided to spend some of the income on a community project, such as a grinding mill, then each head of household returns the agreed portion of the cash for this purpose. They all see and hold in their hands the cash that was generated from wildlife and fully realise that wildlife has a monetary value. Further, each head of household, having assigned money to a purpose, is bound to want to ensure that it will be actually used for that purpose, thus promoting accountability.

Striving for equity

Effective and sustainable co-management organisations pay attention to equity and human rights issues for both ethical and practical reasons. It is crucial to recognise that the top-down management of wildlife or protected areas can maintain a degree of effectiveness even in the face of injustices and the impoverishment of people.[47] Co-management, however, has little chance of success if benefits are not distributed fairly among the relevant parties. Or, let us say, has little chances of remaining "co-management" and not being transformed into yet another top-down body at the service of the powerful. As discussed in Chapter 2, "equity" in natural resource management entails the fair sharing of information among the parties, the chances for everyone to participate in discussion and negotiate agreements that are understood and appreciated by all, and the sharing of resource management benefits and responsibilities in a way that is commensurate with the varying capacities of the parties, the sacrifices and contributions they made and/ or the damages they incurred in the process.[48]

In all societies, the composition of decision-making bodies is likely to reflect and reinforce imbalances of power, with the weaker and underprivileged social groups being least represented in decision making structures.

Achieving a balanced representation of actors and interest groups in co-management organisations is also an important element of an equitable co-management setting, and it is all but an easy task. Most communities show internal inequities and differences, based on ethnic origin, class, caste, economic endowments, religion, social status, gender and age. In all societies, the composition of decision-making bodies is likely to reflect and reinforce such imbalances of power, with the weaker and underprivileged social groups being least represented in decision

---

[46] Bainbridge et al., 2000; Pimbert, 2004.
[47] Brockington, 2003.
[48] For instance, through lost access to resources, damage to crops and through the physical danger presented by many wild animals. See also Pimbert and Pretty, 1998.

making structures. And, of course, what benefits one group and meets some conservation goals, may harm other parties and other goals. Inequities in the composition of the co-management bodies can create profound resentments among the parties and ultimately defeat co-management as a whole. Institutions striving for successful outcomes develop special arrangements to bring to the fore the views of all relevant parties, and particularly the views of gender, caste, racial or religious groups, in ways that are culturally appropriate.[49] A powerful way to do so requires that not only the least powerful actors are represented in decision-making bodies, but also that decisions in such bodies are taken by consensus. Through time, this can generate entirely new skills, collaborative capacities and mutual respect in a local society.

Ensuring fair and equitable representation of different stakeholders is key to the success of co-management institutions. If co-management bodies are created in regions where the demographic composition of the affected communities is quite homogeneous, the decision-making could involve only government and representatives of the communities as a whole, sometimes holding the majority of seats. This occurs in some northern Canadian co-management organisations. On the other hand, where the local communities are highly differentiated internally, their representatives in the participatory management body need to reflect that diversity. Identifying the most appropriate representatives of indigenous communities connected with a particular area may be difficult, especially if there are intra-group conflicts over titles and responsibilities.[50] Clarity over the types of representation and criteria used to identify primary and secondary actors is crucial to ensure the CM success. And care must also be taken not to weaken or damage the traditional community organisations (such as Councils of Elders) that are often the last (and best) resort to represent the interests of communities and negotiate on their behalf.[51]

Many co-management organisations sooner or later find the need to invest time and resources in reforming policy and legal frameworks to ensure more equitable benefit sharing among the parties involved in co-management.[52] Similarly, innovations to promote more equitable benefit sharing need to be encouraged at the local level. A particularly good example of local level practice that evolved with equity in mind is described in Box 9.26. Working through their sanghams, women adapted social mapping and wealth ranking methods to decide on how to allocate food grains in the fairest possible way under a Public Distribution System they co-manage in south India.

---

49   See some examples in Boxes 5.15, 5.16 and 9.1.
50   Sullivan, 1997.
51   Experience shows that such entities can adapt themselves to modern challenges such as gender and equity concerns; attempts at "improving such systems" from the outside can backfire, however, if help is not offered with sensitivity and respect.
52   This point is explored in Part IV of this volume.

Box 9.26   Women design, manage and distribute the benefits of an alternative Public
Distribution System in Andhra Pradesh, India
(adapted from Satheesh and Pimbert, 1999)

Like elsewhere in India, a Public Distribution System (PDS) operates in the villages around Zaheerabad in Medak district of Andhra Pradesh. Every month each family having access to this system (about 50% of the rural population) can buy 25 Kg. of rice at a subsidised rate. Although this ration is the lifeline of poor rural families, the rice sold in the PDS is an alien grain for the women of Zaheerabad. They never grew rice on their dry lands. It was always sorghum, pearl, finger and other millets mixed with a wide range of pulses that made up the crops on their lands and the meals in their pots. With more and more PDS rice coming from the resource rich areas of South India, dry land farmers and their food crops were being gradually displaced. Their lands were being put to fallow and local biodiversity important for food and agriculture was eroded. The PDS rice was economically attractive but was nutritionally inferior to traditional coarse grains. Being reduced to consumers, dependent on purchased food for their own survival, undermined the women's self-esteem and self-respect as food providers and keepers of seed.

The women organised into sanghams– voluntary associations of Dalit women, the lowest social rank in the village– and discussed possible alternatives to the government's PDS. They decided to reclaim their fallow lands and grow their traditional dry land crops again. They aimed at setting up a completely community-managed PDS system based on coarse grains, locally produced, locally stored and locally distributed. Meetings were held in villages and the modalities of running an alternative PDS were worked out together with the Deccan Development Society (DDS), an NGO supporting the work of the sanghams. Formal agreements were signed between the DDS and the village sanghams to specify the roles, rights and obligations of each party in the joint management of the alternative PDS. Working through the DDS, the sanghams also approached the Government of India's Ministry of Rural Development, which saw the merit of their case and approved funding for a Community Grain Fund.

In the very first year, this jointly managed scheme involved over 30 villages, brought about 1,000 hectares of cultivable fallows and extremely marginal lands under the plough, produced over three million Kg. of extra sorghum (at the rate of about 100,000 Kg. per village) in a semi-arid area, grew extra fodder to support about 2,000 cattle; created an extra 7,500 wages and provided sorghum at 2 Rupees per Kg. for about 4,000 families. Grain storage took place in a decentralised fashion, using indigenous storage techniques that minimised pest damage and health hazards. Biological diversity significantly increased in the area as traditional crops and varieties were reintroduced as part of complex and diverse farming systems.

At the end of the storage period, during the food-scarcity seasons, the sanghams grains are sold at a subsidised price to poor households. The sanghams identify around 100 poor households in each village. Using participatory methods, the Dalit women decide who among the villagers are the poorest and qualify for community grain support. In each village, social maps indicating all the households are drawn on the ground by villagers themselves. Criteria for rural poverty are evolved by the villagers themselves and each household is judged on a five point scale of poverty. Each level is identified by a different colour (e.g., black=destitute, red=very poor, green=poor, etc.) and each house marked by a specific colour after careful deliberation in an open and transparent way. Households thus selected are issued a sorghum card by the sangham. Instead of the subsidised rice of the government PDS, which costs 3.50 Rupees per Kg., this card entitles a family to an amount of sorghum at the subsidised price of 2 Rupees per Kg. for each of the six months that make up the rainy season. The poorer the family, the larger their entitlement. In recognising each person's fundamental right to food, the sanghams thus put in practice their own concepts of equity and solidarity as they distribute the benefits of the co-managed Public Distribution System.

Part IV. TOWARDS AN ENABLING
SOCIAL CONTEXT

Chapter 10. NATURAL RESOURCE POLICY AND INSTRUMENTS

Environmental degradation and inequitable access to natural resources are, to a large extent, the result of political choices and processes and cannot be addressed without significant and durable changes in the distribution of power in society. Thus, making co-management "work" at the local level requires overcoming constraints on local conservation and development that have to do with the regional, national and international contexts and are shaped by a variety of forces, processes and instruments. Crucial determinants of such contexts are national legislation and policies.

Many would affirm that locally negotiated and implemented co-management agreements are likely to be ineffectual unless supported– or at least not impeded– by coherent legislation and policies. While this is generally true, it is also observed that co-management experiments generated in absence of supportive policies have demonstrated aliveness and effectiveness. Importantly, they have demonstrated a capacity to influence existing policy and to generate new and more appropriate ones. In this sense, even co-management experiments practiced on a small scale at the local level can serve as a vehicle for social change. They can, for instance, give a taste of empowerment to groups and communities that were previously marginalised. They can increase the accountability of organisations. They can build local capacity. And they can be motivating and inspiring for processes of decentralisation and democratisation at the national level.

Policy implies a purposeful course of action taken by social actors to address particular issues and advance towards specific objectives. Policy is a good part of what many organisations do. Policy involves process, in the form of policy making, implementing and reviewing, and it involves content, in the form of objectives, statements and instruments (Box 10.1).

Box 10.1   Policies defined

In the broadest sense of the term, policy can be defined as discourse, i.e. as an ensemble of norms, rules, views, ideas, concepts and values that govern practice and behaviour, and interpret social and environmental realities.[1] This suggests that the expressions and instruments of policy can be both formal and informal, and that the manner in which policy issues are discussed and framed in discourse is in itself significant.

Public policy refers specifically to the deliberations and directives of actions taken by governments of nation states, including local government agencies and institutions. By extension, public policy also refers to the deliberations and directives of action established and adopted by inter-governmental agencies and institutions, including international conventions. But policy is more than a set of goals and procedures. It encompasses instruments and processes such as mechanisms of resource allocation; institutional arrangements and procedures for public and non-governmental institutions; legal and regulatory frameworks applied by the state; and access, quality, efficiency, and relevance in the delivery of public services.[2]

Policy is not synonymous with public policy. Other actors such as medium and large scale businesses and transnational corporations have their own policies. This private sector policy can have a significant influence on environment and development. And policy is also made by indigenous peoples and local communities of fishing folks, peasants and farmers, nomadic pastoralists and hunters and gatherers. This "community policy" also affects natural resources and their use.

Importantly, public, private and community policy do not always shape, or effectively affect, outcomes, and the difference between rhetoric and reality should be always borne in mind.[3] In this respect, Barraclough and Ghimire[4] provide a useful typology for policies that do not deliver expected outcomes:

● policy failures (they fail to achieve what they were expected to achieve);

● policy perversities (they have unintended negative consequences);

● policy hypocrisies (they ostensibly have one objective but actually aim at other, even contrary, objectives); and

● policy absence (benign neglect results in negative social and environmental impacts).

Policy-making and implementation are inherently political processes, which define a society and reflect its fundamental values and structures. The process of policy-making (who makes policy and how it is made) determines and mirrors the functioning of that society. Policy-making is the privilege of the dictator in an autocratic society, while each and every citizen is expected to participate in policy making in the case of a utopian democratic society. Between these two extremes, there exists a diversity of systems of governance and policy making processes that are more or less participatory.

---

[1]   Keeley and Scoones,1999.
[2]   Norton, 1998.
[3]   Stiefel and Wolfe, 1994.
[4]   Barraclough and Ghimire, 1995.

CM-supportive
policy deals with
ecological
sustainability,
livelihoods,
democratic and
accountable
institutions, social
justice and equity in
the political and
economic arena.

Policies that create environments favourable to co-management seem to pursue three types of goals. The first goal is sustainability, seeking human activities and resource use patterns compatible with ecological sustainability. The second goal is equity, securing the rights of people and communities, enhancing social and economic benefits, and combating inequalities, such as the ones responsible for poverty and exclusion. The third goal is good governance, empowering civil society in decision-making and democratising government institutions and structures, and markets. Ideally, these goals should be pursued in an integrated and coherent fashion. In the real world, however, this is more the exception than the rule. Yet, co-management approaches can still be fostered and supported by limited and sectoral policies, such as policies that address only one of the above goals, or even just a sub-area within any one of these broad concerns, such as:

● building the capacities of any relevant actor in a variety of ecological and social aspects of natural resource management;

● promoting social communication initiatives and soliciting the active participation of disfavoured groups;

● facilitating equitable access to natural resources by recognising and preserving rights, securing tenure, or allocating entitlements through devolution mechanisms;

● managing resource use conflicts, and harmonising conservation with resource use and human development;

● optimising, securing and fairly sharing the social and economic benefits generated from the use of natural resources;

● strengthening the identity and culture of indigenous peoples and local communities, in particular regarding customary rights on natural resource management and conservation;

● fostering the appreciation of cultural diversity, in particular through different ways of satisfying human needs and managing natural resources respectful of customary laws and practices;

● strengthening inclusive democratic processes at various levels including for culturally sensitive issues and customary practices;

● placing limits on the concentration of economic power, both nationally and internationally, and promoting corporate and state responsibility;

● safeguarding local communities, institutions and economies against the negative impacts of unchecked globalisation.

It is thus clear that the policy instruments that are of relevance for co-management extend beyond the regulation of institutional partnerships or the "protection" of the environment. CM-supportive policy deals with ecological sustainability, livelihoods, democratic and accountable institutions, social justice and equity in the political and economic arena.

This chapter focuses on national and international policies that can facilitate and strengthen the co-management of natural resources at different scales. Rather than presenting a fixed menu of policy instruments, it describes a range of policy options and directions for national governments and other actors who seek to mainstream co-management. As democratic participation and citizen empowerment are increasingly proving to be crucial for the design of supportive co-management policies throughout the world, issues related to the process of policy formulation will be addressed in the subsequent, closing chapter.

10.1   Enabling policies at the national level

Co-management requires a policy environment that avoids and departs from extremist and simplified approaches to governance. Aware of the failures and inequities of state-dominated models, of the dangers of approaches that give supremacy to the market and its forces, and of the limitations of exclusive community authority and action, advocates of co-management see the benefits of approaches that recognise the strengths and weaknesses of various social actors and institutions. The ideological foundation of co-management is one that places people unambiguously at the centre of the development process, but it is also one that understands that the state, the market and civil society— including local communities, NGOs and individuals— all have a positive role to play in that process.

Ideally, formal policy frameworks would stem from a broadly shared national vision and provide guidance and direction for the sound governance of natural resources. These frameworks should be the products of internally driven participatory processes that generate broad-based commitment and ownership. In an ideal policy environment, such laws and policy instruments would derive from, and be consistent with, a national vision of development, society and environment. In many parts of the world, however, and especially in the South, environment and development policies are directly influenced by external agencies. For instance, the most explicit statements of public policy on issues and sectors relevant to co-management can be found in such instruments as the World Bank-sponsored National Environmental Action Plans (NEAP) and Poverty Reduction Strategy Papers (PRSP), some country strategy papers assisted by bi-lateral and multi-lateral agencies, or policy statements developed in accordance with the provisions of international conventions (e.g. National Biodiversity Strategies and Action Plans). This pattern of external influence can put into question the ownership of policy statements and of the measures they contain. Also noticeable is the case of external agencies actively colluding with national elites and commercial interests to promote the interests of powerful actors.[5] In general, co-management arrangements are best established in a political context that respects basic freedoms and provides for the rule of law. In the absence of such a context, the promotion of co-management may frankly prove unrealistic (see Box 10.2).

> **Box 10.2** Co-management of forests and protected areas in Haiti
>   (adapted from Renard, 2002)
>
> Between 1996 and 2001, the World Bank and the Government of Haiti implemented a project called Projet d'Appui Technique à la Protection des Parcs et Forêts, which aimed at conserving and managing the last remaining forests of this impoverished Caribbean country. The project had a number of compo-

---

[5]   Hancock, 1991; Sogge, 2002.

nents, including capacity-building and institutional strengthening for government agencies and civil society organisations, promotion of social and economic development activities within and around forests and protected areas, preparation of management plans for individual protected areas, and establishment of co-management institutions and agreements at the local level.

This project was designed and initiated at a time when the political situation in Haiti presented signs of hope. A new President of the Republic had been elected with overwhelming popular support, a relatively stable government was in place, and critical policy reforms were being initiated. This project was part of a broader vision based on the restoration of democracy and the protection of the basic rights of citizens, the improvement of governance through decentralisation and community empowerment, and the reduction of poverty through economic diversification, social protection and improved environmental management.

Co-management of forests and protected areas fitted well in this vision. Through co-management arrangements, this project aimed at strengthening local authority and responsibility over the management of critical natural assets, at giving a prominent role to community organisations, at promoting sustainable use of resources, and at protecting the last remaining areas of forests, in a country renowned for its extreme poverty, and for the extent of its deforestation and overall environmental degradation.

While the project had a number of positive impacts before being interrupted in 2001, as a result of the sanctions imposed on Haiti by the international community, it was not able to achieve its objectives of establishing viable co-management agreements. Specifically, three factors militated against the achievement of these objectives: (a) the state and its civil society partners remained unable to protect citizens and community organisations against corruption and against political and economic violence imposed by powerful interests (the "rules of the game" that prevailed on the ground remained basically unchanged), (b) people did not trust government agencies and officials, and were not prepared to collaborate with them in matters of importance to their livelihoods and survival, and (c) the state and its agencies remained unwilling to delegate formal authority to non-governmental and community partners.

In many respects, it was futile to attempt to establish co-management institutions in a country where basic human rights were not respected, state institutions were largely perceived as corrupt and unreliable, and community empowerment was bound to be perceived as a threat to dominant groups and interests within and outside government.

Constitution and basic civil law

The first and most fundamental expression of public policy in any country is found in its national constitution. Some constitutions directly and explicitly facilitate co-management as they fully and straightforwardly recognise the right of peoples, citizens and civil society in general to participate in decision-making processes and in the governance of national and local institutions. Some constitutions also recognise the rights of communities and indigenous peoples as collective bodies (collective versus individual rights). In Argentina, for example, the constitution stipulates that Congress has the power to recognise the legal status of indigenous peoples and of community property rights over their traditional lands. In Colombia, the constitution states that the law guarantees the participation of communities in the decisions that may affect them. In the Czech Republic, the constitution includes protection for national and ethnic minorities, guaranteeing rights to development, culture, language diversity, participation and association. The constitution of Ecuador is, in many ways, remarkably progressive in its recognition of the collective rights of indigenous peoples (Box 10.3). Recent constitutional amendments in India are also leading to empowered forms of local direct participation (Box 10.4).

Box 10.3   Extracts from the Constitution of Ecuador

Article 84. In accordance with the Constitution and with the law, respect for public order, and human rights, the state shall recognise and guarantee to indigenous peoples the following collective rights:

1. To maintain, develop and strengthen their spiritual, cultural, linguistic, social, political and economic identity and traditions.

2. To protect the imprescriptible ownership of community lands, which may not be alienated, confiscated or broken up, except by the state with its power to declare public utility. These lands will be exempt from payment of property tax.

3. To maintain ancestral ownership of community lands, which will be freely awarded in accordance with the law.

4. To participate in the use, usufruct, administration and conservation of renewable natural resources found on their lands.

5. To be consulted about any plans and programmes to prospect and exploit non-renewable resources found on their lands which may have an environmental or cultural impact on them. To share in the benefits accrued by these projects wherever possible, and to receive compensation for any social or environmental damage they may cause.

6. To conserve and promote their biodiversity and natural environment management practices.

7. To conserve and develop traditional ways of life, social organisation, and creation and exercising of authority.

8. As a people, not to be displaced from their land.

9. To have collective intellectual property rights over their ancestral knowledge, and to the valuation, use and development of these intellectual property rights according to the law.

10. To maintain, develop and administer their cultural and historical heritage.

11. To access quality education, and to an intercultural and bilingual education system.

12. To their traditional medical systems, knowledge and practices. This includes the right to protection of ritual and sacred sites, plants, animals, minerals and ecosystems of vital interest with regard to traditional medicine.

13. To decide on and prioritise plans and projects for the development and improvement of economic and social conditions, with adequate funding from the state.

14. To participate, through representatives, in official bodies determined by law.

15. To use symbols and emblems which identify them.

> **Box 10.4** Constitutional amendments encourage more devolution and subsidiarity in India
> (adapted from McGee et al., 2003)
>
> India's 73rd and 74th Constitutional Amendments gave local governments (the panchayati raj system) the task of planning for economic development and social justice. In theory this process begins with the gram sabha (village assembly) at the village level, though this varies in practice across states. In the state of Madhya Pradesh, a new law was passed in 2001 that virtually transferred all powers concerning local development to the village assemblies, including powers related to village development, budgeting, levying taxes, agriculture, natural resource management, village security, infrastructure, education and social justice. In Kerala, as part of the People's Planning Campaign, local governments received 40% of the state budget allocation for local services. Grassroots planning processes were carried out in thousands of villages and later approved by direct vote in popular village assemblies.

One of the crucial ways in which constitutions and basic laws provide backing to co-management is by recognising communities as legal entities.

While some inspiring examples exist, in many countries the constitution and the basic civil laws fail to recognise community rights over natural resources. Some important elements of legislation (e.g. civil code, rural code, and pastoral code) often do not even recognise indigenous and local communities as legal entities (according to some legislation only individuals, businesses and the state "exist") and they cannot accommodate collective rights and responsibilities. Rarely is there a simple and effective legal status for communities willing to manage and conserve natural resources. Even rarer is a legal status that allows local communities not only to manage their customary common property resources, but also to derive an economic profit from it.

One of the crucial ways in which constitutions and basic laws provide backing to co-management is by recognising communities as legal entities, by allowing the devolution of natural resource management authority and responsibilities at the

lowest effective level (in application of the principle of subsidiarity– see Chapter 4) and by upholding a broader culture and system of participatory policy-making and governance. When such provisions are enshrined in the national constitution, they have the potential[6] to inform and influence all policies and plans.

Natural resource management policy

Policies on natural resource management are crucially important in directing who will manage natural resources and how, and who will benefit from that management. They do so at the national level but also at the sub-national (regional) and local levels. Particularly significant in this sense are policies that decentralise, delegate, devolve and secure control over natural resources, as well as policies that reconcile protection and use.

---

[6] It is not automatic that legal provisions are implemented, especially when they involve sensitive concerns to states.

Some countries do not have formal public policy statements that govern social development and natural resource management. In these situations, co-management can rarely take place on a large scale. In other countries policy statements exist but are narrow and fail to provide a comprehensive framework to integrate and harmonise different sectoral policies. In too many cases, policy-making on environmental issues and natural resource management comes in response to a crisis or to external influences, not as a result of endogenous processes of analysis and decision-making. In addition, laws are not always guided by, or derived from, clear objectives. Therefore there is often an unmet need for a comprehensive framework of formal policy in the field of natural resource management. Such a framework would include:

● National Strategies for Sustainable Development (NSSD): all countries of the world are now committed, since the World Summit on Sustainable Development (WSSD) held in South Africa in 2003, to the formulation of such national strategies. Whatever the title used (e.g. National Strategy for Sustainable Development, National Development Plan, and National Development Strategy), the heart of such statements should ensure that national development is guided by strategic directions and instruments that include concerns for sustainability, provide adequate policy direction for natural resource governance and management, and define a suitable framework for integrated development planning.[7]

● National Biodiversity Strategies and Action Plans (NBSAP): these instruments have been or are currently being developed by most countries of the world, in accordance with the provisions of the Convention on Biological Diversity (CBD). They provide an excellent opportunity for nations to express formally their commitment to participatory governance and co-management, and to put in place the specific policies and instruments required to realise this commitment (see Box 10.5).

Box 10.5   The National Biodiversity Strategy and Action Plan (NBSAP), India
(adapted from Kohli and Kothari, 2003)

From 2000 to 2004, the Government of India, through its Ministry of Environment and Forests, has been involved in the formulation of a National Biodiversity Strategy and Action Plan (NBSAP). This has been the result of a broad process that involved a number of studies and reviews and dozens of strategies and action plans prepared at local, state, eco-regional and thematic levels. This process has been participatory and decentralised, involving a wide range of actors in the analysis of data, issues and options, and in the formulation of policy recommendations and specific instruments. Its coordination has been carried out by the NGO Kalpavriksh.

One of the basic goals of the draft NBSAP is "equity in the conservation and use of biodiversity, including equitable access to biodiversity and control over decision-making about it, as well as equitable distribution of the costs and benefits associated with its conservation and sustainable use". In particular, that includes "creating democratic spaces for the voices of dis-privileged women and men in defining conservation and use priorities." The measures provided by the draft NBSAP include "community tenure rights, in particular the rights of women, children and other dis-privileged sections within them", as well as "balancing local, national and international interests".

Specific provisions of the draft NBSAP include the strengthening or revival of customary governance

---

7   Dalal-Clayton and Bass, 2002

structure, the documentation, encouragement and integration of customary law into statutory laws, and a reconciliation of "the contradictions between the laws of conservation, on the one hand, and those relating to decentralisation and social justice, on the other". In the mechanisms for implementation of the recommendations of the draft NBSAP, specific provisions are being made to facilitate and strengthen co-management and community-based arrangements.

● National Action Programmes (NAP) for Combating Desertification: this is another national obligation under international law– the UN Convention to Combat Desertification (UNCCD). Many countries have already prepared their NAP[8] which is meant to incorporate public and community participation in resource management. Very interesting pilot initiatives have been included in some of these national plans.

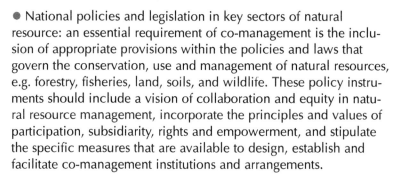

● National policies and legislation in key sectors of natural resource: an essential requirement of co-management is the inclusion of appropriate provisions within the policies and laws that govern the conservation, use and management of natural resources, e.g. forestry, fisheries, land, soils, and wildlife. These policy instruments should include a vision of collaboration and equity in natural resource management, incorporate the principles and values of participation, subsidiarity, rights and empowerment, and stipulate the specific measures that are available to design, establish and facilitate co-management institutions and arrangements.

● National protected area legislation and policies: in addition to their national policies in key sectors, many countries have formulated and adopted development plans and programmes to govern the establishment and management of national systems of protected areas. These plans and programmes are usually supported by national legislation, which should incorporate the principles and instruments of co-management, including specific provisions for shared and delegated management authority (Box 10.6).

Box 10.6   Reforming national protected area systems
            (adapted from Ghimire and Pimbert, 1997)

In many cases, a review of national PA category systems and classifications may be a logical and necessary step to bring new strength and coherence to a national conservation policy. For instance, existing protected areas under co-management with indigenous peoples and local communities may still be classified in categories incompatible with current uses and situations. Often, National Parks fit to be managed as protected areas under IUCN Category V or VI are run by legislation that forbids all human presence and NR uses and impedes all sorts of co-management agreements. It is therefore important to dispose at the national level of a comprehensive range of categories and governance types that fully reflect the varying degrees and forms of human use and intervention on the environment.[9] This is slowly being recognised also in international documents.[10]

Examples of co-management of natural resources and protected areas inscribed in national policy and legislation include:

Marine protected areas legislation in Tanzania
National legislation defines the rules under which participatory management of

---

8   www.unccd.int/actionprogrammes/menu.phb
9   Borrini-Feyerabend, 2004.
10 For instance see the UN List of Protected Areas (2003).

natural resources can take place. The case of the Tanzania Marine Park and Reserves Act of 1994 is a good example. Several local initiatives were started for the co-management of coastal areas, and local government authorities established by-laws and regulations to legalise these activities. It soon became apparent that the national legislation on marine parks and reserves was deficient, and did not formally allow for participatory management processes involving the Division of Fisheries and Village Councils.[11] A new legislation was thus drafted and ratified in 1994 to define the rules for the involvement of village councils in the participatory management of marine parks and reserves. The new national legislation provides an adequate statutory framework for local initiatives to be fully incorporated into national policy, and for village-based resource management systems to be formally recognised as a legal option.

The National Conservation Strategy of Pakistan

Pakistan's National Conservation Strategy, which was ratified in 1994, emphasises public involvement in the management of natural resources and of protected areas in particular. Under its umbrella, provincial and territorial governments embarked in developing regional conservation strategies. The Sarhad Provincial Conservation Strategy[12] includes specific guidelines for the involvement of communities in co-managing protected areas, such as the need to set up a co-management structure where local communities are to be directly represented, as well as specific mechanisms to facilitate their participation, protect their cultural identity, effectively share information and to distribute fairly the benefits deriving from each specific protected area.

Provisions for devolution of protected area management in El Salvador

In El Salvador, the National Park Service has issued a policy document stipulating the official procedures for NGOs and CBOs interested in joint management of protected areas. The relevant agreements take the form of a memorandum of understanding between El Salvador's Park Service and the organisation requesting to co-manage a protected area. A series of requisites are established for an organisation to qualify, such as possessing legal status, and having administrative capacity and prior experience in managing protected areas. Once the organisation qualifies, the Park Service requires it to submit an operational plan, which details the objectives and goals as well as the activities designed to meet them. As in many other instances, the state reserves the right to revoke the agreement that, as a memorandum of understanding, has clear time limits and evaluation periods. If the organisation complies with the requirements and is successfully evaluated, the participatory management of the protected area can continue over longer periods of time.

Civil society management of protected areas in Lebanon

In Lebanon, important conservation initiatives emerged in the 1980s, when there was no effective national government and the country was under Israeli occupation. The initiatives were developed endogenously– one could even say spontaneously– by civil society groups, at times based on progressive religious leadership by Druze and other Moslem groups and Christians, who "declared" and managed a number of protected areas. When Israel was forced to withdraw from Lebanon and a legitimate government was established, it allowed the civil society groups and NGOs that had established the protected areas to continue to manage them, now under the authority of the government and under contract with the Ministry of the Environment. Up to today this arrangement continues more or less

11   Magnus Ngoile, personal communication, 1996.
12   GONWFP and IUCN Pakistan, 1996; Oli, 1998. See also Box 5.14 in Chapter 5.

unchanged in all 9 protected areas of the country, including marine and coastal zones. Yet, states have by nature a monopolistic tendency and the conditions for the management of protected areas are getting tighter for the NGOs– despite their excellent results and their proven capacity to engage local communities and other stakeholders. Unfortunately, the co-management setting of Lebanese protected areas appears in jeopardy.

Joint Forest Management in India

On 1 June 1990, a Joint Forest Management (JFM) programme was officially launched in more than 14 states of India, largely in response to the fast deterioration and uncontrolled exploitation of their forests. The goal of the programme was "to secure the willing cooperation of the people through their active participation for the conservation and development of forests on a sustainable basis".[13] Through co-management agreements, local forest protection committees received the formal authority to control forest resource uses. In the best cases, the agreements have managed to define a fair share of the rights and responsibilities of local user groups and the forest department, and have led to impressive forest regeneration.[14] In other cases, complex controversies related to equity and real versus token participation in forest management decisions have arisen leading to the failure of several local attempts.[15] In 2002, nearly 64,000 Forest Protection Committees were registered in 27 Indian states.[16] Similarly in Nepal, over 3,400 forest user groups have been formed that currently manage 2000 community forests. These legally registered groups work with government forestry staff to develop a five year operational plan. Upon approval of the plan, conditional management rights are handed over to the user groups. The operational plan spells out the rights and obligations of the parties involved in the forest management agreement.[17]

> ...through co-management agreements, local forest protection committees receive the formal authority to control forest resources uses....

Provisions for claiming land and resource rights in Canada

Under the Federal Government Policy of Canada, a comprehensive claim process enables the negotiation and recognition of indigenous rights and interests in areas where earlier treaties did not involve the surrendering of aboriginal titles. Comprehensive claims processes involve negotiations over indigenous peoples' claims to land and resource management, determination of development strategies and indigenous self-government. Claimant groups can secure title to lands covered by the settlement, wildlife harvesting rights, participation in land, water, wildlife and environmental management in the settlement area, financial compensations, revenue-sharing rights, access to measures to stimulate economic development, and a role in the management of heritage resources (Box 10.7). Agreements are protected under the Canadian Constitution and cannot be amended without the concurrence of the claimant group.[18] The comprehensive claims have evolved over time. In 1984, they mostly dealt with rights to harvest wildlife, harvesting methods, native employment in the parks, business considerations and the like.[19] More recently, the boards established under land claim settlements have gained more encompassing and authoritative roles.[20]

> ...legal agreements at the national level offer enabling frameworks for the co-management of natural resources.

---

[13] Palit, 1995.

[14] Poffenberger, 1994.

[15] Sarin, 2003.

[16] RUPFOR. 2002; see also http://envfor.delhi.nic.in/divisions/forprt/jfm/html/eval.htm

[17] McDermott, 1996.

[18] Siddons, 1993.

[19] Kovacs, 1984.

[20] Morrison, 1997. The first modern comprehensive claims treaty in Canada was the James Bay and Northern Quebec Agreement of 1975. It set the precedent for co-management provisions in the subsequent agreements in British Columbia, Yukon, the North West Territories and others. See also Richardson, Craig and Boer, 1994a; Richardson, Craig and Boer, 1994b.

Box 10.7   The Inuvialuit Agreements in the North West Territories of Canada
            (adapted from Government of Canada, 1993)

The Western Arctic Claim Settlement gives the Inuvialuit priority in the harvest of marine mammals in
the settlement region, including first access to all harvestable resources. This means that the Inuvialuit
have the right to harvest a subsistence quota of marine mammals, to be set jointly by them and the government. The Inuvialuit also have a preferential right to harvest fish for subsistence within the settlement
region; this includes trade, barter and sale to other Inuvialuit. Subject only to restrictions imposed by
quotas each year, Inuvialuit are issued non-transferable commercial licenses to harvest a total weight of
fish equal to the largest annual commercial harvest of that species taken by Inuvialuit from those waters
over the preceding three years. Access to commercial harvests above that level is granted on the same
basis to Inuvialuit as to other applicants.

In the Yukon Final Agreement, signed in 1993, self-government arrangements and special management
areas have been negotiated and included in the comprehensive claims settlement for that area. Each of
the four First Nations can exercise law-making powers over land-management, hunting, fishing, trapping and fishing, and business regulation. A new national park, a special management area and a
national wildlife area have also been created. The Vuntut National Park is encompassed within the special management area, much of which will be owned by the Vuntut Gwitchin people, who also retain
harvesting rights. Renewable Resource Councils are established with First Nation representation, and
representation is granted on a range of other land and resource management bodies.[21] The National
Wildlife Area is a jointly managed waterfowl habitat.

Fisheries management in Vietnam
In Vietnam, the Government has developed a Master Plan for Fisheries (1997-
2010). This plan is particularly relevant to the development of coastal and marine
protected areas as it emphasises user rights over resources, addresses policy for
marine capture fisheries, and promotes the need to adopt and implement more
effective conservation measures. The plan emphasises accelerating the process of
establishing a rational system for the exploitation and use of the country's natural
marine resources and habitats, including the introduction of management systems
and structures aimed at supporting resource and habitat protection while recognising the need for an equitable allocation of resource use rights and obligations of
the people and coastal communities. Within this policy framework, both fishery
co-management and marine protected areas find their complementary places.[22]

Fisheries legislation for co-management in the Eastern Caribbean
In the 1980s, all countries that are members of the Organisation of Eastern
Caribbean States participated in a review of their fisheries legislation that resulted
in the inclusion of a provision for the establishment of Local Fisheries
Management Areas. It is this provision that was followed in Saint Lucia to establish the Soufriere Marine Management Area (see Box 3.9 in Chapter 3) and thus
provided the institutional basis for its co-management regime. In the absence of
this provision, the Soufriere Marine Management Area may not have been able to
realise the positive results that it has obtained over the past few years.

Policies for multi-stakeholder boards for protected areas in the Philippines
In the Philippines, new policies and legal instruments provide for local representation on multi-stakeholder protected area management boards. These
boards comprise representatives of national and local governmental agencies,

---

21   Such as the Yukon Water Board, Development Assessment Board, Surface Rights Board, and the Territorial Fish and Wildlife Management
      Board.
22   Vo, 2001.

non-governmental organisations, indigenous peoples and other local cultural communities. They have primary responsibility for protected area management and they call for the participation of community and other civil society actors. With increased capacity-building for community and indigenous people's representatives, some of these boards have become models of participation in protected area management.[23] When combined with the respect of the principle of Prior Informed Consent these policy shifts potentially allow local communities to actively shape protected area policies.[24]

Enabling legislation for local fisheries management in Turkey
The small-scale fishery in Alanya, on the Mediterranean coast of Turkey, is located on the edge of a deep basin, and the inshore zone for setting nets is very limited. The fishers have organised among themselves a system of rotating fishing areas so that each fisher receives equitable access to the more productive fishing spots. There are some 40 named fishing spots in Alanya's trammel net fishery, which takes place between September and May. The overall system of access rights and rules for taking turns is quite complicated but, starting in the 1980s, it has reduced conflict among fishers. Fishery management in Turkey is centralised. There are no local government jurisdictions or local village jurisdictions over fishing, as for example one finds in Japanese coastal fisheries. This created a dilemma for the fishers in Alanya: how to provide legitimacy for the system they designed? They decided to draw legitimacy by using the Aquatic Resources Act as enabling legislation. The Act states that local co-operatives have jurisdiction over "local arrangements". Thus the rules were drawn up under the letterhead of the local fisheries co-operative, endorsed by the fishers at the coffee house where they were formulated, and copies were deposited with the local mayor and police.[25]

Forest policy for co-management in Nepal
As Nepal emerged from a feudal regime during the early 1950s, the incipient state established a basic forest policy. Initially, this policy distinguished three categories of forests, including "community forests" meant to satisfy community needs. Their management and protection was entrusted to village Panchayats. This policy remained on paper and was not truly implemented until the late 1970s. During these two decades, Nepal's forest policy followed the Western model, by which forest ownership was vested in the state and management authority placed in the hands of the Forest Department. The forests were nationalised in 1957, actually not– as many have erroneously remarked– to take them away from the communities, but rather to break the feudal tenure arrangements by which three quarters of the forests and agricultural lands in the country were held by a single family. After nationalisation, the Forest Department was responsible for performing all policing and licensing functions, a nearly impossible task in light of its limited staff capacity. The Forest Act of 1961 provided the first legislation that contemplated transferring government forest lands to village Panchayats for community use. Unfortunately, these legal provisions were never implemented, and the issue was not addressed until 15 years later. Meanwhile, the Forest Preservation Act of 1967 strengthened the role of the Forest Department as policy and law-enforcement agency. A Forestry Plan was established in 1976, including provisions for creating Panchayat Forests to benefit local communities. Finally, in 1978, specific rules

[23] Worah, 2002.
[24] See, however, Ferrari and De Vera, 2003. See also Box 10.16.
[25] Berkes, 1992.

and regulations governing the transfer of limited areas of state forests to the Panchayats were enacted. Formal recognition had thus been given to the rights of villagers to manage their own forest resources with provisions for technical assistance by the Forest Department, as necessary. In 1990, the Government of Nepal stressed its engagement about community forestry by inscribing it as a key component in its major master plan for the forestry sector. This included provisions for:

- handing over of all the accessible hill forests to the communities to the extent that they are able and willing to manage them;

- entrusting the users with the task of protecting and managing the forests, with the users receiving all of the income;

- re-training the entire staff of the Ministry of Forests and Soil Conservation to enable them to perform their new role as advisers and extension workers.

Investigations in forest management have shown conclusively that a great many village communities have been managing their forest resources effectively, creating institutional arrangements to ensure the basic protection of hill forests and the enforcement of access and use rights. Many of these local management systems evolved over the past 35 years, and proved more effective than management by the Forest Department, which had been plagued by constant budget and staff cuts.[26]

Despite the diversity of situations, one broad general lesson emerges from working with natural resource policies throughout the world. While it is essential to establish an appropriate policy and legislative framework at the national level, the purpose of such frameworks is to provide an adequate policy environment, not to impose specific and rigid systems and models of co-management on the ground. Appropriate legislation allows a measure of flexibility in its interpretation and some site-level decision-making to fit at best the specificities of different contexts. It is therefore important to remain aware of the distinction between the CM provisions that more appropriately belong to national law and those that more appropriately belong to specific management agreements, as proposed in Box 10.8.

...through co-management agreements, local forest protection committees receive the formal authority to control forest resources uses....

---

[26] Gilmour and Fisher, 1991; Kothari et al., 1997.

Box 10.8 Provisions made in national legislation and specific co-management agreements	
Provisions normally made in national legislation	**Provisions normally contained in specific co-management agreements**
● Authority and process in favour of local stakeholders to govern the negotiation and allocation of rights and responsibilities ● Mechanism for participatory monitoring, evaluation, reporting, arbitration and dispute resolution ● Guaranteeing the respect of the rights of "rightholders", most especially indigenous peoples (including mobile indigenous peoples), tribal and local communities ● Delegation of authority to local rights– and stake-holders for enforcement ● Delegation of authority to local rightholders for revenue generation ● General conditions for termination of contractual agreements	● Purpose and scope of the agreement ● Specific allocation of rights, responsibilities and resources among co-management partners ● Duration of the agreement ● Termination and amendment procedures ● Transparency and accountability ● Specific benefits ● Specific conditions for termination of contractual agreements

Decentralisation, delegation and devolution policies

Co-management is almost synonymous with local governance, because it requires local power and capacity to exist and succeed, but also because it is, by its very nature, an instrument of local empowerment. The institutional landscape of local governance is complex and varies greatly from country to country. In most respects, local governance is much more than local government; it encompasses a wide range of organisations and institutions, both formal and informal, all of whom have a role to play in the allocation and use of rights and responsibilities at the local level. Local partners in co-management processes and agreements can be of various types, and policies are required to facilitate their participation in management.

> The principle of "subsidiarity" calls for a government to decentralise, delegate or devolve authority and responsibilities to the lowest possible level with capacity to take responsibility for the relevant tasks.

An important innovation for the sustainable management of natural resources is a component of broader policy principles that goes under the name of "subsidiarity". Basically, this calls for a government to decentralise, delegate or devolve authority and responsibilities in several branches of social life to the lowest possible level with capacity to take responsibility for the relevant tasks (see Boxes 10.9 and 10.10). The subsidiarity principle has been re-affirmed by several national and international documents and agreements (see also Chapter 4).[27] Devolving rights and responsibilities in natural resource management, enhancing local autonomy in defining landscapes and seascapes, managing natural resources and planning and implementing development and conservation initiatives are powerful means to awaken the capacities of civil society (see Checklist 10.1 and Box 10.11).

---

27   See for example the basic principles of the ecosystem approach adopted by the Convention on Biological Diversity (CBD): www.biodiv.org, and reported in Box 10.22.

Box 10.9   More perspectives on decentralisation and devolution

As already mentioned in Box 4.1, the words "decentralisation"and "devolution"are sometimes used inter-changeably. Yet, they connote very different processes.

The term decentralisation is used to refer to the physical dispersal of operations to the local level, but also to describe the delegation of a greater degree of decision making authority to lower levels of government administration. Decentralisation thus refers to the distribution of functions and powers from a central authority to regional or local authorities, but the latter are essentially part of the same structure as the central authority. A federal structure with strong provincial control, for instance, is more decentralised than one that is solely controlled by the central government.

Devolution is more radical, involving the transfer of authority and control from one agency to a completely different one, usually more "local" and of a different origin. Effective devolution is as yet rare in the world, for the simple reason that those in power do not want to give it up, or do not believe that local institutions can perform! Even governments willing to devolve the rights to manage and use local resources, tend to retain conflict management functions, budgetary controls, and other functions that keep the local institutions effectively under their control.[28]

Checklist 10.1   Devolving to whom? What kind of organisations can manage common property resources?
(adapted from Shackleton et al., 2002)

A recent compilation and analysis of case studies of natural resource governance examined experiences in three Asian and eight southern African countries and from those derived the following typology of organisations found to exercise local authority over common property resources:

● District organisations. These included local government organisations such as Rural District Councils in Zimbabwe and Panchayats in India, and multi-stakeholder district structures aligned to line departments such as Wildlife Management Authorities in Zambia and forest farms in China.

● Village committees. These are typically initiated and encouraged by government agencies, e.g. the Village Natural Resource Management Committees in Malawi and Forest Protection Committees in India.

● Corporate, legal organisations. These are composed of all rightholders and/ or residents, as Trusts (Botswana), Conservancies (Namibia), Communal Property Associations, Villages and Range Management Associations.

● Households and individuals. In these cases, households and individuals are found to exercise varying degrees of authority over species selection, wildlife harvesting practices, sale and consumption, and the distribution of benefits.

● Indigenous and traditional rule-making institutions. These are largely self-initiated organisations that operate outside the state hierarchy, and include traditional leaders, resident associations and shareholding schemes. Examples include the Councils of Elders in the Solomon Islands or the traditional adat village governance institutions in Sumatra that have re-emerged after the New Order period. Throughout the world, such traditional organisations still play important roles in natural resource management and represent local voices to external agencies.[29]

While the specific policies and arrangements for local governance vary greatly between countries and regions depending on social and political history and conditions, many co-management bodies include representatives of local government

---

28   Parodi, 1971; Burns et al., 1994.
29   Esman and Uphoff, 1984.

structures (see some examples in Box 10.11). Local administrators and government agencies are important actors in co-management for a number of reasons, including the following:

- local administrators should be elected bodies and thus provide a measure of local representation;

- local government agencies are expected, at least in theory, to provide a measure of public accountability;

- local government agencies are also expected to advance "fair rules" in institutional arrangements.

Yet, we should refrain from assuming that local administrators and agencies always and effectively represent the interests and concerns of their local constituencies. On the contrary! In situations where the electoral process has been recently introduced, is poorly understood, unfairly practiced and/ or limited to making a choice among candidates who have little to do with the local environment, the experience is not flattering for local governments as natural resource managers. Customary NRM bodies or even local civil society organisations would have much better chances to succeed. As a matter of fact, it is good to promote the involvement of both local governmental agencies and traditional authorities in co-management bodies, to introduce a good measure of transparency and to promote local communication and mutual learning.

Box 10.10 Examples of government decentralisation policies

With the overthrow of long-time dictator Moussa Traore in Mali, a new constitution was framed, providing for the empowerment of local communities. A process of widespread consultation with various sectors of the population resulted in the demand to grant land tenure and resource management rights to local communities. In 1992, these demands were included in a rural development policy, and in 1993, a law on decentralisation was passed, granting to the local Communes sizeable independent administrative powers, including the right to manage the resources in their territories. The state retained overall tutelage, i.e. the right to intervene to enforce the law and public interest. Benjaminsen[30] refers to this setup, in which governments delegate considerable responsibility and powers to manage local resources, while providing the policies, laws, and technical support, as "the core of co-management". Yet, some have been doubtful about the real reasons behind this policy and its sustainability, as it was at least partly a result of the urging of the World Bank and International Monetary Fund, whose structural adjustment model requires loosening of governmental controls.

In India, two constitutional amendments of far-reaching consequence have been adopted in 1992, one granting village bodies (Panchayats) several powers, and the other doing the same for municipal bodies. A follow-up law in 1996 has extended considerable autonomy to tribal areas, though not the self-rule that some of the tribal movements have been asking for. Later, however, state governments provided their own interpretations, usually highly watered down, to these changed constitutional provisions. When it comes to actual implementation, a considerable control seems to remain with centralised bureaucracies and politicians, unless grassroots movements force actual devolution.

In Uganda, the deposing of Dictator Idi Amin in 1979 marked the beginnings of a hesitant move towards democracy. But it was not until the National Resistance Movement (NRM) took over in 1986 that extensive decentralisation of political functioning started. Through constitutional changes and new legislation (such as the Local Councils Statute, the Local Governments Act, and a new Constitution in 1995), greater power to decide about natural resources has been granted to parishes and other local-level bodies.

---

[30] Benjaminsen, 1995.

Policies that support the organisation of civil society

Partnerships with civil society necessarily demand that civil society be organised, which requires some form of legal or policy basis for:

- the constitution, registration and operation of groups and organisations;

- the ability of these organisations to generate, manage and invest funds;

- the possibility to vest authority for the management of publicly-owned assets, including natural resources, to these organisations;

- the involvement of these organisations in specific management activities and programmes, including planning, monitoring and research, information management, enforcement and sustainable resource use;

- the provision of technical and capacity-building support by state agencies to these organisations;

- the facilitation of networking and communication among civil society organisations, as a mechanism for organisational strengthening, capacity-building and advocacy.

While local administrators and government agencies are important actors in co-management, one cannot automatically assume that they effectively represent the interests and concerns of their local constituencies.

Research carried out in nineteen countries by a global network of civil society organisations and research institutes has identified legal frameworks that have the potential of enabling and strengthening civil society.[31] While the legal frameworks are not sufficient by themselves, they can provide an enabling context. Such enabling legislation will often need to be combined, in mutually supporting ways, with reforms in economic and fiscal measures to regenerate local livelihood assets (natural, financial, physical, human and social) and create safe spaces to express interests and concerns and discuss options for action.[32]

Policies that strengthen cultural identity and customary governance systems

Cultural strength and integrity generate credible institutions, which perform their governance duties, including negotiating and enforcing resource use regulations, with confidence and public support. This is true for a wide range of contexts, but particularly so for indigenous peoples and many rural communities, for whom cultural identity, a living native language and collective practices help conserve a shared body of traditional ecological knowledge. Many co-management processes are thus smoothed and made more sustainable when all or some of the involved parties are bonded by a strong shared culture.

Policies and legislation in support of co-management of natural resources can take advantage of this, and build upon cultural identity and customary governance systems. This requires, most of all, a sizeable measure of flexibility, necessary to accommo-

---

31 For more information see www.ids.ac.uk/logolink. The LogoLink web pages contain a number of resources on ways to help civil society to organise, including recent research on legal frameworks for citizen participation, participatory planning, and participation in local budgets and resource decisions.
32 See Banuri and Najam, 2002. This is further discussed later in this Chapter and in Chapter 11.

date for the complexity of ethnic governance systems. Ethnic governance usually includes a body of norms (e.g., customary law and practice), procedures (e.g., decisional processes, conflict management and dispute settlement), specific knowledge, and individuals playing specific roles (often the traditional leaders). In ethnic governance, land and resource tenure are normally ascribed at the same time to several actors, which include households, extended families, villages, lineages, clans, etc. Overlapping claims are recognised on a same territory, defining different types of rights and specific rules (norms on circulation of people and access to resources, decisional councils, rituals, myths, etc.) that ensure livelihoods.[33] Conflicts are generally solved by local traditional authorities. When traditional authorities have lost the capacity to maintain the respect of rules (at times because they have been officially disempowered and "dismantled") conflicting claims on the same land and resources may generate open clashes among local communities and the state, private developers and migrants. Aware of this, some countries are reversing past policies and slowly recognising traditional institutions for natural resource management as potential powerful allies (see Box 10.11).

Box 10.11 Back to the marga? Reversing destructive forestry policies in Sumatra (Indonesia) (adapted from Brechin et al., 2003)

In the early 1980s the central government of Indonesia decided to outright replace the traditional local authorities (the clan-based margas) of Lahat district (Sumatra) with bureaucrats of the modern state. With decisions taken in "far away offices", they also greatly expanded the lot of protected areas in the region, transforming many local people into illegal residents "with a stroke of pen". It was right at that time that the price of coffee also rose significantly in world markets and more and more people, including many opportunistic migrants, started entering protected forests in order to grow coffee.

The original marga system was very effective in protecting timber and non-timber products from outside exploiters and in dealing intelligently with environmental resources (e.g., farming was commonly banned within 100 metres from springs). Unfortunately, the system was first seriously weakened by the Dutch colonial powers that established a policy of "shooting on sight" for people who would disobey their formal, top-down prohibitions (e.g. would enter a protected forest). Later, after a brief period of resurgence at the time of independence, the system was formally dismantled by national law in 1979. Locally, this was perceived as an attempt by the Javanese elite in the government to gain overall control over the natural resources of the country. In practice, a weak, inexperienced, poorly funded and bureaucratic apparatus abysmally failed at controlling access to the natural resources and only succeeded in transforming the old communal forests into an open access regime. More and more people invaded the protected forests to take advantage of the lucrative coffee markets and deforestation rapidly ensued.

With the fall of the Suharto regime, in the late 1990s, Indonesia has adopted a new forestry management policy that sets in motion opportunities to devolve forest management responsibilities to the local level. Management responsibility can be taken up by local communities organised in either traditional forms (such as the marga) or modern cooperatives. The forestry authorities retain an important role as providers of technical advice. This new devolution policy is not likely to become a panacea, and especially so in a context of weakened civil society and shrewd local politicians that can quickly gather benefits for themselves. It is, however, a major innovation– an experiment that many should very closely watch.

The formal recognition of customary governance systems is more of a challenge in countries deriving their legal tradition from Roman law than in common-law

---

[33] See, for instance, Box 3.5 in Chapter 3, and Baird and Dearden, 2003.

countries. Where national legislation does not "formally recognise" and "allow" indigenous peoples and local communities to play their role in natural resource management, co-management advocates may wish to lobby for policy reform. Even where favourable legislation exists, however, its proper implementation may need to be specifically demanded and supported. Embracing cultural diversity in the co-management of natural resources often implies a radical transformation in the organisational culture of government departments and changes in professional beliefs, behaviours, attitudes and practice.[34] For instance, the tendency to impose "rational" organisational models on local communities[35] is often counterproductive, and even financial and technical "support" may leverage the worst rather than the best in them, spreading internal conflicts and corruption.[36] Most communities can best organise by choosing themselves the models that best suit their culture and needs. If those will change, they should do so from within and not because of external imposition. Examples of broad policy directions supporting cultural diversity for co-management include the promotion of culture-sensitive curricula in basic education and professional training,[37] appreciation and support provided to local languages and local cultural initiatives and, in general, the recognition of the cultural dimension of natural resource management (see Box 10.12).

> The tendency to impose "rational" organisational models on local communities is often counterproductive, and even financial and technical "support" may leverage the worst rather than the best in them, spreading internal conflicts and corruption.

Box 10.12 Discovering and recognising the cultural dimension of natural resource management

Policies in support of the cultural dimension of conservation are based on generating and disseminating information on community values, knowledge, skills, resources and institutions and promoting awareness about the natural resource management capacities embedded into local cultures. For instance, in Morocco the place where botanists still find the few existing patches of "original vegetation" in the country are not the official protected areas but the "marabous cemeteries"– conserved in a nearly pristine state because of the traditional respect and care by the local communities. These local forms of conservation are only beginning to be recognised as part of the patrimony of the country. In India, traditional water harvesting systems that had been left to decay for a long time have been revitalised in recent decades with wonderful success.[38] In Peru, the maintenance of agro-biodiversity is closely related to the maintenance of customary patterns of resource use and exchanges, and some community-originated initiatives are attempting to get this recognised at the national level.[39]

Policies can encourage and support activities (e.g., ceremonies, festivals, fairs) where the people celebrate their cultures, enjoy their artistic manifestations, and show their pride for their lands and the beauty and wealth of their environments. These activities not only have strong impact locally, but also contribute to positioning the local cultures as a vital part of a national heritage. A simple but powerful poli-

---

[34] See Chapter 9.

[35] This has origins in colonial impositions, as for the Cabildo of Ecuador and the Capitania of Bolivia.

[36] Lack of sensitivity for the local context may bring agencies to "assign" positions of authority and financial advantages that amount to local revolutions. In Bénin, a conservation initiative assisting communities in the southern periphery of Parc W has provided jobs, social status and financial advantages to local poachers, in the hope that they abandon their practices and assist the governmental agencies instead. Such interventions are poorly sustainable (they are totally dependent on project resources), dubiously effective (the poachers now understand all the ways by which the agencies carry out their surveillance work) and capable of engendering profound social disruptions in the local communities (the poachers, who were among the least capable and respected members of local societies, are now incomparably wealthier than the rest and even considered as primary referents to the external project).

[37] An example is a GEF initiative currently (2004) engaged to revise the entire training curriculum of protected areas personnel in Morocco, seeking a better and more sensitive understanding of the unique characteristics and capacities of communities for the conservation of biodiversity (M. Rashid, personal communication, 2004).

[38] CSE, 1997.

[39] This is true for the Potato Park, in the region of Cusco (Alejandro Argumedo, personal communication, 2003).

cy decision is to maintain, respect, and restore, as necessary, the local, ethnic names of species and places. Traditional knowledge, customary laws and institutions, biodiversity names and uses, and local languages and dialects are all interconnected. In this sense, a revival of indigenous and local languages helps to maintain alive a body of knowledge that is indiscernible from the language in which it is expressed and may be critical to landscape and natural resource management. In general, it has been a deplorable trend of protected area managers and agencies to change traditional names of places with other names that mean little or nothing to people of the region. For instance, in Ecuador, protected area managers changed the name romerillo that people use to give to their local forests, with Podocarpus, which is the Latin name for the same species. The Park thus became " Podocarpus National Park"– a name that means nothing to people. Fortunately, these practices are becoming less common, and local names and languages are increasing their national and international visibility. Examples of protected areas that conserve their traditional names in local languages exist for Australia, Colombia, Malaysia, South Africa, Mexico and several other countries.[40]

Policies that secure natural resources access and tenure rights

Throughout history, conquerors subjugated the conquered by confiscating their lands or otherwise limiting their access to property. Especially in agrarian societies, control of land, water and other natural resources by ruling elites has been the principal mechanism employed for consolidating the monopoly of political, economic and social power throughout society. Present-day rights that regulate access and tenure of resources among diverse social actors are extremely varied from country to country and within a country among different localities. Generally, the rules regulating the use of, and control over, land and other natural resources reflect the interests of dominant social actors at the time these rules were institutionalised by custom or law. These rules, however, are not static and immutable. They evolve in response to social change and it is not unthinkable that-as human rights hopeful-ly become better understood, recognised and protected-the ones hitherto excluded from the control of natural resources will better come to the fore. Indigenous peoples, landless workers, small producers, mobile communities as well as low-income consumers and all others who are dependent on natural resources but without property rights over them, may hopefully acquire some form of rights entitling them to an equitable participation in their management and benefits.

Effective collaborative management agreements are a step in this direction, in particular when they manage to provide clear and secure rules to regulate the access to and uses of natural resources. If diverse social groups do not have a sense of security of their individual and collective rights over natural resources, they cannot participate effectively in their management.[41] Novel legal arrangements can be explored and developed at the national level to provide that. For instance, some formal recognition of "primary" rights to land (property or permanent usufruct) could be provided to communities with a long-standing local history and practicing an ecologically sound model of sustainable resource use. This could help them re-affirm their rights versus newcomers and opportunistic users.[42] As mentioned in the preceding section, this also implies that national legislation and policies accommodate for a fair degree of local peculiarities and complexity. In particular, they should refrain from imposing organisational models to communities but seek to recognise what exists and is locally legitimate. The explicit formal

---

40 Borrini-Feyerabend et al., 2004 (in press).
41 Barraclough and Pimbert, 2004 (in press).
42 See Bassi, 2003. In all cases, institutionalising the rights of the hitherto excluded is a conflictive endeavour, depending on the purposeful organisation and mobilisation of those who stand to benefit (Barraclough and Pimbert, 2004, in press).

recognition of customary law, collective rights and customary regulations and bodies dealing with NRM conflicts are likely to be particularly important.

A number of resources not specifically related to land rights may have crucial relevance for communities within their wider productive and livelihoods systems, for example mobile resources (e.g., water, wildlife and fisheries) or resources located in areas firmly owned or occupied by the state or other social actors. The identification of such resources requires the involvement of traditional knowledge holders, as most of them are used in a customary way and may not be known to everybody in the communities, and even less to government agencies and outsiders. Some of these resources may not be of critical importance for the physical survival of the people but vital in a cultural sense. Other resources may be essential only in times of drought or special scarcity, and thus critically important for the long-term survival of certain communities. Typically, this has been the case for water, pastures, game, fuel wood, building materials and other resources now included in official protected areas, which communities would still like to access in difficult circumstances.

Tenure and resource access security and rights in such special circumstances imply complicated legal challenges, especially when having to reconcile community, private and state interests, but are not out of the realm of creative institutions.[43] In fact, it may be useful that communities involved in mapping and inventory exercises identify the resources they traditionally use even outside the boundaries of their customary lands. In Mexico, the state of San Luis Potosi recognised use rights over a long pilgrimage route used by the Huichol indigenous people outside their traditional lands, facilitated agreements with owners and other users, and declared the area a Natural and Cultural Reserve, where traditional uses by the indigenous population are legally allowed.[44] In the North of Russia, the Kytalyk Reserve, established on the basis of an agreement with the Even people on their traditional lands, was extended over an area that the communities considered sacred far from their traditional grazing and hunting grounds.[45]

Related to the above, the Intellectual Property Rights (IPRs) of indigenous and local communities need to be clarified and protected. Countries members of the World Trade Organisation (WTO) are under strong pressure to adopt the US model of intellectual property rights. This model strongly favours the rights of global corporations to claim patents on medicinal plants, agricultural seeds, and other aspects of biodiversity, even in cases where the biological material has been under cultivation and development by indigenous people or farming communities for millennia. By eroding secular rights over biological resources, informal innovations and collective knowledge, the risk is that IPRs will shift the control over production, livelihoods and environment from local communities to the corporate sector through the following interrelated processes:

● Erosion of farmers' rights. Traditional livelihood and survival strategies of small farmers based on saving, exchanging, breeding or replanting seeds are under threat from globally uniform IPR rules adopted by governments.[46]

● Privatisation of traditional knowledge. IPRs privatise, commercialise, plunder and erode traditional knowledge without any rewards for custodians (women,

Some of these resources may not be of critical importance for the physical survival of the people but vital in a cultural sense... or essential in times of drought or special scarcity.

---

43 National protected areas in the UK, France, Italy and Spain have such characteristics, and yet manage to develop viable management plans.
44 Otegui, 2003.
45 Oviedo, 2003.
46 GRAIN, 1998.

healers, indigenous peoples…).[47]

● Research and innovation re-directed from the relevant needs of poor people to the demands of companies (focus on high-profit, high-yielding varieties and medicinal drugs).

The loss of control of information is a major concern for people whose political and spiritual power may derive from their traditional knowledge.

For many farmers and indigenous peoples, the enclosure of genetic resources and knowledge through IPR regimes also threatens the diversity of common property cultures by which the rights of local communities over natural resources and community knowledge are ensured. Most of these communities have traditionally viewed plants and seeds as part of the community commons, not subject to ownership and fee structures imposed by outside corporations. This is becoming more of an issue when the communities share their knowledge in the context of co-management processes and agreements. The loss of control of information is a major concern for people whose political and spiritual power may derive from their traditional knowledge.[48] "One size fits all" IPR law should be abandoned to permit reassertion of rules that respect and favour the needs of local and domestic communities as well as the protection of innovations and knowledge developed over time.[49] Even in the absence of specific national legislation that recognises and protects the knowledge and innovations of local communities and indigenous peoples, there are ways of safeguarding these through specific agreements and procedures,[50] which are of particular relevance and value in case of co-management arrangements.

Policies that recognise and respond to the rights of indigenous peoples

The right to self determination is important for indigenous peoples throughout the world. Starting during colonial domination and continuing with independent states, the overriding policy objective vis-à-vis indigenous peoples has been their integration into the national society while denying them their rights to use and regulate access to their resources, to exercise their customary laws and to control decision-making concerning their future. Many of their traditional lands have been taken over by the state and later exploited by extractive industries and for "development" projects, or set aside for protected areas. Those who resisted these trends were marginalised and castigated, and often treated as "anti-development" or subversive. Indigenous peoples have consistently argued that they are not against development per se, but cannot accept a kind of development that leads them towards social disintegration and ecological wastelands. They wish a different kind of development, related to their needs and aspirations. In this sense, their call for the "right to self-determination" can be interpreted as their wish to decide what type of development shall happen in their communities and to retain control over their lives, which is intimately related to their land and natural resources. For many indigenous peoples the right to self-determination thus appears a fundamental condition towards re-assuming responsibility for natural resource management. This would imply that national governments discontinue their integrationist poli-

---

47   GRAIN, 2004
48   Dermot Smyth, personal information, 2003.
49   Crucible, 1994; GRAIN, 2003.
50   Posey and Dutfield, 1996; Laird, 2002.

cies and related practices, first of all involuntary or induced resettlements,[51] and rather provide scope for people to make informed decisions about their future through a variety of participatory processes for assessing, planning and evaluating development and conservation initiatives. New enabling policies could stipulate and ensure just that.

Enabling policies, however, cannot limit themselves to looking towards the future. In many cases, they also need to ensure that past right violations are also addressed, for instance via land restitution and other fair compensation processes. There is overwhelming evidence of the negative impacts inflicted upon indigenous land and resources because of government-led or private operation. This has included community displacements for a variety of reasons, including the establishment of large dams, plantation forests, protected areas, intensive shrimp farming and rangeland development schemes. Mandatory provisions can be made in national law to redress such impacts and damages, providing fair compensation for the damages suffered and restitution for the territories expropriated.[52] As changes have often occurred since the time of expropriation, communities may need some form of specific support to re-establish their livelihoods even when lands are "restituted". In certain cases, a sense of community ownership can be rekindled through affirmative policies that make possible effective attribution and security of tenure, building upon traditional management practices and grassroots-based dialogue on desired futures.[53] Other compensation schemes, such as eco-tourism ventures, may be newer for local communities and require technical assistance to be established effectively. Importantly, a legal representative and/ or a legal team specialising in land rights should be on hand if not permanently representing the communities' case for reparation. Through clear policy commitments "to level the playing field", government agencies can play important roles to assure that indigenous and local communities are fully informed about their rights to land restitution and the equitable compensation of other suffered damages[54]... although this facilitation role may be better suited to NGOs.

Initiatives at various levels can help ensure the respect of rights over traditional and common lands and the redressing of past injustices. At the national level, enabling policies can support communities to demarcate and protect their territorial or marine boundaries against external threats and political impositions. Either as a precondition for legal recognition of ownership and access rights, or as a provisional alternative to it, area demarcation is a central requirement for tenure security of indigenous and local communities engaged in co-management (Box 10.13). In the last few years, especially in the Amazon region but also in other regions, there has been a strong engagement in demarcation of collective territories, in most cases carried out by indigenous organisations with the support of external organisations. In traditional land tenure, permanent physical boundaries are less important than resource boundaries, which are changing and adaptable. Under modern legal systems, however, the recognition of land rights requires the identification of permanent physical boundaries. In this sense, demarcation provides the basis for the legal recognition of natural resources and landscapes valued by local actors. Demarcation implies not only the physical identification and signalling of borders, but a complex process of recognition and mapping of a territory, often including a rapid biodiversity inventory as well. Once demarcation is done, steps need to be taken for its legal recognition. This

...past right violations also need to be addressed, for instance via land restitution and other fair compensation processes.

Demarcation implies not only the physical identification and signalling of borders, but a complex process of recognition and mapping of a territory, often including a rapid biodiversity inventory as well.

---

51 Cernea and Schmidt-Soltau, 2003.
52 See some examples in Table 4.3 and Boxes 4.3 and 7.11.
53 A very interesting example is described in Wilshusen, 2003.
54 See Box 9.1.

is particularly important in areas where there are conflicts over lands and resources, and where external forces could resort to violence, abuse and encroachment into community lands. National policies are crucial to allow and support such processes.

Box 10.13 The demarcation and titling of indigenous land: a duty of the state? (adapted from ILRC and IHRLG, 2003)

On August 31, 2001, the Inter-American Court of Human Rights issued its ruling in the "Case of the Mayagna (Sumo) Awas Tingni Community versus Nicaragua" concluding that Nicaragua had violated the rights of the Mayagna community by granting a logging concession within its territory without the consent of the community and by ignoring the consistent complaints of the Awas Tingni for demarcation of its territory. According to an "evolutionary interpretation", the Court noted that Article 21 of the American Convention on Human Rights, which recognises the right to private property, also protects "the rights of members of the indigenous communities within the framework of communal property." Establishing an important precedent for the defence of indigenous rights within the international system, the Court affirmed that indigenous territorial rights arise from the communities "possession of the land" as rooted in their own "customary law, values, customs and mores." These rights are not dependent on the existence of a formal title granted by the state. The Court recognised the importance that indigenous peoples place on their relationship with the land, highlighting that "indigenous groups, by the fact of their very existence, have the right to live freely in their own territory; the close ties of indigenous people with the land must be recognised and understood as the fundamental basis of their cultures, their spiritual life, their integrity, and their economic survival."

The Awas Tingni decision declares the duty of states to demarcate and title indigenous communal land to make effective the rights recognised by the American Convention. The Court ruled that the lack of demarcation of indigenous territories prevents indigenous peoples from the free use and enjoyment of their lands and resources. As such, the lack of effective juridical mechanisms for demarcation constitutes a violation of the judicial protection and property rights of indigenous peoples as guaranteed by the Convention.

Policies that set the rules and conditions of participation and co-management

In order to provide effective direction for and support to co-management, natural resource policy and other supporting policy instruments often go beyond the mere expression of objectives and desired situations. For instance, they stipulate specific provisions to promote the development and functioning of successful co-management arrangements and agreements. This section presents the main areas where appropriate legislation can help to empower, stimulate and engage local stakeholders.

Requirements for access to information, transparency and accountability
Effective "participation" requires the provision of adequate information to stakeholders in advance of consulting with them. In doing so, planners need to remember that different stakeholders will have different levels of technical expertise and local knowledge. Biologists, for example, may know very little about the socioeconomic situation in an area, while local and indigenous communities are likely to have little background in conservation-related sciences. Efforts in effective social communication would provide many occasions for people not only to receive information but to share it, discuss it and make sense of it in a collective

context. In many cases, language may be a barrier, and materials will need to be presented in appropriate local languages. Many of these requirements can and should be guided by policy statements. Whenever possible, they should also be guaranteed by legislation. The Convention on Access to Information, Public Participation in Decision-Making and Access to Justice in Environmental Matters, usually referred to as Aarhus Convention, is particularly noteworthy in this regard (Box 10.14).

Box 10.14   The Aarhus Convention– promoting access to information, public participation and environmental justice
(adapted from www.unece.org/env/pp; WRI, 2003)

The Aarhus Convention was negotiated in 1998 at the Fourth Ministerial Conference on the "Environment for Europe" in Aarhus (Denmark) and sponsored by the United Nations Economic Commission for Europe. Since then, 24 nations in Europe and Central Asia have become parties to the treaty, and 40 have signed it. The treaty entered into force in October 2001, and is now open to signature by all nations of the world.

The Aarhus Convention links environment and human rights. It acknowledges that this generation has an obligation to future generations and establishes that sustainable development can only be achieved through the involvement of all actors. Thus, it focuses on enhancing interactions between civil society and public authorities in a democratic context and on forging a new process for public participation in the negotiation and implementation of international agreements. At heart, the Convention is about government accountability, transparency and responsiveness. It grants rights to civil society actors and imposes on parties and public authorities obligations regarding access to information, fair and transparent decision-making processes, and access to redress.[55] For example, the convention requires broad access to information about the state of air and atmosphere, water, land, and biological diversity; information about influences on the environment such as energy, noise, development plans, and policies; and information about how these influences affect human health and safety.

There is growing interest in endorsing the Aarhus principles in Latin America, southern Africa, and the Asia-Pacific region, but many other countries perceive the Convention's concepts of democratic decision-making about the environment as too liberal or threatening to commercial confidentiality.

Besides access to information, and as rightly linked in the Aarhus Convention, effective participation in co-management also requires transparency and accountability and a fair recourse to justice available to all. This can be achieved through:

- public reporting requirements stipulated within the provisions of co-management agreements;

- third-party monitoring of the implementation of co-management agreements, by non-governmental organisations, governmental agencies, media houses or independent bodies;

- mechanisms for sanctions when there is a lack of compliance with the provisions of co-management agreements (one key challenge in this regard is to ensure that the mechanisms for sanction apply to all parties in co-management agreements, and not only to civil society and community partners);

- the involvement, whenever required, of active political bodies and civil society pressure groups;

- a reliable and fair judicial system that includes provisions for legal recourse by

---

[55]   See www.unece.org/env/pp

partners in co-management agreements; the system should provide for arbitration in cases of conflict, and guarantee the equality of advocacy in case of dispute.

Related to access to information and transparency is the legal recognition of the right to information and Prior Informed Consent (PIC) of local communities and indigenous peoples. The countries that ratified the ILO Convention 169 and undertook to implement the Convention on Biological Diversity are increasingly considering incorporation of the right to prior and informed consent (PIC) on matters beyond traditional knowledge. This trend is to be supported and encouraged, as it has evident benefits for the lands and resources of indigenous peoples and local communities. PIC should be a central tenet of policies and practices for the co-management of natural resources. In the Philippines, for example, local communities on Coron Island have used the principle of PIC effectively to assert their rights and their own vision of the future (Box 10.15).

Box 10.15 The Tagbanwa strive for the recognition and maintenance of a Community Conserved Area in Coron Island (The Philippines)
(adapted from Ferrari and De Vera, 2003)

The Tagbanwa people of the Philippines inhabit a stunningly beautiful limestone island for which they have established stringent use regulations. The forest resources are to be used for domestic purposes only. All the freshwater lakes but one are sacred. Entry to those lakes is strictly forbidden for all except religious and cultural purposes. The only lake accessible for tourism is Lake Kayangan, which has regulations concerning number of people allowed in, garbage disposal, resource use, etc. Until recently, the Tagbanwas' territorial rights were not legally recognised, leading to encroachment by migrant fishers, tourism operators, politicians seeking land deals and government agencies. This caused several problems, chief among whom was the impoverishment of the marine resources, essential for the local livelihood. In the mid-1980s, however, the islanders organised themselves into the Tagbanwas Foundation of Coron Island and started lobbying to regain management control over their natural resources.

They first applied for a Community Forest Stewardship Agreement, which was granted in 1990 over the 7748 hectares of Coron Island and a neighbouring island, Delian, but not over the marine areas. In 1998, they managed to get a Certificate of Ancestral Domain Claim for 22,284 hectares of land and marine waters and finally, in 2001, after having produced a high quality map and an Ancestral Land Management Plan, they managed to obtain a Certificate of Ancestral Domain Title (CADT), which grants them collective right to their land.

Despite their successful management achievements, the Tagnabwa CADT was later reviewed, as the national policies and systems were being restructured. A governmental proposal was then advanced to add Coron Island to the National Integrated Protected Area System. Despite the fact that the government proposed to set in place a co-management system for the island, the Tagbanwas opposed the move, as they feared that they would lose control of their natural resources, and those would be less and not better protected. Very importantly for them, they wish to remain "rightholders"– the owners and protectors of their territories– and refuse to be classified as one "stakeholder" among others. Another reason mentioned by the Tagbanwa for their refusal to accept the government proposal is the fact that Coron Island was selected as one of the 8 sites to be part of the programme without any consultation with them and thus without their prior informed consent. The refusal to comply with the co-management programme, however, does not mean that Coron Island is less well managed than other environments protected by the state. Possibly even the contrary, as the indigenous right holders have set in place restrictive measures for resource access and use, including a strong curbing of tourism.

Requirements for participatory planning and capacity building support
Co-management is not about any partnership or identifying the minimum common denominator of the wishes of everyone. It is about partnerships that give power, rights and responsibilities to those who have a primary stake in the use and management of natural resources, and who are in the position to contribute to and guarantee their sustainable and equitable use. Legal instruments should not tightly specify who the partners should be, but lay out the procedure that should be followed to identify such partners and to allocate rights and responsibilities within specific management instruments and agreements. In particular, natural resource policy and legal instruments can and should provide safeguards against the marginalisation and exclusion of some of the potential partners. For example, national parks legislation can stipulate that municipalities adjacent to protected areas should automatically be represented on that protected area's management body. Similarly, forestry legislation can stipulate the roles that user groups play in co-management institutions.

"Affirmative" (proactive) national policies are often needed to promote equity in capacity building at the community level. Indigenous peoples and local communities, both rural and urban, comprise groups with different interests and agendas, including some with relatively more power and greater access to resources than others. Women or ethnic minorities may play a more marginal role and may be greatly interested in mechanisms to secure a more meaningful involvement in co-management decisions. One way governments can address this concern is to ensure that relevant information reaches everyone and that all community members can openly participate in discussions over co-management agreements. This may be more feasible in some cultural contexts than in others. In some villages, for instance, women may prefer influencing decisions within the household rather than speaking in public. In general, greater equity in capacity building initiatives may help marginalised or weaker actors such as women, ethnic minorities and poorer social groups to regain some power and standing within their communities and co-management bodies.

It is not always the case that a particular stakeholder group is clear about its own interests and concerns regarding a particular situation or environmental option, including the establishment of a protected area or its relation to it. It is also not often the case that such stakeholders have figured out how to get themselves "represented" in discussions with others. At times NGOs claim to speak for local communities, indigenous leaders claim to speak for their peoples, or private sector industry association representatives claim to speak on behalf of their membership but these forms of "internal organisation" are more top down than genuine. This can cause problems, when, for example, protected areas authorities claim to have "consulted" with indigenous peoples or a local community, but the community does not in fact feel that it was fairly represented in the planning process. As a matter of fact, most if not all co-management arrangements involve some form of representation in governing bodies and management organisations. Legal instruments for natural resource management must therefore specify the mechanisms by which the representatives of people and civil society organisations are selected. These mechanisms should be as much in line with participatory democracy as possible, for instance by involving some form of open discussion of issues followed by an election and/ or a selection through customary community decisions as well as mechanisms for follow up and accountability. And yet, policy makers

> Legal instruments should not tightly specify who the partners must be, but lay out the procedure that should be followed to identify such partners and to allocate rights and responsibilities within specific management instruments and agreements.

should be careful to avoid imposing externally-conceived organising systems on local communities, and rather respect as much as possible their culture-embedded institutions.[56]

A more mundane but similarly important element of capacity building for all rightholders and stakeholders is the possibility to overcome time and travel constraints.[57] Participation is expensive, particularly for local communities and indigenous peoples. Taking time off work for meetings is not an option for many rural people, unless the process is designed with their particular needs in mind, such as avoiding harvest or fishing times, key religious or cultural events, and finding some means to meet the difficulty and expense of travelling, particularly in the remote rural areas where many protected areas are located. Local officials of poorly funded protected area agencies and local government units face similar problems. Policies in support of co-management need to make provisions to cover at least some of the costs of meetings.

Financial and economic policies

One of the fundamental assumptions of co-management is that community-based and collaborative approaches reduce management costs. In a typical co-management arrangement, several of the functions that would otherwise be performed by state agencies are delegated to local government agencies, civil society organisations, community groups and users of natural resources. This is bound to reduce the costs borne by the central management agency. But this does not mean that the costs have been eliminated. They may have been reduced, as it would indeed be more efficient for a local agency to carry out, for instance, a monitoring function, instead of having a team of technicians travelling from the national or provincial capital at regular intervals to collect samples or interview informants. Yet, most of the costs required for management would not be eliminated but simply transferred from the central to the local level.

This observation underscores the need for fair and complete assessments of the costs of management, and for clear rules that govern the allocation of responsibility in this regard. In instances where collaborative arrangements place responsibility for the management of resources in the hands of local communities or agencies, this should be accompanied by a transfer of financial resources through a direct budget allocation, a rental fee, or the transfer of authority to generate financial resources from management.[58]

---

56 See various considerations and examples in Chapter 5.
57 See Box 9.1 in Chapter 9.
58 An example is described in Box 9.2 in Chapter 9.

Very useful policies also establish the right and capacity of local co-management partners to generate revenue, and provide both autonomy and accountability in the use of that revenue. One of the specific instruments that can bring tangible benefits to local actors is the sharing of revenue from tourism and other commercial concessions, hunting and fishing licenses and permits, trade licenses, and sales of timber and non-timber forest products. In Botswana, for example, the Wildlife Conservation and National Parks Act provides communities with the opportunity to apply to the government for rights to manage the wildlife in their area, including the enforcement of regulated hunting.[59]

Indeed, co-management practices on the ground are supported and fostered by national policies that combat poverty and attempt to reduce social and economic inequality. At a general level, it is the broader national and international political and economic context that presents major opportunities or obstacles for co-management. For instance, neo-liberal policies such as trade liberalisation, privatisation and the predominance of competitive market forces in the regulation of access to resources impact negatively on co-management, as they favour the more powerful economic interests at the expense of poor people and communities.[60] An important economic phenomenon that impacts on the outcomes of co-management is the increased commoditisation of goods and services, accompanied by rapid changes in production, information and communication technology. This means that many resources critical to people are now easily governed by market rules and placed outside of the control of their primary users. Globally defined rules such as the WTO-TRIPs agreement (e.g. patents on seeds and medicinal plants) and privatisation (land, water, forests, public services) are undermining the control that local resource users have over their environments, knowledge and institutions.[61] Globalisation and the concentration of economic power in the hands of trans-national corporations and finance markets proceed with a simultaneous process of devolution and decentralisation. But the power to define the content and purpose of policies, institutions and systems is concentrated in the hands of ever fewer trans-national corporations (TNCs).[62] In this light, widening economic democracy and equity appear as a key overarching condition for the mainstreaming of co-management.

...co-management agreements backed by proper legislation could become instruments of protection of special local needs and interests.

For instance, co-management initiatives would be strengthened by policies that protect local interests, placing selected resources beyond the reach of competitive bidding processes, and protecting local markets whenever necessary.[63] In this manner, co-management agreements backed by proper legislation could become instruments of protection of special local needs and interests. National governments, acting alone or in groups, may also need to introduce specific policies to protect domestic markets for natural resources from cheap imports and the negative impacts of competition in international trade. Subsidised imports have often destroyed environments and sustainable livelihoods throughout the South, and many people now working for poverty wages in factories are refugees from local economies based on fishing, farming, pastoralism or forest-based livelihoods. For instance, India's domestic edible oil industry (i.e. oilseed crop producers, millers, processors and retailers) has been undermined as highly subsidised soya from the US and palm oil from Malaysia have flooded the market. Moreover, the dominant paradigm that exports from the South to the North are a major route for economic

...many people now working for poverty wages in factories are refugees from local economies based on fishing, farming, pastoralism or forest-based livelihoods.

[59] Winer 1996.
[60] UNRISD, 2002.
[61] George, 2001.
[62] Korten, 1995; Menahem, 2001.
[63] Passet, 2000.

development ignores the inevitability of adverse competition between poor exporting countries and its hijacking of national priorities to the provision of the cheapest exports. To reverse this trend, countries could develop international trade rules that allow them to introduce constraints on their exports and imports.[64]

Trade rules that favour export production and dumping of cheap imports can be replaced by rules that permit the use of trade tariffs and quotas to regulate imports of food, timber, fish, fibres and other natural products that can be produced locally. This means applying the principle of subsidiarity: whenever production can be achieved by local social actors, using local resources for local consumption, all rules and benefits should favour that option, thus shortening the distance between production and consumption. This is not to suggest that there should be no trade at all in food, fibre and other natural resource based products, but to recognise that trade should be confined to whatever commodities cannot be supplied at the local level, rather than trade being the primary driver of production and distribution.[65]

Governments also need to carefully assess the compatibility of newly evolving international environmental, labour and safety standards with national policies designed to support co-management. For example, in the name of food safety, many international rules, such as the WTO's Agreement on the Application of Sanitary and Phytosanitary Standards and the Codex Alimentarius, have enforced an approach to food processing that works directly against local and artisanal food producers, whilst favouring the global trans-national corporations. Among other things, they require irradiation of certain products, pasteurisation, and standardised shrink-wrapping of local cheese products. Such rules tremendously increase costs for small producers as these homogenised global standards primarily benefit TNCs that trade on global markets. Where co-management schemes seek to retain wealth closer to where it is generated, there is a strong case for food production standards (and other NR standards) to be localised, with every nation permitted to set its own high food safety and other standards related to natural resource management.

Similarly, national governments will increasingly need to work together to put limits on the concentration of economic power in supply chains that link natural resource based producers with consumers. Trans-national corporations involved in natural resource management include suppliers of commercial inputs and services to the farming, fisheries, timber, bio-prospecting, mining, tourism and protected areas sectors. They also include corporations that disproportionately benefit from the processing, distribution and retailing of natural resources (food, timber, minerals, medicinal drugs, genetic resources, new natural products such as oils and cosmetics) as well as TNCs offering services or partnerships for eco-tourism and protected area management.[66] A relatively small number of trans-national corporations are strategically placed along these supply chains, influencing both the nature of production, the terms of trade and who benefits from natural resource based goods and services on the global market.[67] The concentration of corporate power in the global food system is illustrative of these emerging trends (see Box 10.16).

...applying the principle of subsidiarity: whenever production can be achieved by local social actors, using local resources for local consumption, all rules and benefits should favour that option, thus shortening the distance between production and consumption.

[64] Hines, 2003; Mazoyer and Roudart, 2003; Mazoyer, 2003.
[65] International Forum on Globalisation, 2002; Hines, 2003.
[66] Baumann et al., 1996; Ghimire and Pimbert, 1997; Utting, 2002; Vorley, 2001; Vorley, 2004.
[67] Garreau, 1977; Pimbert et al., 2002; George, 1981.

> **Box 10.16 Concentration in agri-food business sectors**
> **(adapted from Vorley, 2001)**
>
> 1. In farm inputs. Concentration in the input sector proceeded at breakneck speed in the 1990s. Six companies now control 80 percent of pesticide sales, down from 12 in 1994.[68] In the period 1995-2000 the amalgamations in the US seed industry alone were worth USD15 thousand million. From a food systems perspective, input manufacturers, as suppliers to the least profitable sector of the agri-food system, namely farming, are in a strategically weak position. The level of concentration in the business is in part a desperate drive to maintain profitability against declining strategic value of chemicals, seeds and biotechnology. Value chain thinking rather than technical justification or innovation is the key to the sustainability of these industries. Survival will depend on strategic alliances with processors and retailers around food quality, safety and quality.
>
> 2. In processing. Partly out of necessity to exercise countervailing economic power to retailers, processing industries are also rapidly consolidating their economic and market power. The economic power of the top eight food multinationals has been compared to that of half of Africa. In 2000, USD 87 thousand million in food industry deals were announced, with Nestlé, Philip Morris and Unilever emerging as the Big Three of global food makers. The justification for such massive accumulation of market power is "to have more clout in the consolidating retailing environment". We are likely to see a growth in networks and cross-ownership between food processing and the seed sector, in which the farmer is contractually sandwiched, just a step away from the farmer as renter rather than owner of contracted crops or livestock.
>
> 3. In retailing. In both the European Union (EU) and the United States of America (USA), it is retailers who determine what food processors want from farmers. Retailers are the point of contact between the majority of OECD (Organisation for Economic Cooperation and Development) citizens and the rural economy. The supermarket sector is most concentrated in the EU, but is also rapidly consolidating in the US. In the nine years since the Earth Summit, USA food retailing chains have concentrated dramatically, with the five leading chains moving from 19 percent control of grocery sales to at least 42 percent. Since 1992, global retail has consolidated enormously and three retailers– Carrefour, Ahold and Wal-Mart– have become truly global in their reach. In 2000, these three companies alone had sales (food and non-food) of USD300 thousand million and profits of USD8 thousand million, and employed 1.9 million people. It is predicted that there will be only 10 major global retailers by 2010.

The growing power of TNCs is a major challenge for governments committed to an enabling policy environment for co-management based on a fair sharing of costs and benefits. TNCs exert inordinate and unaccountable influence over public policies;[69] many corporations involved in the marketing of natural resources have annual revenues that dwarf the Gross National Products of many countries. Newly emerging initiatives, however, may help governments regulate corporate activities for the public good. For example, an increasing number of corporations are working towards a "corporate responsibility agenda" through such instruments as codes of conduct, certification, reporting, stakeholder dialogues and partnerships. This approach to promoting corporate social and environmental responsibility emphasises the role of "voluntary initiatives", in which TNCs themselves define the boundaries of the corporate responsibility agenda. In more recent attempts to move away from corporate self-regulation, trade unions, NGOs and multi-lateral organisations have become involved in standard setting, certification and independent monitoring of codes of conduct.

A "corporate responsibility agenda" can use instruments such as codes of conduct, certification, reporting, stakeholder dialogues and partnerships.

---

68   Kuyek, 2000; see also http://www.pan-international.org/index.html
69   ATTAC, 2001; Balanya et al., 2000; Kneen, 2002.

These are promising developments, but evidence from a range of case studies suggests that there remains a considerable gap between the rhetoric and practice of corporate responsibility. Change has tended to be piecemeal and is fraught with contradictions.[70] Compelling evidence indicates that the regulation of business and TNCs cannot be left to companies and their shareholders, industry associations and service delivery NGOs. More often than not, lukewarm voluntary initiatives have edged out important mechanisms and institutional arrangements that are key to national sovereignty and policy coherence.[71] New policy initiatives and forms of international cooperation are therefore needed to regulate corporations within countries and globally. Several ideas and proposals involving the UN system have emerged that could serve to correct the imbalance of power between TNCs and governments (see Box 10.17). Institutional arrangements involving state and international regulation, watchdog activism, collective bargaining, and complaints procedures that allow different social actors to identify and deal with breaches of agreed standards are all part of the menu of political choices open to governments and civil society.[72] UN agencies such as the UN Conference on Trade and Development (UNCTAD), the UN

Development Programme (UNDP), the UN Environment Programme (UNEP) and the World Health Organisation (WHO), as well as the International Labour Organisation (ILO), can also play a central role and should not shy away from critical research and policy analysis on TNCs and their social, environmental and developmental impacts, and on regulatory initiatives at both national and international levels. And yet, with few exceptions, the current vogue in most international agencies is to appease the TNCs with policies and programmes that integrate private sector interests. We are far from seeing the UN agencies play a critical supervisory role.

Box 10.17   Regulating corporations involved in natural resource sectors: some initiatives (adapted from Utting and Abrahams, 2002)

● The Sub-Commission on the Promotion and Protection of Human Rights has set up a Working Group on TNCs, which is considering a code of conduct for TNCs and has drafted a set of Human Rights Principles and Responsibilities for TNCs and other Business Enterprises. The Working Group has also proposed the creation of entities to assist with the implementation of the principles and to monitor compliance.

[70] Utting, 2002.
[71] Utting, 2002.
[72] Fitzgerald, 2001; Utting, 2002.

- There have been calls for a Special Rapporteur on TNCs to be established by the Human Rights Commission and for some existing Special Rapporteurs to deal with problems involving TNCs. The need to extend international legal obligations to TNCs in the field of human rights and to bring corporations under the jurisdiction of the International Criminal Court has also been suggested.

- Friends of the Earth International proposed that the World Summit on Sustainable Development consider a Corporate Accountability Convention that would establish and enforce minimum environmental and social standards, encourage effective reporting and provide incentives for TNCs taking steps to avoid negative impacts.

- The International Forum on Globalisation has advocated the creation of a United Nations Organisation for Corporate Accountability that would provide information on corporate practices as a basis for legal actions and consumer boycotts. Christian Aid has put forth the idea of a Global Regulation Authority that would establish norms for TNC conduct, monitor compliance and deal with breaches. Others have called for the reactivation of the defunct United Nations Centre on Trans-National Corporations, some of whose activities were transferred to UNCTAD a decade ago.

In practice, a levelling of the economic playing field for the co-management of natural resources calls for mutually reinforcing and radical structural reforms. Among these, the regeneration of more localised economies and culture– in short more effective local governance– merits closer attention. The idea here is to re-localise pluralistic economies that combine both subsistence and market oriented activities.[73] Several mutually reinforcing enabling policies have been identified to bring about such transformation for diversity and democracy (see Box 10.18).

Box 10.18   Policy for local governance
(adapted from Hines, 2000; ATTAC, 2000; Pimbert, 2001; IGH, 2002; Merlant et al., 2003)

Economic reforms

- Re-orientate the end goals of trade rules and aid, so that they contribute to the building of local economies and local control, rather than international competitiveness;

- re-introduce protective safeguards for domestic economies, including safeguards against imports of food and other natural resource based goods and services that can be produced locally;

- promote a site-here-to-sell-here policy for manufacturing and services domestically and regionally;

- "localise money" so that most of it stays within communities and neighbourhoods and helps rebuild local economies, rather than being siphoned off to distant actors and financial markets;

- promote local competition policy to eliminate monopolies from the more protected economies and ensure high quality food production, and natural resource based goods and services;

- restrict the concentration and market power of the major food and other natural resource based corporations and retailers through new national competition laws and international treaties;

- provide mechanisms to ensure that the real costs of environmental damage, unsustainable production methods and long distance trade are included in the cost of food;

- fund the transition to more localised economies and environmental regeneration by introducing taxes on resources and on speculative international financial flows (USD 1,500 thousand million is traded every day on foreign exchange markets alone– most of which is purely speculative and has nothing to do with the real economy).

---

[73] Gorz, 1997; Passet, 2000; Pimbert, 2001; Merlant et al., 2003.

Natural Resource Policies

● Redirect both hidden and direct agricultural and other natural resource subsidies towards supporting smaller scale producers to encourage the shift towards diverse, ecological, equitable and more localised food systems in pastoral, fishing, farming and forest-based communities as well as in urban and peri-urban contexts;

● ensure land reform and property rights to redistribute surplus land to tenants and sharecroppers and to secure rights of access and use of common property resources;

● protect the rights of peasants, farmers and pastoralists to save seed and improve crop varieties and livestock breeds, also through a ban on patents and IPR legislation on genetic resources important for food, health and agriculture;

● increase funding for and re-orientation of public sector research and development (R&D) for agriculture and natural resource management towards participatory approaches and democratic control over priority setting and technology validation;

● introduce a two-tier system of environment and health safety regulations: stricter controls on large-scale producers and marketers and simpler, more flexible, locally-determined regulations for small-scale localised enterprises generating wealth from natural resource transformation;

● enhance research and development and financial support for decentralised and sustainable energy production based on renewable energy.

10.2 Enabling policies at the international level

In a context of political, economic and cultural globalisation, and in light of the power and influence of supra-national institutions and processes, it is important to consider the role of international policy frameworks and instruments. Indeed, the past three decades since the 1972 Stockholm UN Conference on the Human Environment have seen the growing importance of global governance in several ways:

● trade liberalisation agreements have led to the emergence of powerful new institutions and corporations that are based on trans-national markets;

● regional political and economic groupings have been expanded and strengthened, including the European Union, the Free Trade Area of the Americas and the Asia Free Trade Association;

● global standards and commitments have been formulated and adopted, particularly through a number of international conventions and agreements; and

● institutional arrangements have been put in place for the management of the global commons, particularly through the United Nations Convention on the Law of the Sea and the Climate Change Convention.

International instruments and agreements impact directly on co-management at the local level, particularly because:

- requirements for participation and co-management are stipulated in several of the conventions and other binding or non-binding instruments;

- several multilateral and bilateral donor agencies have introduced provisions, guidelines and conditionalities aimed at promoting co-management and other participatory approaches; and

- trade and other international policies impact on the conditions of and capacities for resource use and management at the local level.

In many respects, the most fundamental international instrument in support of co-management remains the Universal Declaration of Human Rights. Adopted by the General Assembly of the United Nations on 10 December 1948, the Declaration is not legally binding but is considered as an international instrument of tremendous political and symbolic importance. After the adoption of this Declaration, the UN Commission on Human Rights began drafting legally binding documents. The International Covenant on Economic, Social, and Cultural Rights (ICESCR) and the International Covenant on Civil and Political Rights (ICCPR) were adopted in 1966.

Articles 1.1 of both the ICESCR and ICCPR uphold the right of all peoples to self-determination:

"All peoples have the right to self-determination. By virtue of that right they freely determine their political status and freely pursue their economic, social and cultural development".

Articles 1.2 of both covenants similarly support the right to development:

"All peoples may, for their own ends, freely dispose of their natural wealth and resources without prejudice to any obligations arising out of international economic co-operation, based on the principle of mutual benefit, and international law. In no case may a people be deprived of its own means of subsistence".

Other international conventions are of particular relevance to marginal social groups who live in areas rich in biological diversity, and who may engage in co-management processes. For example Convention 169 Concerning Indigenous and Tribal Peoples in Independent Countries, commonly known as ILO 169, was adopted in June 1989 by the Conference of the International Labour Organisation. ILO 169 specifically stresses the need for the participation of indigenous peoples in the decision-making process regarding resources and lands on which they have claims of dependence. Article 2.1 affirms that:

"Governments shall have the responsibility for developing, with the participation of the peoples concerned, co-ordinated and systematic action to protect the rights of these peoples and to guarantee respect for their integrity".

According to ILO 169, the protection of indigenous rights is the responsibility of governments, but only with the cooperation and participation of the indigenous peoples themselves. Similarly, many of the principal rights described in the United Nations Draft Declaration on the Rights of Indigenous Peoples[74] can use-

In many respects, the most fundamental international instrument in support of co-management remains the Universal Declaration of Human Rights.

---

[74] The Draft Declaration on the Rights for Indigenous Peoples was agreed upon by members of the United Nations Working Group on Indigenous Populations at its 11th session in Geneva, Switzerland, in 1993. The declaration is expected to be finalised in 2004 or 2005.

fully guide co-management processes and negotiated agreements over the use of natural resources (Box 10.19).

Box 10.19   Key rights affirmed by the UN Draft Declaration on the Rights of Indigenous Peoples

- Right to self determination, representation and full participation;

- right to collective, as well as individual human rights;

- recognition of existing treaty arrangements with indigenous peoples;

- right to determine own citizenry and citizen obligations;

- right to live in freedom, peace, and security without military intervention or involvement;

- right to religious freedom and protection of sacred sites and objects, including ecosystems, plants and animals;

- right to free and informed consent (prior informed consent);

- right to control access and exert ownership over plants, animals and minerals vital to their culture;

- right to own, develop, control and use the lands and territories, including the total environment of the lands, air, waters, coastal seas, sea-ice, flora and fauna and other resources which they have traditionally owned or otherwise occupied or used;

- right to special measures to control, develop and protect their sciences, technologies and cultural manifestations, including human and other genetic resources, seeds, medicines, knowledge of the properties of the fauna and flora, oral traditions, literatures, designs and visual and performing arts;

- right to restitution and redress for cultural, intellectual, religious or spiritual property that is taken or used without authorisation;

- right to just and fair compensation for any such activities that have adverse environmental, economic, social, cultural or spiritual impact.

Agenda 21, adopted at the 1992 UN Conference on Environment and Development, called for effective participation in all the elements of planning and development. In particular:

- Chapter 8 (Integrating environment and development in decision-making) states that "an adjustment or even a fundamental reshaping of decision-making, in the light of country specific conditions, may be necessary if environment and development is to be put at the centre of economic and political decision-making, in effect achieving full integration of these factors."

- Chapter 23 (Strengthening the role of the major groups) identifies, in the "specific context of environment and development, the need for new forms of participation" and notes "the need of individuals, groups and organisations to participate in decisions, particularly those that affect the communities in which they live and work."

- In Chapter 26 (Recognising and strengthening the role of indigenous people and their communities), active participation is called for to incorporate their "values, views and knowledge."

- Chapter 33 (Financial resources and mechanisms) stresses that "priorities should be established by means that incorporate public participation and community involvement providing equal opportunity for men and women. In this respect, consultative groups and round tables and other nationally-based mechanisms can play a facilitative role."

- Chapter 37 (National mechanisms and international cooperation for capacity-building) states that, "as an important aspect of overall planning, each country should seek internal consensus at all levels of society on policies and programmes needed for short and long-term capacity building to implement its Agenda 21 programme. This consensus should result from a participatory dialogue of relevant interest groups and lead to an identification of skill gaps, institutional capacities, technological and scientific requirements and resource needs to enhance environmental knowledge and administration to integrate environment and development".

The 2002 World Summit on Sustainable Development (WSSD) reaffirmed many of the commitments and principles adopted in Rio, and promoted the concept of partnerships. In the strict sense of the term, a partnership is no different from co-management, but the dominant discourses at the Johannesburg Summit applied the concept to all forms of collaboration, including those where industry remained the primary factor and actor. Nevertheless, the Summit's emphasis on partnerships only serves to underscore the value of collaboration and participation, and the need to bring all actors into the management process.

The 2002 World Summit on Sustainable Development (WSSD) promoted the concept of partnerships.

One of the most significant developments that have taken place recently on the international scene in the field of natural resource governance is the adoption of the Convention on Biological Diversity (CBD). This significance lies in its focus on traditional knowledge and practices, in the fact that it is legally binding, and in an approach that goes beyond indigenous groups and includes all local communities. The Convention stresses the need to involve indigenous and other local communities in the conservation of biological diversity, and in the sharing of benefits derived from the use of these resources. Article 8(j) of the Convention commits parties to:

"subject to [their] national legislation, [to] respect, preserve and maintain knowledge, innovations and practices of indigenous and local communities embodying traditional lifestyles relevant for the conservation and sustainable use of biological diversity and promote their wider application with the approval and involvement of the holders of such knowledge, innovations and practices and encourage the equitable sharing of the benefits arising from the utilisation of such knowledge, innovations and practices".

Similarly, Article 10(c) stipulates that each country should:

"protect and encourage customary use of biological resources in accordance with traditional cultural practices that are compatible with conservation or sustainable use requirements; support local populations to develop and implement remedial action in degraded areas where biological diversity has been reduced; and encourage cooperation between its governmental authorities and its private sectors in developing methods for sustainable use of biological resources."

More recently, the Conference of Parties (COP) of the Convention on Biological

Diversity has adopted the ecosystem approach as the primary framework for the implementation of the Convention. The COP has approved operational guidelines, and these are based on twelve broad principles. Particularly noteworthy among these are principles 1 and 2, which stress the need for societal choice and decentralisation of management to the lowest possible level (Box 10.20).

Box 10.20   Ecosystem approach principles adopted as part of the Convention on Biological Diversity

The following 12 principles are complementary and interlinked and they are at the basis of several decisions approved by the Conferences of the Parties to the Convention on Biological Diversity.[75]

Principle 1: The objectives of management of land, water and living resources are a matter of societal choices.
Different sectors of society view ecosystems in terms of their own economic, cultural and society needs. Indigenous peoples and other local communities living on the land are important stakeholders and their rights and interests should be recognised. Both cultural and biological diversity are central components of the ecosystem approach, and management should take this into account. Societal choices should be expressed as clearly as possible. Ecosystems should be managed for their intrinsic values and for the tangible or intangible benefits for humans, in a fair and equitable way.

Principle 2: Management should be decentralised to the lowest appropriate level.
Decentralised systems may lead to greater efficiency, effectiveness and equity. Management should involve all stakeholders and balance local interests with the wider public interest. The closer management is to the ecosystem, the greater the responsibility, ownership, accountability, participation, and use of local knowledge.

Principle 3: Ecosystem managers should consider the effects (actual or potential) of their activities on adjacent and other ecosystems.
Management interventions in ecosystems often have unknown or unpredictable effects on other ecosystems; therefore, possible impacts need careful consideration and analysis. This may require new arrangements or ways of organisation for institutions involved in decision-making to make, if necessary, appropriate compromises.

Principle 4: Recognising potential gains from management, there is usually a need to understand and manage the ecosystem in an economic context.
Any ecosystem-management programme should:
  a) reduce those market distortions that adversely affect biological diversity;
  b) align incentives to promote biodiversity conservation and sustainable use;
  c) internalise costs and benefits in the given ecosystem to the extent feasible.
The greatest threat to biological diversity lies in its replacement by alternative systems of land use. This often arises through market distortions, which undervalue natural systems and populations and provide perverse incentives and subsidies to favour the conversion of land to less diverse systems. Often those who benefit from conservation do not pay the costs associated with conservation and, similarly, those who generate environmental costs (e.g. pollution) escape responsibility. Alignment of incentives allows those who control the resource to benefit and ensures that those who generate environmental costs will pay.

Principle 5: Conservation of ecosystem structure and functioning, in order to maintain ecosystem services, should be a priority target of the ecosystem approach.
Ecosystem functioning and resilience depends on a dynamic relationship within species, among species

---

[75]   http://www.biodiv.org/programmes/cross-cutting/ecosystem/decisions.asp

and between species and their a-biotic environment, as well as the physical and chemical interactions within the environment. The conservation and, where appropriate, restoration of these interactions and processes is of greater significance for the long-term maintained conditions and, accordingly, management should be appropriately cautious.

Principle 6:   Ecosystems must be managed within the limits of their functioning.
In considering the likelihood or ease of attaining the management objectives, attention should be given to the environmental conditions that limit natural productivity, ecosystem structure, functioning and diversity. The limits to ecosystem functioning may be affected to different degrees by temporary, unpredictable or artificially maintained conditions and, accordingly, management should be appropriately cautious.

Principle 7:   The ecosystem approach should be undertaken at the appropriate spatial and temporal scales.
The approach should be bounded by spatial and temporal scales that are appropriate to the objectives. Boundaries for management will be defined operationally by users, managers, scientists and indigenous and local peoples. Connectivity between areas should be promoted where necessary. The ecosystem approach is based upon the hierarchical nature of biological diversity characterised by the interaction and integration of genes, species and ecosystems.

Principle 8:   Recognising the varying temporal scales and lag-effects that characterise ecosystem processes, objectives for ecosystem management should be set for the long term.
Ecosystem processes are characterised by varying temporal scales and lag-effects. This inherently conflicts with the tendency of humans to favour short-term gains and immediate benefits over future ones.

Principle 9:   Management must recognise that change is inevitable.
Ecosystems change, including species composition and population abundance. Hence, management should adapt to the changes. Apart from their inherent dynamics of change, ecosystems are beset by a complex of uncertainties and potential "surprises" in the human, biological and environmental realms. Traditional disturbance regimes may be important for ecosystem structure and functioning, and may need to be maintained or restored. The ecosystem approach must utilise adaptive management in order to anticipate and cater for such changes and events and should be cautious in making any decision that may foreclose options, but, at the same time, consider mitigating actions to cope with long-term changes such as climate change.

Principle 10: The ecosystem approach should seek the appropriate balance between, and integration of, conservation and use of biological diversity.
Biological diversity is critical both for its intrinsic value and because of the key role it plays in providing the ecosystem and other services upon which we all ultimately depend. There has been a tendency in the past to manage components of biological diversity either as protected or non-protected. There is a need for a shift to more flexible situations, where conservation and use are seen in context and the full range of measures is applied in a continuum from strictly protected to human-made ecosystems.

Principle 11: The ecosystem approach should consider all forms of relevant information, including scientific and indigenous and local knowledge, innovations and practices.
Information from all sources is critical to arriving at effective ecosystem management strategies. A much better knowledge of ecosystem functions and the impact of human use is desirable. All relevant information from any concerned area should be shared with all stakeholders and actors, taking into account, inter alia, any decision to be taken under Article 8(j) of the Convention on Biological Diversity. Assumptions behind proposed management decisions should be made explicit and checked against available knowledge and views of stakeholders.

> Principle 12: The ecosystem approach should involve all relevant sectors of society and scientific disciplines.
>
> Most problems of biological-diversity management are complex, with many interactions, side-effects and implications, and therefore should involve the necessary expertise and stakeholders at the local, national, regional and international level, as appropriate.

Last but not least, the CBD Programme of Work on Protected Areas approved at the 7th Conference of the Parties to the Convention (February, 2004) includes an entire programme element on "Governance, participation, equity and benefit sharing".[76] The programme promotes equity and benefit-sharing and the full and effective participation of indigenous and local communities in the establishment and management of protected areas. It recommends the parties, inter alia, to:

2.2.1 Establish policies and institutional mechanisms with full participation of indigenous and local communities, to facilitate the legal recognition and effective management of indigenous and local community conserved areas in a manner consistent with the goals of conserving both biodiversity and the knowledge, innovations and practices of indigenous and local communities.

2.2.2 Implement specific plans and initiatives to effectively involve indigenous and local communities, with respect for their rights consistent with national legislation and applicable international obligations, and stakeholders at all levels of protected areas planning, establishment, governance and management, with particular emphasis on identifying and removing barriers preventing adequate participation.

2.2.4 Promote an enabling environment (legislation, policies, capacities, and resources) for the involvement of indigenous and local communities and relevant stakeholders[77] in decision making, and the development of their capacities and opportunities to establish and manage protected areas, including community-conserved and private protected areas.

Another critical international instrument is the Convention to Combat Desertification, which provides for the formulation and adoption of national action programmes that specify the respective roles of government, local communities and land users, and the resources available and needed. The Parties to the Convention shall,[78] inter alia:

(e) promote policies and strengthen institutional frameworks that develop cooperation and coordination, in a spirit of partnership, among the donor community, governments at all levels, local populations and community groups, and facilitate access by local populations to appropriate information and technology;

(f) provide for effective participation at the local, national and regional levels of non-governmental organisations and local populations, both women and men, particularly resource users, including farmers and pastoralists and their representative organisations, in policy planning, decision-making, and implementation and review of national action programmes.

Like the emphasis on partnerships, a second important trend of the past few years has been the adoption, by most multi-lateral, bi-lateral, governmental and

---

[76] For more comprehensive analysis and guidance on the implications of the CBD Programme of Work regarding indigenous peoples and local communities, see Borrini-Feyerabend et al., 2004 (in press).

[77] In this context nomadic communities and pastoralists are given special reference.

[78] See http://www.unccd.int/main.php

non-governmental agencies, of the discourse on communities and participation. Yet, beyond the apparent homogeneity of this discourse, there are differing ideologies and perspectives even within individual organisations[79] and, even more importantly, the practice does not always correspond to policy discourse and rhetoric.[80]

For example, non-governmental organisations from 26 countries have federated in the Pan-European Eco Forum to promote the Convention on Access to Information, Public Participation in Decision-making and Access to Justice in Environmental Matters (Aarhus Convention).[81] The Aarhus Convention has been ratified by 17 countries (only Denmark and Italy among western European countries) and came into force in October 2001. The convention concerns in particular issues related to the installation of industrial plants (for energy– including nuclear, mining, chemical and genetically modified organisms, or industrial meat production and waste management facilities that have environmental effects). The Aarhus Convention has been promoted mainly by non-governmental organisations in Eastern Europe but poses a serious challenge to nominally democratic Western European governments, which have shown particular resistance to its ratification.[82] It seems that, once again, civil society needs to organise and take action to secure and consolidate its rights.

As seen in this rapid survey of policies that can foster or impede co-management regimes, inclusive participation and citizen engagement are key to getting such policies right. This is miles away from the meek "consultation" and "dialogue" on terms largely decided by others often proposed by environment and development agencies, governments and corporations. To get to the heart of the matter, the very process of policy-making (who makes policy and how) needs to be understood and transformed. The themes "empowerment of peoples", "democratic participation", "citizen voice", "inclusion in policy making" and "information democracy" should be explored in great detail. As some would say, a non negotiable principle is that participation is a basic human right.

> The Aarhus Convention poses a serious challenge to nominally democratic Western European governments, which have shown particular resistance to its ratification.

---

79 Jeanrenaud 2002.
80 Pimbert, 2004a; Pimbert, 2004b.
81 See www.unece.org/env/pp and Box 10.14 earlier in this Chapter.
82 Finger-Stitch and Finger, 2003.

Chapter 11. EMPOWERING CIVIL SOCIETY FOR POLICY CHANGE

11.1 The politics of policy

...it is to be expected that the dominant policy reflects and reinforces the interests of the powerful, be they the political parties, individuals or aristocracies in control of government and/ or influential corporations, financial giants and key market forces.

A policy is the result of numerous interactions among the social actors who, directly or indirectly, shape its content, interpretation and implementation. In general, thus, a "policy-making process" reflects the power relations that exist in society. In other words, it is to be expected that the dominant policy reflects and reinforces the interests of the powerful– be they the political parties, individuals or aristocracies in control of government and/ or influential corporations, financial giants and key market forces.

A few questions help to shed light on the policy making process: "Which actors are involved? Where is "policy-making" actually taking place? Who has the final control and say? Whose knowledge is included and whose excluded? Whose interests are served? Is someone held accountable? If so, to whom, and how?" Asking these questions helps to shift attention from an analysis of policies per se ("Are policies addressing the relevant issues? Are policies good or misguided? ") to the analysis of the policy process ("Whose perspectives, knowledge, values, and aspirations are embedded in policies, and whose are excluded? Through which avenues can policies be improved?").

Issues of power and knowledge are at the heart of negotiations and agreements on natural resource management and co-management practitioners have frequent encounters with them. Broadly speaking, knowledge and values get established or embodied in policy through three main pathways[1] which may be used alone or in combination, namely:

- as a reflection of structured political interests, which happens when policy change results from open interactions and struggles among groups with differing political interests (examples include different classes, factions within the state, the state and society);[2]

- as a by-product of the initiative of specific actors, which happens when some actors have discretion over the policy process[3] and exercise their own interests, capacities and responsibilities;

- as part of the power-knowledge relations that frame practice, which happens when, for instance, political issues and choices are recast in the "neutral" language of science and hidden behind the symbols of scientific authority; in this sense, policies are part of a dominant "discourse" that defines the world and, in the process, excludes alternative interpretations.[4]

Despite the difficulties inherent in deciphering the language of policy studies, a good understanding of what actually happens in policy-making processes can be very useful for people engaged in co-management and for civil society in general (see Box 11.1). This understanding can nurture a critical analysis of "the rules of the game" and promote fairer representation systems and better social inclusion in the policy process.

Box 11.1   What do we mean by "civil society"?
(adapted from Edwards, 2004; Howell and Pearce, 2001)

There are two broad ways in which "civil society" can be understood. The first– and the one encountered most commonly– is civil society as made up of non-market organisations that exist between the household and the state. Civil society may thus comprise non-governmental organisations (such as those involved in natural resource management and agricultural development interventions),[5] social movements (such as indigenous peoples and farmers' movements), membership organisations and trade unions (such as peasant unions)[6] and customary, informal organisations. This understanding is sometimes known as the "associationalist" view of civil society.

A second interpretation understands civil society as the arena within which public debate occurs and in which dominant ideas about how society ought to be organised are discussed and formed by citizens. This might be referred to as a "public sphere" or "deliberative" view of civil society. At a national level, civil society would be, for instance, the social milieu that develops propositions about safeguarding the interests of small scale resource users and farmers. At a more local level it might comprise the people and groups that develop decisions about environmental care or public health through a participatory budgeting process. Within a community it may be the sphere in which ideas about women's role in local leadership are debated, reproduced or modified.

Both interpretations of "civil society" are used in this volume.

---

1   Keeley and Scoones, 1999.
2   Hill, 1997.
3   Long and van der Ploeg, 1989.
4   Hajer, 1995; Grillo, 1997.
5   Farrington et al., 1993.
6   Bebbington, 1996.

Four emerging trends[7] provide a strong rationale for the direct participation of citizens[8] in the formulation and implementation of policies throughout the world:

1. Increased citizens' demand for more direct forms of democracy. In many countries representative democracy has been heavily criticised for its inability to protect citizens' interests. Marginalised groups in both the North and the South often do not participate effectively in such representative democracy. The poor are often badly organised and ill-served by the organisations that mobilise their votes and claim to represent their interests. The crisis of legitimacy faced by institutions in the eyes of the poor, and a growing number of middle income citizens, is widely documented. Drawing from participatory research in 23 countries, the recent "Consultations with the Poor" report,[9] prepared for the World Development Report 2001, concludes:

The poor are often badly organised and ill-served by the organisations that mobilise their votes and claim to represent their interests.

"From the perspectives of poor people world wide, there is a crisis in governance. While the range of institutions that play important roles in poor people's lives is vast, poor people are excluded from participation in governance. State institutions, whether represented by central ministries or local government are often neither responsive nor accountable to the poor; rather the report details the arrogance and disdain with which poor people are treated. Poor people see little recourse to injustice, criminality, abuse and corruption by institutions. Not surprisingly, poor men and women lack confidence in the state institutions even though they still express their willingness to partner with them under fairer rules."

Civil society organisations, in the North and the South, have also been demanding that citizens' voices be heard during the formulation of government policies to meet human needs in environmentally sustainable ways. Many of them argue that citizen deliberation and inclusion can improve the quality of decision-making and make the policy process more legitimate, effective and efficient.[10]

2. Increased policy complexity and uncertainty of results. Policy-making processes involve a good deal of decisions based on imperfect knowledge of their consequences. As policy-related issues and socio-environmental systems become more complex and unstable, such uncertainties increase.[11] Active management interventions and technological risks are particularly noteworthy in this connection. For example, variation within and among ecosystems is enormous. Daily, seasonal and longer term changes in the spatial structure of ecosystems are apparent—from the landscape level to the small plot of cultivated land. Uncertainty, variability and non-equilibrium conditions demand flexible responses and adaptive management practices. Managers must be able to monitor and respond to ecosystem changes and be central actors in analysis, planning, negotiations and action.[12] Local co-management bodies or platforms are well placed to monitor environmental change and deal with the unpredictable interactions between people and ecosystems. Like adaptive management, they involve iterative processes, based on feedback and continuous learning. Adaptive management thus calls for local actors to participate in deliberating and acting on the basis of local feedbacks from the environment.

---

[7]   This section is based on Pimbert and Wakeford (2001a and 2001b) and references therein.

[8]   We note that the concept of citizen is at times understood to exclude indigenous peoples and minority ethnic groups and refugees who are not considered to be part of the Nation State. Yet, the word "citizen" was in use before the emergence of the Nation State (it derives from the Latin civis) referring to all individuals involved in the management of community affairs. In this volume the word citizen is used in this broad sense to include all people living and working in a given country.

[9]   Quote from page 172 of Narayan et al. (2000).

[10] Calame, 2003.

[11] IDS, 2003.

[12] Gunderson, Holling and Light, 1995; Berkes and Folke, 1998; Röling and Wagemakers, 1998.

This call is only amplified by the sweeping changes that currently affect the world. Climate change and the interactions between genetically modified organisms (GMOs) and the environment are characterised by high levels of local uncertainty. Same is for predicting the local impact of, let us say, releasing new types of industrial waste (e.g., nanoparticles) or endocrine-disrupting chemicals into the environment. Conventional risk management approaches and cost benefit analysis are inadequate when we know neither the probabilities of possible outcomes nor the phenomena that can affect those outcomes in significant ways ("we do not know what we do not know"). Given such uncertainty in the face of complexity, perceptions of both problems and solutions are essentially value-laden. And "experts" are no better equipped to decide on questions of values and interests than any other groups of people[13]– another powerful argument for more inclusive forms of participation and deliberation in the policy process.

3. More critical perspectives on "science" and professional expertise. "Science" plays a central role in determining much of the content and practice of policies that shape people-environment interactions, as "experts" (foresters, agronomists, rangeland specialists, economists….) decide about social, economic and environmental issues. With respect to democratic politics, these are much more opaque pathways, as the roots of decisions can supposedly be understood only by small elites of scientists and fellow experts. Increasingly, however, one can perceive mistrust and cynicism and a sense of declining legitimacy vis-à-vis professional and scientific expertise. This is particularly true in countries where poorly trusted government institutions are tightly associated with scientific expertise in policy-making. Some of the reasons for this eroded trust include:

- People are exposed to a wide range of opinions from experts and counter experts in scientific controversies. This undermines the positivist view of knowledge with its claim that any group of experts faced with the same problem should arrive at the same conclusions. Many people in industrialised and post-industrialised countries no longer view "Science" as representing knowledge that is certain and unique.[14] They rather see a plurality of sciences– each offering a different perspective upon the world, each gifted with internal debates and controversies.

- At least a part of the public has also been informed by radical critiques that present science as an embodiment of values in theories, things, therapies, systems, software and institutions. As all these values are part of ideologies (world views), scientists appear immersed in the very same cultural and economic conflicts, contradictions and compromises as all other citizens.[15]

- Citizens feel "at risk" from science-based social and technological developments. For example, the recent crisis in European countries over bovine spongiform encephalopathy and GMOs has undermined public confidence in scientific expertise. This has been compounded by evidence of collusion between some key government experts and the commercial interests of industry. Citizens are increasingly sceptical of scientific solutions when the "experts" who recommend the solutions have contributed to creating the relevant public health and environmental crises in the first place.

Again, in both the North and the South, more deliberative and inclusive policy-making processes seem to be an important pathway to overcome low confidence in government institutions and scientific expertise. In such processes, the value of

Policy by scientific expertise is an opaque process... the roots of decisions can supposedly be understood only by small elites of scientists and fellow experts.

...scientists appear immersed in the very same cultural and economic conflicts, contradictions and compromises as all other citizens.

13   Irwin, 2001; Stirling, 2001.
14   Irwin, 1995; Irwin, 2001.
15   Levidow, 1986; Levidow and Young, 1981; Young, 1977.

formal science is recognised, but so are the citizens' perspectives.[16] In fact, advocates argue that more deliberative and inclusive processes involving citizens and the "lay public" generate a much better understanding of all science-policy questions[17] and, in particular, of the uncertainties that surround them.

4. Enhanced advocacy for human rights, social justice and local empowerment. New social movements and peoples' coalitions throughout the world are reaffirming the importance of human rights over economics and the rule of market forces.[18] For these movements, human rights, justice and democratic accountability are enhanced when the formulation of policies and the design of technologies involve "inclusive deliberation". Inclusive deliberation, a process whose key features are described in Checklist 11.2, potentially allows men, women, the elderly and children to exercise their human right to participate, as citizens, in decisions about society, the environment and the organisation of economic life. In this sense, people are not mere users of policies or social entities subjected to them. They are, instead, active makers and shapers of the realities that affect their lives.[19] Much of this argument draws its legitimacy from the Universal Declaration of Human Rights and resonates with political traditions in which direct citizen empowerment and action are the central objectives of a just and free society that celebrates diversity, empathy and virtue.[20]

How best to recognise the legitimacy of a variety of systems of knowledge [and the need for guidance by] the opinions, aspirations and values of the people and institutions concerned with the relevant policies?

The four trends just summarised provide a rationale for "citizen inclusion" and "democratic deliberation" in the policy process and thus suggest the following reforms:

● Opening up policy processes to more diverse forms of knowledge. The issue here is not to choose between popular knowledge and scientific expertise, but to recognise the legitimacy of a variety of systems of knowledge, and to give them all a place in the decision- and policy-making process. The intent is also to demystify scientific knowledge, bringing it closer to the lives and realities of people and making it more transparent and less threatening.

● Recognising that knowledge is not separated from values. The world views and ideologies of those who possess or produce knowledge are woven into it by virtue of the questions asked, the answers provided and the conditions under which the knowledge itself has been generated. In the decision-making process, knowledge must therefore be complemented and guided by the opinions, aspirations and values of the people and institutions concerned with these policies.

● Embracing participatory decision-making approaches. Methods and procedures exist that allow for the involvement of people and organisations in policy making processes. This is particularly important for the people normally excluded from planning and decisions. Creativity and courage are required to use such methods and procedures, and thereby combat exclusion, offering to all concerned people a fair chance to participate

How best to involve in policy making people normally excluded from planning and decisions?

● Understanding that policy-making is more than formulating policies. In order to be meaningful and durable, policy processes ought to introduce monitoring, evaluation and feedback mechanisms and place the responsibility of managing policies in the hands of those who are supposed to be served by them. At all stages in policy processes, there is also a need to enhance transparency, accountability and credibility.

---

16 Mirenowicz, 2001; Satya Murty and Wakeford, 2001; Sclove, 2001.
17 Stirling, 2001.
18 Amin and Houtard, 2002; Le Monde Diplomatique, 2004.
19 Cornwall and Gaventa, 2001.
20 Woodcock, 1975.

Inclusive and participatory processes of policy-making are likely to be more effective, because of their potential to (a) build ownership among participants; (b) encourage change and make implementation easier; (c) result in empowerment through information sharing, capacity building and confidence building; and (d) create space and demand for new policies.

Policy making is complex and power-laden. Throughout the world, exclusionary and narrow policy processes seem to act to reinforce the values and interests of the more powerful social actors and their networks. Nuanced scholarly studies of policy change also show how policy dynamics are influenced by powerful combinations of political interests, dominant policy discourses and narratives, and effective actor networks that span local, national and international levels.[21] What, then, are the realistic prospects for citizen engagement in decision-making processes? How and under what conditions can previously marginalised voices be included in the framing, interpretation and implementation of the policies that affect both people and natural resources?

There are no unique or full answers to these questions. But our collective experience suggests that, at the very least, two complementary pathways exist that can empower citizens for policy change in co-management: i) the use of specific methods and approaches to expand democratic deliberation and inclusion, and ii) the direct and self-conscious strengthening of civil society.

11.2 Methods and approaches for participatory policy processes

A glimpse of history

Experiments in deliberation and participatory decision-making have a long history. In book 7 of Republic, Plato enumerates the subjects that might be useful for the future leaders of the state: music, arithmetic, geometry, astronomy. These subjects have important theoretical aspects and are expected to shape the mind of the future ruler. In this sense, Socrates asks questions such as "What is virtue?" and mocks people who are unable to provide an abstract definition for it. In contrast to ideal concepts and abstract theory, Protagoras stressed that "man is the measure

---

21   See for example Keeley and Scoones, 1999; Mayers and Bass, 2004.

The distinction
between Plato and
Protagoras, between
the perfect but
simplified world of
abstract ideas and
theories and the
imperfect and
messy, but concrete
and extremely rich
world of human
experience, can still
be traced in
contemporary policy
making processes.

of all things", i.e., personal experience and perspective are central to our ways of knowing and what we say always comes accompanied by a sort of "personal guarantee". For him, then, the question becomes "Was the person X virtuous in that particular situation?"

The distinction between Plato and Protagoras– between the perfect but simplified world of abstract ideas and theories and the imperfect and messy, but concrete and extremely rich world of human experience[22]– can still be traced in contemporary policy making processes. In some socio-cultural surroundings, supposedly objective expert capacities, and the "philosophers" delivering them, are top values. In others, what truly counts is the direct experience and participation of citizens. At heart, this already spells out the distinction between representative and participatory, or direct, democracy.[23] Participatory democracy is distinct from representative democratic systems, such as elected members of parliaments or senates, in that it puts decision-making powers more directly in the hands of ordinary people.[24] In this connection, European and Northern American history offer several lessons that may be of relevance today. The following are just a few illustrative examples among many others that could be chosen from all around the world.

In the Social Contract (1763) Rousseau suggested that participatory approaches to democracy had the advantage of demonstrating that "no citizen is a master of another" and that, in society, "all of us are equally dependent on our fellow citizens". Rousseau suggested that participation in decision—making increases the feeling among individual citizens that they belong in their community. As early as 1790s, William Godwin proposed that government should be mainly reduced to a system of juries and assemblies that would deliberate and carry out all the functions that could be carried out voluntarily or enforced informally through public opinion and social pressure.[25] Others have since argued that not only is democratic deliberation theoretically possible, it is, and probably has been, a feature of everyday human existence. There is indeed abundant evidence of deliberation in situations as disparate as the Athenian assembly of ancient Greece, tribal councils all over the world, revolutionary movements in the last century and modern experiences in popular direct democracy.[26]

For example, E.P. Thompson's historical analysis illustrated how the Luddites of nineteenth century England sought to subject new technologies to a public trial, just as they had put food prices on trial in previous generations.[27] Far from opposing all new technology, recent studies have suggested that the Luddites were in favour of certain innovations as long as they did not threaten their quality of life.[28] As historian Steve Woolgar has put it, "The conventional arguments that assert the Luddites to be irrational resisters to progress– because they mistakenly assumed either capitalism or machinery to be irrational– are based on essentialist notions of progress.... The Luddites failed not because they misrecognised the machine [as their enemy] but because the alliance of forces arrayed against them was too great for their interpretation to prevail".[29]

the Luddites of
nineteenth century
sought to subject
new technologies to
a public trial... they
were in favour of
certain innovations
as long as they did
not threaten their
quality of life.

Writing in the United States in 1909, Dewey pointed to the dangers that arose whenever experts become detached from the concerns of the public, or when the

---

22 On this see also Feyerabend, 1999.
23 This section draws on Pimbert and Wakeford, 2001a; Wakeford and Pimbert, 2003 and references therein.
24 Pateman 1970.
25 Clark, undated.
26 Bookchin, 1982; Bookchin, 1996; Bookchin 1998.
27 Thompson, 1963.
28 Sale, 1996.
29 Woolgar, 1997.

public is excluded from the process of long-term social planning.[30] Unless both sides are engaged in continuous and mutually educative dialogue, neither experts nor citizens are, he suggested, capable of utilising the full range of tools available to them. He also proposed that experts could never achieve monopoly control over knowledge required for adequate social planning because of the extent to which "they become a specialised class; they are shut off from knowledge of the needs they are supposed to serve". When insulated and unaccountable, he argued, this "cadre of experts" became not a public resource, but a public problem.

While accepting that citizens must often depend on experts for the gathering of facts and construction of policy scenarios, Dewey attacked those who dismissed the public's capability to participate in policy-making. He suggested that, given the prevailing culture of secrecy and propaganda, citizens had not been given a fair chance to fulfil their potential in this role. It was impossible to presume the quality of contribution citizens might make if balanced information were available. For example both past and present experience with trial by jury do indeed suggests that citizens are quite capable of engaging in deliberations and arbitrating complex issues (Box 11.2).

Box 11.2   A history of trial by jury
(adapted from Wakeford, 2002; Wakeford and Pimbert, 2003; PEALS, 2003)

It is unclear whether the European system of trial by jury originated in Ancient Greece, where various versions were widely practiced, or in more ancient civilisations. What is certain is that systems of "participatory justice" have been found in various societies throughout recorded history.

Whether or not it had existed there previously, the system of jury trial was brought to Britain with the Norman invaders in 1066. Firmly established by the time of the Magna Carta in 1215, the jury involved ordinary people picked from a wide population and allowed them to hear from witnesses, deliberate in secrecy and reach a decision by majority vote that would then be announced publicly. By the Fifteenth Century it had replaced non-rational methods of trial, such as trial by ordeal, and became established as the form of trial for both criminal and civil cases at common law. The perceived justice of the jury system led to it being taken up across Britain as a tool for achieving social justice. In towns around the country, for instance a people's court often set what was a "fair" price for foodstuffs such as bread and grain.

Whilst elected governments make the laws, it is juries that are able to decide the innocence or guilt of anyone charged with breaking many of those laws, making it a key instrument of participatory democracy. Over the centuries they have achieved an importance to many democracies and have had to be fiercely defended. One senior judge surveying the limiting of a government's power provided by the jury over the centuries compared the jury to: "a little parliament.... No tyrant could afford to leave a subject's freedom in the hands of twelve of his countrymen.... Trial by jury is more than an instrument of justice and more than one wheel of the constitution: it is the lamp that shows that freedom lives".[31] Today, jury trials are practised in the UK, USA, and many other democracies around the world, including Australia, Brazil, Russia and Spain. Perhaps no other institution of government rivals the jury in placing power so directly in the hands of citizens, or wagers more on the truth of democracy's core claim that the people make their own best governors.[32]

Contrary to what might be expected from surveys highlighting apparent public ignorance of science, studies of even highly technical court cases have shown citizens able to deal with technical issues at

---

[30]   Dewey, 1927.
[31]   Devlin, 1956.
[32]   Abramson, 2000.

least as well as the judges. Even in cases where it is claimed that trial by jury is inappropriate because of the scientific nature of evidence, potential problems can usually be overcome if the manner of presenting the evidence is given careful consideration.

Studies comparing the decisions reached by jurors compared with those reached by judicial experts found that the same verdicts were reached in 75-80% of cases. Crucially, this proportion did not change in complex as opposed to less complex cases.[33]

A growing number of people today see democracy without citizen participation and discussion as an empty and meaningless concept. This understanding of politics is the starting point for a growing number of experiments and initiatives that create new spaces for citizens to directly influence decisions affecting their lives.

Such innovations go under various labels, ranging from participatory democracy, to deliberative democracy, to "empowered participatory governance".[34] Whilst extremely diverse in style and context, these initiatives share several common features. These include:

...innovations go under various labels, ranging from participatory democracy, to deliberative democracy, to "empowered participatory governance".

● a concern with more active and participatory forms of citizenship. Such views go beyond the notions of citizens as clients or consumers, as articulated during the 1980s and 1990s, to citizens who engage in policies, in agenda setting for research and in the delivery of services. They also profess to go beyond consultation to more empowered forms of involvement that renew or establish traditions of direct democracy;

● an emphasis on inclusion, especially of racial and ethnic minorities, women, youth, older people, and others seen as previously excluded or marginalised;

● a simultaneous emphasis on the involvement of multiple actors in new forms of partnership, which in turn enable wider ownership of decisions, processes and projects;

● a strong emphasis on broader forms of accountability, which enable multiple partners to hold institutions, professionals and policy makers to account through social, legal, fiscal and political means;

● the search for new political forms that realise the democratic ideal of government of and by, as well as for, the people. These political forms are participatory because they rely on the commitment and capacities of ordinary people to make sensible decisions through reasoned and conscious deliberation, and they are empowered because they try to link discussion with action.

33 Abramson, 2000.
34 Fung and Wright, 2003.

Participatory methods for inclusive deliberation

In the 1990s, deliberative and inclusive processes (DIPs) have been increasingly applied to the formulation of a wide range of policies in countries of both the North and the South.[35] These approaches aim to improve deliberation of policy and policy-making practice through the inclusion of a variety of social actors in consultation, planning and decision-making.

Diverse procedures, techniques and methods can be used to engage different actors in deliberative processes. Examples are citizens juries, scenario workshops, public hearings and visioning exercises illustrated in Checklist 11.1. These approaches and methods differ substantially in detail and have been applied to a wide range of issues and contexts. They all, however, seek to adopt to varying degrees the criteria of deliberation and inclusion listed in Checklist 11.2. When these methods and approaches are used well, they are part of a process in which professional expertise, local expertise, negotiation skills, research skills, and democratic values are the basis for creating new knowledge and promoting social and ecological change.

Checklist 11.1 A selection of methods that can be used in deliberative inclusive processes for policy-making
(adapted from Chambers, 1997; Warner, 1997; Clarke, 1998; ESRC,1998; Holland,1998; Lowndes and Stoker, 1998; IPPR, 1999; Stirling and Maher, 1999; del Valle, 1999)[36]

● Citizens juries
A citizens jury is a group of citizens– chosen to be a fair representation of the local population– brought together to consider a particular issue set by the local authority. Citizens juries receive evidence from expert witnesses and cross-questioning can occur. The process may last up to several days, at the end of which a report is drawn up to set out the views of the jury, including any differences in opinion. Juries' views are intended to inform government decision-making.

● Citizens panels
▹ Research panels
A research panel is a large sample of a local population used as a sounding board by a public sector organisation. It is a form of research which tracks changes in opinion and attitudes over time. In Germany for example, these panels are known to consist of 500-3000 participants. Members are recruited either by mail or by telephone as a sample of a given population. Panels have a standing membership and a proportion of their members is replaced regularly. Participants are asked regularly about different issues over a period of time.

▹ Interactive panels
Other models also have a standing membership, which may be replaced over time but basically consists of small groups of people meeting regularly to deliberate on issues and make policy recommendations.

● Consensus conferences
A panel of lay people who develop their understanding of technical or scientific issues in dialogue with experts. A panel of between 10-20 volunteers are recruited through advertisements. A steering committee is set up with members chosen by the sponsors. The panel's members attend two weekends where they are briefed on the subject and identify the questions they want to ask in the conference. The conference lasts for 3-4 days and gives the panel a chance to ask experts any outstanding questions. The conference is open to the public and the audience can also ask questions. The

---

35 Pimbert and Wakeford, 2001a.
36 For a description of other methods that could be used for participatory policy-making see NEF, 1998.

panel's members retire and independently of the steering committee prepare a report that sets out their views on the subject. Copies of the report are made available to the conference audience and panel members present key sections to the audience.

● Deliberative opinion poll
This method measures informed opinion on an issue. A deliberative poll examines what the public at large thinks when it has had the occasion and information to consider the matter carefully and closely. A baseline survey of opinion and demography is carried out and the participants of the poll are then recruited to resemble the wider group both in terms of demography and attitude. Often briefing begins before the event by means of written or/ and visual information. Then, during several days, the participants deliberate in smaller groups and compose questions to be put to experts and politicians in plenary group discussions. Their views on a given subject are measured before the poll begins and again once it has finished. Changes in opinion are measured and incorporated into a report. Deliberative polls are often held in conjunction with television companies.

● Visioning exercises and future search conferences
A range of methods (including focus groups) may be used within a visioning exercise, the purpose of which is to establish the "vision" participants have of the future and the kind of the future they would like to create. Visioning may be used to inform broad strategy for a locality, or may have a more specific focus (as in environmental consultations for Local Agenda 21 or, indeed for all sorts of co-management agreements as described in Section 6.2 of this volume).

The heart of future search conferences is a two- to four-day meeting where participants attempt to create a shared vision of the future. It brings together those with the power to make decisions with those affected by decisions to try to agree on a plan of action. The process is managed by a steering group of local people representing key sections of the community. People who are recruited are asked to form several "stakeholder groups" within the conference. They take part in a structured two- to four-day process in which they move from reviewing the past to creating ideal future scenarios. Each of the stakeholder groups explains its vision and then a shared vision is explored. The conference ends with the development of action plans and policy recommendations. Self-selected action groups develop projects and commit themselves to action towards their vision.

● Innovative development
Innovative development is a methodology consisting of four participatory steps. First, an "action map" is formulated. This is a systematic vision for action of an attainable and desired future that reflects the consensus of participants. Second, there is estimation of the distance from the current situation to the attainable future and of the capabilities that are available. Third, is a study of "potentialities"– the systematic identification and evaluation of each of the prospective actions. Fourth, is the design for action. All methodological steps are carried out through the participation of relevant actors who are convoked by an appropriate and legitimate authority. This, in fact, is very close to the steps of the co-management process described in Sections 6.3 and 6.4 of this volume.

● Participatory Rural Appraisal (PRA)/ Participatory Learning and Action (PLA)
A family of approaches, methods and behaviours to enable people to express and analyse the realities of their lives and conditions, and to plan, monitor and evaluate action that seems appropriate to them. In PRA/ PLA, outsiders act as catalysts for local people to decide what to do with the information and analysis that they generate. PRA methods include participant observation, semi-structured interviews and visual techniques (maps, matrices, trend lines, diagrams).

● Issue forums
These are ongoing bodies with regular meetings, which focus on a particular issue (e.g., community safety or health promotion). They may have a set membership or operate on an open basis, and are often able to make recommendations to relevant council committees or to share in decision-making processes. In India, for example, "issue forums" or "study circles" in villages (see Section 5.2 of this volume) are spaces where villagers gather to discuss specific subjects of interest, e.g., the impact of

non-timber forest produce collection, or honey collection, or hunting. Sometimes they will call in outside experts to help. The understanding and information that they generate is then used in the village assembly decision-making processes.

- Multi-criteria mapping
Multi-Criteria Mapping (MCM) attempts to combine the transparency of numerical approaches with the unconstrained framing of discursive deliberations. The technique involves a rather complex series of steps, including: deciding the subject area, defining the basic policy options, selecting the participants, conducting individual interviews (2-3 hour sessions where additional options are selected, evaluative criteria are defined, options are scored and relative weighting is given to criteria), having researchers carrying out quantitative and qualitative analyses of the opinions of the participants, providing feedback on preliminary results, developing deliberations among participants and, after a final analysis, producing a report and policy recommendations.

Many of the methods described above are combined and used in the co-management process described in Chapters 4, 5 and 6 of this volume.

Checklist 11.2 Some features of deliberative and inclusive processes (DIPs)
(adapted from Holmes and Scoones, 2000; and references therein)

- Deliberation is defined as "careful consideration" or "the discussion of reasons for and against". Deliberation is a common, if not inherent, component of all decision-making in democratic societies.

- Inclusion is the action of involving others. An inclusive decision-making process is based on the active involvement of multiple social actors and emphasises the participation of previously excluded citizens.

- Social interaction is at the heart of the DIPs, which normally incorporate face-to-face meetings among those involved.

- There is a dependence on language through discussion and debate. This is usually in the form of verbal and visual constructions rather than written text.

- A deliberative process assumes that, at least initially, there are different positions held by the participants and that these views are all respected.

- DIPs are designed to enable participants to evaluate and re-evaluate their positions in the light of different perspectives and new evidence.

- The form of negotiation is often seen as containing value over and above the "quality of the decisions" that emerge. Participants share a commitment to the resolution of problems through public reasoning and dialogue aimed at mutual understanding, even if perfect consensus is not being achieved or even expected as possible.

- There is the recognition that, while the goal is usually to reach decisions, or at least positions upon which decisions can subsequently be taken, an unhurried, reflective and reasonably open-ended discussion is required for those decisions to be solidly grounded and "owned".

Several examples of the use of DIPs for environmental policy making are described and analysed in Table 11.1. A recent example from South India shows how citizens juries and scenario workshop methods were combined in participatory assessments of policy futures for food, farming and the environment (see Box 11.3).

Table 11.1 Examples of deliberative and inclusive processes in environmental policy making (adapted from Holmes and Scoones, 2000; Pimbert and Wakeford, 2001a; further case studies and more detailed information on the outcomes of these processes can be found in Holmes and Scoones, 2000)

Case	Why was the process organised?	Who was included?	What procedures and methods were used?
Innovative Development for Air quality in Santiago, Chile[37]	To render manageable a highly complex environmental problem. To get the mutual commitment of the citizens and government to a plan that is legitimate and effective. To produce a metropolitan plan and enable its participative management/ implementation.	Different participants at different stages, including government officers, NGO members, consultants, university researchers and citizens. [About one half of the instruments included in the plan that was produced came from the citizens proposals!]	Workshops and discussion in small groups by representatives and citizens. Action mapping. Participatory formulation of plan. A follow up conference towards participative management.
Land tenure policy change in Madagascar and Guinea[38]	To inform policy decisions at the national level regarding land tenure policy and national resource management legislation.	Direct participation of citizens in information production. National academics, development workers and government staff involved in conducting case studies and rapid rural appraisals (RRAs), trained and facilitated by the Land Tenure Centre at Wisconsin University. In Guinea, the RRA facilitation teams included only government staff.	Case studies prepared using participatory techniques were presented to multiple government and NGO stakeholders at various regional workshops.
Wetland management policy development In Pakistan and India[39]	To assess current impact of protected area policies on local communities. To revise management plans in the light of interaction between local people and outsiders. To initiate dialogue on policy reforms needed.	Direct participation of citizens in information production and alternative management plan for protected areas.	PRA training for government and WWF staff. Appraisals completed in villages in National Parks in both India and Pakistan. Public deliberations on reforms in wetland management regimes.

37 del Valle, 1999.
38 Freudenberger, 1996.
39 Pimbert and Gujja, 1997.

Gestion de terroir (GT – landscape management) process in Mali[40]	To negotiate land use plans (maps of the terroir delineating what resources exist and are to be used for what). To train communities in natural resource management. Possibly, to agree upon investments in natural resources. [These objectives were criticised as having been largely predetermined and bureaucracy-biased.]	Farmers, pastoralists, GT team members, and local government (to a limited extent).	Teams of facilitators bring different stakeholders to reflect on local land use (within the terroir) and to develop plans for improvement through PRA methods. [A criticism to this method is that the frame for deliberation was set from above, thus it may not have been the most relevant unit for local livelihood, it might have been biased against pastoralists, etc.]
Citizens Panel in Switzerland[41]	To locate a waste disposal site in the Canton Aargau.	Citizens of twelve communities that offered potentially suitable locations for a waste disposal site were asked to take part in a citizen panel and met regularly over six months. The Citizen's Panel involved a random sample of the relevant potential site communities.	Within the Panel, four committees were established, they got introduced to the issues, they discussed conflicting interpretations and different options, and they evaluated the options, produced recommendations, discussed them in a supra-committee and made final recommendations available to media and public officials.
National Biodiversity Strategy and Action Plan, India[42]	To prepare a series of action plans at local, state, regional, and national levels, for conservation of biodiversity, and sustainable use of biological resources. To achieve equity in conservation and use of natural resources.	Various rightholders and stakeholders, including indigenous peoples and local communities, NGOs, government officials, academics and students, industry, armed forces, etc. Over 50,000 people have been involved.	Public outreach through various communication media.Planning exercises at local (village), district, state, and inter-state levels. Public participation through workshops, public hearings, rallies, biodiversity festivals, cultural programmes, school competitions, etc. Local, state, and national level consultations to review results and draft documents, and to finalise the action plans.

40   Keeley and Scoones, 1999.
41   Renn and Webler, 1992.
42   Kohli and Kothari, 2003.

Local Agenda 21 in Antalya (Turkey)[43]	To foster a participatory multi-sectored process to strengthen "local governance" for sustainable development.	Everyone invited to working group meetings, and specifically children, women, elders and the disabled.	Citywide consultative mechanisms (city councils and other platforms) and facilitated working group meetings, supposedly non-hierarchical, where people could discuss specific issues. [A criticism levied to this process is that the discourse styles, and the fact of having to make public speeches favoured some participants with respect to others.]

Box 11.3   Prajateerpu– a citizens jury/ scenario workshop on food and farming futures in Andhra Pradesh (India)
(adapted from Pimbert and Wakeford 2002; http://www.iied.org/docs/sarl/Prajateerpu.pdf; Pimbert and Wakeford, 2003; www.prajateerpu.org)

Prajateerpu is an exercise in deliberative democracy that involved marginal farmers and other citizens from all three regions of the state of Andhra Pradesh. The citizens jury was made up of representatives of small and marginal farmers, small traders, food processors and consumers. Prajateerpu was jointly organised by the International Institute for Environment and Development (IIED), the Institute of Development Studies (IDS) at the University of Sussex, the Andhra Pradesh Coalition in Defence of Diversity, The University of Hyderabad, Andhra Pradesh and the all-India National Biodiversity Strategy and Action Plan (NBSAP). The jury hearings took place in Medak District, Andhra Pradesh, on June 25-July 1, 2001. Jury members also included indigenous (known in India as "adivasi") people. Over two-thirds of jury members were women.

The jury members were presented with three different scenarios. Each was advocated by key proponents and opinion-formers who attempted to show the logic behind the scenario. It was up to the jury to decide which of the three policy scenarios most likely provided them with the best opportunities to enhance their livelihoods, food security and environment 20 years from now.

Scenario 1: Vision 2020. This scenario was put forward by Andhra Pradesh's Chief Minister, backed by a World Bank loan. It proposes to consolidate small farms and rapidly increase mechanisation and modernisation of the agricultural sector. Production enhancing technologies such as genetic modification were expected to be introduced in farming and food processing, reducing the number of people on the land from 70% to 40% by 2020.

Scenario 2: An export-based cash crop model of organic production. This was based on proposals from the International Federation of Organic Agriculture Movements (IFOAM) and the International Trade Centre (UNCTAD/ WTO) and was based on environmentally friendly farming linked to national and international markets. This scenario was dependent on the demand of supermarkets in the North for a cheap supply of organic produce, complying with new eco-labelling standards.

Scenario 3: Localised food systems. This scenario was based on increased self-reliance for rural communities, low external input agriculture, and the re-localisation of food production and markets. It included long distance trade only in goods that are surplus to local production or not produced locally.

---

43   Doganay, 2003.

The jury/ scenario workshop process was overseen by an independent panel, a group of external observers drawn from a variety of interest groups. It was their role to ensure that each Food Future was presented in a fair and unprejudiced way, and that the process was trustworthy and not captured by any interest group.

The key conclusions reached by the jury– their own vision of the desired future– included features such as:

● food and farming for self reliance and community control over resources;

● maintaining healthy soils, diverse crops, trees and livestock, and building on indigenous knowledge, practical skills and local institutions.

It also included an opposition to:

● the proposed reduction of those making their living from the land from 70% to 40% in Andhra Pradesh;

● land consolidation in fewer hands and displacement of rural people;

● contract farming;

● labour-displacing mechanisation;

● GM crops– including Vitamin A rice & Bt cotton;

● loss of control over medicinal plants, including their export.

The Prajateerpu and subsequent events show how the poor and marginalised can be included in the policy process. By being linked with state level and international policy processes, the jury outcomes and citizen voice have encouraged more public deliberation and pluralism in the framing of policies on food and agriculture in Andhra Pradesh. The state government that championed Vision 2020 reforms was voted out of office in 2004. The largely rural electorate of Andhra Pradesh voted massively against a government it felt was neglecting farmers' needs, rural communities and their well being.[44] Similarly, the issues highlighted by the Prajateerpu have been partly responsible for the setting up of a UK parliamentary inquiry into the impacts of British bilateral aid to India– and in Andhra Pradesh in particular. At the time of this writing, the inquiry is under way, conducted by the UK Parliament's International Development Committee.[45]

Linking deliberative inclusive processes to broader policy change

No matter how well they are used, participatory methods in and by themselves do not lead to policy changes. DIPs cannot be viewed as the "magic bullet" for enhancing public participation in policy-making and implementation. Despite the key role they can potentially play in framing and defining the boundaries of emerging policies, they are, after all, only a small part of the policy process. In order to be fully effective, participatory methods for inclusion and deliberation must be rooted in the broader context of policy change, where policy change emerges from a variety of sources and where power relations and vested interests are key.

In order to be fully effective, participatory methods for inclusion and deliberation must be rooted in the broader context of policy change, where policy change emerges from a variety of sources and where power relations and vested interests are key.

The experience to date, however, offers relatively few real life examples in which DIPs have been comprehensively applied to policy-making. A recent critical review of 35 case studies argues that there has been little reflection on 1) how DIPs are located within broader policy processes and 2) how citizens involved in

44 http://www.expressindia.com/election/fullstory.php?type=ei&content_id=31318; www.guardian.co.uk/international/story/0,,1212942,00.html

45 www.parliament.uk/parliamentary_committees/international_development/ind040324_21.cfm

...convenors...
determine much of
the style and
content of the
deliberative
process....

participatory dialogue are linked to wider policy networks and the dynamics of policy change.[46] Whilst this study largely ignores the broad historical experience alluded to earlier in this chapter, it does nevertheless offer critical insights on the strengths and weaknesses of DIPs today. Many of the more recent examples of DIPs are only one-off affairs. Few of the actors involved in these experiences have critically analysed whether and how the outcomes of these participatory events were used to influence advisory committees and technical bodies connected to policy making.

Moreover, several examples of DIPs in the North have been convened by government agencies. In some countries of the South, some of these processes have been promoted by international donor agencies working with national policy making agencies. These are examples of DIPs constituting policy spaces created from above, and in which the state has substantial control over how the participatory methods and approaches fit into policy-making. In many of these cases the deliberative processes primarily fulfilled instrumental objectives ("legitimising" decisions already taken from above).

..."deliberative and
inclusive events"
[can even function]
as a pathway of
legitimisation for
commercial or
political interests.

As convenors, the organising agencies determine much of the style and content of the deliberative process through choice of objectives, methods and tools, the allocation of resources and the scale of operation, and the links to the wider policy processes. This is also true for DIPs that have been initiated by organisations outside government policy making bodies. For example there are several instances where "deliberative and inclusive events" such as consensus conferences, citizens juries and future search conferences ultimately functioned as a pathway of legitimisation for the very commercial or political interests that commissioned and informed the process in the first place.[47]

Elsewhere, in policy spaces created from below, the debate about wider questions of ethics, morality and values and their links with matters of justice and rights, is a striking feature. These DIPs organised by civil society organisations, NGOs and radicalised professionals[48] extend the frame of decision-making, although they

often have relatively weak links with the formal policy process. Therein lies a danger that these democratic deliberations will simply be ignored because they are delivering the "wrong message" or information that cannot or will not be accommodated by bureaucratic decision-making, major industrial lobbies and transnational commercial interests. Relations of power within policy-making bureaucracies and their associated networks of influential actors may result in limited opportunities for other voices to be heard. Yet, there are examples where new spaces for action are created by demanding access to information, such as in the case of movements in India to access village records and information on departmental budgets meant for rural development.[49]

---

46 Holmes and Scoones, 1999.
47 Glasner, 2001.
48 Cunningham-Burley, 2001; Pimbert and Gujja, 1997; Sclove, 2001; Satya Murty and Wakeford, 2001.
49 http://www.freedominfo.org/case/mkss/mkss.htm

In all cases, creating a space for more inclusive deliberation, either from above or from below, is an avenue towards potentially more effective, equitable and informed decision-making. Attempts to link DIPs with the broader policy process are more successful when due attention is given to issues of quality of information but also to process validity, credibility and trustworthiness.

Ensuring safeguards for quality and validity

A central challenge for practitioners of DIPs is to ensure the quality and validity of the knowledge and actions generated by the process.[50] In this light, it may be more realistic and honest to recognise from the outset that the subjectivity and worldview of convenors and key actors can always influence actions as well as interpretations of events and outcomes. For this reason, it is important to build safeguards into the deliberative process to ensure it is broadly credible, trustworthy, fair and not captured by any interest group or perspective. Several criteria and indicators of public acceptance and effectiveness of process can be useful in this regard and are listed in Checklist 11.3.

There are examples where new spaces for action are created by demanding access to information.

Checklist 11.3 Criteria and safeguards for public acceptance and effectiveness of a deliberative and inclusive process
(adapted from Rowe and Frewer, 2000)

Criteria fostering the acceptance of a DIP and/ or decision by citizens and the wider public

● Representativeness: representative sample of the affected population

● Independence: process conducted in an independent, unbiased way

● Early involvement: increases sense of ownership and role at the stage when value judgements are important

● Transparency: the public able to see progress and how decisions are made

● Influence: visible impact on policy

Criteria for effective process (effective design and implementation of a DIP process)

● Resource accessibility: access to appropriate resources (information, time, experts, materials) enables participants to engage and carry out their roles effectively

● Clear and well-defined methodological design: the scope of the exercise, its procedures and the expected outcomes are defined at the outset

● Structured decision-making: debate is enabled over the underlying assumptions, how the decisions are made, the extent to which they are publicly supported

● Cost-effectiveness: the investment (time and money) in the process is suitable to the scale and importance of the decisions.

Criteria of validity and quality will obviously differ depending on the context, the methods used (see for instance Table 11.1) and approach chosen to link DIPs with policy processes.

When assessing the quality of a deliberative process, however, the emphasis should be on methodological rigour rather than aiming to satisfy naïve notions of "objective truth". A prime concern should be on meeting safeguards and quality

---

50 This section draws extensively on Pimbert and Wakeford (2003).

criteria. Some such safeguard and quality criteria likely to be appropriate in many situations include:

- Diverse oversight and transparency. Many of the guidelines for DIPs, such as those laid down by the Institute of Public Policy Research,[51] include provision for the process to be overseen by a panel of independent observers. The inclusion of social actors with a diverse range of interests on this panel can be an important means of ensuring the methodology is not captured by a group with a particular perspective or vested interest. However, for this purpose, in most DIPs it is crucially important to widen the concept of social actor and "stakeholder" to include those marginalised by prevailing socio-economic forces. Only if there is a balance on any oversight body between those whose human rights are at risk and those with power, the process is likely to be fair, and perceived to be fair.

The transparency of participatory forms of policy making can be further enhanced by involving social actors who are able to guarantee credibility and trustworthiness. For example, in the citizens jury/ scenario workshop described in Box 11.3, the organisers built several layers of diverse oversight and transparency into their methodological design (see Box 11.4). It is noteworthy that when media is invited to observe and document the process there is usually greater scope for linking local voices into national and international policy processes.

Box 11.4   Diverse oversight and transparency in the participatory assessments of policy futures for Andhra Pradesh
(adapted from Pimbert and Wakeford, 2002; Pimbert and Wakeford, 2003)

The Government of Andhra Pradesh (India) visualises a radical transformation in the way food is produced, distributed and marketed 20 years from now. As a result, all the proposals for the future of food, farming, rural development and environment made in the government's Vision 2020 are controversial, particularly the promotion of genetically modified (GM) crops and the displacement of around twenty million rural people. The two counter-visions explored in the Prajateerpu citizens jury/ scenario workshop (see Box 11.3) also contained controversial elements. It was therefore critical that the deliberative process was transparent and under the control of representatives of organisations with different vested interests and social aims.

Four primary safeguard mechanisms were built into the Prajateerpu process:

1. The Oversight Panel. The Panel had an explicit mandate to assess the fairness, pluralism and credibility of Prajateerpu. The Oversight Panel's composition was sufficiently diverse to represent a broad spectrum of interests. Chaired by a retired Chief Justice from the Supreme Court of India, the panel critically oversaw the entire process, checking for possible bias and inconsistencies. It included representatives of the international donor community, civil society organisations and indigenous peoples. The members of the Oversight Panel shared their observations with the co-ordinating team at the end of each day of the jury's deliberations, ensuring that all parts of the process were agreed by individuals with a diverse range of perspectives. The Panel also made an overall evaluation of Prajateerpu after the formal closure of the event.

2. The media observers and reporters. Members of the press (audio-visual and written) were invited to document the hearings and outcomes of Prajateerpu. The following national newspapers sent their correspondents to observe and report on different moments of the deliberative process: The Indian

---

51   IPPR, 1994; Lowndes and Stoker, 1998.

Express, The Times of India, The Hindu, and The Deccan Chronicle. A variety of state newspapers written in Telegu also sent their correspondents. Reporters and camera crews from two Indian television news channels (Star News and Doordashan) were present, with Doordashan returning three times to film and interview participants at the beginning, middle and end of the event. The semi-continuous presence of the press ensured another level of control and vetting of the jury process. The wide reporting of the event in the national media highlighted the credibility and impartiality of the deliberations that led to the jury's verdict. Interestingly, a small minority of journalists were eager to demonstrate that jurors had been briefed and tutored into stating pre-formed positions. In interviews with these journalists, however, jurors strongly dismissed these doubts and implicit accusations. In the words of one juror, "These are life and death matters to us. We will not let anyone tell us what we should say."

3. The silent observers. Several other observers were invited to witness the jury process on the understanding that they should remain silent during the specialist presentations and the deliberations of the jury. These observers included other farmers from Andhra Pradesh, NGO representatives, agricultural researchers and planners, trade union representatives and corporate sector representatives. These observers were from both India and Europe. Most of them stayed only two to three days but some witnessed the whole event. All formed opinions on the strengths and weaknesses of the process and were able to communicate their views to members of the Oversight Panel, the co-ordinating team and the press. The presence of the silent observers further enhanced the transparency of Prajateerpu.

4. The video archives. The entire citizens jury/ scenario workshop along with interviews of various participants was recorded on digital video by a team from the Sarojini Naidu School of Performing Arts, Fine Arts and Communication of the University of Hyderabad. These comprehensive video archives were compiled to:

● provide a clear and accurate record of the event, including the location, the jury setting, the participants, the nature and quality of the debates, the process and its outcomes; and

● allow any party or external agency to learn from this experience or check for shortfalls in balance, fairness or failings in the deliberative process.

Two duplicate sets of 26 videotapes were prepared along with a detailed index of the video archives and English/ Telegu transcripts for Prajateerpu. The first set of duplicate tapes was left in the custody of the International Institute for Environment and Development, London (UK) and the second with The University of Hyderabad, Andhra Pradesh (India).

Diverse control and transparency were thus embedded in the very design of Prajateerpu. Moreover, control and scrutiny over the dynamics of Prajateerpu took place in real time and in situ, allowing many different participants to validate their own knowledge, and contest the validity of that of others in an open deliberative arena. For example, the panel of independent observers acted as an extended peer community that was able to directly witness the dynamics of knowledge production, action and empowerment. The Oversight Panel, which included representatives of marginalised communities and more powerful institutions, had absolute power to decide which methods and processes (representativeness of jury, video scenarios, balance of witnesses, quality of facilitation) were appropriate and what constituted valid knowledge in that context. Through this innovation the organisers sought to decentralise and democratise the knowledge validation process as well as ensure that the Prajateerpu's outputs were as legitimate and representative as possible.

Related to issues of balanced oversight, the safeguard of diverse controls can also be further ensured by relying on several sources of funding. Funding sources with vested interests in conflicting visions and policy choices should be involved in DIPs for the sake of pluralism.

Positive discrimination (affirmative action) may be needed to include marginalised groups who have been historically excluded from policy making and the control of regulative institutions.

- Representation and inclusion. Who is allowed to take part and other issues of representation are crucial for the credibility of a deliberative process. DIPs should engage a statistically representative sample of the population affected by a particular policy. Yet, more valid "representation" may require giving more importance to groups of social actors with particular life experiences or characteristics such as gender, race, age, wealth and type of livelihood-resource base. Positive discrimination (affirmative action) may be needed to include marginalised groups who have been historically excluded from policy making and the control of regulative institutions. Where policies have wider social impacts it is usually necessary to include representatives from key sectors (industry, government, civil society organisations, farmer trade unions, academic institutions...) so that they can feed their views into the process. As mentioned in Part II of this volume with regard to the identification of the parties in the CM agreement, this is better developed as an iterative process, with subsequent refinements.

The extent to which citizens are allowed to interrogate their sources of information is a good indicator of how inclusive a process is in recognising the validity of different knowledge systems.

Convenors and facilitators will always need to exercise their best judgment in the act of "including" some parties in the processes of consideration, decision and implementation (inclusion). Inclusion goes beyond the question of "who is allowed to participate" to issues of recognising knowledge and different ways of knowing. This is particularly important in deliberations involving both citizens and experts with scientific or other specialist knowledge. For example, several consensus conferences and citizens juries on the risks of new technologies have demonstrated the competence with which citizens can discuss highly technical issues to which they had no previous exposure. They achieve this by carefully eliciting from each specialist witness the information relevant to their case. The questions of ordinary citizens and resource users have a more holistic quality than the arguments presented by some subject matter specialists. Different ways of knowing are included in the process, as jurors ask questions framed from their own life experience and livelihood contexts.

The extent to which citizens are allowed to interrogate their sources of information, rather than being merely the passive recipients of written briefings and specialist testimonies, is a good indicator of how inclusive a process is in recognising the validity of different knowledge systems.

- Open framing and facilitation. The way discussions are framed by information, witnesses or questions can have an important influence on the extent to which citizens have the opportunity to develop their own policy scenarios and visions for the future. The extent to which assumptions behind issues can be challenged and new questions asked in DIPs is highly dependent on the choice of subject area or/ and the particular way a problem is defined. The initial choice of problems and definition of criteria drives the end results. For example it is noteworthy that assessments of GMOs in the UK were strongly influenced by each participant's early framing of the debate in multiple criteria mapping exercises.[52] Many criteria chosen by the participants lay outside the scope of official risk assessments and for no participant the whole range of criteria was explicitly included in the formal evaluation process of GMOs in the UK. The "sensitivity" of the early framing of issues and questions in DIPs emphasises the importance of ensuring that the entire spectrum of values and interests are represented. The extent to which convenors and organising agencies allow for flexible and open ended "framing" and definition of boundaries

---

[52] Stirling, 2001.

may ultimately prove a good indicator of their commitment to democratic values. It is good practice for the framing of discussions and scope of recommendations to be set by citizens engaged in DIPs rather than be constrained by a question dictated to them by a particular social actor or interest group. The degree to which convenors let go of their power over framing the terms of debate may actually determine whether ordinary people will be able to bring about change or whether DIPs will be merely used to legitimise established power structures and their favoured policy.

- Creation of a safe communicative space. A wide range of different experiences with DIPs have demonstrated the importance of safe communicative spaces. These are opportunities in which people, who might otherwise feel threatened by sharing their knowledge and experience with others, can be placed in carefully thought-out environments of mutual support and empathy in order to allow them to express themselves. Safe communicative spaces are needed for the confrontation of perspectives from the social and natural sciences as well as the knowledge of local resource users, for social actors to negotiate and develop policy futures. The notion of safe communicative spaces recognises that there are differently situated forms of knowledge about livelihoods and the environment, and each is partial and incomplete. Participatory learning, inclusion, dialogue and careful deliberation are needed to bring these multiple and separate realities together, combining the strengths of outsiders' and local peoples' knowledge. Convenors of DIPs who explicitly seek to link local voices with policy change will need to provide safe spaces at a number of different levels.

> ....we need to move beyond uncritical support for assembly-style spaces, where populist attitudes can mask the hidden agendas of the powerful.

Often there is a need to move beyond the uncritical support for assembly-style spaces, where populist attitudes can mask the hidden agendas of the powerful. This is important because the possibility that hierarchy and self censorship might constrain deliberation and inclusion is always present in any space where people come together. Deliberation is, after all, not only governed by rational assessment and dialogue about technical or political options. Feelings like anger, powerlessness, shyness, admiration, fear– all of the emotional side of human beings– are equally important. Like power, emotions are essentially relational phenomena. Personal and collective emotions, the self confidence of individual actors and the level of trust between actors all matter in spaces set up for deliberations on policy change. At a fundamental level, trust and emotions that underlie the self deeply influence the forms and outcomes of deliberations. Communicative spaces for participation, therefore, need to provide a sense of stability and security so that social actors can open up and engage in new struggles for self respect and self esteem.[53] Otherwise learning, understanding and acting for policy change will probably not take place.

> ...anger, powerlessness, shyness, admiration, fear– all of the emotional side of human beings– deeply influence the forms and outcomes of deliberations.

- Emergence of a wide community of inquiry and empowerment. The quality of a process is apparent when there is strong evidence that it has catalysed and informed a broad community of inquiry, with possibly enduring consequences for several of the actors involved. This outcome is often dependent on a methodological design that explicitly links citizens involved in the DIPs to wider policy networks and the dynamics of policy changes.

Whilst there are no universally valid recipes for this, experience suggests that

---

[53] Hoggett, 2000.

reversing dominant trends in policy processes can help engage a wider community of actors for change. Particularly successful reversals from normal roles and locations for empowerment include: a) putting the perceptions, priorities and judgment of resource users and other marginalised citizens centre stage and using appropriate methodologies for DIPs; b) holding the process in a rural or appropriate local urban setting that is familiar to those citizens and resource users more directly affected by the policies; c) getting government bureaucrats, scientists and other specialist witnesses to travel to resource users, farmers and other citizens in order to present evidence on the pros and cons of different choices, technologies, policies; d) using television and video technology to ensure transparency and free circulation of information on the process and the outcomes, both nationally and internationally, and e) going beyond the idea of advocating on behalf of the marginalised to the practice of enabling the marginalised to speak for themselves.[54]

As a general rule, once people involved in DIPs reach their conclusions it is essential that appropriate intermediary individuals and channels link them with those who have the power to create change (e.g., farmer federations, indigenous peoples organisations, advocacy NGOs...). Immediate outcomes of DIPs can be more effective in policy change when they are actively used by civil society actors to influence advisory committees, technical bodies and civil servants connected to policy-making. One option is for groups of actors to use DIPs, when appropriate, as part of a larger set of activities aimed at influencing policy "from below": campaigns, hidden resistance or direct civil action. Another option is to combine formal bodies of representative democracy with the more bottom-up deliberative and inclusive methods and processes. This approach may be particularly effective at the level of local and municipal governments, where citizen participation and government accountability can be mutually reinforcing and supportive.

...once people involved in deliberative, inclusive processes reach their conclusions it is essential that intermediary individuals and channels link them with those with the power to create change (e.g., farmer federations, indigenous peoples organisations, advocacy NGOs...).

All of these criteria and safeguards can help ensure the credibility, efficacy and fairness of DIPs used for policy making. However, ethics, values and intentionality will always remain fundamental to issues of quality and validity. Simply put, participatory methods such as DIPs for policy change can be used either for instrumental ends or for genuine citizen empowerment. Implicit or explicit intentions and underlying values always inform "participation", the framing of issues, the form of any initiative and its operating dynamics. For example, a commitment to democratic values is likely to be expressed by the adoption of design principles similar to those of Checklist 11.4

Checklist 11.4 Broad principles for deliberative and inclusive processes related to policy development
(adapted from Peals, 2003; Wakeford and Pimbert, 2003)

- Participants, not those organising the process, frame and set terms of reference for the whole exercise.

- The group organising, or in overall control of, the process is broad based, including social actors with different interests on the subject being discussed.

- There are safe spaces for participants (usually non-specialist) perspectives to engage in a mutually

---

54 Pimbert et al., 2003; Wakeford and Pimbert, 2004.

educative manner with those of specialists.

● There is full transparency about the activities carried out within the process to those outside it.

● A diversity of information sources is available to participants.

● Those without a voice in policy-making can use the process as a tool for positive change.

● The process contains safeguards against policy-makers using it to legitimise existing assumptions or policies.

● All groups involved in the process have sufficient room for learning, development and change.

● An "audit" trail is designed and set out to explain whether policies were changed as a result of the process, what was taken into account, what criteria were applied when weighing up the evidence from the process and how the views of those involved in the participatory process made a difference to the decision.

Citizens interested in pursuing policy change in favour of co-management of natural resources need to be clear about how this relates to:

● the right to participate at all levels of the policy making process as equal partners regardless of gender, wealth or ethnic origin;

● the right to self representation and autonomy; and

● the right to political, economic and cultural self determination (sovereignty).

11.3 Strengthening civil society

By now it will be evident to the reader of this volume that effective co-management is predicated on a fairer and more balanced sharing of power in society, implying redistribution towards the weaker sectors and civil society in general. While promoting and welcoming this change, we would like to caution against embracing it without a critical approach. For instance, co-management requires some formal organising of civil society, a fact that offers important opportunities but also presents potential problems. Experience has shown that formal organisations, including those that evolve from informal community institutions, can also be dominated by powerful interests, capable of marginalising the poor and the powerless in even more insidious ways.[55] Formal organisations almost inevitably introduce hierarchy and structure, and these can consolidate a sclerotic distribution and use of power within groups and communities. To prevent this, some groups prefer to rely on informal structures and spontaneous, experimental and convivial practices, in other words "a sensible measure of anarchy" at least for the initial experimental phases of the CM process.[56]

> Formal organisations almost inevitably introduce hierarchy and structure, and these can consolidate a sclerotic distribution and use of power within groups and communities.

Secondly, while there is a need to recognise and strengthen local rights and responsibilities, attempts to empower previously marginalised sections of the society can have unintended consequences on local livelihoods, the environment and

55 Bainbridge et al., 2000; Cornwall and Coelho, 2004.
56 Anarchy is meant here in the sense of "absence of fixed governing structures". For instance, some political "parties" in Europe (e.g. the Federalist Party of Italy) prefer to be called a movement rather than a party. They have established automatic and rather frequent rotation of people in positions of authority and preferentially base their action and alliances on specific issues rather than on party positions.

social justice. The social disruption that change could cause, as entrenched groups try to hit back, could in turn upset customary natural resource management patterns. Whether this is ultimately destructive or not depends on the new equations among the social actors and networks involved, interventions by outsiders to stabilise the situation, and other factors. Experience from community-based natural resource management initiatives suggests that greater community engagement combined with supportive outside interventions and incentives leads to better resource management in the long run.[57] Yet, it cannot be assumed that greater democracy in society will automatically and inevitably lead to better resource management at all times and in all places.

Thirdly, the objective of social justice may also suffer, paradoxically, as underprivileged sections are given formal powers and representation on management bodies and DIPs linked to policy processes. This is because they may no longer be willing or able to use their informal, and often more effective, tools of resistance– coming late for work, going slow, minor sabotage, slander, ridicule, pretended ignorance, desertion, etc.– which Scott has called the "weapons of the weak".[58] These tools are quiet and unobtrusive, yet are perhaps more influential in the making of history, in the relations between oppressed people and their oppressors, than open rebellions and revolutions. Scott likens this process of resistance to the creation of immense barrier reefs by the minute actions of millions of coral polyps. Indeed, because of their very nature, such methods of protest are difficult for the formal sector to punish. Yet, if oppressed people are brought out into the open and asked to use formal processes of democracy, at which they may be weak, their relative power might actually diminish. There

> The "weapons of the weak" are quiet and unobtrusive, yet are perhaps more influential in the making of history than open rebellions and revolutions.

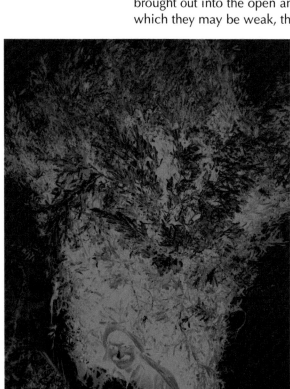

appears to be little way out of this dilemma, however, except to advocate that democratic processes should remain as flexible and open to innovation as possible, that oppressed people should continue to be supported to take all avenues of resistance and protest open to them. And, last but not least, that all processes of empowerment should be sustained over long periods of time.

Finally, and related to the above, there is the danger that some processes of democracy may actually be a means of co-option. People and groups that get engaged in co-management committees, or processes of deliberation and inclusion, often lose their sharp edge and relax their questioning attitude towards authority. They may also become less "representative" of the whole constituency they come from and distort demands or favour some of its sections. This is, of course, by no means an inevitable process, but one that has to be strongly guarded against. Unfortunately, powers affects the attitudes and behaviours of people, and rarely so in a positive sense.

A stronger voice for civil society

As a recent study has shown, there are a number of

---

[57] Many examples are illustrated in this volume. Recent synthesis studies that identified conditions for success include Kothari et al., 2000; Whande et al., 2003; Solis Rivera et al., 2003; and Borrini-Feyerabend et al., 2004 (in press).

[58] Scott 1985.

mechanisms from around the world for strengthening civil society and the engage-ment of citizens and governments.[59] Various approaches may be seen along a continuum, ranging from ways of strengthening "voice" on the one hand, to ways of strengthening "receptivity" by government institutions on the other. The authors of the study argue that the "voice" end of the spectrum must begin with creating the pre-conditions for voice, through awareness-raising and building the capacity to mobilise. As citizens who are outside of governance processes begin to engage with government, there are a series of avenues through which their voices may be amplified, ranging from advocacy to lobbying for policy change and citizen moni-toring of performance in various sectors. Similarly, regarding receptivity by the states, several avenues are available, including government mandated forms of cit-izen consultation, standards through which citizens may hold government accountable, incentives to encourage officials to be responsive to citizen voice, changes in organisational culture, and legal provisions that, in various ways, make participation in governance a legal right.

Broadly speaking, there are three main strategic approaches for the emergence of a strong civil society and the empowerment of "voices from below":

1. Building upon synergies between the state and society. Public sector workers and "champions of change" within governments can help strengthen civil soci-ety and encourage more inclusive policy debates. In the Philippines, for exam-ple, it was the lobbying of radical civil servants along with organisations of pro-fessionals that led to the wide implementation of participatory irrigation man-agement[60] (a model which has subsequently spread to other countries). In Mexico, reformist officials have helped consolidate small farmer marketing organisations[61] and strengthen the role of community organisations in regional sustainable development policy.[62]

Civil society is likely to have a greater potential for influence when civil ser-vants and progressive government officials introduce legislation guaranteeing the right to participation. The legal right to participation is a more empowered form of engagement than participation by invitation of governments, donors, or higher authorities. One area in which rights to participation are being embod-ied into law is that of local governance.[63] A number of pathways have been used:

● Joint approaches to planning. Civil society actors and government bodies work together in planning service delivery and environmental care (see Box 11.5).

● Changing forms of accountability. Innovations have not only emphasised citi-zen involvement with local governments in planning, but also empowered citi-zen representatives to hold government to account for carrying out properly the functions of government (see Box 11.6).

● Empowered forms of local direct participation in the governance of public affairs. While many approaches are looking for new relationships between citi-zens and elected representatives, others are creating forms of direct citizen par-ticipation through legal changes. Representative forms of governance are thus complemented by more empowered, direct involvement of citizens at the local level. Perhaps the most direct and effective example of the latter is the sharing

People and groups that get engaged in co-management committees, or processes of deliberation and inclusion, often lose their sharp edge and relax their questioning attitude towards authority.

Civil society is likely to have a greater potential for influence when civil servants and progres-sive government officials introduce legislation guarantee-ing the right to participation.

---

59 Goetz and Gaventa, 2001.
60 Korten, 1995.
61 Fox, 1990.
62 Blauert and Dietz, 2004.
63 See www.ids.ac.uk/logolink and Chapter 10.

of authority about budget allocation. In Porto Alegre and other municipalities of Brazil, neighbourhood meetings are used to do exactly that in a process called "participatory budgeting" (see Box 11.7).

- Strengthened inclusive representation in locally-elected bodies. A pathway adopted by several countries has been legal change that promoted the inclusion of traditionally excluded populations in local councils (see Box 11.8).

Box 11.5   Mandatory joint planning
(adapted from McGee et al., 2003)

In the Phillippines, the 1991 Local Government Code (LGC) requires citizen participation at all levels of local government through the local development councils. Participation is mandated in the areas of development planning, education, health, bids and contracts, and policing. In theory, the LGC also provides for direct representation of civil society and voluntary organisations on local government bodies, though this has been uneven in its implementation. Legislation also mandates funds for training of citizen representatives in order for them to participate effectively.

In Brazil, the new Constitution of 1988, termed at the time the "Citizens Constitution" affirmed public participation in the delivery of local services as a democratic right. This has resulted in the creation across the country of municipal level councils, which link elected officials, neighbourhood representatives and service providers in almost every sector, including health, education and youth.

Box 11.6   New forms of accountability
(adapted from The LogoLink Network www.ids.ac.uk/logolink)

In Bolivia, the Law of Popular Participation of 1994 mandated broad-based participation, starting at the neighbourhood level, as part of the process of local government decentralisation. It also recognised the importance of social organisations that already existed (including indigenous communities, with their own practices and customs). About 15,000 such "territorial base organisations" are registered to participate in the planning process. In addition to that, the particular innovation of the Bolivian law was to create legal citizens' oversight or vigilance Committees in each municipality, which are empowered to freeze municipal budgets if actual expenditures vary too far from what was agreed in the planning processes.

Box 11.7   Participatory budgeting in Porto Alegre (Brazil)
(adapted from Abers, 1997 and Baiocchi, 2003).

Porto Alegre is a Brazilian town with a population of about 1.2 million people, situated along the polluted Guaiba River in Southern Brazil. There are about 250 favelas (slums) in Porto Alegre, where about 400,000 people live. Since 1989, Porto Alegre has been governed by the Partido dos Trabalhadores (PT, the workers party). This party was founded in 1980, when the military regime first allowed the creation of new parties. The PT emanated from a coalition of labour unions, urban and rural social movements, people from Christian base communities, and formerly revolutionary Marxist groups. The PT has no well-defined ideology, but follows two main tenets: the needs of the poor should get priority and the people should be directly involved in governance.

The original contribution of the PT was the insight that popular control on public spending was the key to real popular participation in governance. To achieve this, the PT introduced the practice of "direct democratic budgeting" from 1989 onwards. This involves a number of phases including assemblies where people can give their views on the way public spending is organised at present; neighbourhood meetings where investment priorities are drawn up; electing delegates for the Regional Budget Forum; holding more assemblies; and, finally, production of a final budget by the Municipal Budget Council, synthesises the demands made in the various meetings.

The result has been increased efficiency in public spending. Before the introduction of the "direct democratic budgeting", the largest amount of sewer line constructed was 17 kilometres, in 1987. From 1990 to 1994, the figure raised to 46 kilometres of sewer line annually. As a result, from 1989 to 1996, the portion of the population with access to sewer lines rose from 46% to 95%. During the three years previous to the PT administration, four kilometres of street were paved each year; after 1990, 20 kilometres of road were paved annually, and the quality of this pavement rose dramatically. Extended favelas, that had only mud roads and tracks, became accessible for buses, garbage trucks, ambulances and police cars. It is estimated that over 100,000 people, representing some 10% of the population of the town, have attended a participatory budgeting meeting at least once over the fourteen years of the initiative in Porto Alegre.

Participatory budgeting has also spread to other municipalities in Brazil. Municipal governments elected to power in several Brazilian cities in the 1990s introduced a participatory budget. The government invests in projects that communities have identified as their priority needs. Given a citizen's right to have information and make demands on the state, government agencies have to consider the feasibility of any request. If a citizen request is judged non feasible, the state agency has to demonstrate why this is so.

In several municipalities, popular participation in this initiative has exceeded the government's expectations and has increased annually. Participatory budgeting has changed public spending priorities, reducing inequalities in places. The improvement of the quality of life in some of the municipalities has been evident, as it is the first time that the local government has taken into account the needs of the poorest sectors of the population. Participatory budgeting has not only meant a much greater involvement of citizens and community organisations in determining priorities, but also a more transparent and accountable form of government.

Box 11.8   Towards more inclusive representation in local government
(adapted from McGee et al., 2003)

The 73rd and 74th Constitutional Amendments of India, described in Box 10.4, mandated that one third of the seats in the local councils should be reserved for women, as well as one-third of the offices of the chairperson. Similar reservations have been made for those of the lower castes and tribes. While making local councils more inclusive, the Constitution also gave them a great deal more power for planning for "economic development and social justice" in twenty-nine separate areas of local development, including forests, education and irrigation. While the implementation of these new representation processes has been uneven, and while the local councils are not always granted adequate financing from central government, the inclusion of new members in the political processes has been vast. About one million women and some 600,000 lower caste or tribal members have now been elected to local government office.

All the above pathways are significant and positive innovations promoted by the state. Through legislation, they create new and stronger roles for civil society in relation to local governance. And yet, the extent to which the legislation itself opens new spaces for participation and citizen voice varies enormously, both

The common
pathway to
strengthening civil
society involves a
collaboration
between
community-based
organisations and
local and national
NGOs, academics
and researchers.

according to the characteristics of the legal frameworks themselves, and the broader context of which they are a part. The actual implementation of these laws also varies, due to differences in understandings, power relations, citizens' awareness, etc. Moreover, state-society synergies are prone to the intermediation of party politics and, at times, corruption.

2. Collaboration between local and external civil society actors. The most common pathway to strengthening civil society involves collaboration between local and external actors within civil society itself. Typically this involves local, community-based organisations and national NGOs, academics and researchers. In the Philippines, for example, scientists and non governmental organisations have collaborated with marginalised farmers to develop a farmer-led network of people's organisations working towards the sustainable management of biodiversity and local control over food systems (see Box 11.9).

Box 11.9   The MASIPAG experience
(adapted from Vicente, 1993; www.masipag.org)

The MASIPAG programme was born out of the Filipino farmer's bittersweet experiences with the Green Revolution. Throughout the 1960s and 1970s, the Philippine government heavily promoted the adoption of high yielding varieties (HYVs) and high input agricultural production systems. The International Rice Research Institute (IRRI) played a key role in researching and marketing the new rice varieties. By 1970, 78% of the country's rice-lands were planted with HYVs and the initial results were encouraging as crop production soared.

However, by the late 1970s many farmers were seriously disenchanted with the Green Revolution. The problems they faced included the rising cost of seed and fertilisers; the increasing concentrations of chemicals needed to keep production up; deterioration of the seed; increasing pest problems; pesticide induced poisoning and deteriorating human health; and environmental degradation. Over the next five years, a farmers' strategy emerged from various formal and informal consultations. The strategy proposed, amongst other things, the launch of an initiative to develop a national agricultural programme independent of foreign support; an agrarian reform programme to address the problems posed by large plantations of bananas, coconut and sugar cane; a review of the government/ IRRI programme with options for nationalising its management or stopping its operation; and building a truly Filipino institution for rice research.

When their proposals were ignored by government, the farmers and their allies in civil society took the initiatives forward themselves. A group of progressive scientists initiated consultations with farmers in different parts of the country (Luzon, Visayas and Mindanao). This culminated in a national convention in mid-1985 dubbed "BIGAS Conference" or Bahanggunian Hinggil sa Isyu ng Bigas. A year after that landmark gathering, a farmer-NGO-scientist partnership was formed and its first project aimed at breaking the control of fertiliser and pesticide companies, multi-lateral rice research institutes and distribution cartels over the rice industry. The Multi-sectoral Forum (MSF), a group of professors, scientists and researchers in the University of Philippines Los Baños, took the lead role in composing the technical pool of what was initially known as "farmer-scientist partnership". By 25 June 1987, the "Farmer-Scientist Partnership for Agricultural Development, Inc." was ready to embark on what is now known popularly as the MASIPAG Project– Magsasaka at Siyentipiko Para sa Pag-unlad ng Agrikultura. For the last 17 years, MASIPAG has been at the forefront of development struggles in the Philippines pursuing, among other things, a holistic approach to development, community empowerment, and people's control over agricultural biodiversity as a contribution in the over-all effort of improving the quality of life of small farmers. MASIPAG's approach to strengthening civil society emphasises social transformation and builds on the following:

1. Bottom-up approach - Any development programme must prioritise the expressed needs, problems and aspirations of the people themselves. The enhancement of knowledge and skills likewise starts with the people's actual capabilities.

2. Farmer-Scientist Partnership - A genuine partnership between the farmers and their organisations, and the scientists/ researchers from the social and natural sciences attempts to put into practice the bottom-up approach in conservation and development. This is apparent in programme implementation and in all activities undertaken by the partnership. This relationship is further strengthened by NGOs from the religious sector and other local organisations of concerned individuals and professionals.

3. Farmer-led research and training - On-farm research and training in different agro-environments and socio-cultural settings start from what the farmers need to learn and develop. They are active participants in plant breeding and in developing technologies such as ecological pest management and biodiversity rich farming systems. They do the research and facilitate training.

4. Farmer-to-farmer mode of transfer - Farmers are animated by a sense of mission to reach out to other farmers. Only in their united and concerted efforts can MASIPAG's vision be realised. Cooperation, not competition is a strong motivating force for the farmers to chart their own destiny.

5. Advocacy towards genuine agrarian reform. In the MASIPAG context, advocacy towards genuine agrarian reform is meant to lead to full ownership, management and control of the land by the farmers/ peasants, and their access to basic support services necessary for sustainable agriculture and livelihoods.

There are indeed very many documented and anecdotal cases of such collaboration. The combined efforts of local and external civil society actors help to bring the concerns of marginalised and excluded people into policy processes from which they would otherwise be absent. A review of twelve federations of rural organisations whose primary concerns related to agricultural development and natural resource management suggests that the strongest organisations, those most able to project members' concerns in negotiations with government, donors and market actors, have each enjoyed an extended period of accompaniment from NGOs or religious leaders.[64] In most cases these external actors were involved in the creation and strengthening of these civil society organisations. Similarly, the emergence of vocal farmer movements in India has often involved non-farmer support or charismatic leadership from other parts of civil society.[65]

All these studies show, however, that how such collaboration occurs is critical. The most fruitful collaborations are those that involve intensive, sensitive and respectful support in which external actors accompany, advise, suggest systems, etc., over a long period. External actors do not intervene in local decision making, respecting and trusting local partners. For example, at the core of one of South America's most successful federation of cooperatives, El Ceibo, has been the longstanding provision of administrative and technical advice from certain volunteer services and donors.[66] Likewise in Indonesia, the emancipatory values and enabling attitudes of external actors (trainers, NGO staff...) were key in facilitating citizen empowerment in Farmer Field Schools and in the wider peasant movement that now seeks to reclaim rights over land and other resources.[67]

3. Independent pathways from below. Strong and representative organisations can emerge from the bottom up. Local organisations with deep roots in traditional

> Strong and representative organisations can emerge from the bottom up. Local organisations with deep roots in traditional arrangements play various roles in local natural resource management and represent local voices to external agencies.

---

[64] Carroll and Bebbington, 2001.

[65] Brass, 1995.

[66] Bebbington, 1996.

[67] Fakih, Rahardjo and Pimbert, 2003; see also Boxes 9.23 and 11.12.

arrangements play various roles in local natural resource management and represent local voices to external agencies.[68] In Sumatra, for instance, traditional adat (customary) village governance institutions which re-emerged after the New Order period have begun to deal with, among other things, tenure issues in the village and represent villager concerns to external actors (see box 10.11). The long lasting traditional basis of many such organisations gives them indisputable legitimacy (see Box 11.10). Yet, these organisations are not always internally democratic and gender inclusive.[69] They can be dominated by leaders in whom tradition or history vests authority but such leaders may not espouse the equity gains recently brought about by historical processes and crystallised in the UN Declaration of Human Rights.

Box 11.10   The Regole of the Ampezzo Valley (Italy) have maintained their autonomous status for a 1000 years
(adapted from Stefano Lorenzi, personal communication, 2004; www.regole.it)

The Regole of the Ampezzo Valley (where the famous Cortina resort is located) is a community-based institution with a known history of approximately 1,000 years. The Regole independently manage the common property resources initially made available by the work of the early Regolieri (extensive pasture creation and maintenance out of the original woods) and, up to today, the Regolieri comprise only the descendants of the early founders of the community and their male sons who remain residents in the valley. Property is held under inalienable and indivisible common title and the general assembly of the Regole takes management decisions after extensive discussion and by a "qualified majority", a procedure more akin to consensus than voting. Through time, the Regolieri maintained their rights of occupation and modes of local production thanks to their skills as diplomats (for instance, they managed to ensure agreements with the Venetian Republic in 1420 and, later on, with the Austrian emperors). In 1918, the end of the First World War saw the Ampezzo Valley incorporated within the Italian state. From then up to today, the Regole struggled to maintain their autonomous status under special exceptions in the national legislation and regional laws, a feat that depended on a combination of personal skills of the Regolieri and importance and visibility of the landscape they managed to conserve. About 15 years ago, the Regole finally received a major recognition as the sole and full legal managers of the Parco Naturale delle Dolomiti d'Ampezzo– a regional protected area established on land and resources mostly conserved by them. They have also obtained a tax-free status from the Italian government and major project funds and subsidies from the European Union, the Italian state and the Veneto regional government.

Old and new social movements provide a variety of examples of civil society organised to reclaim power from below. These include attempts to transform governance structures through political participation, face-to-face discussions, and empowered federations that include people from various local places. Some of these movements have ties with religious beliefs (such as the liberation theology movements of Latin America[70] or the Islamic Brotherhoods that acted as development agents in West Africa[71]), ethnic, caste or kinship associations, and gender or

---

68   Esman and Uphoff, 1984.
69   See Box 7.3.
70   Berryman, 1987.
71   Berhman, 1970.

age-based groups.[72] Others are linked with cooperatives or even the management of natural resources, such as irrigation associations, fishers associations and all sorts of other mutual aid groups. Most typically, these movements include unions, born to uplift the conditions of workers with common interests and concerns and, today, indigenous peoples organisations active in national and international contexts.

Independent pathways from below raise many challenges and risks, as demonstrated by moments in history when citizens have experimented with new forms of direct democracy and confederated power.[73] For instance in Spain, during the Civil War of 1936-1939, the peasants of Andalusia and Aragon established communal systems of land tenure, in some cases abolishing the use of money for internal transactions, setting up free systems of production and distribution, and creating a decision making procedure based on popular assemblies and direct, face to face democracy. A system of self-management for workers was set up in numerous cities, including Barcelona and Valencia. Factories, transport facilities, utilities, retail and wholesale enterprises were all taken over and administered by workers' committees and unions. Much can be learned from these experiments.[74]

Federations, networks and organised policy influence

Civil society organisations exist across a range of scales— from individual through national to international federations, consortiums, networks and umbrella bodies. One reason for linking up and federating in this way is to increase the leverage of organisations in policy and political debates.

Federated organisations have an important role in projecting the voice and concerns of resource users and other citizens in a variety of spheres. Many such federations that aim to influence policy-making are not only natural resource based and agricultural organisations. They may be landless people's movements (the clearest examples being the million strong Movimento dos Trabalhadores Rurais sem Terra (MST) in Brazil and the Kilusang Magbubukid ng Pilipinas (KMP) in the Philippines),[75] federations of the urban poor,[76] indigenous people's movements (such as the Coordinating Body for the Indigenous Peoples' Organisations of the Amazon Basin COICA),[77] peasant movements (such as the Réseau des Organisations Paysannes de l'Afrique de l'Ouest– ROPPA in West Africa), or various national federations of producer organisations, such as those of Benin, Niger, Mali and Senegal.[78] Most of these organisations come to natural resource policy debates with wider agendas– about, say, land redistribution or participatory governance. As a result, discussions may be very wide ranging and complex. Yet, they can lead to important shifts in the balance of power in favour of poor rural people, as the rise of producer organisations in West Africa illustrates (see Box 11.11).

Producers organisations have also been active at the international level. One examples is Via Campesina[79], a broad, worldwide coalition of peasants and farm-

Independent pathways from below raise many challenges and risks, as demonstrated by moments in history when citizens have experimented with new forms of direct democracy and confederated power.

---

72 Ralston et al.,1983.
73 Bookchin, 1996; Bookchin, 1998.
74 Bookchin 1994.
75 MST in Brazil has its own website, with pages in Portuguese, English, French, Spanish and Italian, such is its international prominence. See: http://www.mstbrazil.org/. KMP is a nationwide federation of Philippine organisations, which claims to have "effective leadership" of over 800,000 landless peasants, small farmers, farm workers, subsistence fisherfolk, peasant women and rural youth. See: http://www.geocities.com/kmp_ph/index.html
76 www.iied.org/urban/pubs/eu_briefs.html
77 www.coica.org
78 GRAF/GRET/IIED, 2003.
79 www.viacampesina.org

ers lobbying for land tenure reform, agroecology, and food sovereignty. Another example is the World Alliance of Mobile Indigenous Peoples (WAMIP)– a new organisation whose members are nomadic pastoralists, hunters and gatherers, shifting cultivators and sea nomads. The organisation is made up of tribes, peoples and indigenous nations whose livelihoods, production systems and cultural identity depend on a mobile lifestyle and on the sustainable use (and thus conservation) of natural resources. These peoples are among the most disinherited and discriminated groups in the world.

Box 11.11 Producer organisations, collective action and institutional transformation in West Africa
(adapted from Belières et al., 2002; Toulmin and Guèye, 2003)

Producer organisations (POs) cover a wide range of activities, from management of common woodland or pasture resources to water user associations, collection and sale of a particular crop or providing access to fertiliser, seed and credit. Grouping together through collective action enables producers to take advantage of economies of scale and to make their voices heard in government policy and decision-making. Additionally, producers hope to increase their negotiating power with companies buying their crop, all the more necessary as globalisation is bringing an increased concentration and integration of agri-business throughout the world. In some cases, producer organisations have also provided a valuable bridging function between farmers and sources of technical expertise, such as research and extension structures. Foreign aid funds have often been instrumental in strengthening the role that POs can play despite the associated risk that the leadership may become distant from the interests and needs of the membership.

Over the past decade, a range of POs have become established and have strengthened their positions at local, national and sub-regional levels in West Africa. These organisations are in part the result of government withdrawal from important sectors of the rural economy, including agricultural input supply and marketing. They also have emerged in a context of greater political liberalisation, and now represent a political force of which governments must take notice. This became clear from the strike by Mali's cotton farmers in the 2001 season, due to low prices and continued waste and corruption within the Compagnie Malienne pour le Développement des Textiles. The strike cut output by half, with many cotton farmers switching to maize and other cash crops for that season.[80]

Examples of POs operating at national level include the Comité National de Concertation des Ruraux (CNCR) in Senegal, the Fédération des Unions des Producteurs (FUPRO) in Benin, and the Syndicat des Exploitants Agricoles à l'Office du Niger (SEXAGON) in Mali.[81] The CNCR provides an interesting case, which brings together a series of PO federations in Senegal, and has become a central actor in the dialogue between government, donors, and producers on agricultural strategy and related issues, such as land tenure. Such POs have the advantage of providing a channel to make the case for greater support to agriculture in general, as well as to take account of the particular constraints faced by smallholders. Policy and decision-making in government tend to follow both formal and informal procedures. Smallholders have less easy access to informal mechanisms that operate via "old-boy" (informal friends and associates) networks, and lobbying through high-level political contacts, which are usually the preserve of powerful economic actors, such as large commercial farmers and agribusiness. Thus, POs need to make best use of official channels and opportunities to give voice to the needs of less powerful actors.

At the regional level, there has been increased interest in generating pressure on governments and regional institutions to ensure producer interests are better taken into account in negotiation processes

---

80 Toulmin and Guèye, 2003.
81 GRAF/ GRET/ IIED, 2003.

relating to the WTO, the European Common Agricultural Policy (CAP) reform and Cotonou negotiations. Examples include the Réseau des Organisations Paysannes de l'Afrique de l'Ouest (ROPPA), the Association Cotonnière Africaine and the Union of Chambers of Agriculture for West Africa. ROPPA and its members have been particularly vocal in support of household farming, and opposed to the agribusiness model being promoted by some as the means to "modernise" agriculture. "This vision (in support of household farming) has been inspired by a global perception of the role of agriculture in society, not only for producing food and fibre but also for performing many other economic, social and environmental functions".[82] Thus, the argument being made by ROPPA and others supports broader debates regarding the "multi-functionality" of agriculture and of the land, and the consequent need to avoid a purely economic or market-based approach.[83]

A key goal of the more emancipatory federations and umbrella organisations is to develop a public sphere that allows for maximum democracy in the literal sense of the term. In its present form, this new politics in the making affirms the values of:

● Confederalism — a network of bodies or councils whose members or delegates are elected from popular face-to-face democratic assemblies, in the villages, tribes, towns and even neighbourhoods of large cities. These confederal bodies or councils become the means of interlinking villages, towns, neighbourhoods and ecological units into a confederation based on shared responsibilities, full accountability, firmly mandated representatives and the right to recall them, if necessary.

● Dual power — the larger and more numerous the linked federations and confederations become, the greater their potential to constitute a significant counter-power to the state and transnational corporations. Confederations can eventually exert "dual power", using this to further citizen empowerment and democratic change. For example, they can seek power within local government through strategies of collaboration and political negotiation, while maintaining strong community and municipal organising strategies at the grassroots. Multiple lanes for engagement can also be used to link community based conservation and development, social movements, and political parties with direct local governance strategies. This dual power approach is widely used by the Indonesian Peasant Rights movement (Box 11.12) and the work of the Barangay-Bayan Governance Consortium in the Philippines (Box 11.13).

Box 11.12 The Peasant Rights Movement and policy change in Indonesia
           (adapted from Fakih et al., 2003)

The demise of the repressive Suharto Government in 1997 made it possible for the Indonesian civil society to come out and organise for change on a large scale. New peasant movements have emerged in every region of Indonesia. The Agrarian Reform Consortium and the Peasant Rights Movements launched by the North Sumatra Small Farmers Union, the Friends of Small Farmers movement in central Java as well as the Integrated Pest Management farmers movement created an even bigger alliance in the history of farmers' movement in Indonesia by establishing a Peasant Rights Movement. Organised as a broad federation, the movement is a strong reaction to the neo-liberal approach of trade liberalisation and especially to the corporate takeover of food and farming. The movement is campaigning to protect the livelihoods and culture of Indonesian rural communities, and claiming rights to food and farmer sovereignty. It argues that genuine food security and participation of farmers can only be realised in a system where the sovereignty of farmers organisations and activities are guaranteed. Farmers and

---

[82] Belières et al., 2002.
[83] Toulmin and Guèye, 2003.

people must be able to exercise their human rights to define their food and farming policies as well as have the right to produce their food in accordance with the diversity of their socio-cultural and ecological contexts.

Many civil society organisations are linked into broad federations to exert countervailing power against what they perceive as a largely corrupt centralised government. Networks and federations get actively engaged in policy reforms at the sub-district, district, provincial and national government levels. Civil society organisations facilitate participatory policy processes and co-management settings. A diversity of deliberative and inclusive processes is used by networks and coalitions to gain leverage, exert pressure from below and effect policy changes. Whilst the primary focus is on institutionalising participatory governance at the community level, well organised farmer federations have secured important policy changes by engaging with civil servants at the district and sub district government level.[84]

Box 11.13 Beyond good governance: participatory democracy in the Philippines
(adapted from Estrella and Iszatt, 2004)

It began as a small initiative known as the "BATMAN" project and today it is a movement of NGOs, peoples' organisations, social groups and progressive local officials, loosely known as the Barangay-Bayan Governance Consortium (BBGC)– one of the largest organised consortia working on participatory local governance anywhere in the world.

By using the dual power approach, which "targets civil society, government, and the democratic space in between", concrete gains have been made, including changed attitudes and behaviours, democratised and more accountable local decision-making, strengthened governance institutions, contributions to policy changes, and delivered basic services and livelihoods. Participation in governance has taken on new meanings, as ordinary citizens developed a personal stake in striving for genuine democratic change and transforming power relations and structures that have been acting, and still can act, to perpetuate patronage, injustice, poverty and marginalisation.

Local actors involved in BBGC openly reflect on the obstacles and the challenges they face. They discuss how to change deeply engrained political cultures, including both the "bossism" that persists amongst some officials, and the patron-client culture often found in the community; how to scale up and out from local levels to more national levels, and from rural to urban; how to deal with issues of serious conflict; how to carry participatory work in areas with strong ethnic or religious minorities; and most of all, how to institutionalise and sustain the gains that are made through local community action.

11.4 The challenge of participatory democracy

Empowering civil society for policy change depends on creating an enabling social context at different levels, including within civil society organisations and peoples' movements themselves. At this point in time, three main challenges appear to stand out for civil society, which we will discuss below.

Equity, gender and voice

Throughout the world, the challenge of widening social inclusion and representation is key for most civil society organisations and the federations they are part of.

---

[84] Fakih et al., 2003.

Gender equity and learning how to better include and respect the voices of the very poor and marginalised are both enduring and urgent new challenges for civil society at large. Several discussions of peoples' movements involving farmers and other resource users generally conclude that the demands of these movements are biased to the needs of rich– or at least to those of surplus– producers.[85] Some movements tend not to voice concerns of particular relevance to the rural poor, such as minimum wages and harassment. Similarly, recent reviews of membership organisations have at times concluded that "successful groups among the poor tend to exclude the layers below".[86] This is especially the case for groups whose functions relate primarily to economic service provision, marketing, etc.[87]

And yet, this is by no means a universal phenomenon. For example, Indian farmer movement demands for higher crop prices allow more surplus retention in rural areas, creating investment capital that allow rural industrialisation and thus jobs for the poor.[88] Even if the voices and interests of some layers of the poorest are excluded in such organisations, the voices of less poor (but still poor) people are likely still to be included. The implication here is not to work against such organisations or criticise them harshly, but to support additional organisations that can specifically represent the very poor and the marginalised environments in which they live. It also means that civil society needs to constantly ask: "under what conditions can poor people's voices be heard, and projected by, organisations and social movements that also involve wealthier farmers, fisherfolk, and other resource users?"

Although natural resource management is becoming increasingly feminised, rural organisations still seem to reflect and reinforce the patriarchal relations that characterise many rural societies. Thus if raising the voice of poor people in natural resource policy is a general problem, then raising the voice of poor women in these policy discussions is particularly challenging. Traditional, community level organisations are often biased to men. In Ecuador, for instance, the International Fund for Agricultural Development (IFAD) estimated less than 10 per cent of the members of community assemblies were women, and some estimate that women hold only one per cent of leadership positions.[89] Women also suffer discrimination within many large-scale organisations created by indigenous peoples.[90] Whilst many NGOs have sought to increase women's participation, there are many obstacles to gender sensitivity and inclusion within NGOs. In India for example, broader social relations of caste and class can influence how the NGOs deal with women farmers, reducing any extent to which their work is empowering.[91] In Indonesia, more gender inclusive policies and practices have only just recently started to be introduced in Farmer Field Schools (FFS) and the wider federation FFS are part of.[92]

One important obstacle to women's voice in such organisations is that participation is linked to tenure over land and other natural resources. Tenure rules often privilege male ownership (though not in all cultural contexts). In this connection, the success of women's and indigenous movements in shaping new land use legislation so that it is more inclusive of women's tenure rights is very significant.[93] It

If raising the voice of poor people in natural resource policy is a general problem, then raising the voice of poor women in these policy discussions is particularly challenging.

...under what conditions can women gain more space in organisations and peoples' movements to voice their views on natural resource management, and make their priorities and knowledge count?

85 Brass, 1995.
86 Thorp et al., forthcoming.
87 Bebbington, 1996; Thorp et al., forthcoming.
88 Omvedt, 1994.
89 Cited in Deere and Leon, 2001: 52.
90 Deere and Leon, 2001.
91 Nagar and Raju, 2003.
92 Fakih et al., 2003.
93 Deere and Leon, 2001; Whitehead and Tsikata, 2003.

demonstrates that large-scale organisations can enhance the voice of women in policy and institutions. It also encourages civil society to constantly ask: "under what conditions can women gain more space in organisations and peoples' movements to voice their views on natural resource management, and make their priorities and knowledge count?"

Safe spaces for participation and peoples' knowledge

Spaces, including citizen spaces, are infused with power relations, affecting who enters them, who speaks with what knowledge and voice, and who benefits.

There are important differences between two radically different types of spaces for participation in the governance of natural resources: invited spaces from above and popular or citizen spaces. Government- and donor-led efforts to set up co-management committees and resource user groups are examples of invited spaces from above. In contrast, citizen or popular spaces are created by people who come together to create arenas over which they have more control e.g., indigenous peoples platforms for negotiation and collective action or do-it-yourself Citizens Juries that frame alternative policies.... Whilst there are notable exceptions, popular spaces are arenas within which, and from which, ordinary citizens can gain the confidence to use their voice, analyse, deliberate, frame alternatives and action, mobilise, build alliances, and act.[94]

But not all spaces for participation have the possibility to become spaces for real change. Popular spaces usually offer more opportunities for civil society to develop its agenda than invited spaces by governments. And yet, they are not always welcoming spaces for women, nor inclusive of the weak and marginalised, nor free from manipulation and co-option by powerful insiders and/ or outsiders.[95] Citizen or popular spaces can reproduce subtle forms of exclusion through language and other cultural codes.

Spaces, including citizen spaces, are infused with power relations, affecting who enters them, who speaks with what knowledge and voice, and who benefits. This is particularly apparent, for example, when both professional knowledge and peoples' experiential knowledge are brought together in the same space and discussed. Foresters, agronomists, protected area managers, water engineers, health professionals, architects, land use planners, and scientists all have specialist knowledge that can usefully feed into citizen deliberations and more inclusive forms of participation that strengthen civil society. But the deliberative process, and the political negotiation over what constitutes valid knowledge in a particular context (see Box 11.14), deeply challenges professionals to assume different roles and responsibilities. In particular, citizens with professional knowledge will often need to shift to new roles that facilitate local people's analysis, deliberations and production of knowledge.

Box 11.14 Some quotes on knowledge and power

"Perhaps we should abandon a whole tradition that allows us to imagine that knowledge can exist only where the power relations are suspended and that knowledge can develop only outside its injunctions, its demands and its interests. Perhaps we should abandon the belief that power makes mad and that, by the same token, the renunciation of power is one of the conditions of knowledge. We should admit, rather, that power produces knowledge...; that power and knowledge directly imply one another; that there is no power relation without the correlative constitution of a field of knowledge, nor any knowledge that does not presuppose and constitute at the same time power relations....In short, it is not the

---

94   See Pimbert and Wakeford, 2001b; Cornwall and Coelho, 2004.
95   See Box 7.3.

activity of the subject of knowledge that produces a corpus of knowledge, useful or resistant to power, but power-knowledge, the processes and struggles that traverse it and of which it is made up, that determines the forms and possible domains of knowledge." (Foucault, 1979: pp. 27-28)

"Contests for knowledge are contests for power. For nearly two centuries these contests have been rigged in favour of scientific knowledge by the established power structures. We should ask why scientific knowledge has acquired the privileged status that it enjoys, why it is that scientists' endeavours are not seen to be on a par with other cultural endeavours, but have come to be singled out as providing the one and only expert route to knowledge and guide to action. We need to confront the question of what kinds of knowledge we want to produce, and recognise that that is, at the same time, a question about what kinds of power relations we want to support– and what kind of world we want to live in.... A socially responsible science has to be a science that does not allow itself to be set apart from, let alone above, other human endeavours. In our interactions with the world, we are all involved in the production of knowledge about the world– in that sense, there is no single group of experts". (Kamminga, 1995: 321)

As power and knowledge are impossible to disentangle, the struggle to involve the full diversity of civil society in the production of knowledge is part of the larger struggle for a more equitable distribution of power. The adoption of a participatory culture within organisations, including civil society organisations, and changes in attitudes and behaviour are unlikely to "automatically follow" when new methods for deliberation are adopted or suddenly become fashionable. Chapter 9 of this volume describes the challenge of designing appropriate institutional mechanisms and rewards to encourage the spread of a participatory culture and praxis within government organisations. Civil society organisations and movements that seek to create more safe spaces for participation are similarly challenged to transform themselves, and some ideas about the elements to tackle are offered in Checklist 11.5.

> When does it make sense to engage within "invited spaces", and when is it more appropriate to remain outside?

More generally, civil society will often need to understand better which spaces offer the possibility for meaningful voice and shift in power relations, and which do not; when it makes sense to engage within "invited spaces", and when it is more appropriate to remain outside. Guidelines and criteria for engagement can help citizens and civil society groups decide whether, when, why and how to engage in policy processes.[96] But, in the final analysis, creating safe spaces for democratic participation will depend on civil society's conscious social commitment to a politics of freedom, equity and gender inclusion.

Checklist 11.5 Transforming organisations for deliberative democracy and citizen empowerment
(adapted from Bainbridge et al., 2000; Pimbert, 2003a)

Key actions for reformers working for more accountable organisations (local and national government, NGOs, civil society organisations) include:

● diversify the governance and the membership of budget allocation committees of public sector planning, services and research institutes to include representatives of diverse citizen groups and procedures to ensure transparency, equity and accountability in the allocation of funds and dissemination of new knowledge;

● encourage shifts from hierarchical and rigidly bureaucratic structures to "flat", flexible and respon-

---

96   PLA Notes, 2002.

sive organisations;

● provide capacity building for technical and scientific personnel to foster those participatory skills, attitudes and behaviour needed to learn from citizens (mutual listening, respect, gender sensitivity as well as methods for participatory learning and action);

● ensure that senior and middle management positions are occupied by competent facilitators of organisational change, with the vision, commitment and ability to reverse gender and other discriminatory biases in the ideologies, disciplines and practices animating an organisation;

● promote and reward management that is consultative and participatory rather than verticalist and efficiency led, and establish incentive and accountability systems that are equitable for women and men;

● provide incentives and high rewards for staff to experiment, take initiatives and acknowledge errors as a way of learning by doing and engaging with the diverse local realities of citizen's livelihoods in urban and rural contexts;

● redesign practical arrangements and the use of space and time within the workplace to meet the diverse needs of women, men and older staff as well as their new professional obligations to work more closely with citizens and other actors (time tables, career paths, working hours, provision of paternity and maternity leave, childcare provisions, mini sabbaticals, promotion criteria…);

● encourage and reward the use of gender disaggregated and socially differentiated local indicators and criteria in monitoring and evaluation as well as in guiding subsequent technical support, policy changes and allocation of scarce resources.

Deepening democracy in the age of globalisation

A strong civil society, enabling government policies, pressure from below, organisational change and professional reorientation are all necessary preconditions for shifts towards more policy making by and for citizens.[97] However, at this time in history, the "power to define reality" rests less and less with governments and professionals engaged in planning, service delivery and in the design of technologies to meet human needs. Globalisation in its present form induces huge power differentials as a small minority of economic actors seek and often obtain control over markets, technologies, policies and institutions, imposing a one dimensional homogenising reality on diversity. Of the top one hundred economic entities of the world, 51 are corporations and only 49 are states. The top 200 trans-national corporations (TNCs) are responsible for about 25% of all measured economic activity in the world. Since the early 1990s, in the United States, average corporate profits have increased by 108% and the compensation packages of Corporate Chief Executives have increased by a massive 481%. During the same period, average annual wages for workers have risen only 28%, barely keeping abreast with inflation. In 1960 the combined incomes of the richest fifth of the world's population were 30 times greater than the poorest fifth. By 1991 it was over 60 times and in 2003 the UN's latest figures estimate it as 80 times as high.[98]

Powerful TNCs use a variety of official and unofficial instruments to impose three basic freedoms central to the neo-liberal credo of international competitiveness and comparative advantage: freedom of investment, freedom of capital flows, freedom of trade in goods and services.[99]

TNCs rely on unofficial, non transparent and discrete bodies to influence governments and opinion makers such as:

Globalisation induces huge power differentials, as a small minority of economic actors seek and often obtain control over markets, technologies, policies and institutions, imposing a one dimensional homogenising reality on diversity.

97 This section draws extensively on Pimbert (2001), Pimbert (2003b) and references therein.
98 UNDP, 2003.
99 George, 2000.

- the European Round Table of Industrialists (ERT) made up of the Chief Executive Officers (CEOs) of 47 of the largest European TNCs; the ERT works closely with the European Commission and individual heads of states, often writing some of the Commission's most important "White Papers";[100]

- the Trans Atlantic Business Dialogue (TABD) composed of CEOs from North America and Europe. Through regular dialogue with top politicians and international agency leaders, the TABD strongly influences international trade negotiations; it also maintains permanent expert committees on a range of topics including standard-setting for goods and services so that products may be freely sold in all markets.

As an official organisation, the World Trade Organisation (WTO) is particularly responsive to the demands of TNCs for internationally binding rules in favour of total freedom of trade in goods and services. With little or no public oversight, corporations actively shape WTO negotiations on the liberalisation of trade on goods, agricultural products and intellectual property. Areas such as health, education, culture, the environment, and energy are corporate targets under the emerging General Agreement on Trade in Services. The decisions of the WTO's Dispute Resolution Mechanism (panels of trade experts, meeting behind closed doors) are enforceable through sanctions and apply to all 136 member-countries, both developed and developing. This is where WTO's greatest power lies: during the first five years of its existence, the rulings of the dispute settlement body have generally upheld corporate interests over those of people and the environment.

Corporate led globalisation is increasingly dis-empowering many more citizens on an unprecedented scale, both in the North and the South. Increasing job losses, fractured livelihoods, economic marginalisation, fear and anxiety about the future are all induced by the drive for comparative advantage and international competitiveness via:

- relocations of industry and services, often from countries with higher labour costs and regulatory standards (environmental, working conditions) to countries with lower ones;

- mergers and acquisitions, with post acquisition rationalisation;

- deployment of new cost and labour saving technologies (computers, robotics, automation, biotechnologies) in the restructuring of manufacturing, agriculture, forestry, fisheries and, increasingly, service sectors such as banking, insurance, airlines, accounting, retailing, hotels and environmental agencies;

- reductions in public sector spending and privatisation;

- spread of a culture and vision emphasising the inevitability of the neo-liberal agenda, the public has to accept that There Is No Alternative (the TINA syndrome).[101]

---

[100] Balanyà, 2000.
[101] International Forum on Globalisation, 2002.

...feminist
economists have
shown how the
gendered structure
of the economy and
male bias in
national and
international
economic policies
constrain gender
and inclusive
participation in
development.

In this regard it is important to note that women are more harmed than men by the growing inequalities, insecure employment, and social unrest that have marked the last two decades of neo-liberalism (1980-2000). Throughout the world, women are the first hit by displacements induced by "modernising" forest and agricultural development, and by the mass redundancies associated with the current frenzy of mergers, acquisitions and re-locations of industries. In both developed and developing countries, women's average wages continue to be significantly lower than men's– in all professions and across all social groups. Women are under-represented in all of the world's governments and parliaments where they are often used as tokens in processes of political participation. Moreover, there is some evidence that the degradation of living conditions in poorer households everywhere has translated into an increase in levels of violence, particularly in domestic and sexual violence in which women are the first victims. For example, as many as 40 per cent of adult women are now subjected to domestic violence in Europe (58 per cent in Turkey...). And it is estimated that in 2002 alone, over 4 million young girls and women were sold for use as slaves, wives or prostitutes throughout the world.[102]

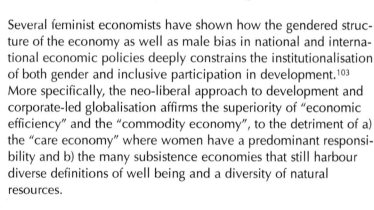

Several feminist economists have shown how the gendered structure of the economy as well as male bias in national and international economic policies deeply constrains the institutionalisation of both gender and inclusive participation in development.[103] More specifically, the neo-liberal approach to development and corporate-led globalisation affirms the superiority of "economic efficiency" and the "commodity economy", to the detriment of a) the "care economy" where women have a predominant responsibility and b) the many subsistence economies that still harbour diverse definitions of well being and a diversity of natural resources.

Whilst clearly important and necessary, a strong civil society does not only imply an expansion of political democracy to include more people and places in shaping the policy process, technologies and institutions. An analysis of how power is increasingly exercised and mediated today suggests that economic democracy and information democracy are also fundamental for change.

a strong civil society
does not only
imply an expansion
of political
democracy... the
issue of economic
democracy and
information
democracy are
also fundamental
for change.

Widening economic democracy is a key overarching condition for the mainstreaming of participatory forms of policy making in this globalising world. In its deepest sense, "economic democracy" means free democratic access to the means of life and the guarantee of freedom from material want. More specifically, there is a need for economic arrangements that offer enough material security and time for citizens (men and women included) to exercise their right to participate in shaping policies for the public good and ecological sustainability. Only with some material security and time people can be "empowered" to think about what type of policies they would like to see and how they can contribute to obtaining them.

Similarly, only with full access to information and liberation from active brainwashing by economic, political and cultural advertisements and the diffusion of sheer lies can people develop some forms of critical consciousness. It is not possible to have message-free media and purely objective information services. But it

---

[102] Le Monde Diplomatique, 2003.
[103] Jahan, 1995; Miller and Razavi,1988; Kanji, 2003.

is possible for media to respect different views and encourage investigative journalism. It is possible for a national legislation to include safeguards against economic powers dominating the political scene, and against various forms of media agglomeration. And it is possible for formal education to promote critical thinking, rather than mere absorption of notions, and to expose children to pluralist views as early as possible.

In this context, the challenge for civil society organisations and social movements is to take the lead in making other worlds possible.[104] In recent years, civil society as a whole has supported not only alternative thinking, practices and innovations for widespread transformation that promote democratic participation, but also economic and information democracy, alternative education systems and gender equity. Examples of proposals for structural reforms aimed at "re-embedding the economy in society"[105] and more are shown in Box 11.15. These are far from being a North-based affair. Both southern and northern actors are now discussing such reforms and proposals throughout the world. These newly emerging views are relevant in the context of our policy analysis because they speak directly to the wider social conditions in which co-management and adaptive governance of natural resources can (or cannot) thrive. And yet, more civil society dialogue and initiatives are clearly needed to further elaborate, test and implement such proposals in the coming years. Indeed, throughout the world, civil society is challenged to give new meaning and content to the "good life", "development" and society's relationship with nature.

Box 11.15 Civil society imagining other possible worlds
(adapted from a variety of sources, including Chomsky and Herman, 1988; Gorz, 1994; Mies and Bennholdt-Thomsen, 1999; McChesney, 1999; Passet, 2000; Pimbert, 2001; Méda, 2001; ATTAC, 2004; Gollain, 2004; Pimbert, 2004 (in press); http://globalpolicy.igc.org/socecon/glotax/currtax/; www.france.attac.org; www.cidse.org/pubs/cttenpt2.htm; http://www.thirdworldtraveler.com/index.html)

In practice, levelling the economic playing field for democratic participation calls for radical and mutually reinforcing structural reforms. Among these, the following merit closer attention because of the broad directions they suggest for societies increasingly involved in the dynamics of globalisation:

1. A tax on financial speculations. The proposal, first launched in 1972 by James Tobin, calls for an internationally uniform tax on all conversions of currency (in the original proposal it was set at 1%). This tax would discourage speculation and encourage exchange rate stability. At the same time, with annual estimates of the tax revenue ranging from a few tens of thousands of million to a few hundreds of thousands of million US dollars, this globally-raised revenue could create a global fund to meet global challenges of human and social development and conservation. Responding to a number of technical criticisms, this initial proposal was transformed into a two-tier tax, levied as a national tax but introduced through an international agreement, with a minimal-rate levied on all transactions (the "basic tax"), and a high rate (an anti-speculation device) triggered during periods of exchange rate turbulence and on the basis of well-established quantitative criteria. Other variations on the theme have also been proposed.

2. The full application of the "polluter pays" principle. The principle allocates costs of pollution prevention and control measures to encourage rational use of scarce and environmental resources and to avoid distortions in international trade and investment. The principle requires, therefore, that the polluters bear the expense to achieve this. Where adopted, the principle helps to prevent or minimise polluting processes and internalise the costs of doing so as part of the cost of production and the cost

---

[104] Amin and Houtard, 2002.
[105] On the concept of embedded economy in society see Polanyi (1944).

for the consumer. A carbon tax can be included as part of a global package of the measure and could be one of its most momentous applications.

3. A guaranteed and unconditional minimum income for all. The Citizen Income proposal is based on the notion that the productive capacity of society is the result of all the scientific and technical knowledge accumulated by previous generations. This is a common heritage of humankind and all individuals regardless of origin, age or gender have a right to benefit from it, in the form of an unconditional basic income. An equitable distribution of the existing world product would allow each person on earth to benefit from such a basic income. Apart from offering a measure of security, a Citizen Income would allow people– men and women– to find more time to engage in caring activities, civic affairs and democratic decision-making over the means and ends of social life.

4. A gender redistribution of roles and responsibilities. This proposal would allow women to work for a decent wage outside the home and men and women to share more evenly in domestic, parenting and caring activities within their households and neighbourhoods. This implies gender equitable property rights over resources as well as redesigning practical arrangements and the use of space and time within the workplace to meet the diverse needs of women, men, dependent children and elderly people (time tables, career paths, working hours, provision of paternity and maternity leave, childcare provisions…). It may also imply a cultural shift affirming the importance and values of the non-monetary reproductive sphere as much as the monetary productive economic sphere– with men and women deriving their identities through a plural anchoring in both spheres of social life.

5. A generalised reduction of time spent in wage-work and a more equitable sharing of jobs. This proposal is about finding ways to a) change the sexual division of labour so that men do as much unpaid work as women and engage in caring activities within the domestic/ reproductive sphere, b)  ensure that wage-work is more evenly distributed so that everyone can invest in other activities, outside the wage economy, c) defend the rights associated with wage-work, and d) move towards a post-wage society and introduce new rights de-linked from wage-work. An important goal here is to free up peoples' time for self-chosen and autonomous activities, whilst ensuring freedom from economic necessity.

6. The re-localisation of pluralist economies that combine both subsistence and market oriented activities. The environments where people live will need to offer more individual and collective opportunities of engaging in many different activities outside– and unmediated by– the market, wage-work and commodity production. These environments could provide the structural means by which citizens could manage their own affairs through face to face processes of deliberation and decision making.[106]

7. The active pursuit of information democracy. If, as in the words of Thomas Jefferson, "information is the currency of democracy", democracy is indeed still in its infancy. Enormous work still needs to be done before the majority of people engage in critical thinking and well-informed decision making. Such work should start from profound reforms in formal education curricula, where pluralist perspectives should be substituted in place of monolithic interpretations of history and uncritical perspectives on "science". And it could continue with appropriate regulation of the media business, safeguarding against power agglomerations, enforcing strict codes of conduct with regard to the implicit or explicit diffusion of false information, establishing appropriate procedures to subtract electoral politics from the grip of economic power and encouraging investigative journalism.

---

106 Bookchin, 1971; Gorz, 1997; Biel and Bookchin, 1998.

The growth of democratic participation in the policy process depends on expanding spaces for autonomous action by civil society, the regeneration of diverse local economies, technologies and ecologies, commitment to deliberative democracy and robust ways to make global and national institutions accountable to those excluded from decision making,[107] and engagement towards ways of thinking that are, at the same time, more critical and more respectful of the self and others.

The unprecedented imbalances of power induced by corporate-led globalisation challenge all co-management practitioners to engage with these new frontiers, and to work towards the strengthening of civil society, both in the North and the South. In the final analysis, only a strong civil society can get people meaningfully involved in the work of the United Nations, shape the international policy arena, lobby for international safeguards and accountability, reform national policies on environment and development, and achieve local solutions that value the wealth and diversity of the world's cultures, communities and environments.

The unprecedented imbalances of power induced by corporate-led globalisation challenge all co-management practitioners to engage with these new frontiers, and to work towards the strengthening of civil society, both in the North and the South.

---

[107] Rahman, 2004.

CONCLUDING REMARKS

The closing words of this volume are written while its authors are scattered in various continents attempting to do, in practice, what this volume has advocated and described. From the variety of our experiences, a few points seem evident to us:

● The wonderful and arresting complexity of each real-life context makes each "co-management case" unique and requires, each time, unique study and care. An appreciation of this complexity, a grounding in history and the experience of local communities, and a basic awareness of the relevant biological diversity and ecosystem functions are the necessary starting point for anything that hopes to be effective.

● On the basis of this appreciation and understanding, the most important ingredients to get co-management moving are humane qualities rather than intellectual qualities or technical proficiencies: a positive attitude, good will, curiosity, attention, care, honesty, appreciation, respect, patience... even humbleness, but also conviviality, perseverance, determination and, more often than not, courage. It is only by building upon these qualities that people can effectively respect and recognise each other's arguments and entitlements, listen, think and organise together, and take new and effective action.

● A further crucial ingredient is the concrete ability of people to become

involved. It may be hard for some of our readers to imagine this, but some powerful obstacles to co-management include being perennially sick– weak with parasites and malaria, light-headed because of lack of food, depressed because of a succession of disasters in the family. They include being unable to reach a meeting because of lack of means of transportation or sheer time, as... if one goes to a meeting, who else will tend the field, fetch the water, care for the children or the sick? These are important considerations to keep in mind when we compare cases in resource-rich and resource-poor environments and when we set forth to "save biodiversity" in the midst of the downtrodden of this world. There are prerequisites for co-management, and those begin with adequate local capacities, from the most basic to the sophisticated.

- Then there is what in this volume we have referred to as a "learning attitude", the openness to novelty, the willingness to experiment, and the curiosity that motivates people to carry out action-research and not be satisfied with easy explanations, platitudes and common scapegoats. We believe that one of the powerful advantages of co-management is the wise merging of local and non-local knowledge and skills– those grounded in the tradition and the accumulated experience of indigenous peoples and local communities and those extracted by formal scientists through a careful analysis of different cases and contexts. We have referred to this wise merging as syncretic solutions– they appear as made up of bits of incompatible nature, but prove surprisingly fresh and effective. A learning attitude is essential for adaptive management, but it must concern more than environmental interventions and their results. Adaptive management has to include adaptive governance– striving for lively institutions, capable of responding through time to the changing conditions that embed both conservation and livelihoods in a given environment....

- A learning attitude and the willingness to merge knowledge from various sources and origins are a good part of what constitutes a "co-management process" but not all of it. Fortunately, one does not need to reinvent hot water at every turn, as much has been learned about experiences, methods, tools and institutions that help people to exchange ideas in constructive settings and effectively understand, plan and act together. We believe that much of the usefulness of this volume rests on the fact that it offers a variety of lessons and tools distilled from experience, and many examples from the field. The lessons and tools are not meant to be "applied" but considered, adapted, modified and used only with wisdom and under intelligent surveillance. Similarly, the examples are not meant to be "copied" but taken into consideration as a pool of ideas and insights. We have gone into some depth to describe issues to be examined and dealt with in preparing partnerships, negotiating agreements, developing co-management organisations, and learning by doing, and we hope that the relevant descriptions, checklists, tools and examples will be useful and inspiring. Indeed, we trust to have convinced at least some of our readers that co-management depends upon on-going learning, and that the best results can be achieved by developing policies and programmes on the basis of lessons learned in practice. The ball is now in the court of communities, field-based initiatives, policy-makers, professional networks and training institutions... and much needs to be accomplished.

- A crucial role is played by the context in which the specific situation we would wish to see evolving into co-management happens to exist. A web of political and socio-cultural ties and economic opportunities and constraints is what makes it possible or impossible to work, reap just returns and invest in a better future. It is what makes the difference between building upon quicksand or on solid ground, acting in fear or security, sustaining results or seeing them wither because of lack of recognition and support. All of us engaged in field-based initiatives have to recognise, first and foremost, whether we are not attempting to co-manage... a handful of dust. Is there a sufficient economic basis for local livelihoods? And, if yes, is there a way to secure the conditions that make such livelihoods possible? Too often, the local producers carry out most of the work and bear most of the risks and yet receive minimal returns, dictated by wholesalers and market speculators.... Too often the ones who dare speak the truth and organise for change are the first ones to pay. Practitioners should make an honest assessment of whether the necessary conditions for co-management are in place. If the answer is no, those conditions should be tackled first.

● Ultimately, the success of a co-management setting is determined by what local actors see as important, and affecting their lives. The results of co-management should be tangible in the sense that the relevant parties should be able to figure out whether the agreement they have developed actually solves their problems. And yet, the satisfaction of a group of parties or even a "local majority" is not all. A balance must be struck between local meaning and values and broader, nationally or internationally declared, liberating principles. Such principles enrich and improve the life of everyone and preserve values greater than any one of us, such as respect for biological diversity and human rights. In this sense, co-management may offer safeguards against both the narrow-mindedness and selfishness that can accompany localised decision-making, and the abstract rhetoric and impositions possibly related to decision-making on a large scale….

The reader of this volume will have noted that, while discussing co-management, we often focused on the role of indigenous peoples and local communities. We did so as we believe that the "community mode" of being in this world– as compared with the "individual mode" intertwined with the "market mode" and the "state mode"– has much to offer for our sanity as people and for the integrity of our environment. As discussed in several places in this volume, the present and recent centuries have seen a world-wide interface, and often a clash, between traditional, localised, communally owned and community-based systems of natural resource management and "modern", "scientific", expert-dominated and a-local systems, based on individual, corporate or state property. This is part of a great transformation by which markets, trans-national corporations and state techno-bureaucracies have come to dominate our lives, a transformation that is neither necessary nor overall positive. Stressing the constructive role, creativity and unique cultural features of communities is a form of resistance to this sweeping transformation, as communities can embed alternative values and lifestyles. Some communities have proven incapable of resisting the modernising onslaught, but others– including many indigenous and mobile communities– have shown impressive strength and resilience. We have offered some of their stories and

examples in this volume, which are both refreshing and inspiring for us.

Discussing co-management has brought us to touch upon other, more encompassing subjects, such as culture, identity, development, democracy, human rights and the need to preserve the integrity of the planet for future generations and for other species. This is at the heart of our motivations in writing this volume. We hope that, in the decades to come, cultural diversity will be fully revealed as the great value that it is, and human rights will be paid increased attention and be much more actively pursued. We also hope, however, that all this will find a counterpart in some recognition and declaration of human responsibilities. Possibly, the real meaning of freedom will be found through a more in-depth understanding of the practice of "sharing power"... curbing some of our prerogatives and privileges to recognise the ones of others– the downtrodden and dispossessed of today, the human generations of the future and even the other species on this planet– all of whom are bearing the costs of much of what the powerful are doing and profiting from today. In this sense, "sharing power" means finding our place in the world, giving as much as receiving, and valuing all we have been given– nature in particular– entirely and meaningfully....

Possibly never before in history have the words "freedom" and "democracy" been used so often and in so many contexts. Yet, have we truly understood what they are about? In this volume we have discussed negotiation processes and inclusive deliberation– ways for people to critically review issues, think together and take common decisions. These seem to be the best we have so far, and surely beat the distant and poorly informed– if not actively brainwashed– exercise of voting rights in today's representative democracies. Yet, we may find that freedom and democracy can go deeper than our immediate "desires" and "opinions" crafted by overt and covert advertisements and stage-set politicians speaking in slogans.... We may find that they depend on regaining that part of us that fuses the human and the biological, the part that redeems the feeling of being one with nature and compassionate (in the original etymological meaning of "feeling together") with all other members of our species. It is in the heart of that feeling of oneness and compassion that awe and respect for the environment and capacity for mutual aid and collaboration are born. In that, we believe, rests the highest privilege of our individual and collective freedom– caring for our fellow beings and the wonders of nature.

> Love, sympathy and self-sacrifice certainly play an immense part in the progressive development of our moral feelings. But it is not love or not even sympathy upon which society is based in mankind. It is the conscience– be it only at the stage of an instinct– of human solidarity. It is the unconscious recognition of the force that is borrowed by each man from the practice of mutual aid; of the close dependency of everyone's happiness upon the happiness of all; and of the sense of justice, or equity, which brings the individual to consider that right of every other individual as equal to his own.
>
> Petr Kropotkin, 1902

REFERENCES

Aalbers, C., Use of Contractual Approach in the Project "Management of Forest Resources in the Kita District, Mali", Case study for the Development Policies Department, International Labour Office, Geneva (Switzerland), 1997.

Abbot, J. and I. Guijt, Changing Views on Change. Participatory approaches to monitoring the environment, SARL Discussion Paper 2, International Institute for Environment and Development, London, 1998.

Abers, R., "Learning democratic practice: distributing government resources through popular participation in Porto Alegre, Brazil", pages 39-65 in Douglass, M. and J. Friedmann (eds.), Cities for Citizens. Planning and the rise of civil society in a global age, John Wiley and Sons, Chichester (United Kingdom), 1997.

Abrams, P., G. Borrini-Feyerabend, J. Gardner and P. Heylings, Evaluating governance. A handbook to accompany a participatory process for a protected area, report for Parks Canada and CEESP/CMWG/TILCEPA presented at the Vth World Parks Congress, Durban (South Africa), September 2003.

Abramson J., We the Jury. The jury system and the ideal of democracy, University of Harvard Press, Cambridge, Massachussets (USA), 2000.

Absalom, E., R. Chambers, S. Francis, B. Guèye, I. Guijt, S. Joseph, D. Johnson, C. Kabutha, M. Rahman Khan, R. Leurs, J. Mascarenhas, P. Norrish, M. P. Pimbert, J. N. Pretty, M. Samaranayake, I. Scoones, M. Kaul Shah, P. Shah, D. Tamang, J. Thompson, G. Tym and A. Welbourn, "Sharing our concerns– looking into the future", PLA Notes, 22:5-10, International Institute for Environment and Development, London, 1995.

Aburto, J. and W. Stotz, "Una experiencia de co-manejo de bivalves en el marco de una nueva herramienta de administración pesquera en Chile: las areas de manejo", Policy Matters, 12:200-204, September 2003.

ActionAid, "Transforming Power, Participatory Methodologies Forum", ActionAid February, ActionAid, www.actionaid.org, London, 2001.

Adams, J. and T. McShane, The Myth of Wild Africa, Norton and Company, New York, NY (USA), 1992.

Adams, L., A Gender Analysis of Community Resource Conservation and Development Institutions: the Case of Morovo Lagoon, Solomon Islands, WWF Forest Study 1, WWF International, Gland (Switzerland) 1996.

African Charter for Popular Participation in Development and Transformation, Statement by a Conference sponsored by the United Nations Economic Commission for Africa (ECA), Addis Ababa (1990), IFDA Dossier, 79, International Foundation for Development Alternatives, Nyon (Switzerland), 1990.

Agarwal, A. and S. Narain, Towards Green Villages, Centre for Science and the Environment, New Delhi, 1989.

Agarwal, C. and S. Saigal, Joint Forest Management in India. A brief review, draft discussion paper, Society for Promotion of Wasteland Development, New Delhi, 1996.

Agersnap, H. and M. Funder, Conservation and Development: New Insights and Lessons Learned, Environment and Development Network, Copenhagen, 2001.

Alcala, A.C. and F.J.V. Vusse, "The role of government in coastal resource management", in Pomeroy, R.S. (ed.), Community Management and Common Property of Coastal Fisheries in Asia and the Pacific: Concepts, Methods and Experiences, International Centre for Living Aquatic Resources Management, Manila, 1994.

Alcorn, J., "Indigenous resource management systems", pages 203-205 in Posey, 1999.

Alcorn, J.B., A. Luque and S. Valenzuela, Understanding global change: institutional and governance factors, draft manuscript for the World Resources Institute, Washington D.C.,

2003.

Alden Wily, L. and S. Mbaya, Land, People and Forests in Eastern and Southern Africa at the Beginning of the 21st Century. The impact of land relations on the role of communities in forest future, Natural Resources International and IUCN, Nairobi, 2001.

Allali-Puz, H., E. Béchaux and C. Jenkins, "Gouvernance et démocratie locale dans les Parcs Naturels Régionaux de France", Policy Matters, 12:225-237, 2003.

Altieri, M.A., Agroecology, the Science of Sustainable Agriculture, Westview Press, Boulder, Colorado (USA), 1995.

Amadou B., G. Vogt and K. Vogt, "Developing a community conserved area in Niger", Parks, 13(1):16-27, 2003.

Amend, S. and T. Amend, National Parks without People? The South American Experience, IUCN, Quito, 1995.

Ames, S.C., "Community Visioning. Planning for the future in Oregon's local communities", http://www.asu.edu/caed/proceedings97/ames.html, 1997.

Amin, S. and F. Houtard, Mondialisation des Résistances. L'état des luttes, L'Harmattan, Paris, 2002.

Anderson, J.L., "Agreements between conservation agencies and tribal neighbors in South Africa", pages 261-269 in McNeeley, 1995.

Appfel Marglin, F. and S. A. Marglin (eds.), Dominating Knowledge. Development, culture and resistance, Clarendon, Oxford (United Kingdom), 1990.

Archer, D. and K. Newman (comps.), Communication and Power: reflect practical resource materials, www.reflect-action.org, Books for Change, Bangalore (India), 2003.

ATTAC, Une Économie au Service de l'Homme, Association pour la Taxation des Transactions Financières pour l'Aide aux Citoyens et Mille et une nuits, Paris, 2001.

ATTAC, Le Développement a-t-il un Avenir ? Pour une société économe et solidaire, Association pour la Taxation des Transactions Financières pour l'Aide aux Citoyens et Mille et une nuits, Paris, 2004.

Augustat, K., Rapport d'activités de la cellule socio-économique de la première phase du projet PRO-FORNAT au sud-est Cameroun (Janvier 1997-Mars 1999), GTZ Cameroun, 1999.

Bahuguna, V.K., Collective Resource Management. An experience of Harda Forest Division, Regional Centre for Wastelands Development, Bhopal (India), 1992.

Bainbridge, V., S. Foerster, K. Pasteur, M.P. Pimbert, G. Pratt and I.Y. Arroyo, Transforming Bureaucracies. Institutionalising participation in natural resource management: an annotated bibiography, International Institute for Environment and Development, London and Institute for Development Studies, Brighton (United Kingdom), 2000.

Baiocchi, G., "Participation, activism, and politics: the Porto Alegre experiment", pages 45-76 in Fung and Wright, 2003.

Baird, I.B., "The co-management of Mekong River inland aquatic resources in Southern Lao PDR", www.co-management.org/download/ianbaird.pdf, 1999.

Baird, I.G. and P. Dearden, "Biodiversity conservation and resource tenure regimes: a case study from Northeast Cambodia", Environmental Management, 32(5):541-550, 2003.

Baland, J.M. and J.P. Platteau, Halting Degradation of Natural Resources. Is there a role for rural communities?, FAO, Rome and Clarendon Press, Oxford (United Kingdom), 1996.

Balanyá, B., A. Doherty, O. Hoedeman, A. Ma'anit and E. Wesselius, Europe Inc. Regional and Global Restructuring and the Rise of Corporate Power, Pluto Press, London, 2000.

Baldus, R., B. Kibonde and L. Siege, "15 years seeking conservation partnerships in the Selous Game Reserve and buffer zones of Tanzania", Parks, 13(1):50-61, 2003.

Baldwin, M. (ed.), Natural Resources of Sri Lanka: Conditions and Trends, Natural Resources, Energy and Science Authority of Sri Lanka and USAID, Colombo, 1991.

Banuri, T. and F. Amalric, Population, Environment and De-responsabilisation. Case studies from the rural areas of Pakistan, Sustainable Development Policy Institute, Working Paper POP 1, Islamabad, 1992.

Banuri, T. and A. Najam, Civic Entrepreneurship. A civil society perspective on sustainable development, Vol. 1: a global synthesis, Stockholm Environment Institute, UNEP and RING, Gandhara Academy Press, Islamabad, 2002.

Barraclough, S. L. and K. B. Ghimire, Forests and Livelihoods. The social dynamics of deforestation in developing countries, Macmillan Press Ltd., London, 1995.

Barraclough, S. L. and M. Pimbert, Property Rights and Participation in Natural Resource Management, International Institute for Environment and Development, London and UNRISD, Geneva (Switzerland), 2004 (in press).

Barton, T., G. Borrini-Feyerabend, A. de Sherbinin and P. Warren, Our People, Our Resources. Supporting rural communities in participatory action research on population dynamics and the local environment, http://www.iucn.org/themes/spg/opor/opor.html

(available also in French and Spanish), IUCN, Gland (Switzerland), 1997.

Barzetti, V. (ed.), Parks and Progress, IUCN and Inter American Development Bank, Washington D.C., 1993.

Bassi, M., I Borana: una Società Assembleare dell'Etiopia, Franco Angeli, Milano (Italy), 1996.

Bassi, M. "The making of unsustainable livelihoods: an on-going tragedy in the Ethiopian drylands", Policy Matters, 10:7-13, 2002.

Bassi, M., "Enhancing equity in the relationship between protected areas and local communities in the context of global change: Horn of Africa and Kenya", TILCEPA report, http://www.iucn.org/themes/ceesp/Wkg_grp/TILCEPA/community.htm#A, 2003.

Baumann, M, J. Bell, F. Koechlin, and M.P. Pimbert (eds.), The Life Industry. Biodiversity, people and profits, Intermediate Technology Press, London, 1996.

Bebbington, A., "Organizations and intensifications: small farmer federations, rural livelihoods and agricultural technology in the Andes and Amazonia", World Development, 24(7):1161-1178, 1996.

Bebbington, A., Capitals and capabilities. A framework for analysing peasant viability, rural livelihoods and poverty in the Andes, Policies that work series, International Institute for Environment and Development, London, 1999.

Behnke R.H., I. Scoones and C. Kerven (eds.), Range Ecology at Disequilibrium. New models of natural variability and pastoral adaptation in African savannas, Overseas Development Institute, London, 1993.

Behnke, R. H. and I. Scoones, "Rethinking range ecology: implications for rangeland management in Africa", in Behnke et al., 1993.

Behrman, L., Muslim Brotherhood and Politics in Senegal, University of Harvard Press, Cambridge, Massachussets (USA), 1970.

Belières, J.F., P.M. Bosc, G. Faure, S. Fournier and B. Losch, What Future for West Africa's Family Farms in a World Market Economy?, Drylands Issues Paper 113, International Institute for Environment and Development, London, 2002.

Beltrán, J. (ed.), Indigenous and Traditional Peoples and Protected Areas. Principles, guidelines and case studies, http://iucn.org/themes/wcpa/pubs/pdfs/Indig_people.pdf, IUCN and WWF International, Gland (Switzerland) and Cambridge (United Kingdom), 2000.

Benjaminsen, T. A., Natural resource management and decentralisation, towards co-management in Mali?, paper presented at "Reinventing the Commons", the Fifth Conference of the International Association for the Study of Common Property, Bodø (Norway), 24-28 May 1995.

Bennet, A.F., Linkages in the Landscape, IUCN Gland (Switzerland) and Cambridge (United Kingdom), 1998.

Beresford, M. and A. Phillips, "Protected landscapes, a conservation model for the 21st Century", The George Wright Forum, 17(1):15-26, 2000.

Berger, P., Pyramids of Sacrifice, Anchor Press Doubleday, Garden City, New York (USA), 1976.

Berkes, F. (ed.), Common Property Resources. Ecology and community-based sustainable development, Belhaven Press, London, 1989.

Berkes, F., "Success and Failure in Marine Coastal Fisheries of Turkey", in Bromley, D.W., Making the Commons Work, Institute for Contemporary Studies Press, San Francisco, California (USA), 1992.

Berkes, F, P. George and R. J. Preston, "Co-management", Alternatives, 18(2):12-18, 1991.

Berkes, F. and C. Folke, Linking social and ecological systems, Cambridge University Press, Cambridge (United Kingdom), 1998.

Berkes, F., J. Colding and C. Folke (eds.), Navigating Social-ecological Systems. Building resilience for complexity and change, Cambridge University Press, Cambridge (United Kingdom), 2003.

Berryman, P., Liberation Theology, Pantheon Books, New York, NY (USA), 1987.

Berry, W., What are People For?, North Point Press, San Francisco, California (USA), 1990.

Bertrand, A. and J. Weber, From state to local commons in Madagascar: a national policy for local management of renewable resources, paper presented at "Reinventing the Commons", the Fifth Conference of the International Association for the Study of Common Property, Bodø (Norway), 24-28 May 1995.

Bertrand, A. and L. Kalafatides, OMC, Le Pouvoir Invisible, Fayard, Paris, 2002.

Bhatt, S., "Conservation through community enterprise", pages 270-286 in Kothari et al., 1998.

Biel, J. and M. Bookchin, The Politics of Social Ecology, Black Rose Books, Montreal (Canada), 1998.

Blackburn, J. and J. Holland (eds.), Who Changes? Institutionalising participation in development, Intermediate Technology Publications, London, 1998.

Blaikie, P., The Political Economy of Soil Erosion in Developing Countries, Logman, New York, NY (USA), 1985.

Blauert, J and K. Dietz, Of Dreams and Shadows. The

case of the Mexican regional sustainable development programme (PRODERS), IIED-IDS Institutionalising Participation Series, International Institute for Environment and Development, London, 2004.

Blomley, T. and A. Namara, "Devolving rights or shedding responsibilities? Community conservation in Uganda over the last decade", Policy Matters, 12:283-289, 2003.

Bocoum, A., K. Cochrane, M. Diakite and O. Kane, Social inclusion: a prerequisite for equitable and sustainable natural resource management, Securing the Commons 7, International Institute for Environment and Development and SoS Sahel, London, 2003.

Bodley, J.B., Victims of Progress, Benjamins and Cummings, Menlo Park, California (USA), 1982.

Bookchin, M., Post-Scarcity Anarchism, Wildwood House, London (United Kingdom), 1971.

Bookchin, M., The Ecology of Freedom, Cheshire Books, Palo Alto, California (USA), 1982.

Bookchin, M., To Remember Spain. The anarchist and syndicalist revolution of 1936, AK Press, Edinburgh (Scotland), 1994.

Bookchin, M., The Third Revolution. Popular movements in the revolutionary era, Volume 1, Cassell, London, 1996.

Bookchin, M., The Third Revolution. Popular movements in the revolutionary era, Volume 2, Cassell, London, 1998.

Borrini, G., Enhancing People's Participation in the Tropical Forestry Action Plan, FAO, Rome, 1994 (2d reprint).

Borrini-Feyerabend, G., Collaborative Management of Protected Areas. Tailoring the approach to the context, http://www.iucn.org/themes/spg/Files/tailor.html (available also in French, Spanish and Portuguese), IUCN, Gland (Switzerland), 1996.

Borrini-Feyerabend, G. (ed., with D. Buchan), Beyond Fences. Seeking social sustainability in conservation (2 vols: "Process Companion" and "Reference Book"), http://www.iucn.org/themes/spg/Files/beyond_fences/beyond_fences.html, IUCN, Gland (Switzerland) and Cambridge (United Kingdom), 1997.

Borrini-Feyerabend, G., Livelihood security and natural resource management in Wenchi District, Ghana, Project Document prepared for CARE Denmark and CARE Ghana, manuscript, 2000.

Borrini-Feyerabend, G., "Governance of Protected Areas, Participation and Equity", pages 100-105 in Secretariat of the Convention on Biological Diversity, Biodiversity Issues for Consideration in the Planning, Establishment and Management of Protected Areas Sites and Networks, CBD Technical Series, 15, Montreal (Canada), 2004.

Borrini-Feyerabend, G., "Participatory democracy in natural resource management: a Columbus' egg?", in Representing Communities, University of Atlanta, Altamira Press, Georgia (USA), 2004 (in press).

Borrini-Feyerabend, G., M.T. Farvar, J.C. Nguinguiri and V.A. Ndangang, Co-management of Natural Resources: Organising, Negotiating and Learning-by-Doing, http://nrm.massey.ac.nz/changelinks/cmnr.html (also available in French and Spanish), GTZ, Kasparek Verlag (Germany), 2000.

Borrini-Feyerabend, G. and M.T. Farvar, Participatory evaluation of the participatory management of the Galapagos Marine Reserve (Ecuador), 14 August — 5 September 2000, mission report for Galapagos National Park, manuscript, November 2001.

Borrini-Feyerabend, G., T. Banuri, M.T. Farvar, K. Miller and A. Phillips, "Indigenous and local communities and protected areas: rethinking the relationship", Parks, 12(2):5-15, 2002.

Borrini-Feyerabend, G. and T. Sandwith, "From guns and fences to paternalism to partnerships: the slow disentangling of Africa's protected areas", www.iucn.org/themes/ceesp/Publications/TILCEPA/Editorial-13_1.pdf, Parks, 13(1):1-5, 2003.

Borrini-Feyerabend, G., A. Kothari and G. Oviedo, Indigenous and Local Communities and Protected Areas. Towards equity and enhanced conservation, IUCN/WCPA Best Practice Series, 11, Gland (Switzerland) and Cambridge (United Kingdom), 2004 (in press).

Boserup, E., Population and Technological Change. A study of long term trends, University of Chicago Press, Chicago, Illinois (USA), 1981.

Brass, T., New Farmers' Movements in India, Frank Cass, Ilford (United Kingdom), 1995.

Bravo, M. and P. Heylings, "Sistema de manejo participativo de la Reserve Marina de Galápagos–actividades en 2001 y resultados de la primera evaluación participativa", Policy Matters, 10:115-120, 2002.

Brechin, S.R., "Wondering boundaries and illegal residents–the political ecology of protected area deforestation in South Sumatra, Indonesia from 1979 to 1992", pages 59-72 in Brechin et al., 2003.

Brechin, S.R., P.R. Wilhusen, C.L. Fortwangler and P.C. West (eds.), Contested Nature. Promoting international biodiversity with social justice in the twenty first century, State University of New York Press, Albany, New York (USA), 2003.

British Columbia Claims Task Force, "The Report of the British Columbia Claims Task Force, June 28, 1991", http://www.gov.bc.ca/tno/rpts/bcctf/toc.htm, 1991.

British Columbia Treaty Commission Act, C. 45. http://laws.justice.gc.ca/en/B-8.5/8596.html, 1995.

Brockington, D., "Injustice and conservation: is local support necessary for sustainable protected areas?", Policy Matters, 12:22-30, 2003.

Bromley, D.W. and M. Cernea, The Management of Common Property Natural Resources. Some conceptual fallacies, World Bank Discussion Paper 57, Washington D.C., 1989.

Brown, J.L. and B.A. Mitchell, "Stewardship: a working definition", Environments, 26(1):8-17, 1998.

Brown, M. and B. Wyckoff-Baird, Designing Integrated Conservation and Development Projects, Biodiversity Support Program with PVO-NGO/NRMS and World Wildlife Fund, Washington D.C., 1994.

Bruch, C. and M. Filbey, "Emerging global norms in public involvement", in Bruch (ed.), The New "Public": the Globalisation of Public Participation, Environmental Law Institute, Washington D.C., 2002.

Burbach, R. and P. Flynn, Agribusiness in the Americas, Monthly Review Press, New York (USA), 1980.

Burns, D., R. Hambleton and P. Hoggett, The Politics of Decentralization. Revitalising local democracy, Macmillan, London, 1994.

Cairngorms Partnership, Managing the Cairngorms—a Consultation Paper, Draft Management Strategy, Grantown-on-Spay (Scotland), 1996.

Calame, P., La Démocratie en Miettes. Pour une révolution de la gouvernance, Charles Léopold Mayer/Descartes & Cie, Paris, 2003.

Campbell, A., Community First. Landcare in Australia, IIED Gatekeepers Series 42, International Institute for Environment and Development, London, 1994a.

Campbell, A., Landcare. Communities shaping the land and the future, Allen and Unwin, Sydney (Australia), 1994b.

Canada Royal Commission on Aboriginal Peoples, Restructuring the Relationship, Vol. 2, Part 2, Ministry of Supply and Services, Government of Canada, Canada Communication Group Publishing, Ottawa, 1996.

CANARI, The Sea is Our Garden. A report on a study of institutional and technical options for improving coastal livelihoods in Laborie, Saint Lucia, CANARI Technical Report 322, Caribbean Natural Resources Institute, Laventille (Trinidad and Tobago), 2003.

Cao, G., and L. Zhang, "Innovative forest management by the local community in Dongda village, Yunnan Province in Forests", Trees and People Newsletter, 34, September 1997.

Carroll, T. F. and A. Bebbington. "Peasant federations and rural development policies in the Andes", Policy Sciences, 33(3/4):435-457, 2001.

Castellanet, C. and C.F. Jordan, Participatory Action Research in Natural Resource Management, Taylor and Francis, New York, NY (USA), 2002.

CBDC Programme, The Protocol for the Community Biodiversity Development and Conservation Programme. Barcelona accord and MOU, The CBCD Programme, Wageningen (The Netherlands), 1994.

CENESTA, The Qanat System in Iran: a Globally Ingenious Agricultural Heritage System, report prepared for the GIAHS project, UN Food and Agriculture Organisation, 2004.

Cernea, M. (ed.), Putting People First. Sociological variables in rural development, The World Bank, Washington DC, 1985.

Cernea, M., "Culture and organisation. The social sustainability of induced development", Sustainable Development, 1(2):18-29, 1993.

Cernea, M. and K. Schmidt-Soltau, "The end of forcible displacements? Making conservation and impoverishment incompatible", Policy Matters, 12:42-51, 2003.

CGIR, Uniting Science and Participation for Sustainable Livelihoods and Adaptive Natural Resource Management, Earthscan, London, 2003.

Chambers, R., Challenging the Professions. Frontiers for rural development, Intermediate Technology Publications, London, 1993.

Chambers, R., Whose Reality Counts?, Intermediate Technology Publications, London, 1996.

Champagne and Aishihik First Nations and British Columbia, Tatshenshini-Alsek Park Management Agreement, manuscript, 29 April 1996.

Chandrakanth, M.G. and J. Romm, "Sacred forests, secular forest policies and people's actions", Natural Resources Journal, 31(4):741-756, 1991.

Chandrashekara, U. M. and S. Sankar, "Tribals and conservation: Chinnar Sanctuary, India", pages 467-480 in Kothari et al. 1998.

Chatelain, C. and B. Ehringhaus, "Le Mont Blanc peut-il s'élever au rang de Patrimoine Mondial sans processus participatif?", Policy Matters, 10:120-125, 2002.

Chatelain, C., M. Taty and G. Borrini-Feyerabend, Tchim Tchieto: Fierté de la Cogestion, IUCN CEESP Occasional Paper 2, IUCN, Gland (Switzerland), January 2004.

Chatty, D. and M. Colchester (eds.), Conservation and Mobile Indigenous Peoples. Displacement, forced settlement and sustainable development, Volume 10, Studies in Forced Migration, http://www.berghahnbooks.com/toc/ChattyColche

ster_toc.htm, Berghahn Books, Oxford (United Kingdom) and New York, NY (USA), 2002

Chester, J. and C. Marshall, "Aboriginal land management - indigenous protected areas", presentation in the Governance Stream of the Vth World Parks Congress, Durban (South Africa), September 2003.

Chhetri, P., A. Mugisha and S. White, "Communities resource use in Kibale and Mount Elgon National Parks (Uganda)", Parks, 13(1):28-38, 2003.

Chhetri, R. B. and T. R. Pandey, User Group Forestry in the Far-Western Region of Nepal. Case studies from Baitadi and Achham, International Centre for Integrated Mountain Development, Kathmandu, 1992.

Chidhakwa, Z., "Traditional institutions manage their Nyakwaa and Chizire forests in Chimanimani, Zimbabwe", Policy Matters, 12:132-140, 2003.

Child, B., Origins and efficacy of modern community-based natural resource management (CBNRM) practices in the Southern Africa region, paper presented at the regional workshop on Local Communities and Conservation: Issues and Challenges Towards a More Equitable and Sustainable Future, Pretoria (South Africa), 26-28 February 2003.

Clark, J., "Municipal Dreams : A Social Ecological Critique of Bookchin's Politics" http://raforum.apinc.org/article.php3?id_article=1038#nb2, undated.

Clark, R., "Community issues groups", UKCEED Bulletin, 55:19, 1998.

Clarke, J.P., The Philosophical Anarchism of William Godwin, Princeton University Press. Princeton, New Jersey (USA), 1977.

Colchester, M., Salvaging Nature: Indigenous Peoples, Protected Areas and Biodiversity Conservation, World Rainforest Movement and Forest Peoples Programme, Moreton in Marsh (United Kingdom), 2003.

Colchester, M. and C. Erni (eds.), Indigenous Peoples and Protected Areas in South and Southeast Asia, IWGIA Document 97, Copenhagen, 1999.

Conservation Corporation Ltd., The Conservation Corporation, an integrated approach to ecotourism, manuscript, undated.

Cordova y Vazquez, A., Planeación Colaborativa para el Uso del Territorio y de los Recursos Naturales en la Sierra Tarahumara, Cornell University, Ithaca (New York), 1998.

Cornwall, A. and J. Gaventa, "Bridging the gap: citizenship, partnership and accountability", pages 32-35 in Pimbert and Wakeford, 2001.

Cornwall, A., and V. Coelho, "New democratic spaces?", IDS Bulletin, 35(2), 2004.

Cousins, B., A Role for Common Property Institutions in Land Re-distribution Programmes in South Africa, Gatekeeper Series, 53, International Institute for Environment and Development, London, 1995.

Crengle, D.L.,"Perspectives on Maori participation under the Resource Management Act", in Report of the IUCN Inter Commission Task Force on Indigenous Peoples, 1997.

Crosby, A. W., Ecological Imperialism. The biological expansion of Europe, Cambridge University Press, New York, NY (USA), 1988.

Crucible, People, Plants and Patents. The impact of intellectual property on trade, plant biodiversity and rural society, The Crucible Group, IDRC, Ottawa, 1994.

CSE, Dying Wisdom. Rise, fall and potential of India's traditional water harvesting systems, Centre for Science and the Environment, New Delhi, 1997.

Cunningham-Burley, S., A. Kerr and S. Pavis, "Focus groups and public involvement in the new genetics", pages 36-38 in Pimbert and Wakeford, 2001.

Dalal-Clayton, B. and S. Bass, Sustainable Development Strategies. A resource book, International Institute for Environment and Development and United Nations Development Programme, London, 2002.

Dana Declaration on Mobile Peoples and Conservation, http://www.danadeclaration.org, Policy Matters, 10:16-18, 2002.

de Graay Fortman, B., Beyond Income Distribution. An entitlement systems approach to the acquirement problem, Working Papers, Institute of Social Studies, The Hague, 1997.

De Lacy, T. and B. Lawson, "The Uluru/Kakadu model: joint management of Aboriginal owned National Parks in Australia", pages 155-191 in Stevens, 1997.

del Valle, A., "Managing complexity through methodical participation: the case of air quality in Santiago de Chile", Systemic Practice and Action Research, 12(4):367-380, 1999.

de Marconi, M. and S. Donoso de Baixeras, "Inhabitants of protected areas in Bolivia", pages 73-93 in Amend and Amend, 1995.

de Noray, M.L., Waza Logone. Histoires d'eaux et d'hommes, IUCN, Gland (Switzerland) and Cambridge (United Kingdom), 2002.

de Sherbinin, A. (ed.), Establishing and Strengthening Local Communities' and Indigenous Peoples' Participation in the Management of Wetlands, Handbook No. 5 for the Wise Use of Wetlands, Ramsar Convention Bureau, Gland (Switzerland), 2000.

Decosse, P.J. and S.S. Jayawickrama, Co-management of Resources in Sri Lanka: Status, Issues, and Opportunities, NAREPP/IRG Report, Colombo, Sri

Lanka, 1996.

Deere, C.D. and M. Leon, "Institutional reform of agriculture under neoliberalism: the impact of women's and indigenous movements", Latin American Research Review, 36(2):31-64, 2001.

Dewey, J., The public and its problems, Ohio University Press, Athens, 1991, first published in 1927.

Devlin, P., Trial by Jury, Hamlyn Lecture Series, Stevens, London, 1956.

Diallo, M.S., Communication du projet Land Tenure Center : insécurité foncière et gestion des ressources naturelles, la stratégie adoptée par le projet LTC Guinée, paper prepared for the workshop "Atelier Régional de Labe sur la Problématique Foncière et la Gestion des Ressources Naturelles au Fouta Djalon", 13 -17 Febuary 1995.

Doganay, U., "Democratic inclusion and public deliberations in Turkey. The case of Local Agenda 21", http://www.psa.ac.uk/cps/2003%5CUlku%20Dog anay.pdf, Faculty of Communication, Ankara University, Turkey, 2003.

Dorf, M.C. and C.F. Sabel, "A constitution of democratic experimentalism", Columbia Law Review, 98(2), 1998.

Draz, O., "The hema system of range reserves in the Arabian peninsula", pages 109-121 in McNeely and Pitts, 1985.

Drolet, C.A., A. Reed, M. Breton and F. Berkes, Sharing wildlife management responsibilities with Native Groups: case histories in Northern Quebec, transcripts of 52d Conference on Wildlife and Natural Resources, Canada, 1987.

Dupuy, J.P. and J. Robert, La Trahison de l'Opulence, PUF, Paris, 1976.

Durning, A.B., Action at the Grassroots. Fighting poverty and environmental decline, Worldwatch Paper 88, Worldwatch Institute, Washington D.C., 1989.

Durning, A.T., Guardians of the Land. Indigenous peoples and the health of the earth, Worldwatch Paper 112, Worldwatch Institute, Washington, D.C., 1992.

Dwyer, P.D., "Modern conservation and indigenous peoples in search of wisdom", Pacific Conservation Biology, 1:91-97, 1994.

East, K.M., "Joint management of Canada's Northern National Parks", pages 333-345 in West and Brechin, 1991.

Edmunds, D. and E. Wollenberg, Disadvantaged groups in multi-stakeholder negotiations, CIFOR Programme Report, manuscript, 2002.

Edwards, M., Civil Society, Polity Press, Oxford (United Kingdom), 2004.

Egeimi, O., M.A. Mahmood, and A. M. Abdella, Towards a Local Peace, Securing the Commons 5,

International Institute for Environment and Development and SoS Sahel, London, 2003.

Eghenter, C. and M. Labo, "In search of governance models for indigenous peoples in protected area: the experience of Kayan Mentarang National Park", Policy Matters, 12:248-253, 2003.

Einstein, A., Honored Listeners Present and Invisible!– Original recordings 1921-1951, Supposé, Köln (Germany), 2003, speech delivered in 1940.

Engberg-Pedersen, L., Creating Local Democracy. Politics from above: the "gestion de terroir" approach in Burkina Faso, Issue Paper 56, Drylands Programme, International Institute for Environment and Development, London, 1995.

EPA, "Top Ten Watershed Lessons", http://www.epa.gov/owow/lessons, doc. 840-F-97-001,Office of Water and Office of Wetlands, Oceans and Watersheds, US Environment Protection Agency, 1997.

Escobar, A., "Discourse on power in development: Michel Foucault and the relevance of his work for the Third World", Alternatives, 10(3), 1985.

Esman, M. and N. Uphoff, Local Organizations. Intermediaries in rural development, Cornell University Press, Ithaca, New York (USA), 1984.

ESRC, Strengthening decision-making for sustainable development, report of a workshop held at Eynsham Hall, Economic and Social Research Council, Oxford (United Kingdom), 15-16 June 1998.

Esteva, G., "Development", pages 6-25 in Sachs, W. (ed.), The Development Dictionary–A guide to knowledge as power, Zed Books, London and New Jersey (USA), 1992.

Estrella, M. and N. Iszatt (eds.), Beyond Good Governance. Participatory democracy in the Philippines, Institute for Popular Democracy, Quezon City (The Philippines), 2004.

Fairhead, J. and M. Leach, Misreading the African Landscape. Society and ecology in a forest-savannah mosaic, Cambridge University Press, Cambridge (United Kingdom), 1996.

Fakih, M., T. Rahardjo and M. P. Pimbert, Community Integrated Pest Management in Indonesia. Institutionalising participation and people centred approaches, IIED-IDS Institutionalising Participation Series, International Institute for Environment and Development, London, 2003.

Fals-Borda, O. and M.A. Rahman, Action and Knowledge. Breaking the monopoly with participatory action research, Apex Press, New York, NY (USA), 1991.

Farley, R., Negotiation versus Litigation or Legislation, special address made at the AIC Conference on Working with the Native Title Act. The Political and Commercial Realities, Brisbane (Australia), 17 June 1997.

Farrier, D., "Conserving biodiversity on private land: incentives for management or compensation for lost expectations?", The Harvard Environmental Law Review, 19(2):304-305, 1995.

Farrington, J. and A. Bebbington, with D. Lewis and K. Wellard, Reluctant Partners. NGOs, the state and agricultural development, Routledge, London, 1993.

Farvar, M.T., Participatory Watershed Management Based on Traditional Water and Irrigation Management Systems, manuscript prepared for training programmes of the FAO Project on Watershed Management in Sefid-Rood Basin, Iran, CENESTA,Tehran, 1991.

Farvar, M. T., "Mobile pastoralism in West Asia: myths, challenges and a whole set of loaded questions..." Policy Matters, 12:31-41, 2003.

Farvar, M. T. and J. P. Milton (eds.), The Careless Technology. Ecology and international development, Conservation Foundation and Centre for the Biology of Natural Systems, Doubleday/Natural History Press, New York, NY (USA), 1972.

Farvar, M.T. and F. Berkes, "Common property resources: ecology and community-based sustainable development (introduction and overview)", pages 1-17 in Berkes, F. (ed.), Common Property Resources. Ecology and community-based sustainable development, Belhaven Press, London (1989).

Ferrari, M.F., "Synthesis of lessons learned in the establishment and management of protected areas by indigenous and local communities in South-East Asia", TILCEPA report, http://www.iucn.org/themes/ceesp/Wkg_grp/TILCEPA/community.htm#A, 2003.

Ferrari, M. and D. De Vera, "Coron island and rights-based conservation in the Philippines", Policy Matters 12:166-170, 2003.

Feyerabend, P., Conquest of Abundance, Chicago University Press, Chicago, Illinois (USA), 1999.

Finger-Stitch, A. and K. Ghimire, Travail, Culture et Nature. Le développement local dans le contexte des parcs nationaux et naturels régionaux de France, UNRISD, Geneva (Switzerland) and L'Harmattan, Paris, 1997.

Finger-Stitch, A. and M. Finger, State Versus Participation. Natural resources management in Europe, IIED-IDS Institutionalising Participation Series, International Institute for Environment and Development, London, 2003.

Fisher, L., "Seeking common cause in the commons: opportunities and challenges in resolving environmental conflicts", The Common Property Digest, October, 3-5, 1996.

Fisher, R.J., Collaborative Management of Forests for Conservation and Development, IUCN, Gland (Switzerland), 1995.

Fitzgerald, E.V.K., Regulating large international firms, UNRISD Paper 5, UNRISD, Geneva (Switzerland), 2001.

Foucault, M., Discipline and Punish. The birth of the prison, Vintage Books, New York, NY (USA), 1979.

Fox, J. (ed.), "The challenge of rural democratization", Journal of Development Studies, 26(4), special issue, 1990.

Franke, R.W. and B. Chasin, Seeds of Famine, Landmark Studies, Universe Books, New York, NY (USA), 1980.

Franks, P., What role for communities in PA management in Uganda?, manuscript, CARE Uganda, 1995.

Freire, P., Pedagogy of the Oppressed, Seabury Press, New York, NY (USA), 1970.

Freire, P., The Politics of Education. Culture, power and liberation, Macmillan, London, 1985.

Freudenberger, K and M. Freudenberger, Fields, Fallows and Flexibility. Natural resource management in Ndam Mor Fademba, IIED Drylands Programme, 5, International Institute for Environment and Development, London, 1993.

Freudenberger, M., Community-based conservation and resource management agreements: issues and strategies for the World Wildlife Fund, draft manuscript, WWF-US, Washington D.C., 1996.

Freudenberger, K., "The use of RRA to inform policy: tenure issues in Madagascar and Guinea", in Holland and Blackburn, 1998.

Fuglesang, A., About Understanding. Ideas and observations on cross-cultural communication, Dag Hammarskjöld Foundation, Uppsala (Sweden), 1982.

Fundación pro Sierra Nevada de Santa Marta, Plan de Desarrollo Sostenible de la Sierra Nevada de Santa Marta, Santa Marta (Colombia), 1997.

Fung, A. and E.O. Wright, Deepening Democracy. Institutional innovations in empowered participatory governance, Verso Books, London, 2003.

Funtowicz, S. O. and J. Ravetz, "Science for the post normal age", Futures, 25(7):739-755, 1993.

Gadgil, M., "Peoples biodiversity register: a record of India's wealth", Amruth (the Magazine on Medicinal Plants, India), Special Supplement:1-16, 1996.

Gadgil, M. and R. Guha, This Fissured Land. An ecological history of India, Oxford University Press, Delhi, 1992.

Gadgil, M., F. Berkes and C. Folke, "Indigenous knowledge and biodiversity conservation", Ambio, 22(2/3):151-156, 1993.

Gadgil, M. and R. Guha, Ecology and Equity. The use and abuse of nature in contemporary India, Routledge, London, 1995.

Gadgil, M., "Grassroots conservation practices: revitalizing the traditions", pages 219-238 in Kothari et al., 1998.

Garreau, G., L'agro-business, Calmann-Levy, Paris, 1977.

Garreau, J.M., "Le transfert de gestion dans le nord-est de Madagascar– apprendre à respecter le rythme local et à accompagner l'organisation et l'apprentissage des acteurs", Policy Matters, 10:102-103, 2002.

GBRMPA, Keeping it Great, Great Barrier Reef Marine Park Authority (GBRMPA), Townsville (Australia), 1994.

Geoghegan, T., Y. Renard, N. Brown and V. Krishnarayan, Evaluation of Caribbean Experiences in Participatory Planning and Management of Marine and Coastal Resources, CANARI Technical Report No. 259, Caribbean Natural Resources Institute (CANARI), Vieux Fort (Saint Lucia), 1999.

George, S, Les Stratégies de la Faim, Editions Grounauer, Geneva (Switzerland), 1981.

George, S., "Confronting and transforming the international economic and financial system", www.tni.org, 2000.

George, S., Remettre l'OMC à sa Place, Association pour la Taxation des Transactions Financières pour l'Aide aux Citoyens et Mille et une Nuits, Paris, 2001.

Georgescu-Roegen, N, The Entropy Law and the Economic Process, Harvard University Press, Cambridge, Massachusetts (USA), 1971.

Ghai, D. and J.M. Vivian (eds.), Grassroots Environmental Action. People's participation in sustainable development, Routledge, London, 1992.

Ghimire, K. B. and M. P. Pimbert (eds.), Social Change and Conservation. Environmental politics and impacts of national parks and protected areas, UNRISD, Geneva (Switzerland) and Earthscan, London, 1997.

Gilmour, D. and R. Fisher, Villages, Forests and Foresters. The philosophy, process and practice of community forestry in Nepal, Sahayogi Press, Kathmandu, 1991.

Gladu. J.P., Aboriginal Experiences in Canada. Parks and protected areas, Boreal Footprint Project and Taiga Rescue Network, http://www.taigarescue.org/index.php?sub=2&cat =41, Snabba Tryck, Visby (Sweden), 2003.

Glasner, P., "Rights or rituals? Why juries can do more harm than good", pages 43-45 in Pimbert and Wakeford, 2001.

Goethert, R. and N. Hamdi, Making Microplans. A community-based process in programming and development, Intermediate Technology, London, 1988.

Goetz, A.M. and J. Gaventa, From Consultation to Influence. Bringing citizen voice and client focus into service delivery, IDS Working Paper 138, Institute of Development Studies, Brighton (United Kingdom), 2001.

Gollain, F., A Critique of Work. Between ecology and socialism, IIED—IDS Institutionalising Participation Series, International Institute for Environment and Development, London, 2004.

GONWFP (Government of North Western Province of Pakistan) and IUCN, The Sarhad Provincial Conservation Strategy, Islamabad, 1996.

Goodman, P and P. Goodman, Communitas: Means of Livelihood and Ways of Life, Vintage Books, New York, NY (USA), 1947.

Gorman, M., Report on socio-economic study. Participatory rural appraisal conducted in March /April 1995, IUCN Tanga Coastal Zone Conservation and Development Programme, Tanga (Tanzania), 1995.

Gorman, M. and T. van Ingen, "Learning by listening in Tanga", pages 17-18 in IUCN, 1996b.

Gorz, A., Capitalism, Socialism, Ecology, Verso Books, London, 1994.

Gorz, A., Misères du Présent, Richesses du Possible, Editions Galilée, Paris, 1997.

Gould, S.J., Wonderful Life. The Burgess Shale and the nature of history, Norton and Company, New York, NY (USA), 1989.

Government of Canada and Government of the USA, Agreement between the Government of Canada and the Government of the United States of America on the conservation of the Porcupine Caribou herd, Ottawa, July 17, 1987.

Government of Canada, Council for Yukon Indians Sign Umbrella Final Agreement/Four Yukon First Nations Sign Land Claim and Self-government Agreements, News Release Communiqué, 1-9325, 1993.

Government of West Bengal (India), Appendix 1: Resolution. Forest Regeneration Through Community Participation, Government of West Bengal, Forest Department, WBFD and Ford Foundation, Calcutta, India, 1989.

GRAF/GRET/IIED, Making Land Rights More Secure, Proceedings of an international workshop, Ouagadougou, March 19-21, 2002, International

Institute for Environment and Development, London, 2003.

Graham, J., B. Amos and T. Plumptre, Governance principles for protected areas in the 21st century, a discussion paper, Institute on Governance in collaboration with Parks Canada and Canadian International Development Agency, Ottawa, 2003.

GRAIN, "TRIPS versus CBD. Conflicts between the WTO regime of intellectual property rights and sustainable biodiversity management", Global Trade and Biodiversity in Conflict, Issue No. 1, GAIA/GRAIN, 1998.

GRAIN, "One global patent system? WIPO's Substantive Patent Law Treaty", www.grain.org, August 2003.

GRAIN, "Community or commodity: what future for traditional knowledge?", Seedling, July 2004.

Gramajo, S.E., Autogestión Comunitaria de Recursos Naturales: Estudio de Caso en Totonicapán, Facultad Latinoamericana de Ciencias Sociales, Guatemala City, 1997.

Gramsci, A., Selections from Cultural Writings, Lawrence and Wishart, London, 1985, original works first published in 1947.

Gray, B., Collaborating: Finding Common Ground in Multiparty Problems, Jossey-Bass Publishers, San Francisco (California) and Oxford (United Kingdom), 1989.

Grillo, R., "Discourses of development: the view from anthropology", in Stirrat, R. and R. Grillo (eds.), Discourses of Development. Anthropological perspectives, Berg publishers, Oxford (United Kingdom), 1997.

GTZ, Indicators for sustainable land management for use in development projects, unpublished report, Gesellschaft für Technische Zusammenarbeit, Germany, 1997.

Guèye M. B and S. M. Tall, Les Conventions Locales au Sahel : un Outil de Co-gouvernance en Gestion des Ressources N aturelles, Série sur les Conventions locales de IIED Sahel, International Institute for Environment and Development, London, 2004.

Guijt, I., Participatory Monitoring and Impact Assessment of Sustainable Agriculture Initiatives: an Introduction to the Key Elements, SARL Discussion Paper 1, International Institute for Environment and Development, London, 1998.

Gunderson, L.H., C. S. Holling and S. Light, Barriers and Bridges to the Renewal of Ecosystems and Institutions, Columbia University Press, New York (NY), 1995.

Gunderson, L. H. and C.S. Holling, Panarchy: Understanding Transformations in Human and Natural Systems, Island Press, Washington D.C.,

2002.

Hacking, I., The Taming of Change, Cambridge University Press, New York (NY), 1990.

Hagmann, J. and K. Murwira, "Indigenous soil and water conservation in Zimbabwe: techniques, historical change and recent developments", in Reij, C., I. Scoones and C. Toulmin (eds.), Sustaining the Soil. Indigenous soil and water conservation in Africa, Earthscan Publications, London, 1996.

Hajer, M., The politics of Environmental Discourse, Clarendon, Oxford (United Kingdom), 1995.

Halle, M., Moving the Frontier. The story of the Sarhad Provincial Conservation Strategy, International Institute for Sustainable Development, Winnipeg, Manitoba (Canada), 2002.

Hamerlynck, O., The Diawling National Park, Mauritania. Joint management for the rehabilitation of a degraded coastal wetland, manuscript prepared for the IUCN Social Policy Group, December 1997.

Hancock, G., Lords of Poverty, Mandarin, London, 1991.

Harmon, D., "National park residency in developed countries: the example of Great Britain", pages 33-39 in West and Brechin, 1991.

Hart, R.A., Children's Participation. The theory and practice of involving young citizens in community development and environmental care, Earthscan, London, 1997.

Harvey, D., The Conditions of Post-Modernity, An inquiry into the origins of social change, Basil Blackwell, Oxford (United Kingdom), 1989.

Haverkort B. and W. Hiemstra, Food for Thought. Ancient visions and new experiments of rural people?, COMPAS and Zed Books, London, 1999.

Haverkort, B., K.vant Hooft and W. Hiemstra (eds.), Ancient Roots, New Shoots. Endogenous development in practice, COMPAS and Zed Books, London, 2003.

Heilbroner, R.L., The Making of Economic Society, Prentice Hall, Englewood Cliffs, New Jersey (USA), 1968.

Hemmati, M., Multi-stakeholder Processes for Governance and Sustainability. Beyond deadlock and conflict, Earthscan, London, 2002.

Henderson, D., "Foul play in Cambodia: developing improved policies that affect community forestry development", Asia-Pacific Community Forestry Newsletter, 13(2):51-52, 2000.

Herman E.S. and N. Chomsky, Manufacturing Consent, Pantheon Books, New York, NY (USA), 1988.

Heylings, P. and M. Bravo, "Survival of the fittest? Challenges facing the co-management model for the Galapagos Marine Reserve", CM News, 5:10-13, 2001.

Heylings, P., Mission report for the Parc National du Banc d'Arguin, manuscript, 2002.

Hickey, S and G. Mohan (eds.), Participation: From Tyranny to Transformation, Zed Books, London, 2004 (in press).

Hilhorst, T. and A. Coulibaly, "Formulating co-management agreements for sylvo pastoral zones in southern Mali", in Hilhorst, T. and N. Aarnink (eds.), "Co-managing the commons. Setting the stage in Mali and Zambia", Royal Tropical Institute Bulletin, 346, Royal Tropical Institute, Amsterdam (The Netherlands), 1999.

Hill, M., The Policy Process in the Modern State, Prentice Hall, London, 1997.

Hill, M.A. and A.J. Press, "Kakadu National Park: an Australian Experience in co-management", pages 135-160 in Western and Wright, 1994.

Hines, C., A global look to the local: the case for localisation, IIED Reclaiming Diversity Series, International Institute for Environment and Development, London, 2003.

Hines, C., Localisation. A global manifesto, Earthscan, London, 2003.

Hiralal, M.H. and S. Tare, Forests and People: a Participatory Study on Food, Fuel, Fodder, Fertiliser, Water and Employment in 22 Villages of Dhanora Tahsil (Gadchiroli, Maharastra), unpublished report, undated, quoted in Pathak and Gour-Broome, 2001.

Hobley, M., "Participatory forestry: the process of change in India and Nepal", in ODI, Rural Development Forestry Study Guide 3, ODI Publications, Overseas Development Institute, London, 1996.

Hoggett, P., Emotional Life and the Politics of Welfare, Macmillan Press, London, 2000.

Holland, J. and J. Blackburn, Whose Voice? Participatory research and policy change, Intermediate Technology Publications, London, 1998.

Holling, C. S. (ed.), Adaptive Environmental Assessment and Management, John Wiley and Sons, London, 1978.

Holling, C.S, F. Berkes and C. Folke, "Science, sustainability and resource management", in Berkes and Folke, 1998.

Holmes, T. and I. Scoones, Participatory Environmental Policy Processes. Experiences from North and South, IDS Working Paper 133, Institute of Development Studies, Brighton (United Kingdom), 2000.

Horowitz, M. and M. Salem-Murdock, "The political economy of desertification in White Nile Province, Sudan", in Little, P.D. and M.M. Horowitz (eds.), Lands at Risk in the Third World: Local Level Perspectives, Westview Press, Boulder, Colorado (USA) and London, 1987.

Horowitz, M. and P.D. Little, "African pastoralism and poverty: some implications for drought and famine", in Glantz, M.H. (ed.), Drought and Hunger in Africa: Denying Famine a Future, Cambridge University Press, Cambridge, Massachusetts (USA), 1987.

Howell, J. and J. Pearce, Civil Society and Development. A critical exploration, Lynne Reinner, Boulder, Colorado (USA), 2001.

Hyden, G., Beyond Ujamaa in Tanzania, Heineman, London, 1980.

Iamo, W., "Sustainable development and land tenure in Papua New Guinea", in International Indigenous Commission, Indigenous Peoples' Knowledge and Management Practices, report prepared for the UN Conference on Environment and Development, UNDP, 1992.

IDS, Tales of the Unexpected. Environmental governance in an uncertain age, Policy Briefing Issue 16, Institute of Development Studies, Brighton (United Kingdom), 2003.

IIED, Whose Eden? An overview of community approaches to wildlife management, International Institute for Environment and Development, London, 1995.

Illich, I., Tools for Conviviality, Harper and Row, New York, NY (USA), 1973.

ILO, "Convention 169 concerning Indigenous and Tribal Peoples in Independent Countries", ILO General Conference, International Labour Organisation, http://www.unhchr.ch/html/menu3/b/62.htm, adopted on 27 June 1989.

ILRC and IHRLG, "The Awas Tingni Decision–Fifteen Months Later. The challenges to the implementation of the decision of the Inter-American Court of Human Rights", www.indianlaw.org, Indian law Resource Center and International Human Rights Law Group, 2003.

Inglis, A., Enhancing equity in the relationship between protected areas and indigenous and local communities in the context of global change in Europe, Draft report for CEESP/ CMWG, 2002.

Institute on Governance, Governance Principles for Protected Areas in the 21st Century, Discussion paper for Parks Canada, Parks Canada, Ottawa, 2002.

International Forum on Globalisation, Alternatives to Economic Globalisation. A better world is possible, Barrett-Koehler Press, San Francisco, California (USA), 2002.

IPPR, Citizens Juries, IPPR, London, 1994.

Irwin, A., Citizen Science. A study of people, expertise

and sustainable development, Routledge, London, 1995.

Irwin, A., "Citizen engagement in science and technology policy: a commentary on recent UK experience", pages 72-75 in Pimbert and Wakeford, 2001.

IUCN, Evaluation of the Implementation of the 1984 Action Plan for Biosphere Reserves, paper presented at the March 1995 UNESCO MAB Conference in Seville (Spain), 1995.

IUCN, La Réserve de Biosphère de l'Archipel de Bijagos, IUCN, Gland (Switzerland), 1996a.

IUCN, People in Charge!, special issue on co-management of natural resources of World Conservation, no. 2, 1996b.

IUCN, Indigenous Peoples and Sustainability, IUCN Inter Commission Task Force on Indigenous Peoples, Gland (Switzerland), 1997.

IUCN/WCPA, Guidelines for Protected Area Management Categories, IUCN, World Commission on Protected Areas, Gland (Switzerland), 1994.

Jackson, W., W. Berry and B. Coleman (eds.), Meeting the Expectations of the Land. Essays in sustainable agriculture and stewardship, North Point Press, San Francisco, California (USA), 1984.

Jahan, R., The Elusive Agenda. Mainstreaming women in development, Zed Press, London, 1995.

Jayatilake, A., N. Pallewatta and J. Wikramanayake, "The practice of community-based conservation in Sri Lanka", pages 170-190 in Kothari et al., 1998.

Jeanrenaud, S., People-oriented Approaches in Global Conservation. Is the leopard changing its spots?, IIED-IDS Institutionalising Participation Series, International Institute for Environment and Development, London and Institute for Development Studies, Brighton (United Kingdom), 2002.

Jeanrenaud, S. and J.P. Jeanrenaud, Thinking Politically About Community Forestry and Biodiversity. Insider driven initiatives in Scotland, ODI Rural Development Forestry Network Paper 20, Overseas Development Institute, London, 1996.

Jentoft, S., "Fisheries co-management", Marine Policy, 13:137-154, 1989.

Jentoft, S., B.J. McCay and D.C. Wilson, "Social theory and fisheries co-management", Marine Policy, 22(4-5):423-436, 1998.

Johansson, L. and P. Westman, The Forests, Trees and People Project in Babati District, Tanzania. Experiences from field work and studies, 1987-1990, Working paper 204, Swedish University of Agricultural Sciences International Rural Development Center, Uppsala (Sweden), 1992.

Jones, B., "Lessons learned from the philosophy and practice of CBNRM in Southern Africa", TILCEPA, http://www.iucn.org/themes/ceesp/Wkg_grp/TILCEPA/community.htm#A, 2003.

Jones, B. and M. Murphree, "The evolution of policy on community conservation in Namibia and Zimbabwe", in Hulme, D. and M. Murphree (eds.), African Wildlife and Livelihoods. The promise and performance of community conservation, James Currey, Oxford (United Kingdom), 2001.

Kabuye, C., "Bark cloth in Buganda", pages 371-372 in Posey, 1999.

Kaimowitz, D., A. Faune and R. Mendoza, "Your biosphere is my backyard: the story of Bosawas in Nicaragua", Policy Matters, 12:5-15, 2003.

Kamminga, H., "Science for the people?", in Wakeford, T. and M. Walters (eds.), Science for the Earth, Wiley, Chichester (United Kingdom), 1995.

Kandeh, H.B.S. and P. Richards, "Rural people as conservationists: querying neo-malthusian assumptions about biodiversity in Sierra Leone", Africa, 66(1):90-103, 1996.

Kanji, N., Mind the Gap. Mainstreaming gender and participation in development, IIED-IDS Institutionalising Participation Series, International Institute for Environment and Development, London, 2003.

Karanja, F., Y. Tessema and E. Barrow, Equity in the Loita/ Purko Naimina Enkiyio Forest in Kenya. Securing Maasai rights to and responsibility for the forest, Forest and Social Perspectives in Conservation 11, IUCN, Nairobi, 2002.

Keeley, J. and I. Scoones, Understanding Environmental Policy Processes. A review, IDS Working Paper 89, Institute for Development Studies, Brighton (United Kingdom), 1999.

Keeley, J and I. Scoones, Understanding Environmental Policy Processes, Cases from Africa, Earthscan, London, 2003.

Kettel, B., Protected area, people, and collaborative management: experiences from Nepal, presentation at the IUCN workshop on Collaborative Management for Conservation, First World Conservation Congress, Montreal (Canada), 1996a.

Kettel, B., presentation at the IUCN workshop on Collaborative Management of Natural Resources in Southern Asia held in Murree (Pakistan) on 21 and 22 May 1996, 1996b.

King Mahendra Trust, Annual Progress Report of the Annapurna Conservation Area Project, King Mahendra Trust for Nature Conservation, Kathmandu, 1994.

Kleymeyer, C.D., Cultural Expression and Grassroots Development. Cases from Latin America and the

Caribbean, L. Rienner, Boulder, Colorado (USA), 1994.

Kleymeyer, C.D., "Cultural traditions and community-based conservation", Grassroots Development, 20(1):27-35, 1996.

Kneen, B., Invisible Giant. Cargill and its transnational strategies, Pluto Press, London, 2002.

Koch, E., Reality or Rhetoric? Eco-tourism and rural reconstruction in South Africa, Discussion Paper 54, UNRISD, Geneva (Switzerland), 1994.

Koch, E., "Ecotourism and rural reconstruction in South Africa: reality or rhetoric?" pages 214-238 in Ghimire and Pimbert, 1997.

Kohli, K. and A. Kothari, "A national plan, built from below? The National Biodiversity Strategy and Action Plan, India" Social Change, 33(2-3), June-September 2003.

Konaté, A.B., Local networks as a tool for influencing policy–experiences of the GDRN5 in Mali, Securing the Commons 6, International Institute for Environment and Development and SoS Sahel, London, 2003.

Korten, D., When Corporations Rule the World, Kumarian Press, West Hartford, Connecticut (USA), 1995.

Kothari, A., Protected Areas, People and Participatory Management: the Indian Experience, paper presented at the workshop on Collaborative Management in Protected Areas in Uganda, Mbale (Uganda), October 1995.

Kothari, A., Gram swarajya: decentralised governance and natural resource management in India, R.S. Dubashi Memorial Lecture, University of Pune, Maharastra (India), 16 February 2000.

Kothari, A. "Protected areas and people: participatory conservation", pages 94-99 in Secretariat of the Convention on Biological Diversity (SCBD), Biodiversity Issues for Consideration in the Planning, Establishment and Management of Protected Areas Sites and Networks, CBD Technical Series 15, SCBD, Montreal (Canada), 2004.

Kothari, A., P. Pande, S. Singh, and R. Dilnavaz, Management of national parks and sanctuaries in India, status report, Indian Institute of Public Administration, New Delhi, 1989.

Kothari, A., Singh, N. and S. Suri, People and Protected Areas: Towards Participatory Conservation in India, Sage Publications, New Delhi, 1996.

Kothari, A. and IIPA Team, Joint Management of Protected Areas: an Action Research Project, Indian Institute of Public Administration (IIPA), New Delhi, 1997.

Kothari, A., F. Vania, P. Das, K. Christopher and S. Jha, Building Bridges for Conservation, Indian Institute for Public Administration, New Delhi, 1997.

Kothari, A., R.V. Anuradha, N. Pathak and B. Taneja (eds.), Communities and Conservation: Natural Resource Management in South and Central Asia, Sage Publications, New Delhi and London, 1998.

Kothari, A., N. Pathak and F. Vania, Where Communities Care– Community-based Wildlife and Ecosystem Management in South Asia, Evaluating Eden Series 3, Kalpavriksh, Pune (India) and International Institute for Environment and Development, London, 2000.

Kovacs, T., "Northern National Parks and Native People: The Canadian Experience", in US National Park Service and the Colorado Historical Society, International Perspectives on Cultural Parks. Proceedings of the First World Conference, Mesa Verde National Park, Colorado (USA), 1984.

Kovanen, T., "Liminganlahti Bay LIFE Project: a bottom up approach to management planning", Natura 2000, Newsletter of the European Commission DG XI, 3:4-5, April 1997.

Krishnarayan, V., T. Geoghegan and Y. Renard, Assessing Capacity for Participatory Natural Resource Management, CANARI Guidelines Series, 3, Caribbean Natural Resources Institute, Laventille (Trinidad and Tobago), 2002.

Kropotkin, P., Mutual Aid. A factor of evolution, Extending Horizons Books, Boston, Massachussets (USA), 1955, first printed 1902.

Kuchli, C., Forests of Hope. Stories of regeneration, Earthscan, London, 1997.

Kuyek, D, "Lords of poison: the pesticide cartel", Seedling, 17(2):18-29, 2000.

KWS (Kenya Wildlife Service) and Mbeere County Council, Memorandum of Understanding between Mbeere County Council and Kenya Wildlife Service for the Management of Mbeere National Reserve, manuscript, 1996.

KWS and FD, Memorandum of Understanding for the Joint Management of Selected Forests, Kenya Wildlife Service and Forestry Department, Ministry of Environment and Natural Resources of Kenya, manuscript, 1991.

Laird, S.A. (ed.), Biodiversity and Traditional Knowledge. Equitable partnerships in practice, Earthscan, London, 2002.

Laird, S.A. and E.E. Lisinge, "Sustainable Harvest of Prunus africana on Mount Cameroon: Benefit-Sharing between Plantecam Company and the Village of Mapanja", in Convention on Biological Diversity, Case Studies on Benefit Sharing Arrangements, Convention on Biological Diversity, Conference of the Parties, May 1998.

Larson, P., M. Freudenberger and B. Wyckoff-Baird, Lessons from the Field. A review of World

Wildlife Fund's experience with Integrated Conservation and Development Projects, World Wildlife Fund (WWF-US), Washington D.C., 1997.

Lavigne Delville, P., "Des groupes cibles aux groupes stratégiques: participation et exclusion", http://www.gret.org/index.htm, January 2000.

Law Reform Commission, The Recognition of Aboriginal Customary Laws, Vol. 2, Australian Government Printing Service, Canberra, 1986.

Lawrence, D., Managing Parks/Managing "Country". Joint management of Aboriginal owned protected areas in Australia, Research Paper 2, Department of the Parliamentary Library, Canberra, 1996.

Le Monde Diplomatique, "Femmes rebelles", Manière de Voir, 68, Le Monde Diplomatique, Paris, 2003.

Le Monde Diplomatique, "Altermondialistes de tous les pays ", Manière de Voir, 75, Le Monde Diplomatique, Paris, 2004.

Leach, M., R. Mearns, and I. Scoones, Environmental Entitlements A framework for understanding the institutional dynamics of environmental change, IDS Discussion Paper 359, Institute of Development Studies, Brighton (United Kingdom), 1997.

Leach, M. and R. Mearns (eds.), The Lie of the Land, Heinemann James Currey, London. 1996.

LeBaron, M., M. Romero, K. Clements and C. Darling, Reaching agreement, manuscript, IUCN, Gland (Switzerland), 1995.

Lee, K., Compass and Gyroscope, Island Press, Washington D.C., 1993.

Levidow L. and B. Young (eds.), Science, Technology and the Labour Process, CSE Books, London, 1981.

Levidow, L. (ed.), Radical Science Essays, Free Association Books, London, 1986.

Lewis, C., Managing Conflicts in Protected Areas, IUCN, Gland (Switzerland), 1997.

Lewis, D., "Civil society in African contexts: reflections on the usefulness of a concept", Development and Change, 33(4):569-586, 2002.

Lightfoot, C., C. Alders and F. Dolberg, Linking Local Learners. Negotiating new development relationships between village, district and nation, Agroforum (Denmark) and ISG (The Netherlands), 2002.

Lim, C.P., Y. Matsuda and Y. Shigemi, "Co-management in marine fisheries; the Japanese experience", Coastal Management, 23:195-221, 1995.

Lindblom, C.E., Democracy and the Market System, Norwegian University Press, Oslo, 1988.

Long, A. (ed.), Livelihoods and CBNRM in Namibia.

The findings of the WILD Project, Ministry of Environment and Tourism of Namibia, Windhoek, 2004.

Long, F.J. and M.B. Arnold, The Power of Environmental Partnerships, The Dryden Press, Fort Worth (Texas), 1995.

Long, N. and J. van der Ploeg, "Demythologising planned development: an actor perspective", Sociologia Ruralis, 29(3/4):227-249, 1989.

Lovelock, J.E., Gaia: a New Look at Life on Earth, Oxford University Press, Oxford (United Kingdom), 1979.

Lowndes, V and G. Stoker, Guidance on enhancing public participation in local government: a research report to the Department of Environment, Transport and Regions, DETR, London, 1998.

Luque, A., "The people of the Matavén forest and the National Park System, allies in the creation of a community conserved area in Colombia", Policy Matters, 12:145-151, 2003.

Lynch, O.J. and J.B. Alcorn, "Tenurial rights and community-based conservation", pages 373-392 in Western and Wright, 1994.

Lynch, O. J. and K. Talbott, Balancing Acts. Community-based forest management and national law in Asia and the Pacific, World Resources Institute, Washington D.C., 1995.

Maarleveld, M. and C. Dangbegnon, "Managing natural resources: a social learning perspective", Agriculture and Human Values, 16:267-280, 1999.

Maffi, L., G. Oviedo and P. Larsen, Indigenous and Traditional Peoples of the World and Ecoregion Conservation. An integrated approach to conserving the world's biological and cultural diversity, research report for WWF, Gland (Switzerland), 2000.

Mainspeizer, I., "Ideas, history and continuity in the practice of power–the case of wildlife conservation in Zambia", Policy Matters, 13, 2004 (in press).

Maretti, C., "The Bijagós Islands– culture, resistance and conservation", Policy Matters, 12:121-131, 2003.

Marisol E. and N. T. Iszatt, Beyond Good Governance. Participatory democracy in the Philippines, Institute for Popular Democracy (IPD) http://www.ipd.phi, The Philippines, 2004.

Mate, K., Capacity building and policy networking for sustainable mineral-based development, paper prepared for the UNCTAD Sustainable Resource-based Development workshop, Monterrey (Mexico), March 2001.

Matowanyika, J.Z., "Resource management and the

Shona people in rural Zimbabwe", in IUCN, 1997.

Mayers, J. and S. Bass, Policy that Works for Forests and People. Real prospects for governance and livelihoods, Earthscan, London, second edition, 2004.

Mazoyer, M., "Des échanges agricoles équitables pour des agricultures paysannes durables", La Revue Durable, 6:16-19, 2003.

Mazoyer, M. and L.Roudart, Histoire des Agricultures du Monde, du Néolithique à la Crise Contemporaine, Editions du Seuil, Paris, 2003.

McCallum, R. and N. Sekhran, Race for the Rainforest, PNG Biodiversity Conservation and Resource Management project, Department of Environment and Conservation/ UNDP GEF, UNOPS-PNG/ 93/ G31, Waigani (Papua New Guinea), 1997.

McCaul, J., "Som Thom commune community-based natural resource management project: an example of successful mediation between local communities and provincial government", Asia-Pacific Community Forestry Newsletter, 13(2):21-28, 2000.

McCay, B.J. and J.M. Acheson (eds.), The Question of the Commons, University of Arizona Press, Tucson, Arizona (USA), 1987.

McChesney, R., Rich Media, Poor Democracy, The New Press, New York, NY (USA), 1999.

McDermott, C., User group forestry on a national scale, an example from Nepal, paper presented at the Sixth meeting of the International Association for the Study of Comon Property Resources, Berkeley, California (USA), 1996.

McGee, R. with N. Bazaara, J. Gaventa, R. Nierras, M. Rai, J. Rocamora, N. Saule, E. Williams and S. Zermeno, Legal Frameworks for Citizen Participation, LogoLink Research Report, Institute of Development Studies, Brighton (United Kingdom), 2003.

McIvor, C., "Management of wildlife, tourism and local communities in Zimbabwe", pages 239-269 in Ghimire and Pimbert, 1997.

McNeely, J.A., Economics and Biological Diversity. Developing and using economic incentives to conserve biological resources, IUCN, Gland (Switzerland), 1988.

McNeely, J.A. (ed.), Expanding Partnerships in Conservation, Island Press, Washington D.C., 1995.

McNeely J.A. and D. Pitt (eds.), Culture and Conservation. The human dimension in environmental planning, Croom Helm, London, 1985.

Méda, D., Le Temps des Femmes. Pour un nouveau partage des rôles, Flammarion, Paris, 2001.

Menahem, G., Enquête au Coeur des Multinationales, Association pour la Taxation des Transactions Financières pour l'Aide aux Citoyens et Mille et une nuits, Paris, 2001.

Merchant, C., The Death of Nature. Women, ecology and the scientific revolution, Harper and Row, San Francisco, California (USA), 1980.

Merlant P., R. Passet and J. Robin, Sortir de l'Economisme. Une alternative au capitalisme néolibéral, Les Editions de l'Atelier, Paris, 2003.

Merlo, M., R. Morandini, A. Gabbrielli and I. Novaco, Collective Forest Land Tenure and Rural Development in Italy: Selected Case Studies, FO: MISC/ 89/10, FAO, Rome, 1989.

Metcalfe, S., "The Zimbabwe Communal Areas Management Programme for Indigenous Resources", pages 161-192 in Western and Wright, 1994.

Mies, M. and V. Bennholdt-Thomsen, The Subsistence Perspective. Beyond the globalised economy, Zed Books, London, 1999.

Miller, C. and S. Razavi (ed.), Missionaries and Mandarins. Feminist engagement with development institutions, Intermediate Technology Publications, London, 1998.

Mirenowicz, J., "The Danish consensus conference model in Switzerland and France: on the importance of framing the issue", pages 57-60 in Pimbert and Wakeford, 2001.

Mitchell, B. and J. Brown, "Stewardship: a working definition", Environments, 26(1):8-17, 1998.

Monachesi, A. and C. Albaladejo, "La gestion concertée de l'eau dans un bassin versant pampéen. Apprendre l'hydraulique et la démocratie", Nature, Sciences, Sociétés, 5(3):24-38, 1997.

Morrison, J., "Protected areas, conservationists and aboriginal interests in Canada", pages 270-296 in Ghimire and Pimbert, 1997.

Mumford, L., The Pentagon of Power, Secker and Warburg, London, 1971.

Munk Ravnborg, H., "Protecting Miraflor… or protecting the livelihood of small-scale farmers?", Policy Matters, 12:196-199, 2003.

Murphree, M., "The role of institutions in community-based conservation", pages 403-427 in Western and Wright, 1994.

Murphree, M., Wildlife in Sustainable Development, Centre for Applied Social Sciences, Harare, 1996a.

Murphree, M., "Approaches to Community Conservation", pages 153-188 in ODA, Final Report of the African Wildlife Policy Consultation, Overseas Development Administration, Sunningdale (USA), 1996b.

Murphree, M., "Common property, communal property and open access regimes", pages 59-61 in vol. 2

of Borrini-Feyerabend, 1997a.

Murphree, M., Synergizing conservation incentives: sociological and anthropological dimension of sustainable use, paper presented to the STAP Expert Workshop on the Sustainable Use of Biodiversity, Kuala Lumpur, Malaysia, 24-26 November, 1997b.

Nabham, G.P., A.M. Rea, K.L. Reichhardt, E. Mellinck, "Papago influences on habitat and biotic diversity: Quitovac oasis ethnoecology ", Journal of Ethnobiology, 2:124-143, 1982.

Nagar, R. and S. Raju, "Women, NGOs and the contradictions of empowerment and disempowerment: a conversation", Antipode, 35(1):1-13, 2003.

Narayan, D. C., R. Chambers, M.K. Shah and P. Petesch, Voices of the Poor: Crying Out For Change, Washington D.C., World Bank, 2000.

National Civic League, The Community Visioning and Strategic Planning Handbook, National Civic League, Denver, Colorado (USA), undated.

National Parks and Wildlife (Australia) and Northern Land Council, Memorandum of Understanding Regarding the Control of Aboriginal Cultural Material in Kakadu National Park, manuscript, 1995.

Navarro, Z., Affirmative democracy and redistributive development: the case of participatory budgeting in Porto Alegre, Brazil (1989-1997), manuscript presented at the international workshop on Collaboration between Local Administration and Local Communities in the Age of Globalisation, SID and Institute of Federalism, Murten (Switzerland), 1997.

NEF, Participation Works! 21 techniques of community participation for the 21st century, New Economics Foundation, London, 1998.

Nelson, J. and S. Zadek, Partnership Alchemy. New social partnerships in Europe, The Copenhagen Centre, Copenhagen, 2001.

Nelson, J. and N. Gami, "Enhancing equity in the relationship between protected areas and indigenous and local communities in Central Africa, in the context of global change", TILCEPA report, http://www.iucn.org/themes/ceesp/Wkg_grp/TILCEPA/community.htm#A, 2003.

Nerfin, M., "Neither prince nor merchant: citizen–an introduction to the third system", IFDA Dossier 56, International Foundation for Development Alternatives, Nyon (Switzerland),1986.

Nesbitt, T., "Migratory bird co-management in British Columbia (Canada): a discussion paper for Environment Canada, Pacific and Yukon region", unpublished manuscript, May 1997.

Netting, R.M., Smallholders, Householder. Farm families and the ecology of intensive, sustainable agriculture, Stanford University Press, Stanford,

California (USA), 1993.

Nguemdjiom, A., Description of the Itoh project (Cameroon) for the Equator Initiative, unpublished manuscript, UNDP Cameroon, 2003.

Nguinguiri, J.C., "Collective learning on collaborative management of natural resources in the Congo Basin: the first lessons", CM News, 4:2-3, 2000.

Nguinguiri, J.C., "Gouvernance des aires protégées: l'importance des "normes pratiques" de régulation de la gestion locale pour la faisabilité des réformes dans le Bassin du Congo", Policy Matters, 12:16-21, 2003.

Niamir-Fuller, M. (ed.), Managing Mobility in African Rangelands. The legitimisation of transhumance, FAO, Beijer and Intermediate Technology Publications, London, 1999.

Nietschmann, B., "Protecting indigenous coral reefs and sea territories, Miskito Coast, Raan, Nicaragua", pages 193-224 in Stevens, 1997.

North, D.C., Institutions, Institutional Change and Economic Performance, Cambridge University Press. Cambridge (United Kingdom), 1990.

Northrup, B. and G. Green, Building a national park system: Jamaica's protected areas resource conservation project, paper presented at the Caracas Congress on National Parks and Protected Areas, February 1992, referred to in page 7 of Barzetti, 1993.

North-West Frontier Province, Joint management agreements for the Hazara Protected Forests, Government of the North-West Frontier Province, Pakistan, 1996.

Norton, A., "Analysing participatory research for policy change", in Holland and Blackburn, 1998.

NRTEE, Sustainable Strategies for Oceans: a Co-management Guide, National Round Table on the Environment and the Economy (NRTEE), Ottawa, 1998.

Ntiamo-Baidu, Y., L.J. Gyiamfi-Fenteng and W. Abbiw, Management strategies for sacred groves in Ghana, report prepared for the World Bank and EPC Ghana, 1992.

Oli, K.P. (ed.), Collaborative Management of Protected Areas in the Asian Region, Proceedings of a Workshop organised by IUCN, HMG Nepal and the King Mahenda Trust for Nature Conservation, Chitwan National Park (Nepal), 1998.

Olsson P. and C. Folke, "Local ecological knowledge and institutional dynamics for ecosystem management: a study of Lake Racken watershed, Sweden", Ecosystems, 4:85-104, 2001.

Omvedt, G., "We want the return for our sweat. The new peasant movements in India and the formation of a national agricultural policy", Journal of Peasant Studies, 21(3-4):126-164, 1994.

Osherenko, G., Sharing power with native users. co-management regimes for native wildlife", CARC Policy Paper No.5, Canadian Arctic Resources Committee, Ottawa, 1988.

Ostrom, E., Crafting Institutions for Self-Governing Irrigation Systems, Institute for Contemporary Studies Press, San Francisco (California), 1992.

Ostrom, E., "Local institutions for resource management", pages 14-16 in Vol. 2 of Borrini-Feyerabend, 1997.

Ostrom, E. and J. Walker, "Neither markets nor states: linking transformation processes in collective action arenas" in Mueller, D.C. (ed.), Perspective on Public Choice: a Handbook, Cambridge University Press, Cambridge, Massachusetts (USA), 1997.

Ostrom E. and T. K. Ahn. A social science perspective on social capital: social capital and collective action, paper presented at the European Research Conference on Social Capital: Interdisciplinary Perspectives, Exeter, United Kingdom, 15-20 September 2001.

Otchet, A., "Michael Walzer: a user's guide to democracy", interview with Michael Walzer, UNESCO Courier: 47-50, http://www.unesco.org/courier/2000_01/uk/dires/intro.htm, January 2000.

Otegui, M., Wirikuta, the Huichol Sacred Space in the Chihuahuan Desert of San Luis Potosí, Mexico, report presented at the 5th World Parks Congress, Durban (South Africa), 2003.

ould Bah, H., A. ould Boubout and S. Bouju, "De la restauration des écosystèmes au développement durable : micro-finance et conservation dans le Parc National du Diawling", Policy Matters, 12:270-275, 2003.

Oviedo, G., "Lessons learned in the establishment and management of protected areas by indigenous and local communities", http://www.iucn.org/themes/ceesp/Wkg_grp/TILCEPA/community.htm#A, TILCEPA report, 2003.

Palit, S., "JFM in India, major issues", in Roy, S. B. (ed), Enabling Environment for Joint Forest Management, Inter India Publications, New Delhi, 1995.

Palmer, P., J. Sanchez and G. Mayorga, Taking Care of Sibö's Gifts. An environmental treatise from Costa Rica's KéköLdi Indigenous Reserve, Editorama, San José, 1991.

Pandey, S.K., Collaborative management of forests in India, presentation at the second meeting of the Intergovernmental Panel on Forests, Geneva (Switzerland), March 1996.

Parodi, J.L. (ed.), La Science Politique, Hachette, Paris, 1971.

Parques Nacionales de Colombia, Politica de Participación Social en la Conservación, Ministerio de Medio Ambiente de Colombia, Bogotà, 1999.

Passet, R., L'illusion Néo-libérale, Fayard, Paris, 2000.

Pateman, C, Participation and Democratic Theory, Cambridge University Press, Cambridge (United Kingdom), 1970.

Pathak, N. and V. Gour-Broome, Tribal Self-Rule and Natural Resource Management. Community based conservation at Mendha-Lekha, Maharashtra, India, Kalpavriksh, Pune (India) and International Institute of Environment and Development, London, 2001.

Pathak, N. with A. Islam, S.U.K. Ekaratne and A. Hussain, "Lessons learnt in the establishment and management of protected areas by indigenous and local communities in South Asia", TILCEPA report, http://www.iucn.org/themes/ceesp/Wkg_grp/TILCEPA/community.htm#A, 2003.

Pattemore, V., "Legislation in the Wet Tropics World Heritage Area–tools for protection", in McDonald, G. and M. Lane (eds.), Securing the Wet Tropics?, The Federation Press, Sydney (Australia), 2000.

PEALS, Teach Yourself Citizens Juries, Policy Ethics And Life Sciences Research Institute (PEALS) and University of Newcastle, Newcastle (United Kingdom), 2003.

Peckett, M., Celebrating the circle: incorporating native spirituality into participatory management, paper presented at the First World Conservation Congress, Montreal (Canada), October 1996.

Peluso, N.L., "Reserving value: conservation ideology and state protection of resources", in Dupuis, E.M. and P. Vandergeest (eds.), Creating Countryside, Temple University Press, Philadelphia, Pennsylvannia (USA), 1996.

Phillips, A., "The parks of Europe's people", page 23 in IUCN, 1996b.

Phillips, A., "Turning ideas in their heads", pages 1-28 in Jaireth, H. and D. Smyth, Innovative Governance, Ane Books, Delhi, 2003.

Pierre-Nathoniel, D., Towards the strengthening of the association: the case of the Soufriere Marine Management Area (SMMA), Saint Lucia, paper prepared for the 2nd International Tropical Marine Ecosystems Management Symposium (ITMEMS 2), Manila, 24-27 March 2003.

Pimbert, M. P., Participatory Research with Women Farmers, videocassette, ICRISAT and TVE, Hyderaband and London, 1991.

Pimbert, M.P., "Reclaiming our right to power: some conditions for deliberative democracy", pages 81-84 in Pimbert and Wakeford, 2001.

Pimbert, M.P., Social Learning for Ecological Literacy and Democracy: Emerging Issues and Challenges, Proceedings of the CIP-UPWARD-FAO-Rockefeller International Workshop on Farmer Field Schools, 21-25 October 2002, Yogyakarta, Indonesia, 2003a.

Pimbert, M.P., "Preface", in Kanji, 2003b.

Pimbert, M.P., Institutionalising Participation and People Centered Processes in Natural Resource Management. Research and publication highlights, IIED-IDS Institutionalising Participation Series, International Institute for Environment and Development, London, 2004a.

Pimbert, M.P., "Natural resources, people and participation", PLA Notes, 50, Special anniversary issue of Participatory Learning and Action, International Institute for Environment and Development, London, 2004b.

Pimbert, M.P., Seeking Transformation. Institutionalising participation and people centred processes in natural resource management, IIED-IDS Institutionalising Participation Series, International Institute for Environment and Development IIED, London, in press (2004).

Pimbert, M.P. and V. Toledo, "Indigenous peoples and biodiversity conservation: myth or reality?", Ethnoecologica, 2-3(96), 1994.

Pimbert, M.P. and J. Pretty, Parks, People and Professionals. Putting "participation" into protected area management, UNRISD-IIED-WWF Discussion Paper 57, UNRISD, Geneva (Switzerland), 1995.

Pimbert, M.P and B. Gujja. "Village voices challenging wetland management policies: experiences in participatory rural appraisal from India and Pakistan", Nature and Resources, 33(1):34-42. 1997.

Pimbert, M.P. and J. Pretty, "Diversity and sustainability in community based conservation", pages 58-80 in Kothari et al., 1998.

Pimbert, M.P. and T. Wakeford (eds.), Deliberative Democracy and Citizen Empowerment, Special Issue of PLA Notes, no. 40, IIED, London, 2001a.

Pimbert, M.P. and T. Wakeford, "Overview — deliberative democracy and citizen empowerment", PLA Notes, 40:23-31, 2001b.

Pimbert, M.P. and T. Wakeford, Prajateerpu. A citizens jury/scenario workshop for food and farming in Andhra Pradesh, India, www.iied.org/docs/sarl/Prajateerpu.pdf, International Institute for Environment and Development, Institute of Development Studies, Andhra Pradesh Coalition in Defence for Diversity, University of Hyderabad and All India National Biodiversity Strategy and Action Plan, IIED, London, 2002.

Pimbert, M.P., J. Thompson and W.T. Vorley, Global Restructuring, Agri-food systems and livelihoods. Gatekeeper Series, 100, International Institute for Environment and Development, London, 2002.

Pimbert, M.P, T. Wakeford and P.V. Satheesh, "Des petits paysans et des marginaux ruraux s'expriment sur l'agriculture et les OGM", La Revue Durable, 6: 34-39, 2003.

Pimbert, M.P. and T. Wakeford, "Prajateerpu, power and knowledge: the politics of participatory action research in development. Part 1: Context, process and safeguards", Action Research, 1(2):184-207, 2003.

Pinkerton, E. (ed.), Co-operative Management of Local Fisheries. New directions for improved management and community development, University of British Columbia Press, Vancouver (Canada), 1989.

PLA Notes, "Participatory monitoring and evaluation", PLA Notes, 31, International Institute for Environment and Development, London, 1998.

PLA Notes, "Advocacy and citizen participation", PLA Notes, 43, International Institute for Environment and Development, London, 2002.

Poffenberger, M., "The resurgence of community forest management in Eastern India", pages 53-79 in Western and Wright, 1994.

Poffenberger, M., Grassroots Forest Protection: Eastern Indian Experiences, Asia Forest Network, Berkeley, California (USA), 1996.

Poffenberger, M., "Local knowledge in conservation", pages 41-43 in Vol. 2 of Borrini-Feyerabend, 1997.

Poffenberger, M. and B. McGean, Village Voices, Forest Choices. Joint Forest Management in India, Oxford University Press, Delhi, 1998.

Polanyi, K., The Great Transformation, Beacon Press, Boston, Massachusetts (USA), 1957, first published in 1944.

Poole, P., The Ye'kuana mapping project, manuscript draft, University of Georgia, 1997.

Porcupine Caribou Management Board, Annual Report 1994-1995, Porcupine Caribou Management Board (PCMB), Whitehorse, Yukon (Canada), 1995.

Posey, D. A., Traditional Resource Rights. International instruments for protection and compensation of indigenous peoples and local communities, IUCN, Gland (Switzerland), 1996.

Posey, D.A. (ed.), Cultural and Spiritual Values of Biodiversity, UNEP, Nairobi and Intermediate Technology Publications, London, 1999.

Posey D.A. and G. Dutfield, Beyond Intellectual Property Rights. Toward traditional resource rights for indigenous peoples and local communities,

International Development Research Centre, Ottawa, 1996.

Pradervand, P., Listening to Africa. Developing Africa from the grassroots, Praeger, New York, NY (USA), 1989.

Prasittiboon, A., "Integrated Natural Resources Conservation Project, Northern Thailand", in Blumley, P. and P. Mundy, Integrated Conservation and Development: a Review of Project Experience from CARE, Care Denmark, Copenhagen, 1997.

Pretty, J., Regenerating Agriculture. Policies and practice for sustainability and self reliance, Earthscan, London, 1995.

Price, T. and B. Gaoh, "Local communities and management of the Dallol Maouri and Niger river ron palm groves: an example of the dynamics of sustainable development in Niger", http://www.cdr.dk/sscafrica/p&o-e-ni.htm, 2000.

Price-Cohen, C., The Human Rights of Indigenous Peoples, Transnational Publishers, Ardeley, New York (USA), 1998.

Pruitt, D. and P. Carnevale, Negotiation in Social Conflict, Brooks/Cole Publishing Co, Pacific Grove, California (USA), 1993.

Przeworski, A., Democracy and the Market, Cambridge University Press, Cambridge (United Kingdom), 1991.

Pye-Smith, C. and G. Borrini-Feyerabend with R. Sandbrook, The Wealth of Communities, Earthscan, London, 1994.

Quinault Indian Nation and Jefferson and Grays Harbor Counties, Memorandum of Understanding Establishing a Joint Land Use Regulatory Program and Minimum Development Guidelines between the Quinault Indian Nation and Jefferson and Grays Harbor Counties, The Fourth World Documentation Project Archives, http://www.halcyon.com/FWDP/fwdp.html, 1993.

Rabetaliana H. and P. Schachenmann, "Community-based management of cultural resources in Ambondrombe–a historic site in Madagascar", CM News, 4:14, September 2000.

Rahman, A., "Globalisation: the emerging ideology in the popular protests and grassroots action research", Action Research, 2(1):9-23, 2004.

Rahnema, M., "Participation", pages 116-131 in Sachs, W. (ed.), The Development Dictionary–A Guide to Knowledge as Power, Zed Books, London and New Jersey (USA), 1992.

Raju, G., "Institutional structures for community-based conservation", pages 303-322 in Kothari et al., 1998.

Ralston, L., J. Anderson and E. Colson, Voluntary Efforts In Decentralised Management, Institute of

International Studies, University of California, Berkeley, California (USA), 1983.

Ramírez, R., "Cross-cultural communication and local media", pages 11-114 in Vol. 2 of Borrini-Feyerabend, 1997.

Ramírez, R., "Participatory learning and communication approaches for managing pluralism", Unasylva, 49(194):43-51, 1998.

Ramírez, R., "Understanding the approaches for accommodating multiple stakeholders' interests", Int. J. Agricultural Resources, Governance and Ecology, 1(3/4):264-285, 2001.

Ramírez, R., "A conceptual map of land conflict management: organizing the parts of two puzzles", http://www.fao.org/sd/2002/IN0301_en.htm, Land Tenure Service, FAO, Rome, 2002.

Ramsar Convention Bureau, Ramsar Handbook for the Wise Use of Wetlands, Ramsar Convention Bureau, Gland (Switzerland), 2000.

Rathore, B.M.S., New partnerships for conservation, paper presented at the Regional Workshop on Community-based Conservation, UNESCO/ MAB, Indian Institute of Public Administration, New Delhi, February 9-11, 1997.

Reader, J., Man on Earth, Penguin Books, London, 1990.

Regis, J., Kikori watershed, Papua New Guinea, presentation at the Forum 1997 meeting in Istanbul, Turkey, November 16-21, 1997.

Renard, Y., Civil society involvement in forest management: the case of Haiti's terrestrial protected areas, CANARI Technical Report 311, Caribbean Natural Resources Institute, Laventille (Trinidad and Tobago), 2002.

Renard, Y. and S. Koester, "Resolving conflicts for integrated coastal management: the case of Soufriere, St. Lucia", Caribbean Park and Protected Area Bulletin, 5(2):5-7, 1995.

Renn, O. and T. Webler, "Anticipating Conflicts: Public Participation in Managing the Solid Waste Crisis", GAIA: Ecological Perspectives in Science, Humanities, and Economics, 1(2):84-94, 1992.

Ribot, J.C., Democratic Decentralisation of Natural Resources, World Resources Institute, Washington D.C., 2002.

Richards, P., "Musanga cecropiodes: biodynamic knowledge encoded in mythic knowledge", page 366 in Posey, 1999.

Richards, P., Indigenous Agricultural Revolutions, Unwin Hyman, London, 1985.

Richardson, B. J., D. Craig, and B. Boer, "Indigenous peoples and environmental management: a review of Canadian regional agreements and their potential application to Australia - Part 1", Environmental and Planning Law Journal,

11(4):320-343, 1994a.

Richardson, B.J., D. Craig and B. Boer, "Indigenous peoples and environmental management: a review of Canadian regional agreements and their potential application to Australia - Part 2", Environmental and Planning Law Journal, 11(5):357-381, 1994b.

Risby, L.A., T. Blomley, C. Kendall, I. Kahwa and M. Onen, "Environmental narratives in protected area planning–the case of Queen Elizabeth National Park, Uganda", Policy Matters, 10:40-49, 2002.

Rodas, H., "Una nueva pedagogia del poder en Paute–Ecuador", Policy Matters, 10: 74-75, 2002.

Röling, N., "Communication support for sustainable natural resource management", IDS Bulletin, 25(2), 125-33, 1994.

Röling, N.G. and M.A.E. Wagemakers, Facilitating Sustainable Agriculture. Participatory learning and adaptive management in times of environmental uncertainty, Cambridge University Press, Cambridge (United Kingdom), 1998.

Röling, N. and M. Maarleveld, "Facing strategic narratives: an argument for interactive effectiveness", Agriculture and Human Values, 16:295-308, 1999.

Rosaldo, R., Culture and Truth, Beacon Press, Boston, Massachusetts (USA), 1993.

Rowe, G. and L. Frewer, "Public participation methods: a framework for evaluation", Science, Technology and Human Values, 25:3-29, 2000.

Ruddle, K., "Local knowledge in the future management of inshore tropical marine resources and environments", Nature and Resources, 30(1): 28-37, 1994.

RUPFOR, Joint Forest Management. A decade of partnership, Joint Forest Management Cell, Resource Unit for Participatory Forestry, Ministry of Environment and Forests, Government of India, New Delhi, 2002.

Sabel, C.F;, "Democratic experimentalism", Columbia Law Review, 98, 1998.

Saberwal, V., "Pastoral politics: Gadi grazing, degradation and biodiversity conservation in Himachal Pradesh, India", Conservation Biology, 10(3):741-749, 1996.

Sale K., Rebels Against the Future. The Luddites and their war on the industrial revolution— lessons for the computer age, Addison Wesley, New York, NY (USA), 1996.

Sanchez Parga, J., M. Chiriboga, A. Galo Ramon, A. Guerrero, J. Durston and A. Crivelli, Estrategias de Supervivencia en la Comunidad Andina, Centro Andino de Acción Popular, Quito, 1984.

Sandwith, T., C. Shine, L. Hamilton and D. Sheppard, Transboundary Protected Areas for Peace and Cooperation, IUCN, Gland (Switzerland) and Cambridge (United Kingdom), 2001.

Saragoussi, M., M. Pinheiro, M. Chavez, A. Murchie and S. Borges, "An experiment in participatory mapping in Brasil's Jau National Park", pages 352-364 in Wood, C.H. and R. Porro (eds.), Deforestation and Land Use in the Amazon, Florida University Press, Gainesville, Florida (USA), 2002.

Sarin, M., "Regenerating India's forests: reconciling gender equity with Joint Forest Management", IDS Bulletin, 26:83-91, 1995.

Sarin, M.., Who is gaining? Who is losing? Gender and equity concerns in Joint Forest Management in India, communication at the sixth Common Property Conference, Berkeley, California (USA), June 1996.

Sarin, M., "From conflict to collaboration: institutional issues in community management", pages 165-209 in Poffenberger and McGean, 1998.

Sarin, M. and SARTHI (Social Action for Rural Inhabitants in India), The View from the Ground. Community perspectives on joint forest management in Gujarat, India, Forest Participation Series 4, International Institute for Environment and Development, London, 1996.

Sarin, M., with L. Ray, M.S. Raju, M. Chatterjee, N. Banerjee and S. Hiremath, "Gender and equity concerns in joint forest management", pages 323-348 in Kothari et al., 1998.

Sarin, M. with N. M. Singh, N. Sundar and R. K. Bhogal, Devolution as a Threat to Democratic Decision-Making in Forestry? Findings from three states in India, Working Paper 197, Overseas Development Institute, London, 2003.

Sarkar, S., N. Singh, S. Suri, and A. Kothari, Joint Management of Protected Areas in India, Workshop Report, Indian Institute of Public Administration, New Delhi, 1995.

Satheesh, P.V and M. P. Pimbert, "Reclaiming diversity, restoring livelihoods", Seedling, 16(2):11-23, 1999.

Satya Murty, D. and T. Wakeford, "Farmer foresight: an experiment in South India", pages 46-51 in Pimbert and Wakeford, 2001.

Schmidt, S., G. Gongor, K. Kar and K. Swenson, "Community organising–a key step towards sustainable livelihoods and co-management of natural resources in Mongolia", Policy Matters, 10:71-74, 2002.

Schumacher, E. F., Small is Beautiful. A study of economics as if people mattered, Blond and Briggs, London, 1973.

Sclove, D., "Telecommunications and the future of

democracy: preliminary report on the first US citizens' panel", page 52 in Pimbert and Wakeford, 2001.

Scoones, I., (ed.), Living with Uncertainty: New Directions in Pastoral Development in Africa, Intermediate Technology Publications, London, 1994.

Scott, J.C., Weapons of the Weak. Everyday forms of peasant resistance, Yale University Press, New Haven, Connecticut (USA) and London, 1985.

Scott, J. C., Seeing Like a State. How certain schemes to improve the human condition have failed, Yale University Press, New Haven, Connecticut (USA) and London, 1998.

Scott, P., Assessment of Natural Resource Use by Communities from Mount Elgon National Park, Mount Elgon Conservation and Development Project, Mbale (Uganda), 1994.

Scott, P., People-Forest Interactions on Mount Elgon, Uganda. Moving towards a collaborative approach to management, IUCN Forest Conservation Series, Gland (Switzerland), 1996.

Scott, P., From Conflict to Collaboration. People and forests at Mount Elgon, Uganda, IUCN, Nairobi, 1998.

Sen, A, "Rights and capabilities", in Sen, A. (ed.), Resources, Values and Development, Blackwell, Oxford (United Kingdom), 1984.

Senaratna, S., and E.J. Milner-Gulland, "What affects livelihood sustainability of coastal communities in Sri Lanka?", Policy Matters, 10:104-106, 2002.

Shackleton, S., B. Campbell, E. Wollenberg and D. Edmunds, "Devolution and community-based natural resource management: create space for local people to participate and benefit?", Natural Resource Perspectives, 76, Overseas Development Institute, March 2002.

Shah, A., M. Kaul Shah and M.P. Pimbert, Institutionalising participatory processes: learning from experience, unpublished document prepared for the IIED and IDS Institutionalising Participation Series, International Institute for Environment and Development, London, 1998.

Shah, A., Participatory village resource management: case study of Aga Khan Rural Support Programme (India), unpublished D. Phil. Thesis, University of Sussex, Brighton (United Kingdom), 1996.

Shah, A., and M. Kaul Shah, Impact of local institutions and para professionals on watersheds: case study of AKRSP in India, paper presented at New Horizons: The Economic, Social and Environmental Impacts of Participatory Watershed Development, international workshop organised in Bangalore (India) by the Sustainable Agriculture Programme of IIED, 1994.

Shanley, P. and J. Galvao, "Invisible income: the ecology and economics of non timber forest resources in Amazonian forests", pages 364-365 in Posey, 1999.

Shanmugaratnam, N., T. Vedeld, A. Mossige and M. Bovin, Resource Management and Pastoral Institution Building in West African Sahara, World Bank Discussion Paper 175, World Bank, Washington D.C., 1993.

Shengji, P., "Conservation of biological diversity in temple-yards and holy hills by the Dai ethnic minorities of China", Ethnobotany, 3:27-35, 1991.

Siddons, T., Federal Policy for the Settlement of Native Claims, Ministry for Indian Affairs and Northern Development, Ottawa, 1993.

Siepen G., Landcare: Communities Shaping the Land and the Future, Allen and Unwin, Sydney (Australia), 1994.

Simmonds, K., "Back to the future: rediscovering island values and fisheries management", in Malcolm, D.G. and J. Skog (eds.), Land, Culture and Development in the Aquatic Continent, Proceedings of a workshop, Hawaii, 26-29 May 1992.

Simmons, I. G., Changing the Face of the Earth, Basil Blackwell, Oxford (United Kingdom), 1989.

Smyth, D., "Joint management of national parks in Australia", in Baker, R., J. Davies and E. Young (eds.), Working on Country. Contemporary indigenous management of Australia's lands and coastal regions, Oxford University Press, Oxford (United Kingdom), 2001.

Sneed, P.G., "National Parklands and Northern Homelands: Toward Co-management of National Parks in Alaska and the Yukon", pages 135-154 in Stevens, 1997.

Snowden, D., L. Kusagak and P. MacLeod, The Kaminuriak herd film/videotape project: a case study paper presented in the Methods and Media in Community Participation Workshops, Dag Hammarksjöld Foundation, 19-27 May and 28 September - 7 October 1984, Uppsala (Sweden) and Labrador (Canada), 1984.

Sogge, D., Give and Take. What is the matter with foreign aid?, Zed Books, London, 2002.

Solis Rivera, V., P. Madrigal Cordero, I. Ayales Cruz, M. Fonseca Borras, Equidad entre Áreas Protegidas y Comunidades Locales: Reflexion desde Meso América y el Caribe, Coope Sol I Dar, San José, 2003.

Sowerwine, J., G. Shivakoti, U. Pradhan, A. Shukla and E. Ostrom (eds.), From Farmers' Fields to Data Fields and Back, International Irrigation Management Institute and Institute of Agriculture and Animal Science, Katmandu, 1994.

SPWD, Joint Forest Management: Concepts and Opportunities, Society for the Promotion of Wasteland Development, New Delhi, 1992.

Stanciu, E., "First steps towards collaborative management of Retezat National Park, Romania", CM News, 5:7, 2001.

Statham, D.K., "The farm scheme of North York Moors National Park, United Kingdom", pages 282-299 in Western and Wright, 1994.

Steenkamp, C., "Balancing the powers in Makuleke land", Policy Matters, 10:77-79, 2002.

Steins, N.A., Balancing Fisheries and Nature. Three case studies of fisheries co-management in the Dutch Wadden Sea, Working Papers on Coastal Zone Management 24, Centre for Coastal Zone Management, University of Portsmouth, Portsmouth (United Kingdom), 1997a.

Steins, N.A., From Single Use to Multiple Use. Cooperation and conflict in marine resource management in NW Connemara, Ireland, Working Papers on Coastal Zone Management 22, Centre for Coastal Zone Management, University of Portsmouth, Portsmouth (United Kingdom) 1997b.

Steins, N.A. and V.M, Edwards, "Harbor resource management in Cowes: an analytical framework for multiple use decision making", Journal of Environmental Management, 54(1):67-83, 1998.

Steins, N.A. and V.M. Edwards, "Platforms for collective action in multiple-use common pool resources", Agriculture and Human Values, 16:241-255, 1999.

Stevens, S. (ed.), Conservation through Cultural Survival, Island Press, Washington D.C., 1997.

Stiefel, M. and M. Wolfe, A Voice for the Excluded. Popular participation in development: utopia or necessity?, Zed Books, London and New Jersey (USA), 1994.

Stirling, A., "Inclusive deliberation and scientific expertise: precaution, diversity and transparency in the governance of risk", pages 66-71 in Pimbert and Wakeford, 2001.

Stirling, A. and S. Maher, Rethinking Risk. A pilot multi-criteria mapping of a genetically modified crop in agricultural systems in the UK, Science Policy Research Unit, Brighton (United Kingdom), 1999.

Sullivan, P., Regional Agreements in Australia. An overview paper, Land, Rights, Laws: Issues of Native Title, Issues Paper 17, Government of Australia, Canberra, 1997.

Sullivan, S. and K. Homewood, On Non-equilibrium and Nomadism. Knowledge, diversity and modernity in drylands, International Institute for Environment and Development, London and The University of Warwick's Centre for Globalisation and Regionalisation, Warwick (United Kingdom), http://www.warwick.ac.uk/fac/soc/CSGR/wpa-pers/wp12203.pdf, 2004.

Susskind, L. and J. Cruikshank, Breaking the Impasse. Consensual approaches to resolving public disputes, Basic Books, New York, NY (USA), 1987.

Sutherland, J. "Legislative Options and Constraints", Vol. 1, in Smyth, D. and J. Sutherland, Indigenous Protected Areas: Conservation Partnerships with Indigenous Landholders, Environment Australia, Canberra, 1996.

Tache, B. "Changing patterns of resource control among the Borana pastoralists of Southern Ethiopia: a lesson for development agencies", pages 51-74 in Manger, L. and M. Ahmed Abdel Ghaffar (eds.) Pastoralists and Environment. Experiences from the Greater Horn of Africa, OSSREA, Addis Ababa, 2000a.

Tache, B., Individualising the Commons: Changing Resource Tenure among Borana Oromo of Southern Ethiopia, M.A. Thesis, Addis Ababa, 2000b.

Tache, B. and B. Irwin, Traditional institutions, multiple stakeholders and modern perspectives in common property–accompanying change within Borana pastoral systems, Securing the Commons 4, International Institute for Environment and Development and SoS Sahel, London, 2003.

Taiepa, T., P. Lyver, P. Horsley, J. Davis, M. Bragg and H. Moller, Collaborative management of New Zealand's conservation estate by Maori and Pakeha, paper presented at the Collaborative Management Workshop, World Conservation Congress, Montreal (Canada), 1996.

Tall, S.M. and B. Guèye, Institutionalisation de la Participation dans la Gestion des Terroirs au Sénégal, IIED-IDS Institutionalising Participation Series, International Institute for Environment and Development, London, 2002.

Tang, S.Y., Institutions and Collective Action. Self-governance in irrigation, Institute for Contemporary Studies Press, San Francisco (California), 1992.

Taty, M., C. Chatelain and G. Borrini-Feyerabend, "An impressive yet vulnerable co-management partnership in Congo", Parks, 13(1):39-49, 2003.

Taylor, B., An Introductory Guide to Adaptive Management, Ministry of Forests, Canada, 1998. http://www.for.gov.bc.ca/hfp/amhome/introgd/toc.htm

Taylor, M., "Indigenous communities and biodiversity conservation in Papua New Guinea: promoting cultural and biological survival", paper prepared for the Regional Conference on Biodiversity Conservation, Asian Development Bank, Manila, June 1994.

Thompson, E.P., The Making of the English Working Class, Penguin books, London, 1991, first edition 1963.

Thorp, R., F. Stewart and A. Heyer, "When and how is group formation a route out of chronic poverty?", World Development, forthcoming.

Thrupp, L.A., New Partnerships for Sustainable Agriculture, World Resources Institute, Washington D.C., 1996.

Tiffen, M., M. Mortimore and F. Gichuki, More People, Less Erosion. Environmental recovery in Kenya, John Wiley, Chichester (United Kingdom), 1994.

Toulmin, C. and B. Guèye, Transformations of West African agriculture and the role of family farms, Drylands Issues Paper 123, International Institute for Environment and Development, London, 2003.

Triantafyllidis, A., Linking Local People and Parks, a Participatory Rural Appraisal Study in the Aveto Regional Park, Italy, M.S. Dissertation, University of Edinburgh, Edinburgh (Scotland), 1996.

Turner, M.D., "The role of social networks, indefinite boundaries and political bargaining in maintaining the ecological and economic resilience of the transhumance systems in the Sudano-Sahelian West Africa", pages 97-123 in Niamir-Fuller, 1999.

Turner, S., S. Collins and J. Baumbart, Community Based Natural Resources Management: Experiences and lessons linking communities to sustainable resource use in different social, economic and ecological conditions in South Africa, PLAAS, DEAT and GTZ, Cape Town (South Africa), 2002.

Tylor, P. and A. Woodruff, Cooperation: a conservation tool of compromise or influence?, paper presented at the Sixth South Pacific Conference on Nature Conservation and Protected Areas, Pohnpei (Federated States of Micronesia), 1997.

Uganda National Parks and Kitsatsa Forest Use Committee of Ulukusi Parish, Draft Forest Use Agreement between Uganda National Parks, represented by Mt. Elgon National Park, and the People of Ulukusi Parish, represented by the Kitsatsa Forest Use Committee of Ulukusi Parish, manuscript, undated.

UNDP, Human Development Report 1999– Globalisation with a Human Face, United Nations Development Programme, New York, NY (USA), 1999.

UNDP, Human Development Report 2002– Deepening Democracy in a Fragmented World, United Nations Development Programme, New York, NY (USA), 2002.

UNDP, Human Development Report 2003– Millennium Development Goals: a compact among nations to end human poverty, United Nations Development Programme, New York, NY (USA), 2003.

UNECE (United Nations Economic Commission for Europe), Convention on Access to Information, Public Participation in Decision-making and Access to Justice in Environmental Matters (Aarhus Convention), ECE/ECP/43, 1998.

UNESCO, "The Seville Strategy for Biosphere Reserves", Nature and Resources, 31(2):2-10, 1995.

UNRISD, UNRISD Participation Programme– A glance at the past and directions for the future, United Nations Research Institute for Social Development, Geneva (Switzerland), 1979.

UNRISD, People, Power and the Environment. 15 years of UNRISD research: a synthesis and annotated bibliography prepared for the 2002 World Summit on Sustainable Development, United Nations Research Institute for Social Development, Geneva (Switzerland), 2002.

Usher, P. J., "The Beverly-Kaminuriak Caribou Management Board: an experience in co-management", in Inglis, J. T. (ed.), Traditional Ecological Knowledge: Concepts and Cases, Canadian Museum of Nature and the International Development Research Centre, Ottawa 1993.

Utting, P. (ed.), The Greening of Business in Developing Countries. Rhetoric, reality and prospects, Zed Books, London and UNRISD, Geneva (Switzerland), 2002.

Utting, P. and D. Abrahams, "The global compact and civil society: averting collision course", UNRISD News, 25:31-33, 2002.

Vane-Wright, R.I., "Identifying priorities for the conservation of biodiversity: systematic biological criteria within a socio-political framework", in Gaston, K.J., Biodiversity, a Biology of Numbers and Difference, Blackwell Science Ltd., Oxford (United Kingdom), 1996.

Varela, J., "Contra la expansión de la acuacultura del camaron en Honduras: la historia de Modesto Ochoa", Policy Matters, 12:154-155, 2003.

Viana V.M. and R. Freire, Participatory land use planning: lessons learned for sustainable development in the Brazilian Amazon, unpublished manuscript, Sao Paulo (Brazil), 2001.

Vicente, P., The MASIPAG programme: an integrated approach to genetic conservation and use, in "Growing Diversity in Farmer's Fields", Proceedings of a Regional Seminar for Nordic Development Co-operation Agencies", Lidingo (Sweden), 1993.

Vincent, J.R., "The tropical timber trade and sustainable development", Science, 256:1651-55, 1992.

Vira, B., O. Dubois, S.E. Daniels and G.B. Walker, "Institutional pluralism in forestry: considerations of analytical and operational tools", Unasylva, 49(3)194:35-42, 1998.

Vo, S.T., Country Report: Vietnam, International Coral Reef Initiative (ICRI), 2001.

Voir Media, Le Souci du Sage, video-cassette, Voir Media Productions (France), 1998.

Vorley, W.T., The Chains of Agriculture. Sustainability and the restructuring of agri-food markets, WSSD Paper, International Institute for Environment and Development, London, 2001.

Vorley, W.T., Food, Inc. Corporate Concentration from Farm to Consumer, UK Food Group, London, 2004.

Wakeford, T., "Citizens Juries: a radical alternative for social research", Social Research Update, 37, www.soc.surrey.ac.uk/sru/SRU37.html, 2002.

Wakeford, T. and M.P. Pimbert, Power-reversals in Biotechnology. Experiments in democratization, The "Democratising Biotechnology" Briefings Series 13, Institute of Development Studies, Brighton (United Kingdom), 2003.

Wakeford, T. and M.P. Pimbert, "Prajateerpu, power and knowledge: the politics of participatory action research in development. Part 2: Analysis, reflections and implications", Action Research, 2(1):25-46, 2004.

Walters, C.J., Adaptive Management of Renewable Resources, McGraw-Hill, New York, NY (USA), 1986.

Warren, P., "Mercado, escuelas y proteínas. Aspectos históricos, ecológicos y económicos del cambio del modelo de asentamiento entre los Achuar Meridionales", Amazonía Peruana, 21:73-97, 1992.

Warren, P., "Sapere locale e gestione partecipativa delle risorse naturali tra etnoscienza ed ecologia politica", Antropologia e Sviluppo, 1:4-5, 1996.

Watts, M., "The political economy of climatic hazards: a village perspective on drought and peasant economy in a semi-arid region of West Africa, Cahiers d'Etudes Africaines, XXIII-I-2:89-90, 1983a.

Watts, M., Silent Violence, University of California Press, Berkeley, California (USA), 1983b.

Weaver, S.M., "The role of Aboriginals in the management of Australia's Coburg and Kakadu National Parks", pages 311-332 in West and Brechin, 1991.

Weber, J., "Perspective de gestion patrimoniale des ressources renouvelables", in Lavigne Delville, P. (ed.), Quelle Politique Foncière en Afrique Rurale?, Karthala- Coopération Francaise, Paris, 1998.

Weber, J. and D. Bailly, "Prévoir, c'est gouverner", Nature, Science, Societé, 1(1):59-64, 1993.

Weinstein, M.S., Pieces of the puzzle: getting to the solution for community-based coastal zone management in Canada, key-note address prepared for Coastal Zone Canada 98, British Columbia, 1998.

Wells, M.P. and K. Brandon, People and Parks. Linking protected area management with local communities, World Bank/WWF/US AID, Washington D.C. 1992.

Wes, J, W. Berry and B. Colman, Meeting the Expectations of the Land, North Point Press, San Francisco, California (USA), 1983.

West, P.C. and S.R. Brechin (eds.), Resident Peoples and National Parks, University of Arizona Press, Tucson, Arizona (USA), 1991.

Western, D. and R. M. Wright, Natural Connections, Island Press, Washington D.C., 1994.

Whande, W., T. Kepe and M. Murphree, Local Communities, Equity and Conservation in Southern Africa, PLAAS, Africa Resources Trust and TILCEPA, Cape Town (South Africa), 2003.

Wheatley, M., Leadership and the New Science. Learning about organizations for an orderly universe, Berret-Koehler, San Francisco, California (USA), 1992.

White, A.T., L. Zeitlin Hale, Y. Renard and L. Cortesi, Collaborative and Community-based Management of Coral Reefs, Kumarian Press, West Hartford, Connecticut (USA), 1994.

Whitehead, A. and D. Tsikata, "Discourses on women's land rights in Sub-Saharan Africa: The implications of the return to the customary", Journal of Agrarian Change, 3(1/2):67-112, 2003.

Wild, R.G. and J. Mutebi, Conservation Through Community Use of Plant Resources. Establishing collaborative management at Bwindi Impenetrable and Mgahinga Gorilla National Parks, People and Plants Working Paper 5, UNESCO, Paris, 1996.

Wilshusen, P., "Territory, nature and culture–negotiating the boundaries of biodiversity conservation in Colombia's Pacific Coastal region", pages 73-88 in Brechin et al., 2003.

Wilson, A., Case study from the North York Moors National Park, UK, presentation in the Governance Stream of the Vth World Parks Congress, Durban (South Africa), September 2003.

Wilson, R.K., "Community-based management and national forests in the Western United States: five challenges", Policy Matters, 12:216-224, 2003.

Wily, L., Villagers as Forest Managers and Governments "Learning to Let Go". The case of Duru-Haitemba and Mgori forests in Tanzania, IIED Forestry and Land Use Programme Paper 9, International Institute for Environment and Development, London, 1997.

Wily, L. and L. Haule, "Village forest reserves in the making - the story of Duru-Haitemba", Forests, Trees and People Newsletter, 29:28-37, November 1995.

Winer, N., Collaborative management and community rights: the Chobe Enclave (Botswana), paper presented in the workshop on Collaborative Management for Conservation, First World Conservation Congress, Montreal (Canada), 17 October 1996.

Winer, N., Co-management in Southern Bolivia: a form of territorial recognition for the Guarani Izoceno People, CM News, 5, 2001.

Winer, N., "Co-management of protected areas, the oil and gas industry and indigenous empowerment–the experience of Bolivia's Kaa Iya del Gran Chaco", Policy Matters, 12:181-191, 2003.

Wittenberg D., "In Bonny it never becomes night anymore. Gas factory brings pollution instead of prosperity to the Nigeria delta", NRC-Handelsblad (The Netherlands), issue of 13 July 2004.

Women Sanghams of Pastapur and M. P. Pimbert, "Farmer participation in on farm varietal trials: multi-locational testing under resource poor conditions", RRA Notes, 10:3-8, International Institute for Environment and Development, London, 1991.

Wondolleck, J. and S. Yaffee, Building Bridges Across Agency Boundaries in Search of Excellence in the U.S. Forest Service, School of Natural Resources and Environment, University of Michigan, Ann Arbor (Michigan), 1994.

Woodcock, G., Anarchism. A history of libertarian ideas and movements, Pelican Books, London, 1975.

Woolgar S., "The Luddites: diablo ex machina", in Grint K. and S. Woolgar, The Machine at Work. Technology, work and organization, Polity Press, Cambridge (United Kingdom), 1997.

Worah, S., "The challenge of community-based protected area management", Parks, 12(2):80-90, 2002.

World Bank, The World Bank Participatory Sourcebook, World Bank, Washington D.C., 1996.

WRI, World Resources 2002-2004–Decisions for the Earth: Balance, Voice and Power, United Nations Development Programme (UNDP), United Nations Environment Programme (UNEP), the World Bank and WRI (World Resources Institute), Washington D.C., 2003.

Wright, S. (ed.), Anthropology of Organizations, Routledge, London, 1994.

Young, B., "Science is social relations", Radical Science Journal, 5:65-131, 1977.

Zerner, C., Turning the Tide. Community management of coastal resources in Southeast Asia and the Pacific, unpublished manuscript, World Resources Institute, Washington D.C., 1991.

Zerner, C., Transforming customary law and coastal management practices in the Maluku Islands, Indonesia, 1870-1992, pages 80-112 in Western and Wright, 1994.

Zoundjihekpon, J. and B. Dossou-Glehouenou, "Cultural and spiritual values of biodiversity in West Africa: the case of Benin and Cote d'Ivoire", page 370 in Posey, 1999.

Zuluaga, G. (ed.), El Pensamento de los Mayores–Codigo de Etica de la Medicina Indígena del Piedmonte Amazonico Colombiano, Unión de Medicos Indígenas Yageceros de la Amazonia Colombiana (UMIYAC), Da Vinci Editores, Santafé de Bogotà (Colombia), 2000.

Zuluaga, G. and R. Diaz, Gathering of Shamans in the Colombian Amazons–Ceremonies and Reflections, Unión de Medicos Indígenas Yageceros de la Amazonia Colombiana (UMIYAC), Errediciones (Colombia), 1999.

Zuluaga, G., J.I. Giraldo and M. Gimenez Larrarte, "Un ejemplo de conservación bio-cultural–el Parque Nacional Natural Alto Fragua Indiwasi en Colombia", Policy Matters, special issue on Community Empowerment for Conservation, 12:171-180, September 2003.

INDEX

Note: Co-management is represented in the index by CM, natural resource management by NRM, and DIPs are deliberative inclusive processes. Page references followed by 'n refer to footnotes.

Aarhus Convention 367, 383
Abdoulanzis, Mady 114—115
Aboriginal People 100, 142—144, 308
    CM agreements 247—248, 267—268
accountability 229, 305, 306, 337
    democratic 392, 409, 410, 421—422
    policy support for 366—368
acculturation 142
actors 39
    see also institutional actors; social actors
adaptive management 34, 192, 311, 386
    conditions for 296—297, 326—327, 329, 429
    definition 65
advisory bodies 279, 286—287
affected groups 124
affirmative action 184, 369, 404
affirmative democracy, definition 67
Aga Khan Rural Support Programme 89, 314, 332
age groups 46
Agenda 21 378—379, 398
agendas 181, 191
agreements 234—236
    components 235, 251—262, 356
    crucial issues for government agencies 274—277
    crucial issues for indigenous peoples 265—274
    customary and non-notarised 236—243
    enforcement 240, 270, 306, 309—311, 367
    formal/legal 243—251
    goodwill 325
    implementation evaluation indicators 316—317
    interpretation 308
    legitimisation 202—203, 307—308
    modification 259—260, 313

outcomes 226—231, 302—303
    plans and accords 222—223, 227
    recognition of efforts and commitment 262—265
    on strategic approaches 206—208
agricultural research 75—76
agriculture 71—73
agro-industrial-market system 16—17, 371—375
    interface with indigenous/local NRM systems 17—33
Aheme lake, Benin 292
Alany, Turkey 354
Alaska 91
Albania 161
Algesiras, Bay of, Spain 201
all time protection 257—258, 263
Alto Fragua-Indiwasi National Park, Colombia 116, 201
Amazon Conservation Team 116
Ambondrombe, Madagascar 90
amendment procedures 257, 259—260, 313
American Convention on Human Rights 366
Amigos de Sian Ka'an 82
Ampezzo Valley, Italy 414
ancestral territories 100—101, 115, 140—145, 261, 275
    mapping 147—149
    Tagbanwa people 368
Andapa Valley, Madagascar 154
Andes 4, 13, 112, 144, 236—237
    minga 71
Andhra Pradesh, India 75—76, 339, 398—399, 402—403
animals, customary rules 237, 238
Anishinabe Ojibwa people 173
Annapurna Conservation Area 88—89
Annapurna Sanctuary 102
Applegate Partnership, USA 78—79, 286
appropriators 53
aquatic resources 88, 173, 214—215, 240—241
    see also coastal resources; fisheries
arbitration 368
Argentina 74—75, 112, 346

articulating opportunities and risks 57—58
Asiatic Cheetah 120—121
Association of Indigenous Ingano Councils 116
Assynt Crofters Trust 282
audiovisual presentations 152
Australia 83, 276
    CM agreements 247—248, 267—268, 293
    CM organisations 287—288
    financial support 298—299
    indigenous peoples 100—101, 142—144, 308
    Landcare programme 72—73, 113
    shared vision 201—202
    trade-offs 264
    see also Great Barrier Reef Marine Park
Auyuittuq National Park Reserve, Canada 283
Aveto Regional Park, Italy 45
Awa Ethnic Forest Reserve, Ecuador 159
Awa Federation 242—243
Awas Tingini people 366

Babati district, Tanzania 80
Bagiai Wildlife Management Area, Papua New Guinea
  102
Bahman-Beygi 24
Baka people 185—186
Bali, Indonesia 73—74
Baluch people 169—170
Bamate people 95
Banc d Arguin National Park, Mauritania 83
Bangladesh 238
Bantu people 185—186
Barangay-Bayan Governance Consortium (BBGC) 418
Batangi people 95
BATNA (best alternatives to a negotiated agreement)
  134
Belize 83, 98—99
Beluga whales 91
benefits of co-management 131—132, 144, 218
  for government agencies 274
benefits distribution 103, 118, 235
  agreement packages 189, 218—219, 223, 226
  improving equity 337, 338—339
Beni Halba tribe 9, 177
Benin 238, 292
  Park W 208—209, 361n
  producer organisations 415, 416
best alternatives to a negotiated agreement (BATNA)
  134
Betsileo people 90
Bhopalpatnam-Ichhampalli dams 165
biocultural co-management 189
biodiversity

  in agriculture 76, 339
  link with cultural diversity 141
  remaining 269
Biodiversity Conservation Network 313
Biodiversity Strategies and Action Plans, National
  (NBSAP) 349—350
Biological Diversity, Convention on (CBD) 142, 272,
  349, 368, 379—382
Birdlife 122
bird sanctuaries 84
Blue Mountains National Park, Jamaica 97
Boa Vista do Ramos, Brazil 148—149
Bokwongo, Cameroon 226
Bolivia 145, 158, 266—267, 410
boneh systems 71—72, 120
Bonny Island, Nigeria 268
Bophuthtswana National Park, South Africa 248
Borana people 77
Borassus aethiopum (ron palm) 79
Botswana 371
boundaries between communities 119, 365
brainstorming 204
Brazil 148—149, 216, 410—411
Bri bri peoples 150
British Colombia, Canada 119, 279
British Columbia Claims Task Force (BCCTF) 279
British Columbia Treaty Commission 279
broad participation events 152
Burkina Faso 208—209
Bwindi Impenetrable National Park, Uganda 96, 149n,
  217, 303, 307, 321
by-laws 80, 143, 328, 351

Cabecar peoples 150
CABI (Capitanía del Alto y bajo Izozog) 145, 267
Cairngorms Partnership Area, Scotland 89, 215
Cambodia 102, 168
Cameroon 113, 137n, 156, 280—281
  benefit sharing 226
  conflict resolution 222
  equity 185—186
CAMPFIRE initiative, Zimbabwe 27—31, 91—92, 113,
  271, 337
Canada
  aboriginal fisheries 119
  CM with indigenous peoples 101—102, 112, 173,
    279
  CM organisations 282, 283, 290—291, 292, 294
  conflict resolution 196, 259, 308
  land and resource rights claims 352—353
  Land Trusts 98
  managing migratory wildlife 91, 250

participatory action research 158
capacities of social actors 125—126, 129, 225
   building 167, 168—172, 255—256, 369—370
     see also training
   issues in agreements 256, 263—264
Caracas, World Parks Congress (1993) 93
CARE (Cooperative for Assistance and Relief
   Everywhere) 96, 100
Caribbean Natural Resource Institute (CANARI) 83,
   169
cash crops 32, 416
Caspian Sea, Joint Commission on Environmental
   Protection of 290
cassava 3
CBDC (Community Biodiversity Development and
   Conservation Programme) 241—242
CBD (Convention on Biological Diversity) 142, 272,
   349, 368, 379—382
CCAs see Community Conserved Areas (CCAs)
CECCA (Centro de Educación y Capacitación del
   Campesinado del Azuay) 112
CEESP (Commission on Environmental, Economic and
   Social Policy) 120, 171, 302
CENESTA (Iranian Centre for Sustainable Development)
   120—121, 170n, 175—176, 302
Center for Watershed Protection (USA) 122
Centro de Reconversión Económica del Azuay, Cañar y
   Morona-Santiago (CREA) 19
ceremonies see ritual ceremonies
chairpersons 180, 304, 305
Chapoto Ward, Zimbabwe 27—31, 33
Chesapeake Bay, USA 318—319
Chile 396
China 196
Chipko movement 150
Chittagong, Bangladesh 238
Citizen Income 426
citizens juries 393, 398—399, 402—403
citizens panels 393
civil servants 409
civil society 407—408
   definitions 385
   management of PAs 351—352
   organised policy influence 415—418
   participatory democracy 418—427
   strengthening 359, 409—415
climate change 38, 387
coastal resources 81—83, 105—107, 122
   Tanzania 54, 82, 210
   see also fisheries
Cobourg Peninsula Land and Sanctuary Act 1981 (NT)
   247—248

COGEREN (Comité de Gestion des Ressources
   Naturelles de Conkouati) 202, 303, 335
Coldwell, Joaquin 81
collaboration
   definition 65
   local and external actors 412—413
collaborative management, definitions 66, 67
Colombia 93—94, 116, 155, 346
colonisation 14, 15—16
   Shuar people (Ecuador) 19—21, 33
Co-managed Protected Areas (CMPAs) 270
co-management 103—105
   appropriate circumstances 129—135, 429—430
   definitions 65, 66, 67, 68, 69—70
   models 166
   monitoring and evaluation 320, 321
   policies 345, 355—356, 366—370
   promoting effective 325—329
co-management agreements see agreements
co-management organisations 278—283, 289—295,
   304—305
   building on local resources and systems 299—302
   composition 283—286, 337—338
   establishing 302—303, 306
   powers and responsibilities 258, 306
   scope of authority 286—287
   size and level of operations 287—289
co-management plans 235, 277, 306
Commission on Environmental, Economic and Social
   Policy (CEESP) 120, 171, 302
common good 103
Communal Areas Management Programme for
   Indigenous Resources (CAMPFIRE) see CAMPFIRE initiative, Zimbabwe
communal property 7, 12, 23—24
   wildlife 27—28
communal work 4, 71, 156—157, 219
communication
   about conservation 275—276
   agreement clauses 261
   issues for agreements 255—256
   negotiations 188—189
   see also social communication
community
   definitions 7, 43—44
   see also indigenous peoples; local communities
Community Baboon Sanctuary, Belize 98—99
Community Biodiversity Development and
   Conservation Programme (CBDC) 241—242
community conservancies 89, 92—93
   see also Community Conserved Areas (CCAs)
Community Conserved Areas (CCAs) 121, 144,

269—270, 301—302
    see also community conservancies
community forestry, definition 66
Community Investment Funds 218, 219
community policy 343
comparative advantages of social actors 103, 125—126, 129, 131, 225
comparing alternative options 211—212, 213
compensation 145, 267, 268, 365
complementary accords 223, 235, 306
compliance see enforcement
components of a CM agreement 235, 251—262
concerned groups 124
concerns 40, 44, 46—47, 124, 128—129
conditions of resource use 215, 216
confederalism 417
confidentiality clauses 261—262
conflict
    for control of natural resources 8—9, 13, 132, 189, 270—271
    management in negotiations 192, 193, 196—197, 212—213, 219—222
    see also dispute resolution
Congo Basin 171
Congo, Republic of 156, 202—203, 294, 303, 335
Conkouati-Douli National Park, Republic of Congo 202—203, 215, 294, 303, 335
consensus 69, 213—219, 229, 338
consensus conferences 393—394
conservation
    agreements 243—245, 255, 268—270, 274—277
    cultural factors 6, 11—12, 13, 141, 299
    management partnerships 70
    and nomadic livelihoods 302
    wildlife management 27—31, 270—271
    see also protected areas (PAs)
conservation easements (deed restrictions) 98, 243—244, 257
constitution and basic civil law 346—348
consultants 211—212
contractual approaches 99—100
control of natural resources see property and access
conveners 138, 180, 181, 191
    for DIPs 400, 404—405
Convention on Biological Diversity (CBD) 142, 272, 349, 368, 379—382
Cooperative for Assistance and Relief Everywhere (CARE) 96, 100
coral reefs 105—107, 117, 210
Coron Island, Philippines 368
corporate responsibility 373—374
Corvallis, USA 200

Costa Rica 150
costs of co-management 118, 131—132, 218, 235, 370
cotton plantations 208
Cowes Harbour, UK 292
CREA (Centro de Reconversión Económica del Azuay, Cañar y Morona-Santiago) 19
credit schemes 112
Cree peoples 159
crop-sharing 71—72
cultural diversity
    link with biodiversity 141
    in negotiations 180, 181—182, 188—189
culturally sensitive information see intellectual property rights (IPR)
culture
    and conflict resolution 196—197, 220
    continuity and change 44
    identity 359—362
    and natural environment 5, 38, 77, 236—239, 268—269, 275
    and NRM 5—8, 11—12, 73, 90, 299, 361
    organisational 328—329, 334
    respect for local norms 152, 161, 167
    see also cultural diversity; indigenous peoples
current managers and users 125
customary governance and management systems 253, 302, 359—362
customary and non-notarised agreements 236—243
customary rights 25, 49, 50—51, 124, 158, 259
Czech Republic 346

damage avoidance 277
Darfur, Sudan 9, 176—177
data collection 147, 312, 314
Dayak people 284—285
debate and discussion see social communication
Deccan Development Society (DDS) 339
decentralisation 356—359
    definition 68, 111
decision-making bodies 279
definitions 252—253
de Graay Fortman, B. 49
deliberative democracy 392, 421—422
    definition 68
deliberative inclusive processes (DIPs) 388, 393—399, 408
    and policy change 399—401
    safeguards 401—407
deliberative opinion polls 394
demarcation of boundaries and resources 363, 365—366
    see also maps

democracy 226—227, 386, 418—426
    definitions 67, 68
    deliberative 392, 421—422
    representative and participatory 175, 177, 389—392
    see also deliberative inclusive processes (DIPs)
democratic experimentalism 62, 63
    definition 67
Democratic Republic of Congo 95
democratisation 103
    definition 66
dependent groups 124
Desertification, Convention to Combat (UNCCD) 350, 382
devolution 356—359
Diawling National Park, Mauritania 84
DIPs see deliberative inclusive processes (DIPs)
direct involvement 409—410, 410—411
direction, in good governance 230
direct representation 59
disadvantaged groups see equity
dispute resolution 196, 258—259, 308, 367—368
Dja Game Reserve, Cameroon 185—186
Djawling National Park, Mauritania 175
Djoudj National Park, Senegal 84
Doi Inthanond National Park 100
domestic and sexual violence 424
donor agencies, changes needed 333—335
Drôme river, France 74
dual power 417—418
duration of agreements 257—258
Durban, World Parks Congress (2003) 27, 93, 97, 271—272
Duru-Haitemba forest, Tanzania 80, 323, 327, 328
Dutch Development Agency 280

easements 98, 243—244, 257
Eastern Caribbean, fisheries legislation 353
Eco-development Programme, India 150
ecological analysis 147
economic democracy 424
economic factors
    in defining NRM units 117—118, 123
    feasibility of co-management 133
    see also globalisation
ecosystems 10
    framework for implementing CBD 380—382
    linkages 38
    as NRM units 117, 123
    variation and change 386—387
Ecuador 83, 362
    Awa peoples 159, 242—243
    communal work 157

constitution 346—347
    initiating co-management 112—113
    the Shuar and colonisation 19—21, 33
    see also Galapagos Marine Reserve
education 425, 426
    supporting cultural diversity 361
    to undermine nomadism 24
    see also capacities of social actors; information; training
ejidos (Mexico) 81, 82
El Ceibo 413
elephant 92
El Salvador, policy for PA management 351
emergency situations 130
Emiliano s farm 31—33, 34
employment 256, 267
    indigenous peoples 165, 272—273
empowerment
    enhanced advocacy for 388
    of local communities 266, 330, 331—332, 336
    for policy change 405—406, 407—408, 417, 424—425
Encadenadas lake watershed, Argentina 74—75
enclosure of the commons 14—16
Endangered Species Act (USA 1972) 113
enforcement 240, 270, 306, 309—311, 367
England, enclosure 14—15
entitlements 48—52, 103, 162, 218, 306
    customary rules 239—240
    establishing priority 52—55, 149, 162—163
    recognition of 52, 60—61, 128, 163—164
    see also customary rights
environmental damage 17
environmental education 169—170
environmental impact indicators 312
environmental interests 37—39
environmental partnerships, definition 66
environmental sustainability 130
Environment Australia 201—202
environment—people interactions 4—5, 329—330
equity 52—63, 103, 182—187, 195
    gender see gender equity
    importance for co-management 337—339, 369
    participants commitment to 192
    policy goal 344
    social communication 151, 152, 186
erosion control
    Oued Sbahiya watershed 21—23
    peasant communities 12, 13
Ethiopia
    breakdown of local management systems 300—301
    Forole mountain 77

migration patterns 236

ethnic governance see customary governance and management systems

Europe, traditional land-use 94

European Round table of Industrialists (ERT) 423

European Union (EU) 423
Common Agricultural Policy (CAP) 417
Directive on watershed management 74
food retailing 373

evaluation 179, 184, 227, 231
issues for agreements 256
see also monitoring and evaluation

Even people 363

exchange visits 170

exclusion
from co-management 127
see also inclusion/exclusion rules

executive bodies 279

experience of co-management, sharing 170

experts 212, 387—388, 390—391
see also professionals

facilitators 152, 156, 180, 182, 184
biased 220
developing a common vision 197
developing a strategy 203, 204, 208, 209, 210
for DIPs 404
promoting participatory approaches 330
role in meetings 190, 192, 193—196

failure 134—135

fairness
in good governance 230
see also equity

falaj 14

family portraits 158

FAO (Food and Agriculture Organisation) 22, 161, 302, 333

Farmer Field Schools (FFS) 333, 413, 419

feasibility analysis 133—135

Ficus natalensis 237

Ficus thonningii 237

field visits 161, 216

Fiji 83

financial and economic policies 370—376

financial issues in agreements 256—257
indigenous communities 267—268, 272—273

financial speculations tax 425

financial support 136, 361, 370
attendance at meetings 170, 172, 181, 370
DIPs 403

Finland, Limingalahti Bay 122—123

fire management 276

First Nations Summit 279

fisheries
CM organisations 282—283
customary rules 237—238
as NRM units 119
policy frameworks 353, 354
practicing CM 86—88, 173—174
see also coastal resources

fishing rights 270—271

flexibility 105, 215, 306, 325—326
in agreements 192, 227, 253

flood management 276

focus groups 158, 200

Fonesca, Gulf of, Honduras 201

Fon people 238

Food and Agriculture Organisation (FAO) 22

food processing 372, 373

food safety rules 372

forest management
customary rules 238
local community organisation 165, 186—187
practicing CM 78—81, 99—100
in the USA 113
see also Joint Forest Management (JFM)

forest product uses 46—47, 96, 254—255

Forest and Rangeland Organisation (FARO), Iran 25, 26

Forole mountain, Ethiopia 77

fouggara 14

Four Directions Council 242

France
CM of protected areas 94—95, 246—247
representation of local interests 174—175
water management 74

freshwater wetlands 84—86, 302

Fundación Pro-Sierra Nevada de Santa Marta 93

funding see financial support

future search conferences 394

Gabbra people, East Africa 77

Galapagos Marine Reserve 173—174, 193
consensus 216, 217—218
initiating CM 127, 137, 189
participatory evaluation 323—324

game farming 92

GELOSE (local security of resource management), Madagascar 80—81, 90, 113, 154

gender equity 246, 369, 419—420, 426
cultural differences 46—47, 142, 240
negative impact of neo-liberalism 424
representing women s views 161, 179, 186—187, 214

general covenants 254—257
Geographical Information Systems (GIS) 72, 216
geographical units for NRM 117—123
German Technical Cooperation Agency (GTZ) 156, 171
ghada system 77
Ghana 197—199, 206—207
Gitksan people 119
Global Environment Facility 120
global governance 376—383
globalisation 371—375, 376, 422—427
GMOs (genetically modified organisms) 387, 404
Godwin, William 390
Gola Forest Reserve, Sierra Leone 238
Gond people 165
good governance 229—230, 344
Gorman, M. 53—54
governance
    global 376—383
    good 229—230, 344
    local 356—359, 375—376, 409—412
    participatory see democracy
    customary 253, 302, 359—362
government agencies 225, 328—329
    changes needed 333—337
    crucial issues 274—277
    local 357—358
    protecting investments 256—257
government officials 160, 165, 214—215, 409
    trust building 179, 210
governments see national authorities
graphic conceptual frameworks 205
Great Australian Bight 201—202
Great Barrier Reef Marine Park 100, 105, 150, 168—169, 193, 215
    fishing rights 270—271
Green Revolution (Philippines) 333, 412
GTZ (German Technical Cooperation Agency) 156, 171
Guaraní Izoceño people 145, 267
Guatemala 141, 167—168, 173, 329n
Guinea Bissau 87
Gujarat, India 332
Gurig National Park, Australia 142—143, 247—248
Gwaii Haanas National Park Reserve, Canada 101—102, 283

Hable Rood, Iran 219
Haida people 101—102, 283
Haiti 345—346
Hawaii 200—201
Hazara Protected Forests, Pakistan 293
hema system 76—77

Himalayan Wildlife Foundation 89
historical background 8—9, 13—16, 389—391
    trial by jury 391—392
history 261
    see also oral tradition
Honduras 201
Houedas people 238
Houegbonou people 238
Huichol people 363
human rights 49, 58, 60, 167, 337
    enhanced advocacy 388
    International Human Rights Law 308, 309, 366, 377—378
    participation 407, 409—412
    regulation of TNCs 374—375
hunting, fishing and gathering 10—11, 185—186
hunting rights 270—272
hydraulic states 13—14

IIED (International Institute for Environment and Development) 302, 398
ILO (International Labour Organisation) 99, 113
    Convention no. 169 (1989) 43, 368, 377
IMAFLORA (Institute of Forest and Agriculture Certification and Management) 148
impacting groups 124
Imraguen people 216—217
Inca people 13
incentives 78, 94, 98, 134, 218, 226
inclusion 103, 127, 152, 192, 418—420
    DIPs 404
    in local government 411
    in monitoring and evaluation 321—323
    in policy making 388, 392
inclusion/exclusion rules 7—8, 11, 300
inclusive deliberation see deliberative inclusive processes (DIPs)
income generation 21, 32
    through wildlife management 27—29
India 15, 52, 58, 112
    CM in agricultural research 75—76
    CM of protected areas 97, 131n
    constitutional amendments 347, 348, 411
    customary rules for fisheries 238
    decentralisation 358
    DIPs 396, 397, 398—399, 402—403
    enforcement 310—311
    gender differences 47, 419
    Joint Forest Management (JFM) 60—61, 79, 186—187, 284, 352
    local community organisation 164—165, 240, 294, 332

local knowledge 150, 158, 361

management of freshwater wetlands 84

National Biodiversity Strategies and Action Plans (NBSAP) 349—350

participatory action research 160

Public Distribution System 299, 339

Rajaji National Park 41—42, 125, 168

representation in CM organisations 283—284

yatras 155

Indian First Nations 279, 291, 308

indicators

for assessment 312, 315—321, 322—323

negative for CM 129—130, 131

indigenous knowledge and know-how 155, 157, 158, 361—362

used in evaluation and monitoring 322—323

use in NRM systems 34—35, 149—150

see also intellectual property rights (IPR)

indigenous peoples 43—47, 140—145, 430—431

crucial issues for 265—274

cultural heritage 275, 359, 363

customary and non-notarised agreements 236—243

customary rights 25, 49, 50—51, 124, 158, 259

entitlements 55, 115

formal agreements 246, 247—250, 252—253, 254—255, 261—262

helping to organise 164—168

land restitution 97, 142—143, 145, 365

policies and rights 346—347, 359, 364—366, 377—379, 380

practicing CM with 100—102, 105—107

social communication 155

social movements 415

see also culture; property and access; WAMIP (World Alliance of Mobile Indigenous Peoples)

Indigenous Protected Area model 143—144

indirect representation 59

individuals 114—115, 125, 136, 137n, 156

leadership quality 209, 336

Indonesia

citizen empowerment 413, 414, 417—418

CM organisations 284—285

forest management 360

Integrated Pest Management (IPM) 333

management of freshwater wetlands 85

marine resources management 236

participatory action research 158

industrial waste 387

information 57, 104, 147—150, 223

agreement clauses 260—261, 262

CM bodies 305

democracy 424—425, 426

policy support for 366—368

publicising agreements 307—308

see also indigenous knowledge and know-how; participatory action research; social communication

Ingano people 116

initiating co-management 110—115, 117, 428—429

process and result indicators 315

Start-up Teams 136—138

innovation 104, 151, 317, 326, 394

Institute of Forest and Agriculture Certification and Management (IMAFLORA) 148

institutional actors 39—42, 47, 57, 103

in agreements 252

asymetrical rights 60—61

identification 124—128, 137, 223

see also entitlements; social actors

institutional development and learning 31, 330—335

institutional framework see organisations

instruments, to regulate access to resources 216—217, 273—274

Integrated Conservation and Development Projects (ICDPs) 99—100

intellectual property rights (IPR) 150, 160, 261—262, 271

policies 363—364

see also indigenous knowledge and know-how

interactive learning 152

interest groups 44—47, 127—128

interests 40, 44, 46—47, 124, 128—129, 220

international agreements and organisations 234, 243, 280, 289, 290

see also International Porcupine Caribou Board

International Institute for Environment and Development (IIED) 302, 398

International Labour Organisation see ILO (International Labour Organisation)

international policy 376—383

International Porcupine Caribou Board 91, 250, 290

Inuit people 91, 158, 159, 196, 283

Inuvialuit people 282, 291, 353

investment 125, 132, 256—257

see also Community Investment Funds

Iran

boneh systems 71—72, 120

choosing representatives 175—176

Community Investment Funds 219

conflict management 197

conservation of the Asiatic Cheetah 120—121

developing capacity 169—170

nomadic pastoralism 4, 23—27, 33, 35, 78

Iranian Centre for Sustainable Development (CENESTA) 120—121, 170n, 175—176, 302

Ireland 293
irrigation see water management
issue forums 394—395
Italy 15, 45, 174, 414
Itoh, Cameroon 222
IUCN (World Conservation Union)
    CM of fisheries 87
    CM in mountain environments 89
    Commission on Environmental, Economic and Social
        Policy (CEESP) 120, 171, 302
    local community organisation 167, 185—187, 280,
        303, 314
    management of coastal resources 82, 210
    PA category system 93
    Sustainable Use Initiative 34
Ivory Coast 238

Jamaica 97
Jambudip, India 238
Japan 86—87
Jardhargaon, India 160, 164
Jaú National Park, Brazil 216
Jimenez, Simeon 159
jirgas 178—179
Joint Forest Management (JFM) 79, 284, 352
    asymetrical rights 60—61
    definition 66
    equity in 186—187
Joint Protected Area Management (JPAM) 97
    definition 66
Josephina disaster 112
judicial systems 367—368, 391—2

Kaa-ya Iya National Park, Bolivia 145, 201, 266—267
Kakadu National Park, Australia 287, 293
KaNgwane National Park, South Africa 248
Karen people 269n
karez systems 14, 120
Kayan Mentarang National Park, Indonesia 158,
    284—285
Kenya 78, 85, 237, 329
    CM organisations 291, 295
Keoladeo National Park, India 84, 131n
Kerala, India 348
Kgalagadi Trans-frontier Park Foundation 290
Khong district, Lao PDR 88, 173, 214—215, 240—241,
    311
    learning by doing 326—327
Khosrow Khan Qashqai 25, 26
Kibali National Park, Uganda 96
Kikori watershed, Papua New Guinea 126
Killary Harbour, Ireland 293

King Mahendra Nature Conservation Trust 88
Kita, Mali 99—100
KMP, Philippines (Kilusang Magbubukid ng Pilipinas)
    415
knowledge and skills 125, 388
    community 34—35, 149—150, 155, 157, 158, 160
    see also indigenous knowledge and know-how; pro-
        fessionals
Kruger National Park, South Africa 98, 114
Kuna peoples 150
Kurdish people 169—170
Kwa Zulu Natal 248
Kytalyk Reserve, Russia 363

Lake Naivasha Riparian Association 85
Landcare programme, Australia 72—73, 113, 298
land degradation 72—73, 166, 275, 301, 329
land literacy approaches 72
landowner aristocracies 15
land reform laws, Iran 25
land restitution 97, 142—143, 145, 267—268, 365
land tenure 7—8, 148—149, 159, 419
    see also indigenous peoples; property and access
Land Trusts 98
languages
    shared vision 200—201
    supporting diversity 180, 361, 362
    using local 153, 307, 367
Lao PDR, fisheries co-management see Khong district,
    Lao PDR
law 346—356
    see also regulations and laws
Leach, M. 49
leadership quality 209, 236
learning by doing 105, 192, 296—297, 326—327, 429
    promoting 171, 330—333
    through monitoring and evaluation 311—324
Lebanon 256, 351—352
legal status 58, 284, 346, 348
liberation theology 414
Limingalahti Bay, Finland 122—123
livelihood systems 10—17
    security 130
LMS (local management structures) 224, 225
local agreements and organisations 280, 288—289,
    292—295
local communities 43—47, 55, 430—431
    communication within and between 151—157, 160
    conditions for CM 130—131
    helping to organise 164—177
    as institutional actors 57—59, 127—128
    knowledge and skills 34—35, 149—150, 155, 157,

158, 160
  organisations 357, 359, 413—415
  relationship to natural resources 118—119, 299—302
  see also indigenous peoples; intellectual property
    rights (IPR)
local governance 356—359, 375—376, 409—412
local motivation 168
Lofoten Cod-fishery Co-management 86
logical framework analysis 206
logistics 180—181
Lubuk Larangan system 85
Luddites 390

Maasi peoples 78, 167
McKenzie Watershed Council 314—315
Madagascar 90, 114—115, 154
  DIPs 396
  forest management 80—81
Madhya Pradesh, India 310—311, 348
Maharashtra , India 160, 165
Mahenye, Zimbabwe 337
Makuleke land, South Africa 114, 189
Mali
  CM agreements 254—255
  decentralisation 358
  DIPs 397
  forest management 99—100, 113
  producer organisations 415, 416
management bodies 62
management-centred paradigms, definition 68
management partnerships see co-management
Mandailing, Sumatra 85
Maori people 189, 297—298
Mapanja, Cameroon 226
maps 147—148, 158—160, 200, 339
  see also demarcation of boundaries and resources
market forces 345, 371
mass media 152, 209, 262
material contributions 263
mature societies 116—117
Mauritania 78, 83, 84
  regulating access 216—217
  representation 175
Maya K iché people 141, 167—168, 173
Mbeere National Reserve, Kenya 295
Mbororo people 222
meetings
  final 230—231
  first procedural 191—193
  see also negotiations
Mekong river basin 86, 88, 173
membership of management body 304

  see also representation
Menabé, Madagascar 114—115
Mendha-Lekha, India 160, 165
Merina people 90
Mexico 81—82, 84, 409
  feasibility study 135
  use rights 363
Mgori forest, Tanzania 80, 323
migrations of people 15
Mikupia 106
minga 71, 156
mining interests 131, 159, 165
Miraflor, Nicaragua 114, 201
Miskito people 105—107
missionaries 19, 21
mobile health services, Iran 25
mobile indigenous peoples 43, 253, 299, 416
Mohammad Reza Pahlavi, Shah of Iran 24
Moloka i, USA 200—201
Molucca islands 236
Mongolia 166
monitoring and evaluation 260, 311—324
  policy making 388
  third party 367
Mont Blanc 89
Morocco 361
Mosaddeq, Mohammed 124
Mountain Areas Conservancy Project, Pakistan 89
mountain environments 88—90
Mount Cameroon National Park 122
Mount Elgon National Park, Uganda 46, 96, 149, 195,
  249—250, 293
MST, Brazil (Movimento dos Trabalhadores Rurais sem
  Terra) 415
multi-criteria mapping (MCM) 395
multiple use arrangements 215
multi-stakeholder processes, definition 68
Murphree, M. 39, 52—53
Muthurajawela Marsh and Lagoon Area, Sri Lanka 149
mutual aid
  definition 65
  social movements 415

naam gatherings 71
nafir systems 71
Naivasha, Lake, Kenya 85
Nama people 261
names
  for places 362
  for projects 153
Namib Desert 92
Namibia 92—93

Nantawarrina, Australia 143
Napa Valley watershed, USA 209
NAP (National Action Programmes) for Combating Desertification 350
national agreements and organisations 280, 285—286, 289, 290—292
national authorities 125, 127
    changes needed 333—337
    conditions for CM 130
    jurisdictional disputes 220
National Environmental Action Plans (NEAP) 345
National Environmental Policy Act (USA 1969) 113
National Forest Management Act (USA 1976) 113
national vision 345
Native Title Act 1993 (Commonwealth) of Australia 268
natural environment, and culture 5, 38, 77, 236—239, 268—269, 275
natural resource management (NRM) policy 348—356, 376
natural resource management (NRM) systems see NRM (natural resource management) systems
NBSAP (National Biodiversity Strategies and Action Plans) 349—350
N Dour N Dour, Senegal 246
negative indicators for co-management 129—130, 131
negotiations 188—191
    common vision 197—203, 213
    conflict management 192, 193, 196—197, 212—213, 219—222
    consensus 69, 213—219
    equity in 60—61, 63, 182—187
    first procedural meeting 191—193
    preparing for meetings 178—187
    procedures and rules 178—182, 192
    process and result indicators 315—316
    a productive close 222—231
    role of facilitator 190, 192, 193—196
    strategic objectives 210—211, 212
    strategy development 203—210
neighbours 125
neo-liberal policies 371, 417, 422—424
neo-Malthusian narratives 329
Nepal
    CM in mountain environments 88—89, 131n
    conflict resolution 196
    forest policy 352, 354—355
    indigenous peoples 102, 168
    monitoring and evaluation 313
    Parks and People Project 150
    state control 16
nested systems 119, 123, 282, 283

Netherlands 292
networking, definition 65
new actors 104, 110, 164, 180, 183, 317
new social partnerships, definition 68
New Zealand 189, 264, 297—298
Ngala Game Reserve, South Africa 98
Ngorongoro management plan 167
NGOs (non-governmental organisations)
    changes needed 333—337
    collaboration with local groups 412—413
    conservation agreements 244
    as institutional actors 53, 126, 225
    negative impacts 106—107, 161
    participatory GIS 216
    restitution and compensation facilitation 365
    social communication 155
Nicaragua 105—107, 114, 366
Niger 79, 208—209, 223—225, 415
Nigeria 268
Nisga a people 119
nomadic pastoralism 12—13, 16, 34, 118
    Iran 4, 23—27, 33, 301—302
    Mongolia 166
    subsidiarity 120
North York Moors National Park, UK 94
Norway 86
NRM (natural resource management) institutions 5, 10
NRM (natural resource management) systems 5—6, 9—16, 34
    building on local knowledge 299—302
    effectiveness through CM 129
    equity in 52—63
    feasibility of CM 133—134
    key institutional issues 254—255
    management units 117—123
    national policies 348—356
    as syncretic constructions 33—37, 55
    see also agro-industrial-market system
NSSD (National Strategies for Sustainable Development) 349
Nta-ali forest, Cameroon 137n
Nukhurluls 166

objectives 206—207, 210—211, 212, 269
    evaluating progress towards 312, 317—321
Ob Long National Park, Thailand 269n
obstacles to co-management 132, 133—134, 371, 428
Okavango river basin 86
open-access land 8, 55, 111, 218, 285
    leads to degradation 16, 360
open ended agreements 257—258
opportunities 38—39

recognition 56, 57
oral tradition 155, 157
organisations 359, 407, 412—413, 421—422
    federations and networks 415—418, 419
    see also co-management organisations
organising for action 57—58
    dangers 52, 105
    helping local communities 164—177
    meetings 178—187
    supportive policies 359
Oromo Borana people 77, 236, 300—301
Ostrom, Elinor 53
Oued Sbahiya watershed, Tunisia 21—23
overgrazing 9, 13
oversight, DIPs 402—403
ownership see land tenure; property and access

Pakistan 89, 178—179, 293
    DIPs 396
    National Conservation Strategy 351
    participation of women 161, 179
    participatory monitoring 314
Pa-Kluay community territory, Thailand 100
Panama 150, 158
Pan-European Eco Forum 383
Papua New Guinea 102, 126, 134, 236
Parc National du Banc d Arguin, Mauritania 216—217
Parco Naturale delle Dolomiti d Ampezzo, Italy 414
Parcs Naturels Régionaux (PNR), France 94—95,
    174—175, 246—247
Parks Canada 101—102
Parks and People Project, Nepal 150, 313
Park W, West Africa 208—209
participation
    Agenda 21 378—379
    in agricultural research 75—76
    in decision making 239—240
    definition 65, 66, 68
    in good governance 229
    in local governance 409—412
    right to 407, 409—412
    spaces for 405, 420—422
    support for 297—299, 366—370
        see also deliberative inclusive processes (DIPs);
        financial support
participatory action research (PAR) 157—164, 301—302,
    330, 331
participatory approaches 330—335
participatory budgeting 410—411
participatory exercises 203, 210
    mapping 148—149
participatory governance see democracy

participatory justice 391—392
participatory learning and action (PLA) 330, 331, 394
participatory policy processes 388—389, 418
    historical background 389—392
    see also deliberative inclusive processes (DIPs)
Participatory Rural Appraisal approaches 76
participatory rural appraisal (PRA) 394
parties to agreements 252—253, 266
passive non-compliance 51—52
pastoralists 76—78
    see also nomadic pastoralism
Pathan people 178—179
patrimonial mediation, definition 67
Paute, Ecuador 112—113, 153n
peasant communities 12—13
    Oued Sbahiya watershed 21—23
    participation in research 75
peasant movements 415, 417—418
people-centred organisational cultures 328—329
People s Biodiversity Register, India 150
people—environment interactions 4—5, 329—330
perceptions of environment 37, 269
performance in good governance 230
Peru 31—33, 236—237, 361
pest management 75—76, 276, 333
Philippines 102, 310, 353, 368
    citizen participation 409, 410, 418
    MASIPAG programme 412—413
pigeon-pea, insect pests 75—76
pilgrimages 155
planning, joint approaches to 409, 410
plant and animal species, customary rules 237
Plantecam Medicam 226
platform for collective action, definition 67
Plato 389, 390
pluralism, definition 67
pluralist economies 426
pluralist organisations 228—230, 231
policies 342—346
    for access to information, transparency and account-
        ability 366—368
    constitution and basic civil law 346—348
    cultural identity and customary governance
        359—362
    decentralisation and devolution 356—359
    financial and economic 370—376
    natural resource management 348—356
    property and access 362—364
    rights of indigenous peoples 364—366
    uncertain consequences of 386—387
    see also policy making process
policy making process 384—385

organised influence 415—418, 422—423
    rationale for direct participation 386—389
    see also participatory policy processes; policies
political context 105, 110, 133
    equal entitlement 58, 60, 62
    government organisation 119
    managing protected areas 93—94, 96, 97, 105—106
    representation 174—175
political economy 424, 425—427
politicians 194—195
polluter pays principle 425—426
popular participation, definition 66
population dynamics
    Andapa valley, Madagascar 154
    and environmental degradation 329
    Shuar people (Ecuador) 20
    social regulation of 6, 9, 11
    studies 147
porcupine caribou 91, 250, 292
Porto Alegre, Brazil 410—411
Poverty Reduction Strategy Papers (PRSP) 345
power
    and conflict resolution 220
    differentials among social actors 116, 180, 195, 209
    and environmental entitlements 51—52, 55
    influencing policy making 345
    and knowledge 385, 387—388, 420—421
    sharing 101, 103, 308, 407—408
    supporting marginalised groups 184—187, 337—338
    see also decentralisation; globalisation
powers and responsibilities of CM organisations 258, 306
Prajateerpu 398—399, 402—403
preambles 251—252
preliminary reports 147
prestamano 71
primary actors 163
primary users 53—54
prior informed consent (PIC) 368
private ownership 8, 14, 92
    enclosure 15—16
    and protected areas 94, 98—99, 243—245
    see also property and access
private sector policy 343
privatisation 371
problem analysis 205
procedural justice 189
procedures and rules for negotiations 178—182, 192
process approach 326
process of developing CM 138—139
process indicators 312—313
producer organisations 415—417

professionals
    attitudes and behaviour 336—337
    expertise and policy making 387—388, 390—391
    valid knowledge 420—421
    see also experts
project cycles 31
property and access 7—8, 11—16, 29—30, 271
    Coron Island, Philippines 368
    formal/legal agreements 243—250, 265—266, 272, 273—274, 275
    hydraulic states 13
    policies and rights 362—366
Protagoras 389—390
protected areas (PAs)
    CBD Programme of Work on 382
    CM agreements 246—250
    initiating CM 114, 115, 154
    legislation and policies 350—352, 353—354
    occupied by indigenous peoples 268—272
    practicing CM 93—97, 142—145
    relationships with neighbouring systems 208—209
    representation of rural communities 174
protection, trade policies 371—372
providors 53
Prunus africana 226
public consultations 193
public involvement in governance, definition 68
publicising agreements 227
public opinion, quality of 104
public policy 343
public recognition 262—263
public reporting requirements 367
Pygmy people 95, 185—186

Qashquai people, Iran 23—27, 35, 40, 219, 301—302
quanat system 14
Queen Charlotte Islands, Canada 101—102
Quinault Indian Nation 292

Racken, Lake, Sweden 283, 294
Rajaji National Park, India 41—42, 125, 168
Rajastan, India 84, 240, 283—284
Ramsar sites 79, 85, 161, 201
rangeland management 76—78, 330
Ratanikiri National Park, Cambodia 102
recognition
    of efforts and commitment 262—265
    of entitlements 52, 60—61, 128, 163—164
    of risks and opportunities 56, 57
recording agreements 227
regulations and laws 7, 133
    access to resources 216—217, 273—274

agreements 227, 236—243
    entitlements 49, 50
    nomadic pastoralism 13
    peasant communities 12
    undermining NRM systems 24—26
    see also law; policies
relevant social actors see institutional actors; social
    actors
religion 6, 74, 237—238, 299, 414
    see also sacred sites
reporting lines in CM bodies 305
representation 58—60, 167—168, 174—177
    in CM organisations 283—285, 337—338, 369—370
    DIPs 404
    in local government 410, 411
research
    agreements with indigenous peoples 242—243
    issues for agreements 256
    participatory action 157—164
    practicing co-management of 75—76, 189, 319—320
    to inform CM initiatives 149
    see also intellectual property rights (IPR)
resources for CM 132, 135—136
resource studies 147
responsibilities 431
    in CM bodies 258, 305, 306
    corporate 373—374
    distribution of 189, 223
    in exceptional situations 227
    and rights 103, 239, 270—272
    strategy components 230—231
    see also enforcement
result indicators 312, 317—321
results expected 227
retailers 373
Retezat National Park, Romania 253
revenue generation 371
review of management plan 227
Reza Pahlavi, Shah of Iran 24
Ribereño farming systems, Peruvian Amazon 31—33
Richtersveld National Park, South Africa 228, 248, 261
rights and responsibilities 103, 239, 270—272
    see also human rights
Rio Grande da Buba, Guinea Bissau 87
risks 38—39, 56, 57
ritual ceremonies 74
    to legitimise agreements 202—203, 307
river basins 86
    see also water management
Roman Empire 9, 14
Romania 4, 253
ron palm (Borassus aethiopum) 79

ROPPA 415, 417
roundtable meetings 178—179
Rousseau, Jean Jacques 390
Royal Bardia National Park, Nepal 131n
rules see procedures and rules
Russia 363
Ruwenzori, Uganda 96

sacred sites 77, 90, 102, 116, 238, 299
safe communicative spaces 405, 420—422
Saigata, India 160
Saint Lucia 83, 193, 242, 295, 353
sanduqs 219
Sangsari people 120, 121
Santiago, Chile 396
Sarhad, Pakistan 178—179
Sarin, Madhu 46—47
Sariska Tiger Reserve, India 131n
Save the Seeds Movement 160
Sbahiya peasants 21—23, 33, 35
scenic views 275
science 30, 421
    and policy making 385, 387—388
Scotland 81, 89, 282
seasonal variations 124
seating arrangements 191
    see also roundtable meetings
secondary users 53—54
seed diversity 165
Seed village, India 283—284
self-determination 364—365, 377
self-representation 59
Selous Game Reserve, Tanzania 92
Sen, Amartya 49
Senegal 40, 84, 246
    producer organisations 415, 416
Senghor, Leopold Sedar 155
Seville, International Conference (1995) 93
shared production regimes, definition 67
shifting horticulture see tropical forest hunters-horticul-
    turalists
Shona people 237
Shuar Federation 20—21
Shuar people 19—21, 33, 35
Sian Ka an Biosphere Reserve, Mexico 81—82
Sierra Leone 238, 329
Sierra Nevada de Santa Marta, Colombia 93—94
Sierra Tarahumara, Mexico 135
signatories of agreements 223, 227
situation analysis 205
social actors 40—42, 103, 105
    analysis of 47, 162—163

capacities 125—126, 129, 167, 168—172, 225—226

entitlements 48—55

initiating CM 110—112, 117, 160—164

internal agreement 167, 172—175, 238—239

maturing partnerships 327

monitoring and evaluation by 321—324

new 104, 110, 164, 180, 183, 317

power differentials among 116, 180, 184—187, 195, 209, 220, 337—338

representation 58—60, 167, 175—177, 283—285

see also equity; information; institutional actors

social capital 41

social communication 151—157, 160, 275, 325, 366—367

social contracts, shared vision 200

social impact indicators 312

social information 149—150

social institutions and NRM 7—8, 12, 13—14, 30, 73

social justice 388, 408

social norms 49, 60, 236

Socrates 389

Solomon Islands 239—240

Som Thom, Cambodia 168

Sonora, Mexico 84

SOS Sahel UK 223

Soufriere Marine Management Association (SMMA), Saint Lucia 83, 193, 242, 295, 353

sound governance, definition 68

South Africa 98, 114, 228, 248

South African National Parks (SANP) 114

South Moresby/Gwaii Haanas National Park Reserve 283

spaces
  of anarchy 62
  for participation 405, 420—422

Spain 201, 415

Special Area Management (SAM) processes, Sri Lanka 82—83

sport hunting 98, 271, 371
  see also CAMPFIRE initiative, Zimbabwe

Sri Lanka 82—83, 149, 169

stakeholders see institutional actors; social actors

Start Up Teams 120—121, 136—138, 142, 146—148, 193
  assisting local communities to organise 167, 170, 175, 176, 177
  bias in 220
  first procedural meetings 191—192, 203
  initial contacts 160—164
  preparing for negotiation meetings 178, 180—182
  social communication 151—152, 153

state property 8, 16

Iran 25—26

stewardship 98—99, 166, 274
  definition 67

stockbrokers 4

strategic advice 264

strategic groups 39—40

strategy development 203—210

strengths, weaknesses, opportunities and limitations (SWOL) analysis 204—205

study circles 160, 165, 394—395

subak irrigation societies 73—74

subsidiarity 120, 348, 356, 372

subsistence farming
  Ribereño people 32
  see also peasant communities

success
  building on 306
  see also monitoring and evaluation

Sudan 9, 71, 176—177

Sumatra, Indonesia 85, 360, 414

supply chains 372

surangam 14

sustainability
  ecological and institutional 29, 30, 132
  environmental 130
  policy goal 344

Sustainable Development, National Strategies (NSSD) 349

Sweden 282—283, 294

Switzerland 3, 397

taboos 6, 237—238

Tagbanwa people 368

Takiéta Forest Reserve, Niger 223—225

Tanala people 90

Tanga, Tanzania 54, 82, 210

Tanzania
  coastal resources management 54, 82, 210
  forest management 80, 323, 327, 328
  legislation for PAs 350—351
  wildlife management 92

Tapajós National Forest, Brazil 148

Tatshenshini Alesk Park, Canada 294

tax concessions 244, 263

Tayna Gorilla Reserve, Democratic Republic of Congo 95

technical advice 263—264

technological innovation 14, 16

terminology 65—69

Territorio Comunitario de Origen (TCO) 145

Thailand 82, 100, 269n

Thompson, E.P. 390

timing of meetings 191

titi bird 189

Tiwanaku, Bolivia 158

tools and techniques

    developing a strategy 204—205, 211—213

    mapping 147—149, 158—160

    research 158

    social communication 152, 156—157

Torris people 238

totem animals 237, 238

Totonicapán 141, 167—168

tourism 112, 174

    benefits from 271, 337, 371

    regulating access 264, 274—275

    see also CAMPFIRE initiative, Zimbabwe

trade 371—372, 422—423

trade-offs 264—265

traditional authorities 125, 127

traditional groups

    entitlements 55, 115

    as institutional actors 41—42, 58—59

    relationship with natural resources 118—119

    see also indigenous peoples

traditional wisdom see indigenous knowledge and
know-how

training 134, 152, 171, 263—264, 332, 410

    collective learning 171

    indigenous peoples 272—273

    in partnership approach 134

    as social communication 152

    see also capacities of social actors

Trang province, Thailand 82

transaction costs 103, 132

Trans Atlantic Business Dialogue (TABD) 423

trans-national corporations (TNCs) 371, 372—375,
422—423

transparency 104, 179, 191, 221, 262

    in benefits distribution 337

    DIPs 402—403

    in good governance 229, 304

    policy support for 366—368

travel expenses 170, 172, 181, 370

trial by jury 391—392

tropical forest hunters-horticulturalists 11—12

    Shuar people (Ecuador) 19—21, 33, 35

trust

    developing 209—210, 325

    government agencies 328

    individuals 125, 137, 161

Tukanoan peoples 237

Tunisia 21—23

Turkey 354, 398

Uganda 3, 193

    CM agreements 149, 249—250, 293, 307

    CM organisations 303

    decentralisation 358

    gender differences in forest uses 46

    monitoring and evaluation 321

    party politics 195

    protected areas 96, 97, 217

Uganda Wildlife Authority 96, 97

Uluru National Park, Australia 143, 267, 287

UNCCD (Convention to Combat Desertification) 350,
382

UNESCO, Man and the Biosphere (MAB) programme
201

uniqueness of each context 104, 429

United Kingdom (UK) 89, 94, 174, 292

United Nations Development Programme (UNDP) 120,
168, 176

United Nations (UN)

    human rights 309, 377—378

    principles of good governance 229—230

    role in regulating TNCs 374, 375

United States of America (USA)

    agri-food business 373

    conservation agreements 243—244

    corporate profits 422

    evaluating success 318—319

    foreign aid 24

    forest management 286

    initiating CM 113

    international agreements 250

    Land Trusts 98

    visioning exercises 200—201

    watershed management 78—79, 122, 190—191, 209,
    306, 314—315

units for NRM 117—123

Upper Guinea resource management agreements 245

Utah State University 26

Uttar Pradesh, India 164—165

values 29, 38—39

    in policy making 385, 387, 388, 406—407

Venezuela 158—160

venues for meetings 189, 191

veterinary services, Iran 25

Via Campesina 415—416

video archives 403

Vietnam 353

village confederations 13—14

Visayas islands, Philippines 310

vision

    common 190, 193, 197—203, 213, 252

complementary accords 223
developing a strategy for 203—210
evaluating progress towards 312
in good governance 230
national 345
visioning exercises 197—200, 394
voluntary initiatives 373—374
volunteers 137, 314—315
rangers 166
Vrikshamitra 165
Vuntut Gwitchin people 353
Vuntut National Park 353

Wadden Sea Agreement 292
Waitangi, Treaty of 189
WAMIP (World Alliance of Mobile Indigenous Peoples)
302, 416
water management
boneh system 71—72, 120
Oromo-Borana people 300
Paute 112
peasant communities 12, 13—14, 158
practicing co-management 73—75, 276
USA watersheds 78—79, 122, 190—191, 209, 306,
314—315
Waza Logone flood plain, Cameroon 113
Waza National Park, Cameroon 280—281
wealth inequalities 422
weed control 276
Wenchi, Ghana 198—199, 206—207
West Bengal 294
wetlands see coastal resources; freshwater wetlands
Wet Tropics World Heritage Area, Australia 287—288
Wilderness Act (USA 1964) 113
Wildlife Conservation Society (WCS) 145, 267, 335n
wildlife management 27—31, 120—121, 270—271
CM organisations 282

gender interests 46
migratory species 90—93
Papua New Guinea 102
Zimbabwe 27—31, 91—92, 113, 237
women s groups
in agricultural research 75—76
alternative PDS system 339
fish sellers 87
reconstruction of Paute 112
see also gender equity
workshops 206—207, 214, 223—224, 398—399
World Alliance of Mobile Indigenous Peoples (WAMIP)
302, 416
World Bank 313, 345, 358
World Conservation Union (IUCN) see IUCN (World
Conservation Union)
World Parks Congresses 27, 93, 97, 271—272
World Summit on Sustainable Development (WSSD)
349, 375, 379
World Trade Organisation (WTO) 363, 371, 372, 417,
423
WWF (World Wide Fund for Nature) 99, 285
management partnerships 80, 84, 89, 122, 154
participatory action research 158

Yadfon Association 82
Ye kuana peoples 158—160
Yemen 12
Yukon Final Agreement 282, 353

Zaheerabad, India 339
Zimbabwe
evaluation of CM approaches 319—320
managing wildlife 27—31, 91—92, 113, 237
transparency 337
zoning 89, 215—216, 312
Zoological Society of Milwaukee County 99

International Institute for Environment and Development

The International Institute for Environment and Development (IIED)

The International Institute for Environment and Development (www.iied.org) is an independent, non-profit organisation working in the field of sustainable development. IIED aims to provide expertise and leadership in researching and achieving sustainable development at local, national, regional and global levels. The Institute works with international and Southern partners, primarily in Africa, Asia and Latin America, to transform decision-making at all levels. This is done primarily through research, communication, engagement with actors and their networks, capacity development and advocacy. In alliance with others, IIED seeks to shape a future that ends global poverty and delivers sustainable and equitable management of the world?s natural resources.

The World Conservation Union (IUCN)

Founded in 1948, the World Conservation Union (www.iucn.org) brings together states, government agencies and a diverse range of non-governmental organisations in a unique world partnership: over 1000 members spread across some 140 countries. Its mission is to influence, encourage and assist societies throughout the world to conserve the integrity and diversity of nature and to ensure that any use of natural resources is equitable and ecologically sustainable. Through its six Commissions, IUCN draws together over 10,000 expert volunteers from virtually all countries of the world. The Commissions are networks entrusted by the World Conservation Congress to develop and advance the knowledge and experience of IUCN. The Commissions provide guidance and advice on conservation knowledge and policy and work in partnership with IUCN members and the Secretariat to implement an integrated Programme. The vision of IUCN is: "A just world that values and conserves nature".

The IUCN Commission on Environmental, Economic and Social Policy (CEESP)

CEESP (www.iucn.org/themes/ceesp) is one of the six Commissions of the World Conservation Union. Comprising an inter-disciplinary network of professionals from all over the world, its mission is to act as a source of advice to the Union on the environmental, economic, social and cultural factors that affect natural resources and biological diversity and to provide the Union with guidance and support towards effective policies and practices in environmental conservation and sustainable development. One of CEESP?s key objectives is improved governance of natural resources— achieving more effective and efficient conservation, ensuring equity for individuals and communities, and respecting human rights.

CMWG

The CEESP Collaborative Management Working Group (CMWG)

The Co-management Working Group (www.iucn.org/themes/ceesp/Wkg_grp/CMWG) is the oldest and largest working group within CEESP and comprises about 400 conservation and development professionals with concern and expertise focusing on participatory, multi-stakeholder management of natural resources. The CMWG members are active in applied research and analysis, technical advice to field-based initiatives, policy development, training, and documentation of field experiences. The group supports and strengthens the work of its members through information-sharing and occasions for mutual technical advice, joint activities at the national and regional level, and international policy advocacy.

Centre for Sustainable Development

Centre for Sustainable Development (CENESTA)

CENESTA (www.cenesta.org) is an Iranian NGO dedicated to the conservation of biological and cultural diversity and to community-oriented practices and policies for sustainable livelihoods. Among CENESTA?s major interests are agroecology, food sovereignty, co-management of natural resources, community conserved areas and the safeguards and enhancement of mobile indigenous livelihoods, both in Iran and inter-

International Institute for Environment and Development

The International Institute for Environment and Development (IIED)

The International Institute for Environment and Development (www.iied.org) is an independent, non-profit organisation working in the field of sustainable development. IIED aims to provide expertise and leadership in researching and achieving sustainable development at local, national, regional and global levels. The Institute works with international and Southern partners, primarily in Africa, Asia and Latin America, to transform decision-making at all levels. This is done primarily through research, communication, engagement with actors and their networks, capacity development and advocacy. In alliance with others, IIED seeks to shape a future that ends global poverty and delivers sustainable and equitable management of the world?s natural resources.

The World Conservation Union (IUCN)

Founded in 1948, the World Conservation Union (www.iucn.org) brings together states, government agencies and a diverse range of non-governmental organisations in a unique world partnership: over 1000 members spread across some 140 countries. Its mission is to influence, encourage and assist societies throughout the world to conserve the integrity and diversity of nature and to ensure that any use of natural resources is equitable and ecologically sustainable. Through its six Commissions, IUCN draws together over 10,000 expert volunteers from virtually all countries of the world. The Commissions are networks entrusted by the World Conservation Congress to develop and advance the knowledge and experience of IUCN. The Commissions provide guidance and advice on conservation knowledge and policy and work in partnership with IUCN members and the Secretariat to implement an integrated Programme. The vision of IUCN is: "A just world that values and conserves nature".

The IUCN Commission on Environmental, Economic and Social Policy (CEESP)

CEESP (www.iucn.org/themes/ceesp) is one of the six Commissions of the World Conservation Union. Comprising an inter-disciplinary network of professionals from all over the world, its mission is to act as a source of advice to the Union on the environmental, economic, social and cultural factors that affect natural resources and biological diversity and to provide the Union with guidance and support towards effective policies and practices in environmental conservation and sustainable development. One of CEESP?s key objectives is improved governance of natural resources— achieving more effective and efficient conservation, ensuring equity for individuals and communities, and respecting human rights.

CMWG

The CEESP Collaborative Management Working Group (CMWG)

The Co-management Working Group (www.iucn.org/themes/ceesp/Wkg_grp/CMWG) is the oldest and largest working group within CEESP and comprises about 400 conservation and development professionals with concern and expertise focusing on participatory, multi-stakeholder management of natural resources. The CMWG members are active in applied research and analysis, technical advice to field-based initiatives, policy development, training, and documentation of field experiences. The group supports and strengthens the work of its members through information-sharing and occasions for mutual technical advice, joint activities at the national and regional level, and international policy advocacy.

Centre for Sustainable Development

Centre for Sustainable Development (CENESTA)

CENESTA (www.cenesta.org) is an Iranian NGO dedicated to the conservation of biological and cultural diversity and to community-oriented practices and policies for sustainable livelihoods. Among CENESTA?s major interests are agroecology, food sovereignty, co-management of natural resources, community conserved areas and the safeguards and enhancement of mobile indigenous livelihoods, both in Iran and inter-

For Product Safety Concerns and Information please contact our EU
representative GPSR@taylorandfrancis.com Taylor & Francis Verlag GmbH,
Kaufingerstraße 24, 80331 München, Germany

Printed and bound by CPI Group (UK) Ltd, Croydon, CR0 4YY

08/05/2025

01864542-0001